NORTHERN ENTERPRISE

MICHAEL BLISS

Northern Enterprise
Five Centuries of Canadian Business

McClelland and Stewart

Canadian Cataloguing in Publication Data

Bliss, Michael, 1941-

Northern enterprise: five centuries of Canadian business

Bibliography: p.
Includes index.

ISBN 0-7710-1577-1

1. Canada - Commerce - History. I. Title.

HF3224.B58 1987   380.1'0971   C86-094750-5

This work was written on a Macintosh personal computer from Apple.
Printed and bound in Canada by John Deyell Printing Co. Ltd.
Maps by James Loates Illustrating.
DESIGNED BY RICHARD MILLER.

McClelland and Stewart
The Canadian Publishers
481 University Avenue
Toronto, Ontario
M5G 2E9

Contents

Maps

J.S. Woodsworth, founder of the *CCF,* **on the evils of capitalism**
(Winnipeg Free Press *and the Dale Estate)*

Introduction

THIS BOOK IS THE FIRST to trace the course of Canadian business history over a period of more than fifty years. My subject is the whole history of business in Canada, from the earliest Atlantic fishermen in the 1480s to the pressure for free trade with the United States in the 1980s.

The idea originated when a group from the Manufacturers Life Insurance Company asked my advice about a book the firm might sponsor as part of its 1987 centennial celebrations. I pointed out that there were no overviews of the development of Canadian business. Our discussions led to my agreeing to write such a book, with support from Manufacturers. The support consisted of a grant to cover my research costs and two years of time away from teaching at the University of Toronto. The agreement gave me sole control over the book's contents (Manufacturers could have asked that I not mention its involvement). In a country where little historical scholarship is produced without heavy subsidization, usually by taxpayers, this arrangement has worked exactly as planned and without friction. I am deeply grateful to Manufacturers, and particularly to its chairman and chief executive officer, Syd Jackson, for this support, and I hope that this project can be a model for other private funding of scholarly writing in Canada. The one way in which our agreement differed from grants and fellowships in the public sector is that I made a binding commitment to finish the book in time for publication during Manufacturers' centennial year.

My interest in Canadian business history began in 1966 when I embarked on a doctoral thesis exploring the attitudes of Canadian businessmen to the economic and political issues of their times. The thesis was published in 1974 as *A Living Profit: Studies in the Social History of Canadian Business, 1883–1911*. In 1978 I followed it with an intensive biographical study of a leading entrepreneur, philanthropist, and business statesman, *A Canadian Millionaire: The Life and Business Times of Sir Joseph Flavelle, Bart., 1858–1939*. A number of colleagues then suggested that I attempt to write a survey of Canadian business history, but I found the prospect too daunting, and in any case had developed a second area of interest relating to the discovery of insulin and medical history in general. Without Manufacturers' stimulus, the business history idea would have been in limbo for many more years, probably the rest of my life. There were times during the research and writing that I wished it had stayed in limbo, but the project has

7

rekindled my interest in the subject. I hope to revise this book periodically in the light of new scholarly knowledge and the ongoing history of Canadian enterprise.

———————◆———————

I see business history as the interplay of enterprise and opportunity. Businesses are organizations of people risking capital in the hope of profit. Entrepreneurs are the individuals who spark the risk-taking with their determination to exploit the opportunities they perceive. The modern world is heir to two great national achievements in enterprise: British leadership in the Industrial Revolution of the early nineteenth century, and the development of the key managerial institutions of modern capitalism in the United States during its long period of world industrial dominance. Perhaps a third mighty contribution is still in the making in the evolution of the Japanese economy. Canadian business history, by contrast, gains its distinctiveness not so much from pioneering in the forms of enterprise, which have usually been derivative of British and American practice, but as an account of the attempt by enterprising spirits to create wealth in the sprawling, thinly populated northern half of the North American continent. Thus the book's title, *Northern Enterprise*.

These nineteen chapters present a long, increasingly complex, and multi-faceted story of wealth-seekers' struggles to find ways of getting the most out of the opportunities they have perceived to exist in the lands that became the Dominion of Canada in 1867 or joined it later. The book is written to be read by any intelligent reader – from a high school student to a chief executive officer or an economist, and especially those in between. In a single volume I have only been able to map the highest peaks and deepest valleys in the range of Canadian enterprise, while at the same time trying to sketch the general contours of the terrain. Problems of selection – of individuals, firms, industries, and themes to highlight – have been almost overwhelming. Many readers, especially those with specialized knowledge of Canadian business in the far-off or recent past, will be struck by the brevity of my treatment, or even my total neglect, of firms, themes, issues, that interest them.

Naturally I could have expanded practically every paragraph to far greater length, and could have added volumes of new material. The history could have become two, five, fifteen, or fifty volumes. In these few chapters the selection and depth of coverage represents my judgment of the relative importance of the material within the limits of one 600-page volume. Reviewers of the book who believe I should have said *more* about something are also obliged, I think, to say what I should have said *less* about. The most serious distortion caused by the format, which I deeply regret, is that it forced me to exclude more than passing references to what historically was Canada's most important single industry, the business of farming. Agriculture is traditionally slighted in the writing of business history, and has been short-changed in most other areas of Canadian historical writing in the last few decades, so its neglect here might have gone unnoticed. But if the study had been two or three volumes, and there had been several more years to do it in, I would have thoroughly re-cast it to include the evolution of farming and its commercial and political consequences.

There are many more than 680 tons of business documents in Canadian archives, not to mention the archives of head offices abroad. During the past twenty years I have used a number of these collections in the research for my previous books and for other projects. Some of that archival work is reflected in these chapters. But for 85 per cent of the factual contents of this book I have been dependent on other people's research and writing: on a huge, growing, and remarkably diverse body of books and articles written by economic historians, general historians, business historians, journalists, businessmen, economists, investment analysts, and many others. It was decided not to encumber the book with footnote references, but to indicate my indebtedness both in the text and in the bibliographical essay at the end of the book. In some ways the book is a pulling together of facts, themes, and ideas generated in a fascinating, specialized literature, one which has been greatly enriched recently by the work of the first generation of academic historians in Canada who have a special interest in business history. I hope many readers who sample Canadian business history here will have their appetite whetted for more, and will use the discussion of sources in the bibliography to plunge into a literature whose existence and riches have not been given enough publicity. Perhaps the book will also encourage more interest in the writing of Canadian business history, if only to set me straight.

The difference between a synthesis and a hash or rehash lies in the author's choice of material and his use of it to weave an original pattern. I do not believe the pattern can be extracted from the cloth – which is to say that the guiding themes, interpretations, and conclusions of this study are shaped by and give form to the material on each page. This is true not only of the factual content, but of organization and style. To find the conclusions, I'm afraid, you have to read the book.

Well, you can cheat a little bit. The chapters are fairly self-contained, making it possible to sample certain themes or periods of Canadian business history. The book's unusually detailed index should be useful. Most business people are present and future-oriented, and might be inclined to start reading at the beginning of the last chapter. To prevent this I have made its first pages difficult to understand without knowledge of the preceding couple of chapters. I most definitely do not believe that Canadian business history begins with C.D. Howe and his boys in the Second World War, but I can understand that readers whose only interest is today's Canada might dive into the book at the beginning of Chapter 16.

You will find throughout the book a heavy emphasis on the fact of competition in business: its presence, everyone's attempts to escape from it or limit it, and its immense strength. Of course, everyone has to find some competitive niche or advantage to survive, and the ultimate niche is to have a monopoly. But, apart from the fact that many entrepreneurs never find their niche and the history of business is littered with failure, even the most successful competitors cannot close their market for very long. That was as true for fishermen and fur traders four hundred years ago as it has proven for OPEC and Inco and General Motors and IBM and the whole Canadian resource economy in the 1980s. The invisible hand grinds on, sometimes slowly, always inexorably, and its power always wears down the structures created by human hands.

In Canada, far more than in the United States, the competitive strategy of working with or through government, or otherwise making use of it, has coloured the evolution of enterprise, the economy, and government itself. Therefore this book pays more attention to the relationship of business and the state, and to the assumptions of politicians, than might be found in other national business histories.

The Canadian political climate has been particularly important in the way it has been affected by assumptions about the potential wealth of the northern community. Through its history the Canadian land mass has been seen sometimes as a useless northern wilderness, sometimes as a cornucopia of raw wealth ready to pour out its bounty. Perceptions of the opportunities available in Canada have ranged from a notion that there was nothing there worth bothering about, to wild excitement about a land of golden opportunity. The bias of governments, which have a natural tendency to wish to encourage growth and job-creation, has tended to be in the direction of the cornucopia view of Canada. That has been particularly true through much of the twentieth century, which has been characterized by a series of natural resource-driven booms, the latest of which came in the 1970s.

Yet the roots of the enthusiasm are very deep. When Queen Elizabeth I lent Martin Frobisher a ship to bring back the gold he thought he had found in the New World, or when the government of France tried to create industries of all kinds in its acres of northern forest, they were reflecting Europeans' deep belief that the North American possessions were storehouses of wealth. It was a belief reinforced by Frobisher and other explorers and promoters whose boundless enthusiasm played to the hopes of rulers. The rulers tended to encourage the men of great faith in their dreams and visions. Thus began a developmental partnership between the state and certain optimistic entrepreneurs which has recurred at intervals and in various guises at many times in the nation's history. Its most recent manifestation was the National Energy Program of 1980.

The disastrous failure of the NEP, like many of the grand development projects before it, occurred because the politicians and their promoter allies in Canadian business were completely wrong in their estimate of Canada's real energy wealth as determined by world markets. Anyone can have visions of great opportunities, and many people possess enormous energies and drive. The difference between success and failure in business is that only a few people are able to assess opportunities realistically and focus their energies on realizing that assessment. Students of Canadian history still occasionally pay serious attention to a totally wrong-headed notion of a fundamental clash between the conservatism of merchants and bankers in Canada and the enterprise of manufacturers. There was a clash, and a fundamental one that continues today, but merchants and manufacturers had nothing to do with it *per se*. It was and is a conflict between those who know that an enterprise has to be sound to succeed, as measured in profit-and-loss statements, and those who believe Canada's opportunities justify ever greater risks, investments, and levels of debt, because it will all work out in the future.

Many observers of Canadian business have been inclined to share what I call the Martin Frobisher view of Canada as a rich land whose people would have been much wealthier if only its businessmen had been more enterprising. My studies in Canadian business history lead me to the opposite view. There has been no shortage of enterprise in Canadian history, one important reason being the openness of the country to immigrants and foreign entrepreneurs. But it has been a harsh land, difficult to extract wealth from, and gravely handicapped by its small population and its peoples' and governments' great expectations. Their desire to force the pace of Canadian development faster than the real resource base has been able comfortably to sustain has tended to burden Canadian business and Canadians generally with very high costs. In the post-NEP, post-inflation world of the late 1980s, the weight of these burdens appears menacingly high. I hope future history proves me wrong in this judgment.

Certainly past history is not a safe guide to the future, and I cannot think that readers of this book will profit financially from the experience. The Scots school teacher in *The Apprenticeship of Duddy Kravitz*, who has no influence at all on his students, finally tears up and burns their history tests, and they hardly notice the loss. On the other hand, we all feel a need from time to time (especially on hundredth birthdays), to look back on our origins and achievements and failures. After all, as Yogi Berra should have said, "How can you make second base if you don't remember the way to first?"

My debt to Manufacturers Life Insurance Company and to the scholars and writers whose works are cited later has been mentioned. This has been a difficult book to complete in the term allotted, and nothing has sustained me more in the effort than the wonderful tolerance, support, and good humour of my wife Elizabeth and our children, Jamie, Laura, and Sally. I received important practical help in the form of specialized research studies prepared by Ben Forster, Joe Lindsey, and Gene Allen. Spot research assistance came from Katharine Ridout, Brad Cowls, Peter James, and Suzanne Zeller. All our requests for help from libraries, companies, and other institutions were met generously and enthusiastically, except by one prominent business family.

The first draft of the manuscript was read critically by Ian Drummond of the University of Toronto and by Duncan McDowall and Sandy Campbell in Ottawa. Specific chapters were read by Andrew den Otter, Ben Forster, and Joe Lindsey. Readers' comments led to hundreds of changes, most of which could only have been for the better. Of course, all the remaining mistakes and misjudgments in the book are my fault. For advice, encouragement, access to unpublished materials, and other support, I am also indebted to Christopher Armstrong, Edward Borins, John Bosher, Doug McCalla, Viv Nelles, Ted Regehr, Paul Rutherford, Joy Santink, Jack Scott, Jim Spence, Albert Tucker, Gerald Tulchinsky, and Sylvia Van Kirk. Apologies to anyone who has been inadvertently omitted from these acknowledgments.

Editors and publishers never get all the thanks they deserve. Diane Mew has edited this and my previous three books, and it helps immeasurably. McClelland and Stewart were involved from the beginning; the firm's president in 1983, Linda McKnight, saved the project in its darkest hour. In the midst of the work I was loaned an Apple Macintosh computer from McClelland and Stewart, had my writing habits revolutionized, and put away the fountain pen and typewriter for ever.

Michael Bliss
Toronto, September 1, 1986

"The image of Time brought thoughts of mortality: of human beings, facing outward like the Seasons, moving hand in hand in intricate measure: stepping slowly, methodically, sometimes a trifle awkwardly, in evolutions that take recognisable shape: or breaking into seemingly meaningless gyrations, while partners disappear only to reappear again, once more giving pattern to the spectacle: unable to control the melody, unable, perhaps, to control the steps of the dance."
ANTHONY POWELL, *A Dance to the Music of Time*

"You lying sons-of-bitches with your books and your socialism and your sneers. You give me one long pain in the ass. You think I never read a book? I've read books. I've got friends now who read them by the ton. A big deal. What's so special in them? They all make fun of guys like me. Pusherkes. What a bunch you are! What a pack of crap-artists! Writing and reading books that make fun of people like me. Guys who want to get somewhere."
DUDDY KRAVITZ in Mordecai Richler's *The Apprenticeship of Duddy Kravitz*

"There is little to be gained from looking backward with disapproval at the consistency of human folly except to notice how each generation thinks itself immune to its predecessor's mistakes"
JOHN H. MAKIN, *The Global Debt Crisis*

Part One: Foundations

Fishing, curing, and drying cod *(Public Archives of Canada, #C3686)*

1

The Original Business: Fishing

*Bristol fishermen keep the New World a trade secret . . . nothing but fish . . .
methods of harvesting and curing . . . specialization . . . worthless land . . .
Cartier deluded . . . Frobisher's mining follies . . . uncontrolled competition
in the fishery . . . Cupids Cove failure . . . Kirke and the planters . . . West
Country merchants resist settlement . . . the industry evolves anyway . . .
monopoly and "foreign" control defeated.*

Practical men seeking profit were the first to sail to the New World. Explorers, who had heard rumours about these earlier ventures, came later. The explorers who thought they were finding a new route to China and the Indies turned out to be wrong. Enthusiasts who claimed that the northern part of the New World was a land of gold and diamonds were also wrong. As those who dreamed of colonies and resource development in the New Found Land were to discover, the northern land mass was forbidding and virtually useless. There is a fanciful legend that the country's name is rooted in Spanish explorers' disappointment as they sailed north from the rich southern lands they had discovered only to find a *cap de nada*.

As the first European visitors to Canadian shores – men in the business of fishing – had realized, the country's wealth lay in the seas. Canada's first great business, conducted for many generations entirely by Europeans based in Europe, was fishing. Its second business, fur-trading, did not develop until the Europeans had come into sustained contact with the first Canadian traders, the native Indians.

THE NORSE VOYAGES TO AMERICA were long forgotten when European countries began their spectacular burst of westward expansion in the late 1400s. But European navigators who probed the western reaches of the North Atlantic, usually under royal sponsorship, were not sailing blindly into the unknown. Fishing ships, on voyages financed by small groups of private risk-takers, had already sailed these waters in their wandering, restless search for better sources of supply. And they had found those supplies in new fishing grounds of wonderful abundance. The fishermen were like businessmen in other times and places in trying to keep quiet about the source of their profitable catch. Those who knew about the existence of a New World tried to keep it a trade secret.

Icelanders may have retained their knowledge of the western land and waters through old connections with Greenland. Perhaps Portuguese fishermen sailing west from the Azores knew where new fish and land could be found. The first concrete evidence of European activities off the coast of present-day Canada concerns merchants of Bristol, England, who from at least 1490, perhaps a decade earlier, were sending expeditions west toward the legendary "Island of Brasil." A reference in the documents to the quantities of salt purchased for one of these voyages gives away the purpose: to collect and cure fish.

The Bristol men may have been following in others' wakes, or they may have first crossed by accident in gales which blew them away from Irish or Icelandic fishing grounds. Or the fishermen may have been more purposeful: their catch in the waters near Iceland, which had become an important source of supply for Britain during the 1400s, was being hindered by various attempts at regulation. The Bristol fishermen may simply have sailed away to find waters where they could carry on a free enterprise. They found the waters, the fish, and the eastern edge of modern Canada.

In 1496 Henry VII of England commissioned the Italian seaman, John Cabot, to sail west on a voyage of discovery. Cabot knew what the Bristol merchants had been doing. After he returned in 1497 and began popularizing his discoveries, one of the Bristol merchants, John Day, wrote to a Spanish "Lord Grand Admiral" (probably Columbus) that Cabot had reached the land "found and discovered in the past by the men from Bristol who found 'Brasii' as your Lordship well knows." Cabot "found" the land the fishermen already knew about. Almost immediately after his return, men interested in geographical and commercial discoveries spread the news of the discovery of a sea "swarming with fish, which can be taken not only with the net, but in baskets let down with a stone. These same English, [Cabot's] companions, say that they could bring so many fish that this Kingdom would have no further need of Iceland."

Cabot should have paid more attention to the sensible Englishmen who realized the value of the fish. Instead he "has his mind set upon even greater things," a resident of England wrote back to Milan. Cabot thought he had found the coast of Asia and that he only needed to sail further along it "until he reaches an island which he calls Cipengo, situated in the equinoctial region, where he believes that all the spices of the world have their origin, as well as the jewels." Cabot managed to raise money from Henry VII and from some London and Bristol merchants to equip an expedition of five ships. It sailed for "Cipengo" in 1498. Four of the ships, and Cabot himself, never returned. The fifth did not find

Cipengo. This first recorded Canadian business venture ended in dismal failure.

Some of Cabot's backers and sons kept the dream of discovering and colonizing wealthy new lands alive. In the early 1500s one ship after another left Bristol for the "newe founde launde," some of them under a royal patent given to men who organized as a corporate body, the Company of Adventurers to the New Found Land. Fishing soon became the only justification for such expeditions, for the land was not Asia and contained nothing of value to the Europeans. The 216 barrels of salt fish brought back to Bristol by Hugh Elyot's *Gabriel* in 1502, however, fetched £180,* which was probably close to the cost of the voyage. Two years later Elyot began doing his Canadian business on credit when he borrowed £50 for one year from Henry VII, arranging to have a prominent London goldsmith guarantee his note. The *Gabriel* and the *Jesus* brought back 240 barrels of salt fish and 7 tuns of oil-rich fish livers. This loan was repaid from the profitable voyage, but Elyot soon found that fishing could not carry the costs of exploring on the side. He failed to pay his outfitters and the Company of Adventurers disintegrated in lawsuits.

The English soon stopped trying to explore the new lands they had found. For about seventy years they even seemed to have stopped fishing there. The fishermen's westward diversion from the traditional Icelandic fishing grounds was apparently premature. English demand could be met adequately and at lower cost from waters much closer to home.

The economics of fishing were different for other European nations, whose entrepreneurs sailed in to exploit the new resource. By 1512 Normans, Bretons, and Basques were fishing in the New World. In 1517, only twenty years after Cabot's voyage, it was estimated that one hundred European vessels visited the Newfoundland fishery annually. On 3 August 1527 there were eleven Norman, one Breton, and two Portuguese fishing vessels in the harbour which became St. John's. When the French explorer Jacques Cartier voyaged to the Gulf of St. Lawrence in the 1530s, he was following well-travelled fishermen's routes.

In the late 1570s an English merchant, Anthony Parkhurst, who had been to Newfoundland, estimated that the fishery involved four hundred Portuguese, Spanish, French, and English ships. Having had more problems with the rulers of Iceland, the English themselves were back in the New World, sending out scores of vessels from their West Country ports. By the end of the century some twelve to seventeen thousand men were crossing the ocean to fish every year. The Newfoundland fishery was the vital centre of New World economic activity in the northern hemisphere. There were no permanent settlements north of Florida, but Europe was making a huge investment in the task of harvesting North American wealth.

* On a rough calculation, one British pound in the sixteenth century had the purchasing power of $10 Canadian in 1914, or about $150 today.

The fishery was as free as enterprise could be. Nobody owned or controlled the fish. The small venturer was not excluded by his lack of capital (a man who risked his money, sometimes along with his life, was a venturer or adventurer; thus the designation of early risk-taking groups as companies of adventurers). It was not prohibitively expensive to charter and outfit a small ship – of perhaps seventy to one hundred tons – capable of crossing to the fishing grounds. The ship was worth about £200; victualling an expedition, including fishing gear and salt, cost about £425 for a nine-month voyage. The captain and crew, about forty men, were paid from the proceeds of the catch, dividing a one-third share.

The risks of a sixteenth-century fishing venture were unthinkably high by our standards. For people whose daily lives were not far from being nasty, brutish, and short, they were more tolerable – "scarce one man in fifty dying whilst on the fishery" – and were much less than the perils of the longer deep-sea voyages to the East or West Indies. In England the Atlantic fishery was soon recognized as a kind of training ground for seamen, who could be pressed into the navy in time of war.

The investor or merchant adventurer could limit his pecuniary risk in several ways. Ownership of a vessel was commonly divided into as many as sixty-four parts, with merchants limiting and spreading their commitments. In France or England an owner or victualler who wanted to make a substantial investment in a voyage might borrow money "on bottomry." He would effectively mortgage his interest in the voyage to the lender, but the lender would take the loss if the ship failed to return. As early as 1580 Englishmen had created complex financial networks to spread the risk still further:

> In the West countrey . . . the fishermen conferres with the money man, who furnisheth them with money to provide victualls, salte & all other needefull thinges to be paied twentie five pounde at the shippes returne, upon the hundreth pound in money lent. And some of the some money men doth borowe money upon ten pounde in the hundreth pounde, and put it forthe in this order to the fishermen. And for to be assured of the money ventured, they will have it assured, gevying six pounds for the assuring of every hundreth pounde to hym that abides the venture of the Shippes returne.

Marine insurance was developing as a specialized business during the sixteenth century. By the 1600s it had become common for British ships to be insured. The earliest known copy of an insurance policy was written to cover fish brought back from Newfoundland by the *Hopewell* of London in 1604. The insured risks were "of the Seas men of warre, Fier, Enemies, Pirates, Robers, Theeves, Jettesons, Letters of mark and counter Mark, Arrestes, Restraints and detaynements of kinges and princes and of all other persons. . . ." The premium was 7 per cent of the cargo's value. The early marine insurers spread their risks, and they seldom insured to full value, believing that an adventurer should bear some of the risk himself.

The fishermen came to North America for the cod that feed and flourish where the Labrador current and the Gulf Stream create favourable conditions of temperature and food supply. Cod was replacing salmon and herring as the staple fish of the European diet, "the beef of the sea." Its flesh was rich and high in protein, and could be easily preserved by some combination of salting and drying. Along the Atlantic seaboard for many centuries the word "fish" meant cod.

It was possible for fishermen to cross the ocean, salt the fish in their holds as it was caught, and sail home without catching sight of land. This was the practice of what came to be called the *green* or *wet* fishery. Another method developed by which fish were brought to shore and spread out to dry, then preserved with a much lighter salt cure. This was the basic technique of the *dry* fishery. British fishermen soon came to specialize in dry fishing, using the southeastern bays and coves of Newfoundland's Avalon peninsula as their base. Economic historians have argued that the lack of cheap domestic salt supplies forced the British to use this method.

Another factor stimulating the dry fishery seems to have been the need to match product to markets. There was not always a steady demand for New-foundland fish in Protestant, meat-eating Britain. The British presence in the Newfoundland fishery came to depend on the development of foreign and specialty markets. British fishermen found outlets for their cod in southern Spain and Portugal, Catholic and warm countries where the dry-salted product kept well. Dry-cured fish also became an important ration for Elizabethan seamen on their not always pacific voyages to warmer climates.

After the defeat of the Spanish Armada in 1588 and with the decline of Por-tugal as a maritime power, the Newfoundland fishery became dominated by English and French seamen. For the next century a huge British fleet of two to five hundred ships a year, most from a handful of West Country ports, migrated west in the spring, worked the Newfoundland fishery all summer, and raced home in the autumn gales. The French fleet was perhaps a bit larger, but came from more scattered ports and tended to disperse itself more widely along the shores of Newfoundland, the Gulf of St. Lawrence, and Nova Scotia.

Specialization and diversification developed quickly, particularly in the British dry fishery. West Country ships came across carrying many small boats and extra hands to man them. The mother ship put up for the season in a Newfoundland cove; the men set to work building fishing stages (wharfs), whatever shacks and sheds they needed, and the long wooden flakes (platforms) for drying fish. Then they would take to the small boats and go fishing, using hand lines. When the boats came in at the end of each day, a primitive disassembly process began. It involved a division of labour, the collecting of by-products, and the automatic disposal of waste:

> They bring the fish to the stage head, the foreshipman goes to boil their kettle, and the other two throw up the fish on the stage-head by... a staff with a prong of iron in him, which they stick in the fish and throw them up. Then a boy takes them and lays them on a table in the stage, on one side of which stands a header, who opens the belly, takes out the liver, and twines off the head and guts (which fall through the stage and into the sea) with notable dexterity and suddenness. The liver runs through a hole in the table, into a coole or great tub, which is thrown into the train fatt.
>
> When the header has done his work, he thrusts the fish to the other side of the table, where sits a spilter or splitter, who with a strong knife splits it abroad, and with a back stroke cuts off the bone, which falls through a hole into the sea.
>
> When the fish is split, he falls into a drooge barrow, which, when full, is drawn to one side of the stage, where boys lay it one on top of another. The salter comes with salt on a wooden shovel and with a little brush stews the salt on it. When a pole is about 3 foot high they begin with another.

The fish were spread out on the flakes to dry, turned, salted, and piled, turned and piled again.

A crew of West Country fishermen could catch more fish in a season than the mother ship could carry back. By the mid-1600s big "sack" ships, freighters which originally carried wines from Europe to England, would put into Newfoundland harbours to take on cargoes of fish. Sometimes the fish was bought in England while it was still in the New World. These cargoes never got to England, but were taken directly to Iberian and Mediterranean ports to be exchanged for sugar and spices, tropical fruits, wines, and other products. Thus the fishery "earned" valuable goods for England. At the end of the season the fishermen would relaunch their main ship, fill it with the last few weeks' catch, and scurry home.

French fishermen pioneered the systematic exploitation of the great offshore banks, shallows of the continental shelf as far as two hundred miles offshore. Hundred-ton bankers left the ports of Normandy and Brittany as early as January and never touched land. The sight of flocks of birds told the seamen they had arrived on the Banks. Soundings confirmed the location, and a ship would simply drift with the wind and currents while the men fished. Harold Innis, the noted economic historian who first emphasized the role of fish in Canada's economic evolution, described the activity:

> Outboard staging was built along one side of the vessel, on which each fisherman placed a half hogshead reaching to the waist. A large leather

apron from the neck to the knees projected over the edge of the half hogs-head. The line was attached to it and the hook allowed to drop to about a fathom from the bottom and the lead to about two fathoms. With two lines, one cod was pulled up while the other was being put over the side. The tongue was taken out and kept as a means of counting the number caught by each man. Pieces of herring or cod entrails were used as bait. The catch might vary from nothing to between 15 and 200, or, exceptionally 350 or 400 a day, about the limit of a fisherman's capacity. Boys took the fish to those who dressed them . . . . With the approach of Lent, ships with as little as half or two thirds of a cargo set out with the fish for the Paris market, for the first arrivals got the best prices for the new cod. They might, by arriving early, return for a second voyage and still be in time for the Lenten sale. The Bank fishery was usually completed by the end of May.

The French also engaged in dry fishing, but had lost the best drying locations to the British. Much of Newfoundland, though, as well as the coasts of Cape Breton and Nova Scotia and the Gaspé (land known to them as Acadia) was visited by French fishermen. From at least the 1540s, Spanish and French Basques specialized in whaling, establishing their tryworks for producing whale oil at stations in the Gulf and along the Labrador shore of the Strait of Belle Isle. These early oilmen used some of the largest ships afloat to transport their product back to Europe. Single cargoes brought to Spanish Basque ports consisted of five hundred to two thousand barrels of whale oil, each barrel weighing three hundred pounds. With the decline of Spain in the sixteenth century, though, the Basque whaling stations effectively disappeared.

It was a migratory industry, men coming in the spring, gathering their products in the summer, and going home in the fall. The wealth was in the sea. Most of the land, especially the New-found-land nearest the fishing grounds, had nothing to offer in the way of resources other than fresh water and wood. In Central and South America the Spanish conquistadors were finding fabulous hordes of gold and silver. The earliest English description of the resource potential of any part of the modern Canadian land mass was written in 1541 by Roger Barlow of Bristol. He dismissed Newfoundland as being too far north to have any wealth:

What comoditie is within this land as yet it is not knowen for it hath not been labored, but it is to be presupposed that there is no riches of gold, spyces nor preciose stones, for it stondeth farre aparted from the equinoctiall whereas the influens of the sonne doth norishe and bryng fourth gold, spices, stones and perles. But whereas our englishe marchantes of brystowe dyd enterpryse to discover and discovered that parte of the land, if at that season thei had folowed toward the equinoctiall, no dowt but their shuld have founde grete riches of gold and perle as other nations hathe done sence that tyme.

Cold facts did not chill the ardour of men seeking wealth. Fishing should not be the be-all and end-all. Throughout the sixteenth century promoters in the Cabot tradition continued to dream of other resources on or near those northern shores. If the westward passage to the riches of the Orient was blocked by the land mass, for example, why not find a northwest passage around it? John Cabot's son, Sebastian, was the first to seek the Northwest Passage. He failed, as did everyone who followed him during the next four hundred years. Jacques Cartier discovered the St. Lawrence in the 1530s and sailed a considerable distance up it looking for the westward passage to China. Cartier reported favourably on the lands he discovered in the area the Indians called Kanata – that they contained abundant wildlife and friendly natives with whom it was possible to trade. Better still, Cartier thought he found "a goodly Myne of the best yron in the world," "certain leaves of fine gold as thicks as a mans nayle," "stones like Diamants, the most faire, polished and excellently cast that it is possible for a man to see." And more: the natives told Cartier about a fabulous Kingdom of the Saguenay, apparently not far up one of the northern rivers "where there are infinite quantities of gold, rubies and riches and where there are white men, as in France, dressed in woollen cloth." It seemed that the northern lands were not barren at all.

Cartier's mineralogical knowledge was non-existent. So was the Kingdom of the Saguenay, an invention of Indians playing intricate games with the gullible whites. We have memorialized Cartier's high hopes in the names of Cape Diamond at Quebec City, and the Lachine Rapids, which block the westward passage up the St. Lawrence.

The most extravagant English hopes were raised by the first voyage of Martin Frobisher, a privateer/pirate in the grand Elizabethan tradition who obtained merchant backing for a 1576 search for the Northwest Passage to Cathay. Frobisher returned to announce that he had found the route, a new strait leading to the East, *and* gold along its shores. When an assay apparently confirmed gold in Frobisher's stones, venturesome Englishmen quickly formed a Company of Cathay. The crown contributed £1,000 plus the loan of a ship, the *Ayde* (the beginnings of state aid to enterprise?). Frobisher was appointed Admiral of Cathay. When the second expedition brought back two hundred tons of ore, the company immediately planned a large-scale development and organized a fifteen-ship expedition costing £20,000. Some 120 colonists, bringing with them a prefabricated building, were going to found a permanent mining settlement.

Losses of supplies on the voyage across made it too risky to leave the colonists, but the two thousand tons of ore brought back by Frobisher's fleet seemed to justify the investors' hopes. When they reached England, however, Frobisher and his miners learned that no gold or silver had been extracted from their earlier rocks. Previous assays had apparently been faked; all the ore was worthless. The Cathay Company went bankrupt, and Frobisher's principal merchant backer went to debtor's prison.

Frobisher had fathered the first speculation in Canadian minerals, the first Canadian mining fraud, and the first failure of the northern rocks. His abandoned mine, also Canada's first, can still be seen in Frobisher Bay – it is not a strait – on Baffin Island. He had not found the Northwest Passage either. Martin Frobisher abandoned mining to resume a profitable career as a pirate.

Other Elizabethan promoters concentrated their enthusiasm on Newfoundland. The merchant Anthony Parkhurst went out each year with his fishing ship and spent most of his time on shore, studying the island "much more than any other Englishman hath done." About the time of Frobisher's fiasco, Parkhurst published two letters urging the settlement of Newfoundland, where he believed crops could be grown and iron could be mined and smelted. More important, Parkhurst argued, was the fact that permanent residents of Newfoundland could make the fishery "twyse, ye thryse, as good as yet yt ys." The settlers could make preparations for each season's fishing, freeing the migrants to do nothing but fish. Moreover, Parkhurst thought that English power concentrated on the island could be used to monopolize the produce of the waters. Competitors could be driven away or taxed. "We shall be lordes of the whole fishing in small time."

Acting on a broad charter from Elizabeth to found a colony in the New World, Sir Humphrey Gilbert made England's first claim to foreign soil when he landed at St. John's in 1583 and formally annexed the land for the Queen and himself. Then he issued fishing licences to each of the thirty-six vessels in the harbour and tried to levy contributions in kind to resupply his ship. The assertion of sovereignty had led immediately to regulations and taxes. But it had no lasting impact, because Humphrey Gilbert, who had grand plans to expand his ventures in 1584, went down with his ship on the way home.

The freedom of the fishery had been taken for granted before government appeared. There was enough fish for all, and at first it seemed there were enough coves on shore, enough beaches and freshwater streams and trees for the fishermen of all nations to supply their wants without interfering with one another. In fact the resources on shore were limited: some coves and beaches were better than others as harbours and sites for stages and drying flakes. The sparse forest cover was quickly destroyed around busy harbours, creating a wood problem. Moreover, fishermen naturally began leaving some of their crude facilities in place over winters, hoping to make use of them the next year. They had no assurance that others would not arrive first, take the best anchorage, the best drying-room on the beach, and use whatever stages and flakes had been left from the year before.

Wide-open competition for onshore facilities created a rush to be first into a cove. Fishing ships would leave their home ports in foul winter weather, dodge icebergs in the North Atlantic, and lower their boats miles from shore to race to a landing. Someone had to begin keeping order because otherwise no one's property – no one's life – would be safe. The custom gradually developed of giving the captain of the first ship into a harbour the right to set rules for the others. These "fishing admirals" provided government on Newfoundland for many generations. It was rough and ready administration, sometimes no government at all according to critics. Richard Whitbourne reported to the Admiralty in 1615, for example, that a state of near anarchy existed in the Newfoundland fishery:

> Many men yeerely... unlawfully convey away other man's fishing boats from the harbour and place where they were left the yeere before; and some cut out the markes of them; and some others rippe and carry away the pieces of them, to the great prejudice and hindrance of the voyages of such ships that depent on such fishing boates and also to the true owners of such boats.... Some arriving there first, rippe and pull downe stages for the splitting and salting of fish... other stages [are] set on fire.... Some who arriving first... take away other men's salt... left the yeere before, rip and spoile the vats.... Some men likewise steale away the bait out of other men's nets by night and also out of their fishing boates by their ships side, whereby their fishing... is overthrown for the nest day.... some men rip and take away timber and rayles from stages and other necessary roomes... fastened with nailes, spike or trey naile, and some take away the rindes and turfe [used as roofing]....

This was what fishermen did to each other. Other menaces to the industry came from pirates, privateers, and foreign navies. During wartime, which was frequent, it became profitable for seafaring adventurers to obtain letters of marque from their monarchs which licensed them as private raiders or privateers. Fishing ships were easy and frequent catches. Occasionally the British navy had to convoy the fishing fleet to or from Newfoundland.

Settlement on Newfoundland was also seen as a potential menace to the fishery. We would expect the fishing ships to have begun leaving men on the island to maintain installations and gear and get a head start on the next season's catch. For many decades, though, year-round occupation of Newfoundland was virtually prohibited by the difficulty and cost of surviving the harsh winters in the bleak land. It was easier, cheaper, and healthier to cross the ocean twice a year rather than try to winter in the New World. Wintering fishermen were also apt to antagonize other fishermen, for men permanently on the spot seemed bound to claim the best of everything for themselves, that is to monopolize resources which customarily were competed for anew each spring. Migratory fishermen were strongly biased against settlement as an infringement on their traditional freedoms.

The West Country fishermen wanted more rather than less freedom. In the early 1600s their leaders became involved in the first serious English debate on free trade versus state regulation when they sided with other provincial merchants to challenge the system of granting trade monopolies to chartered companies. The Mediterranean fish trade was at stake, as big London trading companies were attempting to monopolize the sale of all English products in certain foreign markets. The Londoners complained of destructive price-cutting by independent traders, such as the West Countrymen who sent fish directly from Newfoundland to the Mediterranean at less than half the price the Londoners were trying to get for the same product routed through them. This fight between free trade and monopoly, which pre-dated Adam Smith and liberal economics by almost two centuries, ended in important gains for the West Countrymen, who received complete liberty to trade with France, Portugal, and Spain.

A new threat to their livelihood arose about the same time. Organized capital, taking advantage of the prerogatives available to chartered companies, began moving in on Newfoundland and the fisheries themselves. Parkhurst's idea of a settlement that would support itself by fishing and developing Newfoundland's other resources had persisted. In 1610 it took corporate form with the chartering of the London and Bristol Company for the plantation of Newfoundland. There were forty-eight subscribers to the company, including many prominent London merchants, and the scheme was rooted in the same expansionist impulse as simultaneous colonization attempts in Virginia and then New England. The London and Bristol Company was granted the entire Avalon peninsula of Newfoundland – but was required to respect the freedom of the fishery – and in 1610 sent out thirty-nine colonists and a governor, John Guy. Arriving safely, they built a habitation at Cupids Cove in Conception Bay.

The colonists had ambitious plans to plant crops, build saw and grist mills, and mine and smelt iron. One of their principal backers was a speculator in British coal mines and foundries, Sir Percival Willoughby, who hoped to see great developments based on the iron ore known to exist on Bell Island in Conception Bay. He forced his reluctant, wastrel son, Thomas, to join the business by going out with the colonists.

The whole Cupids settlement soon failed. Its only profitable enterprise was fishing, which succeeded largely because, as Guy wrote, the settlers were "first here every year to take what stage they shall have need of for their own use." Guy also tried to regulate the other fishermen, largely to keep them from despoiling each other's property and the Island's forests, but he and his colonists were themselves roundly suspected and disliked. Most of the colonists eventually fled to England or moved to other tiny settlements, a few of which now eked out a more or less continuous existence. Guy returned to England to continue his mercantile career and grumble about the lack of state support for the Cupids venture. The Virginia Company had been effectively bailed out by the crown, which judged it as a kind of national enterprise. "The plantation of Newfoundland," Guy complained in 1621, "never had penny help, but from the adventurers' purses, nor ever had any lotteries."

The London and Bristol Company disappeared. Among its last traces in history are Sir Percival Willoughby's attempts to get Bell Island granted to himself so he could develop an iron industry. Three centuries premature in his hopes, Willoughby never heeded his son's sensible suggestion – "if efver you looke for money agayne in this country, you must send fisher men."

As other settlements developed on the island, some with the state's blessing, others independently, the migratory fishermen became more determined to protect their interests. They turned to the state to guarantee their freedom, developing a powerful lobby in Parliament against settlement on Newfoundland. They seemed to have won a great victory in 1634 in what came to be called the West Country Charter, guaranteeing freedom of the fishery within a structure of sensible regulations. Already, though, the issues to be handled by regulation were remarkably complex. The need to conserve trees, for example, led to a prohibition on the use of bark "either for the seelinge of shippse houldes, or for roomes on shoare, or for any other uses, except for the coveringe of the roofes for cookeroomes to dress their meate in, and those roomes not to extend above six-teene foote in length at most." Such regulations were palatable because they were patently unenforceable.

The West Country fishermen used their influence to resist the encroachments of other "planters" in Newfoundland. One of the most aggressive of these was David Kirke, an adventurer and privateer who in 1628 had captured Quebec from the French and ruled it profitably for several years. Kirke settled in the southern shore at Ferryland in 1638, having procured a patent from the King. The patent contained elaborate clauses to stop settlers interfering with fishermen. Kirke tried to license English fishermen anyway, and to tax foreign fishing ships. Fishermen's petitions against his "insolences and oppressions" finally led to Kirke's being called back to England. "The victory of the fishermen over monopoly was complete," Innis comments.

In a way it was. But the industry was changing so quickly that it soon became unclear exactly who was interested in free trade and who wanted a monopoly. David Kirke and other settlers began to argue that the West Countrymen themselves were the monopolists, using their political power to keep competitors literally off Newfoundland's shores. Kirke's ventures may have included offensive interference with the fishermen, but he also engaged in new trading practices: selling supplies brought out from England, buying fish on the spot, arranging the export of cargoes to England. And he established Newfoundland's first taverns to slake the thirsts of the fishermen. After Kirke's death his widow lived on in Ferryland where, with her several sons, she became the first female entrepreneur in Canada, employing twelve boats and more than sixty men.

It was proving impossible to prevent the emergence of these and other new approaches to the fishing business. Because the English fishery was based on the land and not done from the ships that came out each season, a new kind of fisherman-entrepreneur gradually developed who was neither settler nor connected with a fishing ship. These "bye-boatmen" were independents who would book passage on a fishing ship, often accompanied by men in their employ, and on arrival in Newfoundland organize fishing ventures of their own, building small boats or using boats put "by" from previous years. They had little trouble selling their catch, and their enterprises often shaded into operations carried out in partnership with the planters.

Captain John Smith reported during the early 1600s that the Newfoundland fishing was being overdone: "New found land dothe yearely fraught neere 800 sayle of ships with a sillie leane skinny poore John and codfish; which at least yearcly amounts to 3 or 400,000 pound . . . yct all is so ovcrlaidc with fishcrs as the fishing decayeth and many are constrained to return with a small fraught." Smith's interest, and that of a growing number of others, was in harvesting cod further south, along the shores of New England. That fishery was originally migratory, too, based on Plymouth, England; but the first settlers, including the Pilgrims, took to fishing as a staple of their economic life. With a better climate and richer land resources than the Newfoundland settlers enjoyed, finding too that they could fish all year round, the New Englanders prospered and their settlements rapidly outpaced the communities to the north. Soon New England seamen were themselves fishing in Newfoundland waters, though often they would simply buy fish in return for provisions and supplies they had brought out from England. This expansion of trade and the growing competition within the industry increased the settlers' competitive advantage over the West Country migrants. So did the disruption of war, whethcr civil as in thc 1640s, or bctween nations on the high seas, which invariably raised the cost of the annual fishing voyages (and also made it convenient for fishermen to winter in Newfoundland well away from the Royal Navy's press gangs).

The old view that there was a sharp, total clash of interests between the West Countrymen and the settlers in Newfoundland neglects the ways in which some of the West Country merchants adapted to new conditions in the business. Some came to specialize in sending out provisions and bringing back fish, or in supplying or employing the bye-boatmen. Others made contacts with planters or developed their own permanent installations on the island (winter caretakers evolved into agents or merchants in their own right). Some moved offshore and continued seasonal transatlantic fishing as bankers.

Many fishermen wanted to carry on the business in the old way, and became ever more determined to rely on political influence to protect them from competition. In presenting their case, these arch-conservative "Western Adventurers" attempted to legitimize their demands for special privileges: pointing to their industry's contributions to the reserve of naval manpower; instancing its importance to West Country industries and employment; urging that the wealth of the fishery should flow to England rather than Newfoundland or New England; claiming poverty, as in 1669: "for many years past few have made 10 per cent on this fishery and last year both Dartmouth and Plymouth lost considerably." For several decades in the late 1600s, the West Country lobby was able to procure one regulation after another aimed at crippling its competition. Ships were forbidden to transport bye-boatmen to Newfoundland; masters were required to bring back everyone they had taken out. Inhabitants of Newfoundland were forbidden to "inhabit or plant within six miles of shore"; they were encouraged to leave the island, and then by an order-in council of 1675 *required* to leave. It was thus official British policy to depopulate Newfoundland in the interests of the migratory fishery.

None of the regulations was effective. The most severe, that of 1675, was suspended two years later. After many representations from the Newfoundlanders and others, the British government gradually realized that the West Country lobby had become a reactionary body whose insistence on inhibiting change in the fishery was not necessarily in any interest but their own. A period of prolonged warfare at the end of the seventeenth century, coinciding with the first years when the catch was not abundant, helped break the residual power of the West Countrymen. The rule of the fishing admirals would continue in Newfoundland ports for several more decades, and there would be many more rounds of conflict between migratory fishermen and settlers. It was not until the 1820s that an indigenous merchant community developed in St. John's to break the power of old country firms in the outports. Dreams of developing other industries on Newfoundland would not materialize for generations, except for the opening of related maritime enterprises in salmon fishing and hunting seals.

Through the logic of the fishery alone, settlement become established on the shores of Newfoundland, and would continue to grow. It took almost three centuries, but the first Canadian industry, originated and controlled from abroad, was gradually taken over by the locals.

UPPER LEFT: **Jacques Cartier** *(Natural Sciences Library (NSL) Archive)*
UPPER RIGHT: **Martin Frobisher** *(NSL Archive)*
ABOVE: **Flensing a whale** *(Metropolitan Toronto Library Board)*

Beaver hunting in Canada, 1760 *(Hudson's Bay Company)*

2

The First Businessmen:
Indians and the Fur Trade

*Close trading encounters . . . whites exploited . . . competition for
furs . . . monopolies fail . . . native traders " trop fins et subtils" . . .
Champlain . . . coureurs de bois . . . failure of state controls and fixed
prices . . . governors in business . . . Frontenac . . . La Salle . . . Cadillac
builds Detroit . . . an approach through Hudson Bay . . . eau de vie disrupts
the balance.*

Jacques Cartier wrote the first account of business transactions on Canadian soil. He described an encounter with a group of Micmac Indians in the Baie de Chaleur in July 1534.

The natives took the initiative in trying to open trade with the Europeans. They made signs for the whites to come on shore, advertising their interest by "holding up to us some furs on sticks." When the whites would not land, the Indians came out in their canoes, so many of them that the frightened explorers, who had no special wish to barter, fired their guns to scare the strangers away. The Indians persisted in their desire to trade, trying again the next day. The Europeans finally cooperated:

> . . . we went with our two long-boats to the point where they were, at the mouth of the cove. As soon as they saw us they began to run away, making signs that they had come to barter with us; and held up some furs of small value, with which they clothe themselves. We likewise made signs to them that we wished them no harm, and sent two men on shore, to offer them some knives and other iron goods, and a red cap to give to their chief. Seeing this, they sent on shore part of their people with some of their furs; and the two parties traded together. The savages showed a marvellously great pleasure in possessing and obtaining these iron wares and other commodities, dancing and going through many ceremonies, and throwing salt water over their heads

with their hands. They bartered all they had to such an extent that all went back naked without anything on them; and they made signs to us that they would return on the morrow with more furs.

The morrow's trade progressed in an atmosphere of dancing, singing, and celebration. The "savages" again traded away everything they owned – "which was, all told, of little value," Cartier commented sourly. Other bands of Indians whom he met later in his voyage were also interested in trading and celebrating. Cartier was more interested in claiming land for France, finding the way to China, and kidnapping Indians to take home with him.

The natives' eagerness to trade with Cartier suggests that trading relations were already established along the northeastern coast. Fishermen and natives had probably met and exchanged goods many times. Thus the Micmac assumption that the whites wanted to trade. Another possibility is that the Micmac band traded regularly with other tribes of Indians and simply assumed this white tribe would want to do the same.

Many explorers' accounts of Indian-white trade, including Columbus's, suggest that the natives gave up a lot (Cartier's Micmacs traded the skins off their backs) for very little – a few knives and iron goods and other cheap trinkets. They surely got the worst of the dealing, we usually assume. Our modern guilt about the plight of the native in white North America leads to a common assumption that European-Indian trade meant cheating or exploiting natives who were ignorant, gullible, or just weak.

This is a patronizing, ethnocentric view, which neglects the elementary fact of economic life that values and prices are relative. The cheap knives, kettles, and hatchets of iron-age Europe were wonderfully effective and valuable implements to people of a stone-age culture. Think about the value of an iron kettle to people who had, at the best, earthenware pots. Think about the cutting power of iron knives and axes, the killing power of the white man's firearms. These were awesome tools and weapons, worth many animal skins. Even Cartier was not sure this first trading had been in his favour, for he did not think the furs he acquired were worth much. The Indians were so happy to trade with these rather timid whites because they were obviously getting the better of the deal. Who wouldn't celebrate at having instant, cheap access to wonderful new tools? And count the other costs later.

———

J ACQUES CARTIER was typical of his century's explorers in having his mind set on finding a route to Cathay or, second best, finding gold, silver, or diamonds. As with the fishing industry, more practical Europeans soon realized the value of the natural products that could be gathered in North America. Fine furs – sable, ermine, fox, marten, otter – had been worn in

Europe for centuries, as trimming and lining for the fine garments that adorned royalty, the nobility, and the high clergy. Fur-bearing animals were in decline in Europe by the 1400s, so skins had to be imported, often from Russia. Fishermen found they could sell the furs they brought back from the New World. So they traded with the natives for more furs, founding an industry which became geographically the most far-reaching in Canadian history. It was a business around which exploration, the mingling of peoples, the course of settlement, and many of the themes of politics, diplomacy, and warfare would revolve for the better part of three hundred years.

Many kinds of furs found uses in the first few generations of trading. A Basque ship captured by the English in 1591 was found to contain a cargo of fish, fish oil, and "greate Store of Riche fures as beavers, martenes otters and many other Sortes." "Sometimes they do bring back black fox skins," a correspondent wrote the Lord Treasurer of England, adding enthusiastically, "no such things to ease the pain of the gout." Skins sometimes became footwear, but by the late 1500s and through the next century and a half the most prized North American article was beaver fur. It was felted and made into fashionable hats.

Beavers abounded almost everywhere in North America. They were easily killed by the natives, who ate their flesh and used their furs for clothing well before the coming of the white man. In pre-contact years some sedentary tribes, such as the Huron nation (located southeast of Georgian Bay), did not gather enough skins for their needs. Instead they exchanged their surpluses of food with other tribes for furs. Trade in these and other goods, including crude copper and a primitive kind of currency, "wampum," seems to have been an established part of Amerindian life. When the white man came the natives were ready to trade with these new tribes that had such excellent products.

They did not feel they were getting the worst of the deal. Indians did not have much initial regard for the white man, who was not even strong and skilled enough to survive winters in the Indians' land; this native superiority complex seems to have included a belief that whites traded foolishly. A Montagnais brave told a Jesuit in 1634, for example, that "The Beaver does everything perfectly well. It makes kettles, hatchets, swords, knives, bread; and, in short, it makes everything." Another time the same Indian remarked on the lack of sense of traders who would offer twenty knives for a single beaver skin. He may have just been commenting on an absurdly high trading price – we will see that the Indians were very price-conscious – but other white preferences also seemed foolish. At most times, for example, the Europeans valued used beaver skins more highly than fresh ones. The trouble with *castor sec*, the fresh pelts, was that the long outer guard hairs were difficult to remove in felting. When natives wore the beaver furs these were rubbed off; the wearer's body oils also softened the short inner hairs, making them more pliable for felting.

Castor gras, or greasy beaver, then, was worth a higher price – which is to say that old clothes were worth more than new ones. Why were the French so greedy for the "old rags and . . . miserable suits of beaver which can no longer be of use to us?" a Micmac mused. Why did the French have to come so far to get fish for food, he also wondered, in the course of a long harangue in which he concluded, "There is no Indian who does not consider himself infinitely more happy and more powerful than the French."

<hr/>

The pattern of the fishery shaped the relative involvement of English and French in the fur trade. In confining themselves to Newfoundland, the English fishermen missed the rich possibilities in mainland furs (they did some fur trading on Newfoundland, but the native Beothuks there were skittish in their relations with whites and were much less aggressive traders than mainland tribes). French fishermen on the shores of the Gulf of St. Lawrence brought home the first valuable fur cargoes, and it was the prospect of furs that lured the French back into the St. Lawrence after the disappointing failures of Cartier's voyages. (The main legacy of the "cargo of illusions" that Cartier brought back from his last voyage was a proverb: "false as Canadian diamonds.")

As with fish, the earliest fur traders probably did all they could to hide the source of their wealth from potential competitors. But trade secrets are never easily kept. In 1582 a Breton syndicate made a profit of 1,400 to 1,500 per cent selling furs their ship had collected in North America to a Paris skinner. Three French ships brought back another fortune in furs the next year. Five trading ships sailed from St. Malo alone in 1584; ten planned to leave in 1585. By 1587 rival French fur traders at the mouth of the St. Lawrence were capturing and burning each other's ships in ferocious competition for the skins.

Governments had a better prospect of controlling the fur business than they did the unfencible, unfortifiable fishery. Cartier had claimed the shores of the St. Lawrence for the King of France, who had granted the explorer and his associates the land as a fiefdom or seigneury. Half a century later, when the fur trade had made the land profitable to visit again, a nephew of Cartier's promptly petitioned the King for a monopoly on the trade and commerce of Canada so he could carry on with Cartier's work and prerogatives.

The fur trade was like the fishery in not necessarily being a stimulus to settlement. Traders met the natives annually at designated places – Tadoussac at the mouth of the Saguenay was the first – did their business, and sailed home. Permanent settlements along the shores of the St. Lawrence were unlikely to be economic in their own right. Their creation was desired mainly for reasons of state. But the only way the state could induce adventurers to create a colony was to give them the incentive of a monopoly on the fur trade. This became the basic French strategy in the attempt to create settlements in New France (or "Canada," as the natives apparently called the land along the St. Lawrence): give a company of risk-takers a charter granting a fur monopoly in return for their commitment to create settlement, perhaps by bringing out a stipulated number of colonists.

Monopolies are seldom popular. The immediate effect of the first grant of monopoly, in 1588, was an outcry by the fur-trading merchants in France, demanding freedom of "traffic and commerce." The state backed away, effectively revoking the monopoly. But the desire to establish a firm French presence in North America was too great not to try again – and again, and again. As at most times in Canadian history, there was an ample supply of entrepreneurs willing to take the risk that a profitable bargain could be struck with the state. As Marcel Trudel comments, "a monopoly was too attractive a prize to be left lying untouched."

Exactly where a company would most advantageously found settlements was not immediately clear. Early attempts to sustain colonies on the Magdalen Islands in the Gulf of St. Lawrence and, of all places, that god-forsaken pile of sand known as Sable Island, seem to have been based on the locations' proximity to fishing grounds. Most of the men left at Tadoussac on the mainland in the winter of 1600–1601 died; a handful survived by living with nearby Indians. In his first trip to Canada in 1603, Samuel de Champlain travelled far enough up the St. Lawrence to realize that the natives used it as a trade route from the interior and to understand the desirability of upriver settlement. But then he was misled by the prospect of a milder climate further south, as well as Indian talk of the existence of mines in the country the French called Acadia. Consequently, when Pierre de Monts organized a substantial company to trade and settle in the New World (he was given a ten-year monopoly, raised 90,000 livres* from merchants in Rouen, St. Malo, La Rochelle, and St. Jean de Luz, and hired Champlain as geographer) the original settlement in 1604 was on the Ste Croix River, which empties into the Bay of Fundy. The first vessel the trader-settlers sighted after crossing the Atlantic belonged to fur traders who had sailed from the same French port and paid no attention to the monopoly.

Royal charters were almost meaningless. De Monts, Champlain, and company were beset by competitors seeking furs: Basque interlopers in Acadia, a Dutch company carrying on an illegal trade in the St. Lawrence, even one of their own shareholders sponsoring a surreptitious trading voyage to Tadoussac. The final blow came when the buyers back in France, the powerful guild of the Hatters' Corporation of Paris, protested against the monopoly. Instead of trying to enforce its commitment to the risk-takers, the French state replied to pressure by cancelling the monopoly.

More monopolies, more uncontrollable competition, more periods of officially free trade. Experiments in permitting colonizers like Champlain and de Monts to

* The French livre was worth about $7 to $10 in modern Canadian currency.

tax their competitors. "It was like trying to drink the sea," Champlain wrote. He and de Monts were back in the St. Lawrence region, where they founded a permanent habitation at Quebec in 1608. Contacts Champlain made in his journeys up the river led to new tribes paddling down to trade with the whites. Competitors promptly appeared, offered the Indians better prices, and sailed off with the bulk of the furs. "Thus had we done them the service of finding new nations in order that they might carry off all the booty without running any risk or taking any trouble," Champlain grumbled in the innovator's eternal complaint.

The phenomenon of the glutted market appeared in Tadoussac that year, 1610. The latest-arriving Europeans offered more trade goods than the Indians would take and suffered serious losses. Canada's pioneer historian, Marc Lescarbot, outlined the effects of excess competition along the Fundy coast in that same year: "so great has been the greed that in their jealousy of one another the merchants have spoiled the trade. Eight years ago for two biscuits or two knives, one had a bever, while today one must give fifteen or twenty and in this very year 1610 some have given away their whole stock in trade in order to obstruct the whole enterprise."

There was even more competition in 1611, with ships from France reaching Tadoussac while snow was on the ground and before Champlain got there from Quebec. The firstcomers' hopes of having won a competitive advantage by risking the Atlantic ice were dashed, for the natives refused to trade until more vessels arrived. The French always called the natives "sauvages," but found it costly to underestimate their capacity as traders: "ces peuples son maintenant trop fins et subtils" was the verdict in 1611.

All the evidence from every era and every location of the fur trade is that clear-headed Indians were shrewd businessmen. There was always a lot of ceremony, including much gift-giving, accompanying the fur trade, but of course a certain amount of socializing has accompanied trade in most cultures, including European. The important fact is that the natives understood the value of both the gifts and the furs they traded, and in the actual trading bargained according to the state of the market. In competitive situations where they had an upper hand they raised the price of their furs (as measured in trade goods). They were quality-conscious, either adjusting their price according to quality or simply refusing to deal in substandard goods. They knew that white men competed with each other, and they would play one trader off against another, even, as we will see, when the traders' posts were hundreds of miles apart. Whites who liked to think of the natives as simply fur-gatherers who killed beavers and brought their skins in to trade gradually realized that some natives were acting as fur merchants or middlemen. It was common for tribes in direct contact with whites to trade with more remote bands, receiving their furs and passing on the white man's goods, always at a profit. The ultimate Indian consumer of a European kettle or blanket might never have seen a white fur trader.

It is wrong, however, to think of the Indians as property-conscious accumulators or a proto-bourgeoisie. Some ethnologists and historians argue that native trading habits were so deeply embedded in their distinctive cultures that it makes no sense to write about fur trading as an activity which can be understood in terms of markets, prices, and competition. They see Indian trading as partly ceremonial, partly political or diplomatic, concerned more with acts of friendship and the forging of strategic alliances than material gain.

The burden of the evidence seems to weigh against parts of this view. Markets, prices, and competition did matter to native traders. But there is no doubt that most Indian perceptions of economic transactions were different from a market-oriented European viewpoint. The distribution of goods *within* most bands of Indians, for example, cannot be understood in conventional economic categories. The Hurons, for instance, were skilled traders with other tribes before contact and with the French from an early date. But there was no barter or trade, as we understand it, among the Hurons themselves. Gift-giving, ceremonies, complex kin and status and sharing relationships were among the factors that controlled transactions within the tribe. Nor were individualism and acquisitiveness evident in the market confrontation with Europeans: Indians of the same band would not compete with one another the way it must have seemed the Europeans did.

The natives obviously valued European products. Some tribes became dependent on the advanced technology now available to them, and soon forgot old skills. It is fair to say that within a few decades of contact some North American Indians were no longer able to survive without the products they obtained in the fur trade. This dependency on trade and technology did not have to be catastrophic to native people, any more than it is catastrophic to North Americans today (who would have trouble surviving without electricity, computer chips, or Japan). So long as the trading relationship – at best a partnership – could be maintained in rough balance, it could continue to be as mutually enriching as it obviously was in the early years of contact. Only if something went drastically wrong in the trade, such as a change in the balance of power or a failure of supply or demand, would doing business with the whites become a losing proposition.

In the early years many Indian tribes seem to have integrated the new partnership into their way of life without extreme disruption. There used to be an economic determinists' argument that virtually everything the Indian nations did after contact can be understood in terms of their lust for trade goods. In one widely read history, for example, all the wars of the Iroquois were explained as manoeuvres to enhance their trading position. In reality, native societies and politics were influenced by other, older considerations and values. These included traditional alliances and feuds as well as the institutionalization of tribal warfare as a rite of manhood. Morever, the native tribes varied greatly in their handling of European products and the fur trade. Beothuks in Newfoundland and Inuit almost everywhere, for example, tended either to avoid the white man or be actively hostile. European material culture did not spread as electrically through the tribes as some historians have assumed: many interior bands did perfectly well with their traditional implements and clothing and hunting patterns for generations after white trade goods entered the network. Similarly, in tribes such as the Hurons some braves were more businesslike than others. Certain families specialized in trading, often as a result of being the first to begin a relationship. Some individual Indians became particularly shrewd and energetic traders; others did not bargain very well. Many Indians, we will see, were tragically vulnerable to other aspects of the white man's ways.

———————◆———————

The most pressing problem for the white fur traders on the St. Lawrence continued to be how to limit competition. The French government wanted some traders to make money and then spend it bringing out settlers. In this situation, Samuel de Champlain introduced the merger to Canadian commerce. He became the leading spirit in a reorganization of the St. Lawrence trade in 1612–14 which saw most merchant-traders joining forces in a new, royally chartered, monopolistic Company of Canada. It was the first in a series of companies, including the Hundred Associates, the Company of Habitants, and the Company of New France, which all tried to make as much money as possible in the fur trade and did next to nothing to advance settlement. In 1663 the crown finally stepped in and turned New France into a royal colony.

Some years were profitable for the companies; other years were not. Historians used to speculate that the fur trade retarded the growth of settlement in New France. In fact there would have been no New France and no settlement without the fur trade, for the agricultural potential of the St. Lawrence valley was far below that of other parts of North America, and the northern climate was terrible. Ordinary Frenchmen had no interest in risking the north Atlantic to sicken, freeze, starve, and die in a howling wilderness. Only subsidies from fur trading, plus perhaps the prospect of getting a share in the fur wealth of Canada, made it possible for the companies to induce a few hundred settlers to come out in the years before 1660. They would not have been enough to maintain the colony as anything more than a string of trading posts. A non-economic development – an outburst of religious enthusiasm in France directed at converting the "sauvages" – was at least as important as the fur trade in drawing hundreds more from France to New France, including the missionary priests and nuns who would create a spiritual and institutional foundation for the new community. In 1642 the religious orders also founded Montreal, which the traders soon found to be better located for doing business than any of the other settlements.

The traders' chief problem was maintaining the flow of furs. The effects of reducing competition among Frenchmen were more than nullified by the growth of competition from English and Dutch traders operating out of New England and New Netherland. The Hudson River was almost as effective a water route into the interior as the St. Lawrence. By the 1620s Dutch traders at Fort Orange on the Hudson were attracting large numbers of skins that might otherwise have gone to the St. Lawrence. Similarly, the New Englanders traded up and down the Atlantic seaboard, mining the fur riches of the continent while gradually establishing their more varied, agriculturally based economy.

The new competitors complicated an already delicate situation between the French and conflicting tribes of natives. Ideally, the French fur traders would have been friends with all tribes, doing business with anyone who had furs to trade, encouraging Indians to spend their time killing beavers instead of each other. But Champlain had succumbed to Huron pressure to become an ally in their nation's campaigns against the Iroquois and had participated in bloody raids south of the Great Lakes. The French soon found they could not easily limit or control this involvement in Indian rivalries, and that it would not always work in their interests.

Champlain's muskets cowed the Iroquois, for example, no longer than it took them to trade for muskets from the Dutch. One reason why the fur trade was erratic and unpredictable in the 1640s and 1650s was the deadly effectiveness of Iroquois warfare on French trading partners, and on New France itself. A Jesuit chronicler in 1653 described the impact of war on the Canadian commerce:

> Never were there more beaver in our lakes and rivers, but never have there been fewer seen in the warehouses of the country. Before the devastations of the Hurons, a hundred canoes used to come to trade, all laden with beaver skins: the Algonquins brought them from all directions; and each year we have had two or three hundred thousand livres worth. That was a fine revenue with which to satisfy all the people, and defray the heavy expenses of the country.
>
> The Iroquois war dried up all these springs. The Beavers are left in peace, and in the place of their repose: the Huron fleets no longer come down to trade: The Algonquins are depopulated: and the more distant nations are withdrawing still farther, fearing the fire of the Iroquois. For a year the warehouse at Montreal has not bought a single beaver skin from the Savages. At Three Rivers the little revenue that has accrued has been used to fortify the place, the enemy being expected there. In the Quebec warehouse there is nothing but poverty; and so everyone has become dissatisfied; there being no means to supply payment to those to whom it is due, or even to defray a part of the most necessary expenses of the country....
>
> But now, if God bless our hopes of peace with the Iroquois, a fine war will be made on the Beavers ... the country is not stripped of Beavers; they form its gold mines and its wealth.

Furs were originally traded at annual shoreside meetings between natives and whites, not unlike European trade fairs. In theory that system could have continued for many years as the most economic way of getting the pelts into European hands. Instead, the impact of war and other impediments, combined with the white man's competitive instincts and the French visitors' growing ability to travel like the Indians, gradually led French traders inland. The pioneering coureurs de bois or "runners of the woods," who travelled a few leagues up the Ottawa River from Montreal, could not have realized that they were beginning a process which would eventually see fur-trading expeditions set out from the same place to cross two-thirds of the continent.

The first Frenchmen to winter in the interior were young interpreters sent by Champlain to live with the natives (one of the symbols of the Indians' early control of the fur trade was the fact that the French tried to learn their language rather than vice versa). They came back with the Indian trading canoes in the spring. The original coureurs de bois seem to have been agents sent out to encourage Indians to trade and let them know where and when the whites could be found. The coureur did no trading himself, merely acting as guide for the native traders. But it was a natural progression to take a few trade goods upstream in your canoe, exchange them with natives who did not want to or could not come down (and would take a lower price to be saved the journey), and bring the canoe back full of furs. Here, in fact, was a perfect opportunity for individual entrepreneurship: any habitant in New France who had learned to paddle a canoe and could scrape together a few trade goods – perhaps through his seigneur – could disappear into the woods looking for Indians. The same phenomenon developed among settlers in New Netherland who came to be called *bosch-lopers*.

The appearance of the coureurs de bois complicated New France's fur business by making it impossible for the chartered company to handle the trade in one annual exchange at a fixed location. Along with Indians coming down to trade at Montreal warehouses, there were Frenchmen themselves seeking to exchange their furs, and the same and more Frenchmen wanting trade goods on credit. It was dangerous to turn away these white middlemen. Not only would they raise an outcry against monopoly, but, like the natives, they would not hesitate to deal with the English or Dutch competition. A monopoly on fur trading out of New France could not be maintained. The chartered companies evolved into buyers and exporters: taking furs from Indians who came down, from coureurs, sometimes from local merchants who had hired or outfitted coureurs, and then disposing of them in France. Like the fishery, the evolving fur trade forced constant adjustment.

Louis XIV made New France a royal colony in 1663 to establish it on a sounder footing. Not only did the aggressive Iroquois have to be beaten back, but the King's talented first minister, Jean-Baptiste Colbert, intended to make the St.

Lawrence settlement far more populous, less dependent on the vagaries of the fur trade, and more prosperous through having developed a balanced, diversified economy. Colbert distrusted the fur trade, believing it was likely to lead to flooded markets in France and expensive expansion in Canada. Instead, he proposed a kind of primitive industrial strategy for the colony of diversifying into agriculture and such other industries as shipbuilding, iron manufacture, and brewing. As in earlier attempts to induce settlement, the state was trying to force the pace of development.

Colbert's non-economic policies succeeded best. Troops from France pacified the Iroquois (for a time). Incentives to immigration and marriage and child-bearing led to rapid population growth, from about three thousand inhabitants in 1663 to ten thousand fifteen years later. Beyond that, there was little development unconnected with the fur trade. It was such an attractive commerce that all settlers became infected with a desire to dabble in furs. Furs were the most common medium of exchange in the colony. Even the Jesuits sometimes were in the business, if only by hiring the occasional coureurs to do some trading to help defray the costs of mission posts. Their enemies accused them of being more interested in converting beaver than Indians. And it was a Jesuit himself who reported the search of the room of an Ursuline nun one year, which yielded 260 pounds of illicit beaver skins.

One reason for the trade's pervasiveness in New France was the stimulus given by the last relic of monopoly, a controlled buying system. When the inhabitants refused to accept yet another monopolistic trading company, the crown opened the fur trade to everyone on condition that all pelts be sold to the royal agent (one-fourth of the beaver and one-tenth of the deerskins would be appropriated to defray the costs of government). Adventurous great merchants, sometimes in France, sometimes in New France, paid large sums of money to purchase the royal agency. It was not a wise investment, for the agent was required to take all the pelts offered in the colony at a price fixed by royal decree. The price-fixing was worked out largely at the behest of the leading colonial traders, and with an eye on the need to offer Indians better terms than the British or the Dutch.

High prices stimulated trading, attracting huge quantities of pelts. Failure to vary prices to take account of differing qualities of furs (in addition to the basic *castor gras* and *castor sec*, there could be *castor demi-gras d'hiver, castor gras d'été*, and other grades, as well as pelts whose weight was fraudulently increased by storage in damp cellars) meant that the King's agent was deluged with low-quality skins. Premium pelts tended to go to Dutch and English traders who would offer selective higher prices.

Canada's furs were sold in France. European demand for beaver had continued to expand as beaver hats reached a peak of fashion, came down in price into a less exclusive market, and were exported by France's skilled felters and hatters. But manufacturers soon found ways to adulterate the beaver used in hats, creating the popular *demi castor*. The tyranny of fashion swung in favour of smaller hats, also reducing the need for beaver. Attempts by royal agents to find new uses for beaver fur – one Paris firm proposed in 1687 to use beaver fur to make woollen clothing – failed. Fur exports were the lifeblood of New France, but the product was a relatively minor item in the French economy; its fluctuations in price and fashion were not of national interest. There was no guarantee, nor could there be, that prices received in France would bear a profitable relationship to the fixed prices being paid in New France.

Those who purchased the royal fur agency seldom did well. Aubert de la Chesnaye, whom we will meet again as New France's first millionaire, nearly lost everything when he bought control of the Canadian beaver trade from the French Compagnie de la Ferme in 1674 for a rental of 119,000 livres per year. Within three years Chesnaye had accumulated a debt of one million livres and had to be bailed out by the Compagnie. Its head, Jean Oudiette, became the first reviled plutocrat of Canadian history, criticized by everyone in New France for trying to obtain relief by buying fewer furs at lower prices. He finally went bankrupt.

French policy was to stop fur gluts and diversify the economy by limiting the activities of the local traders. Sometimes the inhabitants were prohibited from travelling among the Indians. Sometimes a system of licences or *congés* was used to try to limit the number of traders. Nothing worked, not least because hardly any of France's officials in New France wanted controls to work. From the first prominent governor, the Comte de Frontenac, and the first administrator (intendant), Jean Talon, on down and ever afterwards, France's men on the spot became committed to the expansion of the fur trade. The most basic reason for their enthusiasm was the investments that most of them made privately in fur-trading enterprises and then used their public offices to promote.

The idea that people with power should *not* use it to enrich themselves is a very modern notion. In the seventeenth and eighteenth centuries virtually all administrators of government – in Britain, France, and all their colonies – expected to gain personally from possession of their offices. Indeed, the prospect of gain was well understood to be one of the chief incentives to taking on state responsibilities. In New France office-holders were all fascinated by the prospects of involvement in the fur trade.

Louis de Buade, Comte de Frontenac, was a down-at-the-heels aristocrat, soldier, and courtier, whose extravagant lifestyle had put him deeply in debt. In 1672 he escaped from his creditors through being appointed governor general of New France. In two terms as governor (1672–82 and 1689–98, the interruption caused by his being recalled in disgrace), Frontenac spent a fair portion of his time scheming to advance his and his friends' interests in the fur trade, quarrelling violently with everyone who opposed or competed with him, and disobeying royal edicts against the commercial expansion he was directing under the guise of diplomacy and exploration.

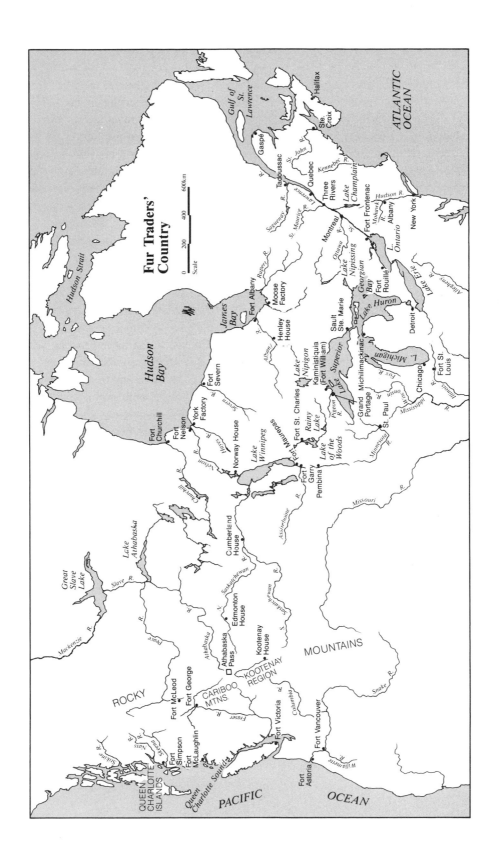

Fur Traders' Country

Scale
0 200 400 600 km

ATLANTIC OCEAN

PACIFIC OCEAN

Hudson Bay

Hudson Strait

James Bay

Gulf of St. Lawrence

Great Slave Lake

Lake Athabaska

Lake Winnipeg

Lake Nipigon

Lake Superior

Lake Michigan

Lake Huron

Georgian Bay

Lake Nipissing

Lake Champlain

L. Ontario

Lake Erie

Lake of the Woods

Rainy Lake

Lake St. Charles

QUEEN CHARLOTTE ISLANDS

Queen Charlotte Sound

ROCKY MOUNTAINS

CARIBOO MTNS.

KOOTENAY REGION

Athabaska Pass

Mackenzie R.

Peace R.

Slave R.

Athabaska R.

Saskatchewan R.

N. Saskatchewan R.

S. Saskatchewan R.

Assiniboine R.

Churchill R.

Nelson R.

Hayes R.

Severn R.

Albany R.

Rupert R.

Missouri R.

Minnesota R.

Mississippi R.

Wisconsin R.

Illinois R.

Fox R.

Snake R.

Columbia R.

Fraser R.

Willamette R.

Skeena R.

Nass R.

Stikine R.

Pigeon R.

Saguenay R.

St. Maurice R.

Ottawa R.

St. Lawrence R.

St. John R.

Kennebec R.

Hudson R.

Mohawk R.

Alleghany R.

Halifax

Ste. Croix

Gaspé

Tadoussac

Quebec

Three Rivers

Montreal

Fort Frontenac

New York

Albany

Fort Rouillé

Detroit

Fort St. Louis

Chicago

St. Paul

Sault Ste. Marie

Michilimackinac

Grand Portage

Kaministiquia (Fort William)

Fort Albany

Moose Factory

Henley House

Fort Severn

Fort Churchill

Fort Nelson

York Factory

Norway House

Cumberland House

Edmonton House

Kootenay House

Fort McLeod

Fort George

Fort Victoria

Fort Vancouver

Fort Astoria

Fort Simpson

Fort McLaughlin

Fort Garry

Pembina

Fort St. Charles

European traders moved farther and farther into what the French called the "pays d'en haut" (high country) after the first series of Iroquois wars was ended by regular French troops in the 1660s. Indian middlemen, who in theory might have brought furs out to market ports indefinitely, began having trouble competing with the coureurs de bois. Some of the trading tribes, such as the Hurons, had been effectively destroyed in war; other tribes were decimated and worse by the white men's most deadly import to North America, a plague of infectious diseases to which the natives had no initial immunity. The coureurs themselves became steadily more adept as travellers and traders in the bush. They journeyed thousands of miles in search of furs, by-passing several series of Indian middlemen, reaching new tribes and bringing furs to the St. Lawrence more quickly and efficiently than their native competitors. In the last third of the seventeenth century, French fur traders penetrated north, west, and south of the Great Lakes, eventually trading into the grasslands of the prairies and most of the way down the Mississippi.

Frontenac often sent out men to pre-empt new fur trading territory under the guise of exploration or military expeditions. As lines of transport and supply lengthened, it was natural to establish permanent posts in the interior, stationing men over the winter and resupplying them each summer. The military outposts of New France were often little more than fur-trading stations camouflaged by the presence of a few soldiers – whose officers ran the trade. Frontenac's first post, at Cataraqui on the eastern end of Lake Ontario, was founded by a protégé, René-Robert Cavelier de la Salle, who gratefully named it Fort Frontenac. The competitor whose business was hurt most by the post was the governor of Montreal, François Perrot. He was outraged by Frontenac's initiative because his own upriver trading post, about which Montreal merchants had complained bitterly, was now being by-passed. Frontenac responded to Perrot's remonstrations by having him arrested.

After Perrot returned from a trip to France to attempt to clear his name, spending time in the Bastille for his troubles, he and Frontenac entered into what W. J. Eccles calls "an uneasy alliance to further their illicit activities in the fur trade." Eccles continues:

> From this point on, when complaints were made against Perrot by the seigneurs and the people of Montreal, Frontenac quashed them. Thus protected, Perrot rode roughshod over the people of Montreal; any who protested against his attempts to garner the bulk of the fur trade for himself were beaten by his guards or thrown into gaol without trial and held there during Perrot's pleasure . . . .
>
> When the Ottawas came to Montreal to trade their furs he stationed his guards to prevent all but his own and Frontenac's men from trading with them. On one occasion he was reported to have traded the clothes off his

back [shades of the Micmacs] to an Indian who then paraded around the town in the governor's garb, and Perrot boasted that he had made a profit of 30 *pistoles* on the exchange. It was estimated that in 1680 alone he had made some 40,000 *livres* illegal profit in the fur trade and two years later it was reliably reported that he had realized 100,000 *livres* on the sale of beaver pelts at Niort in Poitou.

Vaguely familiar names from public school textbooks begin to appear as expansionary entrepreneurs of the fur trade. Cavelier de la Salle became the most famous of Frontenac's associates. Determined to expand from the Lake Ontario base at Fort Frontenac, La Salle built the first Great Lakes ship, the *Griffin*. It brought one great cargo of (illegally obtained) furs from Lake Michigan's Green Bay to Niagara before disappearing with a load of trade goods on its return voyage. In 1682 La Salle led a band of travellers down the Mississippi, claiming the territory he passed through for Louis XIV. France did not consider La Salle's discoveries worth much, but with lies and exaggerations he managed to obtain official support for a grand colonizing venture at the mouth of his river. Approaching it by sea, La Salle could not find the delta, saw most of his companions die during their wanderings around the Texas country, and was finally murdered in the wilderness.

La Salle's expeditions, building on the work of other coureurs and wandering priests, opened an enormous fur-trading area southwest of the Lakes. At the same time, Daniel Dreysolon Dulhut (sometimes called Duluth) was beginning to develop the country north and west of Lake Superior, founding posts on Lake Nipigon and at Kaministiquia at the west end of Lake Superior. The post at Michilimackinac, where lakes Huron and Michigan meet, became the crossroads of the Great Lakes fur trade. One of its first commandants, Antoine Laumet, was perhaps the most single-minded accumulator of all the French officials. He gathered furs by debauching the natives with brandy and fleecing the independent coureurs. The commissary at Michilimackinac wrote of Laumet's tenure, "Never has a man amassed so much wealth in so short a time and caused so much talk by the wrongs suffered by the individuals who advance funds to his sort of trading ventures." Laumet's grandest scheme was an attempt to create a special colony at a place called Detroit. He hoped it would become a fur-trading centre out of reach of New France so he could wholesale furs to either English or French, depending on the market. Laumet, who finished his career as the governor of Louisiana, was one of the most scoundrelly, self-seeking adventurers in the history of New France. Early in his life he assumed a noble alias, a name which survives today as a symbol of North American affluence, when he began calling himself Antoine de Lamothe Cadillac.

Cadillac's habit of trading with the British was not unique. The coureurs de bois were required to sell to a single purchasing monopoly in New France. Few of them had significant scruples about dealing with competitive buyers regardless of nationality. Due south from Montreal was the direction to go – there the British had become increasingly active after annexing New Netherland in 1664. The quantities of furs smuggled into British warehouses at the old Fort Orange, now Albany, New York, and of illicit trade goods flowing north were always substantial. As well, the British had powerful allies in the Iroquois, who kept their middleman role longer than any of the original trading tribes. Still, the volume of furs passing through Albany and out the Mohawk-Hudson system was never much more than a quarter of the St. Lawrence trade, and the quality of pelts taken in the more southernly trading areas was not high. In their rapid movement through the Great Lakes and down the Mississippi, the French had forestalled British trading expansion westward or northward.

Two French-Canadian coureurs de bois who had no qualms about dealing with English traders were the catalysts for the founding of England's greatest fur-trading venture. In 1665 a British commissioner, Colonel George Cartwright, sent out to adjudicate boundary disputes among Britain's American colonies, offered an odd addendum to a routine report:

> Hearing also some Frenchmen discourse in New England of a passage from the West Sea to the South Sea, and of a great trade of beaver in that passage, and afterwards meeting with sufficient proof of the truth of what they had said, and knowing what great endeavours have been made for the finding of a north-west passage, he thought them the best present he could possibly make His Majesty, and persuaded them to come to England.

In 1665 Médard Chouart des Groseilliers and his brother-in-law, Pierre-Esprit Radisson, arrived in London to seek English support for a radically new way of doing the fur business.

Groseilliers went to Canada as a boy in the early 1640s and spent some time as a young man at the Jesuit mission in Huronia. He made his reputation as one of the greatest coureurs with a two-year trip to the "pays d'en haut" at the height of the Iroquois wars in the mid-1650s, finally arriving at Quebec with a flotilla of Indian canoes and a fortune in pelts. The trip made Groseilliers wealthy; having to pay a quarter of his fortune in the tax, or *quart*, left him considerably aggrieved. Three years later he set off again. Now he was accompanied by the younger Radisson, perhaps still a teenager, who had been carried off by the Mohawks during a raid in 1651 and grown up living as an Indian. Groseilliers and Radisson spent the winter of 1659–60 at the far end of Lake Superior, trading and talking with bands of Sioux and Crees. They came down to Montreal with another fleet of Indians and a fortune in furs, saving the then-besieged colony, it is said, from economic disaster. But it had been an illegal, because unauthorized, expedition.

The furs were seized, the partners were fined, and Groseilliers may have been briefly imprisoned.

This bureaucratic stupidity had momentous consequences. Radisson and Groseilliers were infuriated, and decided to get outside support for a daring idea they had developed as a result of their journeys. It was to attempt fur trading out of the great "bay of the north," an inland salt water sea lying close to prime fur country. The English explorer Henry Hudson had found his way into the Bay (and died there) many years earlier while looking for the Northwest Passage. Its shores were a forbidding, apparently useless wilderness, which the English casually claimed as "New Wales" and then ignored. They had no idea of the relationship of the Bay to the Indian tribes in the interior or of trade and travel routes. The genius of the two French coureurs was to realize from their talks with the Indians about the rivers to the Bay that furs might be accumulated and brought out of Hudson Bay more cheaply – at least without the hindrance of marauding Iroquois and greedy governments – than through the Great Lakes–St. Lawrence route.

Like entrepreneurs through the ages, Radisson and Groseilliers began a long, frustrating search for capital and partners. They tried contacts in France; twice they set sail for Hudson Bay with Boston, Massachusetts, support, each time having to turn back; finally Cartwright put them in touch with the court of Charles II. Arriving in England at the time of the Great Plague and the Great Fire of London, the Frenchmen were given a respectful hearing in a court circle consisting of rich aristocrats and merchants, many of whom were deeply interested in geography, discovery, and colonization along the American seaboard. It was a small matter for men of great wealth to subscribe one or two hundred pounds for a trial expedition. It took a couple of years to organize, and was about eight years from idea to execution, but finally in June 1668 the *Eaglet* and the *Nonsuch* sailed from London to test the new approach to the fur trade.

The *Eaglet*, with Radisson aboard, proved "by reason of the deepness of her Wast unable to endure the Violent Stormes they mett with all" and had to turn back. The *Nonsuch* and Groseilliers sailed on, was out of touch with the world for eighteen months, but returned from Hudson Bay in October 1869 with a full cargo of furs. They sold for £1,379 6s. 10d., mostly to a single London furrier, Thomas Glover. It is impossible to know whether Radisson and Groseillier's backers made a profit on their first voyage. In a sense it did not matter, because even before the *Nonsuch's* return, the English adventurers were organizing a company and petitioning for a charter that would confer upon them the sole opportunity to conduct the fur trade out of Hudson Bay. They would have sent out more ships, if only to try and find the *Nonsuch*. A vital and enduring business connection had been made, linking wealthy and resourceful Englishmen, brilliant French coureurs de bois, and the saltwater passage to the heart of North America's fur country.

The first Canadian fur traders, the natives, fared less well as the system developed. The coming of the white man had increased their standard of living. In initial face-to-face bargaining the natives had few problems doing business with the Europeans, who also depended on the trade working well. Whites who came to trade furs were not particularly interested in annexing territory or creating settlements other than crude trading posts. They learned the Indians' language, and they generally respected the native tribes as nations to be treated diplomatically. At first the fur trade was not markedly different from trade among native tribes or among Europeans (who also tended to think of each other as "savages").

The equilibrium did not last. The white traders and missionaries brought non-economic factors to bear on Indian life: devastating diseases such as smallpox and tuberculosis on the one hand, intense religious beliefs on the other. The diseases sharply reduced the numbers of Indians; disease, plus the preachings of the missionaries, plus the evident superiority of the white man's material culture, all combined to assault the spiritual and cultural foundations of the native way of life.

The fur trade itself was not conducive to maintaining an equilibrium. Not much has been written about the trade's impact on the fur-bearing animals, but the consensus of historians, following contemporary observers, is that the great demand for furs led to over-killing and resource depletion. For some tribes the hunt for furs, particularly beaver, led to major shifts in concepts of property. There were significant changes in patterns of animal migration. In general the best furs increasingly came from the west; natives whose own hunting grounds could no longer produce competitive supplies of furs had to become middlemen or reduce their dependence on trade goods or do paid work for the whites or accept their charity. As we have seen, few tribes were able to maintain a middleman's role in competition with the enterprising coureurs de bois. In effect, the coureurs learned how to go about the business from the natives and now were literally by-passing them.

Finally, and possibly most important, there is massive testimony from the documents that the equality and clear-headedness with which Indians and whites confronted one another in fur trading was continuously impaired by the impact of liquor. From the earliest contacts whites offered Indians strong drink, usually brandy, either in trade or as pre-trading presents. Indians drank for the ecstatic experiences drunkenness offered. When they were drunk or thirsty for drink they lost their ability to make rational trading decisions. There seems to be much truth in the stereotype of the unscrupulous European plying the natives with drink and then exploiting their helplessness. The pervasiveness of alcohol and drunkenness when Indians and whites met led in time to addictive dependency and utterly degraded behaviour that appalled observers, including many of the white traders themselves. Drunken natives would sell anything, including their wives and children, for more liquor; murder, violence, rape, and death were everywhere the accompaniments of the flourishing trade in what the French called "eau de vie."

There was a strong movement in New France to ban the use of liquor in the fur trade. It was fuelled mainly though not exclusively by the humanitarianism of the religious orders. But self-interest, along with their own human instincts, also motivated many traders to worry about liquor. Many whites themselves, of course, became drunk, degraded, and violent under the influence of brandy. Some drinking natives lost the physical ability and will to endure the rigours of hunting for furs, becoming degraded and dangerous as they hung around settlements trying to cadge more liquor. At various times the authorities outlawed or tried to license the use of brandy in trade. Bishop Laval, the stern moralist of New France, proclaimed excommunication for anyone offering brandy to the natives. Some Frenchmen were executed for disobeying the liquor regulations.

The use of liquor in the fur business could not be controlled. It was a highly competitive trade, bursting through restraints attempted by spokesmen for Caesar or Christ. Indians, who owed allegiance to neither, wanted liquor. Traders who gave it to them got furs. Attempts to control the flow of brandy to traders simply created another illicit business, bootlegging. And no amount of state control in New France could prevent the Dutch traders on the Hudson, and later the English, from giving spirits, getting more furs, and forcing the French to respond in kind. In 1678 Frontenac, La Salle, and most of the principal traders of New France met to discuss the issue in what was called the "Brandy Parliament." While Louis Jolliet spoke powerfully against liquor, advocating a return to the death penalty for selling it to the natives, the preponderance of opinion went the other way. La Salle argued that it was impossible to keep brandy from the Indians because of the competition and because all regulations would be broken. The majority of traders supported continuing the liquor traffic. Bishop Laval and the Jesuits fought on against a disastrous, dehumanizing business, with little success.

Why would shrewd-trading Indians jeopardize their livelihood by succumbing to drink? To be sure there were many natives who understood the problem, wanted liquor kept out of the trade, and stayed away from it themselves. Hudson's Bay Company records suggest that some tribes of native traders managed to blend drunken celebration into the ritual of the trade by learning not to trade until they had sobered up. This of course was the way that many whites had learned to handle liquor.

The extent to which Indian patterns of life differed from European, particularly in the values possessed by capitalistic traders, made a successful accommodation to liquor difficult. As whites remarked throughout the history of the fur trade, the natives tended to take a limited view of their needs. When their immediate needs were satisfied with trade goods it was almost impossible to induce them to bring in more furs to obtain more goods. In an economic sense this failure to accumulate surpluses which could be "invested" to strengthen natives' presence in the trade (or later to diversify out of it) is another factor explaining why Indians failed ultimately to prosper from the business they could do so well. On the spot, the one good that natives would consume in large and increasing quantities was liquor. Many of them were more attached to the ecstasy, release, and oblivion that brandy induced than they were to accumulating material goods in commercial transactions. It was a commitment to the pleasures of the moment that made survival in a capitalist world difficult.

Fur trading, Montreal, 1700s, by G.A. Reid *(Public Archives of Canada)*

Playing-card money *(Public Archives of Canada, #C14913)*

3

---◆---

Doing Business in New France

*Industrial strategies and northern realities . . . Louisbourg . . . the first
tycoon . . . playing-card money . . . forced growth . . . the St. Maurice
forges . . . Dugard and the negoçiants . . . the need for networks . . . shopkeepers and mobility . . . femmes d'affaires . . . war supply, war profiteering . . . the scandalous "Affaire du Canada" . . . the need for scapegoats.*

New France came into being as a fur-trading and then a missionary outpost.
By the 1670s the ten thousand or so Frenchmen operating out of their St.
Lawrence base – commonly coming to be known as Canada – faced trading
competition from English adventurers in Hudson Bay to their north and
English merchants using the Hudson River system to their south. The
scramble for furs was more important than the salvation of souls in drawing
the French inland through the Great Lakes, then down the Mississippi, then
onto the Great Plains in the heart of the continent. From the shores of Acadia
to the foothills of the Rocky Mountains and south to the Gulf of Mexico, the
French empire in North America came to encompass a vast territorial
domain, dwarfing and shutting in the string of comparatively compact
British colonies along the east coast.

The King of France and his ministers often questioned the whole
American venture. Of course they shared their era's mercantilist interest in
colonies as sources of national enrichment. But a colony that was going to enrich its mother country had to have riches to develop, and the problem with
New France was that even in its most lucrative decades the fur trade was a
fairly minor activity. Canadian furs were a tiny item in France's foreign
trade: much less important, for example, than imports of sugar from the
Caribbean islands of Guadeloupe and Martinique. On its own, the fur trade
did not justify the expense of maintaining New France, particularly the cost
of garrisoning a land much larger than France itself and then actively
defending it against British expansionism.

France stayed in America for largely non-economic reasons. About 1700 a
decision was made to hold the empire the fur traders had created, not be-

cause of its riches in furs, but as part of a grand strategy of enhancing the glory of Louis XIV's France and competing with the British and Spanish empires on a global basis. This policy was maintained for more than half a century. Then it was shattered in one of the first "world" wars, the Seven Years' War of 1756–63. At the end of the war the approximately sixty thousand French inhabitants of a conquered St. Lawrence colony were left to attempt to survive as a minority in British North America. New France disappeared.

Many Frenchmen had hoped that New France could be developed into more than a land of animal skins. Officials in France's Department of Marine, which administered the colony, hoped to spark economic growth that would reduce its cost, possibly even turn it into an economic asset. Profit-seeking merchants sailed to Canada seeking new opportunities. The officials and the merchants were often closely related – sometimes one and the same – for there were few boundaries between commerce and government in the eighteenth century. Like Frontenac and his fur-trading friends, New France's governors and administrators routinely used public office to advance private interests. Merchants and traders worked in partnership with state officials to further their interests and the interests of the colony.

There was no shortage of people with plans for increasing the wealth of New France. But there was a dismal failure of execution. In 1763 Britain took over a bankrupt fur-trading colony, an economic backwater. Its most successful entrepreneurs had taken their money and gone back to France where, somewhat to their surprise, they were thrown into the Bastille and put on trial as unconscionable profiteers.

———————

I T IS SOMETIMES STILL BELIEVED that French colonial policy deliberately retarded the economic development of New France. Suppose that the point of having colonies was to accumulate wealth in the mother country through importing cheap raw materials and exporting expensive manufactured products. Surely, then, colonies existed to export raw resources and import finished products? In such a framework colonial production should remain primitive, lest it compete effectively with the metropolis. In the 1730s Barthélemy Cotton, an enterprising employee of the fur-exporting company in New France (the Compagnie des Indes), began making and selling beaver hats locally. He and a former apprentice, Joseph Huppé, became the principal hatters in Quebec and Montreal respectively, supplying the local market and even exporting semi-finished hats to France. Although the colonials were only making a few hundred hats a year, the Minister of Marine ordered their business closed. At Huppé's Montreal shop, "Au Chapeau Royale," the royal officials smashed his basins and his dyeing and fulling vats and carried off the rest of his equipment to the King's storehouse. The infant hat-making industry of New France, perhaps one of the most "natural" directions in which fur trading could have evolved, was literally destroyed by French fiat. It seems a clear case of French mercantilism stifling the entrepreneurial energies and opportunities of the Canadians.

The crushed hatters were a notorious, but isolated case, in which the real issue was probably the way they diverted furs rightfully belonging to the Compagnie des Indes. The real and constant French policy toward New France, implemented to the point of absurdity, was almost the reverse of doctrinaire specialization on primary products. Practical French officials believed the colony had to have a diversified economic base before it could build any kind of export capacity, that without greater exports it would continue to be a drain on the French treasury, and that almost anything it tried to export, other than furs, would obviously compete with the produce of France. They felt they had to try to stimulate growth anyway, and far from suppressing the entrepreneurial instincts of the Canadians, the King's officials in France and Canada did all they could to encourage colonial development. They supported and subsidized all kinds of wealth-creating schemes and complained bitterly when the Canadians failed to develop opportunities which seemed so alluring.

Jean Talon, the first intendant of New France after the royal takeover of the colony in 1663, tried to implement Jean-Baptiste Colbert's aim of diversifying the economy. The officials founded and funded a host of enterprises. Talon tried to stimulate agriculture, shipbuilding, mining, fishing, local manufacturing of leather, beer, shoes, and other consumer goods, and the export of almost everything, both to France and to the French sugar islands in the Caribbean. Talon's intendancy saw a whirlwind of innovation, as the King's money seeded his pet enterprises and the King's storehouses accumulated their products. Talon usually had a direct interest in the projects, functioning as a combined intendant-entrepreneur. After two years of work he reported enthusiastically to Colbert that the colony was rapidly becoming self-sufficient in a variety of its needs and would soon export substantial surpluses. He sent trial shipments of timber and planks, cod, eels, and seal oil to France and the West Indies, and predicted huge volumes of future exports.

The exporting might be done in Canadian-made ships, for Talon dreamed of exploiting the limitless forest to build ocean-going vessels. He sent inspectors to survey the woods and in 1670–71 began regulating the northern forest with ordnances giving the King's carpenters first claim on oak and other wood used in shipbuilding. In a shipyard on the St. Charles River near Quebec, Talon organized the construction of several sizeable hulls. Some were sold to the crown, some to a private syndicate of which Talon was a member. Supported at first by Colbert's enthusiasm and the Department of Marine's largesse, Talon planned to build huge warships on the St. Lawrence: a 450-ton, 42-gun hull was laid down, and wood was cut for a 600 to 800 ton monster. One of the attractions of shipbuilding as an industry was the belief that it could stimulate subsidiary enterprises, such as tar works, hemp production, and forges to make fittings.

Even before Talon left New France in 1672 it was becoming clear that his dreams were wildly impractical. The only resource the colony could contribute to shipbuilding, for example, was wood – and not even a lot of that, for good-quality oak was scarce along the lower St. Lawrence. Most of the carpenters and other artisans who put together the crude Canadian hulls had to be imported from France. So were all their tools and all the fittings and rigging that went into the ships. Huge construction costs led officials to realize that perhaps it would be more economic to export the wood to France and build the ships there. But timber for shipbuilding from Canada could not compete in France with either local supplies or imports from the Baltic countries.

All of Talon's other enterprises were uneconomic and did not survive their sponsor's departure from the colony. The brewery, for example, which had adequate supplies of local grain (as well as hops grown on Talon's seigneury) and for whose product there would seem to have been an obvious demand in the fur-trading colony, had actually only existed because Talon insisted on a quota limiting the import of wine and spirits from France. As soon as Talon left the regulations were eased; the brewery closed, and finally its owner – Talon – sold the building to the Ministry, which converted it into a residence for future intendants. Brewing never became more than a household industry in a colony that imported huge volumes of French wine and brandy.

Colbert and Talon had failed to understand the immense handicaps in New France to almost anything other than the fur business. This was a tiny colony one thousand kilometres up a treacherous river in a harsh northern land whose soil was thin and the climate bitterly cold. The St. Lawrence River is often seen as the bountiful artery of the north in Canadian economic history. In fact, sailing ships had a devil of a time ascending the artery in summer, and in winter the river was frozen for five months and impassable for a sixth. It was much less costly and time-consuming to do business with the West Indian islands or any of the ports on the Atlantic seaboard than it was to get ships up to Quebec. Not that there was much business to be done at Quebec anyway. The colony's total export of furs in most years would fill only one ship, unless the cargo was broken up for security or other purposes. Other than furs there was hardly anything else at Quebec that could not be bought more cheaply elsewhere.

Canadian wood was uneconomic to export, if only because of transportation costs. All Canadian products were uneconomic in open competition with the British colonies to the south. But since imperial policy usually forbade the French to trade with the English, there did seem to be a potential market for Canadian foodstuffs and other products in the French West Indies. The prospect of creating a triangular trade between Canada, the Antilles, and Europe appealed to generations of merchants and officials. It worked well for the British with their England–New England–Caribbean triangle. Aside from the extra length of the sailing voyages, however, the French triangle was hampered by the fact that the habitants who tilled small farms along the St. Lawrence only rarely produced significant surpluses of wheat, oats, peas, or other products. The land was not very good; the farming techniques were primitive;

whatever profits there might be in the export trade were too small or irregular to stimulate concerted efforts to improve the situation.

The real breadbasket of the northeastern part of the continent was not a few acres of usually snow-covered soil producing a few thousand bushels of this or that grain; it was the fishing grounds downriver, in the Gulf of St. Lawrence, and out on the Banks in the Atlantic. A major geographical gulf between furs and fish had been created when the fur trade moved up the river to Quebec and beyond. Quebec-based entrepreneurs did try to look back eastward and exploit the fishing possibilities of the north shore and Labrador, but it proved almost impossible for the upriver fur-trading colony to harvest the bounty of the sea. Without a second staple product to export, New France was bound to remain a fur-trading backwater, a couple of towns and a few thousand small farmers up a very long creek.

———————

Talon and Colbert had sensed the limits of the St. Lawrence in the 1670s and had considered trying to create some kind of entrepôt or trading centre somewhere in Acadia, a slumbering, much-neglected land, mostly wilderness, only nominally connected to New France. An eastern port would facilitate Atlantic trading on the one hand and the movement of goods in and out of the St. Lawrence on the other. Most planning of this kind was suspended during the long period of bitter warfare first with the Iroquois and then with the British that ended with the Treaty of Utrecht in 1713 – which gave much of Acadia to the British (who renamed it Nova Scotia). Then a French military decision to create a great fortress on Île Royale (Cape Breton Island) had exactly the economic effect that optimists could have hoped for. Within a few years of its foundation, Louisbourg, which included a thriving town on an excellent year-round harbour, was exporting more fish than Canada was exporting furs. Soon Louisbourg had a total maritime trade absolutely greater than Canada's and on a per capita basis many times larger. In the 1720s and 1730s Île Royale was France's busy Atlantic base for legitimate trade with the West Indies, substantial illicit trading with New England and Newfoundland, and, because Louisbourg needed food other than fish, very useful trading with Canada. This later trade declined after the late 1730s, however, because of major crop failures in Canada. From then until the Conquest Canada often had difficulty feeding itself, let alone supplying Louisbourg's needs. New England traders happily filled the gap.*

* For several centuries smuggling was the principal activity in what we now call the "underground" or "black" economy, the network of transactions that take place beyond the ken of the state and therefore never show up in statistics. All of the subjective evidence from the French regime in Canadian history – as well as some hard evidence about the movement of French furs to Albany – suggests a very high volume of illicit trade. It may have been so high as to pose a challenge, some historians feel, to the whole idea of a comparatively poor colony with little to export. The difficulty with this view, aside from the problem of evidence, is that it would have to be applied to all other settlements, whose inhabitants were not likely to be less adept smugglers than Canadians. The comparative disadvantage of New France in the Atlantic trade, licit and illicit, would remain.

There was always a certain amount of Canadian trade, and New France did become host to a few enterprising Frenchmen hoping to make their fortunes in the new world. In certain periods there were considerable fortunes to be made in the fur trade. The greatest fortune was probably the several hundred thousand livres accumulated by Charles Aubert de la Chesnaye, who came to the colony as a young agent for Rouen merchants in 1655. His early transactions are lost in obscurity, but La Chesnaye soon emerged as a grand merchant trader (*négociant* in the French distinction between general shipping wholesalers and the smaller *marchands* who handled goods in later stages of distribution), importing products for his storehouse in Quebec, maintaining a presence in the fur trade, and, typical of his breed, taking an interest in any other venture that looked reasonably profitable. He became involved in the lumbering activities Talon promoted, tried to develop fishing concessions downriver from Quebec, and was interested in a local brickworks. La Chesnaye also became Canada's first important moneylender, advancing cash to both habitants and seigneurs, including such notables as Bishop Laval, who borrowed 10,600 livres from him to help pay for the seigneury of Beaupré. (La Chesnaye made those investments in return for *contrats du rente*, a kind of bond that paid him 5 to 5½ per cent interest, had no maturity date, but was probably negotiable among the handful of other fur traders and merchants making up Quebec's circle of *hommes d'affaires*).

La Chesnaye's enterprises flourished so well and widely that he was able to go home and live for several years in the 1670s in La Rochelle, which had replaced Rouen and St. Malo as the principal source of ships and investors for the Canada trade. Only the death of his Canadian partner obliged La Chesnaye to return to the colony to handle the difficult job of untangling all the estate questions affecting the partnership. He then decided to stay on the spot where so many of his assets were tied up.

La Chesnaye's most frequent investments were in land. He purchased or was granted interests in more of the tracts of land denominated as seigneuries than any one else in the history of New France. Under the semi-feudal seigneurial system a seigneury theoretically generated wealth to its proprietor from the *cens et rentes* and other dues paid by its inhabitants. These "censitaires" benefited reciprocally from some of the obligations incumbent on the seigneur, notably a requirement to help the settlers develop the land by providing such local facilities as a mill for grinding their grain. Historians of New France have concluded that the seigneurial system was close to non-functional, generating little revenue for the seigneurs and having an almost imperceptible effect on the development of farms and settlements. With so much land available for the taking, who would bother with landlords? Canadian seigneurs could not hope to emulate French ancestors whose flourishing estates and letters of nobility meant that they and their children were aloof from the sordid scramble for money. Seigneurial status did not signify much real wealth in the New World.

Upwardly mobile Canadians kept trying. Virtually every successful merchant in New France's history repeated La Chesnaye's progress in becoming seigneur, part seigneur, or multiple seigneur. A few were even able to match his triumph in being granted letters of nobility in 1693, thus becoming a true "gentilhomme." De Chesnaye seems to have aspired to the title, calling himself "noble homme" for years previously. Merchants who chose a path to seigneuries and the aristocracy have sometimes been criticized as following a course of waning entrepreneurial zeal. Perhaps, but the transition was not peculiar to French-Canadian or even French merchants. The passion for landholding and titles affected businessmen from Prussia to New England, and seems to be, as the great French social historian, Fernand Braudel, has argued, a phenomenon of all places and periods.

It was rooted in vague but powerful desires for rest and respectability, and also at many times and places – including even New France – a shrewd sense that land was not a bad investment. Even if the income from a seigneury on the St. Lawrence was slight, it might be a profitable short- or long-term speculation. Trafficking in seigneuries contradicted the feudal notion of grants in perpetuity, but it took place constantly in both New and old France – in other words, a market had developed for real estate. Seigneuries were also a relatively secure investment, in the sense that the land could not easily founder in a storm, be captured by privateers, or be carried off by an invading army. Nor could its value be deliberately debased in the way that gold and silver coinage had been through the centuries and would be many times in the future. Finally, as landed proprietors throughout Europe were beginning to realize in the eighteenth century, improved agricultural and other resource development techniques could produce huge increases in income. Merchants everywhere understood that land was a fundamental source of most wealth.

Aubert de la Chesnaye might have left a greater legacy in Canada if he had limited himself to his seigneuries or a genteel semi-retirement as a noble. At its peak his fortune was estimated at 800,000 livres, about $1.6 million in modern puchasing power, making him easily the richest Canadian businessman of the seventeenth century, perhaps the richest in the history of New France. He appears to have been ruthlessly single-minded in his acquisition of wealth. In 1665 he was fined for having sold shoes from his Quebec store at prices higher than those allowed by the Conseil Souverain in one of its attempts at price-fixing. A trading permit issued to La Chesnaye by the governor of New York in 1684 indicates involvement in the illegal trade with the British. Some of his enemies even accused him, probably falsely, of provoking war with the Iroquois to advance his trading interests.

La Chesnaye's risk-taking was disastrous enough as it was. In the 1680s he was one of the leading spirits in a French challenge to the British fur-trading presence in Hudson Bay. As we see later, the French and Canadian Compagnie du Nord was a strikingly bold and dashing venture – and it failed. The merchants of

Quebec had no more success a few years later when they formed the Compagnie du Colonie to take over the European marketing of their furs from French concessionaires who seemed to be garnering poor returns. The venture was a fiasco because of an extreme glut of furs in France, and the Canadians accumulated heavy debts.

Aubert de la Chesnaye died in 1702. The little we know of the personality of the man who was New France's original *brasseur d'affaires* suggests a man of deep contradictions. He owned one of the larger houses in Quebec, but had some of his curtains made from old tablecloths. He owned a wig and shirts trimmed with lace, but commonly dressed in flannel trousers, a serge jacket, and an old beaver hat. In his will he apologized to those he had wronged, though he could not recall any specific offences, stated that his main interest had been in developing the colony rather than acquiring material goods, and asked to be buried in the paupers' cemetery of the Hôtel-Dieu in Quebec. Perhaps this last request was simple realism, for La Chesnaye's liquid assets at his death were only 125,000 livres. His debts totalled 480,000 livres. The sale of his properties did not bring in enough further revenue to cover the obligations. This premier Canadian fortune had been lost by the time of its accumulator's death.

Many of La Chesnaye's generation of Canadian merchants and fur traders lost their wealth more easily than they had accumulated it. François Hazeur, for example, participated in many of the same business endeavours as La Chesnaye, losing money in lumbering, fishing, and the Tadoussac fur-trading concession. When Hazeur died in 1708, Quebec's governor wrote that he was "missed by everyone because of his merit, his virtues, and his uprightness." He was also insolvent. Dennis Riverin, said by contemporaries to possess "an extraordinary spirit of gain," managed to cling to power and influence only through official favouritism after most of his ventures had failed. Charles Guillimin, another of Quebec's richest merchants, tried to entrench himself with a good marriage and a number of acts of military prowess and good citizenship, including loaning 40,000 livres to the government at Quebec during a financial crisis. Unfortunately Guillimin made the loan in Canada's distinctive playing-card money during a period of inflation and took a severe loss when France decided to redeem the card notes at far less than face value. His biographer concludes: "Guillimin's career had followed a pattern that was not untypical of many of New France's merchants: apparent prosperity and increasing social prestige dissipated almost at an instant by administrative decisions taken in France and by the normal vicissitudes of the Canadian economy." By the early 1700s these vicissitudes had included extreme fluctuations in returns from the fur trade, the collapse of the compagnies du Nord and du Colonie, the erratic development policies of the Department of Marine, the fortunes of war, and, as in Guillimin's case, the problem of the currency.

The currency is always a problem. In the eighteenth-century world the basic medium of exchange was specie, that is, gold and silver coins. There never seemed to be enough specie in circulation and it did not circulate easily enough to meet the needs of commerce. The mercantile world had long since developed various sorts of paper – evidences of debt and orders to pay at some future date – which merchants, shippers, buyers and sellers could and did freely create, circulate, and pass from hand to hand. One form of circulating paper was the simple promise to pay (bon from "bon pour"), the ancestor of the notes that Canada's banks would issue during the nineteenth century. Another was the bill of exchange, an order to pay somewhat resembling today's cheque.

Specie was particularly scarce in New France because chronic trade deficits caused it to move back to France (in payment of debts) and because the French government was often reluctant, sometimes unable, to meet its obligations in hard coin. In 1685, one of the years when the Department of Marine had not shipped out money, and with his unpaid soldiers having to hire themselves out to colonists, the intendant Jacques de Meulles issued distinctive notes by cutting up playing cards, assigning denominations, and signing them. Printed paper currency had already been invented in England and Sweden but had yet to appear in France. The first cards were soon redeemed, but the situation repeated itself and the "monnaie de carte" became a useful local circulating medium. Confidence in the card money was probably increased when an enterprising counterfeiter was fined, ordered to make restitution, publicly flogged, and banished.

The value of the paper debt instruments circulating in New France – bills of exchange, notes, card money, and other variants – depended on the likelihood of their being duly redeemed for the promised amount of specie. Merchants lived or died according to their skill and/or luck at not being caught with paper that had lost its value – such as a bill of exchange drawn on a French merchant who had just failed and could not pay. Uncertainties about redemption tainted almost all notes, including those issued by the government. The greater the uncertainty the greater the impediment to trade. Then, as now, trade flourished best in an atmosphere of confidence in the paper currency.

The greatest impediment to confidence was the French government's reluctance to pay its bills. The practice of issuing playing cards or other government notes became an habitual way of meeting local obligations. But the discovery that specie was not immediately needed meant that a fundamental check on government thrift in the colony had been removed. Local administrators developed a tendency to "spend" more than anyone in the Department of Marine had authorized and afterwards urge the case for the mother country redeeming the debt paper they had issued. The mother country was not always willing to oblige. During the War of the Spanish Succession at the beginning of the eighteenth century, for example, the sheer quantity of paper issued by the King's agents in New France led to significant inflation. Then the realization that France might not, probably could not, redeem the notes at face value led to still more deterioration in the currency's value, causing immense hardship for merchants such as Charles Guillimin. The colonials managed to transfer some of the loss to ignorant French exporters who thought they could safely take payment in bills of exchange drawn upon the Department of Marine. When the treasury of France simply did not produce the coin to redeem these bills, the paper-rich merchants of La Rochelle in 1715 sued the Treasurer General of Marine, who was declared personally responsible for the debt. The crown coolly suspended recourse to the courts and promised to pay the bills "le plus promptement qu'il sera possible." After more delays and uncertainties the Canadian card money and other paper was redeemed at about one-half its face value. Soon there were more issues of card money.

By about 1720 economic conditions in New France had stabilized after several decades of war, inflation, fur gluts, and other problems. The second quarter of the eighteenth century saw considerable population growth, substantial expansion of land under cultivation, and the stimulus to trade and production created by the building of the fortress of Louisbourg. During the peaceful 1720s and 1730s it seemed as though the colony might fulfill some of the aspirations of enthusiastic officials by producing a more diversified range of goods and improving its balance of trade. Elaborate and wildly optimistic plans were drawn up to increase agricultural production in the colony, and there was a renewal of official interest in schemes to produce every imaginable vegetable and mineral product – ranging from domesticated buffalo through developing a trade to the West Indies in Amerindian slaves. Some of the ideas were absurdly far-fetched; others, such as attempts to mine copper near Lake Superior or the coal deposits on Île Royale, were several centuries premature. A few, such as the program to foster hemp-growing and the founding of a local iron industry, seemed as though they almost worked.

Hemp was the fibre used to make rope. The Department of Marine thought it could easily become an export crop for the colony. Surely if the habitants could be encouraged to grow hemp the merchants would develop a good trade in it. In 1720 intendant Michel Bégon began applying the stimulus by offering to buy hemp for 60 livres a quintal. Barrels of seed were imported from France and distributed to interested growers. The hemp plan could hardly fail, in a sense, for the government's price was so high (in France hemp sold at 22 to 24 livres per quintal), that habitants filled the King's storehouses with hemp. Local merchants had too much good sense, though, to take over a trade that required paying more than twice the French price for hemp while ignoring normal quality standards. With 234,000 pounds of hemp in storage in 1730, the government finally eliminated the price subsidy, but had no idea what to do with its unexportable fibre.

Why not make the hemp into rope in the colony, thus adding more value on the spot and creating a new industry? But there were no Canadian ropemakers. Intendant Gilles Hocquart, a particularly enthusiastic promoter of diversification, decided to encourage French ropemakers to emigrate, then help set them up in business so they could train Canadian apprentices while creating a new Canadian industry. Several ropemakers came out in the 1730s. The industry failed. Canadian hemp was of poor quality. So was Canadian rope. Local shipowners and shipbuilders met their needs from France whenever possible. As soon as the department stopped paying exorbitant prices for poor-quality hemp, the habitants stopped growing hemp. Nothing came of proposals to import expert hemp-growers from France. No one is known to have tried to smoke the hemp. Considerable amounts of tobacco were grown for smoking in the colony, but elaborate official attempts to stimulate tobacco production for export also bogged down in problems of quality and price.

The most practical of many proposals for mineral development centred on deposits of soft iron in bogs near the St. Maurice River above Trois-Rivières. Why not take advantage of the ore to build a smelter and forge and make iron products for the colony – stoves, kettles, tools, and so on? Local officials who had been promoting state development of the resource for years were delighted when the fur trader and seigneur of St. Maurice, François Poulin de Francheville, came forward with his own scheme in 1729. The founding of Canada's first manufacturing facility included sending a blacksmith to study methods of iron-making in New England and the obtaining of a loan from the government. Several merchants joined the company Francheville formed, work began, and in the early 1730s a few thousand pounds of Canadian bar iron were produced at the St. Maurice forge.

The sudden death of the founder, Francheville, in 1733 led to suspension of operations, reorganization of the company, and a plea for technical help from France. A French expert, Olivier de Vézin, who was lured out at a high salary, declared that Francheville's installations were absurdly primitive and recommended scrapping them. Vézin drew up a plan for iron works capable of producing 600,000 pounds of bar iron a year, two-thirds of which would be exported to France. An investment of about 100,000 livres, Vézin estimated, would yield a profit of about 60,000 livres annually. "This is an enterprise whose success is assured," Intendant Hocquart wrote to the Minister of Marine after receiving Vézin's report. "As, however, it will be necessary to advance much money before drawing a profit, I have every reason to fear that this project will fail if you, My Lord, are not pleased to support and favour it. . . ."

With substantial state aid and participation, a new Compagnie des Forges du St. Maurice was formed in 1737 to undertake the work. Jean Lunn described the venture in a splendid Ph.D. thesis on New France's economy written long before the parallels to modern Canada were apparent:

Indications of the disaster which was to overtake the enterprise were evident from the beginning.... By October 1737, when the establishment was announced to be complete, the total expenditure was 146,588 livres instead of the 100,000 livres estimated.... In 1737 Hocquart had made over to the company the remainder of the loan of 100,000 livres agreed upon, but the partners declared that they must have an additional 82,642 livres. Their need was so pressing the Hocquart took it upon himself to advance them 25,233 livres to be deducted from the 82,642 livres which he begged the Minister to lend. . . .

The Minister replied in accents of horror and indignation. The King was being gradually more and more deeply involved. First it was only 10,000 livres, then it was 100,000 livres, then delays were proposed in repaying the loan and now it was another 82,000 livres of which 25,000 livres had already been advanced. It seemed clear to the Minister that there had been much waste and extravagance. Nevertheless he did consent to the new loan. . . .

Further shocks were in store for the Minister. In 1738 the company foresaw that it would not be able to meet its first payment due in 1739 and the King had to agree to another year's delay.... De Vézin's estimate had proved completely unreliable, for expenses far exceeded and production fell far short of what had been anticipated.... Constant breakdowns of the furnace interfered seriously with production.... The Forges were operated by a staff of costly, dilatory, insubordinate and discontented workmen.

According to De Vézin's original estimate the Forges should have manufactured 2,400,000 pounds of iron during the four years from 1737 to 1741. Instead total production for the period was about 1,000,000 pounds.... Up to the end of September 1741 returns from the sale of iron amounted to 114,473 livres. The sale of stock on hand and some other assets later produced 39,184 livres. Total expenditure however was 505,356 livres, leaving the Forges with a deficit of 351,699 livres, less the value of the property at St. Maurice. In October 1741 the partners handed in their resignations and declare the company bankrupt. This was the end of the private exploitation of the mines of St. Maurice.

The enterprise collapsed under a burden of technical, administrative and financial incompetence.

The major private entrepreneur who lost his fortune in the St. Maurice fiasco was François-Etienne Cugnet, the only member of the company with access to funds to advance to the firm. It was not clear that all the funds advanced were rightfully his. The crown took over the forges, which continued to make iron goods for local consumption to the end of the French regime and long afterward. The operations were not profitable.

Intendants like Hocquart often complained that the merchants of the colony lacked the resources to invest in such attractive prospects as the St. Maurice forges. Ten years' residence in the sugar islands would be enough to make a man rich, Hocquart wrote in the prosperous year of 1735, "whereas in this colony the greatest individual fortunes, with a single exception, are of 50 to 60 thousand livres. Of these there may be 4 or 5. Common fortunes are not greater than 20 to 30 thousand livres, and are moreover few in number." Historians have echoed his and other complaints in concluding that a lack of investment capital was a major factor retarding the economic development of New France. And just as capital was in short supply, so was labour, leading to endless complaints about shortages of cheap, skilled labour limiting growth.

These judgments confuse cause and effect. If real opportunities for profitable industrial diversification had existed in New France, both labour and capital would have been attracted from Europe, as they were to all the areas in the Americas, South, Central, and North, where greater opportunities existed than could be found in *cap de nada*. The endless and mostly futile attempts to stimulate the development of every conceivable industry in New France – Joseph-Noël Fauteux's 1927 account of them in his *Essai sur L'Industrie du Canada sous le Régime Français* runs to 555 pages – show that there was no shortage of public and private entrepreneurs trying to exploit opportunities. But there was a shortage of opportunities, a lack of products that could be made in Canada and sold profitably in or outside the colony.

Even the fur trade had settled down by the 1720s into a business with little prospect of great rewards. We see later how the French were extending and rationalizing their trade in constant competition with the English to their north and south. As W. J. Eccles has written, they were also "militarizing" it, subordinating economic considerations to their strategic needs vis-à-vis Englishmen and Indians. The men in the trade were beginning to specialize as operators of inland posts, or as Montreal-based outfitters bringing in goods from Quebec and hiring engagés for the trip to the interior. Not many of them accumulated fortunes.

The largest individual investments were made by the import-export merchants moving goods in and out of Quebec, the négociants of the Lower Town who were the biggest fish in the small colonial pond. Most were the agents or factors or partners of French négociants, big shipping merchants of Rouen, Bordeaux, and particularly La Rochelle, who had dominated business from Canada since taking over from Dutch traders in the 1660s.

A single trading voyage was often an enterprise in itself, with a special partnership having been formed in France to finance it and the profits (or losses) being divided at the end. An eighteenth-century merchant "company" was usually a fixed-term partnership, often of members of a family, with unlimited liability and no provision for share transfers. (In Europe the limited liability partnership had gradually developed out of this situation as a way to mobilize capital and conduct business over longer distances and among members of different families. Allowing a partner to transfer his shares in a firm, with or without his partners' consent, increased flexibility still further. It was one more short step, taken as early as the sixteenth century, to the creation of a joint-stock company in which all shares were fully and publicly transferable. The Hudson's Bay Company was the only such organization to operate in Canada before the nineteenth century.) Most of the Canadian trade was done by merchant partners; some tried a voyage or two and sailed on to a more profitable trade; others found success and increased the length, size, and capital base of their partnership agreements to underwrite more ventures.

The best-known French merchant in the Canada trade was Robert Dugard of Rouen, whose investment in a single ship that traded to Quebec in 1730 led to the formation of the Société du Canada, a long-term partnership under Dugard's management. The Société owned and outfitted a fleet of up to eight ships, maintained a warehouse and very active agents in Quebec, and in handling 10 to 20 per cent of the colony's trade was deeply interested in expansion, particularly to the West Indies.

Dugard and company's ships brought a myriad of consumer goods into Quebec. A single cargo included a wide variety of woollen, linen, and cotton cloth, blankets and garments, shoes, hats, gloves, knives, flat-irons, Dutch stoves, weights, locks, bridal mounts, roasting spits, shoe scrapers, combs, mirrors, window panes, plates, mugs, teapots, spoons, salad bowls, garden vases, foot warmers, paper, writing plumes, penknives, pipes, playing cards, pepper, nutmeg, cloves, cheese, salt, vinegar, dried prunes, almonds, and forty-two barrels of red wine, seven of white, ten of anisette, and ninety half-barrels of brandy. The supplies were for the colonists, for trade with the natives, and for the illicit trade with the English. All trade goods were sold at the firm's warehouses to other merchants or middlemen who shipped them up to Montreal, the centre of both the fur trade and the smuggling trade. Retailers and fur traders often purchased on credit extended by the négociants, settling their accounts after the goods had been resold or traded.

The Société's ships left Quebec with cargoes of furs and the occasional surpluses of flour, barrel staves, planks, and fish products that the colony was able to export in the good years. Sometimes the ships came north from or sailed south to the West Indies; Louisbourg was often used as an entrepôt to pick up or exchange cargoes. Even at the best of times trade between Canada and the Indies did not flourish. Canada was not much of a market for rum or molasses or slaves. Worse, as specific studies of individual voyages indicate, it was almost impossible to pick up a cargo in Quebec as valuable as the one brought in: thus the voyage out brought far lower returns than the voyage in. Canadian historians visiting La

Rochelle, France, used to be shown streets whose cobblestones were said to have come across the Atlantic as ballast from a country with nothing else to export. Robert Dugard's Société du Canada earned trading profits of about 10 per cent on its investment, not the fabulously high figures of popular and some scholarly belief, but between two and three times as much as could be earned in interest on less risky ventures.

Dugard and his associates, including the young cousins François Havy and Jean Lefebvre who were sent out to be the firm's factors in Quebec, were interested in any kind of enterprise, French or Canadian, that looked particularly profitable. In the late 1730s, for example, they took advantage of a system of royal bounties on ships built in Canada (another department program to stimulate Canadian industry) to launch the first of a total of six major ships they built in the colony. The last three of these were built after the bounties were ended, and were instanced by Hocquart as evidence that significant private shipbuilding really was feasible in Canada after all. In fact Havy and Lefebvre reported to France that the ships were very expensive to build, and the program seems to have been a kind of loss-leader to support the Société's Quebec trade. New France's card money and some of its other paper was not negotiable outside the colony. An importer accepting payment in the local currency needed to convert it into an exportable product. Shipbuilding was one way of turning Canadian card money into a product that could be sold in France.

Shipbuilding continued in New France, on a small scale for local needs, and as a crown venture after the opening of a royal shipyard, largely at Hocquart's urging, in 1739. The private industry disappeared in the war years of the 1740s and 1750s, but there was fairly constant production of naval vessels at the King's shipyard in Quebec. As in Talon's era, all the skilled shipbuilders, including the director of the works, were brought from France. One Canadian-born blacksmith at the shipyards determined to quit the job, causing the intendant to comment that "comme il est Canadien il préfère sa liberté a estre assujeti à une cloche." In addition to high labour costs, it turned out that the contractors did not deliver properly selected and seasoned wood for the hulls. Neither cost nor quality justified the operation of the royal shipyard. Significant subsidiary industries, such as tar-making, did not develop. The shipyard's demand for labour and material is thought to have contributed to the demise of the more limited but perhaps more economic private sector of the industry.

Both Havy and Lefebvre had an eye for other opportunities in the colony, and soon came to play an important role as both lenders and investors in attempts to develop fishing and sealing operations downstream from Quebec. Like Havy and Lefebvre, most of the men active in Robert Dugard's Société du Canada were Huguenots, French Protestants whose religion was banned in their homeland and its colonies. A fairly large proportion of the merchants trading to Canada in the eighteenth century had overt or covert Huguenot connections. There is no clear evidence, in this or any other period, that such an incidental correspondence can sustain a view of Protestant businessmen as being more "capitalist" or enterprising in their values than Catholics. The old Weber-Tawney hypothesis of a correlation between the Reformation and the rise of capitalism has led to too many simplistic generalizations implying that a Protestant was bound to be a better businessman than a Catholic or that Protestant countries like England were bound to be more enterprising than Catholic ones like France. There is little hard, statistically sound evidence of significant differences in business behaviour between Huguenots and Catholics, in either France or Canada.

A merchant was a merchant, a man trained by experience to assess opportunities, weighing risk against the possibility of gain. Well before Benjamin Franklin's *Poor Richard's Almanack*, austere European merchants were instilling their sons, clerks, and apprentices with a code of hard work, thrift, and the avoidance of personal indulgence. Success in business was never guaranteed to come easily. The eighteenth-century commercial world was fraught with everyday risks, hazards, and insecurities that would horrify a later age, and there were hardly any institutions (such as commercial intelligence services, effective courts, credit-rating agencies, or corporate structures) to help merchants cope with threats to their livelihood.

They tried to minimize risks by creating or becoming part of information, credit, and agency networks – business systems – making possible long-distance and long-term transactions. A man had to have connections he could trust. No wonder that most pre-modern firms – and a good many even in modern times – began as family affairs, and expanded through the recruitment of a web of offspring, nephews, cousins, and in-laws. The next step was from kin to kind, as trusted fellow-townsmen or churchmen became part of a merchant's network of "correspondents," associates, or agents.

Quebec's trade, then, was handled by groups of merchants with family, regional, and religious ties: men whose contacts had alerted them to opportunities and whose networks made it possible to exploit these opportunities with a minimum of defalcation, dishonesty, or other commercial disaster. Historians have recently concentrated on piecing together the links among what J.R. Bosher calls these "clans" or "swarms" of businessmen, tracing the growth, shifts, and declines in the webs of colonial commerce.

Not many purely Canadian-based merchants were prominent in the transatlantic trade. Men operating from the mother country had too many advantages in access to insurers, credit, ships and outfitters, and profitable cargoes to be easily challenged by enterprising colonials. Nor, as the intendants had pointed out, were there many colonial merchants whose local enterprises had profited enough to finance expansion into more costly and more risky ventures. French merchants and their Quebec agents handled about two-thirds of the colony's external trade. Sometimes the representatives of French firms, or French traders who sailed into

Quebec and bought and sold goods on the spot, were criticized as "marchands forains." Locals complained that the outsiders had unfair cost advantages, dumped goods at low prices, competed directly with retailers, and did not have a stake in the colony's well-being. Would the crown please protect them from such unfair competition, they sometimes petitioned.

There were several dozen négociants and marchands in the towns of Quebec and Montreal, and a larger number of small shopkeepers, traders, tavernkeepers, and artisans, engaged in buying and selling, providing services, and producing domestically crafted goods. Trade was often sleepy and apparently non-competitive, but there could be a fierce struggle for livelihoods, particularly on the margin where farming or labouring shaded into commerce. Carting in Quebec, for example, was so vulnerable to unrestrained competition and rate-cutting that intendants fixed the number of carters at ninety (in a town of about five thousand residents), issuing numbered tin tags to be affixed to their horses' collars. Merchants complained about the carters' fixed high rates. Town shopkeepers complained about competition from countryfolk who persistently refused to limit their selling to designated markets. Country shopkeepers had to compete with pedlars, wandering marchands forains, and town merchants who came out to buy directly from habitants, perhaps in hope of cornering the local supply of a product. In a small colony ravaged by periodic crop failures and containing so few producers, markets could so readily produce unattractive prices that intendants issued a host of regulations fixing prices, trying to ensure fair dealing, and otherwise controlling the market.

Accusations of price-gouging, monopoly, and greed were the usual accompaniment of commerce in the eighteenth century and afterwards. Contrapuntally, merchants complained about taxes, customs duties, and all other vexatious regulations. The bourgeoisie of Quebec and Montreal were self-conscious enough to occasionally consider creating a bourse or exchange – a meeting place for trading – and they sometimes appointed one of their number to present a petition to the authorities. The most common subject of petitions was the need for the government to maintain merchant confidence and a sound currency by honouring the cards, bills, and notes issued in its name.

Most merchants in the colony were not specialized, and would dabble in any promising venture. As with La Chesnaye and his like, there were no rigid lines between occupations or classes, nobility and bourgeoisie. Merchants became seigneurs, seigneurs engaged in all kinds of trade, all of the elite intermingled in government positions and councils, and marital bonds linked men and families with common tastes in wealth, power, and prestige. Cameron Nish's designation of the successful merchant of New France as a bourgeois gentilhomme seems fundamentally sound – so long as it is understood (following Molière) that most eighteenth-century merchants were bourgeois gentilhommes. The Canadians differed from type only in being somewhat less prosperous.

Limited opportunities in the colonial economy made it difficult for little men to ascend into the ranks of the merchant bourgeoisie. Of course a few made it: Jean Brunet, a Montreal butcher who was able to retire comfortably after many years in the trade; Jacques Campot, who started as a blacksmith at Detroit and became a substantial general merchant; Ignace-François Delezenne, the most successful of several reasonably prosperous silversmiths in New France, who became a seigneur and in the last years of the colony ran a small industry manufacturing trade silver. Growth at Louisbourg after 1725 probably created more opportunities for mobility there than in Quebec or Montreal. Michel Daccarrette, who began as a small fisherman and sometimes privateer out of Plaisance, Newfoundland, moved to Louisbourg and developed fishing stations on Île Royale that employed as many as 170 men bringing in more than 100,000 livres worth of cod in a season. As the Daccarrette family expanded into shipping, both to France and the West Indies, and to general merchandising, a once-poor fisherman now owned a comfortable Louisbourg house tended by servants and slaves. The *Dictionary of Canadian Biography* memorializes a handful of other men and families who prospered similarly from their skill in capturing the bounty of the new world. Many more tried and fell short, disappearing from history in the mean obscurity of their birth.

Merchants' wives and daughters were sometimes surprisingly active in commerce. With the family unit as the most common basis for a business, in an age of hazardous voyages, long absences, and early death, wives and widows often took an active hand in managing affairs and property. When Francheville of the St. Maurice ironworks died in 1733, for example, his thirty-six-year-old widow, Thérèse, herself the daughter of a prominent Montreal merchant, carried on with his affairs, gradually withdrawing from the forges and investing her inheritance in loans to other merchants. (Her one disastrous mistake was a proposal to sell the family's black slave, Marie-Joseph-Angélique; Marie set fire to the Francheville house in Montreal and fled with her white lover. Forty-six houses and the Hôtel-Dieu were destroyed by the flames; the slave was tortured, hanged, and burned.) Marie-Ann Barbel, mother of fourteen children to Louis Fornel, also managed his businesses during his visits to Labrador sealing stations. After his death Marie-Ann took over the the sealing concession, working with his former partners, Havy and Lefebvre, and adding the fur-trading concession at Tadoussac. "Veuve Fornel et compagnie," as she signed her business documents, tried other ventures, such as founding a small pottery when imports from France were interrupted by war. "The country has a resource in Mademoiselle Fornel," Havy and Lefebvre wrote. "She has a very good craftsman and her earth proves good."

Agathe de Saint-Père, Mme de Repentigny, organized a "factory" to make cloth for the colony during a wartime blockade in 1705. Her workers were nine English weavers whom she had ransomed from Indian captors. They taught

Canadian apprentices the trade, other Montrealers picked it up, and the little industry came to involve twenty looms on Montreal island producing 120 ells of cloth a day. It survived the departure of the English weavers and operated under Mme de Repentigny's control until 1713. This energetic businesswoman, mother of the Canadian textile industry (the one "manufacturer" listed in the early volumes of the *Dictionary of Canadian Biography*), experimented with new materials ranging from bark fibres to buffalo hair and discovered several new dyes. It seems that neither she nor the widow Fornel, however, could compete with French imports in peacetime.

The grand dame of Canadian lumbering was the "very noble young lady" Louise de Ramezy, unmarried daughter of a governor of Montreal, who took over management of a sawmill on one of her family's properties, ran it for three decades – sometimes through a foreman – and became involved in at least two other sawmills and a tannery in addition to her own seigneury. Another female seigneur, owner of the Île d'Orléans, mother of sixteen, was Charlotte-Françoise Juchereau, who styled herself the Comtesse de Saint-Laurent. "People might perhaps have forgiven her vanity and her usurping the title of countess," an intendant wrote, "if she had at least paid her bills." The three Demoiselles Desaunier kept a notorious trading shop on the Caughnawaga Indian lands outside Montreal. Everyone knew it was the centre for the illegal fur trade with Albany, but the sisters fought off repeated state attempts to dislodge them, and stayed in business for a quarter-century. Of course wives and daughters did not normally engage in either licit or illicit commerce in New France, and when women married, their husbands normally controlled their propery. Historians have tended to pay more attention to the strong-minded heroines of the religious communities, Jeanne Mance, Marguerite Bourgeoys, or Marie de l'Incarnation, than to the equally tough femmes d'affaires who occasionally seized opportunities created by the precariousness of life in the little colony.

"We need a good peace," Havy and Lefebvre wrote to a correspondent in France in 1746, "in order to be able to work solidly at increasing the trade of the country. It must be hoped that God will give us the grace soon to see the end of the war." Their hopes were not realized. For most of its history New France was literally embattled, functioning primarily as a military outpost of empire rather than a fur-trading or agricultural colony. The only period of peace and reasonable security in the colony's history ended in the early 1740s; there followed years of war, preparations for war, undeclared war, and war again, culminating in the British conquest of 1759–1760.

For many merchants the wars were disastrous. Robert Dugard's Société du Canada had six ships wrecked or captured during the War of the Austrian Succession in the 1740s. Even through the firm's insurers paid promptly (particularly those based in the enemy capital of London; the Londoners sometimes charged lower rates, some said because they could warn a client of the movements of British fleets), the losses forced the Société to withdraw from Canadian trade. At Louisbourg Michel Daccarrette lost his property and his life during the British siege and capture of Louisbourg in 1745. François Havy's personal fortune and many other merchants' modest accumulations of wealth disappeared in the rubble of Quebec and the destruction of the colony's currency during the Seven Years' War. War destroyed normal trade and many normally conservative traders.

But war also threw up a new breed of risk-takers. It created a huge growth industry servicing the state, supplying troops, provisioning the colony, transporting equipment. The public officials who profited from this opportunity brought the confusion of public and private interests in New France to a climax that finally played itself out in wild inflation, profiteering, scandal, trials and imprisonment, along with military defeat.

Remember that eighteenth-century governments did not expect public officials to set their private interests aside. In an age before the bureaucratization and professionalization of government, part of the compensation for taking the trouble to serve the state was the prospect of using office for private profit. Everyone in Bourbon France did it; every major official in New France was involved in fur trading or other enterprises. Collectors and administrators of the King's revenues kept the accounts in their own name, often investing the money in their own ventures. Consider François Foucault, the King's storekeeper at Quebec from 1715 to 1740. "It was not always clear whether the large credits Foucault extended were from his own or from the king's revenues," his biographer writes. "Consequently, when a creditor proved insolvent, he could shift the loss from his own to the king's ledger." Foucault ran his private store at Quebec in the same location as the King's store, and had a habit of trading with himself, hiding rake-offs through the use of agents or aliases. This was not particularly unusual in the colony. What was the point of holding an office if you didn't make something out of it?

As military business ballooned during the wars of the 1740s and 1750s so did the opportunities available to the holders of strategic offices. Led by François Bigot, the last intendant of New France, the officials seized their chance. A native of Bordeaux, Bigot had served as financial commissary of Louisbourg, engaging in several commercial ventures and investing in privateering on the side, before being posted to Quebec in 1748. During his twelve years as intendant, Bigot was the centre of an elaborate private operation, in which many military officers and senior officials of the colony participated, to supply profitably the colony's wartime needs. One important partnership included Bigot, Jacques Bréard (the financial controller at Quebec), and the Bordeaux shipping firm of David Gradis et fils. It operated as La Société du Canada, but was very different from Dugard's group of peacetime traders. Gradis, a major outfitter to the King of France, sent ships to Quebec where Bigot and Bréard purchased their cargoes on behalf of the government at prices they set; they then collected half the profits from the voyages. The Bigot group's interests included a small fleet of ships in the Louisbourg–West Indies trade and a company formed secretly to buy furs at interior posts which were supposed to be sold at auction in Quebec.

Bigot routinely awarded contracts and concessions to such friends and associates as Michel Péan (adjutant at Quebec), Louis Pennisseaut, Marie-Ann Barbel, Guillaume Estèbe, and others, taking a personal stake in their ventures. His most enterprising crony was Joseph-Michel Cadet, a Canadian-born merchant butcher, who began to prosper selling meat to the crown and expanded into supplying other foods. Bigot made him purveyor general, responsible for provisioning all the garrisons and eventually the civilian population during the desperate war of the late 1750s. Cadet then organized the Grande Société, a partnership in which all of them had an interest, from which he bought most of the provisions. The gang of purveyors and profiteers was knit together by ties of kin, friendship, avarice, and, at the top, the sexual favours of Angélique "Lélie" Péan, Canada's equivalent of Madame Pompadour.

As the noose of British power tightened around the St. Lawrence in the late 1750s, Quebec and Montreal reeked with defeatism, cynicism, and a scramble for booty. Everyone knew the accounts were crooked; the worst swindles were in Indian presents – goods the officials just redirected into private trade. Citizens had nicknamed the Bigot crowd's stores at Quebec and Montreal "La Friponne" – the rogue or rip-off. With the spectre of famine haunting the colony, prices having risen 800 per cent in four years, and paper "money" everywhere, the elite revelled in gambling and balls. The commander of the French troops in North America, Louis-Joseph de Montcalm, saw venality everywhere:

> Everybody appears to be in a hurry to make his fortune before the Colony is lost, which even, many, perhaps, may desire as an impenetrable veil over their conduct. The craving after wealth has an influence on the war, . . . Instead of reducing the expenditures of Canada people wish to profit by everything; why abandon positions which serve as a pretext to make private fortunes? Transport is distributed to favorites. The agreement with the contractor is as unknown to me as it is to the public. 'Tis reported that those who have crowded into trade, participate in it. Has the King need of purchasing goods for the Indians? Instead of buying them directly, a favorite is notified who purchases at any price whatever; then M. Bigot has them removed to the King's stores, allowing a profit of one hundred and even one hundred and fifty per cent, to those whom it is desired to favor. Is artillery to be transported, gun-carriages, carts, implements to be made? M. Mercier, commandant of the artillery, is the contractor under other people's names. Every thing is done badly and at a high price. This officer, who came out twenty years ago as a simple soldier, will soon be worth about six or seven hundred thousand livres, perhaps a million, . . .

Montcalm's own defeatism and incompetence contributed to the British victory on the Plains of Abraham on September 13, 1759. When the colony finally capitulated in September 1760, most of those who had done well in New France's last years sailed back to France, taking whatever wealth they could salvage. For Bigot and Cadet the scavenge was well into the millions of livres. But defeat did not veil misconduct. The French government developed an intense interest in finding someone to blame for the fall of Canada. Bigot, Cadet, and fifty associates were flung into the Bastille, and, in the notorious "*Affaire du Canada*," were convicted of defrauding the crown and plundering the colony. Their penalties included fines, restitution payments, banishment, and the destruction of their reputations. Another penalty paid by everyone with money from New France's last phase was the loss of more than half its value, for France repudiated most of the notes and cards that had been issued in its name.

The supreme irony of the Affaire du Canada was that most of the profiteers and criminals had contributed more to the preservation of the colony than their accusers. Montcalm's opinion notwithstanding, Bigot and Cadet were both brilliant administrators, two of the smartest, most efficient men ever to hold high office in New France. Their private schemes succeeded so well largely because they were so effective in carrying out their public duty to supply the colony. Gradis et fils slipped supply ships into Quebec, for example, more regularly than the French navy got vessels through British blockades. Cadet risked his fortune to get his own ships through in 1758 and 1759 at a time when no one else had the vigour and daring to attempt the feat. He fed the besieged colony to the end, doing well by doing his duty. If the censorious Montcalm had done his job of generalship equally well, the French regime in America might have had a different fate.

The high prices that plagued the colony in its last years were partly due to the Bigot gang's skimmings, but they were mostly caused by inflation. Government spending had soared, war impeded production, and holders of paper shrewdly lost confidence in the French government's promises to redeem it. But everyone needs scapegoats for inflation and defeat. Bigot and company were not unusually villainous by the standards of eighteenth-century France or New France; if anything they were unusually competent products of that century's office-holding system. They did a spectacular job of making the system work. But while they won the battles to keep the civil side of the colony going, the soldiers and the government lost the war.

New France had always been an economically precarious colony, highly dependent on the vagaries of the fur trade, unable to develop other staple products for export. After the boom years of the fur trade, a few Canadian merchants had emerged to trade with the handful of French-based merchants who controlled colonial shipping. The greatest opportunities the colony offered were not to profit from the natural development of a community and its resources, but to get inside the King's purse when it was wide open to finance wars. The risk of exploiting the state and its needs might have been manageable if only the war had been won. When it was lost, the state turned on the risk-takers in its need to find excuses for the loss of Canada.

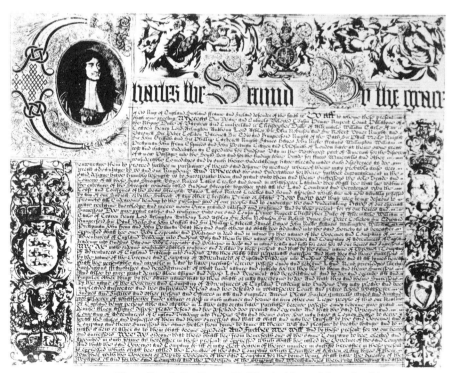

UPPER LEFT: **Pierre Esprit Radisson** *(Public Archives of Canada, #C15497*

UPPER RIGHT: **Sir Alexander Mackenzie** *(Public Archives of Canada, #C2146)*

ABOVE: **Charter of the Hudson's Bay Company** *(Hudson's Bay Company)*

4

"A Mere Business of Fur Trading," 1670–1821

Monopoly in Hudson Bay . . . confused Adventurers . . . interlopers . . . standards of trade; overplus . . . "Give us Good measure" . . . French expansion . . . The HBC's "Sleep by the Frozen Sea" . . . "Pedlars from Canada" . . . "fiery double Distilled Rum from Canada" . . . creation of the North West Company . . . Mackenzie's useless explorations . . . the HBC a "dollhouse company," near collapse . . . the Selkirk grant and the Massacre of Seven Oaks . . . collapse of the North West Company . . . its influence

Ninety years before the British conquest of Canada, the renegade Frenchmen, Radisson and Groseilliers, led Englishmen into the northern wilderness to trade furs on the shores of Hudson Bay. The handful of courtiers and London merchants who financed the 1668 voyage of the *Eaglet* and the *Nonsuch* petitioned for a monopoly on the Bay trade before they had harvested a single beaver pelt. On May 2, 1670, King Charles II issued a "Charter of the Governor and Company of Adventurers of England trading into Hudson's Bay." He gave the company the "sole Trade and Commerce of all those Seas Streightes Bayes Rivers Lakes Creekes and Soundes in whatsoever Latitude they shall bee that lye within the entrance of the Streightes commonly called Hudsons Streightes together with all the Landes and Territoryes upon the Countryes Coastes and confynes of the Seas Bayes Lakes Rivers Creekes and Soundes aforesaid." The grant included exclusive trading rights and property ownership, the Company to be "true and absolute Lordes and Proprietors" of what turned out to be an incredibly vast territory, the drainage basin of Hudson Bay, which stretches from Ungava to the foothills of the Rockies. Payment was according to feudal custom: two elks and two black beavers whenever the monarch should enter the territories.

The monopoly was easier to obtain than to maintain. In the summer of 1670 a renegade Dutchman who had sailed with Radisson told the French government of the British interest in the "Floride du Nord" and got support to journey into the Bay. He failed, but that season natives carried word of the English trading activities across six hundred miles of wilderness to the French settlement at Quebec. In 1672 emissaries from New France reached the Bay overland and claimed the territories for Louis XIV. Within a decade a group headed by Charles Aubert de la Chesnaye formed the Compagnie de la Baie d'Hudson, more commonly known as the Compagnie du Nord, to break the British monopoly on the fur trade out of the northern sea. The French traders maintained a presence – sometimes a foothold, sometimes a near-stranglehold – on Hudson Bay for more than thirty years. When they finally lost it in 1713 they expanded their trade out of Montreal so effectively that the British forts and factories in the north were virtually cut off from the natives.

After the Conquest of 1759–60, a new group of Montreal fur traders, mostly Scotsmen, proved even more enterprising as they drove the boundaries of their business above the Arctic circle and westward to the Pacific. The North West Company was one the most adventurous and expansive firms in Canadian history. It was also the most ruthlessly competitive: a company whose employees and partners sometimes took the idea of "cutthroat" competition literally.

By comparison with the Montreal fur traders, the Hudson's Bay Company was stodgy, cautious, almost anything but adventurous. It was not very competitive either, except in spurts. But it was profitable, in the long run, and it survived, and still survives as one of the world's oldest business organizations. During its first one hundred and fifty years, the time of the great rivalry with Montreal, the Hudson's Bay Company combined conservative business methods with the magnificent advantage of access to the Bay. The Montreal traders – colourful, romantic, ingenious, vicious, and violent – found that no amount of determination and effort could overcome merchants who had lower costs and knew how to keep their accounts.

———

THE COMPANY OF ADVENTURERS began its history with no settled idea of its aims or its future. It was a fairly wild speculation to finance voyages into the frozen north on the word of a couple of Frenchmen. But the speculators – a group of courtiers centring around Charles II's cousin, Prince Rupert, plus a few well-to-do London merchants – could afford to lose a few hundred pounds. When they organized more formally and for the longer term, the investment was still relatively small: £300 each for the eighteen charter subscribers, paid in several "calls"; a few years later total paid-up equity rose to £10,500. The Adventurers formed a joint-stock company, with fully transferable shares, but it was not clear what they would do or how they would do it. Perhaps the company's ships would discover the Northwest Passage to the Orient. They might found a colony in the new land, similar to other British colonies and plantations in America. (The notion of colonizing newly discovered lands – which should belong to their discoverer, like any other patentable discovery – helps explain the sweeping land grant in the Company's charter.) If trade proved the sole reason for trips to the Bay, there might be more than furs to ship back to England. For many years the Hudson's Bay Company hoped to discover minerals in the north, develop a whaling industry, and open profitable sidelines in exotic products like isinglass (from sturgeon glands), seahorse teeth, feathers, and medicines or perfume made from the castoreum secreted in "beaver stones."

The structure of the firm was as unsettled as its aims. Despite the corporate existence or persona created by its charter, the early Hudson's Bay Company operated more like the familiar partnership company of the era than a modern corporation. It lived from season to season, with individual shareholders loaning or subscribing the capital for each voyage, taking back their money, with interest, after each year's fur sale, and then subscribing again, or not, depending on the next year's prospects. At times the Company seemed on the verge of becoming a loose association of private traders operating on their own account (with the employees on the early voyages always engaging in private trading on the side). On the other hand, if it had been able to plant a colony on the Bay, the Company might have turned into just another merchant shipping firm servicing the settlers.

Most of the aristocratic investors, who had apparently expected the Company would be a vehicle for colonization or exploration, withdrew by the end of the 1670s. Their shares were purchased by knowledgeable City merchants plus the occasional shrewd widow or enterprising man about town (such as Sir Christopher Wren and the chemist Robert Boyle).* The company was still small and loosely organized, hiring one or two ships a year to supply a score or two of its "servants" wintering at two or three miserable "forts" in the Bay. There were no dividends until 1784. "We had a List of the Names of the Owners but we have lost it," the principal organizer once wrote the governor of Massachusetts. Perhaps

---

* The Hudson's Bay Company's historian, E.E. Rich, is not sure whether this shift in ownership was rooted in commercial calculations or personal rivalries. Most of the sellers were associates of the Earl of Shaftesbury. Shaftesbury had become malevolently hostile to Sir James Hayes, the secretary to Prince Rupert who was the most active force organizing the Company. Shaftesbury had come to consider Hayes, Rich writes, "a secret Papist, a vice-sodden profligate who had killed his first wife with disease and had run through the fortune of his second wife, a pander who for a mere five shillings would supply 'pretty women' to chance acquaintances – a mean and dishonest rogue." It is not known whether or not this is a true description of the man who deserves to be considered, along with Radisson and Grosseilliers, one of the fathers of the Hudson's Bay Company.

it was lost on one of the many occasions when the directing committee met at Joe's Coffee House rather than the official premises in Cheapside.

Would-be competitors knew the Company could not enforce its grandiose claim to monopoly. In a pattern still common today, former employees were among the first rivals. Significant interloping expeditions into Hudson Bay in the early 1680s were promoted by men who had been on the pioneer voyages. All the freelancers – the *Expectation* from England, the *Bachelor's Delight* out of Boston, the *Mary* from Ireland (captained by John Outlaw) – came to grief, either through being captured by the Company's ships or in the "Mountains of Ice" that the Company warned its competitors they would have to face in the Bay.

French competitors were a more serious threat, for they had financial resources, sometimes the support of the French government, the ability to penetrate the Bay overland from Canada as well as by sea, and an intimate knowledge of both the natives and the fur trade. Canadian merchants, led by La Chesnaye, readily understood Radisson and Grosseilliers's reasons for moving into Hudson Bay. The inland ocean gave access to prime fur areas and new Indians; it offered freedom from taxation and from self-interested governors like Frontenac. Soon Radisson and Grosseillier were telling this to the Canadians in person: in 1675 the old coureurs de bois defected from the Hudson's Bay Company, aggrieved that they had not become its top dogs. Now they would cheerfully assault the company they had founded. Traders in New France sensed it might be a life and death struggle: if the English were left on the Bay, one of the Jolliet brothers observed, "they will render themselves masters of the trade of all Canada inside six years."

Trading posts on the Bay had to be heavily armed – the more cannon the better – and ready to repel invaders. The invaders might be Frenchmen in sailing ships, Frenchmen and Indian allies attacking overland from Canada, or English ships trying to recapture posts from the French. Few of the combatants thought the fur business was worth dying for, so the fur wars on the Bay usually involved more bluster than fighting, ending in face-saving accommodations and years of skirmishing in court. The rivalry and the minor bloodshed were usually dismissed as an "affair of merchants." But when serious soldiers of fortune, such as the dashing Canadian, Pierre le Moyne d'Iberville, became involved, and when warring states offered official support to their companies, the stakes became higher. On September 5, 1697, off Fort Nelson at the mouth of the Hayes River, the rivalry for Hudson Bay came to full-scale battle when Iberville in the 46-gun warship *Pélican* defeated the combined 114 guns of the Hudson's Bay Company's ships *Dering*, *Hudson's Bay*, and *Hampshire*. (The fight's turning point came when the *Hampshire*, a man-of-war borrowed from the Royal Navy, and *Pélican*, both heavily damaged, sailed alongside. The captains called for wine, toasted one another's gallantry, then fired their broadsides. Either the French firepower or a hidden shoal caused the *Hampshire* suddenly to sink with all hands.) The English had just regained several of their posts from the French. Now Iberville captured Fort Nelson and £20,000 worth of furs. The French kept the post (as Fort Bourbon) until the Treaty of Utrecht of 1713.

The French were able to break the Company's monopoly on Hudson Bay, but had difficulty conducting a fur trade there. The Compagnie du Nord did not have the resources to support the costly expeditions it had to mount in the struggle to stay on the Bay. And it was confused about how to do business there, for both the Canadian shareholders and officials of the Department of Marine thought the company should use Quebec as its base for trading through the Bay. The France-based partners in the Compagnie du Nord argued that there was no reason for Canada to engage in the Hudson Bay trade at all: it was far cheaper to trade directly between Hudson Bay and La Rochelle, France (particularly if the exporting agent in Quebec continued to try to tax furs from the Bay, as he did in 1684, causing Radisson to remember why he had originally gone to England and to defect once again). On the other hand, in most years the French fur market was already glutted with pelts from the St. Lawrence, and it was not clear whether the Hudson Bay skins were competitive, complementary, or superfluous.

So there was not one northern fur trade, but two: a Laurentian trade, and a Hudson Bay trade. While it might make sense to control both fur channels from one of the European terminal points, there was no easy way for exporters located in Canada to run a business out of the Bay, especially if they insisted on ships and furs making unnecessary side-trips through Canada. The Compagnie du Nord collapsed in 1700. Its successors, including the short-lived Compagnie du Canada, were overwhelmed by the massive fur glut in France, found navigation to Hudson Bay difficult and expensive, and could not make the trade work. The French were beaten in the Bay in open competition, yielded, and in 1713 formally gave the Hudson's Bay Company back its geographical monopoly.

The Adventurers' fortunes had swung wildly during the first forty years of struggle. A few days after a particularly successful sale of coat beaver in 1684 the Hudson's Bay Company declared its first dividend, 50 per cent on its capital. Four years later another 50 per cent dividend was paid, 25 per cent the next year, and in 1690 a 200 per cent stock dividend was issued on which a further 25 per cent cash dividend was paid. This was a business in which one year's trading, costing about £10,000, might return £20,000 in furs. Acts of God or the French might lead to a £10,000 loss on the same investment the next year. As rivalry increased in the 1690s and European fur markets remained glutted, the company's short series of bonanzas gave way to one lean year after another – twenty-eight successive years without dividends. The Company teetered on the brink of bankruptcy. In 1692 the governing Committee were urged to have their friends "use their utmost Endeavers for the Raiseing of money in order to the payeing of the Tradesmens bills." The Adventurers tapped the purses of anyone willing to lend money, from banker to cheesemonger to spinster. In 1697 the Company had to beg its grocer for more credit and scramble to find £15 to rig a ship. Fifteen years later, as the War of the Spanish Succession ended, it was still close to insolvency, sometimes borrowing to pay the interest on its loans, surviving on the grace of several of its banker-shareholders and the patience of the others.

It did survive. Its rivals did not. The Hudson's Bay Company had three particular strengths. Because of its good standing in rich London circles, it was always able to borrow. Interlopers and the Compagnie du Nord had no similar access to credit. Secondly, the Company was able to maintain its credit by selling enough furs in most years to cover most of its indebtedness: it was able to sell furs on the well-organized London market to buyers for an expanding British industry in years when French markets were glutted and the business was declining. Finally, although voyages into Hudson Bay were intolerably perilous by modern standards, and the Company's men risked their lives constantly in its service, it benefited handsomely from the high standards and comparatively low costs of British seamanship. Year after year the Hudson's Bay Company got ships into and out of the Bay more regularly and cheaply than its competitors, many of whom found that a voyage into those perilous Arctic waters landed them in dire straits. To protect its advantage in knowledge and experience the Company became highly secretive and avoided publicizing its knowledge of Hudson Bay's coasts, rivers, natives, and shoals.

The Europeans at the Hudson's Bay Company's posts did not actually know much about the native people with whom they traded. In contrast to the French, with their coureurs de bois and their missionaries living among the Indians, the English came to conduct a trading business only. They sailed into the Bay and built fortified trading posts or "factories" (and lesser "houses") where they dealt with natives who paddled down the rivers to trade. It was like trading on the coast of India or Africa. The London Committee expected its servants to be proper Englishmen and duly religious, observing morning prayers and Sunday rest, but did not want them to convert, cohabit with, or have any other intercourse with the savages. Of course there were elaborate social ceremonies when natives came to trade each spring, with much gift-giving and fraternal smoking. But trade took place only when natives came to the window of the trading room adjoining a factory's warehouse. Transactions were made across a counter in this "hole-in-the-wall."

Radisson was instrumental in developing the Company's *Official Standard of Trade* – a kind of price list expressed in a unit the Indians could understand, the prime beaver pelt or "Made Beaver." In 1700 at Fort Albany Indians could obtain one kettle for one Made Beaver, two hatchets per MB, one and a half pounds of shot, one pound of tobacco, and so on. A forty-two-inch long gun cost six MB, a fifty-four-inch gun traded for ten MB; one gallon of brandy was given in return for four MB. Other furs and hides were converted into MB values according to the *Comparative Standard*: two fox or four marten equalled one MB, and others were valued similarly.

The Committee adjusted the Standard from time to time in light of its changing costs of trade goods and/or its need for furs. There were slight variations between factories to try to ensure a steady flow of trade at each post. More important, the factors had to be flexible, first in haggling over quality, then in taking account of the competition. At their best the traders stayed close to the Standard, an invaluable reference and accounting device, while making constant local adjustments to meet changing conditions.

Each factor tried to maximize his annual Overplus, a positive balance between his actual receipts and the expected receipts for that quantity of trade goods as dictated by the Standard. Sometimes factors increased by Overplus by simply charging the Indians higher than standard prices for their furs. Often they made "savings" by giving short measures or using crooked scales. Measures of brandy were almost meaningless because liquor could be watered so easily. A trader's ability to maximize his Overplus was usually viewed as a measure of his effectiveness.

Did the factors, then, have a kind of licence to get all they could out of the natives? Yes, but within limits that always constrain traders wanting to do a repeat business. In 1688 the governor of York Factory was instructed to

> keepe to the Standard, that Mr. Radisson agreed to, but withall to give the Indians all manner of Content and Satisfaction and in Some goods Under Sell the French that [the Indians] may be incouraged to Come to our Factory's and to bring their Nations Downe, for Wee are in your minde in the particular, that Wee ought to Trade with the Indians, Soe as that Wee may Trade with them againe, and to make them willing to Come to us and not for Once and never See them more.

The Indians had to be satisfied enough with a season's transactions to want to return the next year rather than go to the French or not trade at all. They understood this, of course, and used it in their bargaining, which was as wide-ranging and cunning as any European's. In 1743 an old chief began the season's trading at York Factory with this speech, uttered slowly and deliberately:

> You told me last year to bring many Indians, you See I have not lyd; here is a great many young men Come with me; use them Kindly! use them Kindly, I say! give them good goods; give them good goods, I say! we Livd hard Last winter and in want, the powder being short measure and bad, I say! tell your Servants to fill the measure and not to put their fingers within the Brim; take pity of us, take pity of us, I say! we Come a Long way to See you; the French sends for us but we will not [hear]; we Love the English; give us good tobacco, black tobacco, moist & hard twisted; Let us see itt before op'n'd; the Guns are bad; Let us trade Light guns small in the winter, and Red gun Cases. . . . Let the young men have Roll

tobacco Cheap, Kettles thick high for the shape and size, strong Ears, and the Baile to Lap Just upon the side. Give us Good measure in Cloth. Let us see the old measures. Do you mind me?

Relations between the Hudson's Bay Company and the natives were generally good. Unlike the French, the Company stayed out of intertribal rivalries and warfare. In the early years its traders did not promote drunkenness or violence, and concentrated on doing their business as well as they could. The aim was to get furs and make Overplus and keep the natives coming back.* Factors were particularly insistent on England supplying them with goods acceptable to the natives, and were intensely frustrated when a committee in England who had never seen an iceberg, Indian, or living beaver misunderstood their needs in the trade. "It is not possible for your Honours to knowe in England by guess what is most convenient for your interest, as it is for me to knowe here by experience," one of the earliest traders wrote.

Head office is often out of touch. The usually shrewd London committeemen handled immense problems of communication and control within their organization with the same mix of rigidity and flexibility that governed use of the Standards of trade. The Company's situation in the Bay, for example, with the factors completely dependent on London for capital, goods, and shipping, made it possible for the shareholders to maintain full control of the enterprise. Their traders remained salaried employees, whose tendency to trade on their own account was carefully controlled. But the Committee had the good sense to allow a limited amount of private trading, experiment with other incentives to aggressive trading,

---

* Natives drove similarly hard bargains when trading amongst themselves. During his great inland journey of the early 1760s, Samuel Hearne wrote a rare description of Indian middlemen at work: " . . . the established rule is to give ten times the price for every thing they purchase that is given for them at the Company's Factory. Thus, a hatchet . . . is sold to those people at the advanced price of one thousand *per cent*; they also pay in proportion, for knives, and every other smaller piece of iron-work. For a small brass kettle of two pounds, or two and a half weight, they pay sixty martins, or twenty beaver in other kinds of furrs. If the kettles are not bruised, or ill-used in any other respect, the Northern traders have the conscience at times to exact something more. It is at this extravagant price that all the Copper and Dog-ribbed Indians, who traffic with our yearly traders, supply themselves with iron-work, etc.

"From these two tribes our Northern Indians used formerly to purchase most of the furrs they brought to the Company's Factory . . . .

"Several attempts have been made to induce the Copper and Dog-ribbed Indians to visit the Company's fort at Churchill River, and for that purpose many presents have been sent, but they never were attended with any success . . . . It is a political scheme of our Northern traders to prevent such an intercourse, as it would greatly lessen their consequence and emolument."

and reward faithful service with promotion and pensions and gratuities. At most times the Londoners paid close attention to criticism from the shores of Rupert's Land. "Wee Cannot be soe well able to Judg of oure Affaires in the Countrey," they wrote a resident governor, "wee being so farr absent, as you can residing there, therefore we must Leave it to your discretion for the management of our Trade." And in 1716 the resident governor, James Knight, wrote a classic declaration of independence within an organization:

> I shall Observe and follow all such Orders as I Receive from you as farr as possible I cann, but it cannot be thought that you that are at that distance can see or know altogether how things goes here so well as I do that am upon the Spott altho' I do take all the care I can to give you what Information I am able that you may not be Ignorant of the State of this country but to tye me up to Close to follow your Instructions I think it will not be for your Advantage but if you please to give me a Little Lattitude. When I were in England I promis'd you I would do what lay in my Power to promote your Interests here which I have in no ways bean wanting as yett in performing of my Duty . . . there is no Man fitt to Serve you, that must be told his Business.

The unfortunate consequence of Knight's independence and enterprise was the voyage he undertook in 1719 up the northwest coast of the Bay to search for legendary copper mines and perhaps the Northwest Passage. Knight and both his ships disappeared. It was later learned that the governor's shipwrecked party was massacred by Inuit. Adventuresome traders such as Knight or Henry Kelsey, who in the early 1690s had made the first important inland journey from Hudson Bay by an Englishman, were not typical or even altogether desirable servants of the Company. Its penchant was for stolid, unimaginative employees, the less given to drink and debauchery (habits that often seemed to accompany an independent disposition) the better. In 1682 Governor John Nixon urged the Committee to hire "Some country lads, that are not acquainted with strong drink, that will woorke hard, and faire hard, and are not debauched with the voluptwousness of the city."

"If England can not furnish you with men," Nixon added, "Scotland can, for that countrie is a hard country to live in, and poore – mens wages is cheap, they are hardy people both to endure hunger, and cold, and are subject to obedience, and I am sure that they will serve for 6 pound pr. yeare, and be better content, with their dyet than Englishmen." It was not long before most of the Company's servants were drawn from north Britain, particularly from the poor crofters and fisherfolk of the Orkney Islands, where ships often stopped for final supplies. The Orcadians normally lived such bleak, hard lives that the numbing isolation of the fur trade on Hudson Bay was no special hardship. For them and most of the other Company servants (a number of whom began their careers as adolescent apprentices), life became so totally bound up with the fortunes of the organization that they developed strong loyalties as "company men." Probing the hierarchical and "household" relationships within the Hudson's Bay Company, fur-trade historian Jennifer Brown sees similarities with the social relationships in corporate organizations in modern Japan.

The Laurentian-based French fur trade never fully recovered from the gluts of the early 1700s and the collapse of the compagnies du Nord and du Canada. French officials were reluctant to unleash the energies of free traders and tried to keep the business licensed and enmeshed in a network of military posts. Commanders at Niagara, Detroit, and Michilimackinac controlled the trade of their regions, sometimes running it on their own accounts, sometimes granting congés to associates or other small traders. French trade relations with the Indians became part of an intricate pattern of diplomatic relations. Economic advantage was sometimes subordinated to political or military requirements, but traders profited from state subsidization in such areas as gift-giving to friendly tribes. The French Compagnie des Indes resumed control of the export monopoly for New France and about one million livres' worth of pelts (about two and a half times the value of furs exported from Hudson Bay) were shipped annually to France.

The French trade centred on the Great Lakes. Slightly more than half the furs were gathered in country south and west of the Lakes, particularly the Ohio valley, where competition came from Anglo-Americans and their Iroquois allies, and, further south, from other Frenchmen based in Louisiana. Traders out of Albany, New York, continued to be aggressive on Lake Ontario in the early 1720s. (Part of the French response was the establishment of a small post, Fort Rouillé, at the end of the Lake Huron–Lake Ontario portage, a place the Indians called Toronto.) Some Albany merchants were content, in the fashion of the Hudson's Bay Company, to let other people, Indians or whites, gather furs and retail trade goods among the natives. In other words, they were doing a wholesale trade, dealing in large quantities and leaving the risks and rewards of retailing to others.

The European nations banned trade between each other's colonies. There was so much smuggling between Montreal and Albany that at times the French traders seem to have been serving as retailers of the highly valued Strouds (blankets), the cheap rum, and the prized wampum that came up from the south. They paid for their goods with skins that the Albany merchants, shipping from New York, could market in London more effectively than the monopoly exporting from Quebec to France. From the days when the coureurs first went into the interior to reach the tribes directly, this drive to extend the trade to the retail level had been a distinguishing feature of the French method. They had displaced Indian middlemen and gone to live and trade and wander with the nomads.

There were no coureurs left in Montreal, for the trade had moved too far west. A Montreal-based trader could not get goods up to the Indians and furs out in a single season. An increasingly sophisticated supply network developed out of the St. Lawrence in which "marchands-équipeurs" outfitted expeditions of big canoes paddled by paid engagés. A voyage might terminate at Detroit or Michilimackinac, where goods were sold and furs bought for the return trip. Perhaps a marchand-voyageur with the expedition would take the goods into the interior and trade them himself. Here he would be competing with the many small traders – the new coureurs or "vagabonds" or "pedlars" as the English called them – who operated from interior posts. French coureurs lived and traded up and down the whole Missouri–Ohio–Mississippi and Great Lakes systems. Michilimackinac was a centre for several hundred "vagabond" traders. "Many of these have inhabited the Indian country from twelve to thirty years, differing little from the Natives except in Colour," a British general reported after the Conquest, "and being more addicted to vice."

Even as they tried to establish a foothold on Hudson Bay, French fur traders realized that they could literally forestall the English by meeting Indians upstream from the Hudson's Bay Company's posts. After they abandoned the Bay, and as competition increased southwest of the Great Lakes, the French renewed their quest for the peltry of the Hudson Bay watershed by developing a trade north and west from Lake Superior. In the 1730s Pierre Gaultier de Varennes, the Sieur de la Vérendrye, along with his sons, extended the French network of postes du Nord from Lake Superior through the western forest to Lake Winnipeg and onto the Great Plains. While doing this, La Vérendrye was continually scrutinized by French officials who endorsed his proclaimed goal of searching for the Western Sea, but suspected that his real interest was in discovering a new "sea of beaver." France would support exploration and expansion for discovery's sake, but worried that the whole venture might, as Père Charlevoix wrote, "degenerate into a mere business of fur trading."

It did. La Vérendrye himself used up his trading profits in his explorations and was insolvent at his death in 1749. But the postes du Nord became a major threat to the Hudson's Bay Company's trade at its leading posts of Albany and Fort York. While the Britishers sat on the Bay waiting for the Indians to come down to trade, the French went into the woods to find the Indians and do the trading. As a result, the furs of the Assiniboine and Saskatchewan regions began to flow through Lake Superior and the St. Lawrence rather than the Bay.

———————————

The Hudson's Bay Company responded cautiously to the competition. After the French had left the Bay in 1713, the Company's business had gradually stabilized. Fur markets improved, the long dividend famine ended in 1718, and through what the Company's historian, E.E. Rich, labels "fortunate ineptitude," a major stock issue to take advantage of history's first great bull market was withdrawn just as the South Sea Bubble collapsed in 1720. For the next generation and more the

Company went about its business, making about £10,000 a year on £20-30,000 worth of trade, paying steady dividends, and building up large financial reserves. The Britishers knew of the French penetration of the interior and the natives' trading response: as one factor put it, the tribes were becoming "so Nice and Dufficult in the way of Trade that I admire to see it."

Realizing that "now is the time to oblige the Indians," the Company's traders offered better prices and more presents, particularly more brandy. The firm tried to open a northern trade out of reach of the French by developing its fort at the mouth of the Churchill River and moving still further north. At the same time its trading presence was strengthened at the Bottom of the Bay (James Bay) where the French influence was most strongly felt. The Company also began exploiting the trading and whaling possibilities of the Eastmain (eastern) coast of Hudson Bay. Credit was extended to Indians in the form of goods payable in furs the next year. The risk that the debtors might not return was balanced by the calculation that they would be attracted by the prospect of further credits.

Some factors wanted to move inland to meet the French on their own ground. Joseph Isbister, the master of Albany, led the way on his own initiative in 1743 by establishing Henley House one hundred miles up the Albany River, just above a French post. The London Committee was not enthusiastic about the experiment, insisting that Henley be no more than a kind of advance advertising depot, displaying wares the Indians could get if they paddled down to Albany. The Company's men at Henley did not adjust well to year-round life among the natives; in 1755 the post's six inhabitants were murdered in a quarrel over women and access to supplies. After a second murder in 1759, probably inspired by the French, Henley House was abandoned as a failed experiment.

The idea of going inland, in effect, to advertise, was pursued. In the 1750s the committee began sending men "a great way up into the Country with presents to the Indians. It may be a means of drawing down many of the Natives to trade." The most impressive of what E.E. Rich calls these "propaganda tours" was Anthony Henday's journey to the Saskatchewan country and the foot of the Rockies in 1754–55. He wintered among the Blackfeet, recorded many details about the customs of the Plains Indians, and returned to York with a flotilla of Indian companions eager to trade.

Henday had trouble getting his fellow travellers past the French posts en route. Over a thousand prime pelts were traded to the French for brandy. He was also surprised to realize that the natives had organized the fur trade to the extent that most of the Crees who came to the Bay regularly were middlemen trading with other tribes. Henday concluded that the Company should by-pass the Indian middlemen, move inland, and compete directly with the French. At home in England there was also criticism of the Company's apparent lack of enterprise, what one assailant labelled its eighty-year "Sleep by the Frozen Sea." The Hudson's Bay Company had failed to explore its territory, found settlements, or allow competitors to do the business properly. Why should such a lazy firm continue to monopolize the trade and government of a northern empire many times larger than the British Isles themselves?

The Company's charter had dubious legal validity. It had been issued by royal prerogative and confirmed only once by Parliament, in 1690 for a seven-year term. There had been no renewal. The Company was not only powerless to keep traders from Canada out of Rupert's Land, but probably could not had excluded determined competition in the Bay (some of its critics did eventually mount disguised fur trading voyages, but little came of them). By the mid-1740s the Company was beginning to lose significant quantities of furs to the French inland posts. "It is surprising to observe what an influence the French have over the Natives," Henday observed. "The French talk several languages to perfection: they have the advantage of us in every shape; and if they had Brazile tobacco, which they have not, would entirely cut off our trade."

French inroads on the Company's trade could not easily have been prevented. The Hudson's Bay Company simply lacked the skills to develop the kind of inland retail trade that the French had mastered. Its seafaring servants had no more idea how to journey up wild rivers than the natives had of crossing the ocean to England. They could not live off the land or pass through the waters. Not five of the Company's one hundred servants could travel by canoe, a former critic wrote in the 1740s, "they are so apt to overturn and drown them." It was not easy to learn canoeing skills on the Bay's shores because the lack of birch trees there made it impossible to make canoes. After Company servants did learn to travel upriver (with much help from hired natives), it was not certain that by-passing their own Indian trading partners would be a productive strategy; the main result of an upriver trade might simply be to ruin the business of the Bayside posts.

For many years there was little sense of urgency. Profits were good, it was not clear that the London market could absorb more furs, and the French supply lines through Quebec, Montreal, the lakes, portages, and rivers, were too long and expensive to support much more than a harrassing competition. The Company knew that many of its British critics, who thought it should be encouraging settlement and developing the natural wealth of its lands, were thoroughly ignorant of the harsh realities of the northern interior. In the late 1740s its defence of its monopoly was supported in the report of a parliamentary investigation. There was no case for interfering with the Company's trade, the MPs concluded, "unless the french was dislodged . . . which is not practicable whilst Canada is in their possession."

The dislodging of the French came sooner than Parliament could have anticipated. In the late 1750s the postes du Nord were gradually abandoned as New France crumbled under British military pressure. In 1759–60 the traders on Hudson Bay found that the whole fur business of the north and west, all the way to the Rockies, was in their control. It had taken ninety years instead of the six that Jolliet had predicted, and the victory was won mainly by force of arms to the south, but the English on the Bay were now the masters of the trade of all Canada.

In 1761 the master of Moose Factory wrote that his commerce was being threatened by "Interlopers who will be more destructive to our Trade than the French was. . . . The French were in a manner Settled, Their Trade fixt, Their Standard moderate and themselves under particular regulations and restrictions, which I doubt is the Case now." This was the first report of competition from a group the Hudson's Bay Company factors soon labelled "the Pedlars from Canada." They were new traders, mostly Scotsmen and Englishmen, who had swarmed into Montreal and the French Great Lakes posts after the Conquest; they were making the old French system their base for bolder, tougher competition than the French had ever attempted. When the leading Pedlars eventually coalesced to form the North West Company, they did cause the Hudson's Bay Company more worry than the French had, for they turned the "mere business of fur trading" into North America's first transcontinental commerce.

The Pedlars came from both Britain and the American colonies and drifted into the St. Lawrence–Great Lakes system at various points. Young merchants came out to represent British exporting houses in Quebec and Montreal, and soon began outfitting canoes. Some of the sutlers or freelance suppliers to the conquering armies stayed in the new province and tried their hands at the fur trade, often going up-country themselves with experienced French Canadians. The old French posts at Niagara, Detroit, and Michilimackinac attracted men from New York and other colonies who traded individually for a season or two and then began forming partnerships up and down the system. The biggest rewards in trading came from big whole-sales made by importers and exporters out of Montreal or London, so the most successful Pedlars tended to leave the high country for the cities. Young Simon McTavish, for example, moved first from Albany to Detroit and then, leaving his lesser partners among the "poor Bearskin catchers" in the interior, moved east to Montreal, with voyages to London, to make his fortune. "I am going home with all our Packs on our own risque," he wrote in 1776: "Fortune has proved so kind a Mistress to me for some years past that perhaps I am too Sanguine; and the Jade may now Jilt me . . . – at any rate I am determin'd to Venture."

James McGill, a Glaswegian trading out of Michilimackinac, moved back to Montreal about the same time, where the Frobishers and Grants and Isaac Todd and other English and Scotsmen were already in business. The new men often outfitted or stood bond for French-Canadian traders, many of whom survived in the business, particularly in the high country. With most of their suppliers gone back to France or ruined by the wars, with the collapse of their currency, and with London now the metropolis for the fur trade, Canadien fur traders had to scramble to form new connections and partnerships. Some, like the Baby brothers, made a smooth transition from French to London correspondents and prospered in a business they had mastered long before most of their new competitors had ever seen a canoe. Many of their countrymen stayed active for a decade or more after the Conquest, but usually as small fish. It was the Scots and Englishmen – kin and kind – who began pooling their resources and integrating their operations up and down the trading network of a colony also governed by kin and kind.

More Pedlars came up from the old colonies when the Quebec Act of 1774 made the whole fur-trading country part of Quebec. Then the American Revolution cut off American fur traders' suppies of British-made trade goods and access to the London market. By the early 1780s Montreal was the uncontested centre of the mid-continental skin trade. The French-speakers who had begun it all were still essential to the process, but usually as the salaried engagés who did the brutal work of moving the goods and furs up and down the vast system.

For more than a generation after the Conquest most of Montreal's furs continued to be harvested southwest of the Great Lakes, even after a border was negotiated and that land became part of the new United States of America in 1783. Major Montreal fur firms, such as the partnership of Isaac Todd and James McGill, flourished for years on the business of the Ohio country. Their competition came from French traders exporting down the Mississippi through New Orleans, and from small but growing networks that American traders were beginning to create. The Montrealers urged British authorities to retain effective control of the Ohio country long after it was part of the United States, and for several reasons the British military presence did linger on U.S. soil for more than a decade. But the encroachment could not last. After the British withdrew from the United States in the late 1790s, and again when the War of 1812 sealed the border with blood, the tendency of the Canadian traders, reinforced by the ambitions and lobbying of their American competitors, was to follow the flag northward. The great rivalry in the Canadian fur trade would be for the pelts of the wilderness north and west of Lake Superior.

The Pedlars from Canada began to trouble the Hudson's Bay Company, and each other, when they started draining furs out of modern Manitoba and the country of the Saskatchewan River. The Hudson's Bay Company factors complained that these "Cursed Pedlars up Country" were trespassers trading illegally and flaunting the Company's chartered rights. You could expect the French to contest the charter, but surely British subjects ought to respect it and stay out of the Company's lands. The Pedlars, who had previously ignored most attempts by British administrators in Quebec to control the trade, paid no attention to HBC complaints. They boasted of their liberty to trade wherever they chose, and the Company was too unsure of the validity of its charter to attempt its enforcement through either home or colonial courts. Writing in those years, Adam Smith concluded that the Hudson Bay fur trade was a rare instance of justified monopoly. But the Company had little political influence in the growing free trade climate in

Britain that the rest of Smith's oeuvre was stimulating. It had to learn to live with the new competition.

Complaints that competition would be the death of the fur trade became more frequent. It could literally be the death of natives because all the traders competed by plying them with more liquor. Traders who gave Indians presents of liquor or other goods, or who had advanced credit to natives, assumed they had a proprietary right to the furs their "clients" trapped. They occasionally asserted their right by using force against the Indians or against competing traders meddling with their Indians. At its worst, in the hands of unscrupulous Pedlars determined to get furs and move on, the fur trade created debauchery and anarchy, limitless competition that was disastrous to natives, fur-bearing animals, and whites alike. In 1787 two worried Hudson's Bay Company traders, William Tomison and George Hudson, complained eloquently to the governor general of British North America:

> Good Sir: – We the Servants of the Honourable Hudson's Bay Company have of late years received very ill treatment from a set of lawless men that has passed from Canada for tradeing in the interior parts of Hudson's Bay; it has been a long standing Custom since the Company's first settling in Hudson's Bay to give large Credits to the Indians, but now of late years by the great quantity of Rum they bring from Canada which this sett of Men despersed amongst the Company's Creditors [debtors] in all parts along the Bay, Debauching the Natives into a state of insensibility and takes from them by force what they cannot obtain with Goods, this I call Robbery and defrauding the Company of their property, but we hope for the time to come that better regulations will be made for such an undertaking, and not to a set of Men that neither regards King or Government.... I myself have been threatened to be shot by Wm. Holmes; it grieves us to see a Body of Indians destroyed by a set of Men merely for self Interest, doing all in their Power to Destroy Posterity, so we hope that your Excellency will make such regulations as will preserve Posterity and not be Destroyed by fiery double Distilled Rum from Canada.

The most fierce competition was always among the Pedlars themselves. The Hudson's Bay Company had the advantage of the shorter Bay route, which produced a significantly lower cost structure for its trade. Traders out of Montreal all had roughly similar high costs. When the Pedlars were vying for the same natives the usual way to outdo one another was to be bolder, tougher, more ruthless. There were so many competing traders by the 1770s that local agreements to limit competition, often by dividing territory in a seasonal partnership, began to form. On the North Saskatchewan near Sturgeon River in 1778–79 there was a recognizable "strip" of fur traders' posts: three major Pedlar houses, half a dozen or more smaller establishments, and a Hudson's Bay Company post, all within six hundred yards. The Pedlars agreed to cooperate that spring in a "General Partnership," forbade the HBC factors to trade with "their" Indians, beat up one who protested, and sometimes locked up natives who were reluctant to trade their furs.

(Violence was even worse further up the Saskatchewan at Eagle Hills that year. A native drinking spree turned violent after a trader gave one of them grog laced with laudanum, "setting him asleep for ever." "This accident produced a fray," Sir Alexander Mackenzie wrote, "in which one of the traders and several of the men were killed, while the rest had no other means to save themselves but by a precipitate flight, abandoning a considerable quantity of goods and near a half of the furs which they had collected during the winter and spring." Native retaliation against white violence was not infrequent. Violence in the fur trade on both sides was probably under-reported. At times the Hudson's Bay Company factors consoled themselves with the thought that violent Pedlars would be destroyed in a whirlwind of native retribution.)

Another competitive strategy was to push into new territory to find new natives with new supplies of pelts. The records seldom show which half-starved, semi-literate Pedlar first pushed over this or that Indian portage into new country. The most famous exploit by a literate, established trader was American-born Peter Pond's leadership of a small expedition, combined from the outfits of several traders, which crossed the height of land into the Athabasca country in 1778–79. Pond wintered on the Athabasca River, part of a vast new watershed, used the "tar" oozing from the banks of the river to caulk his canoes, and accumulated more fine thick pelts in that cold country than his canoes could carry out. He had broken through into the fur traders' Eldorado, the last untapped peltry country east of the mountains.

The Pedlars consolidated their interests partly because there was too much competition, partly because there was too little. The less venturesome traders united to pool their business and reduce a ruinous competition. The more venturesome, like Pond, needed an organization to support and coordinate journeys that took the traders out of range of such established entrepôts as Michilimackinac. (As the traders moved into the Saskatchewan country and on to Athabasca, their basic supply depot had to be advanced from Mackinac to the Grand Portage at the head of Superior; when Grand Portage became American territory, a new depot had to be created at Kaministiquia, soon renamed Fort William. There were not enough traders at the far frontier for these changes to take place naturally in a market response to their demand.) Both to eliminate competition, then, and to coordinate an advanced trade, the leading Pedlars found it advantageous to unite. Wintering traders in the interior as well as Montreal outfitters participated in this merger movement.

Several small groupings operated under the title of the North West Company in the 1760s and 1770s. The first major consolidation under that name was a sixteen-share partnership formed in 1779 by eight of the leading trading firms (Todd and McGill, the Frobishers, McGill and Paterson, McTavish and Company, Holmes and Grant, Wadden and Company, Ross and Company, Oakes and Company). This North West Company was reorganized and expanded in 1783. Benjamin and Joseph Frobisher explained to Governor Haldimand of Quebec in 1784 how the various "Adventurers" had been taught "by experience that separate Interests were the Bane of that Trade." The business was precarious and expensive, and could not be carried on "in opposite Interests, without manifest ruin to some of the parties concerned and the destruction of the Trade. While on the contrary, by a well regulated System in that long and precarious chain of connections which a Company alone can establish and execute, every Advantage may be derived for discovery and improvement." The Frobishers proclaimed high ideals for the new organization:

> The present Company have accordingly adopted the most proper measures to answer those ends, and have entered upon the Business with a determined Spirit, to supply the Natives plentifully with every necessary they require which is the only sure means to extend it and to obtain a perfect knowledge of the Country, so far as it may be done without interfering with the Commercial rights of the Hudson's Bay Company, which on all occassions they will carefully avoid.

They concluded by asking for "An Exclusive Right to the Trade of the North-West" – a monopoly.

The North West Company did not get its monopoly, and in the early years did not even control the Montreal trade. There was always competition in American territory, and there were almost always Montrealers and other small traders operating on their own in the British Northwest. In the mid-1780s the Montreal house of Gregory, McLeod and Company gave particularly strong backing to several winterers, including the cousins Roderick and Alexander Mackenzie, sparking several years of intense competition. The ties of humanity, race, or simple common sense often overcome commercial hostility in the forests, as rivals faced maddening loneliness, starvation, disease, and native hostility. Traders often cooperated. But at other times their competition was savage and bloody, as when Peter Pond's rival on the Athabasca was murdered by two of Pond's men. He was the second trader whose opposition to Pond had ended in violent death. The Gregory, McLeod interests were absorbed by the North West Company in a 1787 reorganization. Alexander Mackenzie described how the merger had come about:

> After the murder of one of our partners, the laming of another and the narrow escape of one of our clerks, who received a bullet through his powder horn, in the execution of his duty, they [the North Westers] were compelled to allow us a share of the trade. As we had already incurred a loss, this union was, in every respect, a desirable event to us.

The North West Company had to be reorganized every few years, but was more or less permanent in form. For the quarter-century after the 1787 coalition the North Westers dominated Montreal and the Canadian fur trade through its greatest years. As soon as the spring ice went out in the St. Lawrence, the North West Company had its brigade of canots du maître ready for the inland journey. Thirty or more eight-to-ten-man canoes, each carrying four tons of freight, set out from Lachine up the Ottawa, crossed gruelling portages to Lake Nipissing and down the French River, battled the winds on Lake Huron past the Sault Ste Marie and across Lake Superior to Grand Portage or Fort William. Here the voyageurs met the company's fleet of the smaller canots du nord bringing the furs and many of the winterers out from the upper country. Amidst relaxation and revelry, trade goods and furs were transshipped while the partners, including those who had come from Montreal, discussed the company's affairs. Early in July the winterers headed back to their posts in canoes packed with trade goods for another season. The "mangeurs du lard" from Montreal headed home with the furs.

While the winterers traded and settled in for months of frozen tedium in their log shacks, the Montreal partners despatched furs abroad, ordered more trade goods, and hired next year's canoemen and clerks. Simon McTavish, whose determined ventures had paid off handsomely, was the most important of the Montreal partners. McTavish, Frobisher and Company held the largest share of the North West Company and was its Montreal agent and supplier, effectively its manager, on a commission basis. The London agents were McTavish, Fraser and Company – that is, Simon McTavish's talented and tireless cousin, John Fraser.

The fur trade involved much more than seasons of canoeing and partying, buying and selling. It took one summer to get a supply of trade goods from England to Montreal. The second summer they moved inland. The furs came out the third year, and were sold in London the fourth. Supplying credit for the business became an important function of the London houses, such as McTavish, Fraser, which began the flow of goods and were the last to handle the furs. As inland transportation routes from Montreal stretched thousands of miles into the northern wilderness, feeding the voyageurs became a major undertaking. Provisions had to be moved from Niagara and Detroit up to Grand Portage. The staple of interior travel was pemmican, a mixture of pounded dried buffalo meat with fat, which was obtained on the plains and cached for the fast-moving canoeist.

There was a high turnover of labour in the trade: freighting by canoe was body-destroying and low-paying, less and less attractive to French Canadians as the growth of agriculture and lumbering in the St. Lawrence region opened up better ways to make a living. The North West Company employed one thousand to fifteen hundred men and its wage bill made up more than half its annual expenditure. Wage pressure caused the North Westers and other Montreal fur traders to replace canoes with flat-bottomed boats on the upper St. Lawrence and sailing ships on the Great Lakes whenever possible. The company made its own canoes and boats and even dug its own canal, complete with locks, to let canoes by-pass the rapids at Sault Ste Marie. The North Westers became involved in road-building in York, Upper Canada, to improve the portage from Lake Ontario to Georgian Bay, ran a sawmill to provide lumber at Grand Portage, and in Montreal in the early 1790s planned to create a bank to facilitate commercial exchanges. A special "Winter Express" courier service rushed commercial intelligence (quantities of furs obtained, trade goods needed, and so on) up and down their interior system. To overcome winter's effect on the St. Lawrence, men and goods moved north and south between Montreal and ice-free New York.

When the Montreal bookkeeping was done, when a partner came down to the St. Lawrence to buy some land and retire after a hard career in the wilderness, when distinguished guests had to be entertained, there were the toasts, songs, stories, and spirits of the Beaver Club dinners in Montreal. "We dined at four o'clock," a guest wrote,

> and after taking a satisfactory quantity of wine, perhaps a bottle each, the married men . . . retired, leaving about a dozen to drink their health. We now began in earnest and in true highland style, and by four o'clock in the morning the whole of us had reached such a degree of perfection that we could all give the war whoop as well as [Alexander] Mackenzie and [William] McGillivray, we could all sing admirable, we could all drink like fishes, and we all thought we could dance on the table without disturbing a single decanter, glass or plate by which it was profusely covered.

The same guest's last memory of another evening was of Mackenzie proposing a toast to fallen comrades – those who had fallen under the table – and pushing a bottle to McGillivray before the two traders slid to join their fellows.

Simon McTavish was apparently not one of the Beaver Club elite, for he had never wintered beyond Grand Portage and so did not meet the membership requirement. But as probably the richest man in Montreal, a connoisseur of good food and fine women (at age forty-three he married an eighteen-year-old French-Canadian belle of an old fur-trading family), the "Marquis" enjoyed the good life his success had brought him. He owned estates in Scotland, and in Montreal was building a grand mansion at the foot of the mountain when he died suddenly in 1804 in his fifty-fifth year.

The huge distances and high costs involved in the Montreal fur trade had the paradoxical effect of making the North Westers more expansive. It was no longer a matter of seeking new Indians and cheaper furs, for no pelts that had to move more than twenty-five hundred miles to Montreal were cheap. Instead, the company explored and expanded in hope of finding new and cheaper routes, above all a way of getting furs out to the Pacific.

Peter Pond's breakthrough into a new watershed at Athabasca in the late 1770s raised the possibility, which Pond understood, that these rivers and lakes drained into the Pacific. Captain James Cook and others were already exploring northern North America's west coasts from the sea, trading some furs with the coastal Indians, and finding a fabulous market for North America sea-otter pelts in China. After the 1787 merger, the North West Company sent Alexander Mackenzie into Athabasca to replace the violence-tainted Pond. Mackenzie was encouraged to find a route to the Pacific. In 1789 he made an epic trip down the new water system to the ocean. It turned out to be the wrong ocean, the Arctic. The frustrated explorer is said to have named the long river he had descended the River Disappointment. Others named it the Mackenzie. "My *Expedition* is hardly spoken of," Mackenzie wrote, describing his partners' attitudes at the 1790 Grand Portage meeting, "but this is what I expected." What was the use of discovering great rivers it they had no commercial value?

Mackenzie tried again in the autumn of 1792, ascending the Peace River into the mountains. He crossed the continental divide, reached the headwaters of the Fraser, and then took natives' advice and headed west by land. This North West Company adventurer was the first white to cross North America north of Mexico, leaving his record on a rock by Bella Coola Inlet: "Alexander Mackenzie, from Canada, by land, the twenty-second of July, one thousand seven hundred and ninety-three." It was another disappointing trip for fur traders because the extremely difficult route had no practical value.

The North Westers remained determined to cross the Rockies and open the Pacific slope for their trade. They pushed posts into the northern regions of British Columbia (which they called New Caledonia); in 1807–18 Simon Fraser explored the great river named after him (another costly, hazardous, and commercially unrewarding trip); and David Thompson, a geographer and adventurer who had come over from the slow-moving Hudson's Bay Company, finally developed a practical route to the sea down the Columbia in 1811. Unfortunately Thompson was not aggressively enterprising and took his time in his travels. When he reached the mouth of the Columbia he found the Stars and Stripes flying over Astoria, a fort established from the sea by John Jacob Astor's American Fur Company.

The North West Company was already attempting trial shipments of furs to China through London and New York. After the War of 1812 it purchased Astoria (which was on jointly held territory) and continued to try to develop the Pacific trade. The proud North Westers used their transcontinental achievement as a lobbying point – they were a company expanding the bounds of empire – against certain of their rivals, notably big companies with huge land grants and monopolistic trading rights. Some of the traders, particularly Alexander Mackenzie, dreamt of a vast inter-oceanic and transcontinental commerce, with trade goods from London being converted to furs in British North America and the furs shipped across the

Pacific where their proceeds would buy cargoes of tea and silks from the Orient. There would be a Northwest Passage by land through Canada.

———————

Where was the Hudson's Bay Company while this grand expansion of Montreal's fur trade was taking place? Its first response to the Pedlars was to stop slumbering by the Bay and realize that its men had to learn how to go inland and compete at what was, in effect, a retail trade. "These little Houses round us send as much furs each out of the Country as Your great factorys have sometimes done," a factor at Moose wrote in disgust on the eve of the change in policy in the 1770s. Slowly, painfully, the Orcadians learned how to get up the rivers from the Bay (developing the flat-bottomed York boat as a substitute for the canoe), set up cheap, portable "long tents" in competition with the Pedlars, and match the opposition dram for dram in debauching willing Indians. The London Committee did its share of yearning for an easy route to the Pacific and China, but had to solve a more immediate problem of getting into Athabasca to challenge the North Westers in what had become prime fur country. Neither goal was achieved, the former being impractical, the latter aim floundering in confusions about route, badly planned expeditions, and a distaste for face-to-face confrontations with the lawless Montrealers.

The Hudson's Bay Company moved more hesitantly and carefully than the Montrealers, exploring and surveying more thoroughly as it went (their surveyors disdained Alexander Mackenzie for seldom knowing where he was), endlessly pondering the pros and cons of strategic manoeuvres. The North West Company's partners in the interior were ambitious and impatient and determined; their Canadian employees could endure almost any hardship and knew how to live as natives. The Hudson's Bay Company's London managers were prosperous, conservative, and unimaginative; during the long Napoleonic wars the quality of men they could recruit fell even further, and their servants were even less enterprising than in earlier generations. When occasional Canadian traders were hired by the Company and began using their normally aggressive methods, their fellow factors were horrified and critical.

The Hudson's Bay Company usually had no taste for all-out competition with the North West Company. Documents indicate that wherever it was feasible the two big concerns encouraged a policy of live and let live, agreeing in certain localities not to meddle with each other's Indians or to tamper with each other's employees. The idea of some kind of merger was often in the air, particularly because the North Westers increasingly realized that their trade was imperilled unless they could share the cost advantage of the Bay routes to the fur country. As costs rose in Montreal (with labour becoming more expensive by the year) and supply lines stretched and stretched, everyone knew that the Bay was the key to the whole situation. It was even the key to the idea of a Pacific trade, for it would be the entry point of the transcontinental route Mackenzie and others projected.

The realization that they possessed the ace in the hole tended to make the Hudson's Bay Company's Committee more conservative and complacent. Its goods were cheaper than those of its rivals. The Indians were bound to keep coming to its posts. Even the Montrealers, proud and tough as they were, would someday come to London to seek an accommodation. That, at least, was the theory.

All the fur traders had benefited from expanding markets and good prices for their skins, not only in Europe but in far-off China and much closer to home in the growing American market. By 1800 the United States was beginning to absorb large quantities of furs of all kinds, including many pelts purchased in Montreal by traders such as Astor. Without effective access to this market, or most other non-English outlets, the Hudson's Bay Company was not able to increase its trade in competition with the North Westers. By the 1790s the Montrealers were selling more than five times the furs exported by their northern rivals – a trade of £70,000 to £100,000 annually versus £12,000 to £20,000 for the Hudson's Bay Company.

After more than fifty years of paying 8 to 10 per cent dividends on the par value of its stock, the HBC paid nothing from 1783 to 1785, resumed at 5 per cent, pushed the payment briefly as high as 8 per cent, but in 1801 cut back to 4 per cent and in 1809 suspended dividends again. With net profits of less than £3,000 in 1806, the Company was in fact paying dividends out of reserves. In 1808 the Hudson's Bay Company petitioned the British government for "that Temporary Assistance which we cannot ask at any other hands" because it had sold no furs in two years. Napoleon's blockade of the United Kingdom had apparently destroyed the re-export market for furs. "The Company was virtually back where it had been in the seventeenth century," its historian writes; it was financing each year's trade on credit, scrambling to pay those of its creditors at the head of the line. Instead of petitioning for a merger, the organized Pedlars in Montreal seemed to be going from strength to strength.

Canadians have a tendency, encouraged by some sloppy history writing, to assume that the fur trade and its companies were of vast economic importance. They were not. In its best years, the total fur trade from British North American territory was in the £200,000 to £300,000 range. These were still significant figures in the northern economy (though far less than, say, the year's catch in the Newfoundland fishery), but a minuscule contribution to British trade. By international standards the fur trade was a tiny industry. The historic Hudson's Bay Company – about a hundred shareholders, a significant number of whom were dead, whose stock was worth £60,000 to £100,000 or less – was still, in the words of K.G. Davies, "a dollhouse company." If it had not survived England would not have missed it.

The Company did not get its government help in 1808. It held on because it was small and had a record of more than a century of fairly steady success. Its modest financial needs could easily be met by such powerful lenders as the Bank of England.

The London Committee wondered at times if the business could be continued. By 1810 it was mulling over a range of options: attempting to exploit the timber resources of the Bay, adjusting its system to give its traders so much freedom that the HBC could eventually become simply their shipping agent; most significantly, making plans to develop the fertile southwestern portions of Rupert's Land. The Hudson's Bay Company was being beaten down by the Montreal competition, but it had important resources left.

The North West Company often found its most severe competition came from other Montreal traders. Good trading years in the 1790s brought rivals into the field and the rival personalities within the partnership sometimes could not be contained. In 1798 several Montreal trading houses and winterers, with backing from Britain, combined to form the Montreal North West Company, soon called the XY Company after the markings on their bales. After a quarrel with Simon McTavish, the proud explorer Sir Alexander Mackenzie joined the organization three years later, and it was renamed Sir Alexander Mackenzie and Company. Repeating their earlier experience, the Montreal traders found that competitive advantage came only through debauching the Indians and intimidating and assaulting both the natives and one another. Posts and employees were multiplied recklessly. Even on a rising fur market, which encouraged their rivalry, both firms lost money in a bitter struggle of stubborn Scotsmen: the established traders of the "old concern" against "those damned starving cats, the potties." "The detail of their proceedings during five years would probably be invidious and disagreeable," an old fur trader/historian wrote. "Instead of providing for their wives and children the wretched Indians lay near a post for weeks together in a state of intoxication; the contending parties and their servants were continually quarrelling, and many acts of violence were committed . . . . In the year 1804, the two contending parties finding that the struggle only exhausted their capitals and made the natives idle, debauched and insubordinate, agreed to unite." The death of Simon McTavish, who appears to have been a domineering, divisive influence among Montreal fur traders, helped ease the union, as did a fear that much more violence might lead to government intervention to maintain law and order. In 1804 Alexander Mackenzie and Company merged into a reorganized North West Company.

The North Westers were not always ruthless competitors. During the firm's several lives the North West Company partners were willing to merge with opponents or divide territory whenever it seemed advantageous. A long series of agreements with both American and Canadian competitors limited activities on the United States' side of the border. After merging with the XY group, the North Westers talked with the Hudson's Bay Company in 1804, exploring alternatives ranging from the lease of rights to use the Bay route through a complete merger of the firms. At the same time they challenged the HBC's charter by sending a trading expedition into the Bay and founding a post there.

The negotiations fizzled out in disagreement about terms for a transit concession. The North Westers probably could have obtained HBC support for a friendly takeover by stock purchase, or they could have continued to interlope in the Bay and fought the Company's charter in the courts. They hesitated to do either (abandoning their presence on the Bay). The problem appears to have been the loyalty that the North West Company had to Montreal and the St. Lawrence–Great Lakes trading route. The Montrealers were caught in the same dilemma as the Canadian shareholders of the Compagnie du Nord a century before: it would be more profitable to use the Bay route, but doing so would necessarily mean abandoning everything that had been built up in Canada. The leading spirits in the North West Company, Montrealers first, decided to carry on the competition rather than turn themselves into Londoners trading into Hudson Bay.

A few years later some of the North Westers again approached the HBC, proposing a partition of the fur territory. They also began to buy Hudson's Bay Company stock with the aim of acquiring control. The partition scheme was rejected by the British firm, and the takeover attempt was frustrated in 1811 when the new dominant spirit in Hudson's Bay Company affairs, Thomas Douglas, the Earl of Selkirk, arranged to purchase, at premium prices, all the loose shares the North Westers were after. This contretemps set the stage for the last and most desperate years of competition between the organizations.

Lord Selkirk was a visionary aristocrat who dreamed of helping impoverished Highlanders create flourishing communities in the rich lands of North America. Undaunted by failures in Prince Edward Island and Upper Canada, Selkirk succeeded in 1811 in obtaining from the Hudson's Bay Company, which he and his family and associates effectively controlled, a grant of 116,000 square miles in the valley of the Red River in Assiniboia. In giving away a domain five times the size of Scotland for ten shillings, the Hudson's Bay Company was not being looted by its owners, but was hoping to develop a new resource, its land (to which it had a better legal claim than to monopoly trading rights it had never been able to enforce). Lord Selkirk was required to found an agricultural settlement and would bear the risks of failure. There would be profitable shipping business for the Company in creating and supplying a community at Red River. In turn the settlers would supply the Company with much-needed provisions and labour. Settlement would not interfere with, but would enhance the HBC's fur-trading activities. It might well interfere with the North West Company's trade, for the Red River country was both the junction of the North Westers' transportation lines and the home of its pemmican supplies.

The Montrealers' alarm at the prospect of the Selkirk grant was one of the causes of the aborted takeover attempt. When it failed, the blunt North Westers made clear their absolute resolve that nothing would be permitted to interfere with their business. This view clashed with the fumbling determination of Selkirk and his agents to get settlers onto the granted lands and assert their legal authority. Quarrels over control of pemmican – the traders called it the Pemmican War – blended into wider issues involving the rights of mixed-bloods (or Métis) in the area, many of whom were the children of employees of the North West Company. There had been dozens of confrontations in the fur forests over the decades as tough, ruthless men had faced each other and literally fought to dominate the trade of a local area. Now the agents and dependants of great organizations faced each other and refused to back down. On June 19, 1816, a party of Métis, some employed by the North West Company, all encouraged by it, killed the governor of Red River and twenty others in a confrontation at Seven Oaks. To the settlers and the Hudson's Bay Company it was the Massacre of Seven Oaks. To the North Westers it was an unfortunate but necessary response to those who would have ruined their business.

Lord Selkirk and a party of constables retaliated by capturing the North West Company's headquarters at Fort William and arresting the leading partners. The traders' wars became a "capturing business," as Selkirk himself was arrested on warrants issued by magistrates friendly to the Montreal company. The battles were refought and fought anew in the courts and in print. Selkirk's health broke and his settlement collapsed. The fur trade continued.

But the North West Company had asserted its impressive will for the last time. Behind the façade of arrogance, pride, and determination, the organization was haemorrhaging from its enormous transportation and labour costs. Because the business records of the North West Company have not survived, there is no authoritative reckoning of its financial situation, only a statement a few years later by one of its principals that the partners had received no returns after 1813. Primitive accounting techniques before and after that date apparently disguised the true seriousness of the North Westers' plight until it was too late to do much about it. Many of the partners, particularly the winterers, had no resources to sustain steady losses.

Most Hudson's Bay Company shareholders, by contrast, did not rely on their dividends as a principal source of income. The Company itself used cash reserves and then its standing on London financial markets to sustain it through the worst years, from about 1806 to 1814. At most times its accounts gave a clearer picture of its situation than the North Westers had of theirs. Even as Lord Selkirk's quixotic colonization scheme was floundering toward tragedy, the Hudson's Bay Company's business, skilfully managed by Selkirk's brother-in-law, Andrew Colvile, was beginning to improve. Using seasoned Canadian traders and such promising new servants as young George Simpson, it finally began challenging the North West Company even in Athabasca, the last frontier of the shrinking fur country.

The North West Company's partnership agreement was due to be renegotiated in 1821. The financial situation was so desperate that no agreement among the partners to continue the venture was possible. The winterers wanted an accommodation with the Hudson's Bay Company, and sent agents to London empowered to negotiate. Realizing that the situation could not be saved, the Montreal partners also began negotiating with the Hudson's Bay Company. Because the North West Company's bold façade still held, with Colvile worrying as late as 1820, for example, that "the scoundrels are too strong and rich for us," the terms of union were generous. Former North Westers were to have at least half, perhaps more than half, the shares in the united enterprise. From June 1, 1821, the whole trade was carried on as one concern in the name of the Hudson's Bay Company. And it was run from London through Hudson Bay.

The accounts of the old North West Company took years to be settled. Its agents – McTavish, McGillivray and Company, the successor firm to Simon McTavish's companies – collapsed in bankruptcy, causing heavy losses to many former partners and creditors. The last accountant of the North Westers' affairs ended his life in a British lunatic asylum.

Simon McTavish's empty, unfinished mansion on the slopes of Mount Royal gained local notoriety as a haunted house. The Marquis lay in a vault on the grounds; it was covered with dirt, as protection from vandals, and its location forgotten. In 1861 the mansion was demolished to make way for another millionaire's house.

The "mere business of fur trading" had been taken from sea to sea by the North West Company, a transcontinental trading organization which preceded a transcontinental political organization, the government of Canada, by more than eighty years. Some comments by H.A. Innis and his disciples suggest that the North West Company created the Dominion of Canada. That is a gross oversimplification. There is not a very close correlation between the boundaries of the fur traders' territories and the Canadian–U.S. border. The border emerged as a result of war, politics, diplomacy, geography, and economic factors, of which the fur trade was one. Nor did the North West Company's history prove that the transcontinental trade tended to monopoly or that the northern economy somehow lent itself to big business. The North West Company was an attempt to create a big business monopoly that failed. It was always a loose, ramshackle, pre-modern partnership, which finally fell apart and was absorbed by a competitor it could not defeat. The new monopoly did not last either, we will see, because the fur trade constantly invited competition.

The North Westers were among the most daring, hard-driving, ruthless, and reckless businessmen in Canadian history. Mackenzie standing on the shores of the Arctic Ocean, then the Pacific; Simon Fraser standing at the mouth of his wild river; North Westers standing over the bodies of the Selkirk settlers at Seven Oaks; red-eyed, unshaven fur traders standing over drunken Indians and dirty packs of pelts in the forest: these were the demonstrations of how far men could go to expand a commerce. The men of the Hudson's Bay Company never went that far, and their organization survived.

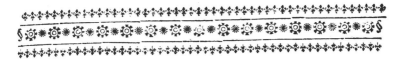

THE
IMPERIAL MAGAZINE,
O R,
Complete Monthly Intelligencer,
For A U G U S T, 1760.

The Importance of CANADA *considered.*
(*An Original Essay.*)

A T a time when it is a point of dispute, whether Canada or Guardalupe will prove the most valuable acquisition to this nation at the ensuing peace, it will not, perhaps, be thought unseasonable to enquire into the importance of the former; I chuse this subject more particularly, as one of your correspondents has already furnished you with an ingenious essay on the latter *.

In considering this subject with the attention it deserves, we must at first remember, that the situation of French America constitutes its greatest importance to this nation. Canada and Louisiana extends on the back of our colonies for near two thousand miles, the southern and middle parts being one of the finest countries in the world, especially if we include that through which the Ohio takes its bending course; consequently, as long as they are in the hands of another nation, Great Britain must be at the continual expence of maintaining a multitude of frontier garrisons; and these must be increased and strengthened, in proportion as the possessions of Canada, &c. multiply and grow wealthy. The present war may convince us, that if garrisons are not maintained on the frontier, in case the country should not be ceded to us at the peace, all the English American settlements will lie at the mercy of our neighbours, on occasion of every difference we may have with them.

It may possibly be objected to what I have said, that the French, if they are left in possession of the country in question, will be obliged to run into the same expence in

UPPER LEFT: **Aaron Hart** *(Jewish Public Library, Montreal)*
UPPER RIGHT: **James McGill** *(Public Archives of Canada #C2873)*
ABOVE: **Canada's attractions,** from *The Emigrant's Guide, 1820)*
(Public Archives of Canada, #C41098)

Wharfs, Warehouses, and Scotsmen:
Merchants' Networks, 1749–1814

Colonies' need for merchants . . . Mauger in Nova Scotia . . . sutlers in Quebec . . . Jewish merchants . . . swarms of Scotsmen . . . fewer French friction with the military . . . "Government is become despicable" . . . merchants' lack of vision . . . Cartwright and Hamilton in Upper Canada . . . shopkeeper aristocrats? . . . more Scotsmen . . . McGill's estate . . . "merchantocracy" in Halifax? . . . "fishocracy" in Newfoundland?

The British took Canada by force of arms. The decisive victory was Wolfe's triumph on the Plains of Abraham in September 1759. That winter his army, commanded by James Murray, held the former French capital, Quebec. Seven thousand British soldiers were accompanied by about one hundred merchants and their servants. "Merchants" was perhaps too dignified a word, for most of these men were camp followers or sutlers, a breed of mean traders and pedlars who followed every eighteenth-century army. Some had won contracts to supply provisions to the troops; others sold whatever they could privately to the officers and men. When the Canadiens laid siege to Quebec that spring the merchants formed an independent company of volunteers to help defend the British gains.

Montreal surrendered to invading British forces a few months later. A call immediately went out for more merchants. General Amherst sent a circular to the governors of New Hampshire, Massachusetts, and New York, urging them "to invite the traders and adventurers of the province over which you preside to transport themselves hither and to Quebec, with quantities of molasses, salt, wines, teas, sugars and all kinds of grocery, as likewise sheep and every thing else that may occur to them to be useful." Amherst promised to give the merchants "good markets and every other encouragement they can in reason wish or desire." The soldiers and civilians of the war-ravaged colony desperately needed the provisions and hard currency that the traders would bring.

Traders thought they needed Canada. "Of all our acquisitions, the conquest of Quebec and consequently of the country of Canada is the most important and most beneficial," a Scots merchant wrote in the *Glasgow Journal* in January 1760, "... for such a source of trade and commerce will be opened to us here, as will be fully sufficient, had we no other, to employ all our trading and commercial people, and find a vent, or constant consumption, for all our goods, products, and manufactures. It is therefore above all things to be wished that the country of Canada may never be relinquished." Deputations of merchants from Glasgow and Greenock urged politicians to ensure that "the French should be totally cleared out of North America."

Greenock was Glasgow's port city. In 1759, 1760, and 1761 its merchants shipped thirty-three full shiploads of provisions for the conquering armies. Soon the Scots merchants began shipping out clerks and apprentices to represent them and start up new ventures in the new colony. The adventurers who came from the south and from the British Isles after the Conquest were of several nationalities, including an important Jewish group. But the Scots became strikingly dominant. The land of Adam Smith was in the throes of a complex social and economic transformation that liberated immense commercial energy and enterprise, much of it into North Atlantic trade. The trading networks created by the first generations of Scotsmen established a grip on the commanding heights of Canadian business that lingered well into the twentieth century.

———————

THE FUR TRADE was the most romantic and far-flung of the colonial enterprises, but was a distant, almost minor, activity compared with basic military and civilian supply problems. Keeping tens of thousands of soldiers fed and clothed and supplied with liquor was a major and long-term job. The conquerors' garrisons were substantial and permanent, for war or threats of war were constant facts of life in Britain's North American territories. The wars against the French were followed in the 1770s by the long, losing struggle against the rebelling American colonists, culminating in 1783 in a new border that required constant defence. In the 1790s Britain embarked on a quarter-century of global warfare against revolutionary France and the designs of Napoleon. Finally the United States fought again, invading British North America in the War of 1812–14. In 1800 it cost the British government approximately £600,000 to supply North American garrisons and another £260,000 to pay the soldiers. The entire fur trade, by contrast, produced less than £300,000 worth of pelts. As W.J. Eccles has argued, war and the threat of war were a staple of the Canadian economy. British defence spending was more critical to the provinces than the goods that traders and farmers could gather for export, more critical, proportionately, than it would be during the arms races of the twentieth century.

Civilians needed to buy everything they could not grow for themselves or make at home. The leaders of the defeated Canadiens returned to France, but ordinary habitants could only stay in the colony, accept the reality of British rule, and get on with farm and family. The extremely high birth rate among these "new subjects" meant that the approximately 60,000 Canadiens at the time of the Conquest became more than 225,000 within half a century. As the rural population of the St. Lawrence valley expanded and virgin land was cleared and came into production, the area's agricultural economy flourished as it never had during the French regime. Grain and flour became important exports.

Crops were harvested by English- as well as French-speakers. In 1783–84 Britain's remaining colonies in North America became a haven for refugee United Empire Loyalists, supporters of the losing side in the American Revolution. The Loyalist influx (to a total of about fifty thousand, 60 per cent of whom went to the Maritimes) swelled Nova Scotia to the point where a separate province, New Brunswick, was created in 1784. Loyalist settlers along the shores of Lake Ontario were also given separate status (not least to escape from the French laws and in-stitutions that Britain grudgingly conceded in the Quebec Act of 1774) when Quebec was divided into Upper and Lower Canada in 1791. The Loyalists' need for supplies created another important commerce. The mother country paid most of the bills, about £6 million, to resettle its loyal subjects.

New World producers gradually began to lessen the imbalance in colonial trade. Europe and the West Indies imported North American fish and grains. The expand-ing British textile industry became a market for colonial ashes – the potash made from burning trees cleared by settlers, which was used in bleaching and dyeing. Wood products ranging from masts and square timbers through barrel staves and shingles gradually found buyers abroad, though this was another area in which government spending, to meet the navy's need for wood, seeded the civilian in-dustry. By the beginning of the nineteenth century these agricultural and forest staples had far eclipsed furs in the opportunities they created for colonial enterprise.

———————

The general or all-purpose merchant (who dealt in merchandise – the term "businessman" was not widely used until the last half of the nineteenth century) dominated the new economy as he had in New France. He imported and exported, handling everything from salt fish to silver spoons, sold at wholesale and retail, operated on credit and gave credit, dealt on his own account and with partners, and invested in adventures and speculations ranging from privateering sorties to the set-tlement of backwoods seigneuries. Merchants' most important fixed investments were in the wharfs and warehouses that lined the shores of every harbour town in British North America. The network of a man's contacts, agents, or correspondents, both in government and in other trading centres, was even more vital to his success in finding and conducting business. It was the same trading world the French had known, fraught with insecurities, debts, risks, market imperfections, lawlessness, and arbitrary political power. It was essential to work with a group of reliable associates, usually relatives or fellow countrymen.

Governments tried to control trade, close borders, and usually enforce non-intercourse during both peace and war. In their restless search for goods to buy and ship and sell, merchants were the natural enemies of trade restriction. They paid no more attention to borders or military regulations than they had to. Thus Montreal's important function before 1800 as entrepôt for large quantities of produce flowing out of Vermont and northern New York through the Lake Champlain–Richelieu River system. Even the War of 1812 was largely an Upper Canadian affair, during which the Lower Canadians, Maritimers, and New Englanders continued their cross-border commerce, buying supplies for the troops in the cheapest market, selling in the dearest. Making war was a job for soldiers; supplying soldiers was the specialty of hard-working merchants and farmers on both sides of the line.

Soldiers and merchants cordially detested each other. As they gained in confidence and importance, British North America's merchants became more aggressive in trying to shape the local environment to suit their activities. They thought of themselves as men of substance, organizers of economic life, who were a community's natural leaders. They had tangible interests to protect, real, calculable stakes in the community, property at risk. To many merchants it seemed perfectly fitting that they or their associates should be the dominant spirits in colonial government and society. Military men, they thought, should have far less to do with governing (or, for that matter, with setting the tone of colonial society).

By contrast, aristocrats and fighting men scorned the venality, the money-grubbing, the lack of valour, dedication, grace, mercy, culture, or sophistication of the traders. Neither they, nor the hard-pressed farmers or fishermen who dealt constantly with merchants, were enthusiastic about the creation of a kind of "merchantocracy" in the colonies. They did not like the tendency of what the malcontented Robert Thorpe called a chain of "scotch pedlars ... linked from Halifax to Quebec, Montreal, Kingston, York, Niagara & so on to Detroit" to form a "Shopkeeper Aristocracy" in British North America.

Merchant power dominated Nova Scotia before the conquest of New France. A British possession since 1713, Nova Scotia remained a sleepy backwater until the Royal Navy decided in the late 1740s to create its own fortress, Halifax, to rival Louisbourg. One of the first civilians into Halifax was twenty-five-year-old Joshua Mauger, a Jersey Islander, a captain by age eighteen, who had somehow mastered the art of obtaining navy victuals contracts. While fulfilling these during the 1750s, Mauger engaged in many private enterprises. The most notable was his establishment of a distillery which became the principal source of rum for Halifax and the other British posts in Nova Scotia. Mauger's distillery existed only because the colonial administration levied duties on imported rum. Molasses and sugar came from the West Indies in exchange for the fish and lumber Mauger exported. He traded with England, Ireland, and New England, and opened a store in Annapolis Royal. He bought ships too, buying captured prizes or other confiscated ships at naval courts in Halifax. Young Mauger became one of Halifax's largest landowners, acquiring real estate in direct grants and from merchants or tradesmen who owed him money. He was a leading force in the development of the German community of Lunenberg, where he had interests in shipbuilding and the timber trade. During the Seven Years' War Mauger invested in privateers; earlier he had apparently traded in slaves. In little more than a decade's intense activity, Joshua Mauger became the first wealthy Nova Scotian. Having made his fortune in the colony, Mauger went home to England in 1760 to enjoy it.

His influence in Nova Scotia was at least as great after he had left the province. A young protégé, Michael Francklin (whom Mauger set up as keeper of a Halifax dram-shop) soon became an important merchant in his own right, prospering in rum, fish, privateering, and contracts to provision the forces at Halifax and Quebec. When Britain granted Nova Scotia an assembly in 1758, it was dominated by Francklin and other Halifax merchants. The Assembly named Joshua Mauger Nova Scotia's agent in London. He proceeded to carry on an extensive, successful lobbying campaign to have the lieutenant-governor, Jonathan Belcher, recalled. A few years later the "Mauger party" used its network – Mauger was now a member of the British Parliament – to stop another governor's attempts to raise excise taxes on rum. A third governor who challenged Mauger's "plan of Dominion" for Nova Scotia was removed from office.

The little band of Halifax merchants dominated the Assembly and the governors, and reached a peak of influence between 1766 and 1776 when Michael Francklin himself was lieutenant-governor. Their power was not unlimited. A competitor was able to establish a rival distillery to Mauger's, for example, and Francklin's attempt as governor to improve his landholdings in the province was frustrated by London. It is not clear whether Nova Scotia's development suffered during these years of "merchantocracy." Naturally some of the merchants did very well out of the colony's growth. Others, like Francklin, over-extended themselves and finished their careers clinging to government sinecures. If the J. Mauger, broker, listed among the bankrupts in Britain's *Gentleman's Magazine* for 1777 was the Joshua Mauger formerly of Nova Scotia, he too had been unable to maintain his success. In the late 1770s and early 1780s all of Mauger's Nova Scotia properties were sold and he disappears from history.

———

Up the St. Lawrence River, scores of would-be Maugers responded to the need for merchants in the inland colony conquered from the French. Almost all of them started in military supply. George Allsopp, for example, worked in the Quartermaster

General's Department during the campaigns against Louisbourg and Quebec. After the Conquest he struck out on his own as the colonial partner of a British mercantile supply firm. He was soon purchasing and shipping wheat, fur, timber, fish, and potash, took an interest in the St. Maurice forges, and was thought to have the most extensive commercial correspondence of anyone in the province. In the late 1760s Allsopp's major supplier in England was another former commissary employee, Brook Watson, who began his career with the military in Nova Scotia, worked in England for the Mauger group, and then took over Mauger's partnership in a firm supplying merchants such as Allsopp in Quebec. In the 1770s Watson was probably the most important British merchant supplying Nova Scotia and Quebec. He became a member of Parliament and developed close ties with Quebec's second governor, Sir Guy Carleton, whose interests he assiduously advanced. Watson continued to serve both the crown and himself, acting as commissary general to the British forces in several campaigns. He eventually became lord mayor of London, chairman of Lloyd's of London, and a baronet, enjoying added prominence because one of his legs had been severed by a shark in Havana harbour.

Through Quebec wholesalers like Allsopp, the firm of Watson and Rashleigh supplied goods to a network of retailers in the growing towns and villages along the St. Lawrence. Two Jewish sutlers, Samuel Jacobs and Aaron Hart, were among the most prominent new shopkeepers. Both came to Canada as followers of the invading British armies. Jacobs, of Alsatian descent, came with Wolfe's troops and first made his home in Quebec. Then he moved to the village of St. Denis and engaged in general storekeeping and grain dealing along the Richelieu River–Lake Champlain route to the United States, becoming the most important merchant in the region. Aaron Hart, apparently an English Jew, followed troops up from New York to Trois-Rivières, settled there as a general merchant, and founded a family dynasty. Hart acquired all the land he could, often from French-Canadian seigneurs who had borrowed from him. When he died in 1800, there was at least one resident of every parish within fifty miles of Trois-Rivières who owed Hart money.

Jacobs and Hart, Canada's first important Jewish merchants, worked closely with the French-Canadian population, the former taking a Canadien wife, many of the latter's descendants eventually becoming assimilated. They maintained business and social contacts with other Jews in New York and Quebec, but did not limit the range of their trading to the old ethnic networks. In addition to buying from George Allsopp's firm, for example, Samuel Jacobs often dealt with one of the first important Scots general merchants in Quebec, William Grant.

Grant came to Quebec in 1759 as agent of a naval contracting firm run by several kinsmen who originally worked the London-Halifax connection. William was only fifteen, but had the advantage of fluency in French. Before he was twenty, he had made major investments in the fur trade, the seal and salmon fisheries, seigneurial properties, and the old French paper currency. He bought city real estate and the homes of departing Frenchmen, and solidified his ties with the conquered by marrying a French-Canadian seigneur's widow. He survived the break-up of the Grants in London who had originally backed him (one of them in 1767 accused William and the other Quebec merchants of paying "less attention to their words characters and credit than the worst thief you ever knew in the High lands of Scotland.") to become possibly the leading Quebec merchant of his generation. Grant often worked closely with Allsopp and through the Watson-Carleton connection, while bringing out his own stock of young Scots clerks and partners. James McGill, a Glaswegian, first appears in Canada as a "deputy" of William Grant's, responsible for organizing the up-country fur trade.

Grant was probably the most successful of the early newcomers (a sometime partner, the quietly acquisitive Thomas Dunn, whose forte was collecting concessions, offices, and contracts from the new regime, was not far behind and ultimately left a larger estate). The advantages of being the first British traders into the conquered colony were considerable. Most of the French merchants were bankrupt or had returned to France or both. A few French Canadians stayed in business, and some made a smooth transition to the new regime. Members of the nimble Baby family, noticed earlier, inquired about possible British trading partners even before the surrender of Montreal: François Baby made his first contacts while a prisoner in England. Pierre Guy, who was winding up his father's affairs in France when the war ended, went to England, made connections with Huguenot expatriates in London, and was soon in Montreal rebuilding the family's affairs.

These were exceptions. Few French Canadians had the contacts, experience, or opportunities to enter the international commercial networks that the new men were creating. Few were able to use the patronage system erected by the new foreign governors. The Canadiens' situation became more difficult with time, for the Babys and Guys had adjusted thanks to pre-existing transatlantic connections. The next generation were not at all equipped to rival the pushing young Scotsmen who poured into the colonies as agents-on-the-make of their parents' and uncles' and cousins' well-financed trading houses.

There was little racial friction at first. "By all that I can find the English and French agree tolerably well and speak well of each other," a newcomer wrote in 1766. "But," he added, "there are great animosities between the English themselves one with another. From what cause this proceeds, other than the mere rivalship of trade, I know not."

It was not so much "rivalship of trade" that was causing problems as rivalry between traders and their governors, most of whom were military men. The division between merchants and the administration of Quebec that developed within a few months of the Conquest began the Canadian tradition of business dissatisfaction with the realities and complexities of governing a diverse community.

The merchants who had adventured into Quebec came into a chaotic situation. It was a war-torn community of sullen Frenchmen under British military rule. It had strange laws, strange customs (such as the Roman Catholic faith), paper currency that might or might not be completely worthless, unpredictable prospects (suppose it was returned to France in the peace settlement? suppose France reconquered it?), and a tradition of political-military control of its principal commerce, the fur trade. Most of the new merchants assumed that these peculiarities would soon disappear and the new province would become thoroughly anglicized, a British North American colony like any other. Surely it would be governed by the usual laws and statutes of England, ruled by a civilian governor with the advice of an elected assembly. After a few years' adjustment, trade and commerce would flourish under liberal British rule. The French and their institutions would fade as British immigrants turned them into a minority. Expections like these, based partly on British policy statements, supported merchants' decision to risk settling in Quebec.

General Sir James Murray succeeded the fallen Wolfe and became Quebec's first governor. He had no particular sympathy for the merchants' point of view. Like most eighteenth-century soldiers and gentlemen, Murray regarded traders as lower-class money-grubbers devoid of breeding, manners, or principles. More important, Murray soon realized that it would not be easy to turn New France into a new New England. The "new subjects" – the French Canadians – would dominate the colony unless or until swarms of English-speakers arrived to outnumber and assimilate them. This could not happen overnight, but until it did no governer could simply sweep away the laws and usages the French had lived by for one hundred and fifty years. Similarly, so long as the Canadiens' Catholic religion barred them from political activity (under British law), any assembly in the new colony would be little more than a council of Protestant merchants. Why should these venal sutlers and adventurers, already starting to clamour about the rights of Englishmen, be given political power over the Canadiens, many of who struck Murray as being more cultivated, urbane, and worthy than his mercantile countrymen?

Military contempt for civilian traders was matched by the merchants' inclination to view soldiers as idlers, parasites, and professional killers. The civilians resented the inconveniences imposed on them under military rule: billets and curfews on the one hand, unworkable ordinances trying to fix currency values or regulate the fur trade on the other. Minor conflicts were blown out of all proportion, as when sentinels tried to arrest George Allsopp for insisting on walking the streets of Quebec at night without carrying a light. Claiming he was free to do whatever he pleased, Allsopp scuffled with the guards, denounced the soldiery as "a parcel of rascals ... from the highest to the lowest, thousands of whom he maintained daily," and charged them in civilian courts. Officers did not invite merchants to their balls. In September 1763 problems with the men's pay led to arguing between merchants and soldiers that ended with the latter throwing stones at the businessmen. Murray described a later incident, as it appeared through his military eyes:

> In a late drunken riot of a few merchants here, one of them entered forcibly, and naked all to his shirt, the bed chamber of the widow of a creditable merchant of this town. The appearance of the man, and the appearance in which he had come in, so frightened the woman as to cause her to make her escape by dropping out of her window, naked as she came out of bed, leaving her room and two of the daughters in the adjacent closet, to the mercy of the drunken merchant. . . . At the desire of the woman, who took refuge in the house where a capt. of the 27th Regt. was quartered, the said capt. went with a file of men to quell the riot and seize the rioters. The said capt. was personally ill-treated, some merchants were confined, released upon bail, a general court martial was ordered, the whole body of merchants took fire at it. Upon a thorough examination, the court martial found some guilty and fined them. I mitigated the fine. Yet the most part exclaimed bitterly, talked strangely, and thought themselves . . . highly offended.

The merchants struck back by refusing to pay New Year's Day compliments to the governor.

In a conciliatory gesture, Murray had appointed some merchants local magistrates. Their rulings often offended the military. One of the merchant-judges, Thomas Walker, made himself particularly offensive in disputes over billeting. He was visited one night by masked men who beat him and sliced off a piece of ear; later that evening it appeared on a regimental mess table. By 1765 there was an almost total breakdown of relations among the military, the government, and the merchants in Quebec, all of them English-speakers.

Merchants organized to exert political power. Their first and most common resort was to petition the home government, presenting their grievances and begging for redress. In October 1764, for example, twenty-one "Quebec Traders" complained to the King about the lack of an assembly in the colony, its chaotic administration (with "Ordinances Vexatious, Oppressive, unconstitutional, injurious to civil Liberty and the Protestant cause") and the "Rage and Rudeness of Language and Demeanour" with which the governor treated the petitioners. They had come to the colony in good faith, the merchants pleaded, "trusting to enjoy the Blessings of British Liberty, and happily reap the fruits of our Industry." Instead they were suffering grievously from maladminstration as well as "the natural poverty of the country." "Our Trade is miserably confined and distressed, so that we lye under the utmost Necessity of the Aids and Succours of Government . . . in the Place of having to contend against Oppression and Restraint."

The Quebec traders used their commercial network to increase pressure by generating a similar petition from their London suppliers. And in 1765 the Quebec and Montreal merchants hired the first paid lobbyist in Canadian history, a London solicitor named Fowler Walker, to advance their interests in the capital for the handsome fee of £200 annually. Barraged by petitions, representations, and accusations from the merchants and their friends, the home government recalled Murray in the autumn of 1765. As in Nova Scotia, the merchant interest seemed predominant. Murray had been driven from Canada by men he considered "the most cruel, ignorant rapacious fanatics who ever existed."

The merchants' charges against Murray were finally dismissed. He did not return to Canada but his successor, Sir Guy Carleton, did not give the merchants much more satisfaction. Carleton soon decided that "barring Catastrophe shocking to think of, this Country must, to the end of Time, be peopled by the Canadian Race," and recommended that the French-Canadians' laws, institutions, and traditions of government be respected. He thought it particularly important to ensure their allegiance because worsening disputes between Britain and her American colonies threatened to erupt in violence. Carleton's recommendations became the foundation of the Quebec Act of 1774, which preserved the French-Canadian civil law, effectively legitimized the Roman Catholic faith in the province, and ended the merchants' hope for an elected assembly.

The prospect of the Quebec Act roused the Quebec merchants to eloquent, pained petitioning. Britain was upsetting the understanding on which they had come into the colony and risked their fortunes: "We have employed our property and credit . . . in a firm belief, that we should have the remedies allowed us by the laws of England for the security and recovery of it; and that if we had supposed the French laws . . . to be still in force there, or to be intended to be revived in the same, we would not have had any commercial connections with the inhabitants of the said province, either French or English." If Britain insisted on passing the act, the merchants argued, implementation should be delayed "until we shall have had sufficient time to withdraw our effects from the said province."

Their bluff was called. The Quebec Act was duly passed and implemented. There was no noticeable exodus of merchants. They stayed and complained about the hardship and injustice of it all. "The Laws and Customs of Canada," George Allsopp wrote, "form the most imperfect System in the World for a Commercial people."

One of the first acts of American rebellion against Great Britain was to send an expedition against Quebec in 1775. A few of the province's most discontented merchants gave the Americans active support. The man who bore the worst scars of the conflict with the military, Thomas Walker, became an outright republican, organizing support for rebellion and the invading armies. Walker was arrested for treason, set free by American forces, and ended his life in Boston. A handful of other merchants left Quebec on Carleton's invitation, some of them joining the rebels. Others, such as Aaron Hart, tried to be neutral, doing business with both sides (although it soon became clear that neither the American army nor the Continental Congress's paper currency were particularly good risks). George Allsopp, for many years the most prominent of the disaffected merchants, apparently remained loyal; but he had caused so much trouble in the past that he was denounced as a rebel and stripped of his minor administrative positions. William Grant, hardly less hostile to the regime than Allsopp, "determined to stand or fall with the King's Government," and was among the most active of the many merchants who joined the militia and contributed to the defence of the province. His loyalism did not cause him to change his view of the administration, which he now condemned for its lack of firmness. "Government from its Supremacy is become despicable," he grumbled.

Some of the merchants' grievances against the authorities in Quebec parallelled the discontents in the American colonies that had coalesced into a determination to strike for independence. As Donald Creighton argued in 1937 in *The Commercial Empire of the St. Lawrence*, however, there were not enough ties between newly conquered Quebec and the older colonies to establish a real community of interest. There were no hard, material reasons for men in Quebec's trade, whether in furs, grain, or general merchandising, to want to cut their ties with Britain. In fact it was positively important to maintain London markets for furs; and the Quebec Act had also favoured the Quebec traders in restoring to the province's jurisdiction the old French fur-trading hinterland in the Ohio and Mississippi valleys.

On the other hand, there is little evidence from the American Revolution or any later period that the merchants possessed the special "Canadian" vision that Creighton grandiloquently assigned to them. Most stayed loyal simply by minding their business. They continued to lobby for their interests, with the fur traders being particularly concerned that the reattached hinterland not pass into rebel hands. Half of it did anyway in the 1783 agreement on a border with the United States of America. The documents do not provide hard evidence to support the literary and nationalist fantasies Creighton spun in calling the Laurentian merchants "the only Canadians in the modern sense of the term," who "alone thought in terms of a distinct and continental northern state." Then, as at most times in Canadian history, the merchants thought first, and often last, in terms of the health of their enterprises. Their economic ideas, such as they were, bore less relation to nationality and northern visions than to the ideas of commercial liberty from all governments being propounded by their countryman, Adam Smith. Trade should be left alone, particularly by soldiers. In addition, merchants should control the political institutions responsible for extending commmerce. Virtually the whole of the merchants' political program was summarized by a fur trader and pioneer banker, John Richardson, writing privately in 1787 that "Government . . . ought to acknowledge commerce as its basis, & the accommodation of the Merchant as one principal means of promoting the national prosperity."

Some of Quebec's new merchants soon failed. In 1767 Carleton wrote that the "Adventurers in Trade" in the province were men who had "set out to mend their fortunes, at the opening of this new Channel for Commerce, but Experience has taught almost all of them, that this Trade requires a Strict Frugality, they are Strangers to, or to which they will not submit." A number of them, he observed, had already left the province, for it was not a land of abundant natural wealth. Those who stayed enjoyed moderate growth and prosperity in the fifteen years between the Conquest and the onset of the American Revolution. Seven years of fighting against the Americans did not seriously interfere with the fur trade; military demand drove up agricultural prices and stimulated production. By the early 1780s some of the larger fur traders, like Richard Dobie and the partnership of Isaac Todd and James McGill, were diversifying into grain and general mercantile activities. The Vermont trade was booming. More important for the long term, clerks and shippers along the fur-trade supply system, from Montreal to Mackinac, began developing new trading opportunities. They became the pioneer merchants in the community which in 1791 became Upper Canada.

Robert Hamilton, one such pioneer, was a Presbyterian minister's son who came out from Scotland in his mid-twenties to serve as a clerk with a fur-trading and provisioning firm. During his apprenticeship at Montreal and upper Lake Ontario, Hamilton developed a small trade on his own account with some of the posts further up the system. His first speculation was "a package of Silk Handerkerchiefs, a pretty good bargain." In 1780 he formed a partnership with young Richard Cartwright, the well-educated scion of a prominent Albany family driven from their home by the rebels. Cartwright had served as secretary to the commander of a Loyalist regiment, the Queen's Rangers, had learned the business of military provisioning, and, most important, had developed excellent contacts. Hamilton and Cartwright founded their partnership on contracts to supply goods to local garrisons and the Indian Department during the Revolutionary War. They got these largely because the military wanted to deal with respectable men of good character instead of merchants who assumed that the army existed to be looted.

Hamilton and Cartwright were supplied and given credit by the well-established Montreal house of Todd and McGill. After the war, Hamilton settled in Queenston on the Niagara frontier; Cartwright moved to Cataraqui, renamed Kingston. They had an important associate at Detroit, John Askin, a former fur trader and sutler, who handled their transactions with the upper posts. In 1785 Hamilton married Askin's daughter.

It was not easy to survive as a frontier merchant in peacetime in the 1780s. The military cow was slowly going dry, and the Indian Department was no longer everyone's gravy train. Speculation in land grants and land bought from natives was a busy game, but the colony had too much land and too few people to make it worthwhile. The United Empire Loyalists who were struggling to clear land along the north shores of Lakes Ontario and Erie needed to be supplied, but their settlements would only support a small commerce. Hamilton and Cartwright found that the key to prospering in this situation was to do a little bit of everything, to be truly general merchants.

They began the postwar era as shippers, and for a few years had a virtual monopoly on the private carrying trade from Montreal through Kingston and Niagara. They were agents, for example, for the first two private ships built on Lake Ontario, by Todd and McGill. In this capacity they moved goods for the fur trade, the military, and the early settlers, all at a 5 per cent commission. Next, their old contacts and their good reputations helped Cartwright and Hamilton win contracts to supply the peacetime garrisons at Kingston and Niagara respectively. Hamilton became the principal contractor operating the Niagara portage, over which all goods for Lake Erie and the up-country had to pass. Both men opened stores in their communities. Each store became the most important in its region, doing both a local retail trade and supplying small shopkeepers in outlying settlements. Hamilton's supplied the whole Niagara peninsula with a huge variety of products. At his death in 1809 some twelve hundred creditors owed him about £70,000. The £7,000 worth of stock in his store included 286 washbasins, 39 dozen pocket knives, and 3,387 yards of cloth.

Goods and settlers moved up the St. Lawrence and the lakes long before there was much return traffic. The volume of furs passing through the southern lakes was first constant and then declining. Farmers in Upper Canada faced years of gruelling land-clearing and cultivation before being able to sell significant quantities of potash, flour, and other products. Growth was stimulated and subsidized by aid to the Loyalists, military spending, and other government largesse – in other words, the British treasury; otherwise Upper Canada would have developed much more slowly. "As long as the British Government shall think proper to hire people to come over to eat our flour, we shall go well and continue to make a figure," Cartwright wrote in 1792, "but once we come to export our produce the disadvantages of our remote inland situation will operate in full force."

Despite his caution, Cartwright, like Hamilton, developed a major stake in Upper Canada's future by acquiring huge tracts of land. They were two of the largest landowners in the province. How much of their property came from calculated acquisition and how much was accepted from debtors is not clear. One way or another Hamilton acquired an interest in more than one hundred thousand acres, mostly in the Niagara peninsula, completing a web of economic power that made him the wealthiest and most powerful man in Upper Canada before the War of 1812. As his biographer, Bruce Wilson, has written, Hamilton's affairs "touched the lives of the inhabitants of the Niagara peninsula more directly and intimately than any government or social institution of their time."

Richard Cartwright was a scholarly and articulate Loyalist, easily the most successful UEL merchant in Upper Canada. Other Loyalists eventually did well in commerce, but in the early years few of them had the necessary downriver contacts to find a niche in the Great Lakes–St. Lawrence trading system. A tendency to rely exclusively on the government to which they had been loyal, or to try to build fortunes on their land grants, was not productive. In the Niagara peninsula Robert Hamilton's ascendency over such Loyalist notables as Samuel Street and the Butler family reflected his canny manipulation of shifting opportunities in the trading system. These became opportunities for a whole clan of Hamilton relatives brought from Scotland to staff Robert's enterprises and establish businesses of their own. The Hamiltons worked closely with the group of Scots fur traders at Detroit into which Hamilton had married. The first "family compact" in Upper Canada, then, was the Hamilton network of Scots merchants.

The first governor of Upper Canada, Lieutenant-Colonel John Graves Simcoe, was typically military in his prejudices. "I am fully persuaded that both the civil & military interests of his Majesty's Subjects in this Colony can never be so well administered as by upright & disinterested Military Men," he wrote. "It is unreasonable to expect Disinterestedness among the Mercantile Part of the Community, nor do their habits or Education in the least entitle them to a shadow of pre-emenence . . . ." At the beginning of his term Simcoe clashed several times with Cartwright and Hamilton, both of whom were members of his Legislative Council and held other judicial and administrative positions. The issues ranged from the merchants' alleged monopoly power as provisioners to disagreements about the operation of provincial courts.

Unlike the earlier merchant-governor struggles in Nova Scotia and Quebec, the governor soon realized that the merchants were men of influence, both locally and along the arteries of British North America. Little backwoods provinces had no pools of aristocrats or officers to draw on for governing. The merchants had to be listened to; their talents had to be used; they were community leaders *faute de mieux*. Simcoe and his successors might still balk at socializing with "men who kept but one table" (that is, dined with their servants), but they all learned to work with men like Hamilton and Cartwright. Upper Canada's leading merchants were not estranged from government – rather, there was a thickening intertwining of commerce and the administration. Robert Thorpe's complaints about the "scotch pedlars" who formed the "Shopkeeper Aristocracy" of Upper Canada were the grumbles of an outsider.

The shopkeepers did not become real aristocrats. None of the early Canadian merchants received hereditary titles, the badge of nobility. They also had trouble with the heirs to their wealth. Both Robert Hamilton and Richard Cartwright took great pains to train sons to take over the family's enterprises and maintain the community standing that the fathers had won. Through mismanagement the Hamilton enterprises in the Niagara region collapsed within a few years of the patriarch's death in 1809. The only lasting achievement of the second generation of Hamiltons was to help found a hamlet that eventually became a big city. In Kingston, Richard Cartwright's last years were scarred by the deaths of his four eldest children, three of them male. The two sons who succeeded the Loyalist merchant went into the ministry and the law. A grandson, Richard Cartwright, became Liberal finance minister in the 1870s, was knighted, and finished a long political career as a senator.

As the population of the St. Lawrence–Great Lakes area became swollen by Loyalists, land-hungry late-Loyalists, and the offspring of the fecund French Canadians, the Quebec and Montreal merchant communities continued to expand. Both the beginning and the end of the Revolutionary War caused more migrations of fur traders north from Albany and other American bases. Some of the merchants who had started in the 1760s vastly expanded. By the 1790s, William Grant, for example, owned mills, bakeries, timber yards, distilleries, ships, and a large handful of seigneuries, in addition to his wharfs and warehouses. Fur traders such as Isaac Todd and James McGill had begun to diversify, moving into distilling, land speculation, provisioning for the army, and supplying such inland merchants as Cartwright and Hamilton. They had both become wealthy men, pillars of Montreal society, as had many of their fellow fur traders and merchants. The plain-living but sociable Isaac Todd was particularly popular among his contemporaries, "he being the only friend, except Mr. Frobisher, who has not changed their dispositions," Alexander Henry wrote, "some from getting rich, others from having obtained places & ca [which] has raised them in their own imagination above their old acquaintances."

The established group's prosperity did not preclude success by newcomers – immigrants from Scotland, England (John Molson will appear in several later chapters), the United States, and even a few resourceful French Canadians rising from obscurity. Joseph Drapeau, a farmer's son who started as a tavern-keeper in Quebec, became an import and wholesale merchant, went into shipbuilding to secure ships for his trade, lent money profitably, and, in the pattern common to both English and French men of property, bought himself several seigneuries. In Montreal young Pierre Foretier started out as a small storekeeper just after the Conquest, did well as an outfitter for fur traders, was unusual among his countrymen in obtaining a government contract to supply the Indian Department, and in the 1780s and 1790s multiplied his fortune many times as a property developer in Montreal. He became the largest property owner in the city in his generation and was, of course, a seigneur.

It was one of the ubiquitous Scots newcomers, however, who achieved the most outstanding success in the second post-Conquest generation. James Dunlop, a well-educated Glaswegian, had an apprenticeship in the Virginia tobacco trade disrupted by the Revolution and was forced to relocate to Quebec in 1779. He set up a small general store selling articles he imported from Glasgow. He moved to Montreal a few years later, expanded his importing and retailing, particularly of rum and whiskys, and developed a flourishing export business in timber and grain. In 1799 Dunlop's new wharf, wharehouses, and stores by the St. Lawrence were apparently the largest such establishment in the colony. Bringing out young Scots to staff his enterprises, Dunlop expanded into ship-owning and became the colony's leading broker of commercial paper (see p. 142) in this pre-bank era. In the early 1800s he nearly cornered the export of potash and grain from the provinces. In the War of 1812 he converted his ships to privateering, and lost only one of them, the *James Dunlop*, which was wrecked in a storm. There was "more good business since the War began than ever I did in the same space of time," Dunlop wrote in 1814. He boasted that he had been "more bold in my speculations than any other person or Company in this Province." Dunlop was thought to have acquired the largest fortune in the history of British North America. He never engaged in the fur trade.

Dunlop never married, and like many of his contemporaries had no male heirs in Canada to carry on his business. Dunlop and Company was wound up after its founder's death in 1815, apparently at sacrifice prices. The approximately £200,000 realized from the estate went to nephews and nieces in the old country and an illegitimate son in Glasgow.

By the 1780s the merchant bourgeoisie of Quebec and Montreal were able to sustain organizations for non-business purposes. Many of the province's leading Scots businessmen could be found worshipping in the Scotch Presbyterian Church on St. Gabriel Street in Montreal. Merchants dominated the Quebec Benevolent Society, formed to support members in need, were prominent in the Quebec Fire Society, and took the lead in subscribing to the Agricultural Society of the District of Quebec, which was dedicated to raising productivity in the province through better farming. They continued to agitate for representative political institutions and against the influence of military governors and would-be aristocrats like the old seigneurs. In 1791, when Britain finally gave the new province of Lower Canada an elected assembly, Adam Lymburner, one of the more political of the merchants, spelled out his group's sense of its importance and future:

> There are now, among the Mercantile Gentlemen of the Province, those whose movable fortunes are perhaps equal, if not superior to any of the Seigneurial Estates; and who, from the Employment and Support they give to thousands of the people, have infinitely more influence in the country than the Seigneurs.... This Honourable House must perceive, from the very small value of the landed fortunes, that the ony means of accumula-

tion in that country must be by the operations of Trade and Commerce . . . . That it is more probable in twenty years, perhaps in ten years, a new set of men may come forward, who may have acquired and realized fortunes much superior to any now in that country; and, it is natural to suppose, will possess a proportional degree of Political Power and Influence.

Several prominent Montreal and Quebec merchants were elected to the first Lower Canadian Assembly. They were often referred to as the "English party" and were in fact largely Scotsmen. Friction between them and the French Canadians gradually developed, bursting into the open in the early 1800s. One of the earliest straws in the wind was the first election for Speaker, a post traditionally given to the most respected member of a legislature. William Grant and James McGill both stood for the Speakership. Both were defeated and a French-Canadian lawyer won the honour. Within a few years the "new set of men" coming forward to lead the Lower Canadian business group would find it very difficult to exercise the political power and influence they considered their due proportion.

By the end of the century Scots firms, agents, and venturing individuals had come to dominate the business life of Nova Scotia and New Brunswick. Through the 1760s Scotsmen had gradually moved into the merchant life of Halifax. Some came as naval contractors during the Seven Years' War. Others had developed an interest in the fishery, first challenging the West Country merchants in the Newfoundland trade, then realizing the potential of Halifax as a great trading centre. Halifax flourished during the Revolutionary War as a naval and privateering base and as a key Atlantic entrepôt for the West Indies trade (from which the Americans were excluded). The old Mauger–Watson, Halifax–London network gave way in the growing city to a Greenock–Glasgow connection.

Several of the Loyalist traders who came after 1783 were Scots agents or merchants moving north, and the Caledonian influx continued to the end of the century. By the early 1800s some fifty-eight Clydeside firms were trading with Halifax. The most important Nova Scotia merchant was William Forsyth, a Glaswegian who since 1784 had created a trading empire, importing and exporting merchandise of all kinds through Halifax in his fleets of ships, invariably using fellow Scots as his agents and correspondents in ports ranging from Grenada and Kingston, Jamaica, through Charleston, Boston, and Saint John, New Brunswick. Halifax's trade had begun in Mauger's days as a business of shipping food and grog and other supplies into a naval base. Now the town was a node in a multi-faceted transatlantic commerce involving movements of fish, grain, salt, molasses, wines, and, from Scotland, manufactured products of all kinds.

The military still had special needs, and these increased in the 1790s as Britain struggled to maintain naval dominance during the Napoleonic wars. The virgin forests of North America were particularly important for the British navy because their tall pines made excellent masts. When Maine became foreign soil, New Brunswick's forests became the empire's most secure preserve for prime masts. Major mast contracts were let by the Admiralty to William Forsyth. One of his key suppliers was William Davidson, who had started in the salmon fishery in Scotland and developed fur-trading and fishing stations at the mouth of the Miramichi River on New Brunswick's wild north coast. Davidson founded the New Brunswick lumbering industry in both the Miramichi and Saint John regions. As a supplier of masts to the Admiralty he competed with another pioneering New Brunswick trader, William Hazen, whose contracts were obtained through the old Mauger–Brook Watson network. Hazen had moved north from Massachusetts to a little settlement at the mouth of the Saint John. It, too, came to be dominated by merchants from the north of Britain; by the 1790s Saint John's main commercial street was known as Scotch Row.

——————◆——————

Successful colonial merchants owned great stone wharfs adorned by solid stone warehouses. Their handsome mansions graced suburbs flowing back and up from the Water Streets of all the port towns. Some owned farms or seigneuries or country retreats. The most cultured among them had private libraries and spent liberally to educate their children, often in old country private schools. It was not uncommon for a man to make his fortune in the colonies and retire to Scotland. In 1801 Alexander Brymer, for years the head of Halifax's North British Society, went home worth an estimated £250,000. His wealth was unusual: £20,000 to £100,000 was the more likely accumulation in a successful career of trading and speculation. James McGill's 1813 estate was probably about £100,000. His will was unusual in his bequest of £10,000 and his forty-six-acre Montreal property to a provincial commission as an endowment for a university in his adopted country. After legal battles with relatives trying to stop the donation, McGill University emerged as the first important creation of Canadian merchant philanthropy.

Great merchants were usually honoured as builders and pillars of colonial communities. Most held public offices, both elective and appointive, serving as magistrates, assemblymen, councillors, commissioners, and in many other capacities. Some participated in public life from a sense of civic obligation, others to advance their interests or as security against the collapse of their private ventures. By about 1800 the merchant groups in most of the British North American provinces were important enough that much of the social standing and political power first exercised by the military had passed into their hands. The "ledger influence" that merchants exercised over those who owed them money was not inconsequential, and has been used by thoughtful historians like David Sutherland, writing of Halifax, to see the community as a "merchantocracy" well into the 1800s.

Newfoundland was perhaps an even clearer case. It had become a one-industry island, settled by poor fishermen and a slowly increasing number of merchants, many the agents of West Country firms, who supplied the inhabitants with goods in return for their fish. While there were enough people in St. John's for market forces to operate more or less constantly, monopolistic situations in the outports created stark instances of economic power by the local "fishocracy." A similar situation existed along the shores of the Gulf of St. Lawrence, particularly the Gaspé, where Channel Island merchants had a number of fishing stations whose inhabitants were often at the mercy of the company for provisions to get them through the winter and equipment for summer fishing. In 1797 Newfoundland's governor described the situation in fishing ports:

> Unfortunately both the Clergy and Faculty [professional men] of this Island are so completely dependent on the merchants that should either of them as a Magistrate, decide a case in favour of an arrested servant against an Unjust Merchant, he would be certain to lose his Easter offering if a minister, or his Practice as an Apothecary and Surgeon should he be of the Faculty. The power of the merchants in the Out-Harbours is so great that they rule as perfect despots, being the sole possessors of the meat, drink and clothing by which their wretched subjects are supported.

Already by that date, however, the merchants of Lower Canada were beginning to sense the limits of their political power. During the next forty years Reform movements in most of the provinces would succeed in expanding the base of popular participation in government. Merchants' direct involvement in politics would shrink and wither almost continuously throughout the nineteenth century. One reason for this withdrawal from politics was the fact that in an expanding and diversifying economy it became increasingly important to attend to the demands of trade.

ABOVE: **Timber slide, Ottawa River** *(Bartlett's Canada)*
BELOW: **An 1819 note of the "Pretended" Bank of Upper Canada**
(Metropolitan Toronto Library Board)

6

Wood, Banks, and Wholesalers:
New Specialties, 1800–1849

*Ashes and masts . . . timberers . . . forest kings of New Brunswick . . . the
Ottawa valley . . . "Grandfather Price" . . . boom and bust . . . "Shoot
Cunard" . . . cheap ships . . . haggis money . . . the Montreal Bank . . . its
competitors . . . the first corporations . . . bank wars . . . bank
failures . . . merchant specialization . . . the Buchanans of Upper
Canada . . . political reform and merchant decline . . . free trade . . . the
desire to join the United States*

British North America prospered for two decades after the end of the
Napoleonic wars in 1815. Industrializing England, the world's mightiest
economic power, was hungry for North America's wood, cotton, tobacco, and
flour. Talented, ambitious Britons poured into the colonies, seeking their fortunes. By the late 1820s immigrants were arriving by the tens of thousands,
many of them fleeing rural overpopulation in Ireland and the United
Kingdom. Most went on to the United States, a tumultuous republic whose
growth, already a wonder of the world, at almost all times outstripped that of
the northern colonies. Enough stayed to reinforce the distinctively British tone
of life and politics – and commerce – in the Canadas and the Maritimes. The
border usually meant little where trade was concerned, though, so when the
mother country decided in the 1840s to let the colonies go their own way, and
when the colonies did not seem to be going well any more, it was not unnatural
for many merchants to wonder about joining the United States.

The merchant's world was drastically changed by the growth of new industries and specialities. The timber trade rose spectacularly to become the
leading colonial industry and spawned dozens of shipyards as it grew. Increasing volumes and complexities of commerce caused general merchants, who had
dealt in anything and everything, to start sorting themselves out as retailers or
wholesalers, importers or exporters, forwarders, brokers, or auctioneers,
drygoods or hardware men, grocers or jewellers, or specialists in some other

commodity or trade. Trading in money itself – offering financial services – was one of the most important of the new specialities, as the first bank appeared in 1817 and five more opened in the next five years. The banks' powers and policies caused immediate controversy.

Government contracting was not as important to mercantile success as in the years of conquest and war. Fewer merchants meshed their affairs with the business of the state. In any case, the dimensions of colonial politics were expanding. Just as a growing economy created new business opportunities, so a growing society developed new political groupings that had to be conciliated and incorporated into the system. Politics was an arena for reformers and radicals, rebels and religious groups, imperial governors and civil servants, as well as for tory merchants. The merchants knew there were vital economic issues at stake in the political game – land sales, bank charters, transportation questions, and other issues – and by the 1840s the very future of the country seemed in question as Britain dismantled the preferential tariff system under which the provinces had flourished. The imposition of free trade, and the coming of its political correlative, responsible government, testified to the inability of the northern merchants to get what they wanted from either the Imperial or their own governments.

———————

THE COLONISTS LIVED IN A WORLD OF WOOD. The pine forest was everywhere on the mainland; only Newfoundland had to make do with stunted trees poking up from the rock. Settlers cut trees to clear land for farming, made all of their homes and furniture and most of their tools and containers and vehicles out of wood, and burned wood to keep warm in winter. Fire destroyed homes, communities, and huge forests. When every man was his own axeman and carpenter and every farm had its own woodlot there were not many opportunities for trading in wood. Soon after the Conquest, though, markets developed at the extreme ends of a forest products spectrum. Colonists literally turned forests into marketable ashes, shipping potash made from burning and lixiviating hardwood. Or they went hunting for the tallest and straightest trees, felled them as carefully as possible, and delivered them to tidewater to be shipped three thousand miles to the Royal Navy's shipyards and made into masts for the fleet.

The potash and mast trades, plus a few shiploads of barrel staves or rude shingles, were about all the wood exports British North America could manage before 1800. Most colonial wood was not competitive in other markets. Great Britain got most of its wood – huge square timbers or thick deal planks – from the countries bordering on the Baltic Sea instead of from far-off North America. Basic transportation costs were much lower and many more trips could be made in a season.

The navy turned to North America for a more secure, long-term supply of vital, scarce masts than the Baltic could guarantee. During the Napoleonic wars Baltic supplies of all wood products became increasingly unreliable; in 1808 they were cut off completely by Napoleon's interdiction of trade with Great Britain. As in mast procurement, British importers looked westward for new sources of supply. To guarantee that the new trade would not be ruined by the outbreak of peace, they lobbied successfully for heavy tariff preferences for the colonial product. After about 1808 the combination of war and huge differential duties against Baltic wood made it economic to ship semi-processed colonial timber across the North Atlantic to Glasgow, Liverpool, and other British ports. A major new British North American industry was called into being.

Its early growth was spectacular. In the early 1790s about 2,500 fifty-cubic-foot "loads" of square timber were exported annually. By 1803 the trade had grown to 10,000 loads. Then it took off, reaching 66,000 loads in 1808, 175,000 in 1811, more than 400,000 in 1825, and a peak of over 750,000 for several years in the mid-1840s. The deal or plank trade was far less important than the timber business, but grew proportionately. By the 1820s timbering provided British North America's staple export and had become an occupation woven into the seasonal fabric of colonial life. Along the Miramichi and Saint John and St. Croix rivers in New Brunswick, the Richelieu and Saguenay and Ottawa and Gatineau in the Canadas, and dozens of their tributaries, tens of thousands of "timberers" moved into the bush every winter to haul down virgin stands of white pine, red pine, oak, and even spruce, hewing the big logs into roughly squared timbers, preparing for the drive to market. As soon as the ice went out the timber began to move on spring freshets, tumbling down little streams to big rivers where it was assembled into cribs and rafts and moved down to seaboard. At Quebec, Saint John, and dozens of lesser ports the big sticks were loaded onto special ships for the Atlantic crossing.

As with the mast trade, British naval contractors and their agents were the first into the North American forests. The contracting firms of Scott, Idles and Company and Henry Usborne and Company set up Quebec branches in the early 1800s, and were soon followed by established private timber merchants moving out of the Baltic trade. The most important of these was Pollack, Gilmour and Company, founded in Glasgow in 1804 to import from the Baltic. In 1812, after Allan Gilmour had visited North America, the firm decided to begin operations on the Miramichi. James Gilmour (brother of Allan) and Alexander Rankin were sent out as "cadets" to begin the business. The Miramichi became the Canadian staging area for a clan of young Gilmours, Rankins, Ritchies, and Fergusons, all graduates of the same parish church and school in Scotland, who then fanned out across the provinces as timber merchants. Capital from the parent house launched Gilmour, Rankin and Company of Miramichi (Chatham) in 1812, Robert Rankin and Company of Saint John in 1822, Allan Gilmour and Company of Quebec in 1828, William Ritchie and Company of Montreal in 1828, Arthur Ritchie and Company of Restigouche in

1833, Ferguson, Rankin and Company of Bathurst in 1835, and other branches in the United Kingdom and United States.

The Pollack, Gilmour "family" of timber trading houses, all organized as standard (and frequently changing) partnerships, was originally directed from Glasgow, but in time the colonial branches developed individual identities. The Chatham company and the other houses on New Brunswick's sparsely settled north shore, for example, had to organize their own felling operations. A large part of their business involved importing provisions and supplies and moving them up to the camps. By 1835 the Pollack, Gilmour group in New Brunswick employed about five thousand men a season and shipped approximately three hundred cargoes of wood. The Quebec house was also a major exporter, but purchased most of its timber from independent producers who brought their rafts down to Quebec.

In both New Brunswick and Quebec the Pollack, Gilmour partnerships diversified into shipbuilding. By the 1830s the family's fleet of one hundred or more timber ships was one of the largest merchant navies under the British flag. The overall business was spectacularly profitable in the decades of expansion. Allan Gilmour senior invested £1,000 in the partnership in 1804. For many years he lived comfortably on the annual returns from the trade and then, complaining about being hard done by, sold out to the Pollacks in 1838 for £150,000.

British timber traders and contractors were first into the business because they knew the market, anticipated the demand, and had the capital to get started. Resident British North Americans soon joined the commercial assault on the forest. Many of the general merchants of Montreal, Quebec, and Halifax dealt in wood products from time to time and invested in shipyards. Abraham Cunard, for example, came to Halifax in 1783 as a master carpenter with the army, gradually acquired properties and began general trading, and by 1812 was engaged in widespread mercantile business with his oldest son, Samuel. Timber cut from lands the family acquired in Nova Scotia became a major item in A. Cunard and Son's trade with the West Indies and England. About 1820 one of the younger boys, Joseph, was sent to Chatham, on New Brunswick's Miramichi, where he opened a branch house, Joseph Cunard and Company. By 1832 the Cunards owned several sawmills in Chatham, stores, a counting house, and two shipyards, as well as mills and stores in other north shore ports and a major establishment in Bathurst. Joseph Cunard had become one of the wealthiest and most powerful merchants in New Brunswick. Much of his trade passed through the Halifax firm run by brother Samuel.

The Cunards of Chatham competed bitterly with Gilmour, Rankin, and Company, located across the river in Douglastown. The firms fought over timber reserves, politics (they backed rival candidates in local elections, mobilizing mobs of loyal workers whose axe-handle enthusiasm finally had to be quelled by troops), and customers. Cunard became obsessed by the competition; when asked about prices he is said to have commented, "We don't care a damn so long as we sell more deals than Gilmour, Rankin & Co."

It was easiest for local entrepreneurs to enter the production rather than the exporting end of the industry. In settled or semi-settled areas of the provinces most of the timbering was organized by locals, often working on a very small scale. In New Brunswick, Graeme Wynn has found, many farmers and small merchants launched themselves on "lumbering speculations": they got supplies on credit from a trader further up the chain, led their gangs of men into the woods, and worked furiously to "make" the timber and get it out to a buyer. In a bad year for weather, a bad year for timber prices, or with poor leadership, a speculation could be a disaster, leaving the organizer deep in debt. In a good year the profits gave the entrepreneur a little more independence, perhaps to get his farm on a solid footing, perhaps to speculate again on a larger scale, perhaps to throw up a sawmill and begin to manufacture deals and other kinds of lumber for the local market (which the big boys usually neglected) as well as export sales.

Timberers in the Canadas ranged from cut-and-run adventurers, stripping the woods and disappearing, to a group A.R.M. Lower calls "pioneer industrialists," respectable men who organized cutting and milling activities year after year in their districts, built on past experience and credit-worthiness, and sometimes achieved great wealth. The history of Ottawa valley lumbering effectively begins with the speculations of Philemon Wright, an ambitious Yankee who led a group of settlers to Hull Township in the late 1790s. Wright built a sawmill for local trade and in 1806, needing cash, decided to make a timber raft and float it down to Quebec – "much as a farmer might bring a load of hay to market," Lower observed. Wright did not have an easy time negotiating the currents and rapids, especially around the island of Montreal, and he raised cash by peddling wood to riverside purchasers as he went ("450 pces of bords to the priest of South Buck parrish at six dolers per hundred" . . . "966 to Moses Hart of 3 Rivers . . . £18.5.0"). He had an anxious time waiting for a purchaser at Quebec, but finally sold his wood and went home satisfied.

Within a few years Philemon Wright and Sons were employing two hundred to two hundred and fifty men a year driving up to twenty rafts to Quebec. They remained content to sell to the exporting merchants there. Their main competitors as Ottawa raftsmen, the Hamiltons of Hawkesbury, who worked mostly the deal trade, sent sons into business in Quebec and Liverpool to keep the whole trade in the family. For hundreds of miles up the Ottawa and its tributaries, gangs of timberers hacked and stripped and hewed and sawed the pine, drove it in the spring, and raised havoc in taverns and bawdy houses all the way to Quebec – especially in muddy, godforsaken Bytown, an otherwise benighted settlement at the mouth of a canal across from Hull.

Rafting and milling families like the Wrights and Gilmours bought timber from independent operators as well as doing their own cutting. As in New Brunswick, a tough, nimble organizer of men who could find a willing supplier (all you needed was a few barrels of flour and pork and some sharp axes) and could have a few good seasons would probably rise quickly in the forest. By the 1840s the founding families had been joined and in some cases eclipsed by newcomers such as Joseph-Ignace Aumond, formerly a general storekeeper in Bytown, now a shipper of forty rafts a year, or Peter Aylen, the reformed "King of the Shiners," who for a time in the 1830s had specialized in systematic violence (by brawling Irish labourers known as "Shiners") as a competitive tactic. One poor Irishman, John Egan, who came to the Canadas in 1832, used a specialization in scarce red pine to turn himself into the largest timberer in the country by the 1850s, employing some thirty-five hundred men in one hundred camps and mills, spending $2 million a year on supplies and wages. Egan, the leading citizen of Aylmer, Lower Canada, was known variously as "The King of the Ottawa" and "The Napoleon of the Ottawa."

The industry lent itself to creating kings and barons because of the power accumulated by single individuals like Egan or Joseph Cunard – hirers of thousands of men, puchasers of hundreds of thousands of dollars' worth of farmers' products, providers of work and wages and contracts in dozens of settlements where there was often no other significant source of employment. These were men whose enterprises meant life or death for vast regions of the provinces. They were as important to their communities, and seemed at times almost as powerful, as the feudal barons of old England. Thus, the citizens of Chatham fired cannon and rang church bells to celebrate the return of their benefactor, Joseph Cunard, from trips to England. He lived in a splendid mansion, its grounds adorned with wandering peacocks, and drove to church in a coach with liveried footmen. Aristocratic splendour in a raw colonial timber town.

William Price arrived in Quebec in 1810, aged twenty-one, to clerk for Scott, Idles and Company, the naval mast suppliers. He learned the Canadian forest and the business while inspecting timber for masts. He was promoted to manager of Idles' Quebec house, then went on his own in 1815 as the William Price Company. While Scott, Idles disappeared from Canada, Price enjoyed steady success. He specialized in exporting wood for Admiralty shipyards (these were excellent long-term contracts, which minimized a merchant's risks) while developing the first important export business in spruce deals. By the mid-1820s Price had given up earlier experiments in general merchandising and was concentrating on the wood trade. He shipped eighty to one hundred cargoes of wood a year by 1834 and employed a thousand men, laying out about £400,000. His profits were about £20,000 a year – 5 per cent on the capital he employed, a much larger percentage on his own capital.

Price differed from many of the established timber merchants in realizing that the long-term Canadian future lay in deals and other sawn products. He invested his profits in sawmills, backing small mill operators, buying mills, taking over debt-ridden mills. He increasingly concentrated his activities on the north shore of the St. Lawrence below Quebec and the Saguenay River country; the £130,000 he had invested in sawmills by the early 1840s gave him a virtual monopoly in the region.

The other big firm in the area, the Hudson's Bay Company, failed in its attempts to compete with Price in the wood trade. By the 1850s William Price's sawmills extended up the Saguenay past the village of Chicoutimi to Lac St. Jean.

The old man was an energetic supporter and investor in schemes to open up the region through "colonization" from more established areas. Through the whole of the Saguenay country, which had about twelve thousand settlers by the end of the 1850s, Price was the sole provider of paid employment. "Grandfather Price," read one of the humble testimonies to his power, "I came here with my wife, my eight children, and barely enough to eat. Now I am all right, thanks to you." Others resented his power. "Price ruled the region," concludes Louise Dechêne. "Charitable when his men were docile, he was ruthless towards those who disputed his dominion." William Price liked to visit his fiefdom, but made his permanent home at Wolfesfield on the Plains of Abraham. After his death in 1867 the firm of William Price and Sons carried on. A statue of "le père du Saguenay" was erected on high ground in Chicoutimi by the people of the region. Few Canadian entrepreneurs have been so immortalized.

Consistent with its feudal overtones, timbering was one of the few British North American businesses which can fairly be said to have been founded largely on theft. Most cutting was done on crown land. The trees belonged to the crown. In the early years timberers simply went into the woods and took the trees they wanted. Occasionally the crown tried to assert its suzerainty over the forests, notably with its policy of reserving prime mast trees by marking them with the "broad arrow" symbol. Broader state claims to the woods were ignored. The forest was everywhere and it was literally limitless. "The sheer magnitude of the landscape, the trees to the horizon on all sides, made timberers impatient of artificial restraints upon their exploitation," Michael Cross has written. "And the inability of government to enforce its regulations only heightened the feeling. The Wrights, like other woodsmen, were angered when they saw valuable timber standing untouched on vacant crown land. Why waste time and money penetrating the forest seeking good sticks, if they were available close at hand, and the only obstacle was artificial rules? The laws made hundreds of miles away mattered little against such commercial logic."

From the 1820s government gradually asserted itself against the timber barons. Since it could not stop their taking of trees, and had no particular reason to want to anyway, it began taxing their output. Then it was able to take advantage of woodsmen's competition for trees by dividing the forests into limits and selling licences to cut on a limit to the highest bidder. Forest policy soon became tangled in conflicting interests, with almost unlimited possibilities for favouritism, corruption, and the exploitation of loopholes or lax enforcement. Few lumber barons were above suspicion of having occasionally bent the law or the boundaries of their limits to get an edge on competitors. Like fur trading, timbering was rough business. You took what you wanted and fought anyone who got in your way. The state's considerable success in taxing and regulating the libertarian woodsmen is more surprising than the problems and failures on the record. In both New Brunswick and the Canadas forest revenues by mid-century had become vitally important to provincial treasuries.

No one wanted to spare the trees. Did trees have any value standing in the forests, waiting to rot, die, or burn? Who could say that any value they might have twenty, forty, or a hundred years in the future would be greater than their value right now? Cash in the pocket was worth a lot more than wood in the bush. Should those extremely valuable mast trees, worth about £100 a stick, be left standing, say to serve the twentieth century's need for masts? The timber trade was an exploitive, destructive assault on the virgin forest. But it was creative destruction, for forest income gave rise to linkages and a pace of development that the colonies would otherwise have been unable to sustain. Settlers, farmers, immigrants, labourers, as well as all the merchants and woodsmen, shared in the prosperity that timber brought. The old idea that the rape of the forests was simply a using up of natural wealth, with no compensating benefits, is a romantic mockery of the realities and difficulties of colonial development. When A.R.M. Lower wove that theme into his writing about Canadian forest industries, with particular reference to New Brunswick, he was parroting some of the industry's least-informed critics. It was far more accurate to observe, as a contemporary did for New Brunswick, that by mid-century the timber trade "has brought foreign produce and foreign capital into the Province, and has been the chief source of the money by means of which the country has been opened up and improved; by which its roads, bridges and public buildings have been completed; its rivers and harbours made accessible; its natural resources discovered and made available; its Provincial institutions kept up and its functionaries paid."

The timbermen themselves often wanted to slow down the pace of cutting. It was a classic boom-and-bust industry: high prices and unlimited access to the forest created huge timber gluts, spectacular market collapses, and disastrous years in which even the biggest operators faced insolvency. Doing business in an industry that operated on long credits, in which forecasting was next to impossible, and that had few ways of adjusting production to market needs, meant risk-taking to a high degree, not far from simple gambling. One reason why established lumbermen were not adverse to the crown's presence in the industry was a hope that licence fees and other duties would limit entry, keeping out the "fair-weather" lumberers whom they blamed for the gluts. During one particularly difficult year in the late 1840s the major Ottawa valley timbermen signed a formal agreement to limit production. They apparently abided by it, but demand was particularly weak, stock from previous years had not moved, and the combine failed to raise prices.

The British North American timber trade's very existence seemed to hinge on state action in the form of the British timber duties. From 1815 to the 1840s the trade's prosperity was based on the differential duties in favour of the colonial product against Baltic wood. They were so high that for a time in the 1830s some

British importers shipped Baltic timber to North America and then re-exported it to qualify for the preference. Most timbermen thought their industry was doomed without this imperial protection. They and their British partners and agents mounted an intense lobby to preserve the preferences. Even whispers of uncertainty about the tariffs tended to disrupt the industry, for each rumour led to a frantic effort to get timber across before the duties toppled, another glut on the market, and poor prices. As free trade sentiment permeated intellectual and then political circles in Britain, the timber interests gradually lost their tariff battle against the Baltic. The timber preference was finally abolished in the late 1840s, causing several years of wrenching dislocation in British North America.

Even the biggest timber barons were overwhelmed in the bad years. Philemon Wright never liked the business, was usually in debt, and believed the family should get out of timbering and concentrate on farming. During the Wrights' financial crisis of 1827, Philemon's son Tiberius wrote to his brother Ruggles, "The store is empty. I am out of money. How we shall get on God only noes. Don't hire any more Irishmen . . . . We have no paper no quills." Ruggles had already been consigned to debtor's prison by a creditor. The family went broke, but recovered in a few years. The Hamiltons of Hawkesbury endured their annus horribilis in 1822, when, coming off a bad season, they had two deaths in the family, a bankruptcy, and a fire. It took seven years to recover. For four years in the 1840s William Price had to fight desperately to hold his creditors at bay, keep his mills working and his cutters in the woods. He told a partner that he would sell his home and live in the office rather than give in.

Price pulled through and rose to new heights. Joseph Cunard did not. His reckless competition with Gilmour, Rankin, and Company so weakened his firm that it collapsed in hard times. The Cunard empire on the Miramichi closed down in November 1847, throwing five hundred to a thousand men out of work. An angry mob confronted the fallen hero in the streets of Chatham. There were cries of "Shoot Cunard." He is said to have stood firm, a pistol in each boot, and called for "the man who will shoot Cunard." He eventually left New Brunswick and worked for his more successful brother, Samuel. In 1871 Samuel cleared the last of Joseph's debts.

———◆———

You could reduce the risk and costs of shipping raw wood to Britain by converting some of it to ships. The wood was everywhere, semi-skilled shipwrights and carpenters could be found in every port after 1800, and, as W.S. Wallace explained in his classic *Wooden Ships and Iron Men*, it was possible to make and sell ships very cheaply:

> An enterprising merchant would secure a foreman shipwright and draft out the plans for a ship or barque from 500 to 1000 tons. The promoter would

secure a little ready money for initial and necessary expenditures, and stock in the proposed vessel would be given in return. The men who supplied the timber, the blacksmith, the block-maker, sail-maker, and ship-chandler would supply materials on the same basis, and even the labour would be secured in return for shares in the ship. Into a good many such craft went the cheapest and flimsiest materials. Launched, rigged, and loaded with the ubiquitous and ever-ready cargo of timber, the ship would be sent to Great Britain consigned to brokers who made a specialty of selling such vessels. Being new and considerably cheaper than the hard-wood ships of British yards, they sold without much difficulty, and the various shareholders received their money and often made a handsome profit upon their investment. Hundreds of vessels were built and sold in this manner and in many cases not a single dollar in cash was paid out for the construction of the ship. Such vessels were only fit for carrying timber. Most were not fit to sail in after a year or two afloat, and many were purchased by unscrupulous shipowners for the purpose of profiting on the insurance.

Most of the early timber exporters from New Brunswick and Quebec went into shipbuilding, operating the best vessels themselves, selling the others. A few builders were skilled professionals, such as the Scotts of Greenock, who had a century of experience behind them when they sent out young Christopher Scott to New Brunswick in 1799 to see what could be done to ease the wood shortage in Scotland. Scott was also instructed to build or buy colonial ships, for the firm knew that British demand was soaring. In two years he organized a major transfer of technology and skills from the old world to the new, smuggling where necessary, building or buying twenty-seven vessels with eleven others under construction. Orders and a stream of Scots shipwrights, blacksmiths, caulkers, carpenters, and sailors flowed across the Atlantic. Christopher Scott became a leading Saint John merchant, organized other shipbuilding ventures in Nova Scotia, and eventually retired to country estates in New Brunswick and Scotland, an honoured pioneer of the Maritime economy.

Other Scots shipbuilders were even more innovative. John and Charles Wood of Port Glasgow on the Clyde calculated that it would be profitable to convert square timber into ships for the Atlantic crossing, avoid duties by importing the wood as a ship, then break up the vessel and sell the timber. At Quebec in 1824 they launched the mammoth *Columbus*, a three-hundred-foot, four-masted timber raft masquerading as a sailing ship. Loaded with yet more timber, the *Columbus* reached Britain. The owners pressed their luck by trying a second voyage on which the *Columbus* broke up at sea. An even larger sister ship, the *Baron of Renfrew*, got as far as the English Channel on its maiden crossing; then a combination of winds and pilot error littered the beaches of France with fine Canadian squared timber. The Woods gave up, apparently without loss, for they had managed to buy full insurance on the sailing timber rafts.

Colonial shipyards eventually became capable of producing high-quality craft, and there was always a steady domestic demand for sturdy, well-built ships for the coastal trade (the few beautiful clipper ships built in Maritimes yards were exceptional). In the heyday of the timber trade, though, shipbuilding was a high-volume, low-quality industry, relying on cheap raw materials and ready foreign markets for cheap ships to sail for a few seasons. Canadian softwood vessels had a poor reputation at Lloyds of London, which seldom gave them a high rating. The quality of ships used in the timber trade itself was never particularly high, for neither elegance nor speed nor particularly strong hulls were required to ferry the wood across. The lack of return cargoes in the early years may be another reason why so many ships were built in Canada for one-way crossings. By the 1820s it was possible to get some westbound business, at cut rates, bringing out immigrants. The timber trade thus became one of the reasons why Quebec and Saint John were host ports for the most destitute, diseased immigrants, especially famine Irish, who came to North America in the nineteenth century.

By the 1840s the heyday of the square timber trade seeeemed to be passing. When Britain abolished all timber duties in 1846 the Baltic countries came back on the British market. Canadian producers suffered several horrible years of gluts and low prices. To the surprise of many, though, the woodsmen weathered the storm. Their timber was still competitive at normal prices, and the more far-seeing invested heavily in sawmills to produce deals for both Britain and the burgeoning American market. When some of the established firms despaired of operating in the new environment or stagnated in old age or conservatism, new producers appeared to take their place.

The Ottawa valley families thought of themselves as progressive entrepreneurs. Within their region they indeed seemed to be, as they cooperated to invest large sums in timber slides and river improvements and steamboats. Rooted by their rivers, though, they tended to miss opportunities in new areas of the provinces. So it was left to a Yankee lumberman out of New York, for example, to seize the strategic moment when steam technology made rafting on the Great Lakes feasible. Delano Dexter Calvin moved his small St. Lawrence rafting business upstream and to the Canadian side in the late 1830s, finding that tiny Garden Island near Kingston was a perfect transshipment base for Great Lakes–St. Lawrence wood movement. The Calvins were soon rafting to Quebec timber cut on all the rivers flowing into Lake Ontario. They eventually brought out wood from the drainage areas of lakes Michigan, Huron, and Superior. They traded on their own account, rafted on contract, and diversified into general shipping and forwarding. By the 1850s Garden Island had blossomed as the bustling home of one of the largest operations in the industry.

Excessive reliance on the old Scots ties of kin, village, and school could turn a formula for growth into a recipe for stagnation. Most of the New Brunswick houses of the Pollack, Gilmour group, for example, ran short of commercial zeal by the 1840s. The firm's own historian writes of "a process of distintegration, a general inertness of management." Old country partners stopped bothering with arduous, regular inspections of the North American operations. Junior partners did the business as they had learned it, making no changes. One employee left an unusually candid account of decay: "In the St. John winter the clerks read magazines and sent me downstairs for brandy when Ferguson [the manager] left. He came late, did nothing, and left early.... Drink began before breakfast, whisky and gentian, and after 11 a.m. continued."

When the firm could not make money on deals from its big Nashwaak River mill it sold the mill and its timber reserves to young Alexander Gibson, a native New Brunswicker who had started in the woods as an axeman. "Boss" Gibson reorganized the method of shipping deals down the Saint John, making significant economies; he acquired new limits, and in territory that the previous owners had written off, built New Brunswick's biggest sawmilling empire, cutting 600 million feet of deals at his Marysville mill alone between 1862 and 1900. Gibson grew as the Scotsmen of the Pollack, Gilmour group faded from Canadian history.

The sole exception was Allan Gilmour of Ottawa (nephew of Allan Gilmour the founder, cousin of Allan Gilmour of Quebec), who had been sent upstream to handle production at Bytown. Gilmour correctly read sawmilling as the industry's future, developed big mills on the Gatineau and other sites, survived the lean years, and by the 1860s had achieved great wealth as a second-generation Ottawa valley lumber king. Back in Britain the Gilmour, Pollack houses slowly withdrew from the square timber trade, which shrank to insignificance by the end of the century. The parent company finally became a shipping firm; its routes specifically excluded Canada because the St. Lawrence was too hazardous.

Another new industry begins:

> By an advertisement in this paper the public will learn that a meeting of the citizens is called at the Court House on Monday morning to deliberate upon a proper plan for immediately establishing a Bank in this City, without legislative sanction.... The utility of banking establishments, has been so generally acknowledged in every civilized country, that any argument against having them in this country, should have little or no weight. Some solitary objections might indeed be started, but those could only originate in little or prejudiced minds; or, among those whose ignorance would always be a sufficient apology, for placing them below notice. The best institutions may be perverted, and a bank conducted without most consummate prudence, might be made the instrument of many evils and even calamities. But wherever such effects have been produced, the causes have been dis-

covered; and can easily be guarded against, by prudent men (*Montreal Herald*, May 10, 1817).

Banks appeared in British North America when merchants realized that an opportunity existed to convenience themselves and their communities and probably make a profit by improving the medium of exchange. Obstacles and objections were put in their way by those who feared the power that banks – the first provincially chartered limited liability corporations in British North America – might exercise. It was not clear what powers banks should have or how to prevent abuse of power. Would restraints on bankers flow most effectively from government or the competitive marketplace? The colonial banking system sprouted in an environment of constant criticism, controversy, and considerable entrepreneurial achievement.

Currency after the Conquest was a confusing, inefficient mess. French, British, Spanish and Portuguese coins of all shapes, sizes, and weights circulated as specie. But there were never enough guineas, livres, dollars, crowns, pistareens, louis, coppers, and other gold or silver pieces, so paper notes were also circulated. These included merchants' "bons" and bills of exchange, the notes of early U.S. banks, treasury notes in Nova Scotia after 1761 and Prince Edward Island after 1790, British army bills issued to pay for purchases during the War of 1812, leather notes issued by a Charlottetown merchant in the 1830s, and innumerable printed or handwritten paper obligations.

Merchants had to know the weights and relative values of all the coins (both their official, regulated exchange values and the real values of pieces that had been under- or overrated), and give painstaking attention to the intricacies of exchange. Every merchant's rooms contained a good set of scales to weigh coins (they lost value with wear, filing, or deliberate debasement), an iron chest to store them, and a stout cudgel the clerks carried when they transferred specie to complete a transaction. Paper was much easier to handle physically, but next to impossible to value. How good was a paper note signed by Hedekiah Barnabus of Port Outport, or the cashier of the Bank of Baltimore? Would it be redeemed in full? How long would redemption take? What discount should be levied to cover the risk in accepting the note and the cost of arranging redemption? Money (ex)changing was time-consuming, tricky, risky.

The smallest transaction illustrated the monetary chaos. An 1820 letter in the *Acadian Recorder* described the problem of making change:

This morning, I went to the green market to buy a bunch of carrots, one of turnips, a squash, and two cabbages, and I carried with me a province [treasury] note for 20s. – after I had made my bargain I offered my note in payment. First, one said he could not change it; another shook his head and shrugged his shoulders, uttering with a foreign accent "me no small money, will keep my cabbage till you pay them"; a third who had the squash, began to fumble in his waistcoat pocket, and emptied out of it, coppers, ragged bits of paper and one solitary seven-pence-half-penny in silver; "my squash, sir if I change the note is 6d. but only 3d. if you give me coppers – change the note, said I, and the d—l take it; for I am tormented . . . ." For the information of others, and probably for the benefit of posterity, I shall faithfully set down what I received in this trifling transaction: –

1st.	George Leggett and Wm. Lawson's note each 5s	£0	10	0
2d.	H.H Cogswell's team boat note for	£0	1	0
3d.	Adam Esson and John A. Barry, each for 1s. 3d	£0	2	6
4th.	Wm. Smith, for three 7 ½d. in his notes	£0	11	0½
5th.	In silver	£0	0	7½
6th.	In coppers.	£0	3	6
		£0	19	6

I had thus 8 paper notes, 1 silver piece, and 84 coppers – in all 93 separate things before I could get vegetables for my family's dinner. . . . Our currency is now like a Scotch haggis, made up of contradictions, of things good and bad, oatmeal, onions, hog's lard, butter, crumbs of bread, salt, pepper, garlic, leeks, parsely, &c, &c.

A common medium of exchange would obviously be a leap forward in daily commercial life. As well, merchants needed to transport and exchange coin and paper over long distances and between countries. And, of course, they often needed credit, that is, someone willing to exchange easily negotiable notes for their promissory notes. *Faute de mieux*, merchants moved specie and notes through private networks and channels and the hands of specialists in exchange. Colonial commerce was energized by long chains of credit extending from London supply houses through Quebec and Montreal importers, and then up-country to the general storekeepers and farmers who might not see coins for years on end. Timbering and fishing operated similarly; shortages of coin or negotiable paper often led to men being paid in notes or chits redeemable only at an employer's store. These barter or "truck" transactions have been criticized as inherently exploitive. In some instances exploitation might indeed occur. But in fact they were fundamentally no more than accommodation to circumstance, unsatisfactory to both sides in the transaction because it was so hard to know the real level of compensation. But there was little choice: without widespread, almost universal reliance on barter and credit, the colonial economy could not have functioned.

By 1800 British North American merchants knew that specialized money-changing institutions could alleviate the problems of the system, or, rather, the lack of system. After centuries of gestation, commercial banks had appeared in England and Scotland a hundred years before, and in the 1790s were opening by the score in the United States. The first proposal to organize a British North American bank originated in the international transactions of fur traders, notably the exchange network created by the house of Phyn, Ellice and Company, originally of Schenectady, New York. In the 1770s this partnership opened London and Montreal offices and developed considerable expertise moving coin and notes from city to city and country to country, in both war and peace. The original aim was to facilitate the fur trade, but Phyn, Ellice found there was often profit in buying up surplus bills or coins in one market and exchanging them in another. The firm also learned to move large sums of money as military contractors and as the agency chosen by the British government to handle compensation payments to Loyalists after the Revolution.

In 1792 the partnership's remaining houses, Phyn, Ellice and Inglis of London, and Forsyth, Richardson and Company of Montreal, joined with their old associates, Todd, McGill and Company, and announced a plan to found a Canada Banking Company at Montreal. It was to operate on well-understood principles of banking, the published announcement said, issuing notes in exchange for cash (specie) deposits, and discounting bills and other paper notes. To protect its customers the company would limit itself to a banking business; it would do business in all the principal towns of Upper and Lower Canada.

The Canada Banking Company was probably inspired by the founding of Alexander Hamilton's first Bank of the United States a year earlier. For the Canadas the proposal was premature. Two surviving printed notes suggest that the CBC may have lived briefly, but it quickly disappeared. The provinces' experiences with worthless notes, including the old French and American paper issued during the Seven Years' and Revolutionary wars, plus some valueless U.S. bank notes that found their way north, may have doomed the scheme. Or, as Denison speculates in his history of the Bank of Montreal, the hostility of other fur traders, particularly Simon McTavish and the North West Company, may have been critical. To the merchants of Montreal, there was no point founding a bank until the public, or at least the merchant public, was ready to accept and circulate its notes.

John Richardson of Forsyth, Richardson waited for many years before deciding in 1808 that the time was now ripe for banks, and introduced in the Lower Canadian Assembly a bill to incorporate a Bank of Lower Canada. It would be a limited liability joint-stock corporation with a monopoly on the right to issue notes (with limited liability a member of a corporation firm would no longer be held responsible for its debts to the full extent of his resources). The provincial government would participate as a stockholder. A group of prominent Halifax merchants made a similar request of the Nova Scotia legislature in 1801 and again in 1811. Groups of Quebec and Kingston merchants also tried to incorporate banks. It is not clear why the efforts failed in the Canadas, but in Nova Scotia the sticking-point seems to have been the petitioners' request for a monopoly. Colonial legislators hesitated to confer vast powers and privileges on a group of merchants without a clear understanding of how their schemes would work.

British army bills (promissory notes issued by the military) circulated easily and conveniently through the Canadas in the War of 1812. Good paper, it seemed, could be trusted. When peace and prosperity set in after 1815 (and the army bills were withdrawn), the need for organized financial intermediation in the colonies was palpable. The opportunity to found a banking business was so promising that merchants decided not to wait for legislators to work out their scruples regarding charters. Several groups of British North American merchants entered into banking as private partnerships without monopoly powers and without limitation of liability.

In Montreal the persistent John Richardson and his associates, direct heirs of Phyn, Ellice and the Canada Banking Company, were first into the field. On November 3, 1817, the Montreal Bank, a co-partnership formed under articles of association – that is, a complex partnership whose binding principles included limits on shareholder liability – opened for business at 32 St. Paul Street. Within a year it had two competitors, the Quebec Bank, formed by Quebec City merchants, and the Bank of Canada in Montreal. A Bank of Upper Canada began operating in Kingston in 1818. In 1820 the first government-chartered bank in British North America, the Bank of New Brunswick, opened in Saint John to serve the city's prominent merchants and Loyalists. In 1822 the three Lower Canadian banks received provincial charters (with the oldest now becoming the Bank of Montreal). A year earlier in Upper Canada a new Bank of Upper Canada was chartered at York. The Kingston group was shoved aside, but tried to carry on privately, running the "Pretended" Bank of Upper Canada. It collapsed in 1822, in Adam Shortt's words "the first of Canada's broken banks." Still unable to obtain a Nova Scotia charter, in 1825 Halifax merchants led by the wealthy trader and privateer Enos Collins, launched a private partnership known as the Halifax Banking Company.

The boom of the early 1830s caused a second wave of bank formation, including the chartering of the Bank of Nova Scotia in Halifax in 1832. Banks were formed in other ambitious trading centres, including Hamilton (the Gore Bank) and Kingston (the Commercial Bank of the Midland District). Banks designed to accommodate "outsiders" came into being: the private Banque du Peuple in Montreal, intended to have a French-Canadian appeal; the Farmers' Banking Company, Bank of the People, and Agricultural Bank in Upper Canada, all oriented toward constituencies neglected by the elitist Bank of Upper Canada. Another institution, the trustee savings bank, had appeared in Montreal and Quebec in 1819 and 1821 respectively, and was soon imitated in the other provinces. These were small branchless banks, semi-philanthropic in their origins, designed to serve as safe depositories for the savings of the lower classes; they had little functional relation to merchants' banks. Other kinds of financial intermediaries, notably marine and fire insurance companies, were also beginning to appear in the colonies; we see the system evolve in later chapters.

―――――◆―――――

British North America's commercial banks sprang from indigenous and American roots. Local merchants who experienced the inconveniences and opportunities of the currency confusions, and the risks and uncertainties of private credit networks, pooled their capital to found banking houses. Some of the Bank of Montreal's organizers, such as John Richardson and the former American Horatio Gates, both of whom dealt extensively in cross-border trade, expected the bank to engage in continuous currency transactions to the United States. They interested a considerable number of Americans in their banking project: New England and New York subscribers bought 47.2 per cent of the Montreal Bank's original five thousand shares. The charter of the first Bank of the United States was the basis for the Bank of Montreal's articles of association and then its charter. The first bank employees in both Montreal and Halifax travelled south to learn the business in the United States, where two hundred and eighty banks existed before British North America had any. The first colonial bank notes were engraved and printed in the United States.

(The most striking example of continental banking solidarity was the sovereignty of the dollar. Spanish pieces-of-eight or "dollars" were the most common silver coins in all the North American colonies before the Revolution. Afterwards, the Americans issued bank notes denominated in dollars. So did the Bank of Montreal and all other Canadian banks (as even the British army had during the War of 1812). Transactions in pounds, shillings, and pence were used as a matter of form and record in the colonies, and adjustments for North American values were made by the use of a special "Halifax" value for the pound. The home government failed, however, in a mid-1820s attempt to impose a sterling currency. Currency bedlam was finally ended in British North America with official adoption of dollar/decimal denominations in the late 1850s.)

During the 1830s the mother country began having a greater impact on Canadian banking practices in several important ways. Imperial authorities demanded a toughening of colonial bank charters just as the Americans were becoming much more liberal. Immigrant banking entrepreneurs introduced such advanced practices as the Scottish system of paying interest on deposits. In 1836 the Bank of British North America was chartered in London, specifically to do business in the colonies. It soon established agencies in all of the provinces, bringing in skilled Scots staff whose appetite for hard work at small wages was noticed by the other banks. Scots tellers and clerks became a staple of the Canadian industry for the next century.

Banks exchanged their engraved paper notes for deposits of specie and other paper notes. A bank would accept a wide range of coins and notes, but would discount most of these to cover the risk and costs of handling and provide a profit. By accepting a merchant's note in exchange for its notes, a bank effectively made a loan. Having taken in assets in return for its notes, the bank made, or lost, money on its ability to realize the assets for more than their cost in notes. A major benefit to the community came from the easy circulation of bank notes, an accepted, convenient, efficient mode of exchange, simplifying all commercial transactions. Many new transactions were possible for those who got credit, because they had exchanged their personal notes for the freely circulating bank notes.

The growth of money transactions also effectively increased the money supply. The risk in banking was that either party might exchange worthless notes. If bankers took in gold and silver coin and good paper, and then failed to honour their promises to redeem their notes in gold or silver coin, they would be effectively loot-ing a community. How could abuse of the banking function be avoided? An anonymous critic of Lower Canada's banks asked in 1820 how the public could be protected from "the fraudulent imposition of advertising individuals, who with an ostentatious appearance of fictitious capital, might pillage the credulous, and by an invented prospectus of anticipated gains, induce the sanguine to hazard their hard-won savings?"

Private individuals and unincorporated partnerships that engaged in banking, such as the Halifax Banking Company, were liable for their notes in the same way anyone was liable for his debts. People who did business with private banks had to judge whether or not the bankers could be trusted to redeem their notes. Rich and prominent merchants, such as these Halifax bankers, were more likely to honour their notes than unknown strangers. The acid test of any banker's honour, of course, was whether or not he could pay up, on demand, in real coin.

Unincorporated banks lasted well into twentieth-century Canada, but had difficulty mobilizing pools of capital and soon after Confederation lost all remaining rights to issue their own notes. For most merchants the unlimited liability of all members of a standard partnership was a disincentive to invest in any secondary en-terprise, particularly one involving small profit margins and large liabilities. Most early banking schemes were not practical unless legislatures limited the investors' (shareholders') liability. So the desire to found banks produced pressure on legis-latures to issue charters creating special banking companies.

The creation of these corporations, with their special privilege of limited liability, instantly raised the question of their special responsibilities. In return for the weakening of normal liability (plus other privileges, such as clauses in bank charters prescribing the death penalty for counterfeiters), the banks had to accept compensating limits or regulations on their business. Early charters usually required that a bank's notes be redeemable in specie, limited the note issue in relation to paid-up capital, specified minimum capital requirements, and confined the institu-tion to a banking business. Notes were not to be exchanged for pledges of real estate (the banks dealt in specie and specie-based notes, not in land or mortgages). For greater security, shareholders' liability need not be limited to the face value of their investment: beginning with the charter of the Bank of Nova Scotia, the colonial practice was to hold a chartered bank's stockholders liable for twice the par value of their shares. These first corporations arose, then, in a bargain by which the state reduced investors' risk in return for limiting their freedom.

Critics immediately complained that the corporations had too many privileges, amounting to a licence to exploit the community. The deepest strain of concern about banks sprang from those who distrusted all paper money. To them paper was paper, almost valueless. Gold and silver were real money. A bank charter gave a group of merchants the power to buy a community's gold and silver in return for nothing but paper promises for which the issuers would not even be normally liable! The deeply conservative Radical leaders in the Canadas, William Lyon Mackenzie and Louis-Joseph Papineau, both distrusted banks for this reason. As Papineau wrote, banks "had it in their power, at the expense of a few shillings for engraving a note, to create vast fictitious capital, and send out large quantities of paper, which might in the end turn out to be blank paper in point of value." Mackenzie was opposed to all limited liability corporations and almost all forms of paper money.

Those who understood the uses and efficiencies of paper currency could still find glaring loopholes in bank charters (the early banks could open before the capital was paid up, could lend on the security of their own stock, could lend all their capital to their own directors, and so on). More fundamentally, there was a deep suspicion that the "money power" conferred on banks could be used to advance certain commercial interests at the expense of others. Were the banks interested in offering their services to everyone in the community on an equal footing? Or were they little more than pools of private capital created for their owners' convenience? Perhaps the real aim was to use discounting and other exchange transactions to advance the principal enterprises of the shareholders?

The men who clubbed together to form banks certainly expected to benefit, not merely as dividend-receiving stockholders, but from the use of a bank's services, particularly its discounting (lending) function. And nothing was more natural than for the directors and cashiers of the early banks to accommodate the needs of men they knew and trusted, men whose promises they believed were good. Bank credit naturally flowed along established networks to directors and shareholders. At first, it was too risky to accept the notes of unknown outsiders (unless, perhaps, they were endorsed by a director or someone of equal prominence).

Merchants' appreciation of the value, in fact the competitive necessity of access to banking facilities, explains the rush to form banks once the crust of conservatism broke. Major merchants in different cities formed competing, place-named banks. Then other groups in the provinces came to understand the uses of banking and wanted accommodation. Small men who believed that their promissory notes, based perhaps on the land they owned, ought to be exchangeable for bank notes, felt that the banks should be more accommodating or there should be more banks. If the Bank of Montreal was not interested in serving the needs of small French-Canadian storekeepers, for example, why not create a Banque du Peuple to meet the people's needs? If the Bank of Upper Canada would not serve the farmers of the province, why not create a Farmers' Banking Company or an Agricultural Bank? The idea that there should be more banks to meet a wide variety of needs was particularly attractive to those who believed that bank notes represented new wealth. The simple equation of more banks, more credit, more money, and more prosperity was beguiling. So was "the impression abroad in the minds of the general public," Victor Ross writes in the history of the Canadian Bank of Commerce, "that the principal advantage or object of being connected with a bank as director or officer was the facilities provided thereby for paying one's debts by borrowing from the bank."

Who would accommodate governments, which had by far the largest financial requirements and generated a huge amount of banking business? How would a government's banking business be allocated? Would all banks be treated equally in the competition for government business? Or would political power and networking come into play as in all other government business? Would politically powerful banks get government business? Would powerful banks use their political strength in other ways, say to deny charters to competitors? Would powerful governments create their own banks and run them as vehicles for printing and peddling paper that they could not redeem?

The Americans were already experimenting with models of how to deliver more – and better, and often much worse – bank service. One view, which stressed the desirability of a uniform note issue and equity in discounting, was to create a single, state-controlled bank to issue all notes and perhaps exercise a supervising function over lesser banks. Or there could be wide-open banking, "free banking," in which anyone who met minimum requirements could issue notes. The public would judge the notes in the marketplace. The founders of both the Bank of Montreal and the Bank of Upper Canada toyed with concepts of monopoly and government participation in their affairs, and from time to time manoeuvred toward a partnership with the state to dominate provincial banking. But by the mid-1830s free banking seemed to be the wave of the future in British North America as surely as it was in Andrew Jackson's United States. In 1836–37 the Upper Canadian legislature passed nine new bank charters.

Competition made the early bankers careful. No bank wanted to be stuck with someone else's worthless notes, so the banks tested one another from time to time with demands for redemption. Bank "wars," like the 1829–30 clash between the Bank of Montreal and the Bank of Upper Canada over the former's penetration of Kingston, led to heavily guarded kegs of specie moving from Montreal to York and back and back again as the rivals demanded payment. Normally, of course, the banks found it convenient to accept each other's notes, clearing accounts at the end of each week. They discouraged small customers from redeeming bank notes by paying in coins like the old French half-crowns or pistareens, which everyone knew were officially over-valued and hard to circulate.

The Bank of Montreal so dominated Lower Canadian finance that its competitors tended to complain to the legislature rather than engage in note wars. The most important critics in the bank's formative years were a group of its own directors who became alarmed at heavy losses the bank suffered when the old North West Company trading firm of McTavish, McGillivray and Company went under in 1825. George Moffat, a major Montreal merchant and one of the bank's founding directors, charged that the president, Samuel Gerrard, had practised unethical, self-interested favouritism and had exceeded his legal authority in discounting the failed firm's notes. Simon McGillivray countered with charges that Moffat was carrying on a vendetta to ruin him. Moffat's group managed to force Gerrard out of the presidency, hold him personally liable for notes he should not have discounted, and toughen the bank's regulations. It took heavy losses during the difficult year of 1826 and did not resume dividends until 1829. The directors gradually restored internal harmony, ending "the evil tendency of disagreement among the officers of the Bank" only to have to face outside critics. Quebec merchants were aggrieved at the Bank of Montreal's habit of locally buying claims on Britain with notes issued in Montreal. It then refused to redeem these notes in Quebec except at a discount and thus seemed to be trafficking in its own notes. These complaints about the Bank of Montreal's Quebec office began an enduring tradition of customer dissatisfaction with the hidden charges and complexities of branch banking (the Bank of Montreal was discounting its notes to cover the cost of moving the specie).

Moving money and notes from city to city in a planned way was apparently a more important source of earnings than the note issue for the Bank of Montreal in its early years. Its founders had sensed the opportunity to tie together the separate money markets of Montreal, Boston, New York, and Quebec. The bank purchased specie or notes in cities where they were in surplus, sold them where the demand was higher. It was an "arbitrage" operation (trading across markets to exploit price differentials), principally along the well-travelled north-south routes between the Canadas and the United States (the same routes that had been used to smuggle furs out of New France when prices were more attractive in the other market). Canada's first bank was not founded to facilitate the Great Lakes–St. Lawrence trading system so much as it was to break down barriers between Canadian and U.S. markets. It soon discovered, too, that the best place to keep its reserves of specie was in New York. The coins could be loaned on demand and recalled and rushed to Canada only if necessary.

The more bankers, merchants, and other traders succeeded in knitting markets together, the more interdependent the North Atlantic triangular trading system became. In good times money and confidence invigorated markets, producers, and lenders along filaments leading from the financial capital of the world, London, through the busy North American port cities, up rivers and lakes to hinterland towns, and out on improbable corduroy roads to general storekeepers in three-shack hamlets. Prospects of good trade caused merchants to exchange paper notes freely, crediting one another in climates of optimism and risk-taking. But then there would come whispers of doubt, a nagging feeling that credit was being overdone. A crop failure in America might trigger the reconsideration; so could a bank failure in London. Suddenly a new mood infected the credit network: time to pay up, time to honour the commitments, redeem the notes. Where is the hard cash? We have to have it because we are being squeezed ourselves. Sorry, we are not making discounts at the moment.

Cyclical spasms in the international trading and credit systems became a recurrent feature of the nineteenth century. One of the earliest and worst was the "panic" of 1836–37, a credit contraction that flashed from Britain to North America where it devastated the free and easy U.S. banking system, which had issued barrels of paper based on bushels of optimism. Most American banks had no hope of redeeming their notes. Many failed. Others suspended specie payments until they could become more liquid. With specie everywhere in demand and runs on banks an everyday occurrence, all but one of the British North American banks suspended specie payment in 1837–38. The suspension was a gross failure of the banking system: the men who ran the banks could not pay their debts to the people who had accepted their notes. Legislatures came to their rescue by temporarily sanctioning the default.

It was better to abandon the specie standard temporarily than to watch the overextended banks fall like dominoes. During the suspension bank notes continued to circulate because they were the most convenient medium, private merchants (like the Molsons of Montreal) issued new paper, and the currency shortage was not crippling. In Upper Canada, however, Lieutenant-Governor Sir Francis Bond Head believed that honourable British banks *must* honour their promises to pay. For several months he forbade suspension. Hard-pressed Upper Canadian bankers bore down on their debtors, increasing the monetary stringency, until the governor relented. The Agricultural Bank failed before it could suspend, leaving shareholders and noteholders with nearly worthless paper. The commercial hardships of the depression were accentuated in both Upper and Lower Canada by the outbreak of armed rebellions led by the most radical of the reformers, Papineau and Mackenzie. The rebellions were quickly suppressed. The capsized Atlantic economies righted themselves because of their natural buoyancy, confidence gradually returned, and banks resumed payment in hard coin.

The first decades of banking in British North America were modestly profitable for the Bank of Montreal, the Bank of Upper Canada, the Halifax Banking Company, and some of their younger competitors. Two banks failed, several others had been or were about to be swallowed up in mergers. The colonial banks were still small and most were conservative in their policies. Most had few branches, or none at all. One or two clerks in head office under the supervision of a cashier, plus perhaps some part-time agents in a few other towns, were all the staff a bank needed. Committees of directors attended to the discounting (lending) themselves. Discount rates were high enough on an expanding market, and confidence in bank notes was usually strong enough, that a reasonably prudent money-changing company had little trouble making 8 to 10 per cent dividends for its shareholders.

Others were not so satisfied with the banks' performance. Their notes, issued in as many varieties as there were banks and in a jumble of denominations, had not yet proven an adequate answer to the currency problem. The coinage in the colonies was as chaotic as ever. "The silver and copper coins we have in circulation are a disgrace to any civilized nation," a critic claimed in the 1830s, "and have more the appearance of the fifteenth than the nineteenth century. All the antiquated cast-off rubbish, in the whole world, finds its way here, and remains. This Colony is literally the Botany Bay for all the condemned coins of other countries; instead of perishing in the crucible as they ought to do, they are banished to Canada."

British authorities thought they could rationalize the colonial currency by establishing the predominance of sterling and setting up a single, state-operated provincial bank to issue all notes. Lord Sydenham, the governor sent out to unite Upper and Lower Canada after the rebellions, strongly favoured the idea. He dismissed the colonial banks as "unlimited paper mills" like the American banks, and believed it would be safer and more efficient to have the money power in the hands of the state. It would also be a profitable service for the state to offer.

Neither the banks nor the colonial legislators supported Sydenham's scheme. The former had no desire to give up the most profitable part of their business. The latter, whose numbers included people such as George Moffat and Benjamin Holmes of the Bank of Montreal, were undoubtedly influenced by governments' record of poor monetary stewardship, particularly their habit of issuing worthless paper to pay their debts. Why would a bank controlled by politicians be any more trustworthy than a chartered bank run by merchants? There was probably a better chance of exercising real control over privately owned banks than over state banks, both through regulation and as a result of competition.

In 1841 the Province of Canada extended the banks' charters for another ten years, but tightened them to prevent trafficking in a bank's own stock, excessive loans to directors, and other abuses. More elaborate reporting was also required. The idea of a government bank to control the note issue was put in limbo, to be revived and talked about every decade or two, and fully implemented ninety-four years later.

A distinctive pattern of British North American economic life emerged between the 1820s and 1840s. It was based on exchanging the raw and semi-processed wealth of the provinces' forests, farms, and fisheries for manufactured goods from the mother country and sometimes the United States. Wood, flour, potash, fish moved down the St. Lawrence or the Hudson systems, the Miramichi and the Saint John, out of the ports of Saint John, St. John's, Halifax, Quebec, or New York, and across the Atlantic. Drygoods, hardware, fancy groceries, wines and spirits, musical instruments, machinery, and thousands of other items were imported through the same ports and moved upriver and along coasts to supply the staple producers.

The volume of trade gradually caused many merchants to specialize. Functional specialization occurred along the distribution network as big importing merchants stopped storekeeping and became wholesalers. Some only imported, just as others began limiting themselves to exporting. It remained more common to both import and export, just as the country storekeeper was still both a buyer and seller. He sold everything that farmers needed and bought, or bartered, and shipped everything a farmer had to sell: potash, grain, salt pork, butter, eggs, whatever. In the cities a few retail storekeepers did a selling business only. Some gradually found it profitable to limit their stock to certain broad lines. Drygoods, hardware, and groceries were the basic retail specialities. Wholesalers sometimes divided their offerings along these lines, with some of them specializing in one or two of the three.

There were still many general merchants in the provinces, but the very use of "general" as a qualifier showed that specialization was becoming normal. Fairly narrow functional specialists had appeared in entrepôts like Montreal: jobbers and brokers who bought and sold goods already shipped, often trading in odd lots; auctioneers and commission agents and manufacturers' agents who bought and sold for fees; the financial specialists we have seen in this chapter, the forwarders to come in the next; a host of millers and distillers and brewers and manufacturers like John Molson of Montreal, of whom more will be heard; not to mention thousands of artisans and tradesmen, some beginning to prosper as businessmen. The world of colonial commerce was becoming more complex every year.

The port cities were the hubs of British North American commerce, centres of lines of trade radiating into their hinterlands. Halifax, Saint John, St. John's and the much smaller Charlottetown were the dominant cities of the Atlantic colonies. Their hinterlands corresponded roughly to provincial boundaries, except for the competition between Halifax and Saint John to control the trade of New Brunswick's north shore and Nova Scotia's Fundy coast. Timber coves (where the rafts were received and sold, and the wood loaded onto ships) lined the shores of the St. Lawrence for miles on both sides of Quebec City, the capital of the square timber trade. But Montreal had finally emerged as the trading metropolis of the Canadas, the transshipment centre for goods destined west up the St. Lawrence to the Great Lakes, north up the Ottawa valley, and south up the Richelieu to the Eastern Townships and the United States. The city of fur traders and missionaries had become the mercantile and financial capital of an inland empire. It was the home of British North America's most important merchants, the centre of agitation for better transportation in the provinces, more support for commerce, and limits on the parochial politics and power of the French Canadians.

The merchants of Upper Canada had always bought and sold through Montreal houses. Every Lake Ontario village aspired to become another Montreal, or at least the hub of a secondary distribution network for the Upper Canada trade. In the days of Cartwright and Hamilton the forwarding centres of Kingston and Queenston were the busiest commercial villages. Now they were eclipsed by muddy York, which had an excellent natural harbour, sat at the end of the portage to Georgian Bay and the upper lakes, was near to water power on the Don and Humber rivers, and had extra advantages as the provincial seat of government. York's merchants, still a relatively small group (the town had fewer than ten thousand inhabitants when it was incorporated as the City of Toronto in 1834), serviced expanding farm communities strung north along Yonge Street to Lake Simcoe and west along Dundas Street into the fertile southwestern peninsula.

Toronto had no preordained right to become Upper Canada's commercial metropolis. On the one hand, Kingston merchants had no intention of surrendering their early predominance. On the other, the villages around Burlington Bay at the west end of Lake Ontario were better situated than Toronto to organize and dominate the trade of the southwest country between the lakes and along the Erie shore. Exactly which village would leap into prominence – Dundas, Ancaster, or tiny Hamilton – was still not clear. The competition of merchant against merchant in these ambitious communities became a war of all towns against all other towns for commercial dominance. This urban or metropolitan struggle for control of hinterlands became a staple theme of economic and regional development as the country grew.

The ebb and flow of merchants into, out of, and around specialties and regions, restlessly seeking competitive advantage, has been authoritatively traced in Douglas McCalla's study of the businesses of Peter and Isaac Buchanan in *The Upper Canada Trade*. Their father was a moderately prosperous Glasgow merchant who had done most of his trading with the Caribbean. The family became interested in Canada when Isaac, the younger brother, was sent to work in the new Montreal wholesale house of another Glasgow firm, William Guild and Company. Finding the established wholesalers difficult to compete with, Guild and Company decided to leapfrog that city and open a wholesale drygoods house in York. Isaac started the business there in 1832, as did several competitors, all rushing to be in on the ground floor of wholesaling in the provincial capital.

Isaac became so enthusiastic about Upper Canada's prospects that he bought out the more cautious Guild and formed a partnership with his brother Peter, who had taken over the family's Glasgow house. "We have means . . . ," Isaac argued to Peter. "These means will not increase . . . unless put into some dangerous Business or Speculation which as regards the Family would never answer. While *if brought to this country now* they are quite certain if laid out with common prudence to secure a large independency for all of us for life."

The brothers put about £12,000 into the business, founded in 1834. They shipped drygoods from Peter Buchanan and Company of Glasgow (and soon of Liverpool) for wholesale by Isaac Buchanan and Company in Toronto. They got credit, about as much as their capital, from members of their family, the Glasgow Banking Company, and the Bank of Upper Canada. One of the problems with their trade was that it was specialized beyond the Buchanans' expertise. They needed someone with a thorough knowledge of drygoods to manage the business, particularly the buying. In an early instance of clannishness giving way to merit, the Buchanans hired Robert W. Harris, an Ulsterman who had worked for Guild and Company, to be their buyer and manager. Isaac's comment about Harris is rich in changing concepts: "I am very much pleased with Him altho' I have never known an Irishman here before whom I could put implicit faith in."

Isaac Buchanan was an irrepressible enthusiast, eager to try almost anything. Peter was a shrewd investor, sometimes able to keep his brother under control, and understood the imperatives of costs and balance sheets. In the early years Isaac experimented with retailing, but Peter persuaded him to drop storekeeping and accept the fast-hardening division between wholesalers and retailers. They found excellent business in concentrating on being the exclusive supplier to a select group of retailers with whom they worked carefully, in season and out, to strengthen their trade and credit-worthiness.* The Buchanans soon brought the valuable Harris into their partnership. In other personnel matters Isaac still retained his ethnic preferences:

> The wonderful success of my operations in Canada may be to a great extent attributed to my solemn determination not to trust Yankees and my exercising the most vigorous scrutiny before doing business with a man Canadian born – this drove me to a system of rearing up a new set of customers for myself who are generally two young Scotchmen associated as partners and every such concern that we supply in the Colony is now doing well.

The bias may have been sound; McCalla suggests that British-born storekeepers and clerks probably had much better commercial training than the North Americans.

The Buchanans prospered in Toronto, making annual sales of about twice their capital. Ten per cent profit on sales produced 20 per cent on capital. Most profits were reinvested and the firm enjoyed exponential growth; the brothers effectively doubled their wealth every four years. Determined to stay ahead of the competition,

---

* "Every winter," McCalla writes, "once the roads had frozen and while the wholesale trade was least active, partners and, later, senior employees toured the hinterland. In summer, when weather permitted, shorter journeys were often made as well. On such trips, the partners met customers and inspected their businesses, investigated new retail opportunities, looked for new activities by competitors, sought information regarding local retail stocks and farmers' crops, and tried to spur payments on accounts . . . .

"The partners did not hesitate to demand to see the customer's books, aiming to judge his assets and liabilities, his sales, and his managerial abilities. They inspected his stocks and assessed the strengths and weaknesses of his employees. Thus, they served as the equivalent of today's management consultant, offering advice on the whole range of business problems encountered by the retailer, including personnel, accounting, display, premises, business and political trends, and techniques of pricing, selling, and collecting. Yet even so there was much room for error and oversight. Accordingly, the partners sought above all to judge the man's character and integrity, and they looked especially for signs of weakness such as alcoholism and serious neglect of business details."

Isaac decided in 1840 to relocate in Hamilton. It seemed to have a clear locational advantage over Toronto, and Toronto was about to lose its role in government as the Canadas were united into one province.

There were good prospects for doing a more general wholesale business in the less competitve Hamilton region, so groceries and hardware were added as new departments. A Montreal office was opened to facilitate imports. This connection became important as the brothers developed a return trade as grain dealers and exporters, moving farm products downstream while bringing tea, sugar, and other provisions up to Hamilton. But like many other Upper Canadian traders, they knew that tea and other products were cheaper in New York City than in Montreal. In the 1840s, the brothers opened a New York agency, bringing goods up the Hudson–Erie Canal system to Upper Canada. The grain they exported started going down that route to New York, for shipment to Britain. Other Upper Canadian merchants in these years were similarly abandoning the Montreal–St. Lawrence system for the cheaper American trade route.

The Buchanans' partnership arrangements multiplied as they added branch houses and associates, and as Isaac's comings and goings became increasingly erratic. Sales kept growing in times of rebellion, commercial recession, and other colonial crises. By far the largest wholesalers in Hamilton, the Buchanans were price leaders, obtaining better markups than in more competitive centres. Profits were about 11 per cent of sales on drygoods, 6 per cent on groceries. Occasional mistakes, such as a £10,000 loss in grain speculations in 1847, were easily absorbed. In sixteen years the Buchanan's capital grew from roughly £12,000 to £130,000, and they had Isaac's "large independency." There were bigger and wealthier wholesale houses in Montreal, but not many. The combination of Isaac Buchanan's optimism, Peter's careful accounting, and Harris's skilful management, enabled the firm to find and exploit competitive advantages and become one of the Province of Canada's largest businesses, the envy of many a struggling merchant. It was the Upper Canada trade at its most successful. It was not, of course, its most typical: the best are never typical.

Isaac Buchanan's generalist instincts helped the partnership grow while others were specializing. They also led him into politics. For a time in the early 1840s he represented Toronto in the legislature of the united Province of Canada. Buchanan worked hard to thwart Lord Sydenham's proposal for a provincial bank, which he felt would tighten the money supply and restrict growth. He was also a voluble participant in the momentous debate on free trade versus colonial preferences, the great commercial issue of the 1840s.

Buchanan was among the many British North American merchants who believed the colonies' economies could not survive without the advantages they received in the British market thanks to the Corn Laws, the timber duties, Navigation Acts, and other restrictions on foreign commerce. He was part of a massive merchant lobby, on both sides of the Atlantic, against the growing doctrine of free trade and the numbing uncertainties caused by London's vacillations on tariff policy. The mother country seemed maddeningly unresponsive to the needs of its growing but fragile colonies.

Many politically interested merchants had already learned how little they could influence colonial events. During the 1820s and 1830s they saw spokesmen for reform movements in the Canadas and Nova Scotia demand that governments become more responsive to the popular will. In Upper Canada the Reformers set out to break the power of the "Family Compact," a close-knit establishment controlling the best jobs in government and the judiciary and holding the most prominent social positions. In Nova Scotia the appointed Legislative Council, or Council of Twelve, seemed to be an unduly dominant oligarchy of leading merchants and lawyers. The most serious political conflict took place in Lower Canada where similar tensions between insiders and outsiders became transformed into major ethnic conflict, the phenomenon Lord Durham later characterized as "two nations warring in the bosom of a single state." During the hard times of 1837 bitter conflict between radical Patriotes and the "English party" or Constitutionalists degenerated into bloody armed rebellion in Lower Canada. It was followed by several small uprisings and rebel-sponsored border raids from the United States in 1838–40. William Lyon Mackenzie's 1837 resort to violence in Upper Canada was far less serious, little more than colonial comic opera. In Nova Scotia and the other provinces there was no rebellious violence.

Leading merchants in all provinces were involved in colonial government, often as appointees to the upper houses, the Legislative Councils. In Lower Canada there was a long tradition of Montreal merchants being actively involved in electoral politics. Political merchants often had close links with financial institutions, serving as directors, shareholders, and officers of the Bank of Upper Canada, Bank of Montreal, and Halifax Banking Company. The mesh between commerce and politics caused some reformers and historians to view politics as a class struggle in which the power and privileges of "merchantocracy" were being challenged by common men, the reformers. The people were resisting rule by businessmen.

Political and commercial realities in the provinces were much more complex. Struggles in the political arena were multi-dimensional. Men formed loyalties and took positions on the basis of race (there were Irish, as well as Anglo-Scottish and French factions), religion (Roman Catholics and several kinds of Protestant, the latter seldom united), region (the scramble of all against all, hinterlands often resisting a metropolis), national loyalty (the American-born were a distinct faction, particularly in Upper Canada), personal ambition (the spoils of government office were well worth fighting for), as well as calculated economic interest. Loyalties often cut across simple class lines, creating allegiances inexplicable in purely economic terms.

Even in Lower Canada, where divisions between Montreal's commercial group and the agrarian majority seemed to be straightforward, there were notable divergences as men chose sides on the basis of race rather than commercial interest. And the commercial interest, such as it was, was deeply frustrated in that province, for merchants' attempts to dominate Lower Canada were always thwarted, first by hostile governors, then by the French-Canadian majority in the Assembly. Eventually the stalemate between contending factions in the province led to violence. In Nova Scotia, by contrast, Enos Collins, Samuel Cunard, and the other merchant members of the Council of Twelve exerted much more influence in the province's formative years; yet the democratization of power as reformers appeared on the provincial stage came more easily than in the Canadas. In New Brunswick and Prince Edward Island there were neither recognizable establishments nor reformers; powerful merchants were most responsible for Newfoundland's getting a legislative assembly in 1832, but it was immediately rent by conflict over religion and education. Colonial society was too multi-faceted to be comprehensible in simple terms of class conflict – or to be controlled by merchants.

For every man of property who went into politics to further his interests, serve his community, or do both, there were many more merchants who concentrated solely on their trade. Most would sign petitions occasionally, calling for changes in the customs duties, revision of weights and measures regulations, or improvement in river navigation, and from time to time they banded together in boards of trade or trade associations to express themselves more forcibly and continuously. The 1820s and 1830s, however, saw a slower tempo in the dance of commerce and the state and a perceptible drawing apart of the partners. With the decline of military spending and other government contracting, and the rise of the loosely regulated timber trade and the commerce in agricultural staples, merchants had less need for good political connections. The banks, which relied on government for their charters, were an exception. Timber traders such as the Gilmours or Calvins, merchants such as the Buchanans, would have little or nothing to do with politics. Isaac Buchanan's political career was opposed by his partners, did nothing to advance the business, and eventually contributed to the dissipation of his fortune.

By the 1840s, as well, high office no longer came so easily to the men of property. The rebels were crushed in 1837, but the ideas of the reformers triumphed. With the advent of responsible government in British North America (the doctrine that the executive must be responsible to the controlling group in the legislature) power shifted from British governors and their hand-picked councillors to the organized factions, or parties, which jostled to form majorities in elected assemblies. Any merchant who wanted to go into government in a serious way would have to become a politician. To many men of affairs, the very idea of politics – politicking, vote-seeking – was repugnant. Better to get on with business.

The old Tories were everywhere in retreat by the end of the 1840s. That would not have much mattered to colonial commerce except that old toryism in the mother country was being superseded by liberalism and free trade. Britain's abolition of the remaining preferences on grain and timber, the end of the navigation laws (confining shipping and trade on national lines) and other trade restrictions, seemed to imply a commercial revolution. How could Canadian grain or timber compete in the British market? How could colonial shipbuilding and the carrying trade survive open competition? Could St. Lawrence commerce sustain all the Montreal merchants, especially now that the Americans were aggressively expanding their trading system through New York and into Upper Canada?

The anxieties became self-fulfilling prophecies. In 1846 colonial markets were glutted as dealers rushed to get grain and timber across before the favourable tariff preferences ended. Then trade was wildly erratic. In 1849, with the Atlantic world suffering from another cyclical credit famine, Europe in political upheaval, and Ireland being destroyed by real famine, it seemed simply impossible for honest merchants to continue the struggle. In that year the governor general of Canada, Lord Elgin, wrote that "Property in most of the Canadian towns, and more especially in the Capital [Montreal], has fallen 50 percent in value within the last three years. Three fourths of the commercial men are bankrupt."

Part of Lord Elgin's mandate was to complete the introduction of responsible government, whatever its consequences for old Tory establishments. In 1849, a disastrous year in every respect, he signed a Rebellion Losses Bill, passed by the Reform majority in the legislature, which everyone knew would compensate many of the rebels of 1837. Loyal men and true were being taxed to support former traitors. Conservative, largely English, mobs in Montreal vented their frustrations and their political powerlessness by stoning Elgin's carriage and burning the Houses of Parliament.

British North America had grown up in a protected trading system, enjoying privileged access to the vast British market. Montreal and the St. Lawrence seemed dependent on a system that was collapsing, both politically and economically. Britain was giving its colonies a larger measure of self-government while taking away their trade privileges. For many Montrealers the future seemed a bleak amalgam of economic decline and misgovernment by venal politicians. What could be done?

Perhaps the future lay to the south. The northern provinces needed access to a large market somewhere; the booming United States was very attractive as a seemingly logical alternative to the lost British market. North-south trading had always been important – along the old fur-smuggling route, all across the Vermont border, through dozens of Nova Scotia and New England ports, along the Niagara frontier, and now by the bankers carrying revolvers to guard the money they were moving from one country to the other. It had probably been as important to the "commercial empire of the St. Lawrence" as the east-west flow of goods. And it was increasing very rapidly at mid-century. More Upper Canadian exports reached seaboard through New York than through Montreal. American lumbermen and lumber buyers were moving north to realign the forest industry on a new axis. The railroads everyone was building or planning to build tended to run along the natural lines of crows' flight, ignoring artificial borders.

In that horrible year, 1849, a movement sprung up to start over again as part of the United States. Annexation manifestos circulated in Montreal and elsewhere. Their hundreds of signatories included most of Montreal's merchant establishment and the leading lumbermen of New Brunswick and the Ottawa valley. Isaac Buchanan believed annexation was inevitable and decided to retire to Scotland. His North American countrymen seemed to have decided that with the old economy and political system apparently in ruins, their best hope for lasting prosperity lay under the Stars and Stripes.

Within a year, the annexation sentiment faded away. Commerce revived. Trade with the mother country did not wither in the winds of liberalization; trade with the Americans continued to increase. As merchants regained their solvency, as they adjusted to the new environment, their equanimity returned along with their disinterest in big geopolitical issues. As business turned up, and up, and up, through one good year after another in the 1850s, they concentrated on getting on with those incredible railroads, with manufactories, and more banks and life insurance companies, and layer after layer of new enterprises. Freer trade with the United States, achieved by a Reciprocity Treaty in 1854, was all to the good – so good, in fact, that any closer political relations, such as annexation, were obviously unnecessary. If you played your cards right in North America, you could have your economic logic and your political desires too.

TOP: **John Molson**

ABOVE: **Molson's** *Accommodation*, **Canada's first steamboat** (Both *Molson's Archives*)

7

The Steam Revolution

*An end to confinement . . . the Molson liners . . . Cunard's "ocean
railway" . . . Hugh Allan's line . . . canals . . . the Welland Canal
fiasco . . . the philosophy of railroads . . . railways and land
development . . . first passengers, late . . . MacNab's Great
Western . . . Galt's St. Lawrence and Atlantic . . . "commercial press
gangs" . . . a "glittering colossus," the Grand Trunk . . . a dismal failure,
the Grand Trunk . . . railway ethics . . . undermining
governments . . . promoters and politicians need more railways*

Steam seemed to change everything. It is difficult to exaggerate the impact of
the steam engine on transportation and development in the nineteenth century.
Steam conquered space and time. It seemed to liberate communities from the
tyrannies of geography and climate. It speeded up the pace of business and
spread commerce everywhere. It opened boundless frontiers for entrepreneurs
who knew how to harness iron horsepower.

British North America had been imprisoned by oceans, endless rivers, im-
penetrable wilderness, a forbidding climate. Steam offered an end to confinement. Steamships could link the principal cities and tie the whole bundle back
across the Atlantic to Great Britain. Steam railways could take travellers out of
the narrow, predestined banks of the Laurentian waterways and speed them
over land – anywhere on land, farther and faster than anyone could have
dreamed, at any time of the year, even in the dead of winter. Steam changed the
land itself, for wherever the rails went they gave the land value. Steam tamed
wilderness, and so it was the indispensable instrument for building the northern economy.

Steam transportation seemed to create wonderful entrepreneurial opportunities. Colonial enthusiasts and promoters were as quick off the mark as
anyone in trying to apply the new technology. They operated some of the
world's first steamboats and, in the 1850s, built the world's longest railway.
The transportation revolution in British North America was fundamental to
and was the beginning of the provinces' industrial revolution. Along with steam

came new industries, new concentrations of power, new relationships with government, new methods of doing business. The slow-moving, wind-driven merchant's world faded into the hammering drive of a society organized by capitalists and busy men.

Steam engines were also the precondition for the creation of the Dominion of Canada. Not just in the obvious sense that railways* and steamboats provided the network making the existence of a huge political unit possible. The dialogue between steam and the state was more subtle than this. Steam supported the state, but the state also supported steam. Steamboats and canals and railways were so important to communities and commerce that it seemed justifiable to build or subsidize them as public works. In fact it was necessary to support them with taxpayers' money if a commmunity was going to keep up with other provinces, states, and countries in the scramble to grow. To build railways it was sometimes necessary to build bigger and stronger states. Once railways were built, the paths they took and the commerce they created sometimes undermined the status quo, making it necessary to reorganize the state. When it was created in 1867, the Dominion of Canada had a railway (the Intercolonial) running through its constitution. It was not clear whether the railway was being built to help make the nation, or the nation to build the railway.

The irony was that steam disappointed. Steam's enthusiasts, like the prophets of most new technologies, promised more than they could deliver at the costs they predicted. The beat of the steam piston was for more – more track, more machines, always more and more money. Railroads turned out to be precarious enterprises for their investors; sometimes, as with Canada's great mid-century railway, the Grand Trunk, they were appalling sinkholes. True, they moved the people and the goods as promised (well, those early engines were not quite strong enough for Canadian snowdrifts), but the cost was astronomic, sometimes crippling. The Canadian love affair with railways, destined to last for more than three-quarters of a century, was part national dream, part nightmare.

JOHN MOLSON'S FIRST AND MOST LASTING ENTERPRISE was a brewery, founded in 1785 when the young Britisher decided to risk a modest inheritance slaking Montrealers' thirsts. Molson and his descendants prospered as brewers, creating the longest-lived family firm in Canadian history. More on those aspects of their history later. The Molsons interest us here because of their remarkable side interest in steamboats.

* The terms "railroad" and "railway" were at first used interchangeably. Gradually railroad became American usage, railway British. Canadians officially followed British usage, but actually continued to use both words.

While investigating breweries in London in the 1790s, John Molson probably saw one of James Watt's first steam engines, installed to grind the malt and raise the liquor in Whitbread's Brewery. Molson had no need for steam power in his much smaller Canadian works, but he shipped beer to communities down the river from Montreal and was always interested in new ways of doing anything. Robert Fulton's *Clermont* made its first trip on the Hudson River in 1807; in 1808 a second American steamboat went into service on Lake Champlain. The next year, 1809, the prosperous Montreal brewer, John Molson, in partnership with two Englishmen familiar with steam engines, launched the *Accommodation* to begin steam navigation on the St. Lawrence and in British North America.

The *Accommodation* was a seventy-five-foot wooden paddle-wheeler, driven by a six-horsepower engine made at the St. Maurice forges. Its first passage from Montreal to Quebec took thirty-six hours. The upriver trip was considerably longer. "It is obvious that her machinery, at present, has not sufficient force for this River," the *Montreal Gazette* reported; "but there can be no doubt of the possibility of perfectionating it, so as to answer every purpose for which it is intended; and it would be a public loss should the proprietors be discouraged in their undertaking."

The *Accommodation* was never "perfectionated." It was plagued by engine problems and in the less than two seasons it operated lost several thousand pounds. The proprietors were not discouraged, probably because the St. Lawrence – Lower Canada's main street but not a friendly thoroughfare for sailing ships – offered such splendid opportunities for steam-powered vessels. After consultation with Fulton himself, Molson commissioned a second vessel, its engine made in England by Boulton & Watt, christened the *Swiftsure* in 1812. It did a splendid business carrying troops and military stores during the war which began that year. With the *Swiftsure*'s success, the Molson family were well launched as the "Bourgeois de Steamships" of the Canadas.

Molson's 1810 request for a monopoly on steamship service in Lower Canada was denied. He owned the third steamboat on the St. Lawrence, the *Malsham*, launched in 1814, but the fourth, the *Car of Commerce*, was put into service by a brotherhood of Montreal Scots grocers and tea merchants, the Torrance family. In 1818 the first collision occurred between rival steamboats racing up the river to Montreal. The next season seven boats, four Molsons and three competitors, steamed between Montreal and Quebec. Downriver fare on the *Accommodation* in 1809 was fifty shillings; in 1822 a Montrealer could ride steerage class for less than one shilling. The Molsons merged with several of their competitors that year to form the St. Lawrence Steamboat Company, popularly known as the Molson Line. The Torrances, who stayed out of the merger, sparked another round of competition by purchasing the *Hercules*, the first steamer built to tow ships. There was a fine opportunity for work towing sailing ships up the St. Mary's current to harbour in Montreal. The Molsons responded with bigger and more powerful steamboats. The rivals finally agreed to cooperate and merged their Montreal-Quebec operations.

It was easy to get into the steamboat game. The early wooden vessels were relatively cheap and easy to operate. A group of merchants might take shares in a steamboat company to break someone's monopoly, give themselves cheap rates and better service, or provide service for new towns. In the 1840s, for example, the Pollock-Gilmour timber interests financed the Tate shipbuilding family in a run at the Molson-Torrance combine. The People's Line, out of Quebec, cut prices to get the mail contract on the same route. Steam navigation had by then spread up the rivers and lakes of the Canadas. Established operators like the Molsons expanded their routes and fleets by buying or merging with upriver carriers. Some of the new operators, such as the French-Canadian proprietors of the Société de Navigation du Richelieu, used local trade to finance a run at the mainstream. As Gerald Tulchinsky shows in *The River Barons*, the Laurentian merchants, French and English, moved very quickly in bringing steam to the great river and its tributaries.

What about the ocean? The Molsons tended to concentrate on brewing and distilling and ignored opportunities for steam travel downriver from Quebec City. Were there such opportunities? There was little intercolonial traffic between the major ports of the British North American provinces. The long run across the Atlantic seemed completely impractical for boats whose fuel supply would leave no room for cargo. Mail was the exception. Everyone wanted fast, regular mail service from Great Britain and between all North American towns. Mail was not a bulky cargo and postal revenue was high enough to support generous contracts to carry the mail.

In the 1820s British mail for America crossed by Admiralty sailing packet from Falmouth to Halifax and was forwarded to other ports by whatever ships happened to be sailing. These often belonged to S. Cunard and Company, which was trading everywhere, it seemed, out of Halifax – sending ships to Newfoundland and the West Indies, to Prince Edward Island and to Joseph Cunard's timber kingdom on the Miramichi, to South America on whaling expeditions, and up the St. Lawrence to Quebec carrying tea for the East India Company.

Samuel Cunard was a classic all-purpose merchant and entrepreneur, happy to test new waters, new lines of trade, and new kinds of ships. He became a letter-carrier by contracting to take mail from Halifax to Bermuda, Boston, and Newfoundland on fixed schedules. About the same time, he joined the entrepreneurs who were trying to mine and sell the coal that seemed everywhere in Pictou county and Cape Breton Island, a connection that interested him in the uses of coal. In Britain he rode on steamboats churning from town to town along the coasts, and he rode on pioneer steam railways chugging overland.

The Cunards were among the two hundred merchants of Quebec City and Halifax who took shares in the Quebec and Halifax Steam Navigation Company, formed in 1830 to run a steamer between the cities, principally to carry mail. The Nova Scotia and Lower Canadian legislatures offered generous payments for the mail service. The *Royal William*, launched at Quebec in 1831, was an expensive failure (it did not help that it was quarantined for cholera during much of 1832) and was sold to its mortgage-holders in 1833. The ship's parting voyage from British North America was impressive, though, for the *Royal William* made one of the first Atlantic crossings under steam on its way to resale in England. Samuel Cunard had inspected the ship carefully and become convinced, he wrote, that "steamers, properly built and manned, might start and arrive at their destinations with the punctuality of railway trains on land." In 1832 Cunard-owned steamboats carried weekly mails between Pictou, Nova Scotia, and Charlottetown, Prince Edward Island.

In 1838 the British government, prompted by the pleading of a dynamic colonial politician and postal expert, Joseph Howe of Nova Scotia, decided to try moving the American mail by steam. An Admiralty call for tenders for an England–Halifax–New York steamer service brought three responses, two from England, one from Samuel Cunard of Halifax. None of the supplicants met all the specified conditions. Cunard had many influential friends in high positions in England, including not only the Admiralty's expert on steam navigation but also the prime minister's alleged mistress, Lady Caroline Norton. He got the contract to carry mails from Liverpool to Halifax, Boston, and Quebec, for seven years at £55,000 a year, later raised to £80,000.

While negotiating the contract, Cunard placed orders for the ships he would need. Friends put him in touch with the best Glasgow shipbuilders. Soon he was negotiating with steam-conscious Glasgow merchants who provided most of the capital to buy the ships. Cunard's contribution was the contract. He had a 20 per cent interest, and was one of three managing partners of the British and North American Royal Mail Steam Packet Company, which launched the transatlantic service. It was always known as Cunard's or the Cunard Line. The capital, approximately £215,000, and the mail contract came from the old country, the enterprise from the colony.

Four Cunard paddle-wheelers began providing regular service from Liverpool to Halifax and Boston in 1840. As long as the firm faithfully executed its mail contract, which was renewed without tender until the 1860s, its success was ensured. There was no need to be technologically innovative. It was more important for the Cunard ships to deliver the mail safely and on time. Competing steamship lines, sprouting like Yankee weeds in the mid-1840s, offered bigger, faster, iron-hulled, screw-driven ships. The little wooden Cunarders seemed obsolete by comparison. But Cunard service was safe and reliable. Competitors' ships broke down and worse. When they did maintain schedules their operating costs outran their income. Most cargo and passengers still crossed on sailing ships, which were cheaper than steamers and seemed to be safer. The guaranteed mail business gave the Cunard Line its economic edge. The Inman and Collins lines failed and disappeared from history. The Cunarders splashed on, making steady if not spectacular profits. The company slowly modernized its fleet and by the 1860s was aiming at a larger share of the growing transatlantic emigrant traffic.

Samuel Cunard's income from selling Nova Scotia coal is said to have been greater in the early years than his return from the steamers. He had both minor and major setbacks. Most of his whaling expeditions failed, for example (the crew of the whaler *Samuel Cunard* deserted her in the Pacific; in drunken despair the captain jumped overboard and drowned). Samuel was so over-extended in the early 1840s that he could not face his creditors and had to be smuggled out of England aboard one of his own steamships. After several hair-raising years, Samuel was getting nicely above water in 1847 when brother Joseph's Miramichi empire came crashing down.

As Cunard recouped in the 1850s (the Crimean War was particularly beneficial; the steamers did well-paid service carrying troops and supplies for the military), he spent less and less time in Halifax. The British and North American Royal Mail Steam Packet Company's ships, capital, mail contract, and other two managing partners were based in Great Britain. Lacking colonial shareholders other than the Cunards, it was effectively a British company. Its ships did not spend much time in Halifax, either. From their first voyages the Cunarders had touched briefly at Halifax, dropped some mail and a few passengers, then steamed on to their real terminus in Boston. Then the Cunard Line began serving New York. Mail and passengers for U.S. ports was always more important than traffic destined for British North America. And soon even most of that business moved through the States, for everyone going to the Canadas preferred the short route from Boston or New York rather than the long sea voyage up the gulf and river. In 1845 Cunard stopped offering mail service from Nova Scotia to Quebec. There was not enough business to support a steamship service into the St. Lawrence.

Laurentian merchants wanted direct steamer contact with Great Britain. When it became clear that the mother country would not underwrite separate mail service to Quebec or Montreal, the province of Canada, urged on by interested Montrealers, decide to subsidize a line to keep the St. Lawrence competitive with Boston and New York. After three years of wretched service from the low bidder, an Anglo-Canadian partnership, the contract was reassigned in 1856 to the Montreal Ocean Steamship Company, headed by Hugh Allan of Montreal, a man on his way to becoming a notorious business baron.

The Allan family operated a fleet of sailing packets out of Greenock, Scotland, and began trading into the St. Lawrence in the 1820s. Hugh, one of the founder's five sons, was sent to Montreal in 1826 at the age of sixteen to work his way up in the merchants' world. By 1839 he was a partner in Edmonstone, Allan and Company, which become a prominent firm of shipbuilders, ship agents, and general merchants. The Allans got into steam on the St. Lawrence to tow their sailing ships up to Montreal. Hugh, a pushy, powerful merchant, became one of the city's strongest enthusiasts for the transatlantic service. He launched the Montreal Ocean Steamship Company on capital raised from his family and other investors on both sides of the ocean (the Canadian shareholders included a leading Quebec timber merchant,

George Simpson of the Hudson's Bay Company, and the wealthy brewer, William Dow), and had ordered his first ships in 1852 before learning he would not have first crack at the service. The original Allan liners went into service anyway, reaping a lucky windfall as Crimean War troopships. When they finally got the Canada contract, the Allans could afford screw-driven iron hulls for the service. Unlike Cunard's southerly routes across open seas, the ice and other hazards of the North Atlantic–Gulf–St. Lawrence run demanded tough, powerful steamers.

The risks taken by investors in the Allan Line were no greater than those endured by its sailors and passengers. The firm's carriers ran aground, broke up, and sank with appalling regularity. For seven years the Allans averaged a wreck a season. The first ocean-going steamship to bear the name *Canadian* was wrecked in 1857 in the St. Lawrence below Quebec. The second *Canadian* was gashed by ice in the Strait of Belle Isle in 1861 and went down with a loss of thirty-five lives (other Allan Line disasters took many more lives). The third *Canadian* survived a grounding off the coast of Scotland and was assigned to the safer South American run.

The Allan Line survived storms of criticism, partly by admitting mistakes (Hugh Allan would *not* excuse the wrecks as acts of God: "Providence has not a special grudge against any honest enterprise, nor does it show it by bringing destruction upon innocent people. The fault is in ourselves in some disregard of nature's laws. It is we who must find out what is wrong and put it right"), partly because everyone knew that ocean voyages to Canada were perilous (in the worst year, 1861, 102 vessels were lost, stranded, or seriously damaged in the gulf), almost certainly because steadily increasing mail subsidies from the Canadian government made the operations worthwhile. Hugh Allan courted important politicians assiduously and with an open purse, particularly at election times, becoming a master at exerting political influence. The line's business strength in the 1860s was the growing steerage trade in immigrants. By the 1870s it had mastered the hazards of the Atlantic passage and its safety record markedly improved. Once the business became easy and profitable, of course, serious competition appeared. The wrecks and catastrophes of the Allan Line's pioneering years were part of the cost of establishing a premature, subsidized service through dangerous waters, part of the cost of trying to maintain transportation and technological parity with the more accessible American seaports.

———————◆———————

The sea was free and open to all travellers and traders. It was near land that navigation became complicated. Mariners needed lighthouses on headlands, channel markers in rivers, dredging and other improvements to harbours. It was generally understood that such improvements to navigation were a public good, properly and most efficiently provided by governments, which might recover the cost in customs duties, direct charges (where feasible; lighthouses could not be coin-operated) or other taxes. The hard questions in navigational improvements revolved around situations where natural barriers could only be overcome by building artificial rights-of-way for vessels across land – that is, canals. Who should build these new waterways for merchants and travellers? For that matter, who should build highways over land to facilitate the movement of commerce and people? Who would make internal improvements to the transportation system, providing utilities to the public?

The transportation network could be built by private individuals or companies seizing opportunities for profit. Or it could be built by governments constructing public works or military works. At first neither public nor private enterprise had any particular priority in British North America. It was the tortured history of internal improvements – canals, highways, and then railways – that set the precedents, showed the forks in the way, and raised alarms about the pitfalls en route.

Many roads, bridges, and canals were planned, promoted, started, and sometimes even finished by private companies. Revenue was to come from tolls on users and, of great importance, from the increased value the improvement gave to nearby land, held by the improver. Of course if all landholders stood to benefit from canals or roads, whether they used them or not, it could easily be argued that all should share in their cost and be taxed accordingly. The state could let contracts for these public works. In situations where private individuals stood to benefit from roads or canals, but lacked the money to build them, or had tried and were failing, they became particularly enthusiastic about public works.

The fur traders and early Montreal merchants built a few shallow private canals around some of the St. Lawrence rapids, for example. But it was generally understood that a major canal system would have to be funded as a public work. That one should be built, at almost any cost, was taken for granted by merchants whose trade and properties depended on the St. Lawrence system remaining competitive with the principal American waterway from New York up the Hudson. The thrust to improve the St. Lawrence as a maritime highway of "national" importance predated the steam revolution and was only intensified by the coming of the steamboat.

But the idea of tax-financed public works raised many questions. Would everyone benefit equally from public works, such as Laurentian canals? Or would their construction actually involve taxing the many for the benefit of a few? What about the weight of taxes? Could the high costs of, say, a major canal-building program be borne by fledgling colonial governments without imposing intolerable burdens? Would governments be able to collect the taxes they needed; was their credit good enough to borrow money? Could they build the works efficiently? Then could they bear the burden of operating them at constant losses? Such losses were bound to come, otherwise private investors would have lined up offering to build and run the things.

Many in government and many of the governed were happy to stay away from public works. Let those who stood to profit put up the money and take the risks. If private money was available to finance public works why not turn to it? Certainly private contractors should be used wherever possible to bear risks and assume responsibility. In their Canadian infancy, governments balanced the need to foster material progress against the need to protect a slim and fragile public purse. It was a delicate margin, because the country had to attract immigrants, and they would not come to an unimproved backwoods wilderness. But neither would they come to a bankrupt country or one that levied oppressive taxes. Find the fine line.

The military was a godsend in the way it looked after some early transportation needs. The main highways of Upper Canada, Yonge and Dundas streets, and the overland track between New Brunswick and Quebec, were built and paid for as military roads. The British army took a spectacular interest in canals as well, helping with some of the early St. Lawrence works and after the War of 1812 deciding that communication with Upper Canada could only be guaranteed by completely by-passing the St. Lawrence above Montreal. Between 1826 and 1834 Lieutenant-Colonel John By of the Royal Engineers supervised construction of the 130-mile Rideau Canal system from the confluence of the Rideau and the Ottawa (where Bytown grew up) to Kingston on Lake Ontario. The huge cost over-runs in the canal building were of little concern to colonial taxpayers or governments. This was a British government work. Internal improvements paid for externally were the most desirable of all.

The Rideau Canal – a long, expensive, and time-consuming by-pass – was a complete commercial impracticality, no answer at all to the St. Lawrence rapids problem. It took decades of controversy in the Canadas, mostly between Montreal's merchants and French-Canadian nationalists, to finally reach a consensus in the 1840s on the need for a modern system of canals on the upper St. Lawrence. Even then, the improvements could not have been made without financial help from the imperial government in the form of loan guarantees to the Province of Canada. The Laurentian canals were built almost entirely as public works. When they were finished in the late 1840s it was possible to travel all the way up the St. Lawrence to Lake Ontario in shallow-drafted steamers.

In fact it was possible to steam beyond Lake Ontario. The Welland Canal, by-passing Niagara Falls, had been opened years earlier, in 1829. Its financing and construction were the outstanding initiative of private enterprise in Canadian canal history. And it was a failed project .

Some day there was bound to be a canal across the Niagara peninsula to connect lakes Erie and Ontario. In the early 1820s the military began surveying possible routes, all well away from the U.S. border, all completely impractical. Meanwhile the Americans completed one of history's great transportation coups: in 1825 the State of New York opened the Erie Canal, a four-hundred-mile artificial waterway constructed as a public work from Albany on the Hudson to Buffalo on Lake Erie. Suddenly the Americans possessed the shortest and cheapest way to move goods and people from the Atlantic to the heart of North America and out again. The Erie

Canal threatened the entire Laurentian trading system, and it threatened to split Upper Canada into two sections economically. Without a Canadian canal, the Lake Erie part of the province would become tributary to Buffalo and New York, while the Lake Ontario half looked to the St. Lawrence and Montreal.

William Hamilton Merritt was a young storekeeper, farmer, and mill-owner on Twelve Mile Creek (later St. Catharines), who liked to dabble in grand ideas. He became interested in hydraulics because he needed more water in the creek to drive his mills. It seemed possible to dig a ditch from the Welland River, which drained into the Niagara River above the Falls, through the height of land to the creek. If a ditch, why not a canal? In 1818 Merritt and a group of his neighbours first petitioned the Upper Canadian legislature for support for a canal scheme, arguing that "a communication" could be achieved between lakes Erie and Ontario "at a trifling expense."

"I understood no branch of business in which I was engaged," Merritt later wrote of his early training. He became insolvent in 1819, but managed to recover and in 1823 renewed the canal proposal. He thought the total cost of excavation would be $10,000. Merritt became a typical early nineteenth-century promoter, holding a series of public meetings to talk up (or "agitate") the canal idea and collect subcriptions from those willing to invest in it. Investors *subscribed* for stock, to be issued at so much a share, if and when a company was formed; they did not have to pay until actually called upon, and then it was usually for instalments. Merritt was able to finance a survey (now the estimate was about $50,000), got a charter from the legislature in 1824 for a joint-stock, limited liability company, and set out to raise the money. "I think it will be one of the best speculations offered in the Western Country," he wrote privately, "and at the same time will not embark in it more than the amount of my Mills, and probably $200 and near one Year of my time .... I consider that I will be richly paid in the enhanced value of my property – in case I meet with no other consideration." The Welland Canal Company consisted, in H. G. J. Aitken's words, of "Hamilton Merritt, plus a charter, plus a handful of family friends, plus a collection of rather ill-defined but uniformly optimistic expectations, and very little else."

The wonder was that Merritt was able to raise a cent as he peddled canal company stock to the merchants of York, Montreal, and Quebec. Some of the prominent members of Upper Canada's Family Compact thought the scheme was a good idea and subscribed for a few shares; some became directors of the company. Public meetings in Montreal and Quebec brought in promises of several thousand pounds. Merritt realized his best hope – almost his only hope – rested in getting government support. He needed government money and the added respectability of state endorsement. "Government taking shares would induce many to do so that are now backward." Upper Canada cautiously offered the company a land grant instead – waste land that would become valuable if the canal were ever built.

Realizing that neither private nor public money could be raised in the Canadas, the Welland Canal promoters turned to London and New York. This was the first major attempt by British North American entrepreneurs to raise funds abroad by public solicitation and subscription as opposed to private, family-based financial networking used by earlier fur traders and merchants and later by Cunard and the Allans. The promoters had little luck in London, where there was no interest in a Canadian wilderness canal. But a group of Americans, headed by John B. Yates, agreed to take almost half of the authorized stock. They were residents of the Lake Ontario town of Oswego, New York, which was about to tap into the Erie system. A Niagara canal, they hoped, would bring goods past Buffalo into Lake Ontario and then into the Erie through Oswego. Yates, who became the Welland Canal company's largest shareholder, was a partner in the largest firm of lottery managers in the United States. If the Canadian canal scheme was a bit of a gamble, he was hardly a man to turn away.

There was enough money to begin construction in 1825. The major contractor, an American outfit that had worked on the Erie, agreed to take some of its payment in stock. All the plans and estimates had to be redone, because to be of any use at all the canal had to be wider, deeper, longer, and much more costly than Merritt and his board had ever imagined. It proved much harder to overcome the steep Niagara escarpment than to build the Erie across gently sloping country. The complete inexperience of Merritt's group added to the problems. Accounting practices during construction were particularly bad, Aitken concludes, judging it to have been "literally impossible for anyone, even with the best intentions in the world, to get an accurate picture of the financial operation of the Company as a whole, or to decide with any confidence where money was being economically expended and where it was not."

Merritt searched desperately for more money. He finally persuaded the Upper Canadian government to buy $250,000 worth of shares (authorized capital was up to $1 million) and the British government to loan $250,000 against a mortgage on the canal. The lieutenant-governor of Upper Canada apparently loaned a further $50,000 from his personal fortune. This was enough to keep the work going, and in freezing weather in November 1829 two small schooners scraped through the ditch called the Welland Canal. The company's cash on hand at year's end was $760; arrears to contractors and others stood at $77,335.

The Welland Canal was hopelessly uneconomic. The company could not earn maintenance costs in competition with the Erie system, let alone finance improvements or reward its shareholders. As early as 1830 a committee of the legislature recommended taking over the canal on the ground that it was, like any highway, a "national concern." Most of the directors. including Merritt, came to the same conclusion. The canal needed literal bail-outs, and the shareholders were ready to give up control. Only the American risk-taker, Yates, fought to the end to carry the debt, raise more private capital, and buy back the government's shares. "I am tired out and wish I had never seen the canal, or anything connected. It has embittered my life," Yates wrote a few months before his death in 1836.

The canal débâcle became farcical that year with William Lyon Mackenzie's public charges that the whole project was "a hoax from first to last" in the interests of the Family Compact. Mackenzie was wrong, or at least was confusing incompetence with corruption. The situation was so serious, though, that abandoning the Welland Canal was a real option. In 1841 the Province of Canada took over the Welland Canal Company, requiring the private shareholders to exchange their stock for interest-bearing debentures. None of the sources suggests that any of the shareholders, including Merritt, were enriched by the transaction. They did get their money back, a return that seldom came to the players in Yates's lotteries. There were no windfall profits in the land grant, which eventually reverted to the province, but Merritt's own lands must have increased substantially in value, as mills and other establishments sprang up along the canal to take advantage of the waterpower. In the 1840s and afterwards the province and later the Dominion spent hundreds of thousands and then millions improving the canal and operating it as a provincial or "national" highway.

There were many other proposals for major canals in British North America: schemes in Nova Scotia, for example, to bisect the Isthmus of Chignecto and for a Shubenacadie waterway from Halifax to the Minas Basin, and a recurring agitation in central Canada for a Georgian Bay canal to by-pass the lower Great Lakes. None of these projects made enough sense to attract private money or public participation; their promoters, of course, complained about investors' and politicians' lack of vision. A few more canals, including the long-discussed and largely unnecessary Trent system in central Ontario, were later built as public works. The Welland Canal Company remained a striking case of private investors attempting a work of great importance, failing, and being replaced by the state. Like many other Canadian public works, including the St. Lawrence canals, it might have succeeded as a private work if it had been dug much later, and rather more skilfully. But a development-minded electorate is seldom prepared to wait – nor are private landowners who hope for capital gains.

———————◆———————

By the late 1840s canals seemed like old-fashioned backwaters. Everyone was talking about building railroads instead. The railroad seemed to be the revolutionary development of the age, the invention to top all inventions. As Sam Slick told Nova Scotians in T.C. Haliburton's *The Clockmaker*, "Since the creation of the Universe, I guess it's the greatest invention, arter man." Here is the Canadian engineer T.C. Keefer, a kind of Marshall McLuhan of railways, introducing the *Philosophy of Railroads* in 1849:

> Old winter is once more upon us, and our inland seas are "dreary and inhospitable wastes" to the merchant and to the traveller – our rivers are

sealed fountains – and an embargo which no human power can remove is laid on all our ports. Around our deserted wharves and warehouses are huddled the naked spars – the blasted forest of trade – from which the sails have fallen like the leaves of autumn . . . . The animation of business is suspended, the life blood of commerce is curdled and stagnant in the St. Lawrence – the great aorta of the North. On land, the heavy stage labours through mingled frost and mud in the West – or struggles through drifted snow, and slides with uncertain track over the icy hills of Eastern Canada. Far away to the South is heard the daily scream of the steam-whistle – but from Canada there is no escape: blockaded and imprisoned by Ice and Apathy, we have at least ample time for reflection – and if there be comfort in Philosophy may we not profitably consider the PHILOSOPHY OF RAILROADS.

It was a powerful image, and largely true. With the railway it would at last be possible to conquer winter, to keep on travelling when the waterways were frozen, to keep trade and commerce and movement going all year long. Climate would be obliterated. So would distance and time and all the obstacles geography put in the way of travel over land. Keefer painted word pictures of the "Sleepy Hollows" of British North America coming alive and getting busy and growing and developing and prospering because of the quickening power of the railway. And much, much more:

> . . . land rises in value – the neglected swamp is cleared and the timber is converted into all sorts of wooden "notions" – tons of vegetables, grains, or grasses, are grown where none grew before – the patient click of the loom, the rushing of the shuttle, the busy hum of the spindle, the thundering of the trip-hammer, and the roaring of steam, are mingled in one continuous sound of active industry. While the physical features of our little hamlet are undergoing such a wonderful transformation, the moral influence of the iron civilizer upon the old inhabitants is bringing a rapid "change over the spirit of their dreams." The young men and the maidens, the old men and the matrons, daily collect around the cars . . . . [C]uriosity and emulation are excited and the results are discernible in a general prediliction for improved "modes". A spirit is engendered which is not confined to dress or equipage, but is rapidly extended to agriculture, roads, and instructive societies . . . .

> The civilizing tendency of the locomotive . . . is so fortunately patent to all, that it is admitted as readily as the action of steam.

The metaphors were usually organic. Railways were arteries or they were sinews or they were trunks (with branches) or they were spines or backbones. Hard to have a living community or body politic without them. The fanciful rhetoric was less important, though, than the real benefits railways seemed likely to deliver. Cheap, quick transportation would stimulate every kind of business. Growing business would mean growing property values, increments to everyone in communities touched by the iron roads. "The essence of a railway," stated one early prospectus, "is to add 25% to the value of every farm within fifty miles of it, to double the value of those nearer than that, to quadruple the value of those farms through which it passes."

Think about the land. By European standards the supply was practically unlimited. Uncleared land was a free good in North America and virtually worthless. The crown gave millions of acres away – to seigneurs, loyalists, army officers, to almost anyone who might do something useful with it, such as induce settlement. Generations of French-Canadian seigneurs, Montreal merchants, Upper Canadian speculators, and others learned that real estate in the New World offered no road to wealth. The labour necessary to improve a parcel of land – soul-destroying years of chopping and clearing and stumping and stoning and road-building – was beyond the resources of absentee landholders. Usually there was nothing to do but sell the land at a pittance to settlers who might give it value.

Of course profits could be made even in pittances. Get the land cheaply (free if possible), add some value by organizing surveys or building roads or founding settlements, and then sell it. In the 1820s a few British entrepreneurs began exploring the possibility of land deals and settlement schemes in the colonies. The crown had more land than it needed, needed money, and had no desire to undertake the risks and travails of serious development. In the United States several big land companies had succeeded in developing large tracts. The first Canadian scheme was promoted in Britain by John Galt, a Scots ink-slinger and paid lobbyist whose interest in arranging compensation for some veterans of the War of 1812 developed into a plan to buy crown reserves in Upper Canada and bring out settlers. Galt became the first secretary and superintendent of the Canada Company, chartered in England in 1826 and well supported by British investors who were beginning to look overseas for new opportunities. It bought a million acres of good land in western Upper Canada – the Huron tract – and Galt came out to develop them.

The scheme was premature and Galt was incompetent. The Canada Company suffered heavy losses, Galt was recalled in disgrace. The organization managed to survive and through the 1830s sold enough land to cover its costs (which included developing the towns of Guelph and Goderich). Its nimble founder helped launch a second, Lower Canadian venture, the British American Land Company, in 1831. The aim was to buy, improve, and sell land in the Eastern Townships, south of Montreal. One of John Galt's sons, Alexander Tilloch, was sent out as Canadian commissioner of the firm and faced the difficult challenge of finding ways to develop the domain. His thoughts soon turned to railways.

Railways increased land values like magic. If you were promoting land companies or emigration they had an added advantage: there were jobs to be had right off the boat building railways and canals, the colonies' first big "works." The work was back-breaking and the pay insulting, but newcomers could at least keep body and soul together and even earn a few dollars. Then they could move on to the land. So railways were needed as employers to help attract and keep immigrants, quite apart from their other good effects. The immigrant-railway relationship was symbiotic, too, in that the prospect of immigrant labour helped make railway-building seem viable. Railways made everything come together, it seemed. The colonies could develop as a haven for the surplus population of the British Isles. Bring them out and put them to work building railways, then sell them the land the railways were making accessible, then watch the land's bounty provide traffic and profits for railways.

Even if none of it happened neatly on schedule, British North Americans knew they had to build railways to answer the "daily scream of the steam-whistle" to the south. In the 1830s and 1840s the Yankees galloped off building railways running every which-way. Many ran in a northerly direction, as Boston and New York merchants dreamed of siphoning the trade of the British provinces. The Province of Canada completed a canal system in the 1840s just as railway technology seemed to make all canals obsolete. Waterway rivalries instantly changed to railway rivalries; the Americans' population, wealth, and geography once again gave them a major head start. If Canada was to compete, especially now that north-south trade was growing in an era of freer trade, it had to build railways, develop land, encourage immigration.

Everyone in both countries lusted after railways. Merchants and landowners and politicians agitated for railways long before they had heard the sound of a steam whistle. The *Montreal Gazette* argued the case for railway lines to the U.S. border in 1824, years before the technology had proven itself anywhere. In 1828 promoters in St. Andrew's, New Brunswick, held a public meeting to whip up support and subscriptions for a railroad to Quebec. Settlers called for surveys of lines through their communities and across their properties. In 1832 the Lower Canadian legislature proposed an act for "Making a Railroad from Lake Champlain to the River St. Lawrence." In the same year citizens of the isolated Upper Canadian village of London held a public meeting and resolved to build a railway to Lake Ontario. British North Americans in the 1830s talked about the weather, the crops, and railways.

Promoters thought railways were so promising that they could be financed and built privately. It certainly wouldn't hurt to test the water by calling a meeting, taking up a stock subscription (with only a tiny down payment), maybe getting up a survey or getting a charter from the legislature. If it turned out that townsfolk were too timid or poor or miserly to risk their money, why then the politicians could be approached. *They* knew the value of railways, and would surely lend a material hand to get them going.

Some politicians were more than supportive, believing that railroads were like canals or highways and should be built as public works. Both Joseph Howe of Nova Scotia and Francis Hincks of Canada, the dominant politicians of their generation, talked about railroads as public works, which would return more to the community in jobs, business, and higher property values than they cost. As Sam Slick explained the imaginary economics of railways:

> "I would like to show you Yankee ciphering. What is the entire real estate of Halifax worth, at a valeation?"
> "I really cannot say."
> "Ah, I see you don't cipher, and Latin and Greek won't do; them 'ere people had no railroad. Well, find out, and then only add ten per cent to it for increased value, and if it don't give the cost of a railroad, then my name is not Sam Slick."

It was political and literary bunkum. When the real ciphering was done about railways as investments the figures did not add up easily for anyone. They were damnably expensive. Unlike steamboats, steam engines required special rights of way – iron canals – which cost fortunes and took years to build. Per mile, canals were expensive too. But they were far shorter. Suppose a railroad would cost £5,000 or $25,000 a mile – a rough average for mid-century lines – and would run for one hundred miles. Who had $2.5 million to put into the construction, let alone another spare half million for rolling stock, and still more money for operating costs? Railways burned money the way steam engines burned wood. Who could supply the capital?

A new specialist, the "capitalist" began appearing in the 1840s, most clearly in Great Britain. His function was to provide capital to build railways and pay for other expensive business projects. Capitalists were either wealthy themselves or able to mobilize other people's money. The colonies did not yet have significant capitalists. Most merchants could not free up large sums for railway investments. Steamboat companies were too small – a single mile of railway cost as much as a whole steamboat. Stagecoach operators were even less likely railroaders; they had next to no capital and knew next to nothing about these strange machines that travelled on completely different roads.* The colonial banks were still small and only in the business of supplying well-secured, short-term credit. They might be able to help out investors a little, but dared not make major long-term loans to railroads. The vital instrument for mobilizing capital was at hand in the form of the limited liability, joint-stock company. But could enough shareholders be found to make the roads a reality? Probably not, unless governments helped out.

---

* One exception in stagecoaching was Francis J. Barnard in British Columbia in the 1860s. During the gold rushes Barnard created a monopoly of mainland transportation, carrying mail, passengers, gold, and other freight, which included what may have been the longest stagecoach line in the world. Barnard hoped to use special steam engines on the Cariboo Road, and dreamed of extending his road transit system across the prairies to Lake Superior. Even so, like all the other stagecoach men, Barnard stayed out of railroading.

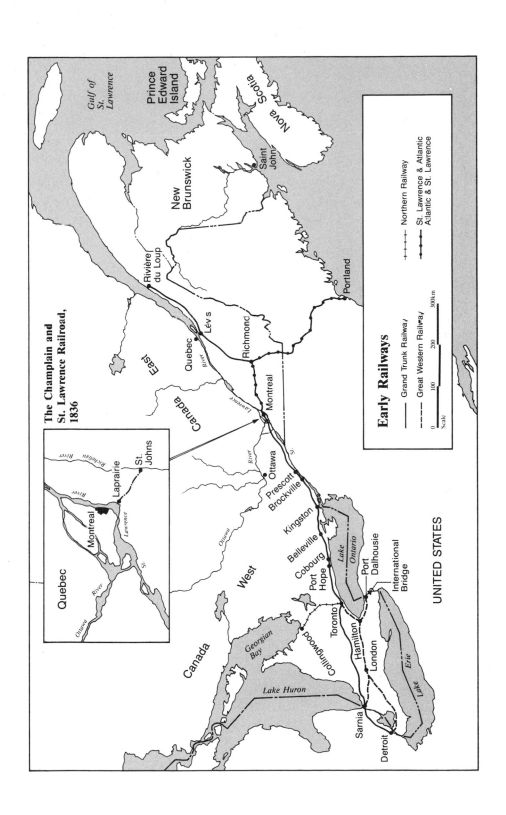

The Champlain and
St. Lawrence Railroad, 1836

Early Railways

Grand Trunk Railway
Great Western Railway
Northern Railway
St. Lawrence & Atlantic
Atlantic & St. Lawrence

Scale
0   100   200   300km

Gulf of
St.
Lawrence

Prince
Edward
Island

Nova Scotia

New
Brunswick

Saint John

Rivière
du Loup

Lévis

Quebec

Richmond

Portland

Canada East

St. Lawrence River

Montreal

Ottawa River

Ottawa

Prescott
Brockville

Kingston

Belleville

Cobourg

Port
Hope

Lake Ontario

Port
Dalhousie

International
Bridge

Canada West

Toronto

Hamilton

London

Lake Erie

Collingwood

Georgian
Bay

Lake Huron

Sarnia

Detroit

Canada

UNITED STATES

Quebec

Richelieu River

St. Johns

Laprairie

Montreal

St. Lawrence River

Ottawa River

St. Lawrence River

Completely private financing was sometimes possible. In the mid-1830s Montreal's merchants found the capital to build a short portage line connecting the St. Lawrence with the Richelieu–Lake Champlain system. A Richelieu valley merchant, Jason A. Pierce, promoted this Champlain and St. Lawrence Railroad, which was Canada's first. Montrealers supplied the money. Old fur traders like George Moffatt and Peter McGill (president of the Bank of Montreal), prominent merchants such as Horatio Gates and young Peter Redpath, and the Molson family invested the £50,000 necessary to build the road. Most took twenty share lots at £50 a share. John Molson Senior was the outstanding exception, investing £9,000. American engineers organized construction of the fourteen-mile line from St. John's on the Richelieu River to Laprairie on the St. Lawrence. This short-cut by rail would save approximately ninety miles of river travel.

On July 21, 1836, three hundred distinguished Montrealers, led by the governor general, boarded the steam ferry *Princess Victoria*, crossed the river to Laprairie, and inaugurated the railway age in British North America. They took two trains, one drawn by the engine *Dorchester*, the other pulled by horses, over the iron-topped pine rails to St. John's. There was feasting and speechifying, but minor trouble later when the *Princess Victoria* ran aground on the way back to Montreal. Canada's first all-steam travellers were late getting home.

The British-made *Dorchester*, one of the great Stephenson's "Samson" engines, was also a disappointment, frequently breaking down on its rough North American roadbed. The horses pulled most of the trains the first year, while the *Dorchester* was being rebuilt. Most later locomotives were made in the United States. Financially, the Champlain and St. Lawrence Railroad Company was steadily successful, carrying many loads of cordwood as well as passengers. The road was conservatively managed and had good steamboat connections at both ends. Dividends to the shareholders averaged 16 per cent per annum on their capital through the 1840s. Such success made the little line highly unusual in the history of Canadian railways.

Several other roads were chartered in the 1830s' wave of railway euphoria. The visionary Londoners of Upper Canada put together a plan for the London and Gore Railroad. Its Lake Ontario terminus would be the ambitious hamlet of Hamilton, where a prominent Tory lawyer and MLA, Allan MacNab, happened to have large property interests. MacNab was a great supporter of internal improvements, believing that the state should go "up to head and ears in debt" to support worthy projects. He took up the London and Gore idea as a railway that would develop Upper Canada's great southwestern peninsula and at the same time be a vital link between American systems at the Niagara and Detroit frontiers. A great lobbyist with his fellow parliamentarians, MacNab won their support for this Great Western Rail Road, as it was now called; rival schemes by a group of Torontonians and by a syndicate led by William Hamilton Merritt, the Welland Canal builder, were rejected. Legislators deemed the Great Western plan so important to Upper Canada that early in 1837 they agreed to loan the company £200,000. "The speculation which has been going on at Hamilton is extraordinary," an observer wrote after the bill passed. "Peter Hamilton has sold off his farm lots to the value of more than £5,000... MacNab has been selling ever since. The Americans have fought to buy in. They all feel confident that the railroad should go on."

Then came the panic of 1837, followed in the Canadas by rebellion, hard times, and political reorganization. All railroad schemes slid into limbo, leaving only the little Champlain and St. Lawrence steaming on busily. Nobody had the capital to back railways. The government of the new Province of Canada gave highest priority to completing the canal system. It was only when the British and American railway networks, which soon totalled several thousand miles, were seen to be flourishing in the mid-1840s, that the British North Americans decided to try again. As late as 1849 there were still only sixty-six miles of railway operating in all of British North America. But that was a misleading statistic, because great colonial railway schemes were finally afoot.

MacNab had revived the Great Western project just as a Lower Canadian promoter emerged with a similar project. The commissioner of the British American Land Company, Alexander Tilloch Galt, had realized that the company's lands had no future unless the Eastern Townships had better communications with the outside world. From his headquarters in the little town of Sherbrooke, Galt became an ardent railway enthusiast. The ideal line would run from Montreal through Sherbrooke to New England, probably Boston. In 1844–45 a smooth-talking Maine lawyer, John A. Poor, persuaded the Lower Canadians to go for a shorter route to seaboard, one with a terminus in Poor's home town of Portland, Maine. Early in 1845 the legislature chartered the St. Lawrence and Atlantic Railroad to build from Montreal through the Townships to the border; it would meet Poor's Atlantic and St. Lawrence Railroad, built in from Portland. The charter-holders were a committee of prominent Montrealers, including Peter McGill, George Moffatt, a Molson, and John Torrance (two of whose daughters would marry A.T. Galt, serially), plus Galt and several other Sherbrookians.

Galt and MacNab went to England in 1845 to try to raise capital for their projects. The timing seemed right because British railway success had created a flourishing market in railway stocks, the first private securities to attract the savings of the Victorian middle class. Railway mania peaked that year, as shares in tracks to the moon would have sold at a premium. The action was stimulated by the way in which readily transferable company shares created short- as well as long-term speculative opportunities. Buy stock as an investment and wait for the dividends or buy it to sell tomorrow on a rising market – and then buy more. The Canadians with stock to sell had good connections (Galt through the land company, MacNab through the Glaswegian merchant trading to Hamilton, Peter Buchanan, who became the Great Western's British agent), were enthusiastically received, and went home with full subscription lists. But then the British railway bubble burst, subscribers simply failed to answer calls on their shares, and the colonials were back where they started.

The Lower Canadians were determined to go ahead and tried local fund-raising by a method copied from Poor in Portland. The directors formed what Tulchinsky calls "commercial press gangs" to go from door to door in Montreal canvassing for subscriptions. They carefully recorded the names of Montrealers who lacked the civic spirit to contribute to the great project. These methods raised enough money to begin construction. Some of the farmer-subscribers in the Townships paid for their shares in kind, delivering food to construction camps.

There simply was not enough private capital. Money would have to come from public bodies if the railways were to be built. MacNab had lobbied for government loans back in the 1830s and the Sherbrooke group's original petition for a charter had included an appeal to "a paternal government" for "that aid and encouragement which is required to warrant a poor community in embarking its all in an undertaking of such extent." By the end of the 1840s, with nowhere else to turn, MacNab, Galt, and other railway promoters were lobbying intensively for state aid to railways in recognition of their value to the community.

Francis Hincks, the Inspector General (the Minister of Finance) and leading figure in the Reform government of Canada, fully endorsed state support of railroads. He realized it would be cheaper, faster, and more efficient to subsidize private railway companies rather than take on the burden and risk of building them as public works. In 1849 Hincks brought in a Guarantee Act under which the province undertook to guarantee the interest on half the bonded debt of railways over seventy-five miles long. Other legislation permitted municipalities to invest in railway company shares. Getting this fledgling level of government involved in railway finance was a way of spreading the burden while appropriately localizing government suport for public works (only the municipalities that benefited from railways would pay for them). The municipal role was further institutionalized in 1852 with the creation of the provincially backed Municipal Loan Fund to finance works supported by local governments.

The Great Western and the St. Lawrence and Atlantic took advantage of all available aid, selling stock and bonds to the cities of Hamilton and Montreal respectively, and to many of the towns and villages along their rights of way. MacNab found important additional funds for his road from American investors led by Erastus Corning, who saw the Great Western as a vital link in the American network of track stretching from New York to Chicago. The Lower Canadians found an angel in Montreal's Sulpician Seminary, which invested heavily in St. Lawrence and Atlantic bonds (the Quebec church always supported railway de-velopment; Montreal's Bishop Bourget was careful to locate his new cathedral near the railway station). More bonds were sold in England, where investor inter-est had recovered (especially after Canada's Guarantee Act was changed to cover principal as well as interest). The contractors for both lines assumed some of the risk by taking partial payment in stock, which they expected to sell when their job was done and the railways became engines of profit.

Ceremonies, banquets, and picnic excursions marked each stage in the railways' progress. In 1853 the first St. Lawrence and Atlantic trains puffed southwest from Montreal to the border. Early in 1854 passengers and freight chugged between the Niagara and the Detroit boundaries of Upper Canada, always stopping in the growing burgh of Hamilton (whose most imposing building was Sir Allan MacNab's residence, Dundurn Castle). The contracts to build both lines went to experienced American firms. Galt had to dismiss his contractor; the line was completed by a talented Polish engineer, Casimir Gzowski, who had drifted to Canada after romantic escapades at home, and compiled a good record building roads for the government before going into construction on his own.

One year after Canada's first two major railways were finished, another important line, the Toronto, Simcoe and Lake Huron Union Railroad, soon known as the Northern, began running trains between the "Queen City" and the booming village of Collingwood on Lake Huron. The Northern also suffered a difficult financial birth: thwarted in a plan to raise money through a lottery, the promoters had to rely on the Guarantee Act and major investments by the City of Toronto and Simcoe County. The Canada Company was also deeply interested in the line, which would add value to its lands. By the time the Northern opened, smaller local railways were being promoted and chartered by the score in British North America. Every little Bytown and Beaverton, Port Hope and Stanstead, dreamed of becoming a booming railroad terminus – or dreaded the certain stagnation if railways passed them by. A few of these lines were even being built, a few miles at a time.

The big lines and the small were dwarfed by the plan for a great Main Line across British North America. The Grand Trunk Railway of Canada was promoted in 1853 as the most magnificent railway project the world had yet seen. The prospectus hailed it as

the most comprehensive system of railway in the world . . . . Commencing at the debouchere of the three largest lakes in the world the Grand Trunk Railway of Canada pours the accumulating traffic through the entire length of Canada . . . . The whole future traffic between the western regions and the east . . . must . . . pass over the Grand Trunk Railway . . . . It comes with the guarantee of the Government of Canada . . . it is supported with the most intelligent, far-sighted men in the colony . . . a combination of railway interests probably never seen before . . . cannot but produce the most satisfactory results.

The Grand Trunk was the greatest enterprise of the age in Canada. Its origins lay in Maritimers' enthusiasm for railway connections with the interior of North America. Every port town from St. Andrew's to Halifax wanted to be the terminus of a major inland railway. T.C. Haliburton and Joseph Howe of Nova Scotia had been boosting railways for years, had helped promote Samuel Cunard's "ocean railway," and believed Halifax had to be the port where steam met steam at dockside to rush mail and passengers inland. By 1851, Howe, now the premier, thought he had agreement from New Brunswick and Canada and the imperial government to build an intercolonial main line (from Halifax to Quebec or Montreal and points west) as a public work. London would guarantee the necessary loans.

Francis Hincks, now Canada's prime minister, went to England to firm up the arrangement in 1852. He found a government having second thoughts about risking millions on colonial railways, and private railway builders with an attractive alternative. The experienced British contracting partnership of Peto, Brassey, Jackson, and Betts persuaded Hincks that they could raise enough share capital to give the Province of Canada the trunk road it needed. It would not be an impractical, unprofitable intercolonial, but rather a line from Montreal to Toronto or Hamilton that would link the St. Lawrence and Atlantic system with the Great Western. Canada would have to support the project under the Guarantee Act, but the risk seemed slight. It would be a 350-mile road, costing about £3 million. No complicated intercolonial agreements or imperial government guarantees were needed. Hincks bought the idea and brought it home to Canada.

The Grand Trunk scheme grew and grew in a climate of boundless optimism about railways and the healthy state of the British capital market. All hitches in the planning were overcome by proposing more track and more capital. The agile Alexander Tilloch Galt was a principal obstacle, for he and two partners, Luther Hamilton Holton and David Macpherson, had obtained a charter for a Montreal-Kingston line. They loudly promised to build better and cheaper railways than any "foreign" contractors. The Grand Trunk had to buy that charter from the Canadians; their terms included also selling control of the St. Lawrence and Atlantic. The St. Lawrence River would have to be bridged at Montreal, so an enormous bridge was planned. To get the system to the sea at Portland the Atlantic and St. Lawrence was leased from its American owners. Branch lines to Quebec City and the New Brunswick border were added because politicians wanted the truncated Intercolonial scheme to survive. When trouble developed over connections with the Great Western, the promoters decided to ignore the Hamiltonians and build a new line from Toronto westward through Guelph to the American border at Sarnia. Casimir Gzowski and Company, a construction partnership which included Galt, Holton, and Macpherson, got the contract to build that section.

No matter that the Grand Trunk would now be three times as long and costly as Peto, Brassey, Jackson, and Betts had originally proposed. The very grandeur of the project would probably help sell it. Most railways were built as patchwork jobs by promoters who invariably discovered that construction costs outran projections. The Grand Trunk would be built all at once by veteran contractors at a fixed price. Shareholders would get a "most satisfactory" annual return of 11.5 per cent. The first limited offering of Grand Trunk stock on the London market was subscribed twenty times over as Britishers clamoured for shares in this "glittering colossus" of railway projects.

Trains began running between Montreal and Toronto in the autumn of 1856. The whole Grand Trunk was finished a year ahead of schedule when the Toronto-Sarnia line was opened in November 1859. The Victoria Bridge across the St. Lawrence at Montreal was one of the engineering wonders of the world. Canadians could take the train from Quebec to Sarnia, and, on American lines, through to Chicago. The Province of Canada had an iron spine. Railwaymen and politicians were already talking about the next big railway jobs: the Intercolonial to Halifax (both Nova Scotia and New Brunswick were building important provincial lines as public works), and, incredible as it seemed, westward extension of the trunk road across the prairies and mountains to the Pacific. Joseph Howe, one of the Main Line's founding fathers, had caught the vision in 1851 when he told an audience that many of them would live "to hear the steam engine in the passes of the Rocky Mountains and to make the journey from Halifax to the Pacific in five to six days."

Construction of the Grand Trunk and many local railroads, in years when Canadian trade with Britain and the United States was booming, contributed to a surge of growth in the mid-1850s. Land values and wages soared wherever railways were being built or planned. Unskilled labourers and many kinds of artisans got work building the Grand Trunk. In 1854 it poured £15,000 a day of British money into Canada in wages alone. Farmers found markets feeding construction gangs; lumberers cut ties and cordwood to feed the engines; manufacturers ranging from iron founders to distillers felt a quickening of trade. And the Grand Trunk's passengers experienced an astounding quickening of the speed of travel: "Literally we are embodying the dreams of youth," a journalist wrote, "when we read of the travels of Sinbad and of the Flying Horse."

———————◄►———————

The Grand Trunk crashed to the ground as a commercial project within months of the start of work. It was a disastrous failure. Peto, Brassey, Jackson, and Betts grossly underestimated their costs of construction and overestimated the value of the existing track they purchased. The wave of British optimism and easy money on which the project had been floated receded within months of the promotion, making it next to impossible to sell more stock. Stuck with large amounts of stock they had taken in part payment for building the Montreal-Toronto line, Peto *et al.* cut every possible corner to save money. Galt and Gzowski and the Americans had similarly skimped on the St. Lawrence and Atlantic track east of Montreal – the Grand Trunk had to spend a small fortune rebuilding it. Only the Gzowski mileage west of

Toronto, over relatively easy terrain and paid for in cash, met expectations. Operating costs, including constantly upgrading the line and endless battles with the harsh Canadian climate, far outran projections.

Traffic was far below expectations. The original forecasts were wild guesses based on non-comparable British and American situations. The idea that the Grand Trunk would "engross" the traffic of the prairies and the American mid-west was particularly absurd, for the system faced crushing competition from existing American lines. It had no advantages over the American systems, for it suffered from higher operating costs, an underdeveloped, little used terminus in Portland (there was hardly any eastbound freight traffic), and poor, sometimes non-existent transshipment facilities at ports along the Great Lakes. The Grand Trunk's disadvantages in continental railway competition were literally widened by the Canadian government's insistence on a special broad gauge for its railway system. The distinctive 5' 6" Canadian width originated with John A. Poor's idea that trains using the line to Portland should not be divertable to Boston-bound tracks. A modern equivalent would be a highway system capable of handling only Canadian cars and trucks. By the 1860s the Grand Trunk and Great Western were spending millions to install third rails to accommodate standard 4' 8 ½" American rolling stock.

More fundamentally, Canada's great trunk line did not fulfill railway gospellers' prophecy that railways would make waterways obsolete. For much of its length the Grand Trunk competed directly with one of the world's greatest waterways, fully canalized and open to steam navigation. Water carriers responded to competition from railways by becoming more efficient, more competitive. Freight cost much less to move by water than by rail. Time savings were important for passengers on trains, but seldom mattered in the movement of bulk goods such as grain or wood products, the main traffic on the Great Lakes–St. Lawrence system. Those commodities which did move by rail often went by American lines.

Steam's mastery of climate was not as important or complete as the promoters had proclaimed. The northern agricultural and forest economy was too geared to seasonal rhythms to generate much winter traffic, a time when operating costs soared. Some branch lines simply shut down for the season. Many winter train travellers experienced times when the irresistible force of the steam engine was overcome by such immovable objects as Canadian snow drifts. For years the imagery of steam power far outran the horsepower of steam railways. The early puffing billies were absurdly small; the pre-1880s railway train has been characterized by railway historian Albro Martin as "little more than a teakettle on wheels pulling a few oblong wooden boxes on spindly iron rails."

The Grand Trunk Railway Company had a desperate struggle to raise the money to complete its line. When the system was finished, at a cost of £13.5 million ($67.5 million in the new dollar currency), its operating income could not cover the fixed charges on its debt, let alone dividends. In 1861 a committee of the bond and shareholders in British North America's biggest and most important enterprise – the colonies' first mega-project – described it as "an undertaking which is overwhelmed with debt, wholly destitute of credit and in imminent danger of lapsing into utter insolvency and confusion."

The British investors expected relief from the government of the Province of Canada. The road had been a joint venture with government from the beginning, they felt, a work considered so important to the Canadian public that part of its debt had been publicly guaranteed. Because of that guarantee, and as a further sign of political support for the line, most of the prominent members of the Hincks government had taken seats on the Grand Trunk's board of directors. The line was endorsed and financially supported by the government. Its construction was obviously in Canada's interest. When private Britishers could not carry the burden of the great work, they assumed that Canada would not let it fall. So they asked for more aid and more, and more, instancing the benefits their money was bringing to Canada, drawing special attention to the failure of Canadian private investors to take shares in the Grand Trunk. Surely the government was morally obliged to counter Canadians' shameful disinterest in the great work.

The Grand Trunk's several petitions for aid between 1856 and 1862 fanned long-simmering questions of business and political ethics. Critics charged that far from being an instrument for conveying wonderful benefits to the Canadian public, the Grand Trunk was really a gigantic "job" or swindle designed to line the pockets of the greedy and corrupt men who promoted it.

Forget about making money by building a good railway and then running it well. Wasn't the real railway money to be made in insider dealing – stock speculation on manipulated markets, land speculation by promoters and directors trading on their private accounts, speculation in the rights conferred by railroad charters? Contractors with inflated costs and chaotic accounts could cream off huge sums of shareholders' money and then move on, leaving meandering, rolling tracks through swamps. Politicians could take their cut, too, ranging from free passes on railways to cash on the barrel-head or under the table in return for voting the right way on railway bills. Politicians often dealt openly in railway stock, land, and contracts. This was because they were the same people as the railwaymen. The leading railway-builders were all politicians. Sir Allan Napier MacNab, chairman of the Canadian legislature's standing committee on railways and telegraphs, was commonly seen weighing the pros and cons of an issue and then coming down in favour of the petition of Sir Allan Napier MacNab, president of the Great Western Railway. The Grand Trunk directors did the same, putting on their legislators' hats to vote public aid to the stricken company they ran. From an early stage in the Grand Trunk's history, the opposition in the legislature, led by the fiery Grit editor of the Toronto *Globe*, George Brown, condemned its directors as perpetrators of every form of malfeasance and most kinds of incompetence in both their political and business capacities.

The reputations of most of British North America's leading railroaders were tarred at the time and in the pages of the history books with allegations of self-interested jobbery. Some charges were highly specific: in 1854 the leading Canadian minister, Francis Hincks himself, was found to have participated with the mayor of Toronto in an insiders' deal leading to a £10,000 profit in City of Toronto debentures being issued to support the Northern railway. "The Ten Thousand Pound Job" helped drive Hincks from Canadian office (to a malarial but otherwise not unpleasant exile as governor of Barbados). Galt's manipulation of charters and contracts to lever himself and the Gzowski syndicate into a highly profitable slice of the Grand Trunk business has always seemed suspect. Revelations of speculation by that group in military lands at Sarnia (their solicitor was a prominent Tory MLA and accomplished land speculator himself, John A. Macdonald) were particularly embarrassing. During fights over Toronto waterfront lands it was said that every lawyer in the city was owned by Gzowski and Company.

Everyone connected with the Great Western was accused at one time or another of corruption, usually by fellow directors. MacNab created an oft-repeated epitaph for the age when he was quoted as saying that "all my politics are Railroads, and I will support whoever supports Railroads." The remark, usually paraphrased as "Railroads are my politics," has been used to characterize years when unscrupulous, buccaneering Canadian politicians and promoters scrambled to board the gravy trains criss-crossing their provinces.

MacNab's statement was actually an epitaph to the politics of his youth, decades of fierce controversy about the constitution, loyalism, rebellion, responsible government, race, religion, and other abstractions. When politicians started spending their time on railway charters (in the early 1850s MacNab's railway committee sometimes had more to do than the legislature as a whole, which may have been another source of his famous statement), it was probably a healthy sign of mid-Victorian communities getting down to business and progress. MacNab's Great Western railway itself soon outgrew his personal promotional style and became in the 1850s one of the first professionally managed companies in Canada. A young Englishman, Charles J. Brydges, sent out by British investors to clean things up in 1852, became one of the country's first career managers, loyally serving his employers.

Corruption is probably too strong a word to describe railway ethics. Some cynical operators did give and take bribes, steal, rig accounts, and otherwise break laws. Many skirted the fringes of illegal and unethical practices, using euphemisms like "commission" or "finder's fee" to camouflage bribes and kickbacks. The euphemisms were often well-meant in the sense that many of today's grey ethical practices were acceptable to the worldly men of the 1850s. Insiders and office-holders were expected to profit from their knowledge and jobs. They always had and surely always would. There seemed nothing wrong with a man having multiple interests, as long as the interests were in confluence rather than conflict. What was good for railroads and railroaders' interests seemed usually good for the country. If profits were bound to be made as land or stock, or City of Toronto debentures rose in value, what was wrong with taking a share of these profits?

Politician-entrepreneurs like MacNab never disguised their pecuniary interests in transactions, so were not hiding anything (the Hincks case was not so open). Other politicians and businessmen naturally courted one another, exchanging small gifts such as free railway passes, and large ones: the easiest way to court influence in the age of the joint-stock company was to give some shares in your company to politicians who might be appreciative. Political-business friendships seemed almost always mutually useful. But even in the 1850s there were fairly well-understood limits on influence-peddling. Gift-taking was acceptable, gift-seeking was not. Outright bribery, say gift-giving that involved cash, was wrong. Businessmen were contemptuous of the few politicians and the rather more journalists whose principles seemed to be for sale. The entrepreneurs bought when they felt they had to – as still happens in most of the Third World – and bemoaned the need to do it. An English lobbyist for the Grand Trunk expressed his regret after a visit to Canada:

> My work was almost exclusively 'lobbying' to get a Grand Trunk bill through the House of Representatives [sic] ... it was clear that some twenty-five members, contractors, etc., were simply waiting to be squared either by promise of contracts or money. As I had no authority to bribe, they simply abstained from voting and the bill was thrown out. £25,000 would have bought the lot but I would rather that someone else had the job than myself .... I confess that I was annoyed at my ill-success and had half a mind to split upon some dozen members who had been indiscreet in their approaches to me .... Upon my word, I do not think that there is much to be said for Canadians over Turks when contracts, places, free tickets on railways or even cash was in question.

For the men in the railway business, ethical lines were always shifting and hard to locate. The stakes in the railway game were much higher than ever before – huge fortunes rose or fell on the passing of a charter or the terms of a contract – and so were the temptations. These complex new enterprises were the first to separate ownership from control; they spun out supporting activities like stock promotion, fund-raising, and land development, and thus multiplied opportunities for quick or incidental dealing on the side and for cutting "friends" in on the action. Hard-driving, ambitious men played a hard game, living with their consciences after they had savoured success or failure. Samuel Zimmerman, the American contractor who became fabulously wealthy building the Great Western and many smaller local lines, lived in cynical splendour in a Niagara Falls mansion and boasted often of his political friendships and influence. Luther Hamilton Holton, one of the partners in the Gzowski contracting firm, on the other hand, was constantly uneasy about the methods the partners might have to use to get a contract. He worried often about being driven by a "less noble impulse which shall be nameless." Holton was pleased when they did not have to pay a kickback to get the big Grand Trunk contract, but would have agreed to one if necessary.

It was not necessary to be corrupt to make a fortune in railways. The Gzowski group did its Grand Trunk work well and carefully, made 12 per cent profit on contracts, and cleared well over $500,000 on the west-of-Toronto operations. These were big winnings for the partners, and were made bigger by profits from land deals. Both Holton and Galt promptly retired from railway work to devote full time to public life. About the same time, the flamboyant Samuel Zimmerman was one of the sixty travellers killed when a Great Western train steamed into the Desjardins Canal near Hamilton.

Railways' impact on commercial ethics was not nearly as important as the way in which they recreated ties between entrepreneurs and government, ties that the development of more prosaic industries had been loosening. Railways could not be private enterprises like wholesaling firms, lumber companies, or even steamship lines. Like chartered banks, railway companies needed rights granted by the state. More than that, in undeveloped British North America they needed the cash and credit ratings only governments, with their taxing powers, enjoyed. Railwaymen petitioned for chartered rights and financial aid as a quid pro quo for undertaking transportation improvements considered to be in the public interest. (From the beginning they also accepted rate ceilings written into their charters; falling costs meant that fares seldom came near the ceilings.)

As the Grand Trunk experience, following the Welland Canal fiasco, indicated, public-private partnership in transportation development did not create sound, well-planned enterprises combining the strengths of government stability and private entrepreneurship. Instead the partnership fed on the weaknesses inherent in a relationship in which each side saw the other as the principal risk-absorber. The illusion of shared or reduced responsibility led to irresponsibility. Freed from the discipline of having to raise the full cost of a venture from skeptical investors, promoters and politicians who saw no limits to the possibilities of the new technology were unleashed to chase their dreams. The reckoning, when directors had to face outraged securities-holders and politicians had to explain themselves on the hustings, came too late to curb the zeal of the high-tech railway enthusiast.

By 1860 the Grand Trunk was a sinking company which had to have state aid to keep going. Aid was being given grudgingly in an atmosphere of mutual recrimination between Canadian politicians and British investors. The British felt the Canadians were receiving all the benefits of a great communications system without having to pay any significant costs. When the Canadians totalled the whole cost of their internal improvements – the canal debts, the grants and guarantees and loans and sweetheart contracts with railways, principally the Grand Trunk – they were almost overwhelmed by the burden of debt they had incurred. In Nova Scotia and New Brunswick government construction of railways was also piling up mountains of debt, and the long-sought Intercolonial line was no further toward realization. In the severe recession of the late 1850s most of the British North American provinces were crippled by their debts and forced to pay stiff premiums for new loans. Involvement with railways had turned governments into poor credit risks.

Railways weakened the British North American provinces geographically as well as financially. They tended to ignore political borders. Canada's "spine," the Grand Trunk, did not really parallel the St. Lawrence waterway, but headed west from Montreal to an American seaport. By the end of the 1850s the old Champlain and St. Lawrence, Canada's first railway, was part of a major system running south from Montreal to Boston and New York. Upper Canada's Great Western railway was little more than a portage line for American traffic avoiding the long haul south of Lake Erie. Other development roads began to snake north from the border to tap the Canadian forest and carry lumber south. A third rail, installed to adjust the Canadian gauge to American requirements, was nicknamed the "annexation rail."

For all the talk there had been about an Intercolonial line linking the Maritimes with Canada, nothing had been done to build one. British North America was such an unnatural conglomeration geographically that the idea of building a railroad from one end of it to another, or just from Halifax to Quebec, defeated even the dreams of promoters and politicians. Not even governments could agree to build it as a public work. Thus that conquerer of nature, the steam engine, reinforced rather than eliminated natural barriers in North America.

Steam navigation had had the same effect. British North America's port cities – Quebec and Montreal, Halifax, Saint John, and St. John's – lived on transatlantic and local trade. There was little commerce, steam or sail, between the St. Lawrence and the Maritimes. Cunard cancelled its Halifax-Quebec steamer service in the mid-1840s because it was easier and faster to deliver Canada's mail to Boston or New York for forwarding by train. It was easier and faster for Canadian-bound passengers and other freight to take the same route, by-passing Halifax and the Maritime provinces altogether. Responding to the logic of their business, the Cunard steamship line stopped serving Halifax in 1867.

Worrisome geopolitical consequences of the steam revolution were easily outweighed by the economic and social benefits conveyed by faster, cheaper transportation. About $100 million was invested in the construction of sixteen hundred miles of railway in British North America during the 1850s. The provinces lagged far behind the United States and England but there was more track in British North America in 1860 than in either Ireland or Scotland. The railway age brought huge amounts of capital into the colonies and it created large ongoing firms and a multitude of opportunities to manage and develop the new technology. Foreign expertise poured into the colonies in the form of railway contractors, engineers, artisans, and managers. Promoted from within the provinces, the railways were financed, built, and then operated by newcomers.

Ironically, the most important opportunity the railway created in British North America was for politicians to reorganize the political entities railways were helping to weaken. Steam power was about expansion – thermodynamically, economically, and geographically. Railway promoters were all expansionists, dreaming of big money and big distances. The solution to a promoter's problem was always more: more money, more track, more territory to open up and more land to develop. More government, too. By the 1860s in British North America the development of the railway had made it possible, some said vital, to look for more territory in the west. It was time to take over the old kingdom of the fur traders: that land beyond the Great Lakes was an imperial expansionists' ideal, virgin country ripe for penetration by steam and settlers.

To build more great railways, even an intercolonial let alone a transcontinental, it was necessary to have more political strength. Governments had to expand; they had to enlarge their visions, their power, and their ability to borrow money. Railway promoters and other expansionists were among the strongest backers of the Confederation movement that led to the creation of the Dominion of Canada in 1867. The men who had cut their teeth on the pioneer systems – the St. Lawrence and Atlantic, the Great Western, the Grand Trunk – were ready to go on to the most ambitious of all nineteenth-century Canadian undertakings, a railway to the Pacific. In 1867 the first successful Canadian contractor, Casimir Gzowski, wrote to Alexander Tilloch Galt, the most skilful railway promoter of the day, that it was time to consider their getting a share in Canada's Pacific railroad, "the only big thing left on this confederated continent."

TOP: **Grand Trunk locomotive, c. 1860** *(Ralph Greenhill Collection, Miller Services)*
INSET: **Collision, Vermont and Canada Railroad, 1864** *(Canadian National Railways)*
ABOVE: **Steam *versus* snow, Grand Trunk** *(Canadian Illustrated News)*

UPPER LEFT: **Sir George Simpson** *(NSL Archive)* UPPER RIGHT: **Donald Smith** *(Canada and Its Provinces)* ABOVE: **F.J. Barnard's stage, Yale, B.C., 1866**
(Public Archives of Canada, #PA61874)

8

Western Empire, 1821 – 1885

Business and Confederation ... the Hudson's Bay Company in the West ... George Simpson, emperor of the fur trade ... monopoly and competition ... the HBC as "imperial factor" ... free trade in Red River ... the founding of British Columbia ... Confederation and railway promotion ... the Pacific scandal ... "Hill's folly" ... the CPR as Canadian epic ... Van Horne and Stephen ... Canada in the grip of Americans and Chinese ... the first western economy ... the HBC superseded by the CPR

The Dominion of Canada was born on July 1, 1867. Its population was about 3.5 million. Some of the politicians in the four provinces – Nova Scotia, New Brunswick, Quebec, and Ontario – talked about Canada's future as a northern transcontinental nation. This hardly seemed credible in 1867. Three years later, in 1870, Canada became more believable when Britain transferred to it the Hudson's Bay Company's territories, an immense kingdom stretching from Ungava and the watershed of the Bay across the northern great plains to the Rockies. With the acquisition of its western empire, the Dominion quintupled in size. It added new provinces – Manitoba in 1870 and British Columbia in 1871 – and became a territorial nation from sea to sea. Dominion land and immigration policies were put in place to develop the new northwest. In the early 1880s a railway, the Canadian Pacific, was pushed across thousands of miles of muskeg and prairie and mountain. With the completion of its transcontinental railway in 1885, the Dominion became a vertebrate nation from sea to sea.

Business groups played a limited, sometimes contradictory, role in the movement for a British North American confederation. There is little evidence that merchants in the principal cities were enthusiastic about political change that held out no immediate prospect of improved trade. Business was generally good during the 1860s, for the Civil War south of the border stimulated demand from the United States while reducing American competition domestically. Conservative traders tended to be wary of political changes that might disrupt established patterns by introducing new competitors, new taxes, or other uncertainties. Halifax and Saint John businessmen were particularly worried that union with Canada offered little more than higher customs duties and Canadian competitors. Montreal and Toronto merchants were too busy serving their established markets to spin out fantasies of future business in the wilderness beyond the Great Lakes; they, too, thought commerce was best fostered by political and tariff stability. In the West itself the men of the Hudson's Bay Company were good citizens of the British Empire, but had no special regard for the dominion of the Canadians. Tiny clusters of independent traders in Red River and far-off Victoria did far more business with Americans in St. Paul, Minnesota, and San Francisco, California, than they ever would with Montreal, Toronto, or Halifax.

Generally, the man in the merchant's counting-house or the bank cashier's cage had little reason to be enthusiastic about politicians' and promoters' schemes for grandiose, expensive projects. The provinces were heavily in debt trying to pay the costs of rapid growth and railway construction. Now the dreamers were proposing more growth and the largest and most expensive railway of all, a line to the Pacific. Confederation and national expansion were not much of a business proposition.

Railway enthusiasts and a few other expansionists argued otherwise. The railwaymen supported Confederation as a way of bailing out the Grand Trunk, getting the Intercolonial built, and as a precondition for a Pacific line. Expansionists had glorious visions of opening up new territories, of bringing value to millions and millions of acres of fertile land on the prairies. The opening of the North American northwest would surely be a project of huge significance for Canada and the British Empire. It would involve building an iron highway across North America to reach the markets of the Orient (the Northwest Passage at last!), peopling the continent's heartland with millions of British immigrants, multiplying the commerce and strength of Canada and the empire beyond measure. It was no accident that Alexander Tilloch Galt, a land agent, immigration promoter, and railway builder, was the politician who most vigorously promoted Confederation in the late 1850s and as finance minister in the Province of Canada helped turn it into practical reality in the mid-1860s. The son of John Galt of the Canada Company was carrying on his father's work on a grand scale, making it possible to develop all of Britain's North American lands.

Or, rather, the Hudson's Bay Company's lands. The British-based fur-trading company was the chief European presence in these territories for many years before the Galts and other Canadians appeared on the scene. After the 1821 takeover of the North West Company it appeared to have no rivals. If ever an organization had a head start on the commerce of an area it was surely the Hudson's Bay Company in the lands that became western Canada. If the Company of Adventurers of the 1860s and 1870s had been as shrewd and supple as its founders had been two centuries earlier, it would have diversified and adjusted its organization to exploit the new order being brought about by Canadian expansion. It would have dominated, if not monopolized, trade and development in the new West. It would have been a leader in transportation – one of the Company's historic strengths.

Central Canadian interests ranging from the Grand Trunk group through the Macpherson-Gzowski contractors to the steamship magnate, Sir Hugh Allan, all wanted to build the great railroad planned for the West. But why shouldn't a western organization, one with intimate knowledge of the country, historic ties to British financial circles, and a long record of commercial success do the job? The fur traders had first crossed the continent in their canoes, and had been the first to talk and write about transcontinental trading systems and lines of communication. Surely it would be fitting, even natural, if the modern fur traders were the men who tied the country together with ribbons of steel. They had made the first Northwest passage by land. Now they might literally build one.

These speculations would seem far-fetched were it not for the fact that the Canadian Pacific Railway was created by westerners and fur traders. But not by the Hudson's Bay Company. The fur-trading concern was not able to maintain the monopoly it gained in 1821 or use its advantages to diversify into new lines. Its adjustment to the new West in the 1860s and 1870s was fitful and cautious. The Hudson's Bay Company would not participate in railway enterprise in the Canadian West. New men, some of whom began as pipsqueak fur traders challenging the mighty Company, became the key to the Canadian Pacific – in alliance with one of the HBC's own former factors. The former fur traders organized the CPR syndicate and built the road after central Canadian capitalists had bungled the job and given up. They succeeded without the help of the Hudson's Bay Company, and by their success they put it permanently in the CPR's shadow.

Even in its beginnings, the western economy of Canada was too big and too dynamic to be dominated by established interests. The rise of new men and new companies was one of the earliest features of western business.

IN 1821 THE WEST WAS LEGALLY the Hudson's Bay Company's kingdom. By its charter the company owned Rupert's Land – that is, all the country drained by the rivers flowing into the Bay. After the merger, when there were no more British North American competitors in the fur trade, the imperial Parliament gave the HBC an exclusive licence to trade with the native peoples in the rest of the Northwest – all the British land west and north of Rupert's Land, stretching to the Arctic and the Pacific coast. From 1821 until the licence lapsed in the late 1850s the Company had a legal monopoly of the region's principal economic activity (and it was often assumed, incorrectly, that the monopoly covered all trade of any kind in the West). In theory the Hudson's Bay Company's enterprise was larger and more secure than at any time in the previous one hundred and fifty years. There were no Frenchmen or Montreal pedlars to contest its sway. No one tried to trade into Hudson Bay. In fact there was no government in the Northwest except that provided by the Company itself. It effectively ruled its trading empire.

Alexis Bailly, a mixed-blood who worked for the American Fur Company, crossed the border in the summer of 1821 driving a small herd of milk cows and oxen before him. He was hoping to sell the animals in the little settlement at the junction of the Red and Assiniboine rivers in Hudson's Bay Company territory. The speculation worked: the community of half-breeds, retired fur traders, and remnants of the Selkirk colonists badly needed cattle and paid Bailly a good price. Yankee cattle traders were in Red River the next season and the next, having driven their beasts from as far south as Missouri. A few years later conditions of supply and demand reversed themselves, and Red River men headed south to sell cattle to fur traders and missionaries in the Minnesota territory. The direction of trade was not important; the fact that commerce was developing along the valley of the Red River of the north was. The Hudson's Bay Company had a practical monopoly on access to its territories by the Hudson Bay route. But it had no practical way to close the southern borders of its lands, no way to prevent the development of competing trading routes.

Cattle traders operated legally so long as they did not deal with natives. Threats from competing fur traders existed everywhere on the HBC's frontiers. In the southeast, where Rupert's Land bordered on Upper and Lower Canada, petty fur traders were constantly encroaching on the Company's business. Many were settlers or lumbermen doing a little trading or trapping on the side. They were the advance parties of a frontier of "civilization" marching up rivers like the Saguenay, St. Maurice, and Ottawa, the onset of which was fatal to the fur trade. Along the north shore of Lake Superior, fishermen set up camps and started to trade in furs and prospectors took time from hunting for precious metals to do a little trading. West of Superior the Red River valley sliced across an Anglo-American border which was no more than a line on diplomats' maps. Neither natives nor Métis paid much attention to any borders across the great plains, and the many American fur-trading outfits south of the line were more than willing to do business with them.

Everyone competed for trade on the Pacific slope. The Russians were in Alaska and expanding south, supplementing their trade with extravagant territorial claims. Independent Yankee trading ships cruised the coast, aiming to skim the finest sea-otter pelts and get away to China or the Sandwich (Hawaiian) Islands. American outfits came up from California or overland into the Snake and Oregon country, centring on the Columbia basin (where the Hudson's Bay Company did not have exclusive rights because the whole Pacific slope south of 44° 40' was under joint Anglo-American occupation until a boundary could be settled). The Company's opponents were everywhere and nothing seemed to stop them. "It is astonishing to see the ruined depart annually," a Hudson's Bay officer wrote of the competitive situation, "but still like the Hydra heads another succeeds."

The opposition was only on the frontiers. In the heartland of its territories the Hudson's Bay Company now enjoyed a monopoly limited only by the natives' sharply diminished bargaining power. After 1821 the Company lowered prices and slashed the number and size of its posts. In four years its complement of servants shrank from almost two thousand to less than one thousand. Wage rates were cut about 50 per cent. Many of the retired traders were encouraged to settle in Red River. Liquor sales to natives were abolished. By refusing trade or applying quotas in some over-trapped interior regions, the Company tried to regenerate the fur-bearing population, particularly the beaver supply. The success of the conservation policies is difficult to judge. In any case, the Company was less reliant on the beaver than in the past, as it adjusted to a shrinking hat market (beaver hats could not compete with silk toppers) and growing demand for furs for coats.

The success of the Hudson's Bay Company's trade in the years after the merger was highly gratifying. Year after year the Company made about £60,000 profit on a trading volume of about £300,000. Its handful of principal shareholders paid themselves dividends of between 10 and 25 per cent per year on their £400,000 capital. Chief factors and traders, entitled to a share in profits as part of the merger arrangement, received £300 to £700 annually, handsome compensation for wilderness living in a country where £100 to £200 was a good year's income for anyone.

The monopoly was maintained and manipulated by a brilliant businessman and bastard, George Simpson. Simpson was an illegitimate son of a Presbyterian minister's son. Born about 1787, he was raised by his grandfather in the manse in Scotland, then sent to London to work in an uncle's sugar-brokerage house. The business was taken over by merchants connected with the Hudson's Bay Company and in 1820 George, noticed for his ability, was plucked from the ranks and assigned to the Company's Athabaska trade in North America.

A little cock of a man, Simpson proved he could stand up to North Westers during the last months of the all-out rivalry. But his real strength was as an economizing manager. He was a master of detail, had a passion for efficiency and economy, was a stickler for "system and regularity," and was utterly ruthless and utterly devoted to the interests of the Company. Simpson was a classic amoralist, uninterested in natives except as fur gatherers and bed partners, a believer in the view that everyone, native and white alike, had a price. He was not only a hard worker, but an obsessive, fanatical traveller, racing back and forth across North America by canoe, pack train, or snowshoe, to tie the HBC's sprawling empire together by his presence. Simpson mastered every operation in every region and measured every one of his traders. He quickly rose to the top of the Company's North American hierarchy and from the mid-1820s until his retirement in 1859 was resident governor, the Hudson's Bay Company's "little emperor" in North America. One of his heroes was Napoleon, and it was said of Simpson that he combined the despotism of a military ruler with the mean parsimony of the avaricious trader. In fact Simpson was usually held in check by the London Committee (which was far more solicitous of the natives' welfare and of the need for good publicity than its resident governor), and his parsimony helped produce handsome returns in every year of his stewardship. In most ways he was a model of the driving, and driven, chief executive officer who considers results the total vindication of his methods.

"Since I have been connected with the Service," Simpson wrote toward the end of his career, "the fundamental principle of our business has been to collect *all the Furs* obtainable within the range of our operations. If we are to retain the control of the Trade, we must prevent other parties getting into it, which can only be done by preventing Furs, in any large quantity, falling into their hands." Simpson engaged the opposition everywhere on the frontiers, paying whatever price in trade goods he needed to keep furs from competitors. Interior trade subsidized the frontier price wars. There were no conservation attempts where competitors might move in, "as an exhausted country I conceive to be the best protection we can have from opposition." Nor was liquor spared in wars with Canadian petty traders or Yankee "grog-shops" on the other side of the line. If the big fur companies abandoned liquor in the trade, John Jacob Astor explained, the Hudson's Bay Company would have the head of the cow, the American Fur Company would hold the tail, and the independents would sit in the middle and get all the milk.

Simpson was always happy to negotiate competitive truces. Astor's American Fur Company was generally willing to oblige, and sometimes the combined resources of the firms were brought to bear on independents in the border area. Occasionally the British firm would buy out independents, but that tactic only encouraged more competitors hoping to be bought out. Better to drive the petty traders to disaster. This was not easily done, particularly in regions where competitors were only part-time traders getting their principal income from other sources. On its border with the Province of Canada, the HBC tried to deny the opposition its advantages by going into lumbering and fishing itself. A less aggressive tactic, used most often in Red River, was to retreat from retail competition and act as wholesaler-supplier-employer to nominally independent traders. Great flexibility could be achieved this way, particularly in surreptitiously entering United States territory; but, as oil companies discovered a century later, such support tended to whet independents' appetites for expansion.

The old trading methods of the North Westers were abandoned. "There are 1,000 ways of annoying and harassing our opponents without having recourse to violent measures," Simpson wrote. But he and the Committee usually did not want to go to court either. Without armed force, of which the Company usually had none, no restrictions on trade could be enforced within its territories. Resort to law within or without the domain would likely lead only to embarrassing publicity and defeat, even disaster if the free traders in Britain's Parliament decided to end the Company's anachronistic privileges. The monopoly rights conferred on the Hudson's Bay Company were so unpopular within and without its territories that even the Company dared not stand on them, except in desperation.

Simpson's methods had their greatest success in the far West, a region in which the HBC had hardly operated before taking over the North West Company's posts. Now it brought Simpson's businesslike methods, the driving energies of former North Westers, and considerable diplomatic clout to bear in the region. The obese, obscene, and brilliant trader-adventurer Peter Skene Ogden destroyed American competition in the Rockies south and east of the Columbia with his six "Snake country" expeditions between 1825 and 1830. Ogden's men did most of their own trapping, wandering wherever they pleased in American and Mexican territory, taking every pelt they could to keep them out of Yankee hands, and making handsome profits from every expedition.

On the Pacific coast the Company was deeply involved in negotiations leading to an Anglo-Russian treaty limiting Russian expansion. South of the Russians, Simpson combined permanent posts with cruising trading ships (including a steamer, *The Beaver*, brought out in 1836). By under-pricing the under-capitalized Yankee traders the Company drove them out of the business. Simpson pressured the Russian traders with competition from the south and from the interior, while holding out olive branches in the form of supply arrangements and offers to sell them the land-based furs they needed. An 1840 agreement with the Russian American Company removed the Russians as effective competitors. The Hudson's Bay Company then reduced prices all along the coast and expanded northwest into Russian Alaska. Setbacks only came when some native tribes it supplied on the coast occasionally managed to out-bid its own interior traders for furs. It was a not unhappy situation when the Company was its own chief competitor.

The Hudson's Bay Company was most clearly an "imperial factor" (in J.S. Galbraith's multiple pun) on the Pacific coast. It maintained and extended a British presence in the face of American and Russian expansionism long before there was the faintest hope of settlement, contact with other parts of British North America, or a significant military presence. Without the energetic commercial activities of the Hudson's Bay Company, the whole area might well have fallen into the hands of the Americans.

Simpson's competitive methods had least success in Red River, the one significant settlement within the Company's territories. The community of a few thousand white and mixed-bloods, the distinctive offspring of generations of interracial contact in the fur commerce, was a spawning ground of adept fur traders. Some of them found an outlet for their energies in the employ of the HBC, but it was well known that half-breeds could not expect to rise to high positions in the British company's service. Many of Red River's young Métis were active in the annual buffalo hunt, a great slaughtering, tanning, and packing operation; some Métis supplied provisions to the hunters and sold their products. The Red River settlement needed wider markets for its products and more imported goods than the HBC could hope to provide. Simpson wisely accepted the growth of general trade between Red River and American posts in the Minnesota territory. Nor did he interfere with the growth of freighting and storekeeping within the colony by the men he called "private adventurers." The Company only wanted to maintain its monopoly on trading furs with the natives.

Through the 1820s and 1830s Simpson's deft competitive tactics kept most of the pelts coming to the Company's stores. Through its wholesaling-licensing approach, the Company bought the fur loyalties of some of the most aggressive of the private adventurers, notably the busy freighters Andrew MacDermot and James Sinclair. But it could not hold their loyalties as the Minnesota trade evolved from occasional season expeditions up the Red River valley into a regular business. The turning point came in 1843 when American fur traders created a new post at Pembina on the U.S. side of the border seventy miles south of Red River. It was run by Norman Kittson, a native of Lower Canada with boyhood links to old North Westers, who had served his apprenticeship with the American Fur Company. Kittson wooed MacDermot and Sinclair and other independent traders. Hudson's Bay Company attempts to crack down on private trade only hurt its image and increased Kittson's business. Competitors the Company sponsored on the American side made no inroads. By 1845–46 "Kittson fever" was raging everywhere in Red River. Illicit trade was openly conducted. The illicit traders openly called for an end to the Company's privileges, labelling it a greedy, oppressive despotism. Kittson himself crossed the frontier to trade in Rupert's Land.

Simpson succeeded in 1846 in having a small detachment of British troops sent to Red River. He got them ostensibly for imperial reasons – to protect against the threat of American expansionism – but really wanted them to cow the smuggling settlers. The mere presence of a detachment of the Sixth Royal Regiment had that effect, but the money spent to maintain the men enormously stimulated Kittson's and the settlers' general business. Regular trains of squeaking, screaming Red River carts made the long northerly trek down the valley from St. Paul through Pembina to Fort Garry, bringing in everything from tea and teakettles to reapers and binder-twine, champagne to toast the troops, and the mail. When the troops left Red River in 1848 Kittson was stronger than ever before. "I shall spare no trouble in giving them the 'Devil'," he wrote his partner after the HBC refused to buy him out.

Red River's chief factor foolishly went to law to try to save the deteriorating situation. In 1849 Pierre-Guillaume Sayer and three other half-breeds were charged with illegal trading. The crowd at their trial included a mob of armed free traders, led by James Sinclair, who also conducted Sayer's defence. The jury (which included Norman Kittson's father-in-law) found Sayer guilty, but recommended that there be no punishment. "Vive la liberté. La commerce est libre!" shouted the crowd of Métis when the result was announced. The HBC accepted reality. Further attempts to enforce a trading monopoly in the settlement would have sparked rebellion.

Norman Kittson was almost driven out of business by renewed Company pressure and a host of whisky-selling competitors at Pembina. "Wish to God I was out [of] the infernal trade or rather that I had never embarked into it," he wrote early in 1851. Kittson held on, retrenched and reorganized, turned the corner and was soon making more money (a clear $10,000 in 1852) than he had thought possible. Scoffing at the Hudson's Bay Company, he opened a post within sight of its Fort Garry – you could get champagne at Mr. Kittson's store – and outfitted and grub-staked independent traders ranging north and west toward the centre of the Hudson's Bay Company's kingdom.

The private adventurers broke the Company's system wide open. In 1853 there were said to be between 150 and 175 individuals in Red River trading on their own accounts. In 1855 the private traders exported some four hundred cartloads of furs from Red River to Minnesota. The next year seventy to eighty Red River traders took three hundred carts with them on a successful expedition to the Saskatchewan country. The Company expected them to go into the Mackenzie country next. St. Paul's Red River fur trade doubled every year, reaching $160,000 by 1857. Simpson advised London that the legal trading privilege was "almost a nullity." Perhaps it was time to "make a merit of necessity," he suggested, and surrender the charter to Her Majesty's Government in return for some kind of compensation.

The Company's hegemony was threatened by more than enterprising private traders. The mortal enemy of the fur trade and the HBC's traditional business was settlement. The growth of settlements meant more competitors, far fewer furs to trade, either the dispersal of natives or their abandonment of the trade, and disrespect for Company authority. Red River was the centre of contamination, but the Company's trade on its border with Canada dwindled steadily as lumberers and farmers moved up the northern rivers. Even in the far West, the HBC had no sooner achieved an effective trading monopoly beyond the Rockies than American settlers began driving into its Oregon heartland. Their presence was a political as well as an economic threat, for the eventual division of the jointly held region would likely be in the settlers' favour.

The Hudson's Bay Company responded to the prospect of a declining fur trade in several ways, not all of them consistent or successful. Often, especially in the east, it simply gave up, closed its posts, and retreated in a northwesterly direction.

Even while withdrawing, the factors found that posts could sometimes do a profitable trade with newcomers or settlers, bartering or selling goods in return for furs or farm products or cash, or even on credit. Diversification was another strategy. If farming or livestock-raising was the manifest destiny of an area, why shouldn't the Hudson's Bay Company organize and develop these new activities? The Company's servants had many years' experience farming around the posts and ought to be able to expand their activities. Lumbering, fishing, mining, and forwarding were other possibilities. The HBC was an organization possessing singular knowledge of northern North America, a staff of highly skilled servants, and ready access to large amounts of capital. Surely it was perfectly situated to seize new opportunities as the fur trade declined.

The Company tried. It went into lumbering in the Saguenay, fishing on Lake Superior, stock-raising and farming in Red River. Sometimes it relied on its traders and factors to found new enterprises. Sometimes it brought out specialists to manage experimental farms or (on Vancouver Island in the 1850s) develop coal mines. New companies were set up, sometimes as subsidiaries, sometimes in concert with settlers. To meet the special situation on the coast, Simpson launched a major colonization venture, the Puget's Sound Agricultural Company. It was a separate joint-stock company, wholly owned by shareholders of the parent firm, dedicated to bringing out settlers who would develop Company lands, produce surplus food for export, and, incidentally, keep the Columbia basin British. "A Fur Trader is now certainly a heterogenous animal," an Edmonton veteran commented in 1848 when he learned the company planned to go into coal mining. "At least the Fur Trade is a most curious compound of professions. Miners, Lumberers, Furriers and the d — l only knows what else besides. By the powers of St. Patrick the Incongruity of the Fur Trade beats an Irish Medley all hollow."

The diversification schemes all failed. Incompetent management was a major problem. The factors and traders understood trading and storekeeping; they handled other ventures badly. When it resorted to outsiders, the HBC was too used to paying low wages for low-grade help to be able to attract first-class managers. Sometimes the London directors, whose knowledge of North American opportunities was no better than their servants', were gulled by smooth-talking promoters – such as the "poor little Drunken Sot" (Simpson's conclusion) who led them into the Buffalo Wool Company fiasco of 1820. Such ventures, including a later attempt to breed cattle with buffalo, were ill-conceived. Others, including most forms of ranching or farming, could only succeed as small family enterprises because the prospect of ownership and independence was necessary to sustain heroic feats of hard work.

The Puget's Sound Agricultural Company supported its farmer emigrants in every way but the vital one: it would not allow them to own their land. Hardly anyone responded to its call for settlers. Who wanted to farm in the interests of the Hudson's Bay Company? The scheme was a dismal failure. And yet many men left the Company's service over the years and succeeded in farming, ranching, or much more ambitious enterprises. "Individuals who would devote attention to raising cattle in the Columbia might make a living by it," a shrewd trader wrote at the time of the Puget's Sound Company, "still it is my opinion the Hudson's Bay Company will make nothing by it."

Part of the problem was that the fur traders could not decide whether they were for or against settlement. The Company half-heartedly cultivated opportunities associated with settlement, accepted failure fatalistically, and fell back on contentment with the fur trade. It soon realized that the coastal situation was untenable – the Americans were bound to get the land south of the 49th parallel, and did in 1846 – and retreated northward, founding a new centre of operations, Fort Victoria, on Vancouver Island in 1843. It seemed a safe haven for fur traders; the Company's secretary wrote George Simpson in 1848 that the island was "*worthless* as [a] seat for a colony. It is about the last place in the globe to which (were I going to emigrate) I should select as an abode." A few months later, in 1849, the Hudson's Bay Company accepted a royal grant of all of Vancouver Island, at an annual rent of seven shillings, on condition that it develop the territory as a settled colony!

The Company had taken Vancouver Island largely to forestall other colonization enthusiasts, but made an honest effort to develop the coast's abundant resources. On the model of the fur trade, it bartered with the natives for salmon, cranberries, shingles, even their labour power in the coal beds at Fort Rupert and Nanaimo (trading one shirt for one ton of coal). It shipped everything from cranberries to ice to California and the Sandwich Islands, but could not develop stable markets for enduring industries: barrelled salmon went bad, ice melted, California started growing its own fruit, and the Sandwich Island shingle market was small and saturated. A few settlers and skilled coal miners came out to Vancouver Island, and Fort Victoria grew into the northern coast's one commercial centre, but the Company priced its land high, lacked the managerial skill to organize serious coal mining, and had no clear view of the Island's future. During the California gold rush Vancouver Island was the last place on the Pacific coast any enterprising man would want to select as an abode. A few independent settlers and visiting naval officers at Victoria in the early 1850s gradually came to resent the HBC's oppressive conservatism and ubiquity.

Gold made California. In the 1850s Hudson's Bay Company men began dreaming of an ultimate substitute for the fur trade, a gold trade. It would be done with natives, who knew where gold could be found in the Queen Charlotte Islands and drove away whites, both Americans and Company servants, who tried to scout the prospects for themselves. The natives expected to trade the gold just as they were trading furs, salmon, shingles, and other products. That would be perfectly agreeable to the Company. "The prospects of the district are really becoming brilliant," a Company man wrote in 1858 as reports came in of mainland gold on the Thompson and Fraser rivers. James Douglas, who doubled as chief factor and the civilian governor of Vancouver Island, planned new mainland forts for gold trading and resolved to keep "motley adventurers" from the United States out of the interior and away from the trade.

The old partners in furs, Company men and natives, were overwhelmed by tens of thousands of gold seekers, most from the United States, who poured into the area in the summer of 1858. Native claims to the gold were ignored, as were Company privileges. Britain would not support Douglas's attempt to exclude outsiders from British territory; it took over the mainland by creating the crown colony of British Columbia. The HBC gave up on Vancouver Island the same year, turning it back to the government to be reorganized as another crown colony. The Company could not control settlers anywhere in its lands, and its trade was collapsing on all frontiers. In England it came under intense parliamentary scrutiny, with every aspect of its operations and stewardship thrown into question. Even the exclusive trading privileges, little more than a paper monopoly, expired forever in 1858 and 1859.

The embattled furriers adjusted to the competition in Red River in at least one important way. Simpson realized that many of his problems with Americans stemmed from their lower transportation costs. The U.S. railroad and steamboat network made it cheaper to move goods in and out of Red River, and much of the northwest, via Minnesota rather than by the company's old, labour-intensive Hudson Bay route. The Bay entrance to the north had bested the St. Lawrence system early in the century (the North West Company's canoe routes were completely abandoned after 1821). Now the American rail-river-steam system was besting the Company's brigades of York boats and sweating teamsters. The cost of modernizing the Bay route with steamers or portage railways seemed prohibitive. So in 1858 the Hudson's Bay Company began shipping goods for the western fur trade through New York, Chicago, and St. Paul, to Fort Garry in Rupert's Land.

The Hudson Bay route was still important for servicing northern posts, but trade through the Bay declined sharply. Company goods were shipped to Montreal or New York, along the Grand Trunk or American lines to Chicago, and then up through St. Paul and the Red River valley. "In its way," wrote Company historian E.E. Rich, "the adoption of the southern route meant the end of the history of the Hudson's Bay Company, properly so-called as a Company based upon the approach to Rupert's Land through Hudson Bay."

The four-hundred-mile trek down the Red River valley was the least improved part of the new route. Cart haulage was slow and expensive. In 1859 the first steamboat appeared on the Red, largely in response to the prospect of Hudson's Bay Company business. When Anson Northrup, proprietor and captain of the *Anson Northrup*, tried to get high rates from the Company, it froze him out, bought his ship, and went into Red River steamboating in a secret partnership with St. Paul forwarders. Its St. Paul agent was the American who had done so much to disrupt its trade, Norman W. Kittson.

The new transportation arrangements helped make the Hudson's Bay Company more competitive in Red River. Its general storekeeping business in Fort Garry increased as the settlement grew, and it was able to hold its own in the competition for furs with private traders. When the trading monopoly expired in the late 1850s it was clear that the HBC's next step would be to surrender the charter. One or more proper crown colonies like British Columbia and Vancouver Island would probably be established for Rupert's Land and the Northwest. The coastal colonies were already overrun by Americans, though, and Red River was fast becoming a hinterland of Minnesota, so it might be just a matter of time until the whole of the Northwest went the way of the Oregon country and became fully American. This would not be of great moment to a Company about to become just another commercial organization, a Company at the end of an era in its history. Its principal shareholders and directors were also about at the end of their careers, having had a fine run since the merger of 1821. In 1859 George Simpson retired after forty years' service to the Hudson's Bay Company. He died the next year.

The Province of Canada's interest in Rupert's Land and the Northwest grew as the Hudson's Bay Company's power declined. Much of the enthusiasm was generated by railway promoters or other transportation entrepreneurs dreaming of shining tracks across fertile prairies, a little skip over gold-filled Rockies, and a Pacific terminus engrossing all the tea from China, all the trade of the Orient. From the days of Lord Durham in the 1830s, who ended his *Report* on the Canadas with a vision of a federation of British North America and a railway from sea to sea, transcontinental communications fantasies were spun by British military men and other imperialist prophets in the motherland. Maritimers such as Joseph Howe had prophesied steam whistles in the Rockies. In the Province of Canada, a little circle of Toronto-based entrepreneurs, centring on Alan Macdonell, a lawyer, mining enthusiast, and former partner of Sir Allan MacNab's, talked up the idea of a Pacific railroad, and in 1851 even applied for a charter. Their proposal was rejected as impractical.

The idea of better Canadian communications with Rupert's Land and the Northwest became more practical with every mile of Toronto's Northern Railway that was built toward Georgian Bay. When it was opened in 1855, the Northern brought the head of the lakes just a steamboat ride away. The next stop might be to build a road or rails from the western end of Lake Superior to Red River and beyond. Macdonell and his group, who had close ties to independent traders and Hudson's Bay Company opponents in Red River, also talked of a new North West Company to renew Canada's challenge for the fur trade. In 1858 they floated a North West Transportation Company, got a mail contract from the Canadian government, and began steamer service from Collingwood to Fort William. Canoes took mail and passengers the rest of the way; work started on a primitive road.

The Canadian route to Red River was ludicrously non-competitive with the Minnesota system. It took one month for the Hudson's Bay Company to get a letter from Red River to Montreal via the United States, five months through Canada.

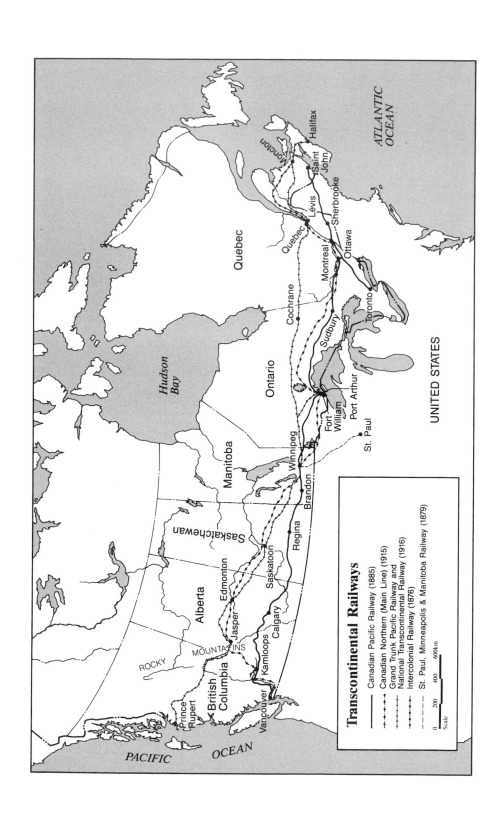

Transcontinental Railways

Canadian Pacific Railway (1885)
Canadian Northern Railway (Main Line) (1915)
Grand Trunk Pacific Railway and
National Transcontinental Railway (1916)
Intercolonial Railway (1876)
St. Paul, Minneapolis & Manitoba Railway (1879)

Scale
0   200   400   600km

ATLANTIC OCEAN

Halifax
Saint John
Moncton
Lévis
Sherbrooke
Quebec
Montreal
Ottawa
Toronto
Cochrane
Sudbury
Port Arthur
Fort William
St. Paul
Winnipeg
Brandon
Regina
Saskatoon
Edmonton
Jasper
Calgary
Kamloops
Vancouver
Prince Rupert

Quebec
Ontario
Manitoba
Saskatchewan
Alberta
British Columbia

Hudson Bay

UNITED STATES

ROCKY   MOUNTAINS

PACIFIC   OCEAN

Simpson estimated it cost the province £100 for each letter that got through. The North West Transportation Company collapsed in 1860; nothing more was heard from Macdonell and his new North Westers.

They had done their promotional job well, though, helping stimulate an intense Canadian interest in the Northwest as a new frontier. Travellers, pamphleteers, newspaper editors, and other expansionists were beginning to write about the Northwest as a frontier of settlement. Canadians had already occupied most of the fertile land south of the Precambrian Shield and east of Lake Huron. Many of them were starting to leave for the American midwest to find new land. Perhaps the Hudson's Bay Company's territories were the answer. Their millions of acres of fine soil, once annexed to Canada and then made accessible by improved communications, would bear wonderfully rich fruit and grain. The old fur-trade kingdom could be a new empire for Canadian settlers and merchants to develop – in fulfilment of Canada's manifest destiny. By the end of the 1850s the Province of Canada was determined to expand westward. It tried to claim the territories, denying the validity of the HBC's charter; but to acquire the Northwest Canada needed – and demanded – the active support of the imperial government.

Railwaymen also wanted the support of the imperial government. It seemed there would never be an intercolonial railroad in eastern British North America without some kind of imperial subsidy. All the railway promoters thought it was time to get on with the subsidy and the road. The Grand Trunk was particularly anxious for intercolonial connections (and accompanying contracts or subsidies) to help salvage its semi-bankrupt system. A visionary British railroader, Edward Watkin, who was sent out to reorganize the Grand Trunk in 1861, became a great enthusiast for the Intercolonial *and* for westward extension of the Grand Trunk to the Pacific. In 1862 Watkin, assorted Grand Trunk bond and shareholders, and other financiers interested in Canadian prospects, formed an informal British North American Association in London to lobby for railways and whatever political changes needed to facilitate them.

Discussions began in England with the Hudson's Bay Company about a land grant to support a telegraph line, a road, and eventually a railroad through its territories. Many of the proprietors had aged along with George Simpson and had no enthusiasm for the costs and other problems that a change in their business would involve. They did realize that the time had come to make what they could out of their chartered rights. The leading shareholders offered to sell the Company. In May 1863, Watkin and his associates agreed to buy the shares of the Hudson's Bay Company for £1.5 million (£300 for each £100 par value share). The deal was consummated a few months later by the International Financial Society, a consortium of London merchant bankers formed to mobilize capital for just such projects. It recapitalized the Company at £2 million, sold the shares widely on the basis of the HBC prospects as a land and colonization company, and exited with a £300,000 profit. The old company of investors in furs had been replaced by shareholders expecting big profits in colonial land. As one newspaper commented, the ancient Hudson's Bay Company had "died of the railroad and the steamboat."

The leading Canadian politicians – Galt, George Brown, George-Etienne Cartier, and John A. Macdonald – surprised and delighted their British friends by hatching a practical Confederation scheme in 1864 and getting tentative Maritime support at the Charlottetown and Quebec conferences. Confederation was highly political in its origins (largely a solution to party deadlock caused by racial and religious divisions in the Province of Canada), and never of burning concern to the ordinary people or merchants of the provinces. It got hearty support from one important business interest, the Grand Trunk Railway. Watkin and C.J. Brydges (hired away from the Great Western as general manager), realized that Confederation would bring both an intercolonial railway and western expansion.

The extent of the Grand Trunk's machinations on behalf of Confederation cannot be determined. Watkin later boasted that he was *the* Father of Confederation, but he was a notorious self-promoter. Brydges was the conduit, possibly the source, of Canadian money used to influence a decisive New Brunswick election. The railroad's role was considerable enough that some of the anti-Confederates saw the whole union as just another Grank Trunk railway job. More accurately, Confederation was partly a political expression of expansionist urges shared by railway promoters and visionary politicians alike. Take advantage of the opportunity to put this political deal together because it might get the big economic projects going.

The new owners of the Hudson's Bay Company were a body of conservative investors who displaced the more aggressive Watkin bunch during the refinancing. They had mixed feelings about Confederation. It was bound to lead to Canadian acquisition of Rupert's Land and the Northwest. The Company found itself negotiating the surrender of its chartered rights with Canadian politicians who had been loudly refusing to recognize the charter at all. The imperial government imposed the final terms: the Hudson's Bay Company was to relinquish its proprietorship of Rupert's Land in return for compensation of £300,000, possession of the land around its posts, and a grant of 5 per cent of the land in the fertile belt. The Dominion of Canada would take over possession of Rupert's Land and the Northwest.

The settlement did not seem particularly generous to shareholders who had just invested £2 million in a company being stripped of 95 per cent of its land. Some of the people who lived on that land and were not consulted about the transfer, the Métis of Red River, were even more concerned. They decided to block the deal, pending settlement of their grievances. The Red River uprising of 1869–70, led by Louis Riel, was a reaction against ham-handed Canadian expansionism. It delayed the closing of the transaction for six months. One of Riel's conditions was that Red River form the basis of a new province, Manitoba. The rest of the acquisition, including modern Alberta and Saskatchewan, was organized as the Northwest Territories.

Ottawa knew it would have to give high priority to improved communications with the western empire. Manitoba could not continue to be a trading hinterland of St. Paul, Minnesota. Settlers and immigrants could not be expected to trek to the Canadian West via St. Paul (they might not make it back to Canadian territory). A certain sense of urgency flowed out of some of the events of the Riel rebellion, too, because a handful of American expansionists had been lurking in the background in Red River. Perhaps the reunited, aggressive United States – which had just bought Alaska – coveted the whole Northwest, or even the whole continent, as part of their republic's manifest destiny. Better communications would obviously help make and keep the Canadian West Canadian.

A delegation of British Columbians came to Ottawa in 1870 to discuss the prospect that their struggling colony – its gold rushes over, its commerce stagnant and tiny population shrinking, Vancouver Island swallowed up by the mainland colony – might join the new Dominion. The Canadians were pleased to offer a faster timetable for building a transcontinental railway than the British Columbians had thought practical. Canada would start a railway to the coast within two years of British Columbia's entry to Confederation and finish it within ten. Generous terms, plus the usual pressure from an approving mother country, enticed British Columbia into Confederation in 1871. Canada had become a political nation from sea to sea. It would not be an economic nation, and the West would not truly be a part of the country, until Canada built the promised railway to the Pacific – perhaps not even then.

———————

The Macdonald government began looking for a company to build the transcontinental railroad. The Grand Trunk was the logical leading candidate, but a shareholder rebellion had ousted the visionary Edward Watkin from the system's management. The new controlling group was more mindful of the perils of expansion; its priority was to consolidate the system, provide service only where traffic warranted, and earn some dividends. The Grand Trunk's lack of interest revealed the dilemma of Canadian transcontinental railway strategy, as imperial dreaming gave way to calculations of real railway dollars and sense. The eastern terminus of the line was set, by the government, at Lake Nipissing in northern Ontario, a point equidistant from Toronto and Montreal and well away from the Grand Trunk's main line. What fools would dare build a railway westward through thousands of miles of empty wilderness and over a sea of mountains to reach a handful of settlers on the Pacific coast?

Well, by making some optimistic assumptions about climate and flows of immigrants you could calculate that the development caused by a railway would eventually create a local traffic in its territories, especially on the prairies. And the government of Canada would certainly sweeten the proposition with substantial subsidies. But would any realistic subsidy be enough to support such an unpromising line? Large chunks of the route would *never* generate any local traffic. The system might support its Rocky Mountain section; all North American transcontinentals had to cross the mountains. But how could an eight-hundred-mile semi-circle across the wild Canadian Shield north of Lake Superior ever be justified? Would an all-Canadian transcontinental ever be competitive with American lines? "I am quite clear," Brydges of the Grand Trunk wrote privately, "that a railway from Fort Garry around the north shore of Lake Superior and Lake Nipissing could not be built except at a frightful cost, when built could not be worked successfully in winter, and if it could be worked would have no traffic to carry upon it."

The Macdonald government probably did not originally intend to sponsor an all-Canadian transcontinental. The prime minister's views are not clear; several cabinet ministers, including veteran politician-promoters Joseph Howe and Francis Hincks, seem to have shared the common view, almost universal in railroad circles, that the northernmost North American transcontinental would have to be an international line. It would have to at least run south of Superior, crossing from Ontario into Michigan at Sault Ste Marie and traversing parts of Wisconsin and Minnesota before heading north. A line south of lakes Huron and Michigan might be even more practical: cross at Detroit or Sarnia, swing north from Chicago through St. Paul and down the Red River valley. There was nothing new in the idea of important rail links crossing international borders. Canada's Grand Trunk itself reached the ocean at Portland, Maine. Such arrangements, which had been touted since the 1850s, were inevitable accommodations to the facts of northern geography. "No continuous railroad route, entirely through British territory, can ever unite Halifax and Montreal with the Pacific," an American railway promoter wrote in 1869. "Nature forbids the banns."

The first proposition was put to the government by Hugh Allan, the Montreal steamship magnate, now said to be the richest man in Canada, worth about $6 million. Allan had been dabbling in eastern Canadian railroads for years and was unhappy with relations between the Allan Line and its principal feeder, the Grand Trunk. This was his opportunity to get into railways on a grand scale. Allan formed a syndicate with a number of the principals in the Vermont Central complex and in the Northern Pacific Railroad, a line chartered to build west from Duluth, Minnesota, across the northern United States. Allan's group intended to give Canada its Pacific connection by building from Lake Nipissing to the Sault, using Northern Pacific track south of Superior to Duluth and up to Manitoba, then building west to the coast. With the Vermont Central, Allan would have a Boston-Montreal-Toronto-Pacific line. The northwestern Canadian-American railway network would be one huge international system, its components cooperating rather than competing, everyone doing well out of it. The Allan interests would buy or build eastern roads to hook up with their transcontinental and the whole network would feed traffic to the steamships. In 1871 Sir Hugh Allan's Canada

Pacific Company seemed the logical firm to build Canada's Pacific railway. Government aid of $30 million cash and 50 million acres of land would accompany the contract.

The Grand Trunk did not relish competition from Sir Hugh Allan, either in eastern Canada or for the traffic of the American mid-western and northwestern states. It now had connections with Chicago and intended to compete with the Northern Pacific and all the other American systems. Brydges of the Grand Trunk became an instant and powerful opponent of the Allan plan, arguing that its real intent was to deliver the trade of the Canadian Northwest to the Northern Pacific group. It would be an American-dominated, American-controlled railway. Brydges had the ear of a prime minister who habitually distrusted Americans. Macdonald and the cabinet were willing to listen to alternatives to the Allan line. Senator David Macpherson, the former Grand Trunk contractor, moved quickly to form the all-Canadian, Toronto-based Interoceanic Railway Company, which put in a competing bid for the Pacific contract. Macpherson's old partner, Casimir Gzowski, was one of his associates. Bitter public and private disputes between the two companies followed. The struggle was further complicated by the regional strength each group commanded, becoming a case of Toronto against Montreal.

The brew of nationalist and regional pressures could not be resisted by the politicians. The upshot of the competition for the contract was the government's insistence that the Canadians form a new company. Allan would be president, but it would have no American directors, the government would monitor share transfers, and the main line would go north of Lake Superior. Early in 1873 the Canada Pacific Railway Company was chartered by Parliament to do the job on this basis. The railway would be a great national project, but it was not really a national dream. Ordinary citizens were largely indifferent. The charter permitted delay of the north of Superior line. In Parliament there was so much skepticism about the railway's feasibility that the government was forced to accept a resolution that taxes would not be increased to fund the Pacific railway. It was a promoters' and politicians' dream.

It would not float in Britain, where the money was supposed to be found. When Hugh Allan went to London to test the market in the spring of 1873, he was met with anything but enthusiasm. The influential Grand Trunk was naturally hostile to a prospective competitor. Experienced railroaders did not believe in an all-Canadian line. British investors had been gulled in the Grand Trunk promotion; this Canada Pacific scheme was less attractive. Hugh Allan was rich and powerful in Canada, but he was not a railwayman or international capitalist of standing. He was a rough-and-tumble acquisitor of the old school, whom Macdonald himself described as "the worst negotiator I ever saw in my whole life," a victim of "intense selfishness."

The unsound Canada Pacific scheme was about to collapse of its own weight when a scandal broke that brought the Macdonald government down with it. The contest for the charter had extended through the 1872 general election. Allan had supported the government with more than $350,000 in campaign funds – the equivalent of several millions today – and in return for this cash had extracted a specific promise from Macdonald and Cartier that he become president of the railroad company. The Conservative leaders eventually admitted that most of Allan's money had been spent in ways "contrary to the statute" (apparently petty bribery). Evidence also came to light that Allan had secretly maintained his American connections. In fact the Americans supplied some of the money funnelled to the Conservatives. Allan had lied to the government and everyone else, including the Americans, during the negotiations, and Macdonald had not known of the continuing connection. But his government had played very fast and loose with the biggest national project in the history of British North America. It seemed to have sold the Pacific charter to Sir Hugh Allan for $350,000.

Macdonald's detailed defence in the House of Commons – Allan was the logical head of the company anyway, the only commitment was the presidency, the Americans were out, everyone raised and spent campaign funds this way, he personally had done no wrong ("These hands are clean") – did not save him from public censure. The "Pacific Scandal" could not be contained. Macdonald's own backbenchers began to abandon him. One of the turncoats was the prominent MP for Selkirk, Manitoba, Donald Smith, a member of the board of Allan's company whose constituency would benefit greatly from railway connections with the outside world. Facing certain defeat in the House of Commons in November 1873, the Macdonald government resigned. A Liberal government, headed by Alexander Mackenzie, took office and was confirmed in power at a general election early in 1874.

Hugh Allan's Canada Pacific Railway Company quietly surrendered its charter and disappeared from history. The international financial panic of 1873 and the onset of several years of worldwide hard times also smashed the Northern Pacific and made it unlikely that anyone would raise money to build transcontinental railways. Given the certainty that Allan would have failed to finish, possibly even to start the road, and that this would have embarrassed the government or worse, it seems clear that the Pacific Scandal was good for Sir John A. Macdonald. It probably saved his career.

The Mackenzie government was inclined to accept the prevailing railroad wisdom that the transcontinental could not be built ahead of settlement, certainly not with an all-Canadian route. The Liberals would have subsidized private capitalists to build by practically any route, but in the international depression of the mid-1870s there was no interest anywhere in frontier railroad building in Canada. Ottawa had to try to meet its commitment to British Columbia, and it did want to encourage western settlement, so the Mackenzie government began building the road in bits and pieces as a public work. The first aim was to give Manitoba better communications with the outside.

Work proceeded slowly. The Intercolonial Railway linking Quebec with the Maritimes was also being built by the government, having been started in 1867 right after Confederation. It, too, was such an uneconomic proposition that no private company was interested in building and operating the line. Government construction of both roads was a mare's nest of politicking, patronage, cost over-runs, and pigging at the public trough. When the Intercolonial was finally finished in 1876 and began operating as a government railroad, it immediately became notorious for bad service and the undue influence of politicians, especially MPs and senators from the Maritimes, in its affairs. It seemed as though everyone would benefit if private capitalists could be found to lift the burden of building and running railroads from the shoulders of government. The appearance of such a group was the result of surprising, but not illogical, transportation developments in the West itself.

The steamboats on the Red River had remained Manitoba's lifeline to civilization during the 1860s. They were operated, fitfully, by Norman Kittson for the Hudson's Bay Company and several American forwarders. Competition appeared in 1871 when another American shipper, James J. Hill, began running his own steamboat. Jim Hill was a former Canadian, like Kittson, who had chosen a future in the United States and, beginning as an agent, mastered the transportation business out of St. Paul. He shared Kittson's interest in the Canadian trade and for a time had acted as the older man's successor handling furs coming out through St. Paul. Now Hill wanted a share of the profits from forwarding goods into Manitoba.

Rate-cutting by Hill and his partners forced Kittson and the HBC to talk steamboat merger. Kittson and Hill became the active partners in the Red River Transportation Company, formed in 1872, which ran steamers regularly and very lucratively for the rest of the decade. The Hudson's Bay Company was a shareholder and got special rates.

The Company's transportation interests in Manitoba were ably handled by Donald Smith, MP, the Hudson's Bay Company's chief commissioner in Canada. Born in the Highlands in 1820, Smith was another in the stream of talented Scots who made their way to Canada equipped with a good education and letters of introduction from relatives at home. His contacts got him a very long apprenticeship with the HBC as a fur trader in the Labrador wilderness. He finally began moving up in the post-Simpson regime, and was in Montreal as head of the Company's eastern Canada operations in 1869 when the Riel trouble broke out in Red River. Sir John A. Macdonald sent him there to negotiate with Riel. Smith did a brilliant job and stayed on in Manitoba as both a prominent politician and the highest Canadian officer of the Hudson's Bay Company.

During his Montreal residence Smith established good contacts with the other business lairds of the island, including his younger cousin, George Stephen, who had come out at the age of twenty-one in 1850 and risen quickly in the drygoods trade. Stephen was now branching out into textiles, finance, and railway equipment. Stephen and the other Montrealers helped Smith raise his sights far beyond the fur trade. In Manitoba he became particularly interested in the western transportation problem and joined several railway speculations, sometimes with Stephen, none of which materialized.

It was clear, though, that railways were coming to Manitoba and the Red River valley. The Mackenzie government wanted to give Manitoba its transportation outlet as quickly as possible by building south to Pembina at the border. The Minnesotans had been talking about a north-south artery for years; a significant beginning had been made by the St. Paul and Pacific Railroad, originally chartered in 1857, which built a couple of hundred miles of track in several sections northwest from St. Paul before collapsing into receivership in 1873. The line had a charter to build to the Canadian border. If that track was ever built, the company would have a strong claim to a land grant of more than 2.6 million acres from the state of Minnesota. The St. Paul and Pacific might have very good prospects – *if* the depression lifted, *if* the Canadians completed their Pembina branch, *if* settlers came to the West, *if* a financial tangle could ever be straightened out (the receiver was operating the road, not very well, on behalf of a syndicate of Dutch bondholders), and *if* enough money could be found to finish it.

The entrepreneurs who were already doing well out of Red River transportation – Kittson, Hill, and, through the Hudson's Bay Company, Donald Smith – were the first to realize the opportunities the St. Paul and Pacific might present. In the mid-1870s they began considering the possibility of getting control of the line by buying out the bondholders. In 1877 Hill, a master of transportation strategy, estimated that it would cost about $5.8 million to buy the St. Paul and Pacific's bonds, foreclose, buy the road, and complete it to the Canadian border. He believed that if the St. Paul and Pacific property were taken in hand and run properly its underlying worth was almost $20 million. If Hill's estimates were right, it was a fantastic prospect.

Hill, Kittson, and Smith needed to raise about $5.5 million of other people's money to buy control of the St. Paul and Pacific. As their financial specialist they brought in George Stephen, whose meteoric rise in Montreal business had taken him to the presidency of the Bank of Montreal. Not that there was the slightest chance of a Canadian bank having millions in risk capital for a railway deal, but Stephen probably had the standing and the skills to interest British capitalists in the St. Paul and Pacific opportunity.

Stephen failed in England. British money had been financing railway development all over the world, but there had been many failures and they had learned to be cautious. Would-be investors did not accept Hill's estimates of that far-off property's value. The group pressed on anyway. Stephen worked out a plan to buy the St. Paul and Pacific from its bondholders on credit and pay up after the road was completed. He got important support from a New York investment house, John S. Kennedy and Company, and, finally, turned to his own Bank of Montreal for cash. Hill, Kittson, Smith, and Stephen signed away all their resources as collateral for demand loans from the bank that eventually totalled about $700,000. The steamboat company was used to provide more support.

The deal was fraught with complexities and risks. It enmeshed people such as Kennedy (who was also acting for the Dutch bondholders) and the general manager of the Bank of Montreal (who soon resigned to work for the railway company) in what today would be considered unacceptable conflicts of interest. At one point they were all sued by the St. Paul and Pacific's receiver, who claimed he had been promised a cut of the profits. His suit failed. All the facts may never be known, but by the standards of the 1870s the St. Paul and Pacific coup was a fairly typical takeover, classic risk-taking by far-sighted entrepreneurs acting on a faith in their judgment that few others shared. The associates' plans to gain control of the line were never secret. Nobody else made a better offer for a property sometimes known as "Hill's folly."

Eighteen seventy-eight was a year of frantic negotiations, last-minute closings, and a race to finish the line in time to get the land grant and link up with the new Canadian line to Pembina. Through trains ran from St. Paul, Minnesota, to Winnipeg, Manitoba, in December 1878, giving Canada's West its railway link with the world. The next spring the associates reorganized their line as the St. Paul, Minneapolis, and Manitoba Railway Company (George Stephen president, Norman Kittson vice-president, James J. Hill general manager), and floated a bond issue which more than covered their debts.

Eighteen seventy-eight was also the last year of the depression. By 1879 the Northwest was booming again and it was soon apparent that Hill had *under*-estimated the property's value. The "Manitoba line," as it came to be called, quickly became one of the most profitable railways in America. By 1885 each of its founding fathers – Hill, Kittson, Smith, and Stephen – had parlayed a $70,000 cash investment in the St. Paul and Pacific into St. Paul, Minneapolis, and Manitoba securities worth $5 million.

"Catch them before they invest their profits," a cabinet minister is said to have told Sir John A. Macdonald about the St. Paul, Minneapolis, and Manitoba group. Macdonald and the Conservatives were returned to power in 1878, their conduct in the Pacific Scandal forgiven or forgotten. They were determined to push on with the transcontinental and it was not long before Macdonald began talking railways with George Stephen, a friend and sometimes political supporter. It was not so much a matter of the Stephen group yet having vast profits to reinvest, as the fact that they owned and operated a western railroad, the only line that actually reached the Canadian West. Here were the railroaders who had faith in the future of the Northwest, were willing to take risks, and, judging by even preliminary results, seemed to know how to make their projects work. These real railway builders and financiers made Sir Hugh Allan appear to be what he really was, a bumbling schemer.

The Macdonald government canvassed other possibilities, but the Grand Trunk was still not interested and no one else wanted to operate a western road, so the politicians came back to Stephen. In October 1880 a new syndicate headed by Stephen signed a contract with the government of Canada to build a railroad from Lake Nipissing to the Pacific with the north of Superior section to be built after the other parts were completed. In February 1881 the agreement was ratified by Parliament and a charter was issued to the Canadian Pacific Railway Company. The principal figures in the syndicate were Stephen, Smith, Hill, Duncan Mc-Intyre, and, very briefly, the old fur trader who had first smashed the Hudson's Bay Company's monopoly in Rupert's Land, Norman Kittson.

Less than five years later, on November 7, 1885, Donald Smith drove the last spike in the Canadian Pacific Railway. The mountain juncture in British Columbia was named Craigellachie after the gathering place of the Scots clan from which Stephen and Smith were descended.

The construction of the Canadian Pacific, at the time the longest railway in the world, was one of the epic feats of nineteenth-century railway building, unmatched until Russia built the Trans-Siberian line at the end of the century. The transcontinental railway's importance to Canada was so fundamental that its history has been celebrated in song and story as a Canadian national epic. Pierre Berton's popular history of the CPR to 1885 broke all Canadian publishers' sales records in the early 1970s. A generation earlier the poet E.J. Pratt celebrated the same events in "Towards the Last Spike," a blank verse epic pitting a race of craggy-browed Scotsmen ("Oatmeal was in their blood and in their names/Thrift was the title of their catechism") against the prehistoric stone reptile of the Canadian Shield. Legions of Canadian school children have grown up on the saga of the CPR. Parliaments of politicians have looked back to it as a model of public-private partnership in nation-building. Labour historians rightly suggest that the men who truly sweated and risked their lives building the CPR were the navvies assembled from all over the world to make the roadbed and lay the track. By today's standards they were driven hard and paid little. The workers who took the greatest risks for the least returns were the Chinese coolies imported by Andrew Onderdonk, the contractor for the government who built the line down the Fraser canyon in British Columbia.

As a business venture the building of the CPR was a magnificent feat of railway financing by George Stephen and railway management by W.C. Van Horne. William Cornelius Van Horne was a native of Illinois who began working on railroads as a fourteen-year-old telegrapher and fifteen years later was general superintendent of the Chicago, Milwaukee and St. Paul Railroad. He was reputed to be one of the best young railwaymen in America. Hill recommended that the Canadian company hire him to tackle the construction job, which had lagged badly through the first year in 1881.

Van Horne was a Renaissance man in the railway business. He possessed prodigious appetites, abilities, and enthusiasms, and in the remainder of his life proved one of the most dynamic achievers Canada has ever seen. Taking over the general managership in January 1882, Van Horne forced the construction of the prairie section at a record pace, driving his contractors and their men with his mastery of the business, determination to get on with it, and personal example in working the longest hours and appearing everywhere on the line. According to Pratt, Van Horne,

> Could straighten crooked roads by pulling at them,
> Shear down a hill and drain a bog or fill
> A valley overnight . . . .
> . . . with a locomotive short of coal,
> He could supply the head of steam himself.
> He breakfasted on bridges, lunched on ties;
> Drinking from gallon pails, he dined on moose . . .
> Only the devil or Paul Bunyan shared
> With him the secret of perpetual motion.

And Van Horne built the line north of Superior, the track that made the CPR an all-Canadian road. At first there was some doubt that these miles would ever be built. Hill was apparently certain that Stephen would postpone the North Shore line indefinitely, and simply use Michigan roads and their St. Paul, Minneapolis, and Manitoba route instead. When it became clear in 1883 that Stephen and Van Horne were going ahead with the all-Canadian route, Hill left the CPR. He went on to turn the Manitoba line into his own American transcontinental, the Great Northern. Originally Hill's protégé, Van Horne replaced him as the CPR's master railway strategist. For the rest of the nineteenth century they were probably the two best railwaymen in North America. Hill's defection from the CPR syndicate was preceded by the retirement of the grand old man of them all, Norman Kittson, who spent the last years of his life as a race-horse breeder and died one night on the train from Chicago.

"My part was easy," Van Horne used to say about the building of the CPR. "I had only to spend the money, but Stephen had to find it when nobody in the world believed but ourselves." He was exaggerating only slightly. Stephen had to tap highly skeptical capital markets for the funds to build a northern development railway. He had to raise more money than he had anticipated in 1880 and do it much faster, for he had under-estimated the line's cost and over-estimated construction time. He had to sell the CPR to investors in the teeth of the active hostility of the leading Canadian railway company, the Grand Trunk. Its initial policy of benign neglect of the CPR (almost certain to fail, you know, but might be a use-ful feeder out of the West) changed when it became evident that Stephen and company were planning to compete all across eastern and central Canada. Far from being a complement to the Grand Trunk, the CPR intended to rival and sur-pass it. As the new company bought and built roads to connect with the main line at Lake Nipissing, the Grand Trunk began squawking about ruinous, wasteful competition; it systematically disparaged the CPR along its international network of financial contacts. Quite unsound; can't be done; bound to fail.

The St. Paul and Pacific adventure taught Stephen how to escape from London investors and their conservatism. He could turn to the growing New York market, a source of capital that Canadians had not yet learned to tap. He also knew how to raise money with instruments finely tuned to the risks of the venture. Earlier North American railroads had proven too erratic in their earning power to support the fixed costs of huge bond or debenture issues. But investors who knew railway bonds were a bad risk might take a flyer in railway stock, issued well below par value and carrying the prospect of much higher returns. Heavy reliance on com-mon stock and the New York market were Stephen's vital innovations in the financing of the Canadian Pacific.

Government support was also essential in the building of the road. Canada's basic subsidy to induce the syndicate to tackle the job was $25 million in cash and 25 million acres of land (valued at $25 million in 1880), payable in stages as con-struction progressed. The company was given all of the track built under govern-ment-let contracts, which included the line from the Lakehead to Winnipeg, the Pembina branch, and the Onderdonk-built mountain lines from Kamloops to the coast. These were valued at $38 million. The total cost of the railway at the time of the driving of the last spike was about $150 million, making the private invest-ment about $62 million. The government made other concessions to attract this money, including tax and import tariff relief, and, most important, a "monopoly" clause in the charter specifying that for twenty years no line could be built south of the CPR's main line without the company's consent. Insistence on the monopoly clause was the syndicate's sensible response to the government's insistence on the uneconomic all-Canadian route.

The subsidy to the CPR was not excessive compared to the terms of the original Allan charter, the aid the Mackenzie government would have given if it could have found private capitalists, or the subsidy the Macdonald government was prepared to give if necessary. It had to be supplemented, however, by emergency loans on two occasions: $22.5 million in 1884 and $5 million in the summer of 1885. The loans were secured by a mortgage on the property in the first instance, which was replaced by bonds during the second crisis. Both crises were triggered by escalating construction costs and bleak capital markets. Stephen and the CPR directors turned to government as a last resort after pledging all of their personal assets, including the furniture and table linen in their mansions. The alternative to government aid was to shut down construction and possibly see the project collapse. A CPR "bust" would have been ruinous to the syndicate and probably to the fortunes of the Macdonald Conservatives. It is not clear that it would have made much difference to the development of the Canadian West.

The Macdonald government reluctantly and hesitantly came to the company's aid. The utility of the road in conveying Canadian troops to put down Louis Riel's rebellion in the Northwest in the spring of 1885 may have had a critical effect in rallying Conservative and public support during the second financial crisis. From the granting of the charter the Liberal opposition in Parliament had attacked the venture as premature and excessively costly. The Liberals would have let the CPR collapse, and then looked to other investors or government to pick up the pieces.

As the line neared completion in 1885 and with the second round of government support, Stephen found he could finally market CPR bonds in England. By July 1, 1886, the debt to the government had been paid. The railroad's directors proceeded to carry out their one continuing obligation under the terms of the charter, to "for ever efficiently maintain, work and run the Canadian Pacific Railway."

The construction of the Canadian Pacific Railway was a national achievement in only a certain, limited sense. The government of Canada did supply more than half the cost of the system and it twice saved the company from impending collapse. The governing Conservatives risked their political destiny in the struggle to build the road. On the other hand, most of the people who risked their own money in the road were Americans. A small group of Canadians, mainly Scots-born, effectively controlled the company, but more than half of the common shares were initially held in the United States. Virtually all of the managerial expertise that went into the construction of the CPR was American – from J.J. Hill and the early engineering staff to Van Horne and the senior managers he imported by the carload. Andrew Onderdonk, the federal government's contractor who built the most difficult mountain mileage, was an American. Most of the labouring men who built the CPR were recent immigrants to Canada; those who handled the most difficult jobs were Chinese.

"We are now fully in the grip of Americans and Chinese," the Toronto *Globe's* British Columbia correspondent wrote in 1882 as more newcomers arrived to build the Canadian Pacific. Canada's "national dream" of a transcontinental railway was realized by reliance on foreign capital, expertise, and labour at every stage of the work. It was a great Canadian national highway, controlled by Canadians, financed, built, and owned largely by Americans.

Western Canadian business had already evolved significantly before the construction of the CPR.

The fur traders had criss-crossed the prairies and mountains and tundra for most of a century. The Hudson's Bay Company's presence had been particularly important in keeping the Pacific coast north of the Oregon country part of British North America. In Rupert's Land the Red River settlement was created by fur traders and their offspring. Between Rupert's Land and the Pacific, the Company had been for generations the only significant commercial and civil organization.

But the Company's dominion had crumbled. Beginning with Norman Kittson and his Métis associates, the fur-trading monopoly was challenged and swept away. Red River became the supply base for independent traders penetrating thousands of miles to the north and west. As agriculture and settlement expanded in the new province of Manitoba, the trading area outside the Company's Fort Garry evolved into the community of Winnipeg. By 1879 it was a bustling town four thousand strong. Merchants such as A.G.B. Bannatyne and James H. Ashdown ran extensive wholesale houses supplying independent traders on far-off frontiers; men such as John McDougall, a hard-working fur dealer and storekeeper, competed with the Hudson's Bay Company at its Fort Edmonton. W.F. Alloway's thousands of Red River carts, the West's distinctive vehicle, creaked from post to post across the prairies, east to Lake of the Woods, south to Minnesota.

The appearance of the Dominion's North-West Mounted Police in the mid-1870s helped create a climate of order across the Canadian plains in which trade flourished without the need for gun belts or circled wagons. The American whisky traders out of Fort Benton, Montana, vanished from their northern outpost, Fort Whoop-Up, before the Mounties arrived to chase them away. But other American traders, often the outfits of I.G. Baker and Company of Fort Benton, were busy turning that semi-arid country south of Fort Calgary into a hinterland of Montana, much as Red River had been a northern market for Minnesota. In fact a separate economy was taking shape in the southwestern prairie and foothill country as ranchmen and cowboys drove herds of cattle up from the States or across the Rockies to graze on limitless ranges – and enterprising easterners, often from Montreal and the livestock farms of the Eastern Townships, began investing in ranches.

In 1871 Victoria, British Columbia, was the only settlement worth mentioning west of Winnipeg. The mainland gold rushes of the late 1850s and early 1860s turned a sleepy Hudson's Bay Company post into a boom town full of prospectors and storekeepers and commission men. The community it was most strongly linked with and hoped to emulate was San Francisco. Then the gold gave out, and the entrepreneurs had to develop new prospects. They were well on their way by the end of the 1870s: primitive sawmills and salmon canneries and collieries kept the British Columbian economy going, not merely as an adjunct of California, but with direct trade links across the Pacific and back to Britain. The men who would become the first generation of British Columbian millionaires – merchant R.P. Rithet, coalman Robert Dunsmuir, shipper John Irving – were on the scene and flourishing before railway construction began making their country a part of Canada.

The pace of western development was too quick and complex for native and Métis traders to exploit. Trading with the natives continued to be profitable in many areas: prosperity and European technology may have stimulated a golden age of cultural expression by the coastal tribes in the second half of the nineteenth century, for example. Some native people, particularly Métis entrepreneurs, went into general trading, freighting, guiding, and any other money-making activity they could find. More often than not, though, they slipped into working for others, becoming wage labour or hired help. Native fur traders had not accumulated capital or contacts or knowledge of related industries and technologies. They tended to stay with fur trading, hunting, and fishing, do some hired manual labour, perhaps try a little farming, or – as in the British Columbia gold rush – simply be pushed aside by aggressive whites. After the fur trade the native people were not on the leading edge of any of the West's new enterprises.

The traders of the Hudson's Bay Company were only moderately more successful than the natives in adjusting to the new order. At most times they had known the fur trade was a shrinking business in a territorial domain that could not be maintained. Perhaps the Company's achievement was to have done so well as it retreated, earning good profits, paying high dividends to its shareholders. Hudson's Bay Company fur traders gradually became storekeepers. After the surrender of its charter in 1869–70, the Company was a major western landholder and land trader, possessor of properties eventually worth many millions. In 1879 it hired its first professional Canadian manager, the ubiquitous C.J. Brydges, who began engineering a major transition to modern storekeeping, government supply contracts, and real estate operations. The Hudson's Bay Company survived a few lean years during its great transition and then it prospered again.

Perhaps it could have done much more. For a few years the Company controlled all of the resources of half a continent. It had opportunity upon opportunity to develop profitable new business, and muffed almost all of them. Of all its might-have-beens, the most intriguing is the decision not taken in Red River transportation in the 1870s. The HBC was venturesome enough to invest in steamboats on the Red River (and on the Pacific coast and eventually on most western waterways). When the real trader-entrepreneurs of the new West, Norman Kittson, J.J. Hill, and Donald Smith, were scrambling for investors in their daring railway projects, the Hudson's Bay Company was nowhere to be found.

Had it become a major partner in the fabulously profitable St. Paul, Minneapolis and Manitoba line, either in its own right or through a subsidiary, the Hudson's Bay Company might have gone on to become a dominant partner or major shareholder in the syndicate that built the Canadian Pacific Railway. It did not. The CPR was created by fur traders and financiers, including the company's own former employee, Donald Smith, who was George Simpson's successor as Canada's leading fur-trader entrepreneur. While these men were embarking on one of the great business adventures in Canadian history, the English shareholders and directors of the ancient, drifting, trading company were hiring an unimaginative manager, Brydges, to mind their stores and land. The transition from Simpson to Brydges was from dynamic, aggressive management to routine conservatism.

The Canadian Pacific Railroad Company became the true successor to the Hudson's Bay Company as the dominant business influence over half a continent. The construction of its main line in the early 1880s set off the first western Canadian land boom, as thousands of speculators, real estate agents, politicians, and bona fide settlers filed, claimed, bought, subdivided, and tilled the soil to get a share of the increase in value that the railroad company's activities were causing. The organization that owned the most town sites, subdivisions, and fertile prairies in western Canada was the CPR itself. It was the largest landowner, the largest employer, the largest carrier in all of Canada. Its directors' actions could and did change the face of the country. Their 1881 decision to relocate the main prairie line some two hundred miles south of the surveyed North Saskatchewan River route changed the pattern of settlement of western Canada and created a new urban landscape. (The company never explained its decision; but the new route was shorter and cheaper, less vulnerable to eventual American competition, and opened up country whose potential seemed newly promising.) The CPR almost destroyed Edmonton; it was the making of Regina and Calgary and hundreds of hamlets, towns, and cities along its main line. At its western terminus on Burrard Inlet, the CPR needed more land and facilities than Port Moody, the first tidewater village, could offer. Its coming led to the incorporation of a new West coast city, which Van Horne named Vancouver (after the explorer).

With the completion of the CPR in 1885, Canada's western empire was ready to be developed. There was an important time lag, a decade of considerable disappointment (see pages 252-309), but eventually the east-west railroad was essential to homesteading and the settlement of the West, the growth of a wheat economy, and the development of most other western resources. Its presence determined the West's future evolution as part of Canada's economy rather than as northern trading extensions of Minnesota, Montana, or California. It also supplied a Northwest Passage from the Orient to the Occident. Neither prairie rivers, nor the prairie canals that were neither built nor proposed, could have done the work that the railway did. The men who created the Canadian Pacific Railway performed a brilliant feat of entrepreneurship and created the most powerful organization in the Dominion next to the national government itself. Successors to the fur traders, the railroaders then began their own struggle to retain their domination.

TOP: **Driving the last spike on the CPR, November 7, 1885** *(NSL Archive)*
ABOVE: **First CPR through train, June 1886** *(NSL Archive)*

Toronto Rolling Mills, 1864, by William Armstrong *(John Ross Robertson Collection, Metropolitan Toronto Public Library)*

9

Protecting the Manufacturers

Healthy infant industries ... ubiquitous Molsons ... millers and merchant
millers ... furniture-makers ... Eddy's matches ... paper mills ...
woollens ... the Manchester of Canada ... shoemakers ... iron-
mongers ... foundries ... rolling mills ... Daniel Massey and farm
machines ... Redpath's sugar ... pea-fed hogs ... the earth oils of
Petrolia ... digging for oil ... manufacturing centres ... shipbuilding's
decline ... markets and tariffs ... hard times and unemployment ...
protection as Canada's National Policy

It was not just a nation of hewers of wood and drawers of water, of farmers, fishermen, and fur traders. The colonials began manufacturing very early in their history. The origins were often humble: in backwoods sawmills set up to cut trees into deals or planks; in seigneurial grist mills for grinding grain into flour, and the tanneries and cooperages and woollen mills that grew up alongside them; in shoemakers' and tailors' shops when machinery was added and new hands were hired; in John Molson's little brewery in Montreal and distilleries everywhere. Growth was uneven, driven by technological leaps and bounds, influences from abroad, and rapid changes in the market. By the 1850s little water-powered country mills existed side by side with big steam-driven factories set up by companies of capitalists to build railway carriages and locomotives, with large furniture factories and foundries and textile operations employing hundreds of workers. It was too soon to say the provinces had "industrialized"; this is a vague, almost meaningless term, especially in a country whose largest "industry" throughout the nineteenth century was farming – but many kinds of industries had arrived.

In the Confederation era, Canadian manufacturers dominated the domestic market in almost all fields, including carrriages, foundry goods, and machinery. As this table indicates, a surprising proportion of the goods sold in Canada were made in Canada.

PRODUCTION AND CONSUMPTION IN CANADA, 1871

Industries	Value of production ($000's)	Production as percentage of domestic consumption and exports
Agricultural machinery	2,685	95%
Boots and shoes	16,134	99
Brewery products	2,141	95
Furniture	3,581	97
Carriages	4,849	99
Cheese	1,602	99
Cottons, denims	782	24
Distillery products	4,093	97
Flour and meal	39,136	94
Glass	293	65
Foundry products	893	79
Machine manufactures	7,326	93
Meats	3,800	88
Oil (coal, kerosene)	3,095	99
Paper	1,072	82
Rope, twine	770	95
Saddlery, harness	2,465	95
Soap, candles	1,324	95
Stone and marble	1,088	97
Sugar	4,133	60
Tanneries (leather)	9,185	91
Tobacco	2,435	98
Woollens	5,508	85
Earthenware	331	39

SOURCE: O. J. McDiarmid, *Commercial Policy in the Canadian Economy.*

Canada's pioneer manufacturers came in various shapes and sizes, and the evolution of their industries does not easily fit the crude moulds historians try to use. Canadian manufacturing did not develop as simple import replacement; it was not simply the transition from household to factory manufacture; nor a matter of a craftsman's society being replaced by the regime of capitalists, proletarians, and dark satanic mills. In only a few cases, like the growth of wooden shipbuilding, was it a response to foreign demand.

Most generally, Canadian manufacturing evolved to meet local demand for processed goods. Imports were expensive, if only because transport was slow and costly. Settlers needed to be clothed, shod, supplied with furniture and strong drink. Primary producers needed tools: ploughs and scythes, axes and saws, nails, horseshoes, and fishhooks. The transportation revolution created an important market for heavy manufactured goods: steam engines, iron rails, wheels, rolling stock, replacements for everything. And the manufacturers themselves needed their machine tools: kettles and grindstones, distilling vats and lathes, sewing machines and steam engines. Wherever Canadian producers found they could meet these needs more cheaply than other suppliers, they got the business.

Change could also be stimulated artificially. Price levels in domestic markets could be raised by tariffs on imports and other monopolistic devices. As early as the 1820s the imperial tariff system gave some colonial producers an important advantage in the home market. As duties rose and fell in later decades (they became governments' most important source of revenue), manufacturers naturally favoured more protection. By the 1870s a near consensus existed among Canadian manufacturers to the effect that the domestic market was theirs as a matter of right. It should be fenced off as the preserve of Canadian producers. Protection from marauding American manufacturers was particularly important. The "infant" Canadian industries needed tariffs to help them grow and provide work and wages for Canadians.

In the depression of the 1870s, manufacturers decided they needed more protection from tougher foreign competition. Canada should have a comprehensive manufacturing policy, they argued – not a policy of responding to this or that special interest, but a broad policy of national development through stimulating all possible kinds of domestic manufacturing. In 1879 John A. Macdonald's Conservative government responded to pressure from manufacturers and their supporters by introducing a "National Policy" of high protective tariffs. Its advent was a spectacular demonstration of the influence that this new manufacturing "class" was able to wield in the developing country. Although it neither created nor sustained Canadian manufacturing in any general way, the National Policy moulded both the structure of the Canadian economy and the course of debate about the society's future for many generations.

J OHN MOLSON MASTERED HIS CRAFT after he used his capital to buy his way into it. An eighteen-year-old orphan from Lincolnshire, skilled in no particular trade, Molson landed in Montreal in the summer of 1782 and pondered his opportunities. He liked what he saw. "There appears far greater opportunities for a person settling in business here than in all probability will in England for many years to come," he wrote home. Molson had a small inheritance, about £1,400. He decided to enter the brewing business and went into partnership with a fellow immigrant, Thomas Loid, to found a small brewery. The partners hired a man to be their brewer, maltster, and labourer.

By 1786 Molson had studied British brewing on trips home, purchased Richardson's *Theoretical Hints on an Improved Practice of Brewing*, and taken over the business as a brewer in his own right. "Bot 8 Bushels of Barley to Malt first this season," he wrote in his notebook on July 28, "My Commencement on the Grand Stage of the World." Stephen Leacock's summary of his success still holds: "Molson built his brewery a little way downstream from the town, close beside the river. Archeologists can easily locate the spot as the brewery is still there."

John Molson realized that the growing British population of Montreal created a permanent market for British ale. Ale was perishable and expensive to ship. A hogshead of imported porter sold in Montreal for £4.15s. sterling. Molson could make good money selling his porter as low as £3.12s., and he developed a line of milder, weaker ales of a sort that was apparently not imported. He also had good connections with government officials anxious to stimulate production of milder spirits than the brandy and rum too often used to debauch the natives. "Good ale is all I want," Molson wrote home in 1786, "plenty of custom & good profits will immediately follow."

The profits followed so quickly that Molson's main need was for more capital to forestall competitors. "There is no doubt but shall meet with an opposition – tis already talked on & the only way to prevent it is to carry the business with spirit." By 1791 Molson was brewing about thirty thousand gallons a year, and had invested about £2,750 in his plant. His gross revenues were about £800 a year, of which some £300 was profit. The brewery continued to expand, slaking thirsts in Montreal and up and down the river. By the early 1800s other breweries had been founded in several Lower Canadian towns. Molson tried to protect his market by agreeing to stay out of competitors' territories. He could not succeed in the long run, and from 1808 faced competition in Montreal. One of his responses was to begin advertising. More competitors appeared; by 1827 Montreal had fourteen breweries.

Molson and his sons were already planning further adventures in alcohol by learning the intricacies of distilling. Grain was dirt cheap, a substantial imperial tariff had raised the price of imported liquor, and colonial demand was strong. But a host of distillers already vied for the market. The industry ranged from farmers and millers who converted grain into potable, portable liquors (often on a barter basis with their customers), to merchant distillers in Halifax and Montreal producing rum from cheap West Indian sugar and molasses. The Molsons were among the first to realize that the demand for liquor in industrial England could profitably be met from the Canadas. In the early 1820s they made large shipments of over-proof rectified spirits to England. Exports were an important component of the Molsons' distilling trade when they began systematically enlarging it in the late 1830s.

Thomas Molson, John's middle son, became a crude industrial chemist and distiller through travel and study. His products were not particularly potent – pioneer whisky was weak by our standards – or flavourful. The spirits were not aged and were often of uncertain gender. "Almost any kind of liquor – whisky, gin, rum, brandy, cognac and liqueurs of various kinds – was produced," Molson's historian wrote, "rather simply and effortlessly, by incorporating various additives or flavorings." On one trip to London, Thomas advertised in the papers his desire "of acquiring knowledge of flavouring a neutral spirit to imitate Holland Gin, Cognac, Brandy, Jamaica Spirits, etc."

The Molsons' Montreal location gave them export advantages over their smaller western competitors. By the early 1840s they were the largest distillers in British North America, and were more interested in whisky than beer. The Montreal brewery was surpassed by William Dow, who in the early 1860s outsold the Molsons four to one (700,000 gallons a year to 142,000). Dow also distilled, but the major competition for Molson's liquors was the "common whisky," "Toddy," and "Old Rye" made made by Gooderham and Worts in Toronto.

James Worts and William Gooderham were brothers-in-law who brought large families and a middling amount of capital (Gooderham had £3,000) to York, Upper Canada, in the early 1830s. Worts established a wind-driven flour mill near the mouth of the Don River. In 1837 Gooderham, who had become senior partner on Worts's death in the mill's well, added a distillery to process waste grain that they had been selling to several small distillers in Toronto. The distillery flourished: like the Molsons, Gooderham and (a second) Worts served a major urban market and participated in the export trade. The firms appear to have worked together and with other distillers to fix prices and allocate markets. The Molsons tried occasional forays into the eastern province, brewing and distilling for some years in both Kingston and Port Hope, but none of their plans to invade Toronto was implemented.

By the 1860s the founding families had radically different distilling strategies. The Molsons were about to abandon the field in the face of growing temperance agitation and higher taxes; Gooderham and Worts increased capacity, mechanized their distillery (by 1861 no human hands intruded between receiving grain at the distillery door and drawing whisky off into barrels), and improved the quality of its product. Other distillers, such as the former baker, Henry Corby, of Belleville, or the Detroit grain buyer and distiller, Hiram Walker, who set up a Canadian branch near Windsor in 1858, or Joseph Seagram, who began distilling a year earlier in a converted grist mill in Waterloo, were as yet of no consequence in the industry.

At one time or another the Molsons explored almost every business opportunity in nineteenth-century Canada. Their interest in steamboats, described earlier, drew them into heavy manufacturing, for example, to service their vessels. When John Molson imported a Boulton and Watt engine for his second boat, the *Swiftsure*, in 1812, he had to import a skilled mechanic to install it. He installed the mechanic in a small foundry next to the brewery to make connecting and replacement parts for the engine. The St. Mary's Foundry, as it came to be called, was sometimes owned by Molson's former employees, sometimes bought back by the family. It made most of the engines for the Molson line and the engine that drove the *Royal William* across the Atlantic in 1833.

By that time Montreal had become a centre for the manufacture of marine engines. Early steam engines and their parts were not interchangeable, making it necessary to have foundries near docks. The engines were not very large or complicated, so it was relatively easy to start a foundry. The St. Mary's Foundry was one of several establishments forming a marine-industrial complex in Montreal. Sailing ships and steamboat hulls for river commerce were built in several shipyards. Engines came from the foundries, notably the Eagle Foundry, created by skilled American engineers John Ward and his brothers. Ward engines became known the length of the St. Lawrence for their quality, and the firm received contracts as far east as Niagara. In the 1820s it employed one hundred skilled workers, sometimes as many as three hundred. Ward himself never liked Montreal, where he felt Americans were discriminated against by Scotsmen. "After we have supplied *John Bull* with all the steam engines that he wants," Ward wrote, he intended to retire to New Jersey. "The reason we stay here now is because steam engines are wanted here more than in Jersey and there are fewer to make them."

The founders who made steam engines also made boilers and paddle wheels and were soon building stationary engines and many kinds of machines for other industries. In the late 1840s the Eagle Foundry, now owned by Canadians, advertised its capacity to make high and low pressure engines, mill gearing, bark mills, bathtubs, cast iron pans and kettles, bar iron, mill and jack screws, and iron tackle. The St. Mary's Foundry was casting car wheels for the St. Lawrence and Atlantic Railroad, and there was talk of the need for a locomotive "works" to supply the railways. As they did later with distilling, the Molson family withdrew from iron founding in the early 1850s rather than face intense competition. They had other irons in the fire, as it were, including the first major attempt to develop the iron ore resources of northern Quebec.

***

The gamut of early British North American manufacturing – spanned remarkably by that one Montreal family – ran from cheap consumer goods like beer to expensive heavy machinery like steam engines. The market was mainly domestic, with occasional valuable opportunities for export. The Molsons were unusual in having entered manufacturing effectively as capitalists, without experience in related industries or special skills. (The family's genius seems to have been its knack for applying advanced technology in trades as diverse as distilling and engine manufacture. John Molson instructed his son Thomas to visit all the manufactories in England he could get into.) Until at least the 1850s it was more natural for primary producers in an industry gradually to add manufacturing processes to their operation, for merchants trading finished products to become interested in their manufacture, or for craftsmen or domestic producers to expand as they discovered a market.

Primitive processing of natural products was the most common form of manufacturing throughout the nineteenth century. Every farming community had its grist mill to grind grain into flour, every settlement its sawmill to turn timber into deals and planks. There were small millers and large: farmers who handled neighbours' grain on a barter basis, seigneurial entrepreneurs whose mills originated in semi-feudal landlord's obligations, the "merchant millers" who lined the Welland Canal and the Humber River by the 1840s and converted Upper Canada's grain to flour for the export trade. One miller often built several mills to make full use of the water-power at his site. At Louth Mills in the Niagara peninsula, for example, George P.M. Ball, scion of prosperous Loyalist farmers, had a flour mill, sawmill, and woollen mill in operation by the end of the 1820s. These became the nucleus of what his biographer calls a "rural industrial centre," the village of Glen Elgin, complete with housing for the workers and a general store, both provided by Ball. The Cooper, Fisher, and Gamble families created similar complexes on the Humber, just west of Toronto, and to the east the Gibbs became the most prominent millers and merchants in Oshawa. In West Flamborough Township in the 1820s James Crooks's complex of a grist mill, sawmill, carding mill, general store, blacksmith's shop, ox-shoeing stall and cooperage was known as "the greatest manufacturing centre in the Western Province." In Lower Canada, Barthélemy Joliette, "seigneur entrepreneur" of Lavaltrie in Jean-Claude Robert's phrase, named the community that grew up around his big sawmill "Le Village d'Industrie," and in the 1840s promoted one of the country's first local railways to link it to the St. Lawrence.

Most of the millers' original business was "custom" work, servicing local needs in return for a share of the raw material. Aggressive millers such as Ball, Gamble, Gibbs, and Crooks then developed a cash trade, buying grain from the farmers and selling their flour through commission merchants in Toronto and Montreal. Distilleries and tanneries and cooperages were common ancillary enterprises, valuable diversification for merchant millers who lost heavily in the volatile grain trade of the late 1840s. When Ball was wiped out in grain he kept going with sawmilling and the "terrible, uphill work" of making woollen cloth and selling it through a retail store in Hamilton.

Sawmills existed wherever farmers cleared their land. Sometimes they were adjuncts of an even more primitive wood-processing operation, the potashery, where wood was burned and the ashes processed, barrelled, and exported. Commercial sawmilling developed most fully in the square timber country of New Brunswick and the Canadas. Sometimes the timberers themselves erected sawmills to cut deals; often they left sawing to little operators, some of whom grew big enough to get their own limits and do their own cutting. In the 1850s the forest industries were revolutionized by the growth of American demand for sawn lumber. As north-south railway lines linked forests to urban markets, the British North American wood manufacturers became very competitive.

A few of the old square timber dealers, such as the Gilmours, adjusted to the new situation. More commonly, the opportunity to saw for the American market was developed by Americans who knew the new market existed. When the Harris and Bronson Company of upstate New York found its timber supplies running short, for example, it sent Henry Bronson north to investigate the Ottawa valley. The opportunity to obtain a superb mill site at the Chaudière Falls near Bytown was instrumental in the firm's 1852 decision to move to Canada. Pattee and Perley, also of northern New York, came to the Chaudière the next year, as did other established American sawmillers. With the development of the big mills at the Chaudière and nearby sites, Bytown was a thriving lumber community before it became Ottawa and a seat of government.

Until late in the century most secondary manufacturing was located near a product's final market, and not uncommonly the manufacturer was also the final consumer. Wooden shipbuilding, described earlier, was a notable and important exception. Usually it was local bakers who turned flour into bread, local carpenters who shaped sawn wood into furniture, local spinners, weavers, and seamstresses – often farmers' wives – who made wool into cloth or cloth into clothing. The farmers' wives often made the bread, too, and the husbands did the carpentering, a reminder that domestic manufacturers were important buyers of semi-processed goods. Because they could not reach the final consumer, most flour and sawmillers were unable to add further stages of manufacturing. It tended to be local artisans or expanding household producers who met the growing demand for wood and grain products.

Bakers, for example, emerged as small businessmen by mid-century. A few, such as the Moirs of Halifax, gradually grew larger, invested in machinery and steam power, and engaged in what the Marxists call "self-exploitation" – that is, grindingly hard work. Cabinet and furniture-makers were common, some of them operating substantial enterprises by the 1860s. In Montreal John Hilton needed six floors of showrooms to display products turned out by eighty hands using the most up-to-date machines. Hilton stressed quality and craftsmanship in the old wood-carving tradition, as opposed to his rival George Armstrong, who specialized in turning out "really good and cheap" woodwork for a mass market. The famous Toronto firm of Jacques and Hay had one of the largest factories of any kind in that city, employing two hundred and fifty hands in 1861, five hundred at times in the 1870s. Jacques and Hay used Ontario hardwoods to make quality furnishings for the well-to-do and standard chairs and desks for schools and institutions. Although he was a big Montreal furniture man, who prided himself on keeping his hands at work all winter, George Armstrong stayed in the funeral business. The steady demand in coffins was bread and butter to many furniture dealers, and a few are still in the funeral business today.

While millers had trouble integrating forward into the final stages of manufacturing because few had access to markets for "store bread," Moir the baker moved "backward" into flour milling in Halifax and Jacques and Hay of Toronto built northern sawmills to cut their own timber. They became prominent timber exporters to the United States. No one integrated as successfully as Ezra Butler Eddy, another of the Americans who drifted up to the Ottawa valley in the early 1850s. Unlike most of the sawmill entrepreneurs, Eddy was just another young man looking for work and wages. He happened to have a craft, for he knew how to make phosphorous matches by hand. Matches were trivial but necessary and a product that the normally handy farmer could not make for himself. Eddy peddled his own matches through the countryside and found a market for other homely wooden products like pails, washbowls, and clothespins. He rented manufacturing facilities, expanded as fast as possible, and by the 1870s had his own timber limits, sawmills, planning mills, sash-and-door factory, and box factory – along with match-making facilities.

Paper-making was not a natural business for early wood-product men. Until the 1860s paper was made from a bleached pulp of ground, cooked rags, usually linen and cotton. Paper mills were often close to towns, which supplied both markets and rags. Pioneer paper-makers were often paper-users seeking cheaper supplies, millers who had water-power and grindstones handy, and a few skilled foreigners who knew how to install and operate equipment that produced paper sheet by sheet, without the continuous-flow machinery that would come only much later. The early paper "mills," therefore, were cheap and simple.

Handbills offering "Cash given for Clean Linen and Cotton Rags" preceded the 1805 opening of the first British North American paper mill, built near Montreal at St. Andrew's, Quebec, by a group of New Englanders. The manufacturers engaged James Brown, a leading Montreal bookseller and stationer, as agent for sales of their brown wrapping paper. "The papermaker being an American, there is little to be expected of him," Brown wrote, "he is determined to take advantage of the times." Brown should have known not to take an interest in the Americans' mill. Soon he was pursuing his partners through the courts. By 1809 the Americans were gone and Brown owned the mill and a newspaper he had purchased and reorganized, the *Montreal Gazette*. Brown could not manage both the newspaper and the mill (there were labour troubles with his American workmen, such as their refusal to make cartridge paper during the War of 1812) and he chose to move to St. Andrew's to concentrate on manufacturing. The St. Andrew's mill was destroyed by ice and flooding in the 1830s.

In Halifax, another early newspaper town, the desire to get cheaper paper than his competitors seems to have caused Anthony Holland, proprietor of the *Acadian Recorder*, to found a mill in 1818 on the Hammond Plains outside of town. He, too, gave up his newspaper to manage the mill and a retail paper store. In Upper Canada, users who were frustrated by irregular deliveries of expensive imported paper persuaded the legislature to offer a $500 bounty to the first domestic paper mill. The offer induced a race to found an Upper Canadian mill; it was won in 1826 by James Crooks, the "industrialist" of Crooks Hollow, West Flamborough. He narrowly beat a group of Englishmen who installed machinery in an old grist mill at Todmorden on the Don River outside of Toronto. The losers claimed Crooks cheated by working on Sundays. Their mill prospered anyway when William Lyon Mackenzie, publisher of the *Colonial Advocate*, gave them his paper contract. Both Crooks and the Don millers had difficulty producing even the crude paper used for wrapping and newsprint; a chief problem was the lack of good linen and cotton rags in the backwoods community. "The paper is detestable," Mackenzie wrote of his new suppliers. "They would refuse it [in England] to wrap up brown sugar. . . . The papyrus from the old mummy of Thebes in Egypt is 'fair' when placed beside the production of my friends at the Don mills."

More mills were founded to meet the growing demand for paper. Toronto's second mill was built upstream on the Don in 1844 to make the paper George Brown needed for his new newspaper, the *Globe*. It became the site of Don Mills. The *Globe* prospered and in the 1860s its hunger for newsprint supported the growth of the Riordon Paper Mills at Merritton on the Welland Canal. John Riordon's decision to risk using new technology to make paper from wood pulp with continuous-flow machinery in the early 1870s was more important in the success of his enterprise; it led to a manufacturing triumph that made Riordon Canada's first real paper millionaire. He also became a publisher when he took over an insolvent customer, the Toronto *Mail*, in 1877 (the merger with the *Globe* came much later). While the Riordons and a few other innovaters did well in the early 1880s, the explosive growth in Canadian pulp and paper came well after the turn of the century. In 1875 Canada's twenty-two paper mills produced a combined total of nine thousand tons.

———————

Everyone needed clothes and shoes. Home manufacture was common, of course, and the big textile mills of England and New England spewed out miles of excellent cheap fabrics. But colonial demand for wearing apparel was so great that garment-related industries were among the earliest to develop and the largest employers.

Millers set up carding and fulling operations to process wool before and after it was spun at home. Often their payment was in kind. Gradually some millers found it economic to organize spinning and weaving at their establishments and began selling woollen cloth. Payment was still often in kind. Early woollen mills were scattered through the central provinces – Cobourg and Sherbrooke were important early locations – but a major centre developed along the banks of the Mississippi River in Lanark County west of Ottawa. The region featured excellent mill sites in good sheep-raising country peopled by skilled Scots weavers; there was good access to markets in Montreal and the lumbering regions. James Rosamond made a particular success of the transition from general milling to woollen manufacture, employing fifteen men in his Carleton Place "cloth manufactory" by 1851 and thirty in his new mill at Almonte a decade later. Almonte on the Mississippi became the metropolis of the industry, priding itself as the Manchester of Canada (even though it wove woollens, not cottons).

As with paper-making, secure markets were crucial to the woollen manufacturer. Partnerships with drygoods merchants were common. Long before he became a wizard of railway finance, George Stephen made his first mark in Montreal as a risk-taker in textiles. During his early years he was a daring buyer abroad, but by the late 1850s he had sensed the growing popularity of Canadian-made tweeds. The doubling of the Rosamond mill's capacity was largely a result of Stephen's success in expanding the market as their selling agent. In 1866 he became a partner in their business. Stephen and his Montreal associates, including Donald Smith, became enthusiastic investors in other woollen mills, buying into both the Cobourg and Sherbrooke establishments. The limited liability company was an appropriate instrument for a joint venture between founding millers and merchant investors. The Rosamond Woollen Company, Bennett Rosamond (the founder's son) president, was formed in 1870 with a capitalization of $300,000, most of which came from the Montreal merchants.

Entrepreneurs began probing the possibilities of cotton in the mid-1840s. The British North American Cotton Company, "being in possession of the most perfect machinery," started production at St. Athenase on the Richelieu about 1845 to "indulge the belief that the Public will appreciate the advantages of consuming a superior article manufactured in this Province, thereby avoiding the Duties, Freights, &c of importation." Of course the raw cotton had to be imported. The only article the mill produced was cotton wadding (probably used as stuffing in quilts), and it did not survive. Other early mills in Sherbrooke, Montreal, Thorold, and Dundas also limped badly. But in the 1860s the disruption caused by the American Civil War temporarily reduced competition in the cheaper lines. In 1861 a leading Saint John, New Brunswick, drygoods merchant and shipowner, William Parks, expanded into manufacturing by setting up the New Brunswick Cotton Mill. The same Montrealers who saw the opportunities in woollens quickly became interested in cottons: in 1872 George Stephen, Donald Smith, Bennett Rosamond, and Hugh Allan were leading founders of the Canada Cotton Manufacturing Company in Cornwall, Ontario. Drygoods men launched two more big mills in Montreal in the next two years.

Housewife manufacture from homespun or store-bought ingredients had its limits. Ordinary boots and shoes were not easy to make; nor were many kinds of shirts, hats, heavy coats, gloves, and fine garments. Most unmarried men needed ready-made clothing; many others preferred it. Any tailor could become a clothing manufacturer, without mechanization, by expanding production. He could hire help for his shop or he could put out or subcontract jobs to women working in their homes. A merchant could similarly organize manufacturing to supply him with clothing for his store or wholesale warehouse. The advent of the sewing machine in the 1840s and 1850s had mixed effects on the industry. It could be used at home, in factories, or not at all. The largest clothing manufacturing firm in the provinces, Moss Brothers, who employed eight hundred people making shirts in the mid-1850s, boasted that all their stock was "hand wrought." English Jews who came to Montreal in 1856, the Mosses started as retailers and importers and integrated into manufacturing. They also exported through family connections to Australia. Other Montreal manufacturers came in all shapes and sizes, some exporting, some shipping to other cities and towns in the provinces, others retailing through their own local outlets.

Machinery led to sharper differentiation among manufacturers in boots and shoes and woollens. Footwear production developed from skilled cobblers and shoemakers doing custom jobs ("bespoke work") in domestic workrooms. Some began to make boots and shoes in assorted sizes for retail sale; some merchants began to market footwear wholesale. Some tanners began making boots and shoes, often along with saddles and harnesses. In the late 1840s shoe manufacturers who could afford new machinery achieved huge advantages in productivity. Two young immigrants from Massachusetts, Champion Brown and W.S. Childs, rent asunder the shoemaking fraternity in Montreal in 1849 by slashing prices thanks to their leather-rolling machinery. Brown and Childs survived a four-month strike by a quickly formed Journeymen Shoemakers' Society and soon became the largest shoe manufacturers in the city, employing three hundred and fifty hands in 1864. By then, development of sole-sewing machines made it efficient to concentrate shoemaking in steam-driven factories. In the early 1860s the four or five biggest shoe manufacturers in Montreal did several million dollars' worth of business annually and were trying to export. The sewn-garment industry never became as concentrated because of ease of entry and the lack of economies of scale. But the invention of knitting machines, which came to the provinces in the late 1850s and 1860s, made it economical for some manufacturers to make underwear, stockings, scarves, and other woollen garments in knitting mills.

The demand for other homely goods, ranging from nails and knives through kettles, scythes, and stoves, was constant and could not be met by household producers. Imports of British hardware were always substantial, ranking next to drygoods in importance. But colonial manufacture of iron products dated from the French regime and the troubled beginnings of the St. Maurice forges. Throughout the early nineteenth century, men interested in iron – blacksmiths, founders, hardware merchants, railway mechanics, and handy farmers – tried to cater to the changing needs of the home market. By the 1870s substantial foundries and machine shops and engine works could be found in many British North American cities, the railways operated huge manufacturing and repair shops, and the production of sophisticated agricultural implements was becoming a major industry. Early in that decade the first Canadian steel works almost came into production in Nova Scotia.

There were various iron deposits in the provinces. Most of the early production was based on small surface findings of pig iron that could be worked with simple charcoal furnaces, such as those at St. Maurice. By adding wood-fired forges or foundries next to the furnaces it was relatively easy to produce iron utensils for sale on nearby markets. So the earliest ironworks tended to be fully integrated, manufacturing raw iron into kettles, stoves, bedsteads, and other simple household products.

At the Conquest the St. Maurice forges were the only significant manufacturing industry in New France. The new crown leased them to various syndicates of private entrepreneurs, most of whom failed. Toward the end of the eighteenth century the forges seem to have reached their maximum production, employing four to eight hundred men for seven months of the year in mining, wood-cutting, smelting, forging, and casting near Trois-Rivières. Many workers lived at the site in company housing; many more were farmers or wood-cutters working seasonally. Production was never very large – perhaps a thousand stoves a year plus other products – but the quality of the iron was reasonably good and there were occasional exports of bar and pig iron and finished products. At best, profits reached about $20,000 annually. For half a century, from 1793 to 1843, the principal lessee was Matthew Bell, a high-living Scotsman who became a grand seigneur of the area and was more innovative as a horse-racer and fox hunter (he raised his own foxes for the Club Tally-Ho's annual hunt) than as an iron manufacturer. In 1846 the crown sold the forges to the highest bidder for $25,000.

Others tried to make iron at several locations in both Upper and Lower Canada in the early 1800s. The most persistent was a young iron-founder from New York, Joseph Van Norman. In 1824 he bought a broken-down furnace in Norfolk County after an Englishman had abandoned it, with partners invested $8,000 in the works, and began producing stoves, kettles, and other ironwares for sale along the Lake Erie shore and into the southwestern peninsula. One of Van Norman's partners, George Tillson, sold out about 1825 and established his own Dereham Forges at a site that gradually grew into the village of Tillsonburg (Van Norman's establishment became Normandale). Tillson discovered that sawmilling and land development were more profitable than iron moulding, but Van Norman diversified in iron, becoming involved with a forge in Port Dover and a foundry in York. When the ore and fuel at Normandale gave out, he moved on in 1847 and bought the bankrupt ironworks at Marmora, near Belleville, which dated from the 1830s. Van Norman was no more successful than previous owners with the high sulphur ore; there was no use making even fairly high quality iron if it could not be priced lower than cheap British wares being brought up through the canal system. Van Norman finally returned to Norfolk County, got a contract to make iron for wheels for the Great Western, and had to abandon $30,000 worth of works when the iron could not meet quality standards. He moved to Tillsonburg and became a road-builder and brick-maker.

Some of the half-dozen other failed founders lacked technical ability; others' costs of production were impossibly high. It was not easy to get skilled, reliable labour. When the General Mining Association, which was developing the coalfields of Nova Scotia, tried an experiment in iron-making in 1829, the experienced furnace-man brought out from Britain had great difficulty making acceptable iron. Then, in W.J.A. Donald's summary, "After fifty tons had been made, the men got drunk one night and left the furnace to take care of itself, which it did for all time to come. In the morning the furnace was cold and the metal a solid mass." Even the semi-successful operations at St. Maurice and Normandale were limited by low ore reserves and their voracious appetites for hardwood charcoal. No iron industry could survive on bog ore: the deposits were too small. There was no coal or accessible high-grade ore in Ontario or Quebec, and as yet no possibility of importing these. The intriguing aspect of the works at Londonderry, Nova Scotia, which operated on a typically small scale from 1850, was that they were close to the coal areas of Cumberland and Pictou counties. In the early 1870s a Steel Company of Canada was formed to buy the works, buy some mines, and begin making steel by the ultra-modern Siemens open-hearth process, overseen by Siemens himself. The method and the company failed, apparently because the ore was hard to smelt. Londonderry iron production continued.

Many blacksmiths and founders made iron goods from imported British bar and pig iron or from melted-down scrap iron. In Montreal in the 1790s an ambitious artisan, John Bigelow, bought big iron hoops to feed the American nail machine he had imported. He headed his nails by hand, passed the business to his son – in 1839 it was the City Nail and Spike Works, employing twenty men on five machines – and it eventually descended through mergers, combinations, et cetera, into today's Steel Company of Canada. In the late 1820s in Saint John, New Brunswick, two skilled edge-tool makers (i.e., blacksmiths with a specialty), James Harris and Thomas Allan, pooled $5,000 to set up a tool works, retail hardware store, and the province's first foundry. Nails, mill castings, and Franklin stoves were the staples of a business that grew steadily despite disastrous fires. Stoves were also the staple of the little business Edward and Charles Gurney, iron-moulders of Utica, New York, began in Hamilton, Canada West, in 1843. They started with $2,800, two employees, and an output of two stoves a day, and almost went under. But Edward was a shrewd, unusually hard-working foundryman who saw the need for patented stove designs, entered into good partnerships, and by the mid-1850s was managing a $200,000 business and still growing. Dozens of other smiths and moulders and founders ran local works or foundries, a few flourishing, some making ends meet, many failing and drifting into other lines of work.

The coming of the steamboat created a sudden colonial market for major machinery. Montreal's big foundries, the St. Mary's and the Eagle, grew up on the demand for marine engines and then diversified into a full line of iron goods. Steamship demand fed other manufacturers, including E.E. Gilbert's Beaver Foundry and Bartley and Dunbar's St. Lawrence Engine Works. By the early 1850s Montreal also had several nail and spike and saw and axe factories – T.D. Bigelow's was still the largest – plus specialized metal-working companies such as the Montreal Brass Works (household fittings) and the Novelty Iron Works (machinery for bakers and confectioners).

Then the coming of the railway meant a large demand for iron wheels, fittings for cars, iron rails (or iron strips over wooden rails), locomotive parts, and whole locomotives. There was little standardization in the early railway years and much equipment failure. As with steamboats, maintenance and manufacturing went hand in hand; most equipment was custom made or re-made. The big Montreal foundries had little difficulty making new steam engines. The iron horses were so small and weak, little more than boilers on wheels, that any established founder could put one together. James Good of Toronto may have been the first off the mark in British North America with his 1853 completion of the *Toronto* for the Northern Railway. He built nine twenty-five-ton locomotives for the Northern at an average price of $5,000.

Some of the Montreal foundries also built locomotives in the 1850s. In Kingston James Morton followed literally in the footsteps of the Molsons: from an apprenticeship in Thomas Molson's brewery and distillery, he became proprietor of his own Kingston Brewery and Distillery (specializing in Morton's proof whisky), and in the late 1850s bought a marine engine foundry which he turned into the Kingston Locomotive Works. Morton lacked the Molsons' business sense and entered into particularly disastrous agreements with Isaac Buchanan. Several locomotives and the furniture in his mansion ("Mortonwood") were eventually auctioned to reduce his debts. The works continued, when there was business. John Molson, Junior, and George Stephen were among the Montreal investors who reorganized them in 1864.

Iron-founders began to integrate back into rolling mills in the late 1850s. A Montreal nail-maker, Mansfield Holland, built the city's first rolling mill, lost control of it to his creditors, then built another mill a few years later on commission from merchants who had prospered as saw and axe manufacturers. A competing nail-man added a third rolling mill. Melted scrap was the usual raw material. In the Toronto Rolling Mills, founded by David Macpherson and Casimir Gzowski in 1860, worn and twisted iron rails were re-rolled into reusable track. No Canadian mill could roll new rails competitively with British imports.

The railway companies' repair shops gave them a nucleus of skilled labour and physical plant. Many outside contractors, like Van Norman, proved unreliable. So the Great Western in Hamilton and the Grand Trunk at Point St. Charles in Montreal established their own car shops, then locomotive works, and then rolling mills. There were lesser works at London on the Great Western and Brantford and Toronto on the Grand Trunk. To us it seems like Toonerville manufacturing: the Great Western's locomotive superintendent reported of the first engine, "the Framing has been made by ourselves from our own scrap iron, the inside and outside connecting rods and the valve motion &c are made from worn out Lowmoor Tyres, and Piston Rods and Slide Bars we have made from old broken springs, and the greater part of the Cylinders consist of old Car Wheels, there being no better metal in the world for the purpose." In its time this was a proud account of an economical use of materials, reflecting cost-conscious standards of efficiency. The two large railways were not only the biggest equipment manufacturers in the country, but probably led the way in manufacturing methods, standardization, and accounting procedures.

Like the Molsons, many iron-founders withdrew from railway work as the company shops grew and the boom of the 1850s subsided. Some adjusted to meet a less spectacular producer demand for iron goods, but one that enjoyed steady growth from the 1840s. This was the farmers' love affair with agricultural implements.

Until the late 1840s, farmers' simple needs for ploughs, scythes, axes, kettles, and other basic tools were met by local blacksmiths and small founders. Expansive farmers cultivated more acres by hiring more labourers and using more horse power. Labour was always expensive. A few mechanically inclined farmers who wanted more "labour-saving devices" enjoyed tinkering around the barnyard with ploughs, cutting tools, rakes, and old wheels. Daniel Massey, founder of Canada's best-known manufacturing dynasty, had an unusually well-developed interest in reducing labour costs because as a young man in Northumberland County, Upper Canada, in the 1820s he specialized in land-clearing: hiring up to one hundred labourers at a time to clear a tract, selling the timber, selling the land, moving on to more land. In the mid-1840s Massey began spending most of his time in a little repair shop on his own farm, then bought into a small foundry in the village of Newcastle, and ran it as a family business from 1849.

Like many other American-born farmers of Upper Canada, the Masseys paid little attention to the border. They often brought back the latest American farm tools, machines of rapidly increasing complexity and importance coming out of the harvesting revolution begun by McCormick and Hussey in the early 1830s. These horse-drawn inventions – reapers, mowers, rakes, seed drills, improved ploughs, and a bumper crop of other implements – were the first complex producers' goods to be made to standard designs and marketed widely. They were not particularly hard to manufacture, the ingenuity lying in the mechanical designs which were usually patented. As the American machines were perfected, as Upper Canadian farmers moved from pioneering hardship to relative prosperity in the late 1840s, and as railroads offered revolutionary distribution possibilities, a significant implement market emerged north of the border. In 1847 the *Canadian Economist* complained that agricultural implements had "but imperfectly engaged the attention of the manufacturers." Six years later a Toronto journalist noted that "manufactories of farmers' tools and implements have been established in all the principal towns and cities in Upper Canada. So great is the demand for improved machinery that even American manufacturers have set up branch establishments in Canada, with very profitable results."

Daniel Massey may have sold some American-made machines from his foundry. His son Hart, who joined the business in 1851, realized it was cheaper to manufacture themselves: they could save transportation and tariff costs and could use cheap British iron and good Canadian hardwood. In the early 1850s the Masseys began making Ketchum mowers and Burrell reapers, having bought Canadian patent rights from the American owners. This became the common practice in Canada. In time the more progressive manufacturers, such as the Masseys, added distinctive improvements.

Many early implement men were immigrants like the Masseys. The earliest American branch establishments have not been identified. In 1858 the Joseph Hall Company of Rochester, New York, attracted attention by taking over the Oshawa factory of a failed Canadian manufacturer; it made several lines of heavy farm implements, including its own Champion mower. Hall's Canadian production of more than seven hundred mowers in 1864, plus other machines, was very large. *

The Masseys and many of their competitors only gradually became specialists in agricultural implements. In 1857 Hart Massey's Newcastle Foundry and Machine Manufactory advertised its ability to make steam engines, brass and iron castings, stoves, and maple sap kettles, along with all varieties of agricultural machinery, including nine types of plough. It made 166 implements that year. In the early 1860s the Masseys dropped non-farm lines, called themselves the Newcastle Agricultural Works, and highlighted their "grass-cutting sensation of the 1860s," the patented Wood's mower.

Many early producers became best known for certain machines – the Veritys of Francestown for their ploughs, John Harris of Beamsville for the Kirby mower and reaper, Wisner and Son of Brantford for seed drills – but all of them still manufactured primarily for local needs. Now and then one would test a new

* The earliest known branch factory in Canada was the Toronto plant of Allcock, Laight and Company, British manufacturers of needles and fishing tackle, established in 1854.

market. In 1870, for example, W.J. Verity's father-in-law began importing Verity ploughs into Winnipeg via St. Paul and the Red River route; W.J. designed a special plough for heavy prairie sod that was soon selling well in the West. Competitors followed considerably later.

———◆———

Alert and agile entrepreneurs, sometimes foolish entrepreneurs headed for failure, experimented with many other kinds of manufacturing, making soap and sails, rope, rubberware, brooms and buttons, baskets and trunks, starch, stoves, sewing machines, pianos, and dozens of other products. Tobacco importers such as W.C. McDonald of Montreal began making their own plugs for chewing and cigars for smoking. (McDonald's plugs were identified by heart-shaped tin labels; his "tobacco with a heart" was an early triumph of branding and packaging. A tough Prince Edward Island Scot, who dealt almost entirely in cash as he built his business, McDonald himself despised all forms of the tobacco habit.) Consumers could not make their own white sugar, a purer, more attractive product than maple sugar, so John Redpath, who accumulated his first fortune as a canal builder, invested $200,000 in a huge seven-storey sugar refinery in Montreal in 1855. Redpath imported raw cane sugar from the West Indies in his own ships, had a healthy tariff advantage to refine in Canada, and sold barrels of refined sugar to the city's wholesale grocers. Within a year he employed more than one hundred hands; in five years he faced competition from a second refinery in the city, promoted by the Molsons.

Domestic food-processing was still primitive – local bakers making bread, local butchers and farmers making sausage, farmers selling butter and cheese at public markets or trading them with country storekeepers. But some interesting export possibilities developed. Ontario cheese-makers, working in farmyard cheese factories, made a good cheddar that the British liked; in the 1860s and 1870s provision merchants who bought in the countryside suddenly found they could export millions of pounds of cheese. In Toronto in the late 1850s a young English butcher and meat-curer, William Davies, noticed that a neighbour was shipping cured sides of pork to England and decided to try his luck too. Toronto area farmers fed their hogs a mash of whole peas, creating finer, leaner bacon than corn-fed American hogs. "I think you will say that the quality of the meat I sent is as good as you ever saw," Davies wrote his brother in England, who sold the experimental shipment in 1860. Within a year William Davies had erected in Toronto the first building in Canada for smoking and curing meats. Later in the 1860s he found he could improve his product and make money on by-products by buying hogs live and slaughtering them at his factory. Farmers began shipping live hogs to the innovative meat-packer in Toronto.

———◆———

Canadians were on the leading edge of innovation in another odd industry in the early 1860s. The "earth oils" in the black guck of the swamps and streams of Eniskillen Township, Lambton County (just west of London) had an increasing number of uses, as medicine, asphalt, lubricants, and, particularly after the development of kerosene by Nova Scotia's Abraham Gesner, among others, as illuminating fluids. Charles Tripp's International Mining and Manufacturing Company, which in 1854 began digging out the gum-like peat and trying to refine it, quickly failed. Others had better luck. A Hamilton carriage-maker, James Williams, took over Tripp's lands, became impatient with collection methods like using blankets to sop up the oil, and decided to increase his supply by digging a well. It was just like digging for water: you dug down, the oil seeped in, and you hauled it up in buckets. By 1857 or 1858 Williams had dug the world's first producing oil well and was refining the muck into illuminating oil. Americans, who were developing interesting deposits near Titusville, Ohio, were a smidgeon behind.

Like farmers searching for water, it was an easy step from digging wells to drilling them. Ram a metal-tipped hardwood pole into the ground, extend it as you go, use a cross-piece over it and human muscle-power (rather like a diving board) to give thrust. The boom at "Oil Springs" in the early 1860s saw about four hundred wells brought into production. Then in 1862 a solitary prospector who had drilled through 158 feet of rock hit the first "gusher" – oil that spewed to the surface without having to be pumped.

Suddenly Canada's problem was having too much oil. At times in 1862 a barrel of the refined product sold for 30 cents, the barrel being worth much more than the oil. (Wooden barrels were used; in 1862 a Toronto merchant, Lewis Samuel, tried exporting casks of oil to England. They swelled and burst on the trip, and the oil arrived in bulk.) Local men and American speculators rushed into the business anyway, buying land, drilling wells, setting up refineries, moving on to more extensive, deeper deposits a few miles away at Petrolia. But the instability of the industry was daunting: the price roller-coaster took the product to $6.50 a barrel by the end of October 1863, and back to $3.50 two months later. And there were real difficulties in keeping the foul-smelling, sulphurous Canadian product competitive with the clean, odourless fluid made in the big new Ohio and Pennsylvania oilfields. Canada was generally self-sufficient in its minuscule oil needs in the late nineteenth century and had occasional surpluses. But no significant new fields were developed in the young Dominion. By the 1870s Petrolia was exporting skilled oilmen to open new fields around the world; the United States was exporting oil.

Manufacturing developed fairly rapidly in the larger British North American provinces after mid-century. The market was so small, of course, that comparisons with the workshop of the world back home or the giant, chaotic republic to the south are completely inappropriate. By world standards the manufacturing achievements of British North America were insignificant. By the country's standards it was almost impressive that in the new Dominion of 1867 hundreds of manufacturers, some pitifully small, a few dozen employing hundreds of workers in huge factories, produced millions of dollars' worth of goods every year and gave work and wages to tens of thousands of artisans and labourers.

Montreal was the manufacturing as well as the commercial centre of Canada. By the late 1850s more than thirty factories lined the Lachine Canal. They employed more than two thousand people, and their products were shipped all over Canada via the Grand Trunk. "The sole difficulties with which they have to contend," it was observed in 1856, "are a restricted market, and the competition of the larger, wealthier, and longer established factories in other countries." Halifax and Saint John were also important manufacturing centres for their provinces. In Saint John before 1850 T.W. Acheson has counted twenty-four tanneries, sixteen flour mills, four iron foundries, two brass foundries, twelve furniture and eight carriage makers, four soap works, two breweries, a paper mill, and several minor industries. In Halifax in 1861 21.8 per cent of the labour force, 1,379 workers, were engaged in manufacturing.

There were clear signs, though, of a westward course in manufacturing growth. The farm implement industry was centred in Ontario because of the numbers and prosperity of the province's farmers. The Atlantic provinces did not have many farmers and Quebec did not have many prosperous ones. By mid-century Ontario's fertile soils supported thousands of farmers whose prosperity would stimulate many industries, beginning with implements. Montreal's prominence as a distribution centre, plus the skills of its merchants and the availability of low-cost labour attracted from rural Quebec, gave the city its early manufacturing growth. This would be difficult to sustain as the population and wealth of the western province continued to increase.

One important manufacturing industry in the east was beginning to falter, almost imperceptibly, by the end of the 1860s. We saw wooden shipbuilding in the Maritimes and Quebec mushroom as an adjunct of the timber trade to Britain. It continued to grow to meet waves of international demand created by the California gold rush and the Crimean War, and the colonial product evolved from floating timber rafts to some of the world's best and most beautiful clipper ships. But in the 1850s some of the patterns on which the industry was founded began to change. The square timber traffic began to decline. So did the immigrant trade into Quebec, and, when steam came to the St. Lawrence, so did the port of Quebec itself, which was replaced by Montreal as a transshipment centre and as Canada's steam- and marine-manufacturing centre. The competitive advantages of the colonial shipbuilding industry had included cheap wood and the timber and immigrant traffic. As these diminished, British North American shipwrights lost their edge on competitors in Britain and the United States. As iron hulls and steam engines became more important in ocean shipping, the expert wooden shipbuilders would soon be at a positive disadvantage.

Maritimers reacted to shrinking export opportunities by owning more ships themselves, and participating actively in both international commerce and the growing coastal trade. Their reckoning with steam and iron was postponed for the better part of a generation. The problems of Quebec shipyards were more serious, and by the late 1860s the industry was clearly declining. Innovative builders such as Henry Dinning responded by trying to build composite iron and wood hulls, or installing iron parts and engines produced in Charles William Carrier's Fonderie Canadienne in Lévis. Other regional entrepreneurs tried to revive the port by promoting improved railway connections with Montreal and central Canada, and by trying to develop a hinterland based on the Saguenay and Lac St. Jean regions. There was little hope that Canadian ocean shipbuilding could make an easy late-century transition to the world of iron, steel, and steam-driven vessels. On the Great Lakes it would be a different story.

In the 1960s and 1970s it was briefly fashionable among historians to try to explain the allegedly slow, unsatisfactory growth of manufacturing in nineteenth-century British North America. Had the northern provinces been caught in some kind of "staple trap," specializing in exporting primary products and thereby neglecting manufactures? Had merchants been imprisoned by their trader's mentality and failed to invest in the fixed plant required to develop industrial opportunities? Had the infant provincial banking system, geared to financing the needs of commerce, been an inadequate vehicle for providing long-term finance for manufacturing? And so on.

In fact there is no evidence that Canadian manufacturing development, given foreign competition and small provincial markets, was slow and unsatisfactory. Just the opposite is true: the speed and breadth of the development of domestic manufacturing by the Confederation years is surprising. Of course the colonial economy was created to exploit opportunities to export fish, furs, timber, and grain. But concentration on major opportunities did not mean that minor ones would be neglected. New men kept coming into the provinces to begin new industries – bringing capital like the Molsons and Gooderham and Worts, starting small without capital, like the Masseys. They joined men like George Stephen and Hugh Allan and Peter Redpath who had done well in traditional industries and eagerly invested in manufacturing. Merchants were no more opposed to industrial development in British North America than they were in the United States or Great Britain.

Some merchants were conservative, of course, tending to put their eggs in one basket and watch it. Many others invested in mills (the term "merchant miller" exactly catches the transformation), foundries, works, any kind of manufacturing likely to be profitable. The limited liability, joint-stock company was by the 1860s a well-understood way to organize capital-intensive new ventures. It gave investors more liquidity than they had in traditionally cumbersome partnerships or in distribution networks with permanent chains of credit. British North American merchants and manufacturers did so well at mobilizing capital through personal and family networks (and, for the big railway projects, on more developed financial markets abroad) that they did not yet need to create new institutions to mobilize investment capital.* Often manufacturers were able to finance expansion from their profits. From early in their history the chartered banks helped by automatically renewing short-term loans to manufacturers and making well-secured loans to merchants making new investments. No one has been able to specify any reasonable Canadian manufacturing opportunity that went neglected because merchants or bankers failed to provide needed capital.

———————————

The real problem in most lines of manufacturing, everyone realized, was how to cope with foreign competition in the small British North American market. Whether or not a market existed for domestic products depended on many factors: comparative raw material costs, labour costs, transportation, and so on. Most of these changed relatively slowly and could not easily be influenced by individual businessmen. One factor was different and has already been noticed in the growth of several industries. Taxes or tariffs or duties levied by governments on imports could have a direct, dramatic effect on prices. Given a high enough tariff, the cheapest foreign wine or widget could become so costly that domestic producers would be able to compete. You could do wondrous things with tariffs: create whole new home industries by a simple tax increase – or, the other side of the coin, wipe them out by adopting free trade. In an era when Canada's governments levied few other imposts, taxed neither incomes nor profits, and did not have much money with which to subsidize or massage private business, tariffs were the variable to conjure with.

Great Britain gave her North American colonies the right to set their own tariffs in 1846. The old imperial tariffs were aimed at maximizing imperial trade (according to mercantilist assumptions about keeping wealth in the family) and raising revenue for the crown. These duties influenced the development of provincial manufacturing industries from the beginning. Duties on spirits had helped make the distilling industry viable. Tariffs of 15 to 30 per cent against American manufactured goods in the 1820s significantly raised their cost. Well before Britain surrendered control of the tariff, colonial producers began petitioning for higher

———————————

* A Montreal sewing-machine manufacturer described his firm's refinancing in 1872: "We had either to shut up or extend and try to get a larger market. I went round to capitalists and showed them my position. We are the largest industry in Montreal. We are engaged in foundry and and wood-work, japanning and sewing machines. I showed them that unless I was able to get them to engage up here with me in this particular branch of business I should be compelled to shut up here and go to the States. I showed them that by manufacturing largely and competing this manufacture would sell well in the foreign markets, and would give a profit with a new tariff." He got his money.

duties to protect them from competition, usually American. The producers included farmers, artisans, and some of the earliest manufacturers. In the 1830s the Assembly of Upper Canada tried to build walls against American farm products and iron goods. In Britain, on the other hand, the triumph of laissez-faire economics caused Parliament steadily to reduce tariffs. In the mid-1840s the mother country opted for free trade and gave its self-governing colonies a free hand to set their own tariffs. Every reduction of imperial tariffs caused colonial protests.

Individual producers wanted protection, but colonial consumers found the low prices of free trade alluring. Import merchants had a natural bias toward free trade, as did exporters who did not want to be taxed in other countries. The prospect that tariff wars might create impossibly high barriers to trade naturally encouraged governments to try to make trade agreements or treaties. By 1851 the British North American provinces had agreed to trade natural (i.e., relatively unprocessed) products freely among themselves. In 1854 a Reciprocity Treaty with the United States was negotiated that created similar free trade across the borders.

Neither of these agreements covered manufactured products. Both before and after Confederation governments looked to customs duties for most of their revenue, so they had to levy some tariffs. In 1847 the British North American provinces established a general tariff of about 7.5 per cent on imports. By 1849 it had risen to 12.5 per cent under the twin pressures of revenue needs and demands for what the *Montreal Gazette* called "incidental protection." The huge increase in U.S. trade during reciprocity did not create a movement for lower tariffs on manufactured products. In 1856 Montreal manufacturers, flexing their muscles, began lobbying for higher tariffs to give them more of the domestic market. A year or two later, during a sharp commercial depression, they lobbied for still higher tariffs, now out of a need to protect existing markets. The Cayley-Galt tariff increases of 1857–58 brought the general level of duties up to 20 per cent, partly in response to the manufacturers' considerable lobbying.

The idea of using tariffs to nurture Canadian manufacturing gradually became an articulated ideology. Various journalists and business spokesmen, most notably the Hamilton wholesaler, Isaac Buchanan, picked up and publicized the protectionist doctrines being preached by such foreign publicists of tariff-induced industrialization as Henry C. Carey in the United States and Friedrich List in Germany. Protectionists promoted a cluster of partly consistent doctrines, some of which took deep root in the Canadian psyche. Many of their ideas echoed a mercantilism most fully seen in Canada in the days of Jean Talon and the bureaucrats who hoped to create industrial diversification in New France.

It was good and natural for a country to have a variety of industries, argued Buchanan and the members of his Association for the Promotion of Canadian Industry. Labour-intensive manufacturing industries were "better" than primary industries, partly because the citizens of a country with lively home manufacturing would not be forced to become hewers of wood and drawers of water. Instead they could choose from a variety of occupations. A growing industrial sector in the economy would provide home markets for farmers' products; flourishing agriculturalists would consume the products of domestic factories. Wealth would be kept in the country, instead of being paid out to foreign producers. If weak, infant industries were given the nourishment of tariff protection, they were bound to grow strong, compete with one another (thus keeping prices down), and gradually emerge to compete on a larger international stage. The natural, organic development of a community was from crude staple production through secondary manufacturing. The growth of manufacturing was evidence of proper national development, growing up. Nations without manufacturing industries could never be mature, whole, or wealthy.

The Confederation movement was already well under way when the Americans decided in 1865 to abrogate the Reciprocity Treaty. The news helped weaken the opposition to Confederation, if only because a united province would have more bargaining power with the United States. A few Maritimers with interests in the coalfields of Nova Scotia thought that Confederation might lead to increased intercolonial trade and industrialization based on their coal. Some central Canadian manufacturers eyed the fairly prosperous Maritime market. Otherwise the manufacturing-protectionist "interest" played little role in Confederation. Even the idea of stimulating east-west trade as an alternative to free trade with the United States was seldom emphasized during the Confederation period because most colonial politicians still dreamed of renewing reciprocity. For manufacturers in Ontario and Quebec the main tariff consequence of Confederation was a slight downward adjustment in 1866, brought in partly to equalize tariffs across the provinces, partly because Galt, the Minister of Finance, believed in maximum trade liberalization. The manufacturers, particularly the iron interests in Montreal, were not pleased.

But the 1860s were generally a decade of expansion for manufacturers, many of whom profited immensely from the American descent into civil war. The disruption of southern cotton production meant a golden fleece for the woollen industry, for example. The Union's manufacturers turned to war production in a climate of rampant inflation and had few surpluses to export to the British provinces. Soaring demand in the war-ravaged country sucked in huge amounts of British North American wood and farm products and even manufactured goods, despite the end of reciprocity. After the Civil War and in the first few years of Confederation, Canadian textile manufacturers and iron producers were particularly optimistic; old mills were recapitalized as public companies, new ones were launched. The Montreal Rolling Mills surfaced from an important merger and recapitalization in 1868, and in the early 1870s Montreal capitalists financed the Dominion's two largest textile mills at Hochelaga and Valleyfield. In 1871 the Pillow-Hersey rolling mills and foundry in Montreal made a 106 per cent profit on its invested capital.

These manufacturers still had substantial protection and did not want to do without it. George Stephen wrote Macdonald that he believed in low tariffs on principle, but "as a manufacturer could not be expected violently to oppose a policy which would tend to secure the more complete control of our own market for my products." Ordinary Canadians would probably have preferred a wide amount of reciprocity with the United States, leading to low prices. The freer the trade the better. But that could not be achieved because the Americans had become protectionist, building higher and higher barriers against Canadian exports. In the early 1870s the Macdonald government considered extending protection, particularly to the Maritime collieries, but also to all industries on an across-the-board or "national" basis. Macdonald wrote a business acquaintance that "a cry for readjustment for Revenue purposes, but affording incidental protection to our own manufactures & products, would go down well," and told his friend David Macpherson before the 1872 election that "our game is to coquet with the Protectionists. The word 'protection' itself must be tabooed, but we can ring the changes on a National Policy – paying the United States in their own coin – incidental protection, etc. etc. etc." In these good times, with domestic production matching total Canadian consumption in so many industries, there seemed no particular urgency about more protection, though, and the lobby was quiet.

An international financial panic in 1873 marked the beginning of five years of severe trade retrenchment, falling prices, and increased international competition in an atmosphere of rapid technological change and transportation improvement. Almost overnight many Canadian manufacturers found their markets threatened by American and British imports. Big, efficient producers in those countries exploited falling transportation costs and the extension of the railway network to try to find new markets or at least dump surplus stock at cut prices. Wave after wave of failures, closings, and layoffs savaged the ranks of Canadian producers. Every significant industry suffered except farm implements, which was still growing to meet unsatisfied agricultural demand. There were very hard times in Canada. "Do you think there will ever again be good times?" a prominent Montreal businessman asked one of his financial friends in 1878.

Protectionist sentiment revived with a vengeance. Parliamentarians who investigated the condition of the Dominion's manufacturing industries and the causes of the depression faced witnesses from industry after industry demanding more protection. New organizations were formed to spread the gospel of protection. The most important was the Ontario Manufacturers' Association, created in 1874 and renamed the Canadian Manufacturers' Association within a decade. Printing presses spewed protectionist literature. Money was available to advance the cause.

The shrill platitudes and convoluted metaphors of protectionist rhetoric were not nearly as important in the debate as the relationship between tariff protection and jobs. Big manufacturers employed hundreds of workers; even medium-sized ones employed dozens. Unemployed labourers and artisans posed many problems, social and political. Sometimes they even demonstrated in the streets, demanding work or bread. One big public meeting of workmen in Montreal in the winter of 1876 was read a letter from George Stephen supporting their demand for job-creating tariffs. Robert Hay, the furniture man in Toronto, had cut his workforce in half and was about to go into politics to get more protection. E.B. Eddy in Ottawa had to suspend payments to his creditors, and declared he could not compete with American wood products. Dozens of other manufacturers across the Dominion were in similar straits, laying off workers, cutting wages, demanding that government come to their aid.

Alexander Mackenzie's Liberal government inclined to doctrinaire free trade beliefs, including a laissez-faire view of the functions of government. The Finance Minister, Sir Richard Cartwright (grandson of the pioneer Kingston merchant), was particularly determined that the state not become involved in propping up ineffi-cient or incompetent firms. He saw no reason why government should tax 95 per cent of the public for the sake of 5 per cent. He would not rob the taxpayers, Cartwright said, "and in particular I decline to do it on behalf of the poor and needy manufacturers who occupy those squalid hovels which adorn the suburbs of Montreal, Hamilton, and every city of the Dominion."

The Conservatives had no such hesitancy about using the power of government to shape the economy and nourish an important (and often highly concentrated) voting interest. When Cartwright refused to bend to pressures for a general tariff increase in his 1876 budget, Macdonald committed his party to a "readjustment of the tariff" which would "not only tend to alleviate the stagnation of business . . . but also afford fitting encouragement and protection to the struggling manufacturers and industries, as well as to the agricultural products of the country."

Prominent manufacturers lined up with the interventionist Conservatives against the laissez-faire Liberals in the 1878 general election. The Tories were fully committed to what Macdonald now called a "National Policy" of aiding home manufactures. His speeches raised issues of employment policy, national develop-ment, and the need for diversification, that would be central to debates on Canadian economic policy and business development for more than a century:

> We have no manufactures here. We have no work-people; our work-people have gone off to the United States. They are to be found employed in the Western States, in Pittsburg, and, in fact, in every place where manufac-tures are going on. These Canadian artizans are adding to the strength, to the power, and to the wealth of a foreign nation instead of adding to ours. Our work-people in this country, on the other hand are suffering for want of employment. Have not their cries risen to Heaven? Has not the hon. the premier been surrounded and beseiged, even in his own Department, and on his way to his daily duties, by suffering artizans who keep crying out: "We are not beggars, we only want an opportunity of helping to support ourselves and our families . . . ."

When the depression is over and times become prosperous, there will be found manufactories in the United States where men will be required to work. The manufactories, and the men are there, but we have not got them here. If we had a protective system in this country, if we had a developed capital, we could, by giving our manufacturers a reasonable hold on our home trade, attain a higher position among the nations. If our factories were fenced round to a certain extent with protection . . . and [we] impose a tariff such as the necessities of Canada may demand, our national prosperity would be enhanced . . . .

No nation has arisen which had only agriculture as its industry. There must be a mixture of industries to bring out the national mind and the national strength and to form a national character. . . . We must, by every reasonable means, employ our people, not in one branch of industry, not merely as farmers, as tillers of the soil, but we must bring out every kind of industry, we must develop the minds of the people and their energies. Every man is not fitted to be a farmer, to till the soil; one man has a constructive genius, another is an artist, another has an aptitude for trade, another is a skilful mechanic – all these men are to be found in a nation, and, if Canada has only one branch of industry to offer them, if these men cannot find an opportunity in their own country to develop the skill and genius with which God has gifted them, they will go to a country where their abilities can be employed, as they have gone from Canada to the United States. . . .

It was grievous to see in Toronto last year, the employés of Messrs. Robert Hay & Co. working at half time, or quarter time, and many dismissed to fight the battle of life as best they could; those, of course being the least competent, and, therefore, the least able to provide for themselves. You saw whole tons of goods marked to be sold for what they would fetch. The sweepings of the manufactories of Buffalo were sold in our markets to crush our people. It was a grievous thing to see, and that was not only one trade, but it applied to every trade in Canada.

Manufacturers contributed campaign funds to the Conservatives in the 1878 election. Some were said to have urged their workers to vote Conservative. Bennett Rosamond, the wool king of Almonte, issued detailed denials of charges of intimidating his workers, but Donald McInnes, one of the textile kings of Cornwall, admitted candidly to Sir John A. that his workers "are all under my thumb." Formerly Liberal manufacturers, such as Robert Hay in Toronto, ran as Conservative candidates. The Liberals were discredited with other groups of voters for other reasons (distillers and brewers, for example, were very worried about the growing, Liberal-backed temperance movement). The Conservatives and their National Policy of stimulating manufacturing with higher tariffs won a resounding victory in the 1878 election.

The triumph of protectionism reflected the powerful appeal of manufacturing in the nineteenth century. Factories gave communities so much employment that they seemed as beneficial as railways. They were seen as agents of progress and prosperity in communities hungry for development. Just as it seemed to be in the public interest to spend taxpayers' money to subsidize railways, surely it was in the public interest to use the power of the state to levy taxes to foster factories. The argument seemed to hold in good times and bad: infant industries needed tariff food to nourish them when healthy and tariff medicine to protect them when sick. There were so many infant industries – there had been so much manufacturing development – by the onset of the depression of the 1870s, that the manufacturers were, as Ben Forster has described them, an "ascending elite." During the hard times they turned to government and got the support they wanted.

A skeptical observer of this business ascendency, A. Skaife, argued at the time that it was a remarkable legitimization of self-interest:

> A brutal outcry would be raised were one individual, or one branch of industry, to demand the exclusion from the country of foreign goods competing with theirs, because they were sold too cheap; but when a great number of widely different interests, spread over the whole country, unite in asking for the same thing, and do it in the name of their destitute work-people, the effect is very different, the demand savours less of monopoly, and it can easily be made to appear that the welfare of the whole Dominion is identified with that of her manufacturers.

Skaife was right. The ambiguities of tariff policy were stunning. The ascendant manufacturers and their worried work people had persuaded the state to rig the business environment in favour of their industries and their incomes. The Canadian consumer would foot the bill, paying the price of protection. It happened in the United States a decade earlier. In Canada the desire to create a great industrial country like the United States was overwhelming. The Canadians believed protection for their manufacturers was the best way to avoid becoming or remaining a nation of hewers of wood and drawers of water, of farmers, fishermen, and fur traders.

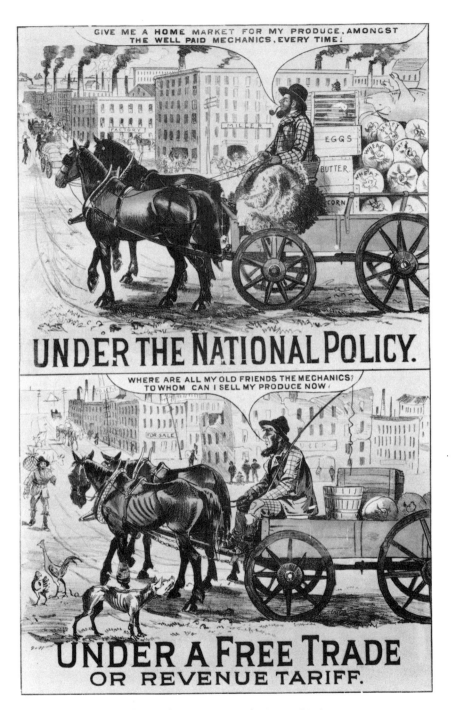

Protectionist propaganda *(NSL Archive)*

THE MANUFACTURERS'

⟶❖ LIFE ❖⟵

Insurance Co.

ACCIDENT

Insurance Co.

HEAD OFFICE: TRADERS' BANK BUILDING, YONGE STREET, TORONTO

CAPITAL, $2,000,000,00 and $1,000,000,00 Respectively.

President:
Rt. Hon. Sir John A. Macdonald, G.C.B., P.C.,

Vice-Presidents:
GEO. GOODERHAM, (GOODERHAM & WORTS, Limited).
WM. BELL Organ Manufacturer, Guelph.
S. F. McKINNON, Wholesale Merchant, Toronto.

Medical Directors:
JAMES F. W. ROSS, M. D., L. R. C. P., Eng.　　　P. J. STRATHY, M. D., M. R. C. S., Eng.

Consulting Actuary:
D. PARKES FACKLER, New York.

These Companies having two separate and distinct charters, Stock Capital, Government Deposits, &c., can issue a combination of Life and Accident Insurance, never before presented to the insuring public, and which can be issued by no other company in this or any other country unless so constituted. To professional men and all others who are likely to incur serious pecuniary inconvenience when laid aside by any casualty, such policies are calculated to prove a great boon. They afford more complete protection than life policies alone, at a very small additional cost, and may be applied to all plans of life insurance.

J. K. McCUTCHEON, Inspector of Agencies,　　　W. H. HOLLAND, General Superintendent.
G. A. STERLING,　　　J. P. MARTIN, Cashiers.

JOHN F. ELLIS, Managing Director.

Sir John A. Macdonald as president of the Manufacturers' insurance companies, 1891
(Manufacturers Life Insurance Company)

10

Moving Money:
The Growth of Financial Services

*Generalists, specialists, and absconders . . . development of the banking
system . . . the "monetary King" of Canada . . . origins of the Bank
Act . . . emergence of big banks . . . "runs" and failures . . . survival of
private banks . . . savings and loan companies . . . preaching the gospel of
life insurance . . . globetrotting insurance missionaries . . . stockbrokers,
the MSE and TSE . . . insider deals necessary and normal . . . the rise of
George Cox . . . Winnipeg's "bank with gold doors"*

One stop at a financial "general store" gave most Canadians all the services
they needed in the mid-nineteenth century. Consider this 1856 advertisement
by a broker/agent/private banker:

John Cameron, Banker
Stocks and Money Broker
Wellington Street Toronto
Cash advances made on produce
Provincial and Municipal Debentures Negotiated
Bank and Other Stocks Bought and Sold
Money raised upon mortgage securities
Agents for London Eagle Life Insurance Co.

There were four or five offices like Cameron's in Toronto and more in smaller
centres lacking competition from chartered banks. On the other side of the
continent, for example, in the awakening village of Victoria, Vancouver Island,
a Scots newcomer, Alexander David MacDonald, decided there was financial
business to be done and in 1859 opened a bank. MacDonald's Bank was a
private institution, backed solely by MacDonald's reputation. It exchanged
currency, shipped gold dust, took deposits, acted as agent for a San Francisco
express company, and issued its own notes – signed by Alexander David Mac-
Donald. It was the first enterprise in western Canada to be called a bank.

MacDonald's business grew nicely, and came to include a branch in the booming Cariboo mining town of Barkerville. His troubles began in 1862 when a chartered bank opened in Victoria. It was the Bank of British Columbia, incorporated in London, England, by capitalists interested in the banking opportunities provided by the Pacific coast mining boom. The Bank of British Columbia had an authorized capital of £250,000 and prominent, well-connected directors. Soon after its appearance in the colony the local legislature passed regulations governing banking, trying to protect the public from fly-by-night "bankers." MacDonald was partially grandfathered by the act, but needed a corporate charter to keep issuing notes. He was planning to get one when his Victoria office was robbed of more than $25,000 in gold and the notes of other banks. The news caused a run on the Barkerville branch; MacDonald, who was there, stayed open, redeemed all the notes presented to him, and restored confidence in his bona fides. A few months later in Victoria, MacDonald found himself pressed by creditors, could not recoup his losses, and decided that it was prudent to leave a colony in which it was still possible to send debtors to jail. He slipped aboard a steamer for California and disappeared. Many of the notes of western Canada's first bank found a final resting place papering the walls of Loring's saloon in Barkerville.

MacDonald's resources were too small to withstand theft and competition from a banking corporation. The Bank of British Columbia almost immediately found itself too big to survive in a weak little colony. Within a year its charter was amended to permit operations in the United States. Soon the Bank of British Columbia's most profitable branches were in San Francisco and Portland, Oregon. The Victoria branch suffered huge losses when the mining boom went bust. In the 1870s and 1880s the British Columbia business gradually overshadowed the foreign branches, not least because of agency work for the provincial government; but through its life the Bank of British Columbia remained a Pacific coast bank. The company's unusual managerial structure of an arch-conservative board in England (who objected, for example, to receiving letters written on typewriters) and semi-independent, often too-liberal branch managers six thousand miles away, did not work very well. Faced with stagnation and decline as the eastern banks invaded British Columbia in the late 1890s, the first Bank of British Columbia merged with the Canadian Bank of Commerce in 1900 and disappeared.

Chartered banks had so many advantages over unincorporated private suppliers of banking services that their dominance in a locality was only a matter of time and growth. Private bankers were often first in the field, but when a community could generate enough business to support an agency and then a branch of a chartered bank, one or other of the closest regional banks would move in. If none of them thought a town was ready for a branch, some of the more aggressive local merchants, perhaps in partnership with a private banker, would form a company, sell shares to raise capital, get a charter from Parliament, and start their own bank.

Other kinds of financial services also came to be offered by specialized firms. Mortgage loan companies met a demand for property-based loans considered inappropriate (and made illegal) for the chartered banks to offer. As aggressive salesmen convinced Canadians to invest in life insurance, distinctively Canadian life insurance companies emerged to compete with the foreign agents operating in the country. By the end of the nineteenth century trust companies were being chartered for estate and other specialized fiduciary work. Private bankers survived in many localities, but many had narrowed their business to selling life insurance, real estate, offering bookkeeping or accounting services, or, particularly in Toronto and Montreal, stock brokerage. Stock exchanges in the two cities had overcome somewhat erratic beginnings and were in full operation. Some brokers were beginning to specialize in stocks or bonds.

The growth of specialized financial services was clearly related to a view of the corporation as an instrument created for a specific purpose. Promoters who hoped to do a general financial business through a corporate vehicle were rebuffed. In 1835 the British Colonial Secretary, Lord Glenelg, offered a classic objection to an Upper Canadian statute incorporating a combined life insurance and trust company:

> It appears that this Bill establishes a corporate body for three distinct objects – the effecting of Life Insurance, the receiving of deposits for accumulation and the acceptance and execution of trusts. These objects, if not, strictly speaking, compatible with each other, could scarcely be carried on so as not to involve the corporation in many dangers and embarrassments. I do not here refer to the circumstance that the time and thought of the Directors would be distracted by their attention to so many branches of commerce (though that is no immaterial circumstance), but rather to the blending together of funds, which justice to the parties concerned and the public's security would alike require to be kept distinct. The trust moneys might be applied to pay off Life Insurance, or the deposits might be used to liquidate the claims of those for whom the Company should be trustees. I find in the Bill no securities whatever against these obvious and formidable dangers.

The crown refused assent to the bill and the company was never created.

The trouble with being a specialized financial company, however, was that excessive concentration of business led to vulnerability. Both the banks and the life insurance companies learned to break out of local or regional cocoons and cultivate new markets for their services. Specialization had a further complication in that the specialized companies seldom operated at arm's length from related firms. What could not be done within a single corporation was achieved by bundling several corporations together. Clusters or families of financial firms developed, channelling business to one other, linked by common shareholders, managers, and directors. The financial generalist did not disappear in this evolution. He mutated into a wizard of finance, the mastermind behind a network of financial service companies. The Canadian Bank of Commerce that went into British Columbia in 1900 was a big bureaucratic corporation at that time. But those who knew the inner workings of Canadian finance knew it was almost as much George Cox's bank as the original western bank had been Alexander MacDonald's.

I N THE EARLY 1840S about a dozen chartered banks, led by the Bank of Montreal and the Bank of Upper Canada, supplied notes and credit to merchants in British North America (for their origins see Chapter 6). The future of the system was still uncertain, for banking evolution had yet to settle two crucial issues: the role of government in banking, and the number and size of banks appropriate to growing, dynamic provinces. For three decades before the passage of the Bank Act of 1871, the system was in almost constant flux as these questions worked themselves out in the special context of the Bank of Montreal's ambition to become Canada's equivalent of the Bank of England.

The first axiom of Canadian banking history is that there was always a demand for more or easier credit than established institutions would provide. No sensible banker could satisfy all the people who came to him for money. Those who went away disappointed wanted the opportunity to go to another bank, and another and another. At first, it was often a question of the inadequacy of private credit networks. When local merchants desired better, more sophisticated, and more secure credit services than anyone in the village offered, they turned to the chartered banks for accommodation. Would a bank open a branch to serve them?

The chartered banks were not originally interested in selling their services widely. Created much like modern cooperatives or credit unions to meet the needs of their founders, they had problems assessing the credit-worthiness of outsiders. How could a prudent banker assess the enthusiasm of the merchants of Farmerston for banks? One major error by a small institution could destroy it. It was necessary to move cautiously, branching out slowly from home ground along familiar geographical or commercial or, in Quebec, ethnic lines.

Through mid-century chartered banks were slow to establish branches. In 1867 the thirty-five chartered banks in Canada had a total of 127 branches. Communities often petitioned a bank to open a branch and they were often turned down. Sometimes a bank required petitioners to prove their seriousness by subscribing for some of its shares; occasionally these local investors formed a subboard to manage the branch. As often as not, frustrated local men were left to prove they could support a bank by founding one themselves.

Those who felt the provinces were underbanked wanted it to be easy to found new chartered banks. They looked to banking practice in many American states. There the enthusiasm for easy credit, tempered by the people's suspicion of impersonal, irresponsible corporations, led to free and easy chartering of small local banks, along with restrictions on branch banking. In the Province of Canada pressures to imitate New York's "free banking" system led to the Free Banking Act of 1850, which made it possible to create small "unit" banks along American lines. Anyone could found a single-branch bank by buying $100,000 worth of provincial securities, depositing them with the government, and receiving customized bank notes in return. Then they were ready for business. The province, which was creating kept buyers for its bonds, guaranteed note redemption if the bank failed.

It was the experiment that failed. Banks established under the Free Banking Act could not compete with the more freewheeling chartered banks, which had control of their own capital, more flexibility in administering their note issue, and unlimited geographical mobility. Despite tax incentives, none of the chartered banks converted to free bank status. Five of the six banks that operated under the Free Banking Act in the early 1850s later became chartered. The act fell into dormancy and was finally repealed in 1880. Canadian banking would not imitate the American pattern.

Governments remained anxious about the chartered banks' control of the note issue. Generous chartering of new banks – thirteen sprouted during the boom of 1855–57 – led to a profusion of new notes and heavy losses for noteholders when some of the hothouse creations died in the hard times that immediately followed. Governments continued to believe that the best way to protect noteholders would be, as the Province of Canada's Finance Minister, A.T. Galt, put it, "to put the currency of the country on a perfectly sound and safe footing by separating it from the banking interests." In 1858 Canada formalized the currency on a dollar/ decimal basis, and the other provinces soon followed (Britain wistfully suggested that the dollar be called a "royal"). In 1860 Galt again proposed a state takeover of the note issue, suggesting that the banks be required to deposit provincial securities in return for government banknotes. His critics, especially the bankers, saw the idea as a debt-ridden government's ploy to sell more bonds. The chartered banks were all opposed to surrendering their note-issuing powers.

Galt could not let the banks go on as before because too many of them were headed for disaster. By 1860 the Bank of Upper Canada, British North America's second largest, was in serious trouble, loaded with a portfolio of over-valued municipal debentures, railway securities, and hypothecated real estate. The bank was so important to the provincial economy that Galt felt he had to keep it in business by maintaining substantial government deposits while new managers tried to save it. The plight of the Toronto-based bank compared sadly with the strength of the Bank of Montreal, which had been much more conservative in its lending practices during the boom of the mid-fifties.

Canada's senior bank moved further away from its competitors' practices and problems by focusing on international operations in the early 1860s. It opened agencies in Chicago and New York and began extensive specie dealing in New York. The Bank of Montreal replaced the Bank of Upper Canada as the principal financial agent of the government of the Province of Canada and secured the largest private account in the provinces by becoming the Grand Trunk's banker. It took a tough line in its transactions with floundering competitors and with Upper Canada generally, becoming much less accommodating. The Bank of Montreal seemed to be withdrawing from ordinary "retail" banking to become a "wholesale" house doing an international business.

These policies reflected the ambition of E.H. King, a tough Irishman who came to Canada in the service of the Bank of British North America, switched to the Montreal in 1857, and become its cashier in 1863 (then, when titles were changed, its first general manager). King quickly won a reputation as one of the most daring and ruthless bankers ever to operate in Canada, "the Napoleon of Canadian Finance," whose aim was to turn the Bank of Montreal into the potentate of the Canadian system. His personal stake was through a unique contract: in addition to his $10,000 salary, King received a special commission in each year the bank's profits exceeded 10 per cent on its capital.

The risks and rewards of the Bank of Montreal's New York gold trading on wild Civil War and Reconstruction markets are still disputed (one of King's New York managers later said the speculations there almost made his hair stand on end, and he resigned in protest). At home King's most daring manoeuvre was his decision to break ranks and support Galt on government control of the note issue. When Galt pushed through a Provincial Note Act in 1866, offering the banks compensation for surrendering their note-issuing power, the Bank of Montreal immediately responded and exchanged a huge load of provincial securities for new provincial notes.

The Bank of Montreal's coup was facilitated by the final collapse of the Bank of Upper Canada early in 1866. Its failure weakened citizen confidence in ordinary bank notes. The Dominion of Canada was created in 1867 in a season of unprecedented insecurity about the stability of the financial system. The early months of Confederation were rife with rumours that the Kingston-based Commercial Bank was about to close, in part because the Bank of Montreal and the government were refusing to come to its aid. The rumours were sound. The Commercial Bank was carrying far too much real estate and western railway securities. It suspended payment in October 1867. Runs on several other banks by noteholders demanding specie only stopped when the government announced it would accept the notes of all banks still in business.

Even as established banks crumbled and fell, important new ones were founded. One of Toronto's leading wholesale merchants, W.R. McMaster, resigned from the board of the Bank of Montreal in anger at its ruthless treatment of Upper Canada and set out to create a new Toronto-based bank. McMaster organized a group of Toronto merchants who bought the dormant charter for a bank to be known as the Bank of Canada, decided to change its name to the Canadian Bank of Commerce, raised capital, and opened in May 1867. "We do not oppose anyone, all we seek is the good of the country," its cashier wrote, and proceeded to say exactly who the Commerce opposed: "We believe that all the floating capital which some banks get hold of is loaned out of the country. Our policy is to benefit our respective localities by employing our own and the floating capital coming under our control in the support of the trade and industry of the place." Moving into the vacuum created by the Montreal's retrenchment and the local bank failures, the Commerce opened branches in the principal towns of southwestern Ontario and in 1869 absorbed Hamilton's weakened Gore Bank.

McMaster got the Commerce going just as King and his supporters in the new Dominion government tried to drop the other shoe. The Bank of Montreal called for a state monopoly of the note issue and a sharp differentiation of banks according to function. The Minister of Finance, John Rose, fresh from the board of the Bank of Montreal, proposed to reform Canadian banking in just that direction. The government would control the currency; as in the United States, a plenitude of small banks would supply local credit; there would be at least one big bank, or perhaps several "greater Banks," to do wholesale banking. As King explained:

> The General Manager believes, that the interests of the country will best be served by the diffusion of Banking interests in different localities, leaving to the greater Banks in a large measure, the care of the mercantile and foreign trade of the country, and to the lesser, in their own districts, the care and support of local enterprise. He sees no reason why, under such a system there should not be perfect freedom and equality in banking nor any reason why the greater and smaller Banks could not exist in harmony, each class within its own sphere . . . .
>
> The General Manager cannot, under such a system, whereby the note circulation and deposits would be secured, see any objection to the establishment of a local Bank in every county.

The "local" banks reacted furiously. The "monetary King of Canada" seemed to be conspiring with the government to destroy the banks' freedom to issue notes and expand. George Hague, cashier of the solid, Gooderham-backed Bank of Toronto, organized a bankers' lobby – their first serious attempt at concerted action – to resist the Rose-King proposals. The group's effectiveness was not hindered by McMaster's strategic location as chairman of the Senate Banking Committee. The broader dimension of the struggle involved regional interests and monetary policy. Would the fast-growing western region of Canada (i.e., central and southwestern Ontario) be held in bondage by a conservative, eastern financial power (the Bank of Montreal)? Would Canada's money supply lose the seasonal elasticity that took place as the banks expanded and contracted their note issue?

The underdog bankers mobilized so much regional political influence against Rose's bank bill in 1869 that the Finance Minister abandoned his scheme and soon abandoned his office. The new minister, Sir Francis Hincks (back from Caribbean exile, forgiven for his railway excesses, still the best business mind in Canadian politics), negotiated a compromise on the note issue issue – the government would issue all of Canada's notes for less than $5, the banks would issue the larger denominations – and brought in a general codification of Canadian banking law, the Bank Act of 1871. With its passage, the imperial pretensions of E.H. King and the Bank of Montreal were finally defeated. Two years later King retired at the age of forty-five, satisfied at having made the Bank of Montreal one of the largest, most powerful banks in the world, despite his Canadian setbacks. King retired to the old world. When he died he was living in Monte Carlo.

The Bank Act set the regulatory environment for Canada's chartered banks. The act and all the bank charters ran for concurrent ten-year periods, then to be renewed or revised in light of experience and changing conditions. New banks would continue to be created by act of Parliament. Petitioners had to meet minimum capital requirements ($100,000 paid-up against $500,000 total). A bank's note issue could not exceed its paid-up capital plus reserves, and it could not pay more than an 8 per cent dividend until a reserve fund had been created. Loans could be made on the security of most kinds of merchandise, verified by receipts or assignments. It was short-term lending, with obligations liquidated when goods were sold. Loans on the security of unstable real estate or mortgages were considered illiquid and were not permitted. Banks had to submit detailed monthly statements, but there was no proviso for government inspection or audit. Nor were there any restrictions on the ownership of bank stock beyond the deterrent of double liability.

The Bank Act was not substantially changed in its early decennial revisions. The capital requirement was raised slightly (to $250,000 paid-up), and better protection was extended to noteholders, judged to be the innocent losers when a bank collapsed. The notes of a failed bank were made a first charge against its assets; in 1891 a special Bank Circulation Redemption Fund was created, each bank contributing, to insure noteholders against loss. These slight changes did not affect the overall stability of the legislative framework for Canadian banking.

The banks, the bankers, and the merchants and capitalists for whom they existed, jockeyed for competitive advantage. Financial services were sold within a matrix of opportunities and constraints similar to the wholesaling and retailing of consumer goods. As the Bank of Montreal was the first to realize, there were special opportunities in foreign exchange dealing, advances to a few large clients (including governments), and other transactions involving percentage charges on large sums. In everyday branch banking, even with much larger margins the volume of business was still too low through the 1860s for the fees, commissions, and profits to mount very high.

From its inception the Bank of Montreal found some of its best opportunities in the United States. There was so much business there. The American banking system had taken the route E.H. King wanted Canadians to follow; the local "unit" banks could not handle the sophisticated transactions that were the Canadians' specialty. When the Bank of Montreal expanded its New York office in the 1860s, it competed with only a few private merchant banking houses. For years it was the largest incorporated bank operating in the United States.

It was soon joined by the Canadian Bank of Commerce. McMaster started the bank in the disrupted Ontario financial climate of the mid-1860s, but his real interest in banking had developed from his wholesale house's long experience in transatlantic and international currency transactions. The fledgling Bank of Commerce did an international business through McMaster's good contacts in Manchester, London, and New York, and soon began currency trading in New York. By 1872 it had an agency there, and developed an extensive business in the bills of exchange financing American cotton exports to Britain. Soon the Canadian bank was doing a worldwide business moving paper generated in the conduct of American foreign trade. Moving the cotton crop became so important to the bank that it opened a New Orleans agency in the late 1890s. Because it had correspondents in Manila, the Canadian Bank of Commerce became principal banker for the United States government during its occupation of the Philippines after the Spanish-American War.

Two Halifax-based banks followed the Montreal and the Commerce abroad. For the first four decades of its history from 1832 the Bank of Nova Scotia remained a fairly sleepy local institution. Its directors' somnambulism was almost fatal. In 1870 the bank found that its faithful cashier of thirty-eight years' standing had systematically embezzled a sum equivalent to almost half the shareholders' equity. A few years later everyone in head office trooped onto the street one day to watch P.T. Barnum's circus parade. The suckers left their cash waiting for the thieves who came in through the basement.

The Bank of Nova Scotia's new general manager, Thomas Fyshe, was out of town that day, but there were few other occasions when he was not complete master of the bank's business. Described by a contemporary as "a Scotchman of cranky disposition but great ability," Fyshe possessed the two contradictory qualities essential to success as a banker – an enterprising spirit and great caution. The fundamentals of business wisdom were condensed in the slogan he wrote inside the Bank's main account book: "BAD TIMES, GOOD TIMES, BULLY TIMES, COLLAPSE."

Fyshe gradually expanded the bank's operations in the Maritimes, taking over the failing Bank of Liverpool and the desperate Union Bank of Prince Edward Island (which was forced to liquidate after its cashier absconded with $400,000, *twice* its paid-up capital), and opening other branches and agencies in Nova Scotia and New Brunswick. In 1882, the bank's fiftieth anniversary year, it made its first excursion out of the region by establishing a branch in booming Winnipeg. When the bully times led directly to collapse in the Manitoba economy, the branch was awash in bad loans ("How such an accumulation of worthless parties could be taken on as customers is yet a mystery," the head office inspector reported) and had to be wound up. The Bank of Nova Scotia stayed out of risky Manitoba for another fifteen years, choosing instead to enter Minneapolis in 1885 and Chicago in 1892. Both ventures succeeded. In 1889 Fyshe went farther afield in a different direction, following Halifax's old trading lines south to Kingston, Jamaica. This was the first Canadian bank branch in the Caribbean, a promising field.

The Merchants' Bank of Halifax was founded as a partnership in 1864 and chartered in 1869. In the early 1880s it too began canvassing possibilities for expansion beyond the region. To be sure, its first foreign office was opened under casual circumstances, according to the minutes:

> Mr. Duncan, the Accountant, having been confined in his house through a severe attack of rheumatism, the President being of opinion that his health was not fully re-established, suggested a visit to Bermuda, to which the Board assented. Mr. Duncan was accordingly advised by his physicians to avail himself of this opportunity, as calculated to do him much good, and he was also authorized by the Board in the event of his finding a suitable opening to establish an agency of the bank at Hamilton.

The Bermuda agency was not particularly successful, but an interest in the Caribbean was maintained. In the late 1890s the bank followed American troops into Havana during the Spanish-American War, developed a thriving business financing Cuban-American trade, and soon opened a New York office. In 1901 the Merchants' Bank of Halifax changed its name to the Royal Bank of Canada. The next year a group of prominent Americans, many of them interested in the Cuban trade, purchased a large block of Royal Bank stock. It continued to expand its Caribbean and American operations, working often with the utility entrepreneurs described in Chapter 12.

Regionally based banks could still do well in certain situations. The Eastern Townships Bank was organized by the prominent English-speaking merchants and farmers of that isolated region in the late 1850s. For four decades it did a solid, gradually expanding business supplying the area's financial needs. Both the Bank of Toronto, chartered in 1853 by a group of prominent Ontario millers, and the Dominion Bank, put together in Toronto in the late 1860s out of the ruins of the suspended Royal Canadian Bank, tended to confine their operations to Ontario, slowly developing networks of branches radiating from Toronto. Both banks profited in the early years from the disgruntlement of some of McMaster's early associates at the Commerce who thought he was expanding too far too fast and too much in the interests of his family connections. None of these banks was at all adventuresome; all did a nicely balanced business in regions where agriculture was flourishing and diverse and growing towns were attracting new industries.

Other regional banks were not as fortunate. The relative decline of the Maritimes after Confederation doomed the less aggressive local banks to stagnation. The Bank of Nova Scotia's old competitor, for example, the Halifax Banking Company, became chartered in 1872, but chose not to follow Fyshe's lead out of the Maritimes. Its earnings, dividends, and stock value all gradually shrank. In 1903 the Bank's aged president and cashier convinced the board to sell to the Canadian Bank of Commerce, which was planning to enter Halifax, rather than try to carry on. Canada's oldest chartered bank, the Bank of New Brunswick, also chose a conservative course, eschewing branches within or without the region. In 1885 the board of this "Old Bank" deliberately shrank the institution by reducing capital and buying up stock. It expanded belatedly in the region after 1900. Too late: in 1910 the Bank of New Brunswick was absorbed by the Bank of Nova Scotia. Actually the *Toronto*-based Bank of Nova Scotia, for in 1900 its board decided to leave Halifax for a city in the mainstream of Canada's current and future business growth. Six years later the ambitious Royal Bank moved to Montreal.

New banks appeared after every few years of good times. They were founded to meet merchants' demands for credit and realize financial entrepreneurs' dreams. A few years into every business downturn the weak sisters went to the wall, weighed down by bad paper, customer distrust, or both. The total of thirty-five chartered banks in the Dominion in 1867 ballooned to an all-time high of fifty-one in 1875 and immediately began to contract. The smallest banks were the most vulnerable, for their business was usually highly concentrated, often in the accounts of a few directors and/or leading shareholders. Formed precisely to serve generous helpings of credit to their founders, weak banks became troubled in proportion to their customers' business troubles. Weaknesses were often disguised by creative accounting, or no accounting at all. The brutal reckoning came when noteholders suddenly demanded specie, or depositors wanted their money back. Seventeen chartered banks failed or were voluntarily liquidated between 1867 and 1900. In that year the much enlarged Canadian economy supported the same number of chartered banks it had in 1867.

The loss of confidence that created dramatic runs on banks tended to be infectious. As in Leacock's "My Financial Career," one rattled customer too often led to more. The worst post-Confederation scare was in the summer of 1879. In May the Mechanics Bank in Montreal stopped payment on its notes. In June the Banque Jacques-Cartier, badly troubled since 1875, suspended for a second time. The Consolidated Bank, based in Montreal but with several Ontario branches, closed its doors at the end of July, about the same time as the shareholders of Quebec's

Stadacona Bank gave up and decided to liquidate. Fear for the whole system developed in the week of August 6–11. The Exchange Bank of Canada suspended one day, the Banque Ville Marie the next; there were runs on the Molson Bank and the City and District Savings Bank in Montreal, and in Hamilton on the Merchants Bank and the Bank of Hamilton. The panic stopped before it became general, and, as usual, did not harm the strong, diversified banks. "The Canadian Bank of Commerce held on its way," its historian wrote, "and apparently profited to some extent by salvage from the wrecks all around it. The deposits at many of the branches increased considerably, and in Montreal, especially, the bank acquired a number of first-class accounts."

Sometimes a bank was able to reorganize and reopen after a run. Both the Banque Jacques-Cartier and the Banque Ville Marie, for example, survived the panic of 1879 (it was actually a year of recovery followed by several very good seasons) and limped on for another two decades. Then they went down forever in similar circumstances in 1899. Ronald Rudin quotes the Montreal *Star's* description of how Montreal's strongest French-Canadian bank, the Banque d'Hochelaga, weathered its own run in 1899:

> Heaps of gold piled up beside the paying teller, of whom three extra were added to accommodate the demands of the situation, were tangible evidence to show that the bank was prepared for all demands upon it. The confident air of the officials and the prompt payment of all claims were factors that could not be disregarded and many who came to withdraw their money went away leaving it in the bank's keeping. And there were also numerous large depositors who in full view of the crowds present, handed their money into the receiving window with an air of confidence.

It is not surprising that the architectural history of Canadian banking is a study in images of classical endurance, strength, and stability. The appearance of permanence was a sine qua non of survival.

Canadians, like other folk, only gradually became accustomed to depositing funds with banks. The chartered banks originated to create a convenient medium of exchange and discount merchants' paper. They sopped up some savings in the act of selling shares and creating their own capital. Except for merchants' temporary deposits of working funds, there was little more need for deposit balances: most people held currency and specie, and kept their total cash and deposit balances as small as they could. The handful of trustee savings banks created to provide a haven for ordinary citizens' surpluses did not grow significantly; eventually their function as a risk-free repository was largely assumed by several provincial schemes and then by the federal postal savings bank.

As the country grew and its economy became more prosperous, businesses and ordinary people became more interested in holding bank deposits, and more able to do so. The spread of the cheque tended to push them in the same direction. Compared with paper currency or specie, a cheque was a convenient and safe way of making a payment. These tendencies were convenient for the banks, because their capacity to make loans beyond their owners' capital and the allowable note issue hinged on deposits. The trouble was that the demand for bank credit fluctuated with the business cycle, and so did deposits, generally in the reverse direction. When trade was bad people were more likely to pay off loans, if they could, and to hold more of their wealth as bank deposits; in good times they would want to expand trade by cutting down on their idle balances and borrowing from the banks. Through the 1870s even the largest banks sometimes complained that they could not find safe domestic investments for all their funds. The same thing occurred in the mid-1890s. Some banks, therefore, were always nervous about encouraging the small depositor, nor did all banks actively seek deposits at all times. They learned to manipulate the attractiveness of deposits, by offering or withholding interest, by offering or withholding permission to write cheques, and in other ways. At the extreme, the Merchants Bank of Prince Edward Island refused for a time to take deposits smaller than $100, and once asked a director to withdraw a deposit of several thousand dollars because it could not continue paying interest on the money.

Bigger, more diversified banks had better opportunities to match deposits and discounts, largely because of the ease with which they could place money where it was remunerative, whether in Canada or abroad. In the late 1860s a few bankers realized they should encourage deposits because of the leverage effect of making money on other people's money rather than just shareholders' capital. As well, the costs of handling deposits were falling as the banks routinized their personnnel and bookkeeping practices. As the costs of "retail" banking fell, opportunities for profit increased. A new deposit/branch-oriented strategy helped such Ontario regional banks as the Toronto, Dominion, and Imperial grow into gaps left by the heavily-capitalized, outward-looking Commerce and Montreal. By the 1880s most of the bigger banks had created savings departments; they solicited savings accounts, paid interest on them, and opened new branches at an accelerating rate partly to tap new savings' pools. Their ability to transfer funds among regions, even among countries, plus their development of accounting and staff controls, meant they had mastered fundamental problems of financial intermediation.

The small chartered banks could not compete on an equal footing. It was theoretically possible to move funds smoothly and efficiently along networks of cooperating small banks – the Americans developed such mechanisms – but in Canada the networks of small banks were too thin, too scattered, and too diverse. The efficient internal transactions of the big banks gave them a major competitive advantage. While the total number of chartered banks in 1900 was the same as in 1867, the number of bank branches had grown from 127 to 708 and a huge new surge of expansion was in full tilt. Big national banks were going to be the strongest and most profitable. They expanded by merger and acquisition as well as by opening new branches. By 1911, in spite of several new charterings, there were seven fewer banks in the country and 1,846 more branches than in 1900.

The day of the private banker was not over. As the market for banking services expanded, new situations emerged in which a private banker could do a "general store" financial business that would not support a chartered bank. In 1882 the *Monetary Times* described opportunities for "private enterprise" in banking:

> The operation of a branch of a chartered bank is . . . a somewhat costly business; and unless the trade, and accumulated wealth of the place rises to [a] certain proportion, a branch bank cannot be made profitable. It is here, then, that the legitimate field for private enterprise is found, that is, in those thriving and well situated villages, which have a certain amount of commercial business, and are situated in the midst of a good farming district. A private banker can carry on his business at much less expense than a branch of a chartered bank. He is, moreover, not bound by any restriction as to the rate which he can charge for money, or the kind of security which he can take. He can practically charge what he pleases for the use of money or its transmission from place to place. And although his charges may be considerable higher than those of a banking institution it may be more economical for residents to deal with him, than to incur the risk and expense of dealing with a branch bank, at a distance, perhaps, of ten or twenty miles.

Some one hundred and eighty private bankers did business in Canada in 1895. Most were in Ontario, with a large handful on the prairies. There were probably many more whose names never appeared in financial directories. This was almost certainly the high point of Canadian private banking. The expansion of corporate financial institutions, offering far better security than any private banker could guarantee, gradually extinguished the private competition.

———————

The chartered banks and their branches at every Main and Division Street came to personify Canadian finance. But they were not the sole purveyors of financial services. In important other realms, where the chartered banks were not allowed to wander, specialists designed new corporate institutions to meet savers' and borrowers' needs.

The mortgage loan company was created to meet the demand for mortgage loans. In 1900 mortgage loan companies ranked second to banks as Canadian financial intermediaries. They existed because prohibitions on real estate lending were written into banks' charters from their Canadian beginnings. Land values were too imprecise and volatile in the early nineteenth century and wealth tied up in real estate was too difficult to liquidate. Dealing in short-term loans and issuing notes redeemable on demand, the banks were simply unsuited to the risk-taking involved in real estate lending. Many Canadian bank failures occurred when profit-hungry bank directors found ways of avoiding the prohibition and lending on real estate anyway.

There was a persistent demand for land-backed credit. Real property was the asset everyone had or wanted to have. There was no good reason why, under the right circumstances, some of the demand could not be met.

In Great Britain building societies evolved to facilitate the savings and borrowing involved in home ownership. Members of a building society saved by regularly depositing instalments on shares they had agreed to take; the accumulating deposits were loaned to other members, on the security of their properties, at good interest. The returns helped all members reach the value of their shares faster. When all shares were fully funded the society was terminated. It was a former officer of a British building society, Robert Skilbeck, who first suggested that the villagers of Sarnia, Lambton County, form one of these cooperatives and pool their money for mutual advantage. The Port Sarnia Syndicate was founded in 1844 to receive members' deposits and loan the money to the member who bid the highest for it. In 1847 the Port Sarnia Building Society was incorporated under a Canadian building society act patterned on British legislation. Other provinces followed, building societies multiplied. Toronto had eighteen of them in 1855.

The original building society was too crude. Auctions were a poor way of placing funds. Closed memberships with term commitments required the organizations to self-destruct, while limiting them in other ways. Skilbeck's group in Lambton County and a young Toronto accountant, J. Herbert Mason, pioneered in reorganizing the societies into permanent corporations combining a savings department with general mortgage lending. Special legislation allowed terminating building societies to become permanent; thus the name, Canada Permanent Building and Savings Society, for the organization Mason created in 1855 out of the Toronto Building Society and the Farmers and Mechanics Building Society. The Sarnia institution became the Lambton Permanent Building and Investment Society. The new companies sold shares and took deposits. They used differential interest rates to encourage term deposits. After investing some of the proceeds in bank stocks or government securities as a liquid reserve, the companies loaned the rest against mortgages.

We do not know enough about the early savings and loan companies that failed. The survivors either had the good fortune to operate in steadily growing areas like Lambton County, or, like the Canada Permanent, they grew away from their home base and took mortgages across their province. If it expanded, a company had to develop intimate knowledge of local conditions and risks. Mason's genius at Canada Permanent was his development of a province-wide network of trustworthy property appraisers, which gave the firm the ability to judge risks far away from head office. Getting out of Toronto was useful, too, in introducing the Permanent to rural business. Ontario's rich farm economy generated both considerable savings and a strong demand for farm improvement loans. Rural Ontario was fertile soil for the Canada Permanent and its imitators. As early as 1869 the *Monetary Times* commented that "What the Banks are to the merchants the Building Societies are to the farmer and mechanic."

The business was a fairly simple form of intermediation between savers and borrowers, with real estate as security. It changed over the years as new savers were tapped in Great Britain, new borrowers in western Canada. Some British savings were already channelled into North American real estate by the Canada Company and other land development companies. As early as 1843 a Kingston group incorporated the Trust and Loan Company to borrow money in the old country and lend it on real estate in Canada. It had mixed success. In the late 1870s the Canadian savings and loan companies, again led by Mason of the Permanent, found they could borrow money in England and Scotland. Canadian and British companies rushed into the field, which was soon much more important to them than Canadians' savings. Issuing sterling debentures at 3.5 to 4 per cent, the capital movers could write mortgages in Canada at 6.5 to 7.5 per cent and do very well. Until the 1890s, there were hardly any losses on mortgages, particularly in prosperous Ontario.

"Perhaps I ought also to refer to another idea which occurred to me in travelling through Ontario," the manager of the North of Scotland Canadian Mortgage Company reported in 1876. "It seemed to me that the farmers in Ontario will by-and-by become so rich that they will not require our money. Should this prove to be the case, we must just make up our minds to move further westward, and in Manitoba, when intersected by the great railway running across the continent, I believe we shall find an outlet for our money for as long a period as it is any use thinking about." A good idea certainly, but it happened that Manitoba was an instance of the perils of innovation. The savings and loan companies that took mortgages on wildly inflated Manitoba land in the early 1880s suffered cruel punishment (along with the mortgagees). Through the mid-1890s it was safer to stick with Ontario, even though interest rate spreads slowly declined.

Life insurance companies were the fastest-growing financial institutions in Canada by the 1890s. A small handful of Canadian firms had mastered the difficult art of selling people contracts payable on their death and, with legislative help, had wrestled control of the Canadian market from their foreign competitors. But, like the big banks, the life insurance companies found the Canadian market too small. In the 1890s Canadian life insurance salesmen travelled the world, opening new markets for their policies, importing capital to Canada where their companies could invest it profitably.

By the 1800s life insurance had outgrown its seedy origins in speculation, gambling, and the tontine contracts (the last survivor got all) that were thought to encourage murder. In Great Britain both joint-stock companies and mutual societies (in which members insured themselves, i.e., the policyholders owned the company) sold life insurance contracts at fixed annual premiums. Britain led the world in the development of the concept and the actuarial science underlying life insurance. British North Americans first bought life insurance from merchants and private bankers acting as agents for British companies. By the mid-1840s some of the outside companies had opened their own agencies in the colonies.

The newcomers were not agile enough to meet the needs of Hugh C. Baker, manager of the Bank of Montreal in Hamilton, director of a local trustee savings bank, secretary of several building societies. It is said that Baker, an asthmatic, had to endure the thousand-mile round trip to New York in 1845 to buy life insurance. On his policy he had to pay an extra premium because of the "climatic hazard of living in Canada." Two years after his trip, in 1847, Baker founded the Canada Life Assurance Company, the first Canadian firm in the industry (and a pioneer by North American standards; the major U.S. companies dated from the same decade). Whatever the truth of the New York story, Baker's endeavour was obviously also influenced by his experience as a one-man financial services industry. The mutual society format he first proposed for the Canada Life had many similarities to a building society. When the legislature rejected the idea because the company would have no capital, Baker found enough investors to subscribe £50,000 in a corporation. They paid 1 per cent down. In August 1847 the Canada Life issued its first policy to its president, Hugh Baker (its charter did not issue from the legislature until 1849). Because of Baker's asthma, the story goes, the directors would only insure him for £500, half the amount he requested. Perhaps someone in New York covered the other £500.

"The practice of life insurance was but little understood among us, while its governing principles were still less generally understood," the Canada Life stated in its first annual report. Baker wrote that the company "encountered coldness where it may have expected cordiality, lukewarmness where there should have been confidence." The half-dozen agents in Hamilton, Toronto, London, and Montreal managed to sell 144 policies totalling $282,500 coverage that year for premiums of $8,250. By 1850 Canada Life had 473 policies in effect totalling $814,903 of insurance; in 1870 its 4,270 policies totalling $6,404,437 were about 15 per cent of all the life insurance in force in the Dominion. None of the twenty-four British and American companies operating in Canada that year was selling as much insurance.

The government of Canada began regulating life insurance in 1868, requiring licences and a deposit (as had previously been required of fire and marine insurers). A wave of criticism of the unsound practices of unregulated life insurance companies in the United States and Canada led to more elaborate controls, including the 1875 appointment of a superintendent of insurance in the Department of Finance to oversee the industry. "A salutory effect of wise governmental supervision would be to impart greater confidence in Canadian companies by giving the public the fullest and most satisfactory assurance of their soundness," the *Monetary Times* editorialized during the debate on regulation. The regulations did create new opportunities for Canadian companies when several British and American firms left the country rather than comply with a requirement to keep sufficient assets in Canada to cover their liabilities. The vacuum was instantly filled by new Canadian firms, including the Ontario Mutual (1871), Sun Life (1871, originally chartered 1865), Confederation Life (1871), London Life (1874), North American Life (1881), the Temperance and General (1886), and Manufacturers Life (1887).

Most of the new companies were organized by financial men much like Baker: experienced bankers, brokers, or agents who knew a little bit about life insurance and had contacts with investors willing to subscribe for a few shares. By 1879 the Canadian life companies were writing more than half of the new policies issued in the country. In 1900 they had about 65 per cent of the business.

Unlike banking, there was little existing demand for life insurance. An insurance contract was still suspect, a no-win deal because the pay-off came only after the policyholder died. It was a strange, almost sacrilegious contract, some felt: life insurance created a pecuniary interest in a person's death (thus it was everywhere necessary to ban life insurance contracts written without consent of the insured). And it was an agreement you made to pay a corporation – an artificial person – a lot of money in return for nothing but a promise that it would outlive you and pay your beneficiaries. How would you know the company paid? From its beginnings, life insurance had to be sold and sold and sold.

The sales pitch emphasized the benevolence of providing for loved ones. Buying life insurance was an act of love, duty, almost religious obligation. Agents preached "the gospel of life insurance," often handing out texts on the subject written by clergymen. Loose livers, on the other hand, were urged to take thought of the consequences of their lifestyle. "Life insurance salesmen soon came to learn that the churchgoers were one market, the unregenerate another," the official historian of North American Life wrote. "The aspects of life insurance that one admired and accepted the other was apt to despise and spurn." On a more down-to-earth note, companies varied the insurance contract to offer elements of reward in the here-and-now: they introduced dividend payments, reduced premiums, savings components leading to endowments and annuities, and other incentives. Within two years of its founding the Canada Life already offered a bewildering variety of products:

> The participation scale, or scale with profits; the non-participation scale, or scale without profits; the half credit system, under which, for a term of years, a reduced premium rate is charged; the decreasing temporary assurance system, which is peculiarly adapted to borrowing shareholders and building societies; endowment assurances; endowment assurances for

children, with or without return of the whole premium paid theron, in case of death occurring before the age is attained, or the endowment is made payable; assurance on joint lives, either upon the death of the first assured, or on the death of the longest liver; immediate annuities, payable during the remainder of life or deferred annuities to commence at a given age and to continue thereafter during life on the payment either of a fixed sum or of an annual premium.

The backsides of most early policies were black with fine print. Policyholders were not allowed to die at the hands of the state, by suicide, or in duels. Various methods of travel were banned. Hazardous occupations were forbidden, as was drinking to excess. It was not necessary to pay a penalty to live in Canada, but policyholders were not allowed to go to unhealthy places like the southern United States in the summer or wild countries like Australia and California. Unlike their British sisters, Canadian women did not have to pay more for life insurance; underweight people often did. The Temperance and General Life Assurance Company did its temperance business with total abstainers at specially low rates, its general business with normal drinkers. For many years the directors of the life companies personally scrutinized all policy applications; some of the firms established regional boards for closer, more informed judgment of applicants.

Government regulation gave customers important assurance that the insurance companies could be trusted. The size of companies' deposits with the government immediately became an advertising point. The superintendent of insurance's annual report, the "Blue Book," became a selling document (whose figures, according to the history of the Life Underwriters Association of Canada, "could be used to prove almost anything"). The other way to give a company the imprimatur of the highest, most public-spirited men in the land was to make them its directors or officers. It was surely safe to do business with the Confederation Life Association of Canada, for while the organizer of the company, J.K. Macdonald, was only a municipal civil servant, its founding president was none other than Sir Francis Hincks, Finance Minister for Canada. North American Life went one better in 1881 by obtaining the presidential services of the former prime minister of Canada, the Right Honourable Alexander Mackenzie. A few years later the organizers of Manufacturers Life achieved the ultimate coup. Their first president was the *current* prime minister of Canada, Sir John A. Macdonald himself. By the end of the 1880s prominent politicians were as thick as blackberries on the boards of the life insurance companies. Politicians had their faults, but it was reasonable to hope they could be trusted to make sure the companies played fair with widows and orphans. They were paid generous salaries for their services. Few criticized politicians' involvement in organizations that seemed almost like public service companies and were either fully mutualized or distributed 80 to 95 per cent of profits to their policyholders.

Many of the life companies flirted a bit with other kinds of financial services. Canada Life bought a trustee savings bank, the Hamilton and Gore, in the early 1850s, and began taking deposits. Heavy and unexpected losses in savings banking posed the question, in the words of an outside auditor, "Whether an institution like the Canada Life Assurance Company should connect itself with a savings or other bank, liable to be run upon, and its character jeopardized by an idle or malicious rumour. It seems to be generally conceded that such institutions should be kept apart, and left to work out their objectives separately." Canada Life left the business.

New life companies often asked for and received the right to do a general insurance business, but soon gave it up. By the 1880s charters were more confining. When a Toronto group proposed to create "The Manufacturers Life and Accident Insurance Company" in 1887, the Senate Committee on Banking and Commerce recommended the founding of separate companies. So The Manufacturers Life Insurance Company and The Manufacturers Accident Insurance Company were incorporated separately – on the same day, with almost identical boards, and with the same prime ministerial president. They did business out of the same office. The important reality behind their paper separation was that their funds were segregated; premium income from life insurance could not be used to underwrite losses in other fields.

Neither prominent politicians nor government inspection guaranteed success or even survival. The life insurance companies were vulnerable to practically every form of mismanagement, ranging from simple theft by poorly chosen agents to poorly selected investments by self-interested promoters, to simple misjudgments by self-made actuaries floundering in the dark ages of their science. In the 1850s Hugh Baker purchased too many unsound mortgages for the Canada Life, as well as the unsound savings bank; a drastic reorganization under a tough, professional manager imported from Scotland followed Baker's early but perhaps not untimely death in 1859. The founder of Montreal's Sun Life, Matthew Gault, and his fellow directors almost ruined the company with unsound investments in the Montreal Loan and Mortgage Company and the Exchange Bank, commitments fiercely opposed by the Sun's professional manager, Robertson Macaulay. London Life's history notes that the residents of London were not a good source of business in the early years "probably because the citizens of London knew too much about the small and struggling Company." The business practices of both London Life and Manufacturers Life impaired the firms' capital: premiums were too low, commissions too high, and neither shareholders nor policyholders paid promptly. At Manufacturers John A. himself was active in ousting the promoter and first managing director, J.B. Carlile, whose day-to-day maladminstration almost ruined the firm in its first two years. Like Canada Life and the Sun, both London Life and Manufacturers finally stabilized their business only when the directors accepted the need for experienced, professional management.

These companies survived. Many did not – the Citizens' Insurance Company, the Toronto Life Assurance and Tontine Company, the Stadacona Life Insurance Company, the Dominion Safety Fund, among others. Lean years in the 1870s saw extreme competition. "The most extravagant estimates of profits and results were given to prospective clients . . ." the Sun's first historian wrote. "It was a common practice to allow a portion of the premium to the applicant as a rebate; bonuses granted to agents to stimulate their production of business were so generous that towards the close of the year it would sometimes pay them to make an allowance to their clients equal to the whole amount of the first year's premium . . . . Officers and agents alike complained of the misrepresentations of their competitors . . . . Threats of suits and counter-suits were common." All the failed companies were apparently able to reinsure policyholders with continuing firms. Only share-holders, agents, and promoters suffered. "There are some things that we never understand until we experience them," J.K. Macdonald, head of the successful Confederation Life, said in 1893: "No living being can ever understand the hours, days, months and years of anxiety through which I passed, especially during the earlier years of this company."

———————

Well-managed Canadian life insurance companies were competitive with British and American firms because they could earn a high rate of return on reasonably secure investments in Canada. As Matthew Gault explained in the 1871 prospec-tus for the Sun Life, "The rates of British Companies are based on an interest return on their invested receipts of three per cent., and as the Dominion Securities afford six per cent., and first-class mortgages may be readily had here bearing seven per cent., it is evident that a lower rate of premium may be charged and an equal profit obtained."

Furthermore, as young, aggressive players in the life game the Canadians were not unwilling to tinker with the product. One of Robertson Macaulay's con-tributions to Sun Life was his introduction of the Unconditional Policy in 1880 – no occupational or travel bans, no grounds for dispute whatever after two years, the simplest policy in the world. "Our canvassers used to merely open out the policy of any competitor," Macaulay said, "then open out ours, point to the mass of conditions in the one and their absence in the other and ask, 'Which do you prefer?'" Manufacturers Life had a similar experience with "Guaranteed Cash Value" policies; their printed tables of cash and loan values were a powerful sales tool when read against British policies that left the holder ignorant of the conse-quences of surrendering or borrowing against his contract. Both North American and London Life were leaders in industrial insurance – coverage aimed at children and the working classes and involving small weekly premiums. All of the com-panies used patriotic sales pitches, stressing that policyholders' money was kept at home rather than exported to a foreign country.

No matter how imaginative the product, no matter how quickly life insurance agents followed the frontier to Manitoba, British Columbia, and the Northwest, the Canadian life insurance market was small and limited. Farmers rarely needed insurance because the value of the farm itself would protect their dependants. In the towns, only the middle and upper classes could afford to purchase enough whole life coverage to generate substantial premiums (London Life's customers in Brussels, Ontario, in 1874 were four carpenters, three clergymen, two harness-makers, two blacksmiths, a woollen manufacturer, a grocer, a music dealer, a mill owner, a lumber dealer, a school teacher, a jeweller, a druggist, and a physician). Industrial insurance was aimed at a mass market, but the five and ten cent weekly premiums made it literally a nickel-and-dime business. In trying to broaden the market, the companies ran into powerful competition from fraternal benefit societies such as the Canadian Order of Odd Fellows, Knights of Pythias, Independent Order of Foresters, and many others, which sold assessment life insurance very cheaply. These contracts included a promise that special circumstances would be met by special assessments on the members. Most were actuarially unsound, but agents for the profit-motivated companies had difficulty fighting low premiums and fraternity.

T.B. Macaulay of Sun Life (Robertson Macaulay's son) solved the Canadian market problem by going outside the country. In 1879 a visiting Trinidadian businessman persuaded him to try selling insurance in the West Indies. It was a successful experiment, which the company followed in the 1890s with forays into the Far East, Central and South America, and finally Africa. These were remarkable expeditions by globe-trotting Canadian salesmen, venturing much farther afield than any of the bankers who were exporting their services at about the same time. "When your work in the Eastern Mediterranean is finished," the company instructed one of its travellers about 1900, "strike down the Red Sea for the east coast of Africa.... You can, if you think well of it, run over to Madagascar. You should certainly take in Mauritius. After leaving Cape Colony, take coasting steamers, again stopping at every little settlement on the west coast, but don't go up the Congo. In this way you will in time reach Senegal." So many foreign customers wanted the address of the company's office in the world capital that the Sun began an English business too, then entered Europe. In 1895 it went into the United States through Michigan, and by 1900 was writing insurance everywhere in the Americas, from the Canadian northwest to Punta Arenas on the Straits of Magellan.

The Canada Life was first into the United States, initiating its Michigan sales in 1889, but otherwise lagged in the development of international business. The much smaller and younger Manufacturers Life came closest to matching the Sun's enterprise. Led by former Sun agents, Manufacturers tried an invasion of Chile in 1892 – aborted at a loss after the agent fell off a horse and went into another line of business – wrote its first foreign policies in Bermuda in 1893, carried on into the West Indies, and in 1897 began scouring the Far East. Six years later the firm opened offices in Great Britain and the United States. As was often remarked in those heady days, the sun did not set on either the British Empire or Canadian life insurance salesmen.

The foreign excursions succeeded because the well-to-do classes in under-developed colonies – often European colonial administrators – wanted to be in-sured by stable companies based in stable countries. The Canadians had the stability and offered premiums and dividends based on higher returns from their investments than most British companies could obtain. At least as important, the Canadian companies were served by a generation of brilliant salesmen – J.M.C. DelesDerniers and the brothers John A. and James C. Tory at the Sun, Robert Junkin and H.H. Horsey of Manufacturers, among others. Their zeal, energy, and endurance was much like that of the missionaries sent out by the churches in those decades to spread a different, vaguely parallel, gospel. The costs of foreign busi-ness were not high. A company's travelling emissary would sign up prominent local merchants or bankers to serve as permanent agents. The need to limit risks in strange countries meant that firms liked to share the business. The innocent Anglo-Saxons had to be cautious, they reasoned: could we tell Orientals apart well enough to protect ourselves from fraudulent death claims? Special perils af-fected both policyholders and agents: "For about six years Bombay had suffered very severely from the Bubonic plague and this had depressed business greatly. Mr. Junkin found Mr. Ellis somewhat discouraged in his rather difficult task of developing the agency," Manufacturers' history relates. "Shortly after Mr. Junkin's departure, Mr. Ellis disappeared mysteriously and no trace of him was ever found." More often the agents survived to tell proud tales of selling a difficult product in far-away lands in competition with the world's biggest in-surance companies. They had left Canada far behind.

In their early foreign operations the life companies were importing capital for in-vestment in Canada. Premium income made them important investors and in the nineteenth century there were few restrictions on their use of the money. The Canada Life bought bank stocks, municipal debentures, and mortgages, then began writing its own mortgages. Shares and debentures of savings and loan companies were common investments for life companies. Railway stocks and shares in the early industrial companies were often considered too risky, though a good dividend record might attract interest. Life insurance money was often loaned to policyholders; increasingly the companies lent on call to brokers and others who were involved in short-term financing, usually underwriting deben-tures or stock issues.

The banks also offered call loans on the security of stock and debentures. By the late 1870s they were experimenting with underwriting. Some of the mortgage loan companies expanded their portfolios to include municipal debentures. Thus, with many financial companies regularly investing large sums of money, an institutional market for securities developed to supplement the investment activities of private individuals. Of course the increased activity expanded the need for brokers to match buyers and sellers of securities. Brokers' own need for a place to meet and do business led to the founding of stock exchanges in Montreal and Toronto.

Brokers were middlemen who facilitated exchanges of commodities. Through the 1850s neither brokers nor their meeting places were particularly specialized: the fellows got together in someone's office or a coffee house invariably named the "Exchange." Often a broker simply operated a private market, using contacts and networks as best he could. Brokers dealt in everything from grain to grindstones. Some specialized in financial deals, acting as agents for buyers and sellers of all kinds of securities. A visionary proposal by some Toronto brokers in 1852 to create a stock exchange had no effect except to mislead historians about the origins of the Toronto Stock Exchange. As J.F. Whiteside showed in a brilliant thesis on the TSE, the 1850s were too early for such a specialized exchange to emerge (the Toronto Exchange, opened in 1854, was a general commodities exchange focused on the grain trade; it, too, was premature, failing in 1863, reopening in 1866 as the Corn Exchange, which merged into the Board of Trade in 1884). The only visible signs of a securities market in Toronto or Montreal in that decade were occasional newspaper listings of "prices current" for a few securities, mostly bank stocks.

The Toronto Stock Exchange was founded in 1861, to serve, according to its first rule, as "a medium of communication between the members, so as to facilitate the negotiation of bills of exchange, stocks, shares, bonds, debentures, mortgages, and other loans: Thus establishing a reliable market for the benefit of the public." This private, informal brokers' association collapsed in 1869 in doldrums of disinterest in bank stocks after the 1866–67 failures. The TSE was revived in the good years of the early 1870s and incorporated in 1878, four years after the Montreal Stock Exchange came into formal existence. The Montreal institution had evolved out of the meetings of a small Board of Brokers, formed in 1863.

The stock exchanges were small and sleepy. Sixty-three securities were listed on the Montreal Stock Exchange in 1874, fifty-two in Toronto. Bank shares and government debentures made up more than half the lists. Trading volume in Montreal of about 800 shares a day in 1874 significantly outpaced Toronto. TSE trading volume reached a record nineteenth-century high of 302,703 shares in the good year of 1883. In a very bad year, 1894, only 92,800 shares changed hands. In 1900 volume had recovered to 223,920. Trading sessions were held twice daily for half an hour, once on Saturdays. The bulk of the action was always in bank shares. Mortgage loan companies became increasingly important in the 1880s. By

1900 utility and industrial shares were beginning a spectacular growth, described in Chapter 12.

A few dozen brokers – about forty-five in Montreal, thirty in Toronto – had seats on the exchanges. As private cartels trying to control stock trading, they restricted admission, creating a market in their own seats, which sold in the $1,000 to $4,000 range. It cost $100 to have a stock listed on the Toronto exchange, $25 annually for brokers to renew their membership. Many of the members were part-time stockbrokers; as general financial agents they dealt in real estate, mortgages, life insurance, loans, and even travel arrangements. Most new stock issues were underwritten privately by brokers, and only later listed on the exchange. Many "brokers" did not bother with stock exchanges. Some were beginning to specialize in debentures or bonds, which tended to trade privately. Others ran private stock-trading dens or "bucket shops," equipped with the new-fangled stock tickers of the 1880s, where "investors" gambled on whether stocks would rise or fall.

The early stock exchanges were primeval, unregulated, insider-dominated markets where investors trod at their peril. Speculators could easily influence share prices by bull and bear raids, attempts at corners, self-dealing, the release of misinformation, and other devices. Trading on large margins was common. Conservative merchants denounced all stock exchanges as little more than gambling dens. In 1888 the federal government tried, for the first time, to outlaw the bucket shops by banning stock sales in which there was not a bona fide intent by the seller to make delivery. Objections in the Senate that the law would prohibit nine-tenths of all stock transactions were met by a government promise not to use the law against the established exchanges.

With real share ownership still limited to a tiny few, most investors were knowledgeable insiders. Insider trading and self-dealing were common, completely unremarkable practices on these imperfect markets. Investors had to work through familiar networks where they could measure risks and gather trustworthy associates. Surely the manager of a life insurance company was putting the firm onto a good thing in suggesting it take shares in the bank he was organizing or the savings and loan company he controlled. The financial companies often operated in clusters, with interlocking owners, directors, and managers. The early financial networks were a myriad of webs spun by energetic promoters and investors. In Montreal the Sun Life, the Exchange Bank, and the Montreal Loan and Mortgage Company were linked through Matthew Gault and one or two associates – and the Sun was almost destroyed by the connection when the Exchange Bank collapsed. More happily in Toronto the prospering Gooderhams were at the centre of a bank (Toronto), insurance (Manufacturers Life and Manufacturers Accident) and mortgage (Canada Permanent) network that was usually sound. London Life and the Ontario Loan and Debenture Company had the same offices and president, Joseph Jeffery, and dealt with the London branch of the Molson Bank, which

Jeffery had managed. "Since many shareholders of the London Life were also shareholders of the Ontario Loan and Debenture Company," the firm's history notes, "investment in the stock of the Ontario Loan was natural. Similarly, when Daniel Macfie became Vice-President of the London Life in 1878, stock of the Dominion Savings and Investment Society, of which he was president, was acquired in substantial amounts."

George Albertus Cox spun the most elaborate financial web. A young telegraph and express agent for the Grand Trunk in the bustling town of Peterborough, Cox signed a contract to become the Canada Life's local agent in 1861. He was a superb salesman – it was said he always had a policy application form in his pocket – and manager, building the eastern Ontario branch of the Canada Life so well that in the late 1880s it was doing almost half the company's business. Having dealt in real estate on his own account in Peterborough for many years, Cox set up two mortgage loan companies in the mid-1880s, the Central Canada Savings and Loan, and the Toronto Savings and Loan (the one raised money in Britain, the other at home). In 1886 he joined the board of the Canadian Bank of Commerce as part of a general reorganization after Senator McMaster's retirement, and in 1888 moved all his operations from Peterborough to Toronto. The busy financier (who had also found time to serve six terms as mayor of Peterborough and president of the Midland Railway) relied on his three sons to help manage their several businesses, and was fortunate in a daughter's marriage to a talented bank manager, Alfred Ernest Ames. Ames took over several family companies and gave the Coxes a stock-trading capacity by founding his own brokerage business, A.E. Ames and Company.

George Cox was already president of the thriving Central Canada Savings and Loan in 1890 when the directors of the Bank of Commerce elected him their president. His $100,000 in Commerce shares, about a 2 per cent interest, made him one of the bank's largest shareholders. But his real target was the Canada Life, whose shares he had been accumulating for years. In the early 1890s he had close to a controlling interest and pushed his way onto the board. In 1899 Cox forced the relocation of the company's head office from Hamilton to Toronto; a year later he became the Canada Life's president and general manager. He and his family and investment companies owned over half the shares in the company.

At the beginning of the twentieth century George Cox owned and ran Canada's oldest and largest life insurance company, was president of its second-largest bank, headed and controlled one of its most successful mortgage companies, had a son-in-law who was a prominent stockbroker. And more: in the mid-1890s he became president of the two leading fire insurance firms in Ontario, the British-America and the Western, both of which did a continent-wide business.*

* Marine and fire insurance companies predated life insurance in Canada, but their early history remains to be written. Canadian shipowners had access to British marine insurance

In 1898 he founded a new life insurance company, the Imperial, and purchased from the Gooderham family controlling interest in both Manufacturers and the Temperance and General (after a few troubled years the companies were merged and the Gooderham family regained control). Also in 1898 Cox moved into a new kind of financial intermediation by founding the National Trust Company to do a general trusteeship business for estates and corporations; it was among the first of its kind. The amount of debenture and bond trading being done at the Central Canada became so great that in 1901 Cox spun out a new company, Dominion Securities, to specialize in that business. Ames, of course, handled stocks. When the Toronto Stock Exchange created a clearing house to facilitate its operations, National Trust received the contract to operate it. For many years the TSE rented its quarters from National Trust.

Fifty years earlier George Cox would have been a private banker and money-broker, doing every kind of financial business he could out of a single office. Now he moved from office to office (often by stepping across the hall, perhaps changing desks, sometimes just opening a different file), superintending separate companies engaged in every kind of financial business. The half-century of financial service growth and development had been mainly in the direction of specialization through corporate instruments. General retailers of financial services continued to exist beside the new corporations, finding a niche where growth created a demand not yet adequate to support the specialists. Many of the old generalists gradually became specialized, working as managers for the new companies, or on their own as stockbrokers, real estate agents and mortgage brokers, insurance agents, or bookkeepers and accountants. A few of the most skilled financial men rose, like Cox, to head the financial corporations.

It is always possible to be superlatively good in a dying line of business. In 1879 William F. Alloway, Charles V. Alloway, and Henry T. Champion, three young men who came to Manitoba as soldiers in the aftermath of the Riel uprising and

---

from the earliest days, and began forming their own companies by the end of the eighteenth century. The Halifax Fire Insurance Company, founded in 1809 as the Nova Scotia Fire Association, appears to have been the first domestic insurer against that hazard; the Quebec Fire Assurance Company was organized in 1816. Marine and fire insurance firms were often mutuals, created as merchants and citizens clubbed together to reduce risks. But they had trouble competing against British and American insurers, whose risks were much less concentrated. For fire insurers, survival and growth depended on branching out of a hazardous regional concentration. There was also an intense struggle to fix tariffs, commissions, and risk classifications through the Canadian Fire Underwriters' Association, formed in 1883. The general nature of the business prevented the accumulation of pools of capital for investment. Latecomers to insurance, the life companies quickly dwarfed the marine and fire firms.

did well in transportation and other enterprises immediately afterwards, formed a partnership to carry on a private banking business in Winnipeg. Alloway and Champion had more flexibility to deal in real estate than the chartered banks; they understood western land so well that they were able to prosper in booms and sidestep the busts. Thanks to Charlie Alloway's mastery of native dialects, the firm dominated trade in land scrip (government warrants for land grants), buying the paper from Métis and other original settlers, selling it to incoming settlers. In hard times Alloway and Champion picked up a lot of cheap land at municipal tax sales.

As immigrants poured into Manitoba after 1900, the private bank developed a staff that served newcomers in their native languages, did the most important foreign exchange business in the city, and became a favoured repository for immigrants' savings deposits, all through the branch office opened near the CPR station. The same office also sold railway and steamship tickets. Alloway and Champion's head office on Main Street was known for its heavy bronze doors, so immaculately polished that newcomers were simply told to find their way to "the bank with gold doors."

The Alloway and Champion bank had a capital of $555,000 in 1906, $1,125,000 in 1912, the year it became incorporated. As the partners became old men they decided the business would have to pass to a chartered bank and sold out to the Canadian Bank of Commerce in 1919. The firm's standing was so high in Winnipeg that the change in ownership was not made public until it was required by law in 1923. Alloway and Champion was probably the most successful private bank in Canadian history. Its doors finally closed in 1930, six months after the death of the last partner, W.F. Alloway. "Winnipeg has been my home, and has done more for me than it ever may be in my power to repay. I owe everything to this community," Alloway wrote in 1921 to explain a gift of $100,000 to the Winnipeg Foundation, another of his creations. Eventually it received the entire Alloway estate. The private banker's gifts totalled $1.7 million.

Part Two: Coming of Age

UPPER LEFT: **Timothy Eaton** *(Eaton Archives)* UPPER RIGHT: **Robert Dunsmuir** *(Provincial Archives of British Columbia)* ABOVE: **Massey-Harris's Toronto Light Binder** *(Massey-Ferguson)* RIGHT: **Max Aitken (Lord Beaverbrook)** *(Maclean's Magazine)*

11

A Nation in Business, 1880–1900

National businessmen . . . Timothy Eaton and the retailing revolu-
tion . . . western wholesalers . . . Woodward's . . . the CPR's struggle to
survive . . . competition and the monopoly clause . . . Stephen
heartbroken . . . the hothouse boom in manufacturing . . . industrial
Maritimes . . . steel comes to Hamilton . . . municipal bonuses . . . the roots
of the branch plant . . . the National Policy encourages ignorant invest-
ment . . . Masseys and Harrises . . . Pat Burns and beef . . . Toronto becomes
"Hog town" . . . F.H. Clergue rolls steel at the Sault

Canada was in business as a nation by the 1880s. The Confederation of 1867 was a hurried, rickety, political unification of two Atlantic and two inland provinces. There was little travel or trade between the Maritimes and the central provinces; west of Ontario there was only wilderness, wandering Indians, and a few miners and fur-traders' posts. But in less than twenty years the Dominion became an economic reality. The Northwest was bought from the Hudson's Bay Company and British Columbia joined Confederation, creating a political-geographic transcontinental nation. Treaties with the Plains Indians, the creation of the North-West Mounted Police, the work of the Dominion Lands Survey, turned the prairies to a land ready for an influx of homesteaders. The completion of the Intercolonial Railway in 1876 began the economic integration of the Maritimes with the central Canadian economy. The completion of the Canadian Pacific in 1885 made it possible to think of a Canadian economy, with truly national firms doing business from the Atlantic to the Pacific. Since 1879 it had been the country's National Policy to use tariffs to protect the home market for Canadian producers.

Ottawa's several national development policies – the railroad, free homesteads on Dominion lands in the West, an open door for immigrants, high tariff walls – were not part of a coherent plan or recipe for nation-building. They only seemed that way later.* At the time the policies were ad hoc,

* The myth of a grand, coherent National Policy was first promulgated by the Liberal scholar and civil servant, O.D. Skelton, in the "General Economic History" volume he con-

confused, and partly contradictory. The one notion that did govern them was a vague desire to see Canada imitate American economic progress. Millions of immigrants would settle the great plains. Population growth would create a large domestic market in which infant manufacturing industries would strengthen and grow. A second powerful industrial nation would gradually emerge in North America. When Sir Wilfrid Laurier said, "The nineteenth century was the century of the United States. I think we can claim that it is Canada that shall fill the twentieth century," he was implying similar stories of economic progress. In numbers, size, wealth, Canada would catch up.

In fact, Canada did not and could not match American growth. The budding nation of the 1880s was pitifully small, a northern fringe of only four and a half million people compared with fifty million Americans. Economically it was little more than a series of regions that railways happened to traverse. Most of the regional economies were troubled: the Atlantic provinces suffered from the decline of the wooden sailing ship, Quebec from rural over-population, the West from under-population. Only Ontario had a flourishing economy and reasonably healthy agriculture, manufacturing, and financial industries. It was a potential breadbasket and smokestack province comparable to states such as Pennsylvania, Ohio, Michigan, or Illinois. But even Ontario had real weaknesses, such as an almost complete absence of coal and quality iron ore, the elements thought fundamental to the industrial revolution. Without them would it be possible to make steel, the heavy metallic symbol of industrial maturity? The raw materials would have to be imported, probably from the United States, probably at high cost.

Business came of age in the United States in the late nineteenth century. Working with a wonderful resource endowment and in an enormous, unfettered market, American entrepreneurs created huge national and international corporations, developed sophisticated managerial techniques, and mounted a display of raw growth and economic power such as the world had never seen, even during Britain's industrialization.

Canadian business activity was much more limited. The northern economy was still being created. New land was being cultivated, mining and forest industries were being founded in the emptiness of the Canadian Shield, national railroad and financial networks were still being filled in. Markets were scattered over vast distances and were minuscule by American or European standards. It was not until 1902 that Canadian heavy industry had the capacity to make a single rail from Canadian steel. The age of Carnegie

tributed to the Canada and Its Provinces series in 1913. It was perpetuated through several generations of standard economic history textbooks, most notably Easterbrook and Aitken's *Canadian Economic History*. One of the idea's implications was that governments had the capacity to plan grand, coherent nation-building programs.

and Rockefeller and J. P. Morgan and young Henry Ford in the United States, from about 1875 to 1910, was in Canada still the age of the general storekeeper on the prairies, sawmills in the Gatineau, shoe factories in Quebec, and textile mills and candy factories in New Brunswick. Between 1880 and 1896 several hundred thousand Canadians emigrated toward better opportunities in the United States; for a time in the late 1880s many Canadians shared the Liberal party's view that the country had to become integrated with the United States in a single continental economy. In 1891 Canada's leading intellectual, Goldwin Smith, suggested in *Canada and the Canadian Question* that full political union with the Americans was the only answer.

Smith's pessimism soon came to seem misplaced. Within limits imposed by geography, natural resources, and demography, Canadian growth was impressive and sometimes spectacular. In the 1880s and 1890s agriculture in the central Canadian heartland generated huge surpluses for export. Prospering farmers were able to bear the extra costs imposed by the National Policy tariff, and new factories sprouted in towns and cities almost as spectacularly as the protectionists had predicted. The West went through many troubled years, but finally began to bloom after 1900 as the tide of immigration at last reached the prairies and rebounded in a flood of golden wheat. One mineral strike after another – in Ontario, and British Columbia, and the Klondike, and Ontario, and Ontario, and Ontario – the development of hydro-electric power, application of the new pulp- and paper-making technology, all meant that the rocks and trees and rivers of the Precambrian Shield and the Rocky Mountains became generators of wealth instead of barriers to farmers and railway-builders. Iron mines in Newfoundland and coal mines and steel mills in Nova Scotia promised industrialization even in the Maritimes, perhaps especially in the Maritimes.

During the headiest years of the Laurier boom, from 1900 to 1912, not one but two new transcontinental railways were built to handle all the business the Dominion's economy was creating, or was expected to create. In the financial heartlands, along King Street in Toronto and St. James Street in Montreal, bankers and bond dealers wrote prospectuses for more and more Canadian electricity and street railway companies: not only for the utilities in their own cities, which were already well launched, but also for enterprises in other countries on other continents – enterprises created by Canadian financial, legal, and engineering ingenuity that continued to spill out of the home market.

The country imported huge sums of foreign capital – still mostly British – and an increasing amount of American technology and enterprise, as branch plants began to flourish and Yankee risk-takers promoted steel and pulp mills up north in God's country. But most of the business leadership in the changing economy was Canadian. In the early 1880s a storekeeper named Timothy Eaton who had started out in rural Ontario learned how to become the country's first national retailer. In 1910 a bond salesman who hailed from a Presbyterian manse in rural New Brunswick, Max Aitken, left Canada for the world's capital, London, in search of new worlds to conquer. He had created all the trusts in Canada, he said. These big industrial mergers, including one that created the Steel Company of Canada, were the last phrase of the Laurier boom. Between Eaton and Aitken flourished a generation of railwaymen, financiers, manufacturers, starry-eyed promoters, and others – even newspapermen – who were the first businessmen in Canada to operate on a truly national scale.

IN 1869, THIRTY-FIVE-YEAR-OLD TIMOTHY EATON purchased the drygoods stock of James Jennings and opened T. Eaton and Company at 178 Yonge Street, Toronto. Eaton was a barely-educated Irish Protestant, a convert to Methodism, who served an apprenticeship in storekeeping and emigrated to Canada in 1854. He kept store in the town of St. Mary's and several other locations before moving to Toronto, and when he opened in the big city he was still troubled by what he referred to as his "past years Difficulties.... How I am to attempt to carry on a business here in the face of everyone in the Whole Sale houses knowing this?" He needed credit from the wholesalers, of course, and worried that the business methods he wanted to try now would cause more trouble. He could not offer "the old excuse I have made use of Many times... that we done So Much Credit and that we could not get our money unless we Sued our customers.... Of the above I cannot now say a Word as I am selling only for Cash." His assets, he said, were his wife, five children, and seven dollars.

Eaton managed to get credit from one important wholesaler, John Macdonald, another devout Methodist willing to support a "brother" in the faith. Macdonald was one of Canada's largest wholesalers, doing a million-dollar-a-year business and employing more than a hundred clerks in his splendid downtown Toronto warehouse. He had withdrawn from retail trade, specialized in drygoods, and further subdivided his house into departments which he used as accounting units. Departmentalization, careful accounting, and cautious use of credit had marked Macdonald's path to the front ranks of wholesaling. Active in politics and church affairs, possessor of a splendid mansion, "Oaklands," overlooking the city, Macdonald became known as Toronto's merchant prince during wholesaling's prominence from the 1860s to the 1880s. The help he gave Timothy Eaton was virtually as prince to pauper.

Wholesalers were still the dominant merchants in the distribution system, but some were much better situated than others. Toronto houses grew steadily through mid-century as the expansion of Ontario strengthened them against the Montreal men. These inland merchants increasingly by-passed Montreal and New York importers and sent buyers directly to England and Europe. Toronto's advantages within the province were also important to its merchants, for the steady development of the railway network, with Toronto the hub, gave the city's distributors an important edge, particularly over wholesalers in rival Hamilton. Isaac and Peter Buchanan had built the province's first great wholesale business in Hamilton in the 1840s. By the mid-1860s it was crumbling under a burden of bad debts from retailers, lack of growth in Hamilton and its hinterland, and Isaac's inept management after Peter's death. The Buchanans' Hamilton and Glasgow houses failed in 1867, limped along in semi-receivership for a few more years, and disappeared in the 1870s. With none of his sons talented enough to rescue the firm or succeed in a new business in Canada, Isaac Buchanan spent his final years as a genteel failure, living on patronage crumbs tossed his way by old political friends.

In the meantime Timothy Eaton slowly built a retail business in Toronto that did not depend on anyone. Cash sales – and a lot of them – were the foundation. The cash itself was a sign of a maturing economy: so many Torontonians now had incomes of coins and bank notes that a storekeeper's dream of no more trade in kind or credit could finally come true. But only for the few retailers willing to give customers extra value for their cash in the form of rock-bottom prices. This, in turn, required a high volume of sales and low overhead. It was no longer worthwhile to bother with the time-consuming practice of haggling with customers; goods had one fixed, low price, take it or leave it. Regular advertising was essential to attract new customers. To counter their fears about the quality of products paid for in cash (could you return it if it was truly paid for?) it made superb sense to offer a blanket guarantee of refunds on unsatisfactory goods. Timothy Eaton was not the first merchant to try to apply any of these policies; many others had experimented with variations on all of them, particularly a cash system. Eaton was the first in Toronto to make the new methods work as a general storekeeping strategy.

Eaton's growing ability to finance his own purchases in cash enabled him to cut the ties binding him to Macdonald and other suppliers. Soon he was by-passing wholesalers, travelling to England to buy direct from manufacturers. Eaton's was originally a drygoods store, but the range of fabrics and clothing was increasing all the time; it also seemed sensible to keep volume increasing by selling any product customers would buy (except alcohol and tobacco, where the Methodist merchant drew the line). Through the 1880s Eaton added one line after another, moving to larger stores, enlarging his stores further, hiring scores of new clerks. He kept on top of the business by sectioning it into departments, each with its own manager, buyers, and separate accounts.

If Eaton's could sell anything, it should also be able to sell to anybody, anywhere, not just those who found their way into the store. In 1884 Timothy Eaton distributed his first "newspaper of merchandise" to visitors to Toronto's

Industrial Exhibition. The flyer soon evolved into catalogues of goods that customers anywhere in Ontario, then anywhere in Canada, could order from Eaton's. The country's railway network and its efficient postal system made quick, safe delivery possible.

By 1890 Timothy Eaton was employing upward of four hundred and fifty clerks (six hundred during the Christmas rush) – far more than any Toronto wholesale house – in a mammoth sixty-department store covering almost a whole city block. John Macdonald died that year, and his firm began a long slide into oblivion. As the wholesalers were eclipsed, the retailing Eatons succeeded them as Canada's new merchant princes. Timothy, a crusty, hard-driving man whose life was little more than business and church, was too busy to ponder the role he was forging in the community. In the early 1890s he integrated into clothing manufacturing, added grocery and pharmacy departments (because bottled patent medicines, canned foods, and packaged bulk goods like crackers and tea now made it possible to do a huge volume in these lines*), and copied the best innovations made in leading British and American department stores. The retailing revolution, based on high volume, low prices, cash payment and the ability of entrepreneurial retailers to break the traditional horizontal and vertical divisions of trade, was an international phenomenon. Timothy Eaton was its Canadian prophet.

———————◆———————

Leading wholesalers were eventually surpassed by mass retailers in other cities and other fields, but their decline was gradual and relative and it was interrupted by major new opportunities, particularly the explosive development of western Canada. As early as the 1870s some of Winnipeg's storekeepers separated their wholesale and retail divisions, then specialized in wholesaling as they became suppliers to the general storekeepers beginning to dot the prairies. Often the merchants did a return grain business, repeating a pattern established years earlier in Upper Canada. The crash of 1883 ushered in many years of hard times for

---

* Many of the most popular branded items, like Pears Soap or Pinkham's Compound, were British or American products. But Peter C. Larkin's success at selling packaged tea under his "Salada" brand made the Toronto wholesaler several millions and a reputation as "Tea King of America." And in the 1890s a Brockville, Ontario, druggist, George T. Fulford, discovered how to market a new patent medicine: use saturation newspaper advertising, stress signed personal testimonials, and coin a catchy slogan to promote a product to cure everything. The product, "Dr. Williams' Pink Pills for Pale People," was an advertising and commercial sensation around the world. Fulford, too, became a millionaire and his great slogan, "pink pills for pale people," was for many years one of the few Canadian expressions deemed memorable enough for inclusion in the *Oxford Dictionary of Quotations*.

everyone on the prairies, but as the new century approached a sizable number of handsome warehouses lined Winnipeg's business streets. The city was the gateway for goods and people coming to the new West. Winnipeg's own merchant prince at the turn of the century, James H. Ashdown, had made his fortune in hardware, mostly as a wholesaler.

Before 1850 most merchants did their own travelling. The country storekeeper visited the big city wholesale house in the off-season, or aggressive wholesalers such as the Buchanans toured the hinterland to work with customers and drum up new ones. As the pace of business quickened, thanks particularly to railways, the wholesalers began to employ specialized travellers, commercial travellers, to keep in touch with their customers. The farther afield the customers, the more important the travellers; so Montreal led by sending travellers into Ontario and the Maritimes in the 1860s. Later the Toronto houses, which had at first been outraged by Quebec salesmen invading their markets, sent travellers to the prairies to compete with the Winnipeggers. Finally the Winnipeg houses hired travellers. Only a few conservative firms – John Macdonald's was one – bucked the trend and advertised a policy of employing no travellers.

Manufacturers soon realized they could by-pass wholesalers by employing their own travellers. Shoe and drug companies led the way. By 1900 the manufacturer's agent was as common a denizen of the pullman and smoker as the wholesaler's drummer. As a third for poker they might bring in a department store buyer going or coming from a trip to England.

Eaton's was the greatest retail success story, but there were many others, not least the good trade Robert Simpson did near Eaton on Yonge Street in Toronto. Simpson copied most of Eaton's methods, kept his thirst for liquor under control, and somehow found the resources to build a bigger and better store every time he was burned out. Both merchants profited from the sales synergy created as their two giant stores stimulated Yonge Street shopping. Like Eaton, Simpson had moved into Toronto from the hinterland. John Northway, who started as a "merchant tailor" in Tillsonburg, also moved into Toronto, but kept the several drygoods stores he acquired in smaller centres. Northway planned to do a wholesale drygoods business in Toronto, saw there was no future in it, and applied his skills to clothing manufacture. By the late 1890s Northway and Sons was one of the largest garment manufacturers in the city; the Northway retail stores in half a dozen small cities were their most important outlet. A few years later Northway opened a major store in Toronto.

Another refugee from Toronto wholesaling was the firm of Ogilvy and Company, which had emigrated from Montreal in the 1870s and went home in the 1890s to concentrate on mass retailing. Ogilvy's, Morgan's, and Dupuis Frères all flourished in Montreal by the end of the nineteenth century. Their growth was limited, though, by the lack of a prosperous Quebec hinterland to supply new customers – for, say, a catalogue business – and to generate talented managers.

Charles Woodward did not do particularly well at storekeeping on the fringes of Ontario's hinterland on Manitoulin Island. His troubles with creditors and debtors persuaded him of the desirability of cash storekeeping, and he tried that method when he sought his fortune at the end of the CPR line in 1891. The city of Vancouver grew so fast that a general storekeeper such as Woodward became a department store general manager without going through the middle stage of specialization. Woodward had several nasty brushes with creditors and partners as he scrabbled through the tough world of Vancouver retailing. By 1905 Woodward's department stores ran soundly and profitably, ready for the founder's sons to take over – if only the domineering old workaholic would retire. Like Eaton and so many of the single-minded storekeepers who made the retailing revolution, Woodward had made the business his life.

The Hudson's Bay Company ought to have sewed up the department store business across western Canada. Just as it was forestalled in Vancouver by Woodward (a sometime fur trader in his northern Ontario days), so it let opportunity slip in Winnipeg. The Eatons stepped in, opening the largest store in western Canada in 1905. It was probably less important to Eatons' domination of western retailing than the tons of Eaton's catalogues distributed across Canada by the dawn of the new century. The catalogue was the ultimate travelling salesman, offering farm folk who saw few humans from one week to the next almost as wide a range of shopping opportunities as the slickest city folk enjoyed. Eatons' buying power, sales volume, breadth of offerings, and distribution system were so well developed that few small retailers could compete with the catalogues. These fat, colourful, and free magazines became legendary as the most widely distributed publication in Canada next to the Bible, and perhaps the better read. Certainly the women in the underwear ads were more stimulating than the story of Onan. Simpson's also did a national mail order business, but never developed the reputation of the leader. At the turn of the century Eaton's proudly advertised itself as "Canada's Greatest Store."

———————

The commercial travellers, the agents and buyers, the department store catalogues, and all the products, went by train. Canada's first blush of railway mania had long since faded. The iron horse was not going to carry a bride for every bachelor, transform every backwoods village into a new Athens, make every farmer a millionaire. But it had become the work horse of the Dominion. By the 1880s the railway network was Canada's overland transportation system. Everyone took the train; everyone shipped by train. Everyone who could not – say a Manitoba farmer located more than ten miles from a branch line – wanted to ship by train. In 1886, when they opened the line, it became possible to travel and ship from one end of Canada to the other via the Canadian Pacific Railway, the largest and most important business in the country, the first pan-Canadian corporation.

On the day the last spike was driven, the CPR's directors must have given little thought to the ceremony in the Rockies. One of their Great Lakes freighters, the *Algoma*, ran aground in Lake Superior in fog and was wrecked with a loss of forty-eight lives. Its sinking was a sickening introduction to the grim side of the transportation business. The CPR's future was not by any means secure in 1885. Shipwrecks were not at all a regular occurrence, nor were train wrecks, but the everyday problems of running a transcontinental railway business were staggering enough.

The Canadian Pacific was still a railway in search of business – a railway in search of a country, actually – for even on completion the CPR was little more than the audacious development line its opponents had criticized as absurd, a railroad built from the edge of civilization through wilderness to reach nowhere. It was expected to link up with other lines at Callander, a village in the northern Ontario forest. Twenty-five hundred miles to the west, on Burrard Inlet, the total population of a few sawmill camps was less than one thousand souls in 1885. Except for the depressed province of Manitoba and a few cattle ranches in the southern Alberta District of the Northwest Territories, there was nothing in between. Where was the railway's business to come from?

Yes, there was the great construction boom as the track-layers moved westward amidst swarms of land speculators, homesteaders, and pedlars of booze, sex, and hardware. The last and best stage of the boom came at the far end when the line was finished. Everyone realized that the Pacific terminus, a few acres of forest named Vancouver, was bound to become an important city. The optimism was self-fulfilling. Merchants and speculators lined up to buy good lots on the site, the CPR made handsome profits on its land sales, and some thirty real estate firms did a thriving business churning raw properties. By 1891 the thirteen thousand people in Vancouver and the Inlet expected perpetual growth and prosperity for their busy Terminal City. "The fact that grain shipments were negligible in the early 1890s, that the trans-Pacific trade was modest, and that no major national demand existed for British Columbia's raw materials could be ignored," Norbert MacDonald has written. "People were convinced about Vancouver's future, and as long as these convictions were sustained, migration continued."

Convictions about the prairies' future had turned sour in 1883, the last year of major CPR construction in the region. A mood of doubt, then pessimism, and finally despair descended on Manitoba and the Northwest, entering even British Columbia in the later nineties, which was not totally dispelled until the early 1900s. Settlers came down to earth on the prairies: dry, hard, cold ground that farmers found damnably difficult to cultivate. The northern plains have always been difficult to farm; through most of the 1880s and 1890s prairie agriculture was simply uneconomic. Homesteaders had trouble growing crops, and when they could ship good northern wheat found they were too far from world markets to get a living return. Westerners learned to live with reduced expectations or gave up and moved on. Fewer and fewer newcomers arrived. Land values collapsed. Towns and cities stagnated, businessmen retrenched or failed. The West was not yet ready to develop: much of the planning of the early 1880s was premature – including, probably, the building of the Canadian Pacific Railway.

The CPR syndicate and the government expected the railroad to generate rapid settlement and agricultural development. Land sales and then steady traffic would make the whole system, including the mountain and Lake Superior sections, profitable. These projections were based on unrealistic estimates of the West's agricultural potential, and were wrong. Built as a development road in advance of settlement, and passing through some of the least attractive prairie country, the CPR was unable to induce the settlement that would have justified the haste to build it. If the CPR had gone bankrupt during construction, or if it had not been built until the mid- or late 1890s (at much less cost in subsidies), the broad history of western Canadian development would not have been greatly different. The epic struggle to push the CPR through the wilderness was based on assumptions about a virgin land pregnant with growth possibilities. It took more years than most people expected for western Canada to be truly born.

Should the CPR have been built, then, at huge cost to the Canadian taxpayer, when it was? Probably not. The railroad could have been built later, with less subsidy. The uneconomic early construction of the CPR was justified only if Canadian fears about an American political or expansionist menace to the West were soundly based. After the early 1870s they almost certainly were not. The myth of the CPR, as a nation-building risk that had to be taken and that worked wonderfully, inspired generations of visionary promoters and politicians during the next hundred years.

How would the CPR survive? Absence of debt plus brilliant management of the system, mainly by Van Horne, helped overcome its handicaps. Promoted to the presidency in 1890 on George Stephen's retirement, Van Horne remained a cyclone of energy, a storehouse of railway expertise, and a master of operational detail. His and the directors' strategy was a nice blend of economizing and expansion. They aimed at having the lowest possible costs, and appear to have succeeded. The CPR's ratio of operating costs to revenue averaged about 60 per cent before 1900. "No important railway in the world was ever operated as cheaply as the Canadian Pacific in its most extravagant year," Van Horne boasted to Stephen in 1894, and explained why: "When the Canadian Pacific was built we had the advantage of the experience of all the railways in North America, and were able to lay out the entire system with a view to the greatest possible economy and convenience in working, and I do not believe that any important railway in the United States can possibly get down to our figures." Van Horne was stretching the truth about economy and convenience, for the CPR's steep grades in the Rockies created horrendous operating difficulties, but management did have a genius at cost control. At the same time, cost-consciousness was balanced by a stategy of expansion. The directors set out to turn a troubled development railway into an integrated international transportation empire – impervious, they hoped, to competition from lesser Canadian and American systems.

The railway company entered the steamship business immediately by buying Great Lakes freighters to move grain. The *Algoma's* black day was the only serious mishap on the Lakes. The more venturesome shipping expansion was on the Pacific, where the Canadian Pacific had to attract ocean traffic to Vancouver. It chartered sailing ships to bring tea from the Orient to Vancouver, then hired three old Cunarders to tramp the Pacific, and in 1891 introduced three brand-new twin-screwed *Empress* liners to oriental service. On their maiden voyages from Liverpool to Vancouver via the Suez Canal, the *Empresses* took passengers "around the world in 80 days" for $600.

The tourists stayed at the CPR's Hotel Vancouver, accommodation the company erected as part of the terms of its townsite grant. In the mountains the company built rest stops because it was too expensive to pull dining cars up the slopes. These restaurants in spectacular settings soon turned into hotels. Van Horne then realized he could "capitalize the scenery" in terrain that had been nothing but trouble for the railway. In 1887–88 the CPR built a major tourist hotel at Banff Hot Springs in Canada's first national park. Ottawa had obligingly created the park at the CPR's suggestion. (Donald Smith named Banff after the county in Scotland where Stephen was born; politicians and railway barons also named several mountains after themselves.) The Banff Springs Hotel immediately became a North American institution. So did the Château Frontenac in Quebec City, a majestic hostelry in one of North America's most spectacular locations, opened by the company in 1893.

Why was the CPR, whose main line did not reach the Quebec border, building hotels in Quebec City? The company never accepted the logic of truncated transcontinental status, and determined from the outset to expand to serve all the populated areas of central Canada. The directors saw no alternative to eastern expansion and competition with the Grand Trunk and all other lines, and insisted that the CPR charter permit ownership and construction of eastern feeder roads. "Had you stopped at the completion of your main line across the continent," Van Horne told the shareholders in 1890, "your enterprise would have come to ruin long ago, or at best it would have existed only as a sickly appendage of the Grand Trunk. Like a body without arms it would have been dependent upon charity – upon the charity of a neighbour whose interest would be to starve it."

While the main line was being built, Stephen, Smith and company leased, bought, and built lines into major cities and through paying countryside. The Grand Trunk Railway had managed to right itself in the 1860s, fight its way into Chicago in the 1870s, and become established as a major North American system. It handled a large amount of international through traffic and intercity Canadian trade. The GTR's board apparently hoped they could use the CPR as an "appendage," but could not have been surprised at the rival's determination to get into

Canada's leading cities, Montreal and Toronto. It was surprised, then alarmed, when it became apparent that the CPR intended to compete everywhere, including rich southwestern Ontario. Van Horne's threat to duplicate every Grand Trunk line drove the point home.

By the early 1880s promoters in the central and eastern provinces had chartered scores of railways, "of which some had even been built," G.R. Stevens writes, "short lines squiggling across the countryside, as casually as cowpaths, as unintegrated as worm casts." The Grand Trunk and Canadian Pacific raced to buy or lease these lines, either as feeders or to string together, building where necessary, into new through routes. The Grand Trunk was the more active consolidator, swallowing both the old Great Western and the Northern, but the CPR still managed to penetrate most of its territory. By 1884 it had completed a line to Windsor to connect with American roads and was running through trains to Chicago.

The CPR's expansion was encouraged by everyone who hoped that more railway competition would mean better, cheaper service. The Grand Trunk complained loudly about the unfairness of competition from such a heavily subsidized system and warned that the CPR was intent on becoming a power stronger than the government. But the Macdonald government was happy to have created a second railway power in the land, one that could pull some hot old railway chestnuts from the political fires. As an unwritten condition for government support in the crises of 1884 and 1885, the CPR agreed to buy the North Shore Railway, linking Montreal and Quebec City. It was a scandal- and patronage-ridden line whose construction had nearly bankrupted the government of Quebec. The CPR also agreed to build a "Short Line" across northern Maine to the Maritimes, meeting the Intercolonial at Saint John. Maritimers now had a much faster route to central Canada than the Intercolonial's all-Canadian main line offered. Ironic, of course, for the national railway to be building shortcuts across American soil.

In all negotiations with the government the CPR's directors protected themselves as best they could by asking for subsidies and protection against losses. Their strategy was to reduce risk, trade quids for quos, try to safeguard the shareholders' interests. The game was endlessly complicated, involving trunk lines and branches across a continent, several layers of government, and powerful competitors at home and abroad. In the West the CPR's struggle to hold its territory was like the Hudson's Bay Company's problems with the fur trade. In both cases Canadian customers developed a burning desire to patronize American companies. The Red River valley was again the hotbed of agitation. As Manitoba's economic problems mounted in the mid-1880s, its farmers were outraged by CPR freight charges of up to 25 cents a bushel on wheat that would only bring 50 to 60 cents. As well, Van Horne bungled his grain elevator policy by refusing to load wheat except from full-service elevators. Most of the elevators fell into the hands of W.W. Ogilvie, of the milling family, whom Stephen labelled "an awful fool both in speech and action" for abusing his monopoly in dealing with the troubled farmers. Manitobans had been delighted to get a railway, but now wanted more than high rates and elevator monopolists. Why not more railways – new lines to link up with U.S. systems, new lines to develop new Canadian possibilities? Why not build to salt water on Hudson Bay, for example? Such a railway would revive the old fur-trade route, save a thousand miles of freight rates, give Manitoba its own seaport, and free westerners from bondage to the east.

The CPR syndicate knew that the white elephant of the Northern Ontario line would make it vulnerable to American competition. So it had insisted on the monopoly clause in its charter, forbidding non-CPR connections across the forty-ninth parallel for twenty years. This was a major blunder because the monopoly could not be enforced. The people of Manitoba would no more accept serfdom to the CPR than to the Hudson's Bay Company in the fullness of its power. Responding to overwhelming popular demand in the mid-1880s, the provincial government began chartering railway lines to the border. The Macdonald government disallowed the charters and Manitoba issued new ones.

The CPR reacted arrogantly and stupidly to the anti-monopoly agitation by threatening to move its repair shops from Winnipeg to Fort William. Van Horne is said to have threatened to make grass grow in the streets of Winnipeg. Westerners only became more angry at CPR "tyranny" and more determined to get railway competition. Their agitation began to hurt the company financially. "CPR shares worth today 49½ against 75 last year," Stephen wired Macdonald in 1887. "The shrinkage is more than Winnipeg is worth with all the people in it thrown in."

Stephen rejected Macdonald's advice to, in effect, bribe the Manitoba legislature into cooperation ("The CPR might get control of the legislature of Manitoba for the next four years if it chose," the prime minister wrote, "and those would be years of comfort") and decided to give up the monopoly clause. As compensation he got a Dominion guarantee for a $15 million bond issue and permission to buy control of American lines south of Lake Superior. By 1889 the CPR controlled a south shore route from Winnipeg through St. Paul or Duluth to Sault Ste Marie, and handled all transcontinental traffic north of the Chicago route.

Many CPR trains used exactly the international route – a western "short line" – most experts had originally preferred to an all-Canadian line. The north of Superior track became, as the experts had predicted, costly surplus mileage, handling little freight, doing its best duty in geography and history texts as encouragement to Canadian chauvinism. The CPR and the people of Manitoba would have been better off without the complex, costly charade created by misguided nationalism. Most western grain did not need a through railway at all, for it was transferred to lake freighter at the head of Superior. The main problem with Manitoba freight rates was that the CPR was serving a frontier region generating little traffic. But this issue and the monopoly struggle owed the seeds of deep anti-CPR sentiment in the West. It was a feeling that would feed on every company mistake and every grievance remotely attributable to the West's largest company and would do the Canadian Pacific inestimable harm.

After the monopoly clause was broken, the government of Manitoba invited the Northern Pacific to operate branch lines in the province. Freight rates did not come down. The main competitive threat to the CPR in the 1890s came from one of its own founders, J. J. Hill. He had withdrawn from the CPR in 1883, and embarked on one of the great adventures in American railroading: in ten years Hill turned the Minneapolis, Manitoba, and St. Paul into an American transcontinental, the Great Northern, and even took over his main American rival, the Northern Pacific. Would Hill threaten the Canadian Pacific? There was a strong community of interest between the Canadian Pacific and the Great Northern because the leading shareholders in both roads were the same two men, Lords Strathcona and Mount Stephen, earlier known as Donald Smith and George Stephen. But the rival presidents, Van Horne and Hill, were two of the world's most aggressive and talented railway entrepreneurs. Mount Stephen, who retired to England and was used by both presidents as a prime confidant, could not keep their competitive energies in check. "He has neither good will nor good intentions to the Canadian Pacific," Van Horne wrote Stephen about Hill in 1891, "whatever his inside feelings toward yourself and Sir Donald may be . . . . I shape my plans on the assumption that he is the most dangerous enemy of the Canadian Pacific."

Hill kept threatening to branch into Canada, especially southern British Columbia, where rich lodes of gold, silver, and copper had been found in the early 1890s. The companies locked horns in the Kootenay in a byzantine game of charters, buy-outs, mergers, and bluffs, often using fronts, sometimes having all their plans disrupted by interloping freelancers. If it was clear enough that the Naskup and Slocan Railway, moving ore north to Canadian refineries, was a CPR creature, it was not certain who owned the rival Kaslo and Slocan Railway, which shipped ore south. Van Horne said the Great Northern owned it, Hill denied it. Hill was lying. The Kaslo and Slocan was the first of eleven spurs Hill eventually built into British Columbia. They were only a prelude, he often threatened, to a new transcontinental on Canadian soil.

Hill's challenge and other pressures to open the country caused the CPR to run a steamship service on the Columbia and the Okanagan lakes, buy mines and refineries in the Kootenay, and finally offer to build a major line into the region from southern Alberta over the Crow's Nest Pass. Needing help to make the branch viable, the company made a deal with the Laurier government in 1897. In the Crow's Nest Pass Agreement, solidified by federal statute, the CPR got a hefty subsidy for its Crow's Nest Pass line in return for reducing its rates on prairie grain moving to the Lakehead and its charges on many westbound items. The statute bound the company never to raise these rates. The agreement was suspended during the Great War, but then reimposed on the CPR and other railways. Long after most of the Kootenay mines were closed, Jim Hill had lost interest in

Canada, and the Kaslo and Slocan was merged with the Naskup and Slocan, the Crow's Nest Pass freight rates were still in effect.

Presidents of the CPR negotiated with prime ministers of Canada as men of roughly equal power. The government of Canada could make laws and levy taxes, but the CPR employed almost as many people and offered an equally vital service. It did business in most political constituencies; the sum of its national influence made the CPR in the 1880s and 1890s the most influential corporation Canada ever created. In elections the company was a helpful friend of the government, a "sleeping partner" Macdonald called it. The hundreds of letters exchanged between Stephen and Macdonald, then Van Horne and a series of prime ministers, richly document the relationship.

The CPR heads were usually aggrieved by the government's failure to recognize the importance of the railway's needs, the justice of their views, and what they saw as the common interests of the CPR and the Dominion of Canada. To outsiders, the CPR appeared to be a leviathan, feeding on lavish subsidies, well in control of government, more powerful than Parliament itself. To Stephen and Van Horne, fighting endlessly against aid to competitors, tangled in Manitoba and the monopoly clause, negotiating interminably over subsidies or grants for half a dozen branches, the government of Canada was too often more hindrance than help. "It is positively heartbreaking the way we are treated," Stephen burst out in frustration in an 1890 letter, "and I am tired of beseeching & begging for fair treatment, & have resolved on giving up all further efforts to secure it, as useless . . . . In almost every transaction we have had with the Govt arising out of the contract we have been taken advantage of and duped and deceived in the most cruel manner. Had I been the worst enemy of the Govt politically I could not have been worse treated than I have been by the Dept. of Railways."

Stephen was so frustrated in this letter that he reminded Macdonald, for the only time in their correspondence, that he personally had contributed more than one million dollars to the Conservative party since 1882 – an enormous sum of money in the 1880s – adding immediately that he would not ask anything of the government "but what is fair, and which ought to be granted even had I never done a thing for it politically." Van Horne tended to be less emotional in his outbursts, more willing to play an overtly political game. He made sure, as he put it, that most CPR workers were "fully-circumcized" Conservatives.

Stephen's frustrations reflected his growing sense that his effort to create Canada's national railway was not appreciated and may not have been worth it. With negligible land sales and less traffic than had been expected, the CPR through its first decade earned only enough to cover its fixed costs and pay a 1 or 2 per cent dividend on the par value of its common stock. It was unpopular with the Canadian people and often frustrated in its dealings with the government. Stephen endured years of intense stress to create the CPR and seemed often on the brink of mental or physical collapse. In 1889 on his sixtieth birthday he told Macdonald of his sufferings since his fiftieth: "I cannot help thinking what a fool I was not to have taken advantage of the opportunity I then had to end my work and enjoy the leisure which I had earned by 40 years of hard work."

The CPR's worst years were yet to come. By 1895 its $100 par value shares, which sold originally at $50 to $60, were worth $33 on the London market. Lord Mount Stephen lost faith in both Van Horne and the CPR and advised his friends to sell out. Van Horne held on through the lean years of the nineties and kept hoping for the best. When earnings picked up after the middle of the decade and the stock began to rise, Mount Stephen is said to have sold out lest he appear to have profited from the bad advice he gave his friends. He lived handsomely in England, a philanthropist and friend of kings, and was over ninety at his death in 1921, but according to Van Horne neither Donald Smith nor George Stephen made money out of their Canadian Pacific adventure. The real basis for their fortunes was their interest in Jim Hill's American railways, dating from the old St. Paul, Minneapolis, and Manitoba.

Fortunes were ready to be made in manufacturing even before the National Policy of high tariffs was implemented in 1879. Duties of 30 per cent and higher on a wide range of imports increased the opportunities, securing the home market for Canadian producers, and inducing a rush of capital into manufacturing. In the decade of the 1880s, years of slow growth in several areas of the economy, the number of manufacturing establishments increased by 52 per cent, the capital invested in manufacturing by 114 per cent, wages by 68 per cent. The tall chimneys of National Policy factories dominated the landscape of industrial towns from New Glasgow, Nova Scotia, to Windsor, Ontario. Iron foundries in Winnipeg and sugar refineries in British Columbia seemed to show that the policy was truly national. Loud grumbling about the costs of the NP by farmers and some lumbermen and by Liberals in Parliament was ignored through the 1880s as the government kept adjusting tariffs upwards. National Policy protection reached a peak level of about 35 per cent on most items in 1887.

Tariff policy was highly political. Before elections Sir John A. used to meet with the members of the Canadian Manufacturers' Association in the Billiard Room of the Queen's Hotel in Toronto to exchange mutual promises of support. Free traders were outraged by the devilish pacts made in this lurid Red Parlour. In the 1891 election a Liberal platform favouring unrestricted reciprocity (i.e., unlimited trade liberalization) with the United States was defeated following Tory charges that freer trade was really a prescription for the destruction of Canada by annexation. The Liberals finally came to power under Wilfrid Laurier in 1896 only after they had let manufacturers know well in advance that they were "safe" on the National Policy. Conservative and Liberal governments in the 1890s both threw some tariff crumbs to free traders, and in 1897 the Laurier government instituted moderate but promising preferences on imports from sister countries of the Empire. But by and large the National Policy was unchanged under Liberalism. The use of high tariffs to foster "made in Canada" manufacturing became bipartisan national policy.

Manufacturers' success at identifying protection and the National Policy with Canadian nationalism (including Canada's very survival in 1891) underlay their political success. It was simple patriotism, surely, to be in favour of building Canada by protecting Canadian industries. The protected manufacturers gloried in a nation-building role that coincided nicely with their self-interest and took credit for every manufacturing job in the country, implying that Canadians would not have sawed a piece of wood or milled a barrel of flour without the NP. Canada's renowed Indian poetess Pauline Johnson put the protectionist creed to rhyme in "Made in Canada," composed specially for the 1903 convention of the Canadian Manufacturers' Association:

> We don't need the marts of Europe, nor the trade of the Eastern isles,
>   We don't need the Yankee's corn and wine, nor the Asiatic's smiles.
> For what so good as our home-made cloth and under the wide blue dome,
>   Will you tell me where you have tasted bread like the bread that is
>   baked at home?

It was the homemade cloth that received the greatest stimulus from the National Policy. Investment soared in every area of the textile industry. Seventeen cotton mills were opened between 1878 and 1885; most were huge red-brick factories employing hundreds of men, women, and children. Quebec was the centre of the industry with about 45 per cent of total production, but the greatest relative expansion took place in New Brunswick and Nova Scotia, as mills sprouted in Halifax, Yarmouth, Moncton, Saint John, St. Stephen, and Marysville. Quebeckers and Maritimers alike hoped their provinces would repeat the experiences of the neighbouring New England states and become cloth-makers to the nation.

Particularly in the Maritimes, the new factories sopped up the funds of merchants diversifying away from such weakening traditional industries as shipbuilding and the timber trade. Now that the Atlantic region was tied by railroads to the central provinces, and with the National Policy in place, it seemed possible to think of an industrial future for the region. Was there any reason why Maritime manufacturers, well situated to receive raw materials from abroad, could not supply the nation's growing interior market? And the big textile mills, the new sugar refineries and glass factories and confectionary houses might all be just icing on the cake if Maritime boosters ever succeeded making their provinces the centre of the most basic of all nineteenth-century manufacturing industries, iron and steel production.

Why not? Nova Scotia had huge coalfields and accessible deposits of iron ore. Newfoundland had more iron. Ontario and Quebec had no coal and no significant quantities of iron ore anywhere near their centres of population. The bog-iron works in the central provinces were almost played out (the St. Maurice forges closed for good in 1883; no furnaces operated continuously in Ontario) at a time when demand continued to rise. Ottawa's commitment to the National Policy implied new, higher coal and iron duties or other subsidies whenever it was clear that domestic industries could be created.

Established merchant families in Pictou County, the Carmichaels and Mc-Gregors, organized the capital needed to begin steel production in Canada behind the NP's tariff wall. In 1882 the Nova Scotia Steel Company was formed by these and other merchant families allied with skilled foundrymen in the area. In 1883 it cast Canada's first steel ingots at Trenton, using the Siemans-Martin open hearth process. Imported pig iron was used at first, but the high "iron tariff" of 1887 – said to be designed to make Nova Scotia the Pennsylvania of Canada and New Glasgow the Birmingham – encouraged several of the steel men to promote a major iron works at Ferrona. Halifax money, organized by the prominent merchant industrialist, John F. Stairs, was important in the financing of this New Glasgow Iron, Coal and Railway Company. Its main Canadian competitor was the Londonderry Iron Company, also of Nova Scotia, but soon controlled by Montrealers.

In the early 1890s the steel and iron producers of Pictou County went from strength to strength, supplying good-quality products to feed a growing regional complex of forges, foundries, rolling mills, and car works. In 1893 they secured an important new supply of ore by buying for $5,000 the huge deposits of hematite on Bell Island in Newfoundland's Conception Bay. In 1895 the steel and iron companies were merged into the Nova Scotia Steel Company, capitalized at $2,060,000. "Containing its own blast and open hearth furnaces, rolling mills, forges, foundries, and machine ships," T. W. Acheson writes, "the firm represented the most fully integrated industrial complex in the country." A few years later Scotia Steel became more fully integrated by buying its own collieries on Cape Breton Island, erecting a new steel plant at Sydney Mines, and reorganizing again as the Nova Scotia Steel and Coal Company, capitalized now at $7 million.

In the meantime a Boston utility magnate, H.M. Whitney, had come north to secure coal supplies for his utilities. In 1893 Whitney and a number of Montreal capitalists organized a major consolidation and refinancing of several Cape Breton collieries as the Dominion Coal Company. In 1899 they launched a new public company, Dominion Iron and Steel, to erect steel works at Sydney. It soon became the largest steel complex in Canada. At the dawn of the twentieth century, Cape Breton Island's great industries – its two big steel mills and dozens of coal mines – gave steady work and wages to thousands of men. Say what you liked about tired Montreal or upstart Toronto, where the money and the banks seemed to be going, the smoking chimneys and the roaring furnaces, the grime and sweat and steel of the new Canada were right here in industrial Nova Scotia.

Secondary iron and steel works – foundries, rolling mills, wire works, nail and screw and nut and barbed wire fence companies and other finishing plants – did blossom near their markets in Ontario and Quebec. But at least half a dozen attempts to found new smelters and steel mills in the upper provinces failed. Steel-making plants were installed in Montreal and London, Ontario, among other cities, only to burn up large sums of investors' money in furnaces that never turned out saleable ingots. For several years it seemed as though the works on Huckleberry Point in Hamilton Bay would have the same fate. The American capitalists who came in 1893 to put up a Hamilton iron and steel mill (the city gave them the seventy-five-acre site and a bonus of $100,000) saw their furnace stack blown down in a gale and their company collapse in the depression of the mid-nineties. A group of Hamiltonians, including hardware merchants, iron-founders, and the publisher of the Hamilton *Spectator*, William Southam, finally got a blast furnace going on the last day of 1895, shut it down for want of skilled iron-makers, had to be bailed out by a personal loan from Toronto's George Gooderham, and could not get a steel plant operating. In 1899 they amalgamated their Hamilton Blast Furnace Company with the Ontario Rolling Mills to form the Hamilton Steel and Iron Company. It imported American technical help and furnaces, as well as American coal and iron ore, and finally began pouring open-hearth steel in 1900, years behind the big Maritime steel companies.

Hamilton's bonus to lure steel-makers was standard municipal practice. The bonus habit was everywhere and was deeply ingrained. It began with the first bank and railroad promotions when public corporate bodies had subscribed for shares in ventures likely to advance their community's interests. By the 1880s every municipality in Canada was willing to bonus manufacturers with some combination of free sites, tax exemptions, free utilities, loans, investments, or outright cash sub-sidies. Manufacturing seemed particularly worth bonusing because of the enormous employment and cash flow opportunities these factories created for communities, benefits that would surely far outweigh the temporary cost of the subsidy. An English immigrant to Hamilton who observed that in the old country townsfolk would pay a company to stay away had no understanding of the North American desire for growth and more business, or of the intense competition among communities hungry for growth. Such policies were miniature National Policies, and they were everywhere. When Sam McLaughlin's carriage works in Oshawa burned in the late 1890s, for example, fifteen other towns offered bonuses if he would relocate. Oshawa helped keep him with a $50,000 loan, repayable "as convenient." Hamilton had outbid a number of other communities to get its iron and steel works going, and it continued to outbid them in the rivalry for other attractive industries. Generous municipal aid a few years later helped convince both Westinghouse Electric and International Harvester to erect their Canadian branch plants in Hamilton.

Getting American companies to erect Canadian branch plants was, of course, a main aim of the National Policy. Politicians hoped the tariff would induce transfers of foreign capital, technology, and expertise to Canada – a policy one journal called "importing industries instead of products." As early as 1879 the young manager of the Windsor, Ontario, branch of the Bank of Commerce, B.E. Walker, reported that the "extra song from the siren" was having its effect in pulling American companies across the Detroit River. Other notes in the siren's song included legislation requiring non-resident holders of Canadian patents to have the article manufactured in the country within two years or lose their rights. These policies, indistinguishable in their influence from the normal economics of regionalization, helped lure scores of American companies into Canada in the 1880s and afterwards.

Overall ownership of manufacturing and most other industries was predominantly Canadian, with important British and European investments from coast to coast. By the early 1900s, however, it was common knowledge that the National Policy had encouraged such major American firms as Singer Sewing Machine, Edison Electric, American Tobacco, Gillette, Swift's, Parke Davis, and Coca-Cola to enter Canada. Many other ostensibly Canadian factories had American investors or American managers or used American-made machinery or made American-designed goods under licence. No one thought foreign ownership of factories in Canada was in any way harmful. On the contrary, the "Canadianization" of American business in this migration was exactly the result economic nationalists wanted. The National Policy helped move jobs, technology, capital, and capitalists into Canada. This was the aim of all the industrial policies, including bonusing. "American firms of every description 'seeking a new site' or 'wishing to extend their business by establishing a Canadian branch' have only to make public their designs and be inundated by letters from Canadian municipal authorities," the *Monetary Times* reported in 1895.

The National Policy none the less created distorted, hothouse growth in manufacturing that had serious, often harmful, consequences in both short and long terms. It seemed easy to get up a company, negotiate a deal for a municipal bonus, import machinery and managers from the States, and start making money. In his study of the National Policy and the industrialization of the Maritimes, William Acheson found that one of the characteristics of the men who launched the region's new industries was "ignorance of both the technical skills and the complexities of the financial and marketing structures involved in the new enterprises." In a case study of Milltown, New Brunswick, where the huge St. Croix cotton mill – thirty-four thousand spindles, five hundred employees – was thrown up in 1882 to take advantage of the National Policy, Peter DeLottinville notes that none of the local promoters had "the slightest knowledge of the textile trade." All of them believed that the project could not possibly fail. While the Nova Scotia Steel Company was more carefully launched, apparently, its main competitor was not. After touring the Sydney steel mill in the early 1900s, an English visitor wrote in the *Times* that "in Canada they have a way, which does more credit to their courage than to their prudence, of taking hold of enterprises without any proper training or experience."

The rush of inexperienced investors produced predictable results in cotton in 1883 when it was suddenly realized there was more capacity in the industry than the Canadian market could bear. For the rest of the decade frantic attempts by mill-owners to divide the market and fix prices alternated with periods of cutthroat competition. Finally the leading cotton barons of Montreal, A.F. Gault and David Morrice, amalgamated most of the country's mills into the Dominion Cotton Mills Company (1890) and Canadian Coloured Cottons (1892). The original investors in the combining mills took heavy losses. Through most of the 1890s the two cooperating firms were able to control prices and production in the industry. Pressure from new competitors in the early 1900s led to another major merger in 1905, creating the Dominion Textile Company. At all times the cotton manufacturers kept a close eye on the tariff, for any significant reduction in the National Policy rates could doom the Canadian industry. There was little hope that the twenty-odd cotton mills scattered from Yarmouth to Hamilton, many more than the Dominion needed, many equipped with obsolete machinery and second-rate managers, could ever mature into a truly competitive industry.

The cotton manufacturers did export sporadically to China and Japan in the late 1880s; some even talked of exporting to England. But this was just dumping, sacrifice selling abroad to clear the Canadian market and hold prices. The National Policy did not encourage the development of Canadian firms fit to export manufactured goods. On the contrary, the tariff existed largely because the Canadian manufacturers that sheltered behind it were not efficient enough to compete with foreigners. The long-term effect of the National Policy was to burden exporting industries with higher than necessary input costs and to discourage Canadian manufacturers from specializing in lines where they might be able to exploit a comparative advantage and become internationally competitive.

In New Brunswick, for example, Boss Gibson's eldest son had urged the old lumberman to build factories that would make wood products instead of the gigantic textile mill he erected at Marysville, near Fredericton. The son lost the toe-to-toe shouting matches about strategy that they used to have on the front steps of their office. He died young and his father lived to see the mill, a red-brick white elephant, drain away much of his fortune. In Ontario the McLaughlins of Oshawa did work with wood, but found themselves producing some 143 different carriages and sleighs for the small national market – Concord bodies for Quebec, boxlike shapes for Ontario, buckboards for the West, Phaetons, Stanhopes, and fringe-top surreys for Maritimers and city folk. The manufacturing sector in the Dominion was encouraged by the National Policy to become a northern replica of U.S. manufacturing. As a general rule, small copies could no more compete with originals in foreign markets than thin branches could with mighty trunks.

Many manufacturers made the most of their opportunities in the home market, becoming leaders in their industries, turning their companies and products into Canadian household names. Bennett Rosamond of Almonte, a Tory MP and a sometimes president of the Canadian Manufacturers' Association, continued to run one of the most efficient woollen mills in the country, employing hundreds of hands in a model company town. Edward Gurney's stoves and furnaces, produced in Hamilton and Toronto, secured considerable market dominance, as did the pots and pans and other kitchenware made by a Montreal hardware merchant who moved to Toronto, A.E. Kemp. Staunch protectionists, both Gurney and Kemp served terms as head of the CMA (and Kemp eventually became a senior minister in Borden's Conservative government). The Heintzmans and Nordheimers in pianos, Wanzer in sewing machines, McClary in ranges, the Ganongs in candy and chocolates, the McLaughlins in carriages, and many others, bested their Canadian competition to create dominant firms in the fields so helpfully fenced off by the National Policy.

A few of the protected manufacturers occasionally tested export markets, and a few of these succeeded very well. The most important export breakthrough was the performance of the Masseys and Harrises in farm implements. During the 1870s A. Harris, Son and Company of Brantford and the Massey Manufacturing Company of Newcastle both began specializing in heavy harvesting tools – mowers, rakes, and reapers. A 17.5 per cent tariff against imported machines was considered satisfactory by the implement men in the seventies. The 35 per cent National Policy levy after 1883 must have made them ecstatic. Canadian imports of mowers, reapers, and threshers fell from 1,068 in 1871 to exactly 6 in 1886.

The perfection of self-knotting devices revolutionized harvesting in the 1870s and 1880s by making it possible to bind grain mechanically. Both Harris and Massey entered the field with patented light binders developed from American prototypes. In 1880 the Masseys moved their operation to a big new factory in Toronto. In the next ten years their Toronto Light Binder, "The Mighty Monarch of the Harvest Field," duelled in fields across Canada with Harris's Brantford Binder, "The Little Brantford Beauty." The two companies broke through into high sales volume, developed national networks of selling agents, and began advertising heavily. They probably did not compete in prices, and the profits from the big, expensive machines – at $200 to $350 they were the first high-priced consumer durable – must have been considerable. No would-be competitor could achieve the two big firms' advantages in quality and volume, so the industry developed not unlike automobile manufacture forty years later: an oligopoly of national firms dominated the market (Massey and Harris had over 60 per cent of the business by the end of the decade), while a shrinking crowd of small men scrambled for the crumbs. The big companies painted their machines like fire engines, distributed four-colour catalogues showing off a host of models and optional extras, held lavish field trials and exhibitions, and on "Delivery Day" hired brass bands to lead the parade of implements down Main Street. The techniques reflected both non-price competition and North Americans' love affair with their machines, and were all used later to sell automobiles. So was the reliance on manufacturer financing, with low down payments and many months to pay.

North America led the world in labour-saving farm implement technology. In the mid-1880s the Masseys and Harrises both began exhibiting and trying to sell internationally. Not unlike the life insurance salesmen at about the same time, the Canadians probed every possible market, trying to find a niche between domestic firms and the big American exporters. The best markets were in England, Australia, and the Argentine. Massey's European business was considerably stimulated by the Mighty Monarch's success in the binder trials of the Paris Universal Exhibition of 1889, when it won the firm both a gold medal and one of the coveted "Le Vainqueur du Coq" trophies.

In 1891 the Harris and Massey companies decided to merge. Both Alanson Harris and Hart Massey had lost the sons they expected to succeed them in the industry, and Harris's development of a revolutionary open-end binder had suddenly upset the competitive balance between the companies. The merger restored stability and created a deeper pool of managerial talent. Massey-Harris Company Limited, capitalized at $5 million, was the largest manufacturing company Canada had yet seen. The harvester firm immediately began to expand by acquisition, taking over the just-formed Patterson-Wisner company to give it a "full-line" capacity, and adding established specialized firms through controlling interests in Verity Plow, the Sawyer steam tractor and thresher company, and, several years later, the Bain Wagon Company. In 1892 Massey-Harris advertised itself as the largest makers of farm implements in the British Empire.

Some farmers criticized Massey-Harris as an attempt at monopoly and the federal government appeased them a little by cutting its tariff protection to only 20 per cent. The 1890s were good years anyway. The company sold more than half of all the farm implements used in Canada. Its export sales grew rapidly during a global agricultural expansion, amounting to 40 per cent of the company's production by 1900. Between 1890 and 1911 Massey-Harris made 15 per cent of all the manufactured goods exported from Canada. The sun never set on fields where Massey-Harris binders were working. A special experimental department of the company, probably Canada's first significant private research facility, was founded in 1892 to improve the products. (The firm's failure to win any glory at the Chicago World's Fair of 1893 was a major disappointment, but was considered a result of corrupt American judging.)

The Massey name was on its way to becoming a household word in Canada: because of the big machines in the barn, because the Massey Cornet Band had been to town, because the household subscribed to *Massey's Illustrated* or *Massey's Magazine* (serious periodicals that grew out of advertising handouts), because at the town fair in 1898 everyone had gaped at the moving pictures of Massey-Harris machines at work – made by special arrangement with Thomas Edison himself – because the family had heard a wonderful concert at the beautiful new Massey Hall in Toronto, because the daring youngsters rode the newest-fangled of all Massey-Harris implements, its Silver Ribbon "wheel" or bicycle. The company went into bicycle manufacturing, competing against several American branch plants, during the cycling craze of the late 1890s. The Silver Ribbons were ridden as far afield as Wellington, New Zealand, where they were standard issue for the police force.

The Massey family advanced in wealth and social status, growing away from its agricultural roots, but remaining devoutly Methodist. Masseys were expected to be deeply committed to the business, to hard work and clean living in all aspects of life, and to Christian stewardship in the community. At the intersection of the family and the firm the most pressing question was whether there would always be enough talented Masseys, with perhaps a Harris now and then, to man the highest ranks of the company.

———◆———

Neither the Masseys nor many other manufacturers prospered on the backs of the western farmer, for there were still relatively few farmers in the West. Canada's agricultural triumphs of the 1890s centred in Ontario, with Quebec catching up very fast, as dairy and livestock farming grew beyond all expectations. The British market for eggs, butter, and cheese from the young Dominion seemed insatiable. Canadians made thousands of tons of cheese and some very big cheeses. (Their indisputable triumph at Chicago in 1893 was the world record "Canadian Mite," a 22,000 pound cheddar cheese made in Perth, Ontario. It was eventually exported to England. Another Canadian export was J.L. Kraft of Stevensville, Ontario, who moved to Chicago in 1905 and became the world's most successful cheesemaker.) Through the 1890s and well into the early 1900s the leading staple export from Canada, next to wood, was cheese. Almost three thousand tiny cheese factories and creameries, most of them little more than household industries, dotted the rural landscape of Prince Edward Island, Quebec, and Ontario, and they were slowly becoming consolidated into dairies. Agricultural research was vital to Canadian productivity and international competitiveness and was stimulated by experimental farms at the Dominion, provincial, and private levels. The president of Massey-Harris, Walter Massey, for example, owned an experimental dairy farm outside of Toronto, Dentonia, which produced some of the earliest pasteurized milk distributed in Toronto. It became the basis of the City Dairy Company, Toronto's first modern supplier of dairy goods.

The first area of food manufacturing to become centralized under corporate management was meat-packing. The centre of Canadian cattle production moved from the Eastern Townships of Quebec to the semi-arid southern ranges of the District of Alberta in the 1880s (because of the Townships' connection, some of the largest ranch-owners were Quebeckers, including Sir Hugh Allan). A semi-literate Irish-Catholic from Kirkfield, Ontario, Patrick Burns, first tried his luck homesteading in Manitoba, then began trading cattle and contracting to supply beef to railway camps. An old Kirkfield chum who ran a contracting outfit, William Mackenzie, gave him good business. In the mid-1890s Burns's railway work led him into the British Columbia interior where he discovered a demand for fresh beef in the mining camps of the Kootenay. Pat Burns developed a large wholesale beef business out of Calgary supplying a chain of retail butcher shops he created in the mountain towns. In 1899 the "Meat King of the North West" opened his first large abattoir in Calgary. The festivities were highlighted by a ceremonial killing of the first steer. "The sight was one, which though gory at times," a reporter wrote, "could not but make one feel that Alberta had at last secured an industry of practically illimitable scope."

Its scope was in fact limited by the domestic market and the difficulties of shipping "dead" beef before refrigeration was perfected. Except in the West, where settlement was so scattered, the beef market could easily be entered by small operators. Cattle were normally driven or shipped on the hoof and slaughtered near the point of final sale. Canadians tried to export their product, but found they could not sell refrigerated or frozen beef in competition with Argentine producers. Live cattle exports to Britain became important for Canadian ranchmen, and for Pat Burns as ranch-owner, but not Pat Burns as meat-packer.

The hog trade was very different. With a salt cure, pork could be preserved almost indefinitely, packed, and shipped over long distances. Many small pork "packers" supplied barrels of fat, salt pork to lumber and railway camps. But there was also the big Toronto pork-packer, William Davies, who had built a handsome export business cutting and curing sides of bacon for the British market. In the late 1880s Davies slaughtered about eighty thousand hogs a year, mostly for export, and grew rich on about $30,000 a year profits on sales in the $700,000 to $800,000 range. Then the good years began.

In the 1890s British demand for foreign bacon soared. New American agricultural tariffs caused hog prices in Canada to decline. Stone-deaf and aging, his sons dying of tuberculosis, William Davies invited an earnest provision merchant who had recently moved to Toronto from Peterborough, Joseph Wesley Flavelle, to become managing director and part-owner of the business. Flavelle was a brilliant, dedicated manager, who improved the Davies product, mastered every aspect of the bacon trade, and presided over an astonishing growth in sales and profits. William Davies's killings rose from 95,000 in 1893 to 446,000 in 1899 (years when Pat Burns was shipping about 10,000 cattle a year and had to import hogs from Ontario to meet western pork needs); export sales rose from $1,000,000 to $3,560,000, by far the largest part of the business. The shareholders in the William Davies Company received dividends of 110 per cent on their $250,000 capital in 1897, 100 per cent in 1898, 120 per cent in 1899, and 82 per cent on $400,000 in 1900.

Davies and Flavelle both became millionaires, proving that there was indeed a relationship between sows' ears and silk purses. Flavelle's rise to riches was particularly noteworthy as a classic saga of Christian virtues and good luck overcoming the handicaps of poverty and a drunkard father. By 1900 the poor Peterborough boy, whose first job had been delivering telegrams for George A. Cox back in the 1860s, was presiding over the largest pork-packing business in the British Empire. During the next decade drovers funnelled millions of pigs from the rich farm hinterlands of Ontario down the Grand Trunk's Don Valley line to the big William Davies slaughterhouse on Front Street in Toronto, and the city got its enduring nickname, "Hog town."

"It is an awful thing to think that all the rails used in our... railways are brought in from other countries," one of the struggling Hamilton steel-makers complained in 1896. For most Canadian manufacturers the export success of the Masseys and the meat-packers was inconceivable. Manufacturing in Canada was domestic, tariff-sheltered, and most promising as an exercise in import replacement. Thanks to the National Policy, most of the Canadian market for manufactured goods remained in Canadian hands by the end of the 1890s. But big steel products, especially the long, heavy rails that symbolized the foundations of nineteenth-century industrialism, were not yet Canadian. Canada's national railway, the CPR, ran on foreign-made tracks, imported duty-free. The Macdonald government had not even tried to use tariffs and the CPR to foster domestic production. No Canadian steel producer could hope to match the great furnaces and hearths of Birmingham and Pittsburgh.

Well, there were a few visionaries who had more faith than this in the northern country and its resources. By the 1890s a handful of true believers in the country's endowment of ore and fuels and waterways and manpower became convinced that the time had come to realize the dream of building the Canadian nation with Canadian steel.

No one believed more passionately in Canada's bounty than Francis Hector Clergue, an American promoter who in 1894 began a series of astonishing developments in the wilderness town of Sault Ste Marie, Ontario. Backed by Philadelphia investors, Clergue started with a hydro-electric power development, harnessing the rapids of the St. Mary's River between lakes Superior and Huron. He used some of the power to grind wood, an abundant resource of the region, in a large pulp mill, developed a machine shop and foundry, and began exploring for minerals. A hematite deposit he purchased for $500 and named the Helen Mine became the largest iron ore producer in the Dominion. He had never thought God had put iron only on the American side of Superior, Clergue liked to say.

Now that he had a mine and was building a railroad (the Algoma Central) and buying lake freighters to move the ore, Clergue began construction of a massive iron and steel works at the Sault. The steel would be used to make rails to feed the surge of railway expansion just getting under way in the Dominion. The Laurier government, believing the new century would belong to Canada, encouraged Clergue with the first steel rail contract given to a Canadian producer; it was to make rails for the Intercolonial. In May 1902, F.H. Clergue's Algoma Steel Company, a unit of his giant Consolidated Lake Superior Corporation, rolled the first steel rail ever made in Canada.

With Clergue's achievement at the Sault, the nation's thrust toward manufacturing sufficiency seemed almost complete. The irony, of course, was that Clergue, an American, had had more faith in Canada than the Canadians themselves. As he explained in a landmark 1900 speech to the hard-faced, rather skeptical Scotsmen who dominated the Toronto Board of Trade, his only plan in his endeavours was to go into Algoma, "take the raw resources which God left there when the world was created, and turn them to the beneficial uses of mankind." Hailed as one of Canada's greatest captains of industry, a pioneer in industrial research and high technology, F.H. Clergue emphasized his link with entrepreneurs of the past by living in a reconstructed Hudson's Bay Company blockhouse next to the rapids.

Building a trestle on the Grand Trunk Pacific Railway *(Public Archives of Canada, #PA38622)* INSET: **Sir William Mackenzie** *(James Collection, City of Toronto Archives, #1298)*

12

"Trusting Somewhat the Future"

*The wilderness blooms . . . King Coal . . . Dunsmuirs, Galts . . . mines in
Sudbury, the Kootenay, Klondike, Cobalt, Porcupine . . . pulp and
paper . . . railways needed everywhere . . . CPR alumni . . . Mackenzie and
Mann . . . new transcontinentals . . . street railways . . . Canada goes to
Brazil . . . electricity . . . Canada's utility imperialists . . . Max Aitken and
mergers . . . "I created all the big trusts in Canada" . . .
newsmagazines . . . the fall of Francis H. Clergue*

The "raw resources" that F.H. Clergue talked about seemed the key to
Canada's twentieth-century growth. It was such a wonderfully rich country,
overflowing with raw materials to be cut, mined, ground, refined, milled, rolled, and sold – all for the beneficial uses of mankind. The farmers had always
tilled what fertile soil they could find and the lumbermen had cut the big trees.
But now there was so much more: the rocks themselves, even those with coal-
black seams, glittered with promise. Rushing, falling water was ready to be
harnessed as "white coal" to light homes and streets and power industries.
Even as the woodsmen began to exhaust the pine forests of eastern Canada
they learned that the incalculably larger spruce forests of the north could be
ground to pulp and rolled out as the world's paper supply. And the millions
and millions of acres of fertile soil on the prairies – kingdoms of rich black sod
– were finally ready to come into their own, as immigrants were ready and
able to make farming in Manitoba and the West a success.

The eighties and nineties were uneven years for Canadian business. The
early 1900s would be much better. Mining, pulp and paper, hydro-electric development all soared. Immigrants poured into the West, and grain began to
flow out of it. Foreign capital poured into every part of the country. Cities
blossomed on the prairies and thrived in the central provinces, and even grew
in the Maritimes. Canada got two new provinces, Alberta and Saskatchewan,
carved out of the Northwest Territories in 1905. The "Laurier boom," evident
from about 1900 to 1913 (two years after the Liberals were defeated on the

reciprocity issue), saw year after year of spectacular growth in almost every area of the Canadian economy, with only temporary setbacks during seasons of contraction and tight money in 1903 and 1907.

Opportunities seemed to be everywhere. The frontiers of Canadian enterprise were out in the wilderness and they were right on the downtown streets. Some of the same entrepreneurs worked both frontiers, digging, building, and scheming to keep the foreign capital coming. They built railways through untamed wilderness and railways down the busiest streets in the Dominion; then they built railways and dams and power outside the Dominion – in Latin America, Europe, even the United States. Canada's utility entrepreneurs, like the bankers and insurance men before them, would not be confined within the Dominion. Their horizons, like their country's, seemed boundless.

———————◆———————

THROUGH MUCH OF THE NINETEENTH CENTURY it seemed that God had short-changed the north when He parcelled out mineral resources. Coal beds in Nova Scotia and on Vancouver Island were too far away to supply the most populous central regions of the country, which had to rely on Pennsylvania bituminous and anthracite. Little iron was found, except the bog stuff used in St. Maurice and the other primitive forges. What riches did Canada's breastplate, the great, granite Precambrian Shield contain? Very little, the early prospectors concluded, as they scoured the north shores of Huron and Superior in the 1850s. There was one bonanza – rich veins of silver in a rock in Lake Superior near Thunder Bay – and nothing else. An American syndicate extracted several million dollars' worth of ore from Silver Islet in the 1860s and 1870s. Otherwise Ontario's rocks seemed barren.

South of the St. Lawrence, in Quebec's Eastern Townships, there was growing interest by the 1880s in several copper deposits and the strange fibrous mineral, asbestos, but development was slow and unpromising. In the far west, Barkerville, British Columbia, boomed for a few years in the 1860s as the centre of gold country, but by the end of the decade the Cariboo creeks, like the Fraser streams before them, were pretty well played out. The little goldfields of Nova Scotia, opened in the same decade, never amounted to much. A brief gold rush in eastern Ontario in 1866 created the boom town of Eldorado and an important Canadian tradition of promoting worthless mining stock; total production from Eldorado's mines was eighty-five ounces. At Confederation mining was not an important or promising Canadian industry.

Coal was the humble king of Canadian mining for the first several decades after Confederation. Nova Scotia's deposits were first developed by the General Mining Association, a British organization equipped with capital, technology, skilled labour, and, until the late 1850s, a monopoly. Other capitalists, both American and Canadian, gradually opened mines, but the soft bituminous fuel was not high quality and for half the year ice prevented shipment by water. Railways such as the Intercolonial had the double attraction of both carrying and burning the coal. Markets gradually developed for the Nova Scotia product in both New England and Quebec (the tariff was the key to Quebec, but was never high enough to keep American anthracite from dominating Ontario). Then the development of iron and steel manufacturing in the region during the 1890s seemed to guarantee the colliers' perpetual prosperity as feeders of the heavy industries of the industrial east.

The West coast deposits created one of the first spectacular British Columbia fortunes. Robert Dunsmuir, out from Scotland as an indentured miner to the Hudson's Bay Company in 1851, discovered the Wellington coal seam near Nanaimo in 1869, and with his son James developed it into a great and prospering mine. The Dunsmuirs cultivated their markets – San Francisco and the British navy – carefully, and emphasized close, hard management of mines in which Orientals toiled for very low wages. As the leading businessmen on Vancouver Island, the family naturally took an interest in railways, gathering more mineral deposits and timber rights as part of a large subsidy for building the Esquimault to Nanaimo railway (a much-lobbied-for Island extension of the transcontinental system) in the mid-1880s. By the time of Robert's death in 1889 the Dunsmuirs were easily the most powerful and controversial family in the province, symbols of raw capitalist achievement to some, naked capitalist exploitation to others. Although markets were limited to the West coast, the Dunsmuir mines were productive into the twentieth century, feeding the family fortune while James served his province as premier (1900–1902) and lieutenant-governor (1906–1909).

The coming of the CPR made possible the development of the coal seams of the eastern slope of the Rockies. The opening of the first mines, at Coal Banks in the southern part of the district of Alberta, was a final business adventure of old Alexander Tilloch Galt, railway-builder and resource developer to the end, who became one of western Canada's most optimistic promoters in the 1870s. Galt and his son Elliott leased huge coal deposits, organized construction of a hundred-mile "coal branch" railway to connect with the CPR's main line, then developed the region's largest mine as well as the town of Lethbridge (named after one of their principal investors, a British bookseller). The Galts did as much to develop southern Alberta in the 1890s as the Eastern Townships in the 1840s. Elliott had become deeply involved in irrigation projects in the area when his interests were finally bought by the CPR. Railways were always the leading consumer of Alberta's coal.

The Canadian Pacific stimulated a somewhat disappointing mineral discovery in northern Ontario, just west of the Sudbury station, when construction workers alerted local merchants and timber cruisers in 1883 to deposits of copper tainted with *kupfer-nickel*," Old Nick's copper." The stuff was hard to refine and there was no obvious market for nickel. The Sudbury claims passed through several hands before they were bought by an American, S.J. Ritchie, who had been trying to revive the iron industry in Hastings County. Ritchie's Canadian Copper Company began mining and smelting in Sudbury, had its ores refined by another American firm, the Orford Copper Company (formed to mine copper in the Eastern Townships), and devoted most of its efforts to finding markets for nickel. By 1900, military demand for nickel-steel in the United States and Germany was stimulating sales of Sudbury nickel, even as the smelting process denuded the countryside with sulphuric corrosives.

There was so much ore in the Sudbury basin that competitors had little trouble opening mines. Its leadership in the difficult arts of smelting, refining, and selling the nickel gave Ritchie's company vital advantages. Several rival nickel companies failed. In the 1890s Ritchie himself, an erratic promoter, was forced out of Canadian Copper, and in 1902 it was merged with Orford Copper and several minor companies to form the International Nickel Company. More competitors appeared – everyone, including even Thomas Edison, seemed to want to try his hand at nickel – but only one other Sudbury firm, the British-owned Mond Nickel Company, survived, largely on the strength of refining expertise. Mond worked closely with Inco and the Rothschild-controlled French company, Le Nickel, to fix prices, allocate markets, and develop new uses for their metal.

Foreigners dominated Sudbury because they had the technology and marketing ability to refine and sell what was otherwise useless rock. Americans were first into the big Canadian strike of the early 1890s, the silver-copper-gold-lead boom in the Kootenay region of southern British Columbia, because the area was a geographic extension of the mineral belt that American miners had been following up the cordillera. The isolated Kootenay camps were originally accessible only through the United States. Butte, Montana, and Spokane, Washington, were the staging areas for the prospectors and the capital that opened the region, created the rush to Rossland and Slocan, and made the big Canadian mines – Centre Star, War Eagle, Le Roi, and Silver King – which for a few years were world famous.

When Canadian investors realized what was happening in the Dominion's own remote mountains and valleys, they wanted opportunities for a piece of the action. Brokers and mine promoters quickly obliged. In May 1896 the *Rossland Miner* had complained that "the absolute indifference of Canadians generally and Eastern Canadians in particular, to the mining developments of their own great country, is enough to make a citizen of West Kootenay tired and weary." Within three months, Toronto markets were deluged by stock offerings of western mining companies.

The eastern brokers were happy to peddle Kootenay stock and were joined in their efforts by veteran promoters moving up from the United States. Mining investment was wild risk-taking, with occasional fabulous pay-offs. Promoters reached out to everyman's propensity to take a small flyer, and became some of the first financial intermediaries to sell stock to the common man. The trick was to issue huge numbers of shares in very low denominations – a dollar a share or even penny mining stock – and then promote the speculation as virtually riskless. The line between selling and swindling was almost non-existent. One notorious technique was to give shares to prominent people and then advertise their names as shareholders, in, say, the Palo Alto Gold Mining Company and the Nest Egg Mining Company, both of Victoria, BC, offering one dollar shares at only twenty cents through ads in the *Toronto World*:

> These two mining properties, owned and controlled and operated by the leading business men and the best known citizens of the Province of British Columbia is [sic] a guarantee that investors in these two mines have great chances of realizing big profits for a small investment . . . .
>
> I have come to the conclusion that British Columbia, and Trail Creek, in particular, is about to develop into the greatest gold producer that this continent has ever known, and that Trail Creek will rival, and most probably surpass, the wonderful gold fields of South Africa. English capitalists have already begun to find out the wealth of this favored region, and they have already begun to buy some of the mines in Trail Creek. When London has once fairly started to buy these mines there will be no chance for Canadian capital to get mining property at low figures. I therefore think that if the people of this province desire to share in the enormous profits that are certain to be realized in British Columbia mines they must invest at once, and for this reason I offer to my clients mining stocks to which, after most careful consideration and investigation, I believe they will have an excellent chance of realizing big profits.
>
> GEO. A. CASE,
10 Victoria St., Toronto
Real Estate and Mining Broker

By 1898 Toronto's financial district housed more specialists in mining shares than there were members of the Toronto Stock Exchange. The new brokers formed two special mining exchanges, which soon merged as the Toronto Standard Mining Exchange. Mining companies and mining brokers tended to be short lived, many disappearing overnight (sometimes on the sleeper to Buffalo). But there had to be enough real evidence of solid pay-offs in western mining to have generated the boom in the first place. Along with the suckers in Toronto, some of the city's shrewdest capitalists, including the Gooderhams, E.B. Osler, and George A. Cox, invested heavily in Kootenay mines and the coal properties being developed as the CPR drove its Crow's Nest Pass branch into that country. As it wrestled business away from J.J. Hill and the Great Northern, the CPR itself became the major force for both development and Canadianization of the area, buying smelters and mines, and in 1906 spinning out a mining subsidiary, the Consolidated Mining and Smelting Company of Canada, or Cominco.

Thousands of prospectors worked the creeks and gravel beds of the northwestern mountains in the 1890s. The more remote the country a man prospected, the better the prospects, it seemed, if only because no one might have been there before. So the advance scouts of the mining entrepreneurs were everywhere. By 1895, according to one estimate, about five hundred of them had pushed north to scour the country drained by the Yukon River in the Northwest Territories and Alaska. In 1896 George Washington Carmack, Skookum Jim, and Tagish Charlie struck it rich on a tributary of the Klondike River named Rabbit Creek. They found a place where a quarter-ounce of gold would sift out from a single pan of gravel. Ten cents' worth of gold in one pan was a good haul; this was $4 worth. Rabbit Creek was renamed Bonanza Creek.

The men already in the Klondike country were the first to stake their claims. When boatloads of the sourdoughs returned to civilization toting their pokes of gold dust in 1897, the rest of the world tried to rush in. The 1898 stampede to the Klondike by thirty thousand prospectors and adventurers, and competing parties of Canadian bankers, was one of history's classic gold rushes. Anyone could try his hand at placer mining, extracting the gold dust contained in gravel deposits. Fancy companies and tons of capital were unnecessary. So at first the Yukon was a place to go to rather than invest in, and there was not a major eastern boom in Klondike mining stock. About the best the stay-at-homes could do, especially on the West coast, was try to make a little profit selling outfits to the men brave or foolish enough to tackle the trails to the Klondike. The well-developed American shipping and prospecting centres, San Francisco, Seattle, and Portland, got most of that business, no matter how loudly the merchants in Edmonton proclaimed the superiority of their overland routes to the Klondike.

From a different angle, the best Klondike mining business could be done back east in Ottawa. As the gold-hungry and greedy rushed in to the Klondike in that first summer, the smartest local entrepreneur, Joe Boyle, rushed out of the Klondike to the nation's capital to talk mining with politicians. Boyle, the son of a Woodstock, Ontario, horse-breeder, had been a drifting devotee of the sporting life, who wandered up to the Klondike with a pugilist he managed, the "Australian Cornstalk," Frank Slavin. Boyle was one of the first to realize in the glory days of the rush that the panners and sluicers would soon exhaust their claims. The long-term future of Yukon mining was bound to lie in massive thawing and dredging and washing operations along miles of riverbank. Boyle went to Ottawa to be among the first to secure concessions of unclaimed or lapsed gold-bearing lands. By 1899, when the swarm of little men was about to fly from Dawson to Alaska and the next Eldorado, Boyle and the other concessionaires were settling in to organize mining companies. It was not a smooth transition: the placer miners fought the big interests, charging favouritism and corruption, and forcing several flip-flops in concession policy. Political favouritism was more common than corruption in Ottawa's Klondike policy, if only because it was not considered corrupt for a member of Parliament to invest in and lobby for a mining company.

Back in the Klondike, Boyle developed lucrative sidelines harvesting lumber and cordwood on his concessions, and became one of Dawson's most prominent sporting men – sponsor, for example, of the Yukon hockey team that played for the Stanley Cup in 1904. He managed to raise money abroad, and in the decade after 1905 his Canadian Klondyke Mining Corporation extracted gold with some of the world's largest dredges. The Klondike's Kipling, Robert W. Service, saw the new methods through a prospector's eyes:

... turning round a bend I heard a roar,
And there a giant gold-ship of the very newest plan
    Was tearing chunks of pay-dirt from the shore.

It wallowed in its water-bed; it burrowed, heaved and swung;
    It gnawed its way ahead with grunts and sighs;
Its bill of fare was rock and sand; the tailings were its dung;
    It glared around with fierce electric eyes.
Full fifty buckets crammed its maw; it bellowed out for more;
    It looked like some great monster in the gloom.
With two to feed its sateless greed, it worked for seven score,
    And I sighed: 'Ah old-time miner, here's your doom!'

                                                    ("The Prospector")

Joe Boyle, whose only competitor, the Yukon Gold Corporation, was a venture of the Guggenheim family, was locally known as the "King of the Klondike." In the First World War he left the region to go adventuring in Russia and Romania, where he dissipated wealth and health. The dredges wallowed on for decades.

The Klondike had to have a railway. By 1899 an Anglo-American company had built the White Pass and Yukon Railway from Skagway over the height of land and on to Whitehorse. The traffic prospects were so good they had even done it without a subsidy. Just as they completed the line, the gold rush declined and most of the traffic disappeared. This was an unhappy example of the symbiosis between Canadian mining and railways, which was normally close and fruitful. In Sudbury the building of the railway led to the discovery of mines; in British Columbia the mines led to railway development. Railways and resources went together.

Ontarians took the general notion of railways as resource developer to a spectacular conclusion in the early 1900s when northerners, promoters, and southern boards of trade convinced the provincial government to open up "New Ontario," as the country north of Lake Nipissing was called, with a development railroad. Its boosters argued that the line would unveil new lumbering country, new agricultural country in the northern clay belts, and who could forecast what wonderful deposits of minerals might be found? – en route, of course, to giving Ontario its own salt-water seaport on James Bay. The province decided to build the railway as a public work.

The dream came true, beautifully. In 1902 the Temiskaming and Northern Ontario began building north from North Bay. One season later tie contractors and some workmen began staking mineral claims along the right-of-way at about Mile 100, where there were traces of copperish-looking deposits. As usual, the original claimants soon sold out, taking a quick profit. A general storekeeper from Mattawa named Noah Timmins bought a quarter interest in Fred LaRose's original claim, and a local lawyer, David Dunlap, got an interest for his services in fighting off claim jumpers. M.J. O'Brien, a lumberman and railway contractor from Renfrew, was soon in on the action, along with Colonel R.W. Leonard of St. Catharines, who had been grubstaking prospectors in the area.

The rest of the world did not pay much attention to these slow-moving mining developments around the Cobalt station on the T&NO. Then in 1906 the realization that this was a major silver-copper strike revived Toronto mining promoters and their printing presses with a roar heard all the way down on Wall Street. In 1906–7 more than five hundred Canadian and American companies were organized to strike it rich in Cobalt. Little people all over North America bought shares to get in on the game.

The silver veins twisted near the surface over a fairly large area around Cobalt, so it was a good prospector's camp where even latecomers could strike it rich. You didn't have to spend a fortune or risk your life packing through wilderness or mushing over muskeg to get to Cobalt either. Just hop on the pullman in Toronto on the line through Mariposa. Ontarians had pots of silver at the end of the railroad, a real Eldorado in their backyard.

And Cobalt was only the beginning. It was the strike that taught a generation of Ontarians about mining and encouraged and grubstaked them to spread out to look seriously at every prospect in the region and points north. One result was a telegram in 1909,

HAVE DISCOVERED THE GOLDEN POLE
BEYOND DESCRIPTION. ANSWER MATHESON
WEDNESDAY HAILEYBURY THURSDAY

from the prospectors who had just staked claims on Porcupine Lake, one hundred miles northwest of Cobalt, which became the fabulous Dome mine. Porcupine was another classic gold rush, veins of real gold just sitting there waiting to be found – like the strike made by a teenage barber from Haileybury, Benny Hollinger: "the quartz . . . looked as though someone had dripped a candle along it, but instead of wax it was gold." Gilbert LaBine and the Noah Timmins group from Cobalt helped develop the Hollinger Mine. The American promoters who bought

Sandy McIntyre's Porcupine claims for drinking money were too interested in swindling investors to realize the riches they stood on. When the McIntyre Porcupine's first president went to jail for crooked stock promotions, the boy wonder of Toronto mining broking, J.P. Bickell, gradually took over the property and turned it into a great mine. The McIntyre Porcupine joined Dome and the Hollinger as Ontario's golden trio. Noah Timmins also developed the townsite at Porcupine that bears his name.

And already there was new action, in the country between Cobalt and Porcupine where they found gold at Swastika on the T&NO and on the little lake named after a stenographer in the Department of Mines, Winnie Kirkland. Two former butchers, William Wright and Ed Hargreaves, made the first big Kirkland Lake strike. It became the Wright-Hargreaves mine. They were soon followed by a college-educated career prospector from New England named Harry Oakes, who had been in the Yukon, Alaska, Australia, and Death Valley before reaching the end of the railway line in Ontario. Oakes was one of the few prospectors in Canada to make a mine from staking to dividends. At first his Lake Shore Mine stock seemed just another dubious promotion, selling for 15 cents a share in 1914. Eventually it was worth $64 a share. The more typical prospector was the hapless Sandy McIntyre, who found the gold that became the big Teck-Hughes mine. He sold out early for $4,500; later his shares would have been worth $1.5 million.

Gold sold for $15 to $17 an ounce, silver about 60 cents in the years before 1914. The miners took about $100 million out of the Klondike in its heyday, another $100 million out of Cobalt in the first decade (mostly in silver; the market for the cobalt in the ore developed later), and in 1914 had just begun to reap the harvest of Porcupine and Kirkland Lake. Over in Algoma, F.H. Clergue had opened up Ontario's first big iron mines, and up north near James Bay there were even huge fields of lignite, a form of soft coal, which the T&NO might someday open up. Was lucky Ontario on its way to becoming the coal and iron centre of Canada, as well as its silver and gold capital?

———————◆———————

The forests of Ontario and Quebec and the Maritimes yielded millions of board feet of lumber every year, most of it exported to the United States. The old square timber trade was dead. A few far-sighted lumbermen could see a crisis coming in the eastern pine supply, too, for the big trees were being hacked down far faster than nature regenerated the forest. The three most prominent lumber barons of the Ottawa valley, E.H. Bronson, J.R. Booth, and W.C. Edwards, became strong advocates of conservation measures to try to protect their wood supply. The more common response in the industry was still just to open up more territory. Following the railways, the lumbermen crossed into the Georgian Bay watershed in the 1870s and began cutting everywhere marketable wood was found on the north shores of Huron and Superior and on into Manitoba. American woodsmen from

Michigan were among the pioneers of the region, taking out saw logs and floating them across to their mills. Ontario stopped the practice in 1898 by requiring that the logs it owned be "manufactured" in Ontario. Some of the established Ontario millers also shipped the logs to their old mills: the Gilmours built a two-mile timber slide to get wood over the height of land and into the Trent system; Ottawa's J.R. Booth, the biggest operator of them all, built a 250-mile railway, the Canada Atlantic, entirely out of his own resources, from Ottawa to Parry Sound to get into the new hinterland. More commonly, the millers migrated to new towns – lake ports like Collingwood and Midland, rail and water junctions like Huntsville, Blind River, Thessalon, and points farther and farther west, until they were logging and sawing on Lake of the Woods and then into the eastern forests of Manitoba. In the twenty years from 1880 to 1900 a country the size of Europe came under the axe and the saw.

Some of the eastern lumbermen had already gone much farther west, all the way to the coast where the tree supply seemed unlimited, and where the shortages of wood that plagued the pioneering mills (because of the difficulty of hauling trees from the forest) were being overcome by the use of steam "donkeys" and short logging railroads. Markets were still a problem because Puget Sound producers dominated the American market, but railway construction and the opening of the British Columbia interior and then the prairies caused a steady increase in demand for BC lumber.

Eastern Canadians were among the leaders in the rush to the British Columbia forests between 1900 and 1914, which saw lumbering surpass mining as the province's largest industry (investment in sawmills jumped from $2 million in 1900 to $150 million in 1913). John Hendry of New Brunswick, who had been a true pioneer in moving to the coast back in 1872, now controlled most of the original Burrard Inlet mills in his British Columbia Mills, Timber and Trading Company. He was a leading technological innovator, and by 1900 had become one of the largest industrialists on the mainland. Ottawa valley money came into British Columbia through the Maclarens of Buckingham, Quebec, who created two big mills and brought a branch of the lumbering-oriented Bank of Ottawa along with them. Many other easterners bought BC timber limits or took an interest in sawmills. In 1907 a group of Lindsay, Ontario, businessmen, organized a typical timber-cruising expedition to British Columbia. It resulted in one of the young members of the Flavelle family starting an important cedar mill, as well as a young forestry student named H. R. MacMillan spending his first summer in the West coast forest. In all of their operations the Canadian woodsmen found themselves competing with Americans, who were just as interested in getting a piece of some of the finest stands of timber on the North American continent.

By 1900 a different and ultimately much more extensive assault on the northeastern forest was taking shape. Paper-makers had learned how to make their product from a pulp of ground wood instead of cooked rags. Manufacturers turned to the forests for their raw material, and, led by innovators such as J.R. Barber of Georgetown, Ontario, began using the new form of water-based power, hydro-electricity, to drive their big grinding machines. While many paper-makers simply shipped pulpwood or ground pulp into their mills near their urban markets, other entrepreneurs realized it would be economical for the industry to move north nearer the new raw materials, forests and falling water. Again, F.H. Clergue was the pioneer. His Sault Ste Marie pulp mill was the first big one of its kind in the north. Its opening in 1896 was seen as the beginning of a new era for the communities on the fringes of the Canadian Shield. For the inaugural ceremonies Clergue hired a band and put on a banquet; the townsfolk of Sault Ste Marie literally danced among the machines. In Quebec similar ceremonies included priests' blessing the mills. The work and wages that came with pulp and paper seemed a godsend to the poor farmers and woodcutters of the inhospitable north country.

Quebec seemed short-changed for minerals, but it had limitless supplies of fast water and spruce forest. Up the St. Maurice River at Grand'Mère, for example, a far-sighted Scotsman, John Foreman, struggled for years in the eighties and nineties with transportation problems, capital shortages, and inadequate technology to get a pulp mill going. His Laurentide Pulp Company was finally able to make pulp, but not money. A consortium of Montreal and American investors, headed by Van Horne and R.B. Angus of the CPR, eventually bought control of Laurentide, squeezed Foreman out, expanded the works, and added paper-making machinery. Laurentide became Canada's first modern newsprint-maker, producing 44,500 tons in 1906, a year when the whole Canadian consumption was only about 27,000 tons. Laurentide exported to the United States, Great Britain, South Africa, and Australia. The company paid steady dividends and continued to expand.

The rush to enter pulp and paper manufacturing came about equally from established lumbermen, local promoters, and foreign paper users. Van Horne's American friends moved into Canada because of a sense that their country would soon run short of pulpwood: the same group soon opened a second mill at Grand Falls, New Brunswick. In the Lac St. Jean–Saguenay region of Quebec, the Price family's lumber kingdom was collapsing (Price Brothers Company was in receivership in 1899) when the prospect of pulp and paper manufacture enabled William Price II to reorganize the firm, raise British capital, and start afresh. But a local promoter, Alfred Dubuc, who managed the Chicoutimi branch of La Banque Nationale, beat the Prices into the business, putting together local and American money to launch the Compagnie de Pulpe de Chicoutimi in 1898. "Je ne suis pas personallement intéressé dans cette compagnie de pulpe pour une raison incontrôlable," Dubuc wrote his bank's concerned president, "je n'ai pas d'argent." As the Compagnie's director general, Dubuc made it one of the largest pulp operations in the world, and was celebrated throughout the Saguenay and Quebec as a hero of French-Canadian enterprise. Several other groups of French Canadians founded small pulp mills, some making good when they were bought out by Dubuc or the Prices, others losing everything when the mills burned down or when they just ran out of money. French-Canadian entrepreneurs were also active in the early development of some of Quebec's most important hydro-electric sites, including Shawinigan Falls on the St. Maurice, but, as in mining, local "claimants" usually sold to outside syndicates that could raise capital.

Big Ottawa valley lumbermen such as E.B. Eddy and J.R. Booth had the money, the know-how, and the timber limits to get into pulp and paper successfully. Further west in Ontario, applicants lined up for pulpwood concessions from the provincial government, offering to invest millions in mills if they could guarantee their supplies of raw material through long-term leases. In 1911 the prospect of the abolition of the American tariff on newsprint caused a pulp and paper rush in Canada; nineteen companies, capitalized on paper at $41 million, were formed that year in Quebec alone. The duty came off in 1913 and Canadian paper-making was poised to enter its golden age.

As Canada moved north and west in the late 1890s, and as the cities grew, the inadequacies of the railway network seemed glaring. To start with, tracks did not run nearly far enough north. Thus a development line to open the riches of New Ontario, for example, fuelled the construction of the Temiskaming and Northern Ontario. Why, the land up there included at least twelve million acres of fertile soil in the Clay Belt, a whole new agricultural kingdom. Quebec had been looking in the same direction for many years; where else, besides the United States, which had certainly taken enough of them, could its young sons of the soil go to make a living? In the 1880s the province heavily subsidized the Quebec and Lake St. John Railway to give transportation to Maria Chapdelaine's family and all the other "colonizers" who would become farmers and woodcutters and tame the north.

Alberta no sooner became a province in 1906 than its government offered lavish subsidies to virtually anyone willing to build north from Edmonton to the Athabasca and Peace River country. The British Columbians wanted railways to link every one of their valleys, railways to develop their north, and railways to link Vancouver with the north and their Peace River country. In Manitoba it seemed perfectly natural to re-establish the old Hudson's Bay Company's trading routes to England and Europe by building a Hudson Bay railroad. Even in isolated, aloof Newfoundland, from the 1870s there was a constant belief that the one way to develop the island's mineral and agricultural riches was to span it with a railway. Agricultural riches? Of course. Newfoundlanders were like other Canadians in believing that all land on which vegetation grew only needed to be cleared to be ready for farming.

More important, by 1900 the needs of the prairie wheat economy seemed to be dictating a huge expansion of the main east-west railway network. The West's prospects were so good that a whole new transcontinental railway might be needed. To be sure, the CPR wanted all the business, and by the late 1890s saw its traffic, revenues, and profits all soaring to golden heights. But the CPR could not provide equipment and new branch lines fast enough to meet western demand – there were crippling car shortages in some busy seasons – and westerners demanded new railway service from anyone but the CPR. Their resentment of the CPR's near-monopoly, its high rates, and its corporate arrogance coloured all their perceptions and decisively influenced the course of Canadian transportation history. The prairies wanted new railroads in the new century to carry grain to market and to offer the life-giving, rate-lowering competition that would humble the CPR and its barons into becoming just another railway.

Finally, Canada's cities all needed railways as people-movers on their main streets. Steam railways would not do, of course. Horse-drawn street railways began in the major cities in the 1860s, with spotty results (Canadian winters were hard on the operators; care and treatment of the horses was a problem in all seasons). By the mid-1880s electrical energy was being applied to street railways in the United States and soon came to Canada. The electric street railway was part of the utility revolution underlying the development of the twentieth-century city. Streetcar wires parallelled those bringing electricity and telephone services into houses and offices and factories. Sometimes wires were buried along with new gas mains or the pipes and sewers of municipal water systems. As railway-builders on a grand scale, Canadian entrepreneurs undertook street railway work and other utilities with an enthusiasm and flair that soon carried them far beyond the bounds of anyone's expectations.

The construction of the CPR in the 1880s trained a generation of Canadian railway-builders and capitalists. The men who built the main line had cut their teeth on local Ontario and Quebec roads, did well out of the big CPR job, and when it was finished were eager for more contracts. There was several years of finishing up to be done – building the Short Line through Maine, working on snowsheds in the Rockies, contracting for the Calgary-Edmonton line and some of the northern branches in Manitoba – then nothing at all. In the early 1890s one CPR veteran, Donald Mann from Acton, Ontario, built a railway for the government of Chile, and sought more work as far away as Manchuria. Robert Reid, a Scots-born stonemason who built much of the north of Superior line, obtained the contract to finish the trans-Newfoundland railway. James Ross and Herbert Holt moved to Montreal, where Ross became interested in Maritime coal and steel while Holt worked with local gas and electricity companies. Another of their associates, William Mackenzie of Kirkfield, Ontario, became interested in the street railway situation in Toronto and put together a syndicate to get the franchise to electrify the system.

Mackenzie's Toronto Railway Company got its contract in 1892, not without spending money to "persuade" some aldermen to change their votes, and quickly became a financial success. It had close ties with its Montreal counterpart, in which James Ross and a consortium of Montreal financiers had a controlling interest. By the mid-1890s these street railway capitalists had expanded to Winnipeg and Saint John and were looking for new franchises or charters wherever they might be found. They also developed promising business connections with the groups of foreigners who preceded them in cities at both ends of the country: the H.M. Whitney group from Boston who promoted the Halifax Tramway Company, and English capitalists led by a young stockbroker, Robert M. ("Monty) Horne-Payne, who merged struggling West coast utility companies into the British Columbia Electric Railway Company.

William Mackenzie was born in a log cabin in Kirkfield in 1849, and briefly became a school teacher before drifting into tie-cutting and then contracting. Mackenzie was a restless, daring, insatiable contractor, ready to build railways in country or city, wherever he thought they would work. In 1895 he formed a new partnership with Donald Mann, who had come back to Canada, and the pair bought up the charter for one of Manitoba's "paper" railways, the Lake Manitoba Railway and Canal Company. Mackenzie and Mann thought they could get government support to finance a line to open rich farming country northwest of Portage La Prairie, and to do this were willing to accept control of their rates by the CPR-scarred provincial government. Rate control did not frighten them, partly because railway rates had been declining for forty years, partly because any government that guaranteed the interest on the bonds they issued would have to let them make a modest success.

Armed with their guarantee from Manitoba and a loan from the Bank of Commerce, building and operating on a shoestring (Mackenzie and Mann usually served as their own contractors, taking their contracting profit in the form of common stock), the partners built the first 125 miles of the LMR&CC in 1896. It was the first branch-line construction in western Canada in five years. When the Lake Manitoba Railway opened in 1897, Mackenzie and Mann were already building a second line, the Manitoba and South Eastern, in a southeasterly direction from Winnipeg.

By 1898 it was clear that the duo would willingly build railways anywhere in Canada – they almost got a government contract for an all-Canadian railway to the Yukon – if governments would only give them the necessary help, usually in the form of bond guarantees. By 1899 they had acquired rights to build from Manitoba to the Lakehead and they began consolidating their system as the Canadian Northern Railway. The government of Manitoba guaranteed the bonds on even the Ontario mileage of the Lakehead line because it seemed so important to create real competition to the CPR. Mackenzie and Mann played to this sentiment by offering more accommodating service and lower rates than the CPR. The august giant hardly took the upstart pair seriously, until in 1901 the Canadian Northern leased the old Northern Pacific branch lines from the Manitoba government, opened its own line to the Lakehead, and cut all its freight and grain rates by 15 per cent. The sole owners of the Canadian Northern, Mackenzie and Mann and Company, were buying charters authorizing lines running everywhere. The CPR finally realized that these audacious, rate-cutting competitors might even be intending to build a second transcontinental.

Or a third! Because by 1902 the government of Canada had also decided to challenge the CPR and had formed a transcontinental partnership with the Grand Trunk. In the late 1890s the Grand Trunk had been invigorated by an aggressive general manager imported from the United States, had its finances and reputation in fairly good condition, and finally set out to get a share of the prairie grain traffic. It was ready to build north of Superior to the West – always assuming, of course, a reasonable amount of government help. Sir Wilfrid Laurier's government was more than willing to help the Grand Trunk – assuming, of course, a reasonable willingness of the company to accept some political realities. Quebec just had to have a development line through its north, for example, but a transcontinental could not end in Quebec City; it would have to have a Maritime terminus, say in Moncton.

Knowledgeable railwaymen, businessmen, and even members of Laurier's cabinet felt that one important reality was the need for cooperation between the Grand Trunk and the Canadian Northern. Canada's growth would probably support a second transcontinental railway (though whether a second northern Ontario line was necessary was a moot point), but would there ever be traffic enough for three? Serious negotiations among the railway entrepreneurs floundered on Mackenzie and Mann's determination not to lose control of the Canadian Northern ("We were too young and too ambitious to sell at that time," Mann said later) and the Grand Trunk's belief that the pair were little more than fly-by-night railway promoters who would soon give up and go away. The final Grand Trunk–Laurier deal was for the government of Canada to build the National Transcontinental railway from Moncton to Winnipeg and a new company, the Grand Trunk Pacific, to build west to the coast. The Grand Trunk Pacific would lease the National Transcontinental from the government and operate the whole system (which was never officially named, but was often called the National Transcontinental). Mackenzie and Mann could do what they liked.

There was considerable public criticism of Laurier's railway policy as a prescription for overbuilding and heavy burdens on the taxpayer. The plan was not based on any estimates of past, present, and future growth, only wild guesses. The critics included Laurier's Minister of Railways, whose resignation might have been more telling had he not been tainted by scandal, and the Grand Trunk's president and some of its directors, who fretted about wild risks they were taking. C.M. Hays, the dynamic general manager, urged the Englishmen, whose timidity had cost the Grand Trunk the first transcontinental line, to make up their minds before the competitors swept the field: "Extremely important that we should come to terms with Government trusting somewhat the future. Otherwise Mackenzie and

Mann... will accept conditions and forestall us with Government." The Liberal prime minister, Sir Wilfrid Laurier, tried to drown his critics with his rolling oratory:

> ... To those who urge upon us the policy of tomorrow, and tomorrow, and tomorrow; to those who tell us, Wait, wait, wait; to those who advise us to pause, to consider, to reflect, to calculate and to inquire, our answer is: No, this is not a time for deliberation, this is a time for action. The flood tide is upon us that leads on to fortune; if we let it pass it may never recur again .... Heaven grant that it be not already too late; heaven grant that whilst we tarry and dispute, the trade of Canada is not deviated to other channels, and that an ever vigilant competitor does not take to himself the trade that properly belongs to those who acknowledge Canada as their native or their adopted land. Upon this question we feel that our position ... corresponds to the beating of every Canadian heart.

Twenty years earlier the Liberals had opposed the CPR contracts and taxpayers' subsidies to railways. The CPR's success seemed to have proven them wrong. Now Laurier and the Liberals threw caution to the winds and set out to duplicate the Conservatives' railway saga of the 1880s. This would be the Liberals' railway epic.

So Canada entered its third and final era of railway construction, the building of two new transcontinentals. Total Canadian railway mileage more than doubled between 1900 and the completion of the Canadian Northern and the National Transcontinental–Grand Trunk Pacific in 1915. With thirty-five thousand miles of operational railway track that year, Canada had more railways per capita than any country in the world.

William Mackenzie and Donald Mann were too young and ambitious to stop, and they too were infected with the belief that by "trusting somewhat the future" they would all be justified thanks to Canada's growth. Their Canadian Northern lines were better located in many areas than their competitors' and Mackenzie and Mann had substantial government support, especially from the prairie provinces. In farming communities railways were the equivalent of today's roads: essential utilities, the more of them the better. All politicians favoured building more trunk and branch lines; most favoured generous subsidies of land, or cash, or, best of all because they didn't seem to cost anything, bond guarantees. All railway companies came under tremendous political pressure, particularly in election seasons, to build or at least announce new branches. None responded more enthusiastically than the Canadian Northern.

In 1909 alone Mackenzie and Mann got guarantees for almost two thousand miles of branch lines on the prairies. Their main line through the Yellowhead Pass and down to Vancouver was built with handsome guarantees from the British Columbia government. Their eastern link, from Port Arthur to Montreal, was made possible when the Laurier government, willing to subsidize anything that would benefit it politically, produced similar guarantees just before the 1911 election. When they were later criticized for overbuilding, Mackenzie and Mann insisted they had never come close to building all the railways that politicians wanted. You could never have too many good (rail)roads.

The Grand Trunk Pacific–National Transcontinental went foward at the same time, with the Grand Trunk organizing most of the work through its subsidiary, the GTP. The CPR, which remained flush with traffic and revenue, concentrated on improving its system: reducing its horrendous mountain grades, double-tracking on the prairies, upgrading its steamship and hotel service. The company's acquisition in 1909 of the Allan Line completed its dominance of Canadian shipping on both oceans (though competition developed immediately: in 1910 Mackenzie and Mann put Atlantic passenger liners into service; in 1911 the Cunard Line started serving Canada again). Van Horne's successor as CPR president, Sir Thomas Shaughnessy, was a careful, colourless manager who financed growth out of profits and new equity issues. Busy with its spiral tunnels and its steamships, the CPR made few mistakes, few burdensome commitments during the most hectic years of the railway circus. It thoroughly disapproved of the new, subsidized competition, but could do nothing to stop the alliance between governments and the new railway entrepreneurs.

The politicians and their pet companies built and bought as though tomorrow would justify any expense. Everyone worked on the most optimistic projections; all the growth curves were projected up and up indefinitely. The country's future was boundless. The northern rocks were storehouses of wealth. Mackenzie and Mann were particularly affected by northern resource visions, had their men scouring the shield for minerals, and bought mines from one end of the country to the other. Railway-building and nation-building seemed indistinguishable. This was having faith, vision, confidence in Canada. The twentieth century would belong to Canada.

Year after year of growth and prosperity gradually silenced most of the critics. A few opposition supporters made the usual charges about graft and corruption and "rails of steal" in federal and provincial railway policies. Some suggested that Mackenzie and Mann's financial methods were a little too frenzied for anyone's good (they formed subsidiary companies to service their system, kept the equity in everything themselves, pyramided bonds and debentures and mortgages beyond normal reckoning, and were thought to be fabulously wealthy). Others argued, and historians tend to agree, that theirs was the frenzy of builders rather than buccaneers, aiming onward and upward in an ultimate entrepreneurial adventure.

For all its boundless size and future, Canada was still too small to contain the builders' ambitions. They had expertise and energy to export, and in the late 1890s began multiplying enterprises abroad, particularly in Latin America. Canadian companies built the electric street railways and installed power plants in far-away places like Sao Paulo and Rio de Janeiro, Brazil. Van Horne built a second trans-national railway, from one end of Cuba to the other, and became the father of Guatemala's main line. A Canadian syndicate owned the Mexican Light and Power Company, the Mexico City street railway, utilities in Pachuca, Puebla, and Monterey, and the Mexican North Western Railway in Chihuahua. There were important Canadian utility interests in the United States, Barcelona, Spain, and half a dozen West Indian Islands. Canadian developers seemed to be everywhere, bringing light, power, and movement to usher communities into the modern century.

The golden age of Canadian utility imperialism emerged from a fruitful conjunction of entrepreneurs and opportunities. Van Horne and the people who had worked under him – Mackenzie, Mann, Ross, Holt – were superb railway-builders and contractors. When they got into street railways, they learned to work with electrical men: engineers, equipment suppliers, and other experts. Contacts between the Toronto-Montreal and Halifax street railway groups generated a vital connection in the person of Fred Stark Pearson, one of the most brilliant and energetic American electrical engineers of his generation. A New Englander, Pearson directed the electrification of Boston's street railways for H.M. Whitney before following the capitalist to Nova Scotia. He soon became the Canadians' favourite consulting engineer, supplying expertise and staff from his cohort of electricity enthusiasts, and gradually taking a leading role in the promotion of new enterprises in Canada, the Americas, anywhere there were jobs to be done by engineers.

For their financial needs the builders drew on the services of an increasingly mature Canadian financial industry, now capable of underwriting and organizing and supporting industrial and utility promotions anywhere in the world. Banks and life insurance companies offered bridge-financing and underwrote securities. Bond and stock dealers marketed securities. The securities were traded on Canada's fledgling stock exchanges. Trust companies handled trustee and agency work.

William Mackenzie formed the most important business contact of his career in 1892 when the Canadian Bank of Commerce, acting with George Cox on his own account, bought $1 million of the bonds of Mackenzie's Toronto Railway Company. A few years later the Commerce gave Mackenzie and Mann vital support in their early Manitoba ventures. It became the Canadian Northern's bank, deeply commited to the railway's fortunes. The Bank of Commerce's general manager, and successor to Cox as president, Byron Edmund Walker, became the truest of believers in Mackenzie and Mann as nation-builders and in a world role for Canadian enterprise. All of George Cox's other companies, the Canada Life, A.E. Ames in stocks, Dominion Securities in bonds, and the National Trust Company, became involved with Mackenzie's adventures.

Canadian financiers could promote a project and carry it through the early stages, but most of the money still had to come from abroad. The Canadian conduit to the British investment community was personified most visibly in Monty Horne-

Payne, chairman of the British Columbia Electric Railway and the London-based British Empire Trust Company. Horne-Payne was a wizard of Anglo-Canadian finance, financial agent in Britain for the Canadian Northern and many of the foreign ventures, super-salesman of hundreds of millions in railroad and utility bonds. He rode the crest of the last great wave of British investment abroad, as the savings of the Victorian era were poured into enterprises in the colonies, the underdeveloped countries, anywhere there was reasonable safety plus a better return than investors could get at home.

Utility entrepreneurs had to have good lawyers. Concessions, franchise agreements, corporate charters and by-laws, trust deeds, and other documents defined the limits and opportunities available to the entrepreneurs in their intricate manoeuvres, often with governments. In earlier generations many lawyers had been intimately involved in corporation work and personal dealing, George-Etienne Cartier and John A. Macdonald being among the most active. Macdonald's immediate successor as prime minister, Sir John Abbott, was probably Montreal's best nineteenth-century entrepreneur at law. But it was Zebulon A. Lash, a senior partner in the Toronto firm of Blake, Lash and Cassels, who took corporation work to new levels of specialization and excellence in the early twentieth century, a time of greatly increased business reliance on the corporate form.

Lash was a native of Newfoundland, educated at Toronto's Osgoode Hall, who served a term as deputy minister of justice before settling in Toronto to practise. Through the Bank of Commerce he became counsel to the Canadian Northern and almost all of the Cox-Mackenzie enterprises, guiding the players masterfully through the rule book and its mysteries and opportunities. He became much more than corporate counsel, serving as a director of the leading companies, taking an active role in developing strategy and tactics. Montreal and Halifax entrepreneurial circles had counterparts to Lash in the success of J.N. Greenshields and C.H. Cahan respectively. The shoals of franchises, corporate finance, and modern capitalism generally, were too hazardous to risk without a skilled legal pilot standing close to the helm.

An obscure Italian-Canadian engineer, Francisco Gualco, who had done some contracting work for the CPR, introduced the Canadians to an interesting South American opportunity in 1898. Gualco was involved in an improbable scheme to induce French-Canadian habitants to migrate to Brazil to work on coffee plantations. Through it he became persona grata with the rulers of the prosperous state of Sao Paulo. On a visit in 1896 Gualco noticed how poorly a mule-drawn tramway serviced the two hundred thousand residents of the city of Sao Paulo, Brazil's second-largest. He toured some interesting water-power sites, and formed a partnership with a well-connected local promoter, Antonio de Souza, to secure the right to build an electric street railway for Sao Paulo city.

Gualco got his concession, tried to interest British and American financiers in the opportunity, and got nowhere. He had no standing in the international financial world and the terms of the concession were problematic enough to make the proposition unattractive – just another Latin American paper promotion, sort of like Canadian mining stock. Finally Gualco turned to the CPR old boys' network and presented the situation to James Ross in Montreal. Ross had just worked with William Mackenzie in two foreign traction ventures, one in Birmingham, England, which was being fouled up by tough municipal politicians, and a freshly obtained concession in Jamaica. The Sao Paulo proposition seemed worth at least a good look.

One of F.S. Pearson's experts went down to investigate and reported enthusiastically on the opportunity to build a modern street railway in a rich, growing, fever-free city, and then go on to supply electric light and power. In Toronto, Mackenzie had Lash set up an Ontario company, Sao Paulo Railway, Light and Power Company Limited, capitalized nominally at $6 million. It bought the Gualco-Souza concession from William Mackenzie, who had bought it from the concessionaires. Pearson himself went to Brazil to organize the start of the work. He was accompanied by Alexander Mackenzie, a bachelor junior partner in Blake, Lash and Cassels, who was assigned to do the local legal arranging. Construction of the new tramway began officially on July 4, 1899.

Mackenzie sold Sao Paulo bonds and stock to a syndicate of his associates. It included George Cox, Frederic Nicholls (president of Canadian General Electric), Pat Burns, the meat-packer from Mackenzie's old home town, J. W. Flavelle, the hog king of Toronto, the Bank of Commerce, and the Central Canada Savings and Loan Company. These underwriters took most of their stock on credit. National Trust and the Bank of Commerce loaned Sao Paulo most of the start-up cash it needed. Sao Paulo was a Cox "family" promotion; the group arranged all the transactions among themselves as they changed corporate hats, and Lash did the legal work for all parties. The Toronto *Globe* noted that in a country "where we still look for outside capital to build our railways and to work our mines, the formation of a local company to operate electric railways and supply electric light in Sao Paulo is decidedly a novelty. We should not, however, fail to appreciate the enterprise of our fellow-Canadians who take the risk of such a venture, nor to congratulate them if they bring home (as they bid fair to do in this case) a 'rich return'."

Members of the underwriting syndicate took early profits, selling Sao Paulo bonds and shares on a bull market in Canada, with some of the securities moving out to England. Long-term returns depended on the achievements of the managers and technical people in Brazil. These soon became impressive. Pearson's engineers were able to harness the Cachoeira do Inferno, or Rapids of Hell, on the Tietê River, bring the power into the city, and begin electrifying track. Alexander Mackenzie proved a superb lawyer-diplomat-manager as he guided the company through the tangles of local politics, protected the franchise from its enemies, and gradually drove the competing mule-team operators out of business. Money must have been spent liberally to secure goodwill, but Mackenzie and Pearson also believed the company should provide good service. It was an enlightened approach to management that was still absent back in Toronto, where William Mackenzie's Toronto Railway Company was hugely unpopular with the city's streetcar riders.

The Paulistanos took to electric streetcars enthusiastically, labour costs and taxes were low, revenues and profits were high. The company moved quickly to supply domestic and industrial electricity to Sao Paulo. Pearson and Alexander Mackenzie began planning a repeat performance in Rio, bought the necessary franchises and concessions, and turned to Canada for financial support. The Toronto group hesitated – the market collapse of 1903 was heavy weather for all of them – but finally came around and in 1904 launched the Rio de Janeiro Tramway, Light and Power Company. The Rio company's profits soon exceeded the most optimistic projections. Canada's Brazilian utility companies were huge successes, and growing more so every year. In 1912 William Mackenzie and Pearson brought all the components of "o pulve Canadenses" (the Canadian octopus) under the control of one holding company, Brazilian Traction Limited.

The instant success of these foreign ventures, F.S. Pearson's gargantuan appetite to build and promote, and the desire of other Canadian entrepreneurs for a share of the action, led to a seemingly endless series of promotions and flotations of domestic and foreign utilities in the early years of the new century. Right in their own backyard, as it were, the Toronto group had one of the world's finest sources of electric power at hand, Niagara Falls. In 1903, Mackenzie, Nicholls of CGE, and Henry Mill Pellatt, a stockbroker-financier who had worked often with Mackenzie and was Nicholls's partner in the Toronto Electric Light Company, obtained a concession at Niagara. They founded the Electrical Development Company to transmit power to Toronto to supply for the light and streetcar companies.

While the Torontonians were busy with the EDC, the Halifax group that had first dealt with F.S. Pearson in Canada decided to back his ambitions in Mexico and were the original promoters of the Mexican Light and Power Company in 1902, another vehicle to bring power into a big city. During the promotion the Haligonians gave way to the big Montreal capitalists – Ross, Van Horne, and the Bank of Montreal – a group already active in Cuba, who could command more resources. A second, domestically oriented group of Montrealers, dominated by the Forget brokerage family and later by Herbert Holt, consolidated that city's utilities in 1901 into Montreal Light, Heat and Power.

Halifax had had its appetite whetted for Latin American utilities, so in 1903 John F. Stairs, scion of one of Nova Scotia's leading merchant families, put together a local syndicate to found Royal Securities, the first bond-trading house east of Montreal. It was created mainly to be a vehicle for a twenty-four-year-old New Brunswicker, Max Aitken. The son of a Presbyterian minister (he was actually born in a manse in Maple, Ontario), Aitken had failed the entrance examination for Dalhousie University, become intoxicated by the game of money-making, and found he had a knack for selling insurance and bonds. By the time he became a protégé of Stairs, Aitken had moved from selling securities on a commission basis to investing and doing small underwritings on his own account, operations he continued while working for the investors in Royal Securities. As head of Royal, Aitken specialized in lesser Latin American promotions, including the Trinidad Electric Company, Puerto Rico Railways, and several Cuban utilities.

Aitken developed the Cuban properties as a result of his honeymoon trip. He spent his honeymoon this way:

> While in Cuba, I bought the Puerto Principe Electric Co., for the sum of $300,000. I bought 200 acres of land in the City of Camaguey, and 217 acres to the north of Sir Wm. Van Horne's car works. I bought the old Mule Tram franchise, and I acquired the electric railway franchise in an almost completed condition . . . . When the tram lines are constructed they will pass through the lands I have purchased. On account of the congested condition of the population of the City, I expect to make a very large profit out of selling business lots.

Aitken aimed at bigger game than the business lots, tram lines, and Canadian sales commissions were able to provide. In 1906 he moved to Montreal, and began rising in investment circles there. He left Royal Securities to take over Montreal Trust, returned by taking over Royal Securities, and by 1909 was exploring opportunities in New York and London.

Canadian utility financiers had to look abroad almost constantly after 1906–7 because their promotions far outran the capacity of the slender Canadian market to absorb new issues, even in primary distribution. Mackenzie's Toronto circle handled its last big operation in 1906, backing F. S. Pearson in the promotion of the Mexico City street railway franchise (Mexico Tramways Company) after the Montrealers in Mexican Light and Power hesitated. But Pearson and the Canadians increasingly looked to investment bankers in London to make the markets in their securities. Horne-Payne's operations at British Empire Trust became central for both the Latin American flotations and the voracious appetite of the Canadian Northern. The great railway, Mackenzie and Mann's masterwork, was able to keep building at a breathtaking pace only because Horne-Payne was able masterfully to feed British investors one paper pledge after another, in return for cash sent over to Canada.

James Dunn, of Dunn, Fischer and Company, was the other Canadian and Latin American specialist in London, having moved there from Montreal in 1905. Dunn, like Aitken, came out of north shore New Brunswick. He finished law school at Dalhousie, then tried his luck in Alberta (along with Aitken and another New Brunswick acquaintance, R.B. Bennett, who stayed in Calgary), but came back to the securities business nearer home. "The west must pay tribute to the east," Jimmy quipped to Max, "and I'm off to the east where I can collect tribute." Dunn's timing in moving farther east to London was superb. His star rose brilliantly in the City. With boundless energy, excellent connections, and a shrewd, ruthless approach to risk-taking, Dunn thrust himself into the centre of the international financial world – and into the nouveau riche world of champagne, French villas, fast cars, and obliging women.

F.S. Pearson's utilities remained central to Dunn's operations, and he was a key broker in the group's last big promotion, the 1912 flotation of the Barcelona Traction, Light and Power Company. It was an attempt to transplant the Pearson group's expertise from Latin America to mother Spain. Most of the Barcelona securities were sold in England and Europe, but it, too, was a Toronto-based company, another Zebulon Lash creation with considerable primary underwriting from George Cox's old companies, especially National Trust and Dominion Securities.

As the promoting and financing grew, Canadian financial circles developed new breadth and sophistication, particularly in the handling of securities and the nurturing of the adolescent domestic capital market. Bank shares and government bonds and debentures had led the way at mid-century, but it was with the mass marketing of railway and utility bonds that significant public participation in industrial development finally took place. Bonds seemed an appealing risk for investors because, unlike stock, they were usually secured by tangible assets. Bond-issuing utilities seemed particularly secure because their franchises or charters apparently gave them long-term freedom from competition.

In 1899 new possibilities developed when it became legal in Canada to break the stock of a public company into preferred and common shares. A person who owned shares of a company's stock held equity, or ownership, but, unlike bondholders, was not owed specific sums. Shareholders might collect dividends, if there were any. Preferred stock, which had first claim on dividends, seemed a more secure investment than ordinary or common stock. In the new dualism common stock became a fascinating speculative "kicker." It was usually next to worthless at issue because current earnings were earmarked for bond interest and dividends on the preferred shares. As profits grew, though, the value of the common stock might soar.

The par values still assigned to shares of stock – usually $100 a share, except in mining – had lost their original function because companies no longer tried to compel shareholders to pay their subscriptions up to par. But the use of par values was retained into the 1920s with confusing results. Big issues of $100 common shares meant that "capitalization" figures ballooned crazily. A $20 million company might have $2 million in real assets, $18 million of worthless common stock. Bankers and promoters found it useful to inflate or "water" share figures this way, partly to impress the unsophisticated, partly for the eventual camouflaging of profits that might seem exorbitant as a percentage of the capital originally employed in a venture. Getting the right mix of solid assets and water in a merger or promotion became something of an art form, complicated by legitimate considerations of profit expectation or the value of such intangibles as goodwill. At least the tools had developed, and the bond and stock dealers could use them to tap the savings of a growing number of investors at home and abroad, taking underwriting profits, sales commissions, and sometimes large capital gains as they went.

By the late 1890s the leading institutional investors, banks and insurance companies, had made a major commitment to industrial securities. Most of them moved their money along the comfortable financial networks described in earlier pages, preferring insider trading and self-dealing to the hazards of the unknown. A few pioneers, such as Sun Life, tried to scour the market more disinterestedly. After some serious mistakes ("Now there was nothing wrong with the Cornwall Street Railway except the lack of population," T.B. Macaulay said later), the Sun made a major commitment to the Illinois Traction Company, a large inter-urban electric street railway network in the American mid-west. More than a third of the company's total bond portfolio went into Illinois Traction. At home, the Sun became deeply involved with an American group financing the Shawinigan power project on the St. Maurice River, taking its bonds and short-term notes. Many of the life insurance companies made short-term money available to brokers, often on call, for underwriting and market "support" activities.

These new investment practices were important to the banks and life insurance companies, but their main source of growth was the general increase in the country's business and wealth in the Laurier period and the ability they both had to tap the savings of middle-class Canadians. Trust and agency work with corporate securities was very important to the early trust companies, which were created partly to meet this need, partly because of the depersonalization of investing that occurred when estates endured over generations. The power that trust companies were given to receive and invest money in trust actually amounted to a deposit-taking function, making these firms partly competitive with banks. Most chose not to compete with big brother banks, usually because of the "family" structure of Canadian finance. National Trust was a sibling of the Bank of Commerce; Royal Trust was a creation of the directorate of the Bank of Montreal; Aitken sold Montreal Trust to Royal Bank people; and so on. Some of the mortgage loan companies evolved into trust companies because of the attractiveness of the estate business. Otherwise, the best way to get into the banking business was just to found a new chartered bank, as financial groups continued to do throughout the Laurier years.

The securities dealers enjoyed the greatest growth after 1900, finally coming into their own as important financial intermediaries. The Forgets and then Aitken in Montreal, Osler Hammond, Pellatt and Pellatt, Ames and Company, and Dominion Securities in Toronto, fattened on the proceeds of big bond and stock issues, and their senior partners became rich, powerful figures in Canadian finance. There were occasional setbacks, of course. A.E. Ames, for example, decided in the early 1900s to go his own way, eschewed George Cox's good advice, set up his own mini-financial family complete with bank and life insurance company, and plunged into American traction issues. In the short financial panic of 1903, A.E. Ames and Company was caught holding too much Twin Cities Rapid Transit as security for loans his American bankers called. Ames had to suspend, accept help from his father-in-law, and struggle for several years to pay his debts before reopening for business, a much chastened financier. His alter ego in the Cox financial family, E.R. Wood at Dominion Securities, was always more circumspect, carefully worked the mainstream of Cox-Mackenzie-Pearson financings, and used his mastery of the bond business to build "DS" into the largest investment house in Canada.

The stock and bond houses rested on dominant individuals, for the "street" was an intimately personal, clubby place. Wood's position at Dominion Securities was so powerful that the firm was not particularly troubled when its original secretary and accountant, G.A. Wood (no relation) and J.H. Gundy, left to form Wood Gundy and Company in 1905. Aitken had better luck keeping talent at Royal Securities, and came to rely heavily on his original employee, young Isaac Walton Killam of the Yarmouth, NS, shipping Killams. James Dunn, by contrast, was not well served by the young men he left in Montreal when he moved to London. The partner mainly responsible for the over-extension of J.H. Dunn and Company and its collapse in the panic of 1907 committed suicide rather than face Dunn.

There was no good reason methods for selling railway and utility securities would not work for other companies. All industries needed consolidating, modernizing, and refinancing from time to time. The tools and the men to wield them had emerged; the public, at home and abroad, seemed ready to buy stocks and bonds. So it was time to apply strategies of amalgamations, public financings, and refinancings to other industries. The Whitney interests in the Maritimes pioneered in industrial flotations at the turn of the century, launching both Dominion Coal and Dominion Iron and Steel as public corporations. They attracted widespread investor interest. In Toronto the Cox group tried the same route with firms ranging from the Crow's Nest Pass Coal Company to the Carter-Crume Company, a merger in merchants' duplicating and triplicating sales books under the brilliant management of S.J. Moore. The group's most interesting promotion was the 1899 creation of Canada Cycle and Motor Company, a merger of five bicycle companies – four branches of American firms plus the Massey-Harris bicycle division – which seemed to have attractive prospects. CCM would dominate the buoyant Canadian market for "wheels," and it had ambitious plans to lead Canada's transportation revolution by building autmobiles.

The CCM flotation was a near-disaster. It was badly timed (the bicycle market collapsed), badly organized (it did not achieve the desired market control), wretchedly managed (the accounts were a mess), and haunted by bad luck (the key executive, Walter Massey, died of typhoid). Although the company survived, the experience spoiled the Cox group's appetite for new Canadian issues outside of the utility field. Others gradually left the industrial financing game, some after being burned in the 1903 or 1907 panics, many of the big institutions after the western Canadian mortgage market took off, offering good returns with little risk. The Mackenzie group concentrated its energies on the Canadian Northern, and most of the rest of the action had moved abroad. As Donald Paterson has shown in his studies of investment in British Columbia, large amounts of industrial capital continued to move into Canada through older, informal networks separate from the investment dealers and public markets.

Yet the flow of new issues continued to grow, fed by the bond houses and the brokers. Furthermore, a few financiers maintained a specially keen interest in the game. The impetus to merge was bound to break out in industries where competition from firms making similar products kept prices down. It existed wherever entrepreneurs saw opportunities for economies of scale, rationalizations, or technological innovations that required more plant, more money, or both. It increased because bond and stock salesmen wanted business and urged companies to merge and sometimes intervened by buying companies themselves, putting them together, and organizing a financing. Above all, the idea of going public, with or without amalgamation, was attractive when the public seemed ready to buy, as it always is in the late years of any boom. In the later Laurier years the pace of growth became more hectic, generating noticeable inflation from about 1909. Prices and profits seemed likely to keep rising for many years. Investors were willing to lend on the strength of growth projections, on future prospects instead of past records. What better time to go to the market?

The normal, almost haphazard, rhythm of public financings and mergers jelled about 1909 into a recognizable merger movement. During the next four years, through 1912, some 275 individual firms were combined into 58 industrial enterprises with a total authorized capital of almost half a billion dollars. There were mergers in flour milling, textiles, paint, coal, lumber, electricity, shipping, baking, cement, and steel. The last three of these were the biggest promotions of the master merger-maker, Max Aitken.

Using the techniques he had learned in Latin American utilities, Aitken sometimes acted on behalf of merger-minded proprietors in an industry, sometimes on his own by buying or taking options on the properties he wished to put together. Both methods were involved in his biggest deal, the creation of the Steel Company of Canada in 1910.

The industry was in a period of restless flux. The giant U.S. Steel Company was poised to enter Canada through Windsor. Excess capacity had developed in steel-finishing firms. Several mergers had taken place and more were being discussed when Aitken optioned the venerable Montreal Rolling Mills and offered to do a big deal with the leading Ontario steel producers. Hamilton Steel and Iron was the other principal firm, interested in merging as part of a plan to integrate from primary steel production through finishing. Canada Screw and Canada Bolt and Nut also came into the combine. The country's two biggest steel mills, those in Nova Scotia, tended to integrate backwards to control their raw materials, and were content to tie their manufacturing to the booming steel rail market. We see below why Algoma Steel had special problems of its own.

The central Canadian merger made good sense on paper and splendid sense in the long run. At the time it was badly flawed. The new Steel Company of Canada was burdened with heavy charges on its senior securities. Its well-being depended on the Canadian boom continuing indefinitely. Its debt was high partly because a lot of money was being poured into expansion, mainly in Hamilton, partly because a heavy price was paid for the merged properties. During the negotiations a heated argument developed about the value of the Montreal Rolling Mills. Should the Steel Company pay more or less than the $4.2 million Aitken owed the old owners? Max agreed to accept the results of an independent valuation. The valuators came up with a figure of $6 million, a cool million more than even Aitken had asked! The smiling financier insisted on taking his full pound of steel dollars.

Aitken and Royal Securities marketed most of the Steel Company's bonds in England, and soon after the merger Max moved there. He established residence in London, bought his way into Parliament and the peerage, eventually becoming Lord Beaverbrook, and began dabbling in newspapers. "I created all the big trusts in Canada," Aitken wrote Winston Churchill, " ... my relation to Canada was in a small way the same as [J.P.] Morgan's relation to America. I'm done now."

Aitken's "trusts" had monopoly power in only a few industries and usually only for a few years. Canada Cement, a merger of twelve of the country's thirteen Portland cement-makers, was the most obvious and most criticized attempt at outright monopoly, and it failed to control its market. Critics of the merger movement began a long Canadian tradition of failing to set specific consolidations in the context of overall growth. In these years, for example, the disappearance of about 200 firms in mergers in four years was far outweighed by the creation of 1,815 new federally chartered corporations, 4,437 Ontario corporations, and 761 Quebec corporations, plus thousands of unincorporated businesses. Still, the public's alarm was real, part of a well-established and growing concern about the machinations of big business which I explore in the next chapter. In Aitken's case as well, his unwillingness to cut a deal with his merger partners in the Montreal Rolling Mills valuation permanently tarnished his reputation in Canadian business circles. Who wanted to do business with a sharpie like Aitken? So it was a good time for Max to leave Canada, quite apart from his desire to play bigger games on the world stage.

Max Aitken moved on at the peak of the Laurier boom, joining his friend Jimmy Dunn in the financial capital of the world. They were products of a Canadian business world that had evolved to the point where it was now spawning raw capitalists – suppliers and organizers of the money consumed by the builders and managers of gigantic twentieth-century industries. The Canadian capitalists were the end products of a period of staggering business expansion and economic growth after 1900. Between 1901 and 1914 Canada's population grew from 5,300,000 to 7,630,000, an astonishing 44 per cent in only thirteen years. Gross National Product more than doubled between 1900 and 1910 and was on its way to doubling again in the next decade. Almost every Canadian industry did spectacularly well in the boom.

Laurier's time as prime minister came to an end with his government's defeat on the free trade issue in the 1911 election, but the boom went on. The future of Canada seemed truly great. The supply of raw resources providence had deposited in the northern rocks and forests was astonishing. The place was a cornucopia of precious metals, base metals, wood, coal, water-power, fertile soil, who could tell what else? Why, way out in Alberta they were discovering natural gas and exploring for oil. The world knew about Canada, too; that was why foreign money and foreign people were pouring into the country in ever-increasing quantities, a full one million immigrants in 1911–13 alone. With such human resources, with capital coming from the money centres of the old world and the new, and with its limitless natural resources, who could imagine limits to Canada's potential? It already had millions of acres of waving wheatfields, great transcontinental railways, belching steel mills, banks everywhere, mammoth stores in very big cities. Think of the fantastic possibilities for the future. Take, for example, the population growth rate of about 40 per cent between 1901 and 1911 and project it to the end of the century: 145 million Canadians by the year 2000! Probably a conservative estimate. Laurier was right. In its growth Canada would be the United States of the twentieth century. It would certainly be a wonderful place for businessmen.

The optimism was captured by the editor of the *Canadian Courier*, John A. Cooper, who in 1906 left the Victorian *Canadian Magazine* to create a lively weekly journal devoted to news of Canada and its wonderful growth. What did modern Canada offer its youth? According to the *Canadian Courier* in 1909,

> ... hundreds and thousands of Canadian boys can hope to trip over a fortune one of these days in the Canadian wilderness. Pots of gold lie hidden there more truly than at the end of rainbows.... Golden opportunities lie all around; and we can never tell that the lad who plays on the street before us will not some day be a railway builder, a bank president, a mighty financier.... Canada is a perpetual Christmas Tree with a present for every son of the house.
>
> ... We are adventurers living the thrilling life of discovery, of daring, of

chance and of conquest. Bare-footed boys become millionaires and live in palaces. In the knapsack of every Canadian schoolboy there is – not a marshal's baton – but a millionaire's bank book. When you part from your school fellow because he must go to work while you go to college, you never know but what you may meet him next when he invites you to dine with him in his private [railway] car.

Cooper's own enterprise in creating Canada's first newsmagazine reflected the explosive growth that newspaper and periodical publishing had been experiencing since the 1880s. At mid-century a small elite had poured over dense reports of legislative debates and ponderously partisan editorials in the *Globe* and a few dozen other four-page weeklies or bi-weeklies, most of them founded and run by men whose real interest was politics. By 1900 a generation of business-minded publishers had developed modern newspapers catering to the interests of the mass reading public in the big cities – bright, brash, brassy, cheap (one cent) dailies like *La Presse* and the *Star* in Montreal, the *Evening Telegram* and the *World* and the *Star* in Toronto. Canadians read their dailies in the big cities, their weeklies in the little towns, handsome church papers on Sundays, and more and more glossy magazines (mostly American, of course) the rest of the week. Some of the Canadian purveyors of news and information for the masses were becoming both influential and rich in the business. In the age of Hearst and Pulitzer in the United States, Rothermere and Northcliffe in Great Britain, Canada too was developing notorious press barons: Hugh Graham of the Montreal *Star*, John Ross Robertson of Toronto's *Evening Telegram*, and the aggressive Southam family of Hamilton who poured the profits from their *Spectator* into enterprises ranging from the steel company to printing plants and newspapers in other cities.

Businessmen needed news, too, and as early as the 1840s specialized journals had sprung up to provide British North American merchants with market reports, commercial intelligence, and comment on the course of affairs. The most successful in the late nineteenth century were Toronto's *Monetary Times*, founded in 1867, Montreal's *Journal of Commerce* (1876), and, for French-Canadian merchants, *Le Moniteur du Commerce* (1881). The trend of the future in business journalism was spotted by John Bayne Maclean, a clergyman's son who became a newspaper reporter in Toronto and developed a beat covering the livestock trade and other commercial news dismissed as unspeakably dull by his seniors. In 1887 Maclean scraped together $2,000 to launch a weekly trade paper, probably the Dominion's first, the *Canadian Grocer*. Within two months Maclean knew he had succeeded. The *Grocer* catered to a large group of small businessmen whose buying was avidly sought by wholesalers, manufacturers, and packers advertising their wares. Maclean began expanding, adding *Hardware and Metal* in 1888,

Books and Notions in 1890, the *Dry Goods Review* in 1891, and *Canadian Printer and Publisher* in 1892. Restless to escape from Toronto, Maclean experimented with a popular art magazine in New York and a "local scene" monthly in Montreal before contenting himself with his trade papers.

In 1907 Maclean's little fleet got a flagship when the first issue of the *Financial Post*, a new paper catering to the investment community, was published. The company was already publishing a magazine of general interest to businessmen, *The Busy Man's Magazine*. In 1911 Maclean decided to try to occupy some of the territory his sometime employee, John A. Cooper, had moved into, and changed *Busy Man's* to a general interest monthly, modestly named *Maclean's*. Neither a brilliant writer nor a very good editor, J.B. Maclean knew how to sell advertising, keep costs down, and reinvest profits. He cultivated the rich and famous and played the stock market well enough to make his fortune independently of the publishing company.

———

But now the story of continuous growth and almost unrelieved success comes to an end. Even as Canadian business reached new heights of prosperity in the Edwardian age before the war, as such "captains of industry" as Van Horne, Mackenzie and Mann, George Cox, William C. McDonald, and others, stood high up polls of "Canada's Ten Biggest Men," and the phenomenon of the genu-wine millionaire and his mansion made its appearance from Halifax to Vancouver Island, and Stephen Leacock satirized them all in *Arcadian Adventures of the Idle Rich*, free enterprise capitalism was reaching several kinds of limits.

One set of limits, dealt with in the next chapter, was the resistance to unfettered enterprise that caused the *Financial Post*, within a year of its founding, to complain bitterly of the "socialism" of the Conservative government of Ontario. These were the anti-business attitudes that caused the some of Canada's most enterprising newspaper publishers to fatten their circulation and profits through "people's journalism," a large component of which was attacking big business as being monopolistic and oppressive.

The other, more basic, limit was in the capacity of the northern economy to support all the enterprises that the enthusiastic promoters and politicians launched. It turned out that there were constraints on Canada's ability to realize its potential, limits to the amount of profitable business that all the raw resources could generate.

One of the earliest developers to discover the hard problems of making the wilderness bloom was Francis Hector Clergue, the much-heralded Napoleon of Canadian industry. Clergue's integrated industrial complex at Sault Ste Marie, so dazzling to think about and talk about, and so impressive to tour through and dance around, turned out to be completely unsound as a business proposition. Expansion had far outrun markets. Clergue's companies did most of their business with each other. Canada's first steel rails, rolled at Algoma, failed to meet quality standards; they were too brittle. Costs were high throughout the Clergue empire; solid managerial control of the businesses was almost non-existent.

In September 1903, a time when the boom was nicely getting rolling in the rest of Canada, the Consolidated Lake Superior Corporation ran out of money. It suddenly shut down, leaving thirty-five hundred men without work or wages. The Ontario government had to rush troops to the Sault to keep order and rush money to the firm to bail it out. Clergue blamed his troubles on foreign competition and inadequate capital. He was gradually pushed aside in the reorganizations and consolidations that followed his débâcle. For the rest of the decade, and most of the next two decades, the Sault industries limped along under the wings of worried governments, marginally profitable at best, usually a drain on the country's taxpayers. The biggest losers were the original Philadelphia investors in this premature development, the Americans who had believed Clergue's vision of what Canada could become.

F.H. Clergue moved to Montreal where he began promoting Canada's fourth transcontinental railway. The North Railway, as he called it, would head up the Ottawa valley to James Bay. Freight and passengers would board ferries that would take them to the mouth of the Nelson River on Hudson Bay where track would recommence. The rails would run due west along the sixtieth parallel – through frozen wilderness.

Federal and provincial politicians took Clergue's plans seriously and were willing to entertain his requests for land grants, subsidies, and guarantees to get the work started. But the onset of hard times in 1913 began putting an end to the North Railway and many other Canadian dreams.

TOP: **Casa Loma, Toronto** *(James Collection, City of Toronto Archives, #4095)*
ABOVE: **Sir Henry Pellatt inspects the Boy Scouts**
(Queen's Own Rifles of Canada, Regimental Museum)

13

At War with Business

*Secrets of success . . . tasteful ostentation . . . philanthropy . . . rich men's
idle sons . . . "La Riche Canadienne" . . . accountability . . . diligent
employees . . . working conditions . . . unions . . . competition . . .
combines . . . capturing government . . . anti-business sentiment . . .
populism . . . public ownership . . . "The Peoples' Power" . . . free
trade . . . the boom ends . . . Mackenzie weeps . . . the impact of war . . . "To
Hell with Profits" . . . a robber baronet*

The rich paid no taxes. Neither did corporations. At least not as we think of income and corporation and sales taxes. The provinces and municipalities were beginning to go after estates and corporate capital by 1900 and experimenting with ways of taxing income, but they still got most of their revenues from land sales, natural resource rents, and Ottawa's subsidies. Ottawa's revenues came mainly from customs duties. There were no national income or corporation taxes for anyone, rich or poor, to pay.

Not all businessmen were rich. Many failed as entrepreneurs or investors; many others achieved modest success – say a thousand or two in income every year from the store or agency. A few became fabulously wealthy. Railway and bank and insurance company presidents who earned upwards of $25,000 a year in 1900 made more than fifty times a factory hand's annual income of about $500, a far greater gap than now exists after taxes. The few businessmen who amassed great wealth belonged to the charmed circle of millionaires. There were four or five dozen of them in all of Canada in, say, 1910. Their money had so much purchasing power that they could afford to live in real castles, employ servants by the dozen, give their children the best of everything, keep on accumulating – and still pay no income taxes. The community had yet to exact the wages of success.

MANY WELL-TO-DO BUSINESSMEN thought they owed their success to following an austere personal code. The "Protestant" values of thrift, sobriety, and hard work – in other words, sustained self-denial – were not a monopoly of any religious group or social class in Canada, nor did they lead inevitably to success. But not many successful men had made their way without a fairly steady commitment to hard work and self-discipline, at least during business hours. Prominent businessmen were often pillars of their local churches, intensely dedicated Christians who moved easily from board meetings to prayer meetings, eschewed drinking, gambling, dancing, and other frivolities, and tried to apply the golden rule in all their business dealings. Success sometimes did not change any of these attitudes, so there were millionaires who lived plainly, counted their pennies, and religiously turned out the office lights all their days (electricity did cost much more in its early years).*

More normally, successful businessmen invested portions of their wealth in the good things of life: a fine house, a few extra servants, first-class travel, the best education for the children that money could buy. Such spending was often not ostentatious. Privacy to the point of seclusion was highly valued in hedge-lined Westmount and Rosedale. If you had money you might as well enjoy some of it (most of it, of course, was always tied up in the business), but you should not be a show-off about your wealth. When Joseph Flavelle, a devout Methodist millionaire, visited the California villa of fellow Methodist millionaire E.R. Wood, he was distressed by the "amount of self-consciousness 'look at me'" attitude displayed in Wood's splendid home and furnishings.

Flavelle himself lived in one of the most splendid and conspicuous mansions in Canada, "Holwood," built in Queen's Park on land belonging to the University of Toronto. But he did not consider his beautiful Beaux Arts home to be ostentatious: he saw it, rather, as dignified, classical, and restrained. He probably had a similar view of the classical façades of Bank of Commerce branches, which were designed by the same architect. Unlike the more ultra-democratic or puritanical among his associates (such as the old packer, William Davies, who found "Holwood" appalling in its ostentation), Flavelle thought wealthy men, those who had

---

* How many of the well-to-do had risen from rags to riches in the classic fashion described in Horatio Alger's novels? A few. But historians have shown that in both Canada and the United States members of the business elites commonly had parents of higher than average socio-economic standing who gave them better than average education. These findings are of little use, though, for proper comparisons would be with members of other elites and would involve working out yardsticks for measuring comparative social mobility. The overwhelming fact about capitalism's early millionaires is that this mobility, measured in terms of the accumulation of wealth, was fantastic by any standard. Some of the rich did start a few rungs up on society's stepladders. Then they transferred to aerial ladders that took them to the sky.

risen to society's top ranks, were obliged to play a suitable role in public life – as owners of mansions, hosts of entertainments, and generous patrons of a broad range of community activities and good causes. Stratification by wealth, in this view, was part of the nature of things, especially in an Anglo-American country like Canada. Aristocracies were renewed by the newly rich, who had a responsibility to learn to behave like aristocrats and raise their children accordingly. Having made your money, you neither sat on it nor worried overmuch about increasing it. You lived well and tried to use your money and talents to do useful things for your fellow man.

Cynical men-in-the-street nicknamed Flavelle's home "Porker's Palace," but there were much clearer examples of nouveau aristocratic posturing. One fairly clear dividing line was between those millionaires who gave their mansions ordinary Anglo-Scottish names like "Holwood," "Oaklands" (John Macdonald), "Glencoe" (Lord Strathcona), "Glen Stewart" (A.E. Ames), or "Deancroft" (A.F. Gooderham) – and those who proclaimed to the world that they lived in Castle Frank (A.E. Kemp), Dundurn Castle (MacNab), Craigdarroch Castle (the Dunsmuirs), and that most gaudily absurd of all millionaires' residences, Toronto's Casa Loma. Casa Loma's owner, the stockbroker and financier Henry Mill Pellatt, was as absurd as his home, a pompous, obese man who had made his millions in mining and utilities promotion and between 1911 and 1914 spent one million dollars building the romantic, pseudo-medieval pile on a hill overlooking the city. Pellatt's obsession with play-soldiering in the Canadian militia as Colonel of the Queen's Own Rifles was common among the more transparent social climbers who believed that military blood was the bluest of all. Scratch a Canadian "colonel" before the military was put through the crucible of the Great War and you often found the rich red blood of a parvenu.

Many of the well-to-do gave generously to good causes, and got no payback in tax deductions. Some conscientiously followed principles of Christian stewardship and gave lavishly to their churches, to other Christian institutions like the YMCA or church colleges, and to fellow Christians needing help. The devout merchant prince of wholesaling, John Macdonald, gave away 20 per cent of his annual income. He was in constant demand to lay the cornerstones of new Methodist churches in Ontario, collecting the ceremonial trowels as souvenirs and contributing handsomely to building funds. Knowledge of Macdonald's generosity led to a stream of supplicants at his office door, ranging from collectors for every charity to tramps in every stage of dilapidation. The merchant treated everyone generously, offering tracts and prayer as well as money. All denominations had outstanding and generous business laymen, but the Methodist Church of Canada, which flourished brilliantly before disappearing into the United Church in 1926, seemed to have more than its share. The Masseys, Eatons,

George A. Cox, A.E. Ames, E.R. Wood, J.H. Gundy, and J.W. Flavelle all gave handsomely to every Methodist appeal. Flavelle was particularly active in the Macdonald tradition, keeping, as one minister put it, almost an "open house for beggars."

Philanthropists' interests broadened at the beginning of the twentieth century to include such semi-secular institutions as hospitals and universities, and, for a few, the cultural institutions conspicuously absent in the young country. Byron Edmund Walker, general manager and then president of the Bank of Commerce in the Cox years, was a scholarly agnostic, who devoted immense energy to advancing art and knowledge in Toronto. He was the effective founding father of both the Art Gallery of Ontario and the Royal Ontario Museum, often raising funds by dunning the city's and his circle's Methodist millionaires.

Most giving was rooted in a sense of stewardship, but was often triggered by claims of friendship and business association as the well-to-do tapped each other for favourite causes. Giving became something of a social obligation of the rich, irrespective of their personal inclinations. When Flavelle was raising money for a new Toronto General Hospital, for example, he put to William Mackenzie the view of the Toronto circle that "we would all be grateful if the scale of his giving would be such that we could feel proud of it . . . one which we can all look at with pride in contrast to what is being done in Montreal by men who hold representative positions such as Mr. Mackenzie holds here."

There was little corporate giving in an age of personal philanthropy (the Bank of Commerce, under Walker's influence, was probably the pioneer; by their nature corporations could never be as generous as individuals). The charitable foundation was an invention of the American super-rich, the Rockefellers and Carnegies who had so much wealth that they had to organize the job of giving it away. The idea came to Canada in a small way in the self-perpetuating trusts established by Hart Massey to administer the $2 million estate he left in 1896, but was not used by others until the 1920s or 1930s. (Fortunately both the Rockefeller and Carnegie foundations operated almost as though the border did not exist and spent millions on good Canadian causes; Carnegie money, for example, built most of the public libraries erected in the Dominion before 1914.) The most conspicuous consumers among the rich, men like Pellatt or the Dunsmuirs of British Columbia, gave little more than token support to good causes, but liked publicity for their donations.

Some self-made men patronized particular institutions, the most visible being their own company towns – Hiram Walker's Walkerville, Alexander Gibson's Marysville, Henry Corby's Corbyville, the Calvin family's Garden Island community – where they took deep paternal pride as givers of schools, churches, hospitals, and Christmas turkeys. Flavelle's comments notwithstanding, Montreal's wealthy businessmen, from the McGills through Molsons, Redpaths, and the CPR millionaires Strathcona and Mount Stephen, had generously endowed the English-speaking city with its university, several fine hospitals, museums, and homes for boys, orphans, incurables, and single women. The lumber barons did the same for Ottawa well in advance of the federal government. Private collecting and personal support of artists was another form of patronage, but had few outstanding Canadian practitioners other than Sir William Van Horne and Byron Edmund Walker. It was not that Canadian millionaires were less cultured than their American brethren, only that there were so many fewer of them with many fewer millions.

The non-smoking tobacco king of Montreal, William C. McDonald, was easily the Dominion's greatest philanthropist. He was a bachelor with few family ties, a strong sense of the need for social betterment, particularly in rural Canada, and, some said, well-developed guilt feelings about the source of his wealth ("I am not proud of my business," McDonald is reported to have remarked, "and that feeling, perhaps, has been the reason for my donations"). From the 1880s until his death in 1917, and through a spelling change to Macdonald on obtaining a knighthood in 1898, Sir William lavished money on programs to consolidate rural schools, introduce practical subjects in school curricula, and train men and women to lead Canada into an age of scientific agriculture and efficient rural living. He gave English-speaking Quebec its equivalent to Ontario's state-supported agricultural college by founding Macdonald College of McGill University and gave women a role at the Ontario Agricultural College by creating the Macdonald Institute as a centre for domestic science. Macdonald's tobacco money ushered McGill's engineering faculty and science departments into international stature, but there was also money to endow chairs of history and moral philosophy, create scholarships, and purchase ten thousand books for the library. (Macdonald drew the line only at professors' salaries, refusing the money needed to retain one scholar for McGill with the comment, "Why, the professors will be giving dinner parties if they get such high salaries.")

Macdonald's giving to McGill alone amounted to more than $14 million, the equivalent of $300 million or more in current dollars. He was not a practising Christian. His desire to have his name on the buildings and institutions he founded perhaps suggests a longing for a kind of secular immortality. The less worldly philanthrophists, like John Macdonald and Flavelle and some we know nothing about, often gave anonymously and without publicity. The extreme of philanthropic bad taste was reached in 1914 with the naming of Timothy Eaton Memorial Church in Toronto.

Most successful entrepreneurs hoped to leave heirs who would carry on the work. Fathers hoped sons would follow in their footsteps, even to the top of large public corporations. Easier said than done, for many rich men worried that their children were handicapped by the old man's money. How could youngsters brought up in ease and affluence, without a material worry in the world, develop the hunger and habits of self-denial necessary to rise to the top – assuming that they had inherited practical ability? Rich men were haunted by the fear of spawning idle sons, wastrel playboys frittering away inheritances, contributing nothing to business or the community. "Young men who inherit riches may become useful citizens," one of Maclean's trade journals fretted: "The chances are against them." "The inheritance tax should have no terrors for the millionaire," Max Aitken wrote. "Wealth without either the wish, the brains, or the power to use it is too often the medium through which men pamper the flesh with good living, and the mind with inanity, until death, operating through the liver, harries the fortunate youth into an early grave."

Some fathers tried to toughen sons with measly allowances, spartan living conditions in private boarding schools, and humble first jobs as office boys or factory hands. Powerful fathers who constantly won tests of will against strong-willed sons were apt to ruin everything by reducing the boys to simpering obedience and insecurity. (The best psychological foundation for entrepreneurial success, reflected in a thousand high achievers' comments about having had "the best mother who ever lived," was apparently instilled by the combination of a weak father and strong mother.) More commonly, fathers vacillated between discipline and lavish generosity, achieving predictably mixed results. The Eaton and Molson families bred able business leaders for generations.* The Masseys and Harrises produced talented offspring, but by the third generation became confounded by the youths' interest in higher education, the arts, politics – anything but farm implements. In 1925 the Oxford-educated head of the family, Vincent, left the presidency of Massey-Harris for a political career that eventually led to his becoming the first Canadian to serve as governor general. He was the last Massey to be president of the company. His brother Raymond became a distinguished actor. The Harrises produced politicians, clergymen, and Lawren Harris, the most spiritual member of the Group of Seven school of painters.

* A kind of Molson family code, typical of patriarchs' aspirations for their descendants, was dictated by John H.R. Molson on his deathbed in 1897:

"The Molson family has maintained and preserved its position and influence by steady, patient industry, and every member should be a real worker and not rely on what it has been. All that is good and great of the family should not be under ground.

"Your private life should be pure. Make no compromise with vice, be able to say *no* in a firm manly manner.

"Character is the real test of manhood. Live within your income no matter how small it may be. Permanent wealth is maintained and preserved by vigilance and prudence and not by speculation.

"Be just, and generous when you have the means.

"Wealth will not take care of itself if not vigilantly cared for."

Massey-Harris was like many family firms in changing from a partnership to a limited-liability corporation years before the family left executive leadership and sold voting control. In other cases, incorporation would occur when the founders ran out of manpower or capital and simply sold out – to competitors, outsiders, sometimes just to promoters or securities salesmen such as Max Aitken. Of course the family name might survive for generations, particularly in industries like brewing or distilling where it identified the good old brands (and some that wanted to be thought of that way).

There were also more disorderly transitions. None of George A. Cox's three sons had the old man's business abilities, but he brought them along anyway in brazenly nepotistic fashion, giving them senior positions at the Canada Life, creating a new insurance company (the Imperial) for one of them to manage, turning a blind eye to associates' complaints about incompetence and moral turpitude. The young Coxes maintained a façade of family success, thanks largely to the loyalty of the old man's friends and the competence of hired managers.

Not so the Dunsmuir heirs, whose dissolute ways became almost a parody of *arriviste* capitalism. Robert Dunsmuir's second son, Alexander, who was in charge of the coal baron's San Francisco operation, became a hopeless drunkard, kept a mistress for many years, and died in alcoholic delirium a few weeks after marrying her (the story came out in the court battle over his estate). The first son, James, was true to his father's spirit and carried the business to new heights. His firstborn, Robert William Dunsmuir, staggered along in Uncle Alexander's footsteps, was disowned and shipped to Argentina. James then placed all his dynastic hopes on young Jimmie "Boy" Dunsmuir, whom he brought up much more strictly. Boy went down on the *Lusitania* in 1915. British Columbia's millionaire coal baron spent the last months of his life secluded in the study of his mansion playing over and over again a recording of "Where, Oh Where, Is My Wandering Boy Tonight?" The Dunsmuir enterprises were sold to Mackenzie and Mann.

It helped to have so many males in the family that third and fourth sons or nephews could take up the challenge. Many entrepreneurs had no children or were dynastically crippled by having given birth to daughters. "Girls," said Mr. Dombey in the Dickens novel, "have nothing to do with Dombey and Son," a simple fact of business life in Canada as well as England. For generations the Canadian business world was exclusively male, more so than in the pioneer days of New France. The odd widow or heiress served on the boards of family companies ("Lalia Chase can sit on the corner of a table and swing her leg as good as any man," Nova Scotia's Roy Jodrey liked to say), but never in an executive or career role. It never occurred to Joseph Flavelle, for example, that one of his daughters, Clara, had the ability to become a brilliant businesswoman. She was fated to spend her life raising children and doing good works, while her one brother failed repeatedly to fill the role his sex and his father had planned for him.

It is not clear whether any of James Dunsmuir's eight daughters could have become businesswomen. Most were notorious social butterflies and spendthrifts, running through their inheritance with driven abandon. It was thought that Elinor Dunsmuir was the most brilliant. Marion and Muriel were content to toss their money away in the "Harem," "Cave Caucasian," and other Paris nightclubs of the twenties, but Elinor was going to increase hers. "La Riche Canadienne," as she was called, was strikingly mannish, wearing short hair and a black velvet smoking jacket as she gambled day after day at Monte Carlo, Nice, and Cannes. After Elinor Dunsmuir had lost her share of the wealth the miners had scrabbled out of the Vancouver Island pits, she was shipped home, like her sisters, to make do with the remnants of trust funds. The youngest daughter, Dola, titillated Victoria society in the 1920s with her habit of playing tennis without panties.

The ability to grow good men was essential to business survival. When talented sons were not there to manage divisions and be ready to take the helm it was necessary to go outside the family. Old friends of the family, and their sons, young men familiar from church or school or club, whose values and moral codes were well known, were often the first choice. Educational attainment beyond basic literacy was not particularly important, for most businesses were mastered on the job. Good men proved themselves by moving up the ladder, from, say, bank teller to bank president. The chartered banks were among the largest employers of ambitious young men; they liked to hire Anglo-Saxon boys, preferably Scottish lads, who had a sound basic schooling and were willing to work. Why risk giving young men of strange ethnic origins, whose character and values were unknown quantities, positions of trust and responsibility, they reasoned. Girls from good families often made good workers (in shops and factories and some offices, not yet in bank branches) but were not thought to have managerial potential or aspirations. What right-minded woman, almost certainly destined for marriage and motherhood, would think of business as a career, even if she did have a head for it?

Having a head for figures and the ability to write them down and organize them was increasingly important as firms grew and their business became more complex. One of the most common causes of failure, then as now, stemmed from proprietors' tendency to lose control of a growing business. Accounting or managerial ability did not always accompany entrepreneurial skill. In promoters like F. H. Clergue or William Mackenzie, who were far more interested in dreams and deals than in details, accounting and entrepreneurship seemed polar opposites. The secret of making the transition from builder-promoter-entrepreneur to manager of a big business was to find ways of bringing the business under accounting control, if only by hiring people who could.

At the turn of the century the key to accountability was departmentalization, breaking the big firm into components of understandable and accountable size.

The aim was not just to produce a clear sense of where each department was going, but to use the accounts as tools to unleash the energies of managers and employees whose responsibility for their performance could be clearly traced and measured, no matter how big the organization. With accountability came control and the ability to expand and integrate rationally. Often you knew what you were doing and where you were going more clearly than the smaller players still buffetted by the vagaries of the market and their guess-and-golly bookkeeping.

The biggest stores were the department stores. Leading banks were becoming departmentalized; railroads, the first big business and pioneers in many managerial techniques, had been for years. The group around George Cox in Toronto made departmentalization and careful accounting the basis of their approach to management. J.W. Flavelle's accounting practices as a meat-packer were the most sophisticated and exacting in the North American industry, and it was no accident that his successor in the industry, J.S. McLean, started as a bookkeeper with one of Flavelle's companies.

Employers in large and small firms alike expected their staff to be sober, hardworking, and thrifty. Believing that most people were naturally inclined to idleness, indiscipline, and extravagance, employers insisted on rigid codes of punctuality, dress, and deportment both on and off the job. Analogies with military organization and discipline were common in commercial organizations; men were expected to exercise initiative and leadership qualities, but mastering the drills and skills of the martinet seemed a precondition to all other advancement. The banks' codes were the most strict. "Officers found guilty of immoral practices, of visiting gambling houses or saloons, will be dismissed," read the Bank of Nova Scotia's 1902 Manual of Rules and Regulations. "We now state it to be our policy to eliminate from the staff all who drink in saloons or use intoxicants in any other way than in strict moderation," head office elaborated. "Some may defend a visit to a bar-room for a friendly drink with a customer on the plea of securing business; and doubtless, the customer seeing that such conviviality makes his banker more pliant, is likewise convinced that a saloon attachment is a desirable addition to a banker's office. However, we have been taught that the customer generally has the advantage in such bibulous financiering." As part of their concern that young staff live within their limited means, banks banned from marriage, except by special dispensation, all who earned less than the "marriage minimum." Many clerks fell below the minimum (it was about $1,000 in eastern Canada in 1912; $1,200 in the West); there were many broken hearts.

Employees were expected to attend diligently to their work, whether balancing ledgers in the office or stuffing cigar moulds in the tobacco factory. Wasted time and frivolity meant money lost, so employers became disciplinarians. In some factories where young children were employed, foremen behaved much like school teachers. One notorious case in the 1880s of corporal punishment and temporary "imprisonment" of young tobacco workers in Montreal was defended as being no different from punishments meted out in home or school. In certain older trades, such as iron moulding, workers maintained considerable personal control over their work routines and rhythms. But the imperatives of mechanization, cost-consciousness, and control within the growing organization all seemed to tend away from worker autonomy.

In the early years of the century some manufacturers flirted with ideas of time-and-motion study, shop floor reorganization, and piecework incentives that jelled into the "scientific management" movement, created in the United States by the engineer and factory organizer, Frederick W. Taylor. The approach came to Canada through branch plants and hired consultants, as well as the brainstorming of energetic managers. In 1901, for example, the general manager of the Bank of Nova Scotia, H.C. McLeod, introduced a "unit system of work" based on elaborate cost analyses of all the jobs in a bank branch expressed as units of labour. The most efficient employees received special bonuses. We do not know enough about innovations like these to be able to generalize about the passion for productivity. Many organizations, including these same banks, were ultra-conservative in other ways. By 1914 the life insurance companies were innovating with the employment of women in head office, and were adopting new business machines that made it easier to do complex calculations. But the banks thought female employees were inappropriate for their branches and also distrusted the early adding machines or "arithmometers" as being likely to undermine clerks' calculating skills.

A clerk who found the grinding conditions of service in a bank objectionable was always free to look for employment elsewhere. So were shopgirls, factory hands, lumbermen, all paid workers. Most employers bought labour on the open market, offering wages and conditions as good as necessary to get help, seldom better. Employers who valued low turnover might offer slightly higher wages, better working conditions, sales incentive plans, or, in a few cases, profit-sharing schemes. By the late 1880s the larger railways and banks were experimenting with pension plans to reward long service. Such benefits were both advanced employment practice and an echo of the old paternalism of the small shop. Some employers carried paternalism to the point of giving their workers more benefits – perhaps at Christmas, perhaps by keeping them on in hard times – than simple market calculations required.

Most employers thought there were elements of paternalism or altruism in their very ability to offer work and wages under any conditions. They told themselves, and they were told by practically everyone in their communities, that it was a fine thing to create employment by founding and operating enterprises. They did not take kindly to criticisms of the wages they paid, hours they required, or conditions of sanitation, ventilation, and safety in their workplaces.

Hostile critics dared to suggest that employers were exploiting workers. It was a refrain heard loudly enough by the mid-1880s for the federal government to appoint a Royal Commission on the Relations of Labor and Capital and several of the provinces to begin regulating conditions in factories. The fear was that the rapid growth of manufacturing, induced by the National Policy, was bringing dark satanic mills to Canada instead of steady, pleasant work at high wages. Perhaps the new industrialism was leading to worse conditions, not better, a lower rather than a higher standard of living.

The royal commission uncovered a few sensational examples of bad working conditions and exploitive use of child labour. From time to time factory inspectors, special commissions, or crusading journalists uncovered other abuses. These were usually in hard-pressed marginal firms in marginal industries. The main finding of the Royal Commission on Labor and Capital, reporting in 1889, was "that wages in Canada are generally higher than at any previous time, while hours of labor have been somewhat reduced. At the same time, the necessaries and ordinary comforts of life are lower in price than ever before, so that the material conditions of the working people who exercise reasonable prudence and economy have been greatly bettered." Concern about child labour and long working hours in the factory system was not a response to declining standards. Factory working conditions and rewards were usually better than farm life offered, particularly in overpopulated farmed-out districts. Real wages rose steadily in most decades and per capita income continued to rise in periods when apparent wage rates remained constant or fell behind inflation.* Work in factories, though not in mines, was easier and healthier than work in the bush or at sea.

Alarm about child labour reflected rising expectations about childhood as a time for school and play. Few employers thought young children were worth the trouble of hiring, even at very low wages. The worst offenders may have been the newspapers in their use of young newsboys. In poor areas of the country, and in industries such as textiles where multiple jobs for a family were traditional, employers complained of parents and children who lied about birth dates in their desire to have the family fully employed. "He indeed would not only be a bold but a bad man who regarded the gradual advance of the laboring class from a condition of indigence and oppressive anxiety and domestic discomfort to a state less degrading, with any other feeling than that of satisfaction and thankfulness," the *Journal of Commerce* editorialized in 1890, summarizing the normal feelings of most of those who hired help.

But there was usually neither the incentive nor the desire to offer wages greatly higher than other employers were giving, to give away profits (except afterwards, to good causes), or to deviate in other ways from the practices of the

* This point is poorly understood by historians whose comparisons of wage rates in selected occupations over time, such as the Laurier years, result in generalizations to the effect that standards of living were declining. No account is taken in these studies of such important variables as changes in occupational structure and frequency of employment.

labour market. There were other times when it was necessary to implement wage cuts, shutdowns, and other regressions in conditions of employment. At the best of times most work was long, hard, and poorly remunerated. The camaraderie of work in the small shop or farmer's field (in the good seasons) was increasingly difficult to sustain in larger operations, where scores of operatives had to be organized by impersonal foremen to follow time- and machine-driven routines. Some owners and foremen and contractors had absolutely no skill in human relations. Employees did not see their interests as always identical with those of the old man. There could be conflict with the boss over any or every aspect of the job: hours, wages, work routines, the introduction of new machines, whatever. Disputes usually led to the abrogation of the work contract as the malcontent quit or was fired. But from the earliest years of Canadian business history there were occasions when employees with grievances combined and took collective action, usually by stopping work.

Labour historians have scoured newspapers and other documents to uncover scores of small unions originating between 1800 and 1850. There were hundreds of nineteenth-century strikes. Many early "unions" were associations of skilled tradesmen, proud of their autonomy, who resisted the erosion of their position by employers, technology, and other forces. From the 1840s there were periodic strikes by unskilled labourers – canal workers, railway navvies, longshoremen – often to protest wage cuts or unpaid wages. Canadian unions had their legal right to exist sanctified by Parliament in 1872. By the 1880s "people's strikes" in coal or lumber or textile towns sometimes engulfed whole communities. In that decade an American-born universal union cum spiritual movement, the Noble and Holy Order of the Knights of Labor, spilled into Canada. It briefly enrolled tens of thousands of workers, became embroiled in strikes and other conflicts (with the Catholic Church in Quebec, for example), and, when its American parent disintegrated, kept a few Canadian assemblies going into the twentieth century.

An ostensibly national Trades and Labor Congress of Canada existed from 1883, but its affiliates had few teeth until the American Federation of Labor began a serious campaign in the late 1890s to increase the Canadian membership of its "international" unions. AFL organizers were the making of the Canadian labour movement. The absolute number of trade unionists remained small – 133,000 in a non-agricultural work force of 1.8 million in 1911 – but most employers knew that the "labour question," (or, in other words, workers' aptitude for forming unions to bargain collectively), was never going to go away.

Bosses were deeply suspicious of the whole idea of these workers' combinations. Prepared to deal with employees on a one-to-one basis, they instinctively responded to collective action by refusing to bargain with or recognize any organization of their men. If that caused men to quit their jobs by going on strike, then the thing to do was to hire new men. People who abandoned jobs surely had no right to interfere with willing workers by picketing or using other methods of intimidation. Whatever happened, the determined employer would not bend. Here is a Galt, Ontario, iron-founder talking to a worker during the bitter strike of 1889:

> There is my factory. It is a large one, it is built of brick and stone. You might begin and take it away piecemeal – one brick at a time, one stone at a time – carrying the particles on your own shoulder over into the next county, going as slowly and deliberately as you please, and then, when all has been taken away, I will be no nearer to yielding the management of my business to your trade union than I am now. I will never do it.

Grim strikers and iron-willed bosses sometimes fought violently, particularly in single-industry towns or other situations where strikers' numbers or the popularity of their cause meant broad community support. When local police, if there were any, proved unable to keep order, the militia or regular troops were called out.

NOTICE

> There is an impression in the community that we are obliged to accede to the miners' demands; but for the benefit of those whom it may concern we wish to state publicly that we have no intention to ask any of them to work for us again at any price.
>
> Dunsmuir, Duggle & Co.

This was Robert Dunsmuir's approach to labour relations at his Nanaimo mine in 1877. When he turned the striking miners out of their company housing, two companies of infantry and a gunboat had to be sent to keep order. A quarter-century later Robert's son James explained to a royal commission his approach to labour relations:

> Q. Do you know of any real cause for the difficulty which the men have now in these mines?
> A. No, I do not. The only trouble is because I won't let them belong to the union. They can belong to the union if they like – I don't care. I have my rights. I can hire them if I like, and they can work if they like . . . .
> Q. You have no other motive for refusing to recognize except – ?
> A. Except, that I want the management of my own works, and if I recognize the union, I cannot have that. Then we are dictated to by a committee of the union as to what should be done and what should not be done. . . .
> Q. Have you not, when you became aware of a man belonging to the

union, got rid of him?

A.   You mean fired the heads of the union?

Q.   Yes.

A.   Every time.

These British Columbians were fairly representative of the tough frontier employers whose confrontations with highly concentrated work forces in mining and lumber camps gave the province a tradition of bad labour relations. On the other hand, another large West coast employer, the British Columbia Electric Railway, avoided disputes for many years in an often troubled industry by following a policy of deliberate, enlightened paternalism. Paternalism often worked, particularly in firms profitable enough to give it a real cash value. In human terms, it often led to a willingness to discuss grievances with committees of men, or, as with the BCER, to get along with a local union, especially a cooperative one. There was much more resistance to negotiating with paid union organizers, outside "agitators" whose income seemed to depend on fomenting conflict between capital and labour and whose organization, employers thought, probably had no real concern for either a company's or its workers' interests.

Many employers gradually learned to live with organized labour, often in a working relationship that proved useful for settling grievances, improving morale and discipline, and dividing the earnings of the enterprise. Some employers even got used to the closed shop. There is very little evidence that the size of enterprises, or the form of their organization, was a significant variable shaping attitudes toward labour or toward unions. Factors ranging from an employer's cultural background through the state of the labour market in his region or industry seem to have been more important. There were wide variations from industry to industry, company to company. Still, the attitude of most businessmen to the power and the levelling tendencies of unions was nicely summarized in the Canadian Manufacturers' Association's journal, *Industrial Canada*, in 1909: "Unionism undoubtedly is a good thing in some ways, but like strychnine, it must be taken in small doses."

Employers' standard reason for being unable to make things better for their men, or for having to make things worse, was the pressure of competition. No firm could let its costs or prices get out of line and stay in business. The real bottom line was always the need to stay competitive – in fact to have a competitive advantage of some kind if money was going to be made. To get and hold business it was necessary to offer lower prices or better-quality products or have better salesmen or service or have some kind of monopoly on portions of the market. The ultimate competitive advantage, of course, was always monopoly.

But who could hold a monopoly, or even keep a good thing quiet long enough to make a fortune on it? There were always new people, it seemed, determined to get in on any good thing, competitors who would force you to cut prices and trim costs, duplicate the goods and services you offered, invade your markets. They might work longer hours than you wanted to work, or be satisfied with lower profits. They might be less ethical, misrepresenting goods, bribing customers or others, finding every possible short cut. They might be just stupid, not realizing how surely they were heading for failure while helping drag everyone else down. But what could be done about them?

In some cases it paid to fight fire with fire, to try to beat competitors so thoroughly that they left the business. Treat business as a war of all against all, a Darwinian struggle for the survival of the fittest. The trouble was that victory might be expensive and could seldom be decisive or complete. There would always be more competitors. The other denizens of the jungle had to be lived with. Often it made sense to at least talk to competitors to try to define the limits of the rivalry. Surely it would be in everyone's interest to outlaw the most harmful, most wasteful forms of competition.

In many larger towns by the 1880s, for example, grocers and other merchants found themselves spending heavily on presents for their customers every Christmas season. It seemed only sensible to agree amongst themselves to end the practice. Business hours were another problem, as competition seemed to be driving storekeepers into ever longer hours. Why should retailers and their clerks have to work six days and six nights of the week, often till ten o'clock or later? Why not agree to all close at the same time, say six o'clock on week nights? Perhaps a half-holiday every week, at least in the summer, could be agreed upon. Early closing movements, broadly supported by merchants and their help, became common in the 1880s. Such organized cooperation was not necessary in earlier times when smaller numbers of merchants limited their hours informally.

If hours could be the subject of merchants' agreements, why not terms of credit, which were usually absurdly generous? Why not prices? The nub of the matter, the ugly heart of competition, was price-cutting. When men were selling essentially the same product, as was bound to happen in most industries, did it make any sense for some of them to ask less than a fair price – a price fair enough to return, say, a "living profit"? Price-cutting was surely counter-productive, for competitors had to meet cuts, leading to price wars. Usually only buyers gained in price wars. Why not agree to eliminate price rivalry, and compete in other ways?

Adam Smith pointed out that people of the same trade "seldom meet together, even for merriment and diversion, but the conversation ends in a conspiracy against the public, or in some contrivance to raise prices." Price-fixing agreements were a staple of nineteenth-century Canadian business. They existed in most lines of business and they evolved as business evolved. Two or three local shopkeepers could agree informally on prices; so could two or three big national distillers or harvester manufacturers. As newcomers set up shop or started shipping into a market, the discussions might have to become more complex, the agreements more formal. Perhaps a trade association was needed to administer price agreements (and any other agreeable limits to competition). When members proved not as good as their word it was necessary to set up an enforcement mechanism. And how could ornery outsiders, who kept on with the bad old ways, be brought to see the light? How do you punish price-cutters? Perhaps their suppliers could be asked to require all resalers to maintain prices. If people were not willing to cooperate with the majority they could be cut off or boycotted.

Ontario's oil producers and refiners were among the first to form price-fixing associations. They began as early as 1862 and tried again in every period of low prices and sharp competition. The salt men of Goderich and Windsor did the same. By the 1880s and 1890s price-fixing trade associations came in all shapes, sizes, and kinds. They ranged from village shopkeepers' coffee klatches to well-funded, professionally managed national organizations. "There are few branches of trade in this or any other country," the *Journal of Commerce* remarked as early as 1887, "which are not represented by associations which seek to prevent unprofitable competition." At a national convention of hardware men in Toronto in 1894, coincident meetings were held of the Wire Nail Association, the Wire Association, Screw Association, Bolt and Nut Association, Rivet Association, Barb Wire Association, Bar Iron Association, Cut Nail Association, Horseshoe Association, Tack Association, and Paint Grinders' Association, all to discuss prices.

One of the most important national organizations was the Dominion Wholesale Grocers Guild, which formed branches in all major cities in the mid-1880s and organized elaborate price-fixing agreements in tobacco, starch, baking powder, pickles, white sugar, and other grocery staples. Enforcement was carried out through manufacturers and threats of boycott. The guild had regulations to limit another disrupting, "demoralizing" form of competition, wholesalers' tendency to burst established trade patterns by selling at retail. Many associations wrestled with similar problems, trying to protect traditional lines of business from those who would upset all the existing patterns and profits.

Price-cutting acquired the dimensions of an ethical issue for many businessmen. Was it right to cut prices below cost in predatory assaults on fellow merchants, in the knowledge that after the weak went down the helpless consumer could make up the losses by paying higher prices? Such forms of competition seemed unethical in the same way that doctors and lawyers considered certain practices unethical. Some businessmen with aspirations to professional standing tried to agree on lists of unprofessional competitive practices to outlaw. "If banking is worthy the name of a profession," claimed a writer in the *Journal of the Canadian Bankers Association* in 1898, "there should be certain things universally considered unprofessional within our ranks. Giving service without profit or at an actual loss should be unprofessional. Solicitation of business by offering to work more cheaply should be as unworthy a banker as we consider it unworthy a doctor." As part of its aim of advancing the interests of Canadian banks, the Canadian Bankers Association, formed in 1891, worked diligently to fix interest rates and reduce other kinds of competition. Many small businessmen compared their price-fixing and other anti-competitive practices with the activities of those combines in the labour market, the unions. If it was just for men to meet and work together to limit competition in the labour market in the interest of obtaining a "living wage," surely it was equally right and just to limit competition in other markets so that honest shopkeepers and merchants could obtain a "living profit."

Combinations to restrain trade were not particularly important or effective in Canada's free society. Whenever an association succeeded in restricting a form of competition it simultaneously created an opportunity for someone to gain a competitive advantage by adopting the banned practice. In other words, every monopolistic situation was simply an invitation to others to come in and get a share of the loot (intelligent restrictionists recognized this, of course, and tried to enjoy quiet, stable prosperity by avoiding gouging). Most trade associations found they could not enforce price agreements. Members would cut prices whenever it seemed in their interest, or newcomers would step in offering lower prices.

It happened classically in the oil industry. Trade associations always failed to hold together, so in 1880 the two leading refiners in Petrolia and London, Frederick Fitzgerald and Jacob Englehart, organized a well-financed ($500,000) combination, the Imperial Oil Company Limited. Imperial bought eleven local refineries and closed nine of them. It became the dominant Canadian company, but was never able to eliminate its domestic rivals. In 1891 it produced 45 per cent of all Canadian refined oil, a much smaller market share than John D. Rockefeller's Standard Oil Company held in the United States. Worse, Standard Oil invaded Canada, and Canadians' demand for cheap, high-quality petroleum products caused the government to reduce Imperial's tariff protection. By 1898 Standard Oil was marketing lower-cost, better-quality American oil across Canada and had begun to refine an odourless Canadian product that Imperial could not match. The competition ended abruptly on July 1, 1898, when Standard Oil acquired 75 per cent of the stock of Imperial. Imperial was reorganized by its American owners and again became the dominant company in the Canadian industry, for a time.

Then there were renegades like Timothy Eaton: classically individualistic entrepreneurs who recognized no limits on their right to engage in any lawful business practice. Eaton and men like him would sell whatever they wanted to whomever they chose at whatever price they could get. They would buy wherever they could, do their own wholesaling, and do their own manufacturing if it paid or if it was necessary to protect their freedom. "We mind our business," Eaton advertised. The fact that the growth of his business meant the destruction of any number of small merchants' livelihoods did not trouble him. The aim was to produce "the Greatest Good for the Greatest Number," to serve the buying public, not the interests of fellow businessmen. "We make a business of looking after the interests of our customers ... you come to us more than you go to anybody else, because you know where your interests lie." Merchants who liked to think fraternally of their membership in a business "community" deluded themselves. Free enterprise was ruthlessly destructive. In the long run only the fittest survived.

There was one critical variable in the competitive struggle, a force that could sometimes destroy other competitors' advantages, including their monopolies, and that could create wonderful competitive advantages, including very powerful monopolies. This variable was government.

Governments were the ultimate secular power. They created the environment, set the rules of the game, had the taxing, bounty-paying, and tariff-setting power. Get government on your side in the struggle and you could increase your competitive edge in any number of ways. If politicians accepted the legitimacy of your cause, their laws and taxes could make all the difference. Think of the difference that, say, the tariff made for Canadian manufacturers. They were able to mobilize the power of government to frustrate the forces of international competition and turn the whole Canadian market over to them.

What role would governments play in the domestic competitive struggle? One of the most legitimate functions of government in economic life, most Canadians thought, was to protect people from oppressive monopolies. By the late 1880s the activities of some of the leading price-fixing associations, such as the Dominion Wholesale Grocers Guild, were getting so much publicity that the House of Commons created a select committee to investigate combines. The committee recommended legislative action "for suppressing the evils arising from ... combinations and monopolies." In 1889, one year before the Sherman Antitrust Act was passed in the United States, Canada's Parliament passed special anti-combines legislation to set domestic competition policy.

The original anti-combines law of 1889 was anything but an onslaught on the combines and other anti-competitive arrangements. During the course of the investigation and law-making, members of Parliament decided they had no quarrel with restraints of trade that did not "unduly" or "unreasonably" lessen competition. The price-fixing trade associations made a persuasive case for their right to associate, just like trade unions or professional bodies, to try to obtain fair living profits. Most of their critics turned out to be veteran price-fixers who happened to be angry at this or that particular combine. The 1889 law was pious anti-monopoly posturing that had no effect on anything. As the Liberal opposition pointed out, a government whose National Policy was to restrict imports was not likely to be enthusiastically committed to free competition in the domestic market.

Some businessmen hoped governments would limit competition further by giving legislative support to their restrictive activities. The vicious price-cutting and other competitive practices of people like Timothy Eaton, for example, could not be stopped by private groups. Small retailers urged governments to agree that the department stores' methods were unfair or predatory, really aiming at creating a monopoly. Special laws could limit their aggression, perhaps by prohibiting the use of loss leaders or the selling of any goods below cost. Perhaps taxes could even the balance: why not levy a tax on each line of goods a store sold? Legal protection for manufacturers who insisted on resale price maintenance might be another approach.

Other competitors used methods amenable to legislative control. Consider grocers who sold those new, powerful patent medicines. Pharmacists did not believe grocers should be in that business and constantly lobbied for tighter laws confining the sale of drugs to pharmacies. What about all those hawkers and pedlars swarming in city streets and from door to door? They took business away from "legitimate" merchants, who had heavy fixed costs, paid local taxes, and surely deserved protection. Merchant organizations petitioned for laws limiting or taxing transient traders. And the early closing movements were too often disrupted by mavericks who insisted on staying open as long as they wanted, making everyone do the same. The way to guarantee early closing was for municipalities to give the force of law to merchants' agreements by passing by-laws limiting the hours of business. For about one hundred years, until the new competitive atmosphere of the 1980s, retail business hours in Canada were regulated on these principles.

Small businessmen and their organizations were the most persistent advocates of legislative restrictions on competition. From 1897 the Retail Merchants' Association of Canada led a series of campaigns against department stores, transient traders, and all other "harmful" forms of competition. In the early 1900s it succeeded in obtaining national legislation outlawing merchants' use of trading stamps as premiums; the claim was that this was a useless, expensive form of competition. A few municipalities discriminated against department stores, particularly in rural areas or provinces where the big stores could be portrayed as outsiders, but with little effect. Small businessmen in weak competitive positions continued to portray department stores as octopuses, leeches, and other life-draining monsters, and lobbied for political succour. The press's sympathy on the issue, they claimed, was paid for in department stores' heavy advertising budgets.

Business jostling for competitive advantage by capturing government was a microcosm of the larger struggle of interest groups to secure government intervention. Many economic actors claimed they were at a competitive disadvantage in their dealings with big business – that they were the victims of monopolies, rings, trusts, and other agglomerations of power – and needed government help to ensure fair play. Unions said this from the beginning as they sought government support in their struggles to organize. They needed legitimization in the most basic way, for unions could not legally exist in Canada until old British statutes banning workers' combines in restraint of trade were repealed. After that happened in the early 1870s, unions stood on guard against any sign that post-1889 competition policy might require unhampered competition in the labour market. Unions lobbied for legislative controls on child labour and the hours females worked, and by the early 1900s were exploring the idea of the minimum wage as a legislated limit to price-cutting in the labour market. Organized labour fought for rights to organize and to picket, and demanded laws against employers' strike-breaking tactics. Utopia would come when governments gave unions the legal muscle they wanted to enable them to monopolize labour markets.

Farmers felt particularly victimized by monopolies. Look at the CPR in western Canada, with a blatant monopoly clause written right into its charter. Look at its high freight rates. Look at the way it supported gouging grain elevator monopolists. Farmers got government help to break that grain buyers' combine in the 1890s, but then a new one got going in the form of the Winnipeg Grain Exchange. It was an ostensibly open market for grain trading where, of course, the traders all charged the same commission and in farmers' eyes seemed to be buying collusively. Why else would dealers all offer the same low prices in the autumn of the year when everyone wanted to sell grain, and high prices in the spring when no one had anything to sell?

Railways and their rates offended almost all farmers everywhere, for rural customers never seemed to get anything like the service or discounts available to big-city shippers. But the even greater offence against honest agriculture was the crime wrought by Canada's National Policy. The high protective tariff raised the price of almost everything a farmer and his family had to buy, from harvesters and hay-rakes to pots and pans and all kinds of pumps. The Masseys may have been good churchmen and philanthropists and made good farm implements, but it seemed clear enough that their mansions and their private railway cars were paid for out of the higher prices the tariff enabled them to charge north of the forty-ninth parallel. The cost of farming in Minnesota and every other American state was a lot lower than in Canada, and yet most Canadian farmers had to sell on the same unprotected world markets as the Americans and everyone else.

Natural conditions made farming in Canada difficult enough without the artifical barrier of the tariff. Why not dismantle it, farmers argued? Trade freely with all comers, and make Canadian manufacturers sink or swim like any other businessman. Let them live or die on the work they did and the value they offered, not on favours tossed their way by government. It was also a myth, agrarians thought, that competition inside Canada drove prices down. They correctly saw the tariff as the mother of trusts, the wall behind which manufacturers formed their rings and combines. The one competition policy Canada needed, most farmers believed, was free trade with the rest of the world.

Farmers were not the only shippers on railways. Anyone who dealt with the big railway companies was apt to wonder about the equity of the railways' hopelessly complicated rate schedules, which seemed to boil down to charging all the traffic would bear. Rates varied widely depending on competition, sometimes leading to crippling discrimination against the locationally disadvantaged. What could be done about it in situations where more railway competition was not feasible? How could a shipper break his vassalage to transportation monopolies that seemed intent on milking his business?

How could customers control any of the essential services they relied on private companies to perform? In Canada's cities, gas, power, light, telephone service, and local transportation were in the hands of franchised monopolies. Suppose the service was inadequate? No competition. Suppose a franchised company, secure for years in its monopoly, paid no attention to complaints and went on a merry high price, high-profit way? Middle-class city folk were at the mercy of the telephone or the power company just as prairie farmers were tied to the bindertwine ring or grain elevator monopoly. Where was competition in the new world of big business? It seemed that the course of modern economic development was toward more and more concentration and monopoly. The big would get bigger, the small would get smaller, and extremes of wealth and poverty would characterize modern life.

These extremes seemed glaringly evident at the dawn of the twentieth century. Those millionaires and their castles and servants and sumptuous entertainments and the raw power of their corporations were highly visible on both sides of the border. Everything was highly visible in the first era of cheap newspapers and mass circulation magazines. Journalists were fascinated by both winners and losers in the economic struggle. Readers whose attention was drawn to life at the extremes of the system – by young William Lyon Mackenzie King's newspaper articles on sweatshops in Toronto's garment district, perhaps, or any one of dozens of other muckraking exposés – were bound to wonder where justice lay. North America's Judaeo-Christian value system, featuring Jesus' attitudes toward money-changers and parables about rich men, camels, and eyes of needles, did not seem to sanction a system of glaring inequities based on sheer money-making ability. Nor did most notions of democracy: Americans and Canadians had not left the old world's aristocratic order behind them only to be governed by a new world regime of capitalist plutocrats.

Who were these money-makers, anyway, and how could any man make a million dollars? Ordinary people could not easily understand the mechanisms and motives of a complex economic order. If competition created small profits, surely big profits only came from monopoly. Or they came from theft, or some kind of gouging, some appropriation of a surplus that other people had created. Wasn't it the common man who made wealth by the sweat of his brow and the strength of his arm? Labour created value. Conniving capitalists used their monopolistic corporations to skim away fat profits, taking the money right out of the pockets of the honest workers and farmers. Was this justice?

These everyday thoughts about wealth and poverty and profits seemed to question the system that farmers, unionists, and urban consumers were beginning to attack for more self-interested reasons. Criticisms of great wealth were increasingly articulated by churchmen, journalists, men of letters, and other intellectuals, a group naturally predisposed to elevate artistic and moral interests over the materialism of accumulators. Many of them believed that Canada needed to be saved from the ravages of unbridled capitalism. The country seemed already too far along the road the Americans appeared to be taking, with their Rockefellers and Carnegies and big trusts and frequent industrial violence. The poet Archibald Lampman nicely captured this sentimental idealism in his sonnet, "To a Millionaire." The millionaire is "A creature of that old distorted dream / That makes the sound of life an evil cry." The poet, on the other hand, has a different consciousness:

> . . . I
> Think only of the unnumbered broken hearts,
> The hunger and the mortal strife for bread,
> Old age and youth alike mistaught, misfed,
> By want and rags and homelessness made vile,
> The griefs and hates, and all the meaner parts
> That balance thy one grim misgotten pile.

Reformers who saw themselves as tribunes of the people against big business monopolists were known as "populists," and were as common as crab apples in the United States and Canada by the end of the nineteenth century. Populism emerged in farmers' anti-railroad agitations in the American mid-west in the 1870s, expressed itself often in people's or populist political parties, and donned distinctive Canadian garb as resistance to the National Policy tariff, the CPR, and the big shots on the Winnipeg Grain Exchange. By the 1890s a new "civic populism" of disgruntled urban utility users sparked big city crusades against electricity rings and power trusts and street railway monopolies. The populists' common enemy, staring out of innumerable, interchangeable political cartoons in the *Grain Growers' Guide, Farmer's Advocate*, Toronto *World*, and *Grip*, was the bloated monopolist, a cigar-smoking stuffed shirt in top hat and formal garb, grinding poor people, workers, farmers, and consumers under his iron heel. Populist reformers set out to challenge rule by plutocracy, rule by robber barons.

The three ways to defeat monopoly were to create new competition, institute government regulation, or operate businesses under public ownership. Most populists advocated all three strategies simultaneously and in all possible combinations. In the railway struggle, for example, westerners had broken the CPR's monopoly and continued to favour the chartering, and subsidizing, of as many competitors as possible. At the same time, years of shipper complaints against railways' often collusive rate structures caused the Laurier government to begin formal regulation of the railway system by establishing a Board of Railway Commissioners (ancestor of the Canadian Transport Commission) in 1899. A few years later, the same goverment embarked on a major experiment in public ownership through its decision to construct and own (though not to operate) the eastern division of the National Transcontinental. To populists the CPR's leaders would always be Canada's archetypal robber barons, to be fought at all times and with all weapons. Not surprisingly, the CPR's directors were among the first big Canadian businessmen to develop a siege mentality.

The urban utility wars waxed and waned in every sizeable city. With almost everyone agreeing that most municipal services were "natural monopolies," reformers called for public ownership as the best answer to bad service, high rates, and corporate arrogance. In a few localities, astute corporate management provided excellent service, low rates, and good public relations, and staved off serious populist outbreaks for many years. The British Columbia Electric Railway was a master of smooth public relations. Herbert Holt's Montreal Light Heat and Power, on the other hand, opted for toughness. It freely used its lawyers, the courts, and all the political influence it could muster, to fend off critics.

In Toronto, William Mackenzie tried to use the same tactics in the Toronto Railway Company's relations with city council and the public, and succeeded in the sense that no one could overthrow the company's thirty-year franchise. The cost of short-term success was steadily increasing resentment at Mackenzie and his circle of utility magnates, who seemed to thumb their noses at the people as they went on piling up money, power, and influence. Some day they would be brought to heel, and it might not take until 1921 either, for the gang was into utilities more vulnerable than the street railway company. In the early 1900s, Toronto was both the capital of the Canadian utility entrepreneurialism and a hotbed of civic populism. By contrast, a city like Port Arthur, Ontario, had few utility struggles because it adopted a policy of public ownership from the beginning.

Most of the targets of populist agitation believed they were unjustly maligned. Service, they maintained, was never as bad as critics charged, profits never as high. Competition was always more intense than most outsiders understood. There might be no competing streetcars in a city, for example, but other forms of transportation, first the bicycle and then the automobile, were a constant menace. Critics often seemed to have a blind prejudice against private companies, profits, and capitalist success. Sometimes these prejudices masked simple self-interest, such as consumers' determination to drive the costs of urban services as low as possible, whatever the consequences to the providers.

Many leading businessmen at the dawn of Canada's century thought of themselves as reformers. They were "progressive" men, interested in many movements for community betterment. They supported a host of private organizations delivering education, health care, and help to the downtrodden. Many businessmen were deeply interested in the problem of good government, became involved in politics at municipal and provincial levels, and earnestly supported movements to limit corruption, patronage, and political inefficiency. Some businessmen were themselves corrupting influences, of course, as they tried to manipulate the political system in their interest; but it was more common for even strongly self-interested businessmen to be contemptuous of the ignorance and venality of the old-fashioned professional politician. As Van Horne of the CPR put it, commenting on the vulnerability of legislatures to corporate buccaneers, "people who put pigs in office ought not to complain if they eat dirt and are bought and sold."

The success of movements to make governments more businesslike and efficient was partly responsible for the growing faith in public ownership as an anti-monopoly strategy. Governments that could run a pretty good post office or fire department, as they did in those days, should also be able to run a trolley line, perhaps even a railway. The trick was to choose good, businesslike politicians and administrators to do the job. Many private businessmen saw no political or ideological threat to their own well-being in public ownership. No one needed worry seriously about the threat of socialism in Edwardian Canada. So businessmen could be enthusiastic supporters of public ownership as a way of delivering cheap services. Why pay tribute to private companies if you can set up a taxpayer-supported public corporation to do the job?

Businessmen's support for public ownership was the determining factor in Canada's greatest fight between public and private interests. The campaign for "people's power" in Ontario in the first decade of the twentieth century led to the creation of the world's first large state-owned integrated electricity company, known today as Ontario Hydro. The most important "people" who wanted the Ontario government to enter the power business were several hundred manufacturers in the cities and towns of southwestern Ontario. These entrepreneurs wanted the cheapest possible "white coal" to drive their factories. They saw no reason why Ontario's municipalities, whose councils many of them dominated, should not form a cooperative to bring hydro-electricity from Niagara Falls at cost. When the provincial government instead gave the most important Niagara concession to the Mackenzie-Nicholls-Pellatt circle and their Electrical Development Company, it seemed that all of Ontario might have to pay for power on these millionaire capitalists' terms. The self-interest of the manufacturers blended with populist anti-monopoly sentiment to create intense agitation for a Niagara alternative. "The waterpowers of Niagara should be as free as air," proclaimed Ontario's

Conservative leader, James P. Whitney, in fine populist demagoguery, marvellously attractive to anyone who might be in the market to buy electricity.

The public power supporters knew they needed expert leadership, "some public man," *Saturday Night* wrote, "who will make himself an expert on the question and give to the public the advantage of knowledge ordinarily possessed by, and used on behalf of, those who desire to monopolize." The populists' first choice to lead them was that visionary industrialist, then at the zenith of his Canadian career, F.H. Clergue. When Clergue indicated his lack of interest in Niagara, another experienced businessman emerged to don the mantle. Adam Beck, a manufacturer of veneers and thin lumber and cigar boxes, had gone into public life as both mayor of London and a Conservative MLA. Now he became one of Canada's first public entrepreneurs as he marshalled the public power forces in a mighty struggle against the monopolists.

It was a complex, bitter fight, involving several years' struggle over prices at which Beck's Hydro-Electric Power Commission might buy either the services or the assets of the Electrical Development Company and the Toronto Electric Light Company. Many private utility companies were finding it convenient to cut a deal with their critics by selling out or agreeing to work for a fixed rate of return on their capital. The imperious Mackenzie group tended to be as uncompromising as their Beck-led opponents were unbending. The HEPC gradually began to compete with the private companies. It bought electricity at Niagara from an American-owned firm that had a previous concession, built its own transmission lines to reach municipally owned distributors, and spawned a new municipal cooperative in the critical market, Toronto, that had been the preserve of the Toronto Electric Light Company. The private power supporters cried foul, and much more, at the way their huge capital investments were being imperilled. The government of Ontario was using taxpayers' money and the full force of the law, at Beck's call, to undermine private companies.

The *Financial Post* and a few other concerned newspapers argued for fair play for the foreign investors who had bought the bonds of the Electrical Development Company and the other utility companies. Certainly the world's investors would shun a province whose treatment of foreign money was more typical of an "outlaw state" than even a South American republic. Nothing like this happened to the Canadians in Brazil. Where was British – or Brazilian-style – justice and fair play in Canada?

No one listened. The "Electricity Ring" of millionaire plutocrats had few friends. Angry British investors were not influential enough to damage Ontario's borrowing ability. Public power marched on. Its most important troops were men in the street with attitudes like these, expressed in a 1906 letter to Premier Whitney:

On every hand and upon every side the people are being bled by all these corporations. Millionaires are being made wonderfully fast in Canada lately . . . while merchants and other honest people have to plod along for a whole lifetime for little more than bread and butter. Mr. Mackenzie a few years ago and his brother were in the bush getting out ties . . . to build railways and see what the public purse has done for Mr. Mackenzie. The public purse should not be milked dry by a few sharpies while the masses of the people have to struggle for a bare existence. The Pellat's, the Coxe's, the Jaffrays and the Frederic Nicholls and the others – have got their greedy hands into the Public Purse and want now to boss the country – The Ross Government gave away everything to the ring of grabbers.

In 1910 Ontario's Hydro-Electric Power Commission had its first "switching on" celebration when power generated at Niagara gave light to the people of Berlin (renamed Kitchener during the Great War). The speeches included glowing praise for Hydro's own "human dynamo," Adam Beck. In the meantime, William Mackenzie consolidated the Electrical Development Company and the Toronto Electric Light Company into the Toronto Power Company, a subsidiary of his Toronto Railway Company, and tried to soldier on.

The Cox-Mackenzie financial circle was assailed from another quarter about the same time. In 1906 a federal Royal Commission on Life Insurance made a detailed investigation of the ownership, management, and investment practices of the leading life companies. The affair grew out of New York State's Armstrong investigation of American life insurance, which revealed a host of dubious practices jeopardizing policy-holders' security. Ottawa appointed the MacTavish Commission to see if Canadian policy-holders were being better served. By and large they were not, for most of the same abuses had infected the Canadian firms.

Many of the problems centred on management's fast and loose investment policies. Although Montreal interests were far from simon pure, the greatest sinners appeared to be the Toronto group of financiers centring on George Cox. Their funnelling of insurance company funds through interlocking company networks to support utility promotions was laid out in exhaustive, embarrassing detail, complete with occasional illegalities, huge doses of nepotism, and ostensible conflicts of interest at every turn. The frenzied financial methods of the monopolists were exposed in all their apparent seaminess, more grist for the populists.

Few of the excesses had imperilled life insurance policy-holders' funds because most of the insider investing *was* profitable for all parties. New federal legislation in 1910 tightened investment and reporting requirements in the industry. Some of the insiders who saw the MacTavish Commission as little more than an anti-capitalist (or at least an anti-Cox) witch hunt, could not understand criticisms of situations which had normally been handled carefully, honourably, and profitably to all concerned. The idea that interlocking investment networks or families of financial institutions should be broken up or regulated seemed hugely impractical. In a small investment world how could you operate any other way?

Cox and the other capitalists failed to understand the growing popular suspicion that no matter how loudly these men proclaimed their personal integrity, they simply could not be trusted. Their tight rings of companies and waves of self-dealing, whatever the outcome, were being condemned as irresponsible techniques of personal manipulation. Normal "family" dealing was now seen by outsiders as incest. State regulation was invoked as a substitute for trust in the judgment and integrity of business leaders – a trust which no longer existed.

The assaults on the Toronto circle's methods, prestige, and power were parallelled by other struggles with real or imagined monopolists. To prairie farmers the financial men who bought and sold their grain in Winnipeg were easily as iniquitous as any eastern monopolist. They determined to break the dealers' ring and take over control of the grain trade. Only the first rounds of a long, bitter fight were completed before the Great War. When the cooperative Grain Growers Grain Company was expelled from the Winnipeg Grain and Produce Exchange (because its patronage dividends represented rate-cutting), it went to court and to the legislature seeking redress. The exchange responded by surrendering its corporate charter and reopening as a private association, apparently beyond the farmers' reach. Farm leaders immediately urged the Manitoba legislature to bring the monopolists back under public control, and demanded that the state go into the grain elevator business to foster more competition in that area. For wheat farmers, grain elevators were as vital a utility as street railways or electricity were to city folk.

A crusade for public ownership of the telephone systems became Manitoba's and Alberta's equivalent of Ontario's hydro struggle. Politicians in both provinces found their farm constitutents eagerly responsive to denunciations of the Bell Telephone Company of Canada as a parasitic monopoly, combined with promises of cheap, universal telephone service to end the loneliness of farm life. Here was something important the politicians could do for the people. In 1907 the governments of both provinces entered the telephone business, working with their municipalities and buying out Bell's systems. A few years earlier the government of Canada had considered national public ownership of telephone lines. Laurier's postmaster general, Sir William Mulock, had wanted to operate the telephone system as a division of the post office. After extensive hearings, the government was content to bring the Bell monopoly under the regulatory authority of the Board of Railway Commissioners.

———————◆———————

Some of the early crusades against monopoly were reasonably selective and sensible. The CPR, arrogant municipal monopolies, and other abusers of corporate privilege were unsurprising targets. Their critics included thoughtful, public-spirited businessmen as well as self-interested customers and ideological populists. J.W. Flavelle, the millionaire packer, thought of himself in the early years of the century as a progressive-conservative businessman and favoured an active, interventionist development role for the state. He would have brought the CPR to heel by having the federal government buy a controlling interest in the line on the open market. Failing that, he supported a second, publicly owned transcontinental, and his views had an important influence on Conservative leader Robert Borden's support for public ownership of major railways. Flavelle also supported public ownership of municipal utilities and provincial distribution of electricity, partly because, as an insider, he knew Mackenzie and company too well to believe that "the predatory actions of unscrupulous men" could be controlled any other way.

By 1906–7 Flavelle and other business leaders realized that the anti-monopoly agitation was turning into a general assault on Canadian big business. In his own meat-packing industry, for example, Flavelle had to defend the William Davies Company against claims in the farm press that it was the leader of a packers' combine holding down the price of hogs. Then city papers began complaining about the high price of meat, probably caused by those same devil packers. The "food trust" had become a target of both rural and urban populist concern.* The cost of living in Canada was beginning to rise by about 1909. There were major mergers in one industry after another. To the populists it seemed that the whole Canadian economy was headed in the direction of monopolies and high prices. The former probably caused the latter. What could be done?

The useless anti-combines law of 1889 accidentally grew some teeth when housecleaning amendments in 1900 removed a key qualifying word, "unlawfully." Several successful prosecutions of price-fixing trade associations suggested that the law could force business to be more competitive. In 1910 the Laurier government passed a Combines Investigation Act creating machinery to look into situations where oppressive combines were alleged to exist.

Many critics of business had been saying all along that Canadian manufacturing was a huge, state-created combine thanks to the tariff. Why not strike at the heart of the monster by going after the National Policy itself? The Laurier Liberals had made their peace with high tariffs as part of the price of gaining power in 1896. At that time it seemed more important to court the manufacturing interests than the declining agrarian free traders in Ontario and Quebec. Fifteen

---

* Thanks to anti-corporate muckraking in the United States, the Canadian packers were already having their products constantly inspected by government agents. The 1906 publication of Upton Sinclair's stomach-turning exposé of lack of sanitation in Chicago's packinghouses, *The Jungle*, caused Canadians to take the precautionary step of introducing federal meat inspection. In the prevailing climate of distrust of private business, the stamp of government approval was welcomed by both the industry and consumers. It was a form of regulation in everyone's interests.

years later the settlement of the prairies had revived farmer power and influence with a vengeance. To protect its western and rural base the Laurier government felt it had to appease free trade sentiment and managed to negotiate an agreement with the United States for reciprocal tariff reductions. The 1911 reciprocity agreement seemed a first-class political coup: it would substantially reduce duties without removing the protection needed by most of the key manufacturing industries. The government was happy to fight an election on the issue.

Businessmen with important investments in the industries that would be affected by reciprocity, and in those that would not, were alarmed by the agreement. They interpreted reciprocity as the beginning of the end of the protection that the Canadian economy required to survive. Weakened industries, they thought, would mean a weakened nation. Under free trade, which might be the next step, the branch plants might go home, jobs would certainly be lost, and east-west trade would diminish. Canada itself would be diminished, perhaps to the point of swallowing its identity and being annexed by the United States. Fiercely protectionist and nationalistic, the Canadian Manufacturers' Association led the fight against reciprocity in the 1911 election. The Liberal party split, as eighteen of its most prominent businessmen, largely Toronto-based, defected to the Conservatives.

Several of the Toronto Eighteen, including E.R. Wood, Zebulon Lash, B.E. Walker, and W.T. White (general manager of National Trust), were central figures in the Cox-Mackenzie circle. The big businessmen wrapped themselves in flags as they argued that national survival depended on the government using its powers to prohibit free competition in the Canadian market. When the Liberals and reciprocity went down to defeat in 1911, Canada's populists interpreted the results as another victory for the forces of big business and monopoly. "The good old patriotic slogan of the CMA, 'Canada for the Canadians', means Canada for 2,500 Canadians," the *Grain Growers' Guide* scoffed. Westerners were increasingly seeing the monopolists as eastern, Toronto- and Montreal-based. What could be done to strike at the source of their power?

***

Depression and war did the job. Canada's great boom expired in the winter of 1912–13. The clearest signal of trouble came from Britain, where surfeited investors decided that Canadian projects had been overdone and a time of settling-down and sorting-out was needed. The business retrenchment began in the spring of 1913, as orders and trade slowed in one industry after another. Within a few months Canadians had to worry about unemployment for the first time in fifteen years and businessmen worried about their solvency. War took almost everyone by surprise. On August 4, 1914, the British Empire declared war on the German Empire. It lasted until November 11, 1918, claimed sixty-two thousand Canadian lives, maimed and crippled many more, and smashed the innocent optimism of the peaceful northern kingdom.

In some ways the war was good for some kinds of business. The urban building boom was over, of course. And so was railway-building after 1915. But armies needed supplies of clothing, horses, food, guns, shells, shells, and more shells. War orders mounted with the slaughter, until by 1916 Canadian factories worked round-the-clock. Most of them filled shell contracts let by the British government through a Canadian agency, the Imperial Munitions Board, chaired by Flavelle of Toronto. The IMB placed all the British orders, helped manufacturers with technological and labour problems, took delivery of the shells, and lobbied both the British and the American governments for more orders. By 1918 the Imperial Munitions Board had overseen Canada's greatest industrial effort – the production of more than $1,250 million worth of shells, fuses, ships, even primitive aeroplanes. War work drove Canadian manufacturing to higher levels of efficiency and technological sophistication than anyone believed possible in 1914. The profits the manufacturers earned on the work more than made up for prewar losses. For them, and for their workers, there was little sacrifice in the war economy.

Financial intermediaries mobilized money for war needs. The banks worked closely with Ottawa, supplying short-term loans and organizing Dominion borrowing on the New York market. As New York shut down, the bankers, brokers, and bond dealers, as well as the government, were all surprised to find that the Canadian people themselves would subscribe to one "Victory Loan" after another. It was the first time the Dominion government floated loans domestically. Fees and commissions on these financings meant a good war for most money-movers. Lesser industries such as advertising did a booming agency business in the bond drives, recruiting, and fund-raising and other campaigns. Food producers fattened on war-swollen demand and high prices, particularly in western Canada, where acreage under crop almost doubled. Farmers' cash on hand meant cash in storekeepers' tills. The fully-employed civilians on the peaceful home front did not have to make significant material sacrifices in the Great War. Families of all classes and incomes sacrificed husbands and sons and brothers on the battlefields of France.

The entrepreneurs who had been building the new railroads did not have a good war. The pace of railway construction kept accelerating in the later Laurier years and the momentum of the final contracts carried work through the prewar depression. By 1915 both the National Transcontinental–Grand Trunk Pacific and the Canadian Northern were finished, more or less. (William Mackenzie drove a Canadian Northern last spike in January, but the line did not meet government standards. A second last spike ceremony was cancelled when a tunnel collapse in the mountains forced the Canadian Northern to seek running rights on the CPR.) They were also insolvent, hopelessly unable to earn their operating costs, let alone service their mountains of debt.

The new transcontinentals were the largest peacetime enterprises in Canada next to the CPR. Each system had swallowed between $250 and $400 million in private and public money, the equivalent of $4-6 billion in later values. Not since the Grand Trunk troubles of the 1850s had Canadians faced business failures of this magnitude. The government was already strained to the limit trying to organize and finance the increasingly ghastly war effort. It found the ongoing railway crisis, as the prime minister put it, a constant "nightmare."

Mackenzie and Mann's Canadian Northern was not a completely unsound railway. It had been reasonably well-conceived, well-located, and efficiently operated to give western farmers an alternative to the CPR. The system was not milked by Mackenzie and Mann, as many believed, for promoters' or contractors' profits. It was built cheaply and staffed by good railwaymen. But the decision to go transcontinental had probably been a fatal error. It burdened the Canadian Northern with hundreds of miles of unproductive mountain and northern Ontario line, and millions in debt, that could only be carried if traffic and rates grew faster than the most optimistic projections.

Traffic did soar during the war, and the business would have been a godsend to the Canadian Northern (which would certainly have collapsed if peace and depression had continued), but rates became an insurmountable problem. All railway rates were controlled, mainly by the Board of Railway Commissioners, with some Canadian Northern rates set by special agreement with the western provinces. Consumers of railway services, particularly western farmers, applied fierce political pressure against rate increases of any kind, even those necessary to keep up with inflation. Mackenzie and Mann had no credibility in the political arena, having long ago been written off as grasping millionaire capitalists who were probably looting their companies. Why should Canada pay more tribute to these people who wanted to take everyone for a ride?

The Mackenzie group's international utility empire was also crumbling. Adam Beck and the public power movement had struck at its underbelly in Ontario. The Brazilian situation remained strong, but the Mexican ventures were all imperilled after 1910 by successive revolutionary governments who had little love for even Canadian gringos. British and continental capital markets were already turning away from F.S. Pearson's development mania when the war shut them down completely. Pearson himself, the man at the vital centre of the whole coil of Canada's Latin utilities, had the misfortune to be aboard the *Lusitania* in 1915. He did not survive.

Governments and their regulatory boards in Canada would not give the Canadian Northern the rate increases that might have enabled it to service its debts. Mackenzie and Mann's gamble that governments which guaranteed their bonds would never let them go down proved only partly true. There was too much populist pressure on governments, particularly on the prairies, for politicians to release the Canadian Northern from its rate agreements. It would be disastrously expensive for provincial governments to have to honour their bond guarantees, but might be less politically damaging than being held responsible for rate increases. And probably those rich guys were just bluffing anyway. How could they possibly fail? And if they did, probably some other rich capitalists would step in and take over.

The federal government could not be so sanguine. A default by a railway the size of the Canadian Northern might weaken foreign confidence in all Canadian securities, poisoning the country's credit standing for years to come. The prairie provinces would not be able to honour their guarantees of Canadian Northern securities and would have to be bailed out by Ottawa. A bank was threatened, too. The Canadian Bank of Commerce had advanced so many millions to the Canadian Northern and Mackenzie and Mann's other partnerships and ventures that its capacity to help the war effort, possibly even its stability, would be jeopardized by a CN failure. These enterprising business partnerships, Mackenzie and Mann and their banking friends, so full of faith in Canada, so willing to cooperate with politicians and governments, had created a mess from which governments dared not withdraw. "It is too bad that individuals go so far that they wrap themselves around national interests to an extent that means widespread damage or national help," a frustrated federal minister commented in his diary.

The government of Canada had created an even worse mess in its partnership with the Grand Trunk to build the National Transcontinental. The Eastern Division, a thousand miles of track through traffic-free wilderness, was probably the poorest planned, most wasteful major construction ever undertaken by the federal government, Mirabel Airport not excepted. Surveys had been almost non-existent; guesstimates of construction and operating costs and of revenues were absurd; waste and corruption were endemic; the 1907 collapse of the Quebec Bridge over the St. Lawrence was one of the worst industrial disasters in the country's history. Nine years later the Quebec Bridge collapsed again.

The Grand Trunk Railway was committed to operating the National Transcontinental through its subsidiary the Grand Trunk Pacific. The Grand Trunk Pacific could barely make its operating costs on the Western Division, which it built and owned, the worst-located of the prairie and mountain main lines. Even without the obligation to operate and pay rent on the Eastern Division, the Grand Trunk Pacific was a doomed company. Its parent, the otherwise solvent and somewhat venerable Grand Trunk, would be dragged down with it. The man most responsible for getting the Grand Trunk into this situation, C.M. Hays, who had urged management to go into the deal "trusting somewhat the future," made a worse mistake in 1912. He decided to cross the ocean on the maiden voyage of the *Titanic*. Hays went down with the ship after putting his wife in a lifeboat.

The Borden government began giving emergency grants and loans to the Canadian Northern in 1913. The Minister of Finance, W.T. White, knew Mackenzie and Mann intimately, for as manager of National Trust he had been on the inside of the financial circle. His knowledge only made White a more formidable critic of the Canadian Northern; in return for support the government insisted on acquiring equity in the road. The emergency aid the Grand Trunk Pacific required in 1914 was secured by a mortgage on its properties. Within two years both systems were being given emergency operating grants while a royal commission pondered their future.

No one in the railway world or the government believed that public ownership through nationalization of the Grand Trunk Pacific and the Canadian Northern was an ideal solution to Canada's railway problem. It seemed the only solution. The one alternative, a private monopoly run by the CPR, was politically out of the question. As the government embarked on a tortuous course toward nationalization and the launching of the Canadian National Railways, it showed little sympathy toward either Mackenzie and Mann or the thousands of British shareholders in the Grand Trunk. They would all pay the price of their reckless optimism. The Prime Minister described the reaction of Canada's most visionary railway promoter to the news that his dream had ended:

> Sir William Mackenzie... was possessed of brilliant initiative, immense resourcefulness and unflinching courage.... On July 14th 1917 I had an interview with Sir William and I definitely informed him that the Government could not grant any further aid and must take over the Canadian Northern in its entirety. Sir William was a man of iron nerve and this was one of the only two occasions on which I saw his self-control desert him. Knowing my decision was final he was silent for a moment and then completely broke down, with audible sobs that were most distressing.

Thousands of ordinary Canadians were paying a far higher price for the future in the summer of 1917 than Mackenzie would ever suffer in losing his railway. In war a community committed itself to more important causes than economic progress, profits, or protection of property. When men were bleeding and dying for their country, the idea that wealth had any special standing or rights seemed ludicrous. It became part of the obligations of wealth to pay a much greater share of the cost of Canada's national profits than ever before.

In 1916 a business profits war tax, retroactive to the beginning of the war, began the levying of direct federal taxes on companies. It was meant to apply only to "excess" profits, those above certain generous levels. One year later the income war tax was a direct federal levy on both personal and corporate incomes. Its rates were steeply progressive, with a married citizen's tax rising from $80 on an income of $5,000 to $43,760 on $200,000. The top rate of the business profits war tax was hiked to 75 per cent on profits of more than 25 per cent of capital. The thresholds were very high and the new revenues were insignificant. There was no significant resistance from business or anyone else to these politically necessary taxes. Flavelle as chairman of the Imperial Munitions Board gave Canadian businessmen blunt marching orders in 1916 when he returned from England and a tour of the front to find manufacturers complaining about low profit margins on shell contracts.

"Profits!" he told a meeting of IMB contractors, "I have come straight from the seat of a nation where they are sweating blood to win this war, and I stand before you stripped of many ideas. Profits! Send profits to the hell where they belong."

———————

Outstanding achievement in British countries was recognized by the granting of a title from the monarch. Leading men in business won at least their share of knighthoods, baronetcies, and lordships. Some, such as Strathcona and Mount Stephen and Van Horne of the CPR, were honoured for their contributions to the Dominion's bone and sinew; others, such as Henry Pellatt, for their support for the militia; others, such as William C. Macdonald, for their philanthropies or public service. A few, including James Dunn and Max Aitken in England, bought their first titles with political contributions. Titled Canadian entrepreneurs sometimes went home to the old country and the House of Lords, sometimes stayed in Canada as the Dominion's certified aristocrats.

In June 1917 Joseph Flavelle of Toronto, a millionaire entrepreneur whose public service had been outstanding, received a baronetcy for his work as head of the Imperial Munitions Board. It was an hereditary title. Another self-made man joined the aristocracy.

Six weeks later Flavelle became the most reviled man in Canada. It was charged in the press that the William Davies Company made a 5-cent profit on every pound of bacon it sold. That figure was false. But the company had done so much war business, so well, filling orders from the British government, that on margins of 0.5 to 1.0 cents a pound it had amassed pretax profits that were large in relation to its recorded capital: 80 per cent in 1916, 57 per cent in 1917. Flavelle received hundreds of thousands in dividends from his company's war business. Canadian soldiers in France received $1.10 a day.

Flavelle was too proud to publicize his donations to charities, which amounted to more than his wartime income. He endured lasting public contempt as the arch-profiteer of the Great War, the robber baronet, the patriotic hog. The affair seemed to have proven everything the populists had always believed about the pork trust in particular, big business in general. It came to be said, completely falsely, that the William Davies Company had shipped spoiled meat.

The excellence of the company's business methods and Flavelle's public service were ignored in the inflationary, egalitarian, and anti-business climate of 1917. The meat-packing industry was placed under tight government control and the excess profits tax levelled the Davies company's profits. Parliament decided that no Canadian should ever again receive an hereditary title. After the war it resolved that Canadians should not get titles at all. There was only one brief reprieve in 1935. Flavelle became the last Canadian domiciled in the Dominion to receive an hereditary title. In the new Canada after the war the rich would pay taxes and no one would be allowed to become an aristocrat.

LEFT: **J.W. Flavelle as chairman of the Imperial Munitions Board, by F.H. Varley** *(Canadian Courier)* BELOW: **Flavelle attacked for alleged profiteering** *(Saturday Night)*

Who Did You Do In the Great War?

TOP: **Salesmen, Kelly Douglas Co. Ltd., Vancouver, 1929** *(Vancouver Public Library, #10655)* ABOVE: **Collision, Vancouver Island** *(Vancouver Public Library, #2568)*

14

The Stuttering Twenties

*The decade doesn't roar . . . wartime inflation . . . postwar collapse . . . the
Home Bank failure . . . BESCO's failure . . . troubled Maritimes . . . troubled
Prairies . . . troubled railways . . . taxes . . . whispers of death . . . the
Model-T revolution and a tinkering tradition . . . booze . . . Bronfmans . . .
resource booms . . . H.R. MacMillan . . . Canada hits her stride . . . bull
markets and little big boards . . . big business and its methods . . . the office
revolution . . . business machines . . . IBM . . . Moore . . .
ticker tape and castles*

Henry Pellatt's medieval castle in Toronto went unheated in the winter of
1923–24. The roof leaked and mildew stained walls where the panelling had
been stripped away. Children snuck into the overgrown grounds and systematically smashed the glass in Casa Loma's windows. In June 1924 Pellatt
held a spectacular three-day auction of the castle's contents, selling everything from exotic Nubian bronzes to his well-used bathroom scales. He liked
to blame the city of Toronto – annual property taxes on the castle had risen
from $600 in 1913 to about $12,000 – for his inability to keep his home. The
truth was that Pellatt in the 1920s was a distinctly down-at-heels millionaire,
most of whose ventures had cracked up. The Home Bank of Canada, which
financed many of Pellatt's speculations, had also cracked up, suspending
business in the summer of 1923. The remnants of Pellatt's wealth were being
liquidated to help pay his debts to the bank, or sheltered to save him a little
dignity in his old age. Casa Loma was for sale, but in the decade Canadians
know from American history as "the roaring twenties" no one wanted to buy
a gingerbread castle in Canada.

Torontonians who went to see the funny building on weekends drove
there as often as not in their Model-T Ford automobiles. The tough black
horseless carriages were even more popular in Canada than in the United
States, often holding more than 50 per cent of the car market. They were
made mainly in Windsor, Ontario, by the Ford Motor Company of Canada, a
corporation in which Canadians held a majority interest. Henry Pellatt and

his Toronto friends had a chance for a front seat in this car business years earlier. The bicycle company they had promoted in 1899, Canada Cycle and Motor, went directly into automobile sales, sold the first Ford in Canada which was the sixth Ford built, and intended an early entry into automobile manufacturing. CCM' s manager, T.A. Russell, organized production of the Ivanhoe Electric, and began planning a Canadian gasoline vehicle. His lack of interest in the possibility of making Henry Ford's cars left the way clear for a carriage-maker in Walkerville, Gordon M. McGregor, to make the approach to Ford that created a hugely successful Canadian subsidiary.

The Toronto financiers were too wrapped up in their world of electricity, street railways, and transcontinental railways, to pay much attention to the development of the internal combustion automobile. Now in the 1920s the electrical companies had been bought out, street railway franchises had expired, transcontinental railways had gone bankrupt, fortunes dissipated and castles emptied, and the Model-Ts rambled right along. The castle and the cars symbolized the two sides of the 1920s for Canadian business: obsolescence and disaster in some vital traditional industries, solid new growth, with considerable help from the south, in important new industries.

The Americans enjoyed a different decade. Latecomers to the Great War, they returned to "normalcy" much faster than Canada or the countries of Europe. Their almost self-sufficient and enormously productive economy was sheltered from most of the confused currents of world trade. Their populist revolt against big business had played itself out years earlier; in the 1920s a series of Republican administrations offered aid and comfort to the leaders of a success-oriented culture in which business seemed to be creating mass affluence. The twenties "roared" in the United States as the promise of American life seemed to be coming true for everyone in a wide-open, growth-oriented, business-influenced society. The decade also roared, of course, with the engines of the fast cars and speedboats bringing illegal booze into the United States, often from Canada.

The Canadian economy was much more troubled, partly because of greater wartime strains, partly because of the excesses of the prewar boom. Canada did not return to normalcy until at least 1926, and perhaps not then: important parts of the country, notably the Atlantic provinces, would never again experience the growth rates and prospects of the Laurier years. The big business leaders of Canada had also seen the passing of their golden age. Even when growth returned with a rush in the decade's closing years, the Canadian people were not inclined to give business pride of place in national priorities. The dominant Liberal party was not unfriendly to business, but it was not unfriendly to any other interest either. William Lyon Mackenzie King intended to govern Canada with the broadest possible popular support.

THE WAR SET CANADIANS on the worst roller-coaster of price changes they had ever seen. In August 1914 the convertibility of bank notes and Dominion notes into gold was suspended – in other words, Canada left the gold standard – and the federal government paved the way for unlimited expansion of the money supply by agreeing to lend notes to the banks as needed. Wartime taxes did not cover the material cost of the war or hold down domestic purchasing power, partly because everyone thought it was fair to require future generations of Canadians to help pay for this war to end wars. With government pumping credit into the economy, and war demand straining most industries to capacity and beyond, prices rose – only 1 or 2 per cent a year in 1914 and 1915, but 8 per cent in 1916, 23 per cent in 1917, and another 20 per cent in 1918.

There was no sudden price break when the war ended, for devastated Europe needed huge supplies of food, clothing, and other goods. Exports, full employment, and inflation continued: the cost of living rose by another 10 to 12 per cent in 1919, close to 20 per cent again in 1920. The happy side of the postwar boom was the ease with which most returned soldiers were able to find jobs (most firms found places for all former employees who had volunteered, and they were so busy that many of the temporary female workers were kept on as well). The darker effects were reflected in the cost-of-living index, which almost doubled between 1915 and 1920; the wholesale price index more than doubled.

Many businesses adjusted to the inflation without apparent difficulty (until it came to an end later). The regulated, faltering railways and other utilities were an outstanding exception. Usually it was a simple matter of raising prices to cover higher costs on markets that seemed willing to bear any price. Often prices could be raised faster than costs went up; wage increases, for example, tended to lag. But wage-earners began to be severely squeezed by inflation, and their resentment was magnified many times over in the wartime climate of sacrifice and egalitarianism and anger at "profiteers" such as Sir Joseph Flavelle. As labour markets tightened, harried workers began demanding catch-up pay increases and more. Unions came into their own and more as organizers enrolled thousands of Canadian workers whose expectations rose even faster than the cost of living.

With even postal workers organizing and staging national strikes, labour unrest was barely contained in 1917 and 1918. In 1919, a year when union membership increased by 50 per cent, the unrest burst out of control in Winnipeg and several other major cities as federations of unions staged general strikes. Winnipeg's was the most serious, a six-week stoppage of almost all industries in the city. It polarized the community, raised fears of Bolshevik-style revolution in classless democratic Canada, and petered out only after bloody confrontations with police. The situation in urban centres ranging from Vancouver to Toronto was not much better. Tensions created by a combination of inflation and war-bred utopianism threatened to rend the fabric of Canadian industrial relations, indeed Canadian life itself, beyond repair. Most businessmen were shocked and frightened by the new climate. The government of Canada's attitude was an uneven mix of conciliation, experiments with price controls to try to hold the lid on inflation (in 1919 a Board of Commerce was created with broad powers to fix prices and profit margins; it careened around the country having little effect, and disappeared when the courts ruled that its powers were unconstitutional), and outright repression of labour radicalism.

Prices finally broke in what merchants called a "buyers' strike" in the summer of 1920, and began heading straight down. The collapse was the most drastic in Canadian history: in one year the wholesale price index dropped from 288 to 198. The cost of living declined by about 15 per cent that first year, a further 10 per cent the next. Much of the force of labour's unrest had already been spent (the Winnipeg general strike was a catastrophic defeat for the city's unions, crippling them for many years); the rest disappeared in the severe unemployment and depression of the early 1920s. Businessmen and workers alike turned to face the problem of survival in the hard times of the new decade.

One group's militancy seemed only heightened by the downturn. During and immediately after the war the organized farmers of Canada had decided to enter politics in their own right. Their rebellion against the two-party system was the result of decades of festering grievances: against the tariff, against the railroads and the grain dealers and the banks and the other big interests, against city-slickers and their ignorant contempt of rural life, against demographic forces which revealed in the 1921 census that Canada was now an urban country. During the war the government had taken control of the marketing of grain (to stop runaway inflation) and prevented wheat farmers from getting the full benefit of rising prices. In the deflation the free market was restored and prices collapsed: from $2.37 a bushel of wheat in 1919 to less than $1.00 in 1922.

Generally, the farmers were fed up with being dominated by big business, by old-line politicians, and, in western Canada, by the East. In 1919 rural Ontario reared up and gave candidates sponsored by the United Farmers of Ontario control of the provincial government. In 1921 the United Farmers swept both Alberta and Manitoba. In the federal election at the end of that year farmer organizations elected sixty-five Progressives to the Parliament of Canada, a group larger than the Conservatives. King's Liberals formed a minority government, and tailored their policies to win Progressive support. The plight of the Conservatives, reduced to a rump of fifty seats in the House of Commons, fairly reflected the country's suspicion of many of the interests connected with the old business establishment. While the King governments had conservative, business-minded finance ministers, Ottawa was much less enthusiastic about businessmen and their interests than Washington in the age of Coolidge and Hoover.

Deflation was far harder to accommodate than rising prices. Thousands of firms were caught with expensive inventory that had to be liquidated well below cost. Prudent businessman normally built enough reserves during good years to be able to hold on through depression. But many were not prudent – they had bet the good times would go on forever, or at least for a few more months – and in many cases the reserves were not enough. Canada experienced the fewest commercial failures in 1918 and 1919 since records began in 1885, only 873 the one year, 755 the next. In 1921, 2,451 firms went down and in 1922, 3,695, a total not exceeded in any year of the 1930s. Other companies absorbed huge losses. Sugar refineries lost millions on their inventories when the world market crashed. Meat-packers saw their war-bloated export trade to Britain and the continent collapse in 1920–21. In 1920 the William Davies Company absorbed the first loss in its history, about $100,000; in 1921 it lost $1,235,000. These losses did not affect the man who built the firm in the good years, J.W. Flavelle, for he sold out at the peak of the boom in 1919. Izaak Walton Killam of Royal Securities, on the other hand, thought the time was right in 1920 to create the largest forest products firm in the world, the Riordon Company Limited, a massive consolidation of the Riordon, Gilmour, Edwards, and Hughson pine and pulpwood holdings. Riordon was no sooner put together than the market collapsed, its security-holders lost millions, and Killam and the management entered years of struggle for survival.

The Riordon mess was part of the death throes of the old lumbering kingdom of the Ottawa valley, now largely bereft of both white pine and heirs to the old logging families. The 1919 merger of the forty-five-year-old Bank of Ottawa, which had risen on timber wealth, with the Bank of Nova Scotia was another symptom of the decline. Two years later another old family bank, the Merchants, created by Sir Hugh Allan of Montreal, became the first to crumble under the burden of depression losses. The Merchants was still Allan-influenced but had grown into a national institution with four hundred branches and about $190 million in assets. In 1916 management decided to support a couple of troubled clients, who needed about $650,000. When Thornton Davidson and Company and the Exclusive Ladies Wear Limited failed in 1920 they owed the bank more than $5 million. With reserves stripped, assets shrinking dramatically, and management in disarray, the shareholders gave up and in 1921 accepted the Bank of Montreal's terms for a merger.

The Merchants' well-publicized problems were only the tip of a foundering iceberg. Behind the doors of more than half a dozen chartered banks in 1921–22 emergency audits were held, reserves tapped, customers dunned, and letters written to politicians and other banks sounding out the possibilities for emergency help. Meanwhile, with the Bank Act due for decennial revision in 1923, important public hearings were held on the future of the system. Many agrarians were convinced that the contraction of bank credit was a cause of the depression. If only the government took control of banking, they argued, say through a central bank, it could expand credit and get the country moving again. At the least, the critics suggested, the government should become more involved in inspecting the chartered banks to avoid the bad management that had contributed to the Merchants Bank's problems.

Leading bankers reassured Parliament and the public that Canadian banking practice was flexible in meeting the needs of the country and fundamentally sound in protecting the savings of depositors. The Bank Act revision went through Parliament in the spring of 1923 without significantly changing the system. The day after it passed third reading in the House of Commons, the Winnipeg-based Union Bank (which moved there from Quebec City in 1912) announced that most of its reserves were being written off to cover bad debts and "certain unauthorized transactions in foreign exchange." Six weeks later the Toronto-based Standard Bank announced that it, too, was slashing its reserve and reducing dividends. Another of the lesser Toronto-centred banks, the Home, was not suspected to be in trouble, for on June 26 it reported net profits of $232,539 and a surplus after dividends of $72,761; it was in "a splendid financial condition," management said early in August, just after the Standard write-down.

On the afternoon of August 17 staff locked the doors of all seventy-one branches of the Home Bank (forty-seven in Ontario, twenty-one in the West, three in Quebec) and posted signs: "Bank closed – payment suspended." Depositors could not get their money out. Nobody had been willing to buy or merge with the Home Bank.

On August 27 the Minister of Finance announced that the 145-branch Bank of Hamilton was being purchased by the Canadian Bank of Commerce. The government of Quebec was propping up the Banque Nationale to avoid what one of its leading customers called "une catastrophe rentissante et une humiliation pour notre race." On October 3 police arrested the president, vice-president, five directors, the general manager, chief accountant, and chief auditor of the Home Bank.

On Friday October 12 a teller in one of the smaller Toronto branches of the Dominion Bank had difficulty explaining to a recent immigrant that he had overdrawn his account. Customers who heard the teller saying loudly "No money in the bank" decided to get theirs out. By closing time the branch was out of cash. The next day, Saturday, there were runs on every Dominion Bank branch in Toronto. On Monday the blind force of financial panic confronted the organized banks, all standing behind the Dominion. The most difficult single problem that day was getting cash to branches quickly enough. "Women were fainting in the line-ups before the wickets," a reporter wrote, "but I noticed they were not overcome till after they got their money out." The bank held firm, the Ontario government announced it was making special deposits, and by Tuesday afternoon embarrassed customers were lining up to re-deposit their money. The year ended with the announcement that the Banque Nationale was being absorbed by the

Banque d'Hochelaga; the Quebec government guaranteed the institution's solvency.

Who would help those who had trusted their savings to the Home Bank? It had evolved out of a Roman Catholic-sponsored savings bank and still held the funds of many Catholic institutions and blue-collar workers. The liquidator found that the Home Bank was hopelessly insolvent and had been misstating its position for years. Depositors would get twenty-five cents on the dollar, no more. They immediately began petitioning Ottawa for relief, claiming that the government had known of the bank's unsound position for years and had done nothing to protect the public. There was no legal case for aid, but a strong moral claim was accepted on the ground that the wartime Minister of Finance, W.T. White, probably should have acted on information given to him in 1916. White had let the situation drift, partly because he had no desire to add a financial crisis to his other wartime troubles, partly because he thought a millionaire like Sir Henry Pellatt would be able to pay his debts.

The depositors eventually divided $3 million in compensation from the government (those with claims of less than $500 got 35 per cent payment on top of the 25 per cent from the liquidator; depositors of more than $500 were compensated according to need, but never more than 35 per cent. No money was given to directors of the bank, public or private corporate bodies, business firms, labour unions, senators, or members of Parliament). Two Home Bank officials were convicted of fraud; convictions against the directors were quashed on appeal on the ground that they had not known what management was doing. In 1924 the government of Canada reversed its position on bank inspection and established the office of Inspector General of Banks. The Canadian Bankers Association also reversed its position and welcomed federal inspection as likely to increase confidence in the banking system.

The system continued to consolidate as weaker banks gave up the struggle. The Standard and Sterling merged and were then absorbed by the Commerce. The Bank of Montreal took over the Molsons Bank, the last and strongest of the "family" banks. The Royal took over the 327-branch Union Bank. By 1928 Canada had only ten chartered banks, down from thirty in 1910. The big three, Montreal, the Commerce, and the Royal, controlled 70 per cent of banking assets in the country. With the branch system and the savings deposit business fully in place, the banking system stopped growing faster than the economy. If the last years of the 1920s had not been so prosperous, the degree of concentration in Canadian banking might have been of greater concern. Each merger had aroused more criticism, along the lines of a *Manitoba Free Press* comment in 1923: "If the smaller Banks find themselves unable to compete with the larger Banks in their appeal for deposits, owing to a public feeling that the larger Banks are safer, there will be inevitably a succession of mergers which will result in the capital of this country being centred in the control of a group of banking magnates so limited in number that it could meet in conclave and settle the business policies of this country around an ordinary table in a club."

———◆———

The single most troubled Canadian corporation in the 1920s was one of the most ambitious industrial organizations the country had ever seen. During the final stages of the war, ambitious industrialists began planning to exploit the huge postwar demand they foresaw for new shipping. So much tonnage had been sunk by submarines. War orders had pressed Canada's shipyards to capacity, and postwar opportunities would surely enable huge expansion. Prospects were particularly exciting in Atlantic Canada, the nineteenth-century shipbuilding centre, for now it would be possible to re-enter the big league of ocean shipbuilding by creating modern steel vessels. The capacity to make steel for new shipyards existed on Cape Breton Island, if only the mills were taken in hand, modernized, and linked with shipbuilding initiatives. A friendly federal government encouraged development with contracts that caused Dominion Steel to open the country's first ship-plate mill at Sydney in 1920.

Vague visions of becoming shipbuilders for the Empire were the rationale for a grand merger and modernization of the steel and coal properties of Nova Scotia, which was announced at the peak of the boom in 1920. The promoters were an Anglo-Canadian syndicate headed by Roy Wolvin of Montreal, an American-born shipping expert who had worked his way to the top of the Great Lakes business and become associated with J. W. Norcross's circle in Canada Steamship Lines. Wolvin's English friends included members of Beaverbrook's circle, who had romantic dreams of tempering the steel of the young Dominion with expertise from the motherland. The British Empire Steel Company – BESCO – was planned as a colossal $500 million merger of all the principal shipping companies and shipyards in Canada plus the Nova Scotia steel and coal companies.

The deal was too big and ambitious to complete, especially after the boom broke in the summer of 1920. The promoters patched together an impressive second choice: BESCO became the holding company for all of the big Cape Breton steel and coal properties (Nova Scotia Steel and Coal, Dominion Coal, Dominion Iron and Steel, Dominion Steel), a major Halifax shipyard, and several smaller operations, and issued more than $100 million (par value) in securities to finance its purchases. Wolvin boasted that BESCO owned "the greatest known deposits of coal and iron ore, splendidly situated," and set out to make the company a major force in the world's industry.

The world's shipbuilding and steel industries were awash in surplus capacity. War losses had been more than overcome before the struggle ended, and there was far less traffic in peacetime anyway. Ocean-going ships were a dime a dozen; every shipyard and steel mill in the United Kingdom was scrambling for orders, as were the Americans. The vital Canadian railway market for steel rails had collapsed with the complete cessation of railway construction and postwar shrinkage in traffic. American coal producers, who had surplus capacity of their own, were more aggressive than ever in their penetration of the central Canadian market. No new markets could be found. Steel and coal production in Nova Scotia stagnated well below the levels of 1913, let alone the good years of the war. But the optimistic promoters of BESCO had created a debt structure involving heavier obligations to bondholders than any of the previous firms had had to carry.

Wolvin and his management tried to make the coal miners and steelworkers of Cape Breton bear some of the burden in the form of wage cuts. Tough, radical unions fought back. The worst industrial warfare Canada has ever seen plagued Cape Breton from 1921 to 1925. In 1922 approximately one-third of Canada's shrunken armed forces had to be sent to Cape Breton to keep order; the commanding officer of the region asked for air support and the contingency stationing of British battleships with plans to land troops. In 1925 at least one man was killed in rioting after a pitched battle for the New Waterford power plant. Canada's glowing postwar industrial future had turned into class warfare between bankrupt, ruthless capitalists and the ragged, starving, proud miners of Cape Breton.

Even businessmen who appreciated the hopelessness of BESCO's financial position and the dilemmas of an industry whose only hope lay in retrenchment turned against Wolvin's inept management and confrontational approach to labour relations. "These industries can never succeed under the active direction of Mr. Wolvin," the Conservative premier of Nova Scotia wrote. "He is one of the most cordially hated men I know." The central Canadian financial establishment, led by Sir Joseph Flavelle as chairman of the Bank of Commerce, intervened to force settlement of the five-month-old 1925 strike. The banks stopped carrying BESCO, its constituent companies began defaulting on their securities, and by 1928 the $100 million British Empire Steel Company was a dead turkey. The National Trust Company of Toronto managed the one surviving steel mill at Sydney while a Toronto and Montreal financial group, led by J. H. Gundy, tried to salvage Nova Scotia's once-great industries. The 1920s was a ghastly decade for industrial Nova Scotia.

The ills of steel and coal were symptoms of fundamental difficulties for the Maritimes. The region's manufacturing sector went into steep decline early in the decade and never recovered. The foundries and machine shops and car works of the dying railway age were unable to find new business; the old National Policy textile mills and similar redbrick factories had no hope of competing with anyone outside of Canada, and inside Canada they were badly situated on the fringe of the country. Maritime ports had the same locational disadvantages. The region had little mineral wealth or hydro-electric capacity, and, except for Prince Edward Island, the Annapolis valley, and the potato country of New Brunswick, marginal agriculture. So little good pine was left in New Brunswick that lumber began coming in from British Columbia via the Panama Canal. Could a prospering twentieth-century future be built on fish and pulp and paper? In the early 1920s one hundred and fifty thousand Maritimers passed judgment on their provinces' future by leaving for the United States.

Spokesmen for the one million who stayed behind began claiming that the rest of Canada was obliged to protect the standard of living in the Atlantic provinces with special subsidies. Railway freight rates became particularly controversial, as leaders of the "Maritime Rights" movement charged that it was discriminatory to have to pay freight rates that might actually cover the real costs of shipping products to central Canada. They began interpreting Confederation to mean an arrangement under which extra economic costs stemming from their region's geographical location should be borne by their fellow Canadians. Highly subsidized railway rates, larger direct subsidies to provincial governments, and special coal tariffs were demanded in the name of equal rights for Maritimers. The political influence of three provincial governments and a gaggle of regional MPs was mobilized effectively in mid-decade to get substantial aid from Ottawa. The King government claimed it was helping the region on a one-time only basis and when the coal and steel industry was back at the trough in 1928 turned down requests for further help. "The whole problem seems a futile effort," the Prime Minister confided to his diary, "to combat geographical & other economic considerations."

Much of the rest of King's country seemed to be having trouble combatting geographical and other economic considerations in the 1920s. For much of the decade the three prairie provinces were little better off than the Maritimes. In the first twenty years of the century the prairies had known nothing but growth and more growth, culminating in a huge expansion of cropland induced by the high prices of the war years. In 1920 the growth ended. Twenty years of depression, retrenchment, stagnation and worse began, interrupted only by three or four good years at the end of the decade. The new reality on the prairies was dollar-a-bushel wheat, no more immigrants, serious winter unemployment in cities and towns, and a steady exodus of failed homesteaders from the semi-arid country of Palliser's Triangle in southern Alberta and Saskatchewan.

There were few other industries in the West to sop up surplus people from the land. Despite Turner Valley gushers and hectic booms in penny stock every few years, the still small oil and gas industry in Alberta did not pump jobs or money. The coal towns on the eastern slope of the Rockies declined with the railroads. No amount of western lobbying for a "national energy policy" could persuade Ottawa to levy tariffs high enough to enable western bituminous coal to break into eastern markets. The West's gateway city, Winnipeg, began to stagnate as people lost interest in coming through the gates.

The far west was happily exceptional, for part of Winnipeg's loss was Vancouver's gain. The opening of the Panama Canal in 1914 shortened the voyage to

Europe by ten thousand miles, making it economic to ship grain, wood, and other products from the West coast to Great Britain and other continental markets. Prairie agricultural products could flow west to export markets as well as east (the "grain watershed" finally settled in western Saskatchewan), and in the 1920s a major grain trade developed through Vancouver. The port city came into its own with a flourish as both Canada's great Pacific terminus and the metropolis for the developing interior. Hard times cut prairie demand for British Columbia wood, but new exports more than compensated. The coastal province sailed through the decade largely oblivious to the troubles of other regions of the country. Some of the memoirs suggest that F. Scott Fitzgerald would have been more at home in Victoria or Vancouver than any other part of Canada in the 1920s (particularly, of course, if he was with the Dunsmuir heiresses).

Canadians still took the train to travel more than a few miles in any direction, but they had more trains to ride on more miles of track than the country would need for decades – even if the automobile stopped making inroads on local and inter-urban street railways. It was now clear that the prewar orgy of railway expansion had been based on absurd, disastrous optimism. The result was at least one full transcontinental railway system, about ten thousand miles of track, that Canada did not need. All these miles were in the hands of that dustbin for failed railways, the government of Canada. In addition to the Intercolonial, which it had owned and operated, inefficiently, since the 1870s, Canada now had the Canadian Northern, National Transcontinental–Grand Trunk Pacific, and the Grand Trunk itself. These were sprawling systems, comprising dozens of divisions, departments, and separate companies, employing a total of one hundred thousand workers, issuers of about a billion dollars in bonds and other securities still in private hands.

Some of the securities, such as Grand Trunk common stock, were worthless (a fact that did not deter angry Grand Trunk shareholders from years of lobbying for compensation on the ground that their Canadian investment had been unfairly expropriated). The bonds and debentures, of course, had to be honoured. And the trains had to be kept running, for neither in war nor peace was it thinkable to close down more than the most obviously redundant lines. (When the railways started trying to close money-losing, apparently redundant branches, they met fierce resistance from shippers, travellers, and politicians.) The cost of the system was going to be staggering: hundreds of millions in taxpayers' money poured into the government railways year after year – $160 million dollars in 1921 alone, more money than the total budget of the government of Canada in 1913.

Could the mess ever be straightened out? The one solvent railway, Canadian Pacific, was deeply alarmed at the prospect of competition with a system bank-rolled from the public purse and almost certain to receive government favours. In 1917 and again in 1921 the CPR proposed the creation of one unified Canadian railway system, government-owned, which the CPR would manage in return for guaranteed dividends. For most Canadians, including most businessmen outside of Montreal, the spectre of railway monopoly in the hands of the CPR was worse than even the prospect of public ownership. The government would have to find a way to operate a national system of railways, in competition with the CPR, as economically as possible and with a minimum of political interference.

Canadian National Railways, the CNR, was created in several stages between 1917 and 1922. The nationally owned railway companies were gradually consolidated into a corporate body wholly owned by the Minister of Finance, who appointed its board of directors. From its inception the CNR was the biggest company in Canada. Its chief executive officer would have the toughest job any Canadian businessman had tackled. In 1921 fellow businessmen and the Conservative prime minister, Arthur Meighen, put strong pressure on Sir Joseph Flavelle to take the job. He refused. In 1922 Mackenzie King went outside the country to hire Henry Thornton, a dynamic American railwayman who had risen to top management ranks in Britain. As first president of the CNR, the largest and most ill-conceived company in Canada, Thornton faced a job Flavelle thought would try the administrative capacity of the Angel Gabriel.

(As both big railways struggled to show a profit in the early 1920s they got a sharp lesson in Canada's new balance of power when the King government insisted on the restoration of the Crow's Nest Pass agreement rates on grain. They had been suspended in 1919 when inflation made them absurdly low. When first the Board of Railway Commissioners in 1922 and then the Supreme Court of Canada in 1925 seemed to limit the scope of the Crow rates, the government imposed the specific 1897 rates by statute.)

Hundreds of millions in taxpayers' money flowed out to keep the CNR going. Hundreds of millions were spent to service war debts and provide veterans' benefits. All of Canada's problems in the 1920s were compounded by levels of taxation that were unprecedented by prewar standards. The excess profits tax was retained for two years after the war. When it disappeared a new federal sales tax of 6 per cent on all manufactured goods was introduced (business spokesmen opposed the tax as cumbersome, suggesting instead a turnover or value-added tax). Some war taxes on luxury goods lingered, blending with a wide range of commodity and excise taxes. In their sphere the provinces began financing increasingly heavy social expenditures with taxes on gasoline and alcohol. Most important for the future, the tax on corporate and personal incomes, introduced to Canadians only in 1917, was not only retained, but increased. The Dominion still drew most of its tax revenue from tariffs and excise duties.

Through the early 1920s Canadians paid substantially higher taxes than American or even British income-earners. Marginal rates for individuals and corporations were above 50 per cent in the top brackets (interest on some issues of Victory Bonds was tax exempt). No deductions for charitable donations were allowed until 1929, but neither capital gains nor dividend income was taxed, the latter because it would be double taxation. The complexities of the tax system were already baffling: in 1923 the first Canadian Tax Conference was told that "it is questionable if there are ten members of Parliament in the Dominion and Provincial Houses throughout Canada, or one business man in five hundred who is able to determine the amount of his income tax without the aid of an expert."

Business spokesmen began a long tradition of complaining that Canada's steeply progressive taxes were a disincentive to investment and enterprise. Thus the Toronto Board of Trade, also in 1923: "The systems of federal taxation at present in force are unduly onerous and complicated; are proving vexatious and ruinous to enterprise and thrift, and are discouraging and will continue to discourage the re-investment in business ventures of the capital in this country and the enlistment of outside capital for this purpose." Insofar as taxation sopped up money that would have been reinvested in the productive resources of the country, the complaints were soundly based, albeit exaggerated. This was part of the cost of the Great War and the prewar railway extravaganza. The fact that some of it was being paid through these unprecedented taxes on well-to-do individuals and corporations also reflected the institutionalization of prewar populist attitudes. In 1926 double income taxation was introduced with the removal of the dividend exemption.

War debts, taxes, bankrupt railways, class warfare in the Maritimes, farmer outrage in the West, business stagnation in the centre of the country – these seemed to be the facts of postwar life in Canada as late as 1925. The splendid growth of the Laurier years, the shining future in Canada's century, sometimes seemed to be old dreams. Population flows were the most damning evidence of the loss of confidence. Not only had immigrants almost stopped coming to Canada (in most years of the 1920s the influx was less than one-third of the 1910–13 average), but Canadians themselves were leaving for better opportunities in the United States. As many as one million emigrated there during the 1920s, including many highly trained professionals and skilled tradesmen for whom the Canadian economy could not provide good jobs. In one year, 1924, an estimated three hundred thousand Canadians emigrated to the United States, both legally and illegally.

The big business circles of Toronto and Montreal seemed infected by a crisis of confidence. In Toronto Pellatt's decaying castle symbolized the collapse of the great utility-railroad ventures. The Cox-Mackenzie empire had gone down in the ruins of the Canadian Northern, the onslaught of civic populism in Ontario (the Toronto Railway Company expired with its franchise in 1921; Beck's Ontario Hydro, which continued its unrestrained, octopus-like growth throughout the 1920s, bought the Toronto Power Company), and the striking inability of that entrepreneurial circle to renew itself. Cox, Lash, Mackenzie were all dead, none of them leaving heirs of outstanding ability (neither Mackenzie nor Mann left much money either, having spent their fortunes trying to keep their railway going). Pellatt was a pathetic buffoon, reducing to trying to peddle Louisiana oil stock to the servants of the castle. Sir Joseph Flavelle carried on as an elder statesmen, fortunate to be out of meat-packing, another troubled industry of the decade. E.R. Wood at Dominion Securities presided over Canadians' interests in their remaining foreign utility ventures: the failing and bankrupt properties such as Barcelona Light, Heat and Power, the happily successful Brazilian Traction, and many in between.

The more conservative Montrealers went into the 1920s with their utilities (especially Montreal Light, Heat and Power) intact and highly profitable, their superbly managed railroad riding from strength to strength, and their two big banks (the conservative Bank of Montreal and the brilliantly aggressive Royal Bank) controlling upward of 40 per cent of Canada's banking assets. Edward Beatty of the CPR and Herbert Holt, now president of the Royal Bank and Montreal Trust as well as Montreal Light, Heat and Power, were the country's two most important business leaders. Sir Charles Gordon, principally of Dominion Textile, J.W. McConnell, the brilliant general manager of St. Lawrence Sugar Refineries who bought the Montreal *Star*, Senator Lorne Webster, who had started out as a coal merchant in Quebec City, the Macaulays of Sun Life, a resurgent I.W. Killam at Royal Securities and his protégés, A.L. Nesbitt and Ward Pitfield, were among the brightest shiners in Montreal's final years of ascendency.

They were also a deeply worried crowd in the early twenties, however, because of their fear that the CPR would be crippled, their dislike of big government and taxes, and their belief that the Conservative opposition was being led ineptly by Arthur Meighen. The nadir of pessimism was reached in Lord Atholstan's 1923 "Whisper of Death" series of editorials in the Montreal *Star*, depicting a country on the verge of national collapse. Influential Montrealers were said to be giving Canada about fifteen more years before it would be absorbed into the United States.

Many of the Toronto and Montreal financiers had operated with close European connections. They had looked to England and the continent for capital to make Canada grow and for the immigrants to open the West and make the railroads viable. Part of their pessimism reflected the decline of war-exhausted Europe, particularly Great Britain, which was no longer going to be a metropolis for Canadian development. Over in London expatriates such as Beaverbrook were concentrating on the domestic scene. Sir James Dunn, lamenting the passing of the turn-of-the-century development days, began dreaming of building a real enterprise of his own back in Canada (he coveted Clergue's old Sault Ste Marie steel mill, which was teetering near bankruptcy because of its inability to sell steel rails or other products competitively). The old "developing days" and the old international growth industries had gone with England's Edwardian summers and the power and prospects of the British Empire.

Businessmen who were locked into traditional assumptions had difficulty coming to grips with the new economic forces of the 1920s. Witness the general manager of the Bank of Nova Scotia writing to a branch manager in 1919:

> Your letter... on the subject of motor cars received. I may say that hearing from some Manager on this subject is now almost a daily occurrence with us. I quite agree with you that "everyone" seems to have a car now-a-days. As I walk down University Avenue in the morning and home at night, myriads of them pass me, and I often reflect on the economic waste, not to mention the impairment in the general health of our citizens, who would be much better off financially and physically if they travelled on foot as their forefathers did. However, the thing is in the air and I suppose it must run its course.... If, therefore, you conclude to purchase a car we will make you a loan, although I would point out that a loan of $2,000 reduced at the rate of $600 a year would hardly be extinguished during the lifetime of the car.

Canada's automobile pioneers were new men, alert to a transportation revolution many of their fellow businessmen barely understood. It helped to have been in carriages and wagons and to be a bit of a tinkerer, like so many of the Americans who made the new industry. Being the proud inventor-designer-manufacturer of a distinctive Canadian automobile in the early years of the century was *not* a prescription for enduring success. The Fossmobile, Maxmobile, LeRoy, Bourassa Six, Mottette, Neff, Redpath Passenger, London Six, Lavoie, and dozens of other Canadian cars left hardly a track in the annals of motoring as their founders went out of business almost as quickly as they invented new prototypes. Almost anyone could put a motor on wheels and make it run. The problem was to make cars that would sell.

Canada Cycle and Motor made a good saleable Canadian automobile, the Russell, named after Tom Russell, the general manager, which was fairly popular before the war. The Tudhope carriage-building family of Orillia offered first a "motor carriage," then a completely redesigned and improved model of an American car, the Everitt. By 1915 the Gray family of carriage- and sleigh-makers of Chatham were in the business, upgrading American designs. The entrepreneurs who made the most important American connections, Gordon McGregor of Walkerville, and Sam McLaughlin of Oshawa, had also grown up in the carriage trade.

The secret of endurance in the industry was price and volume, both of which were hard to come by in the small Canadian market. A certain imaginative leap was necessary to foresee a day when everyman would own his own car. Most of the Canadian auto-makers who did not survive adopted a strategy of high-priced sales to a luxury trade. The Russell was "Made Up to a Standard – Not Down to a Price," CCM advertised. McLaughlin, however, toured American plants and sought advice from the leading manufacturers. Richard Pierce of the Pierce-Arrow told him that the luxury car had no future; Will Durant, head of Buick, "showed me that it was futile to make cars a hundred at a time. He showed me this is a volume business and if you didn't have volume you were dead." McLaughlin bought the rights to Durant's Buick engine and put it in a Canadian body. The early Mc-Laughlin-Buicks were costly, high-quality vehicles, but sold in enough volume – one thousand in 1914, for example – to keep the firm well in the business.

The Canadian auto-entrepreneur who had hitched his wagons to the brightest star was McGregor of Windsor, founder of the Ford Motor Car Company of Canada. It took so little capital to found a Canadian assembly works for Ford products (much cheaper than importing them over the 35 per cent tariff), that bankers' conservatism was no obstacle. McGregor sold shares in the Canadian company to local wine merchants, lawyers, grocers, a bicycle store owner, and a nephew of Hiram Walker, the distiller. Canadians put $56,250 cash into the company, capitalized in 1904 at $125,000. The stockholders of the Ford Motor Company of Michigan contributed all their plans, specifications, expertise, and rights to make and sell Fords in every country in the British Empire except Britain herself. It was easy for the Detroit people to commute to Windsor to help start production in McGregor's old Walkerville Wagon Works.

The advent in 1908 of the Model-T, the world's first people's car, made Ford's fortunes in Canada as surely as in the United States. "Business soared," the company's historians write. "That year saw the declaration of a 10 per cent dividend. In 1909 one for 25 per cent followed. In 1910 sales swelled to astonishing dimensions and went on increasing at what seemed a fantastic rate. A 100 per cent dividend was announced; in 1911 this was repeated, with a 500 per cent stock dividend thrown in. Nineteen twelve saw another stock increase of 33⅓ per cent and a straight 20 per cent dividend out of profits. A man who had bought one share in the company in 1904 for $100, now had eight (worth $500 each), and had received $361 in dividends." In 1913 the Walkerville factory turned out more cars than any plant in the British Empire, including England herself. About 40 per cent of production was exported because of the international rights McGregor had obtained. Ford Canada exported two or three times as many cars as Ford US.

By 1922, the year of McGregor's death, Ford Canada had assets of more than $25 million and operated five assembly plants in the Dominion (in London, Toronto, Winnipeg, and Montreal, as well as Windsor). Half the cars on Canadian roads were Fords. Durant's General Motors of Canada was far behind. It had bought out the McLaughlin family of Oshawa (who became very rich with their GM stock). Several other American firms assembled in Canada, including Studebaker, Chrysler, Dodge Brothers, and Willys-Overland, which had taken over the Russell subsidiary of CCM. When Gray-Dort of Chatham gave up the struggle in 1925 (the Gray-Dort was a classy car, but cost about $1,000 at a time when Fords were under $500), it left Brooks Steam Motors Limited, of Stratford,

Ontario, as the last producer of a distinctively Canadian automobile. Oland J. Brooks was an American promoter who got generous help from the city of Stratford to reopen an old thresher plant, where he organized production of "the Gentle Giant of Motion." The one model of Brooks Steamer listed at $3,885. The company ceased production in 1927.

The tinkering tradition continued, of course, wherever car men or mechanics had time on their hands and parts nearby. Nineteen twenty-seven was also the year when a twenty-year-old garage owner in the Eastern Townships village of Valcourt named Armand Bombardier sold his first "auto-neige," an automobile with skis on the front, built to tackle the region's snowy winter roads.

The auto-makers did not need the help of banks or anyone else, for they expanded by reinvesting earnings, extended credit to their customers, and quickly organized that business by spinning off separate sales finance companies. By 1923 Industrial Acceptance Corporation, Traders Finance, and General Motors Acceptance were all established in Canada. Whether or not the stuffy old Bank of Nova Scotia would lend people money to buy cars hardly mattered – except in our judgment of the banks' entrepreneurial performance in the decade.

In 1926 Canada was second only to the United States in its number of private automobiles. The nation's eleven auto plants were capitalized at $83 million, employed twelve thousand workers, and made two hundred thousand cars. Thousands more workers had jobs in tire and other parts plants, the new service stations, auto-supply dealers, and other businesses created by internal combustion. The automobile had spawned the largest industry in Canada next to pulp and paper, and was still in its infancy. Its long-term impact would be easily as important as the advent of the railway. In the short term the automobile industry was one of the first to have to bear the brunt of serious tariff reductions when the Liberals cut the duties from 35 to 20 per cent in 1925. The car-makers' lack of clout in established financial circles may have weakened their position in the dance of tariff lobbyists. The Prime Minister, Mackenzie King, distrusted them as "the hardest looking lot of manufacturers' promoters I have seen, a genuinely brute force gang from Fords and other concerns." Their industry was strong and profitable enough to adjust to lower tariffs and keep growing.

———◆———

Some of the fastest cars were used by the real brute force gangs who ran Canadian booze into the United States. Between 1919 and 1933 the eighteenth amendment to the U.S. constitution prohibited the domestic manufacture and sale of alcoholic beverages. Canada had no such general prohibition. After a war-induced national drying-out from 1917 to 1919, the provinces set their own liquor policies. Following Quebec's lead, most gradually reintroduced the sale of beer, wine, and spirits under tight government control. There was never any prohibition of manufacture for export, so no Canadian laws were broken by brewers and distillers who upped production to sell to people hoping to quench American thirst. Law-breaking only took place when the stuff was smuggled into the United States. Most of the smugglers – the true rum-runners – appear to have been Americans. Trouble only developed in Canada if provincial liquor laws were broken through illicit sales or bootlegging. It was perfectly possible to carry on a flourishing brewing, distilling, or distribution business through the 1920s without breaking any laws.

The sons of Yechiel and Minnie Bronfman, poor Jewish refugees from Russian anti-semitism who came to Canada in 1889, were beginning to make their mark in prairie hotelkeeping and real estate before the war. Then North America's rapidly changing liquor regulations created a series of new necessities and opportunities. When temperance laws closed the bars in Bronfman hotels, Abe and Harry found they could continue to sell liquor legally as mail-order distributors. Wartime regulations closed that business, but in 1919 they were free to resume on a larger scale as import-export wholesalers, proprietors of the Canada Pure Drug Company in Yorkton, Saskatchewan.

Harry Bronfman, a prominent Yorkton entrepreneur who would probably have succeeded in any line of business, quickly became the largest liquor wholesaler in Saskatchewan, competing with established Montreal houses, the venerable Hudson's Bay Company, and dozens of other little men scrambling for a share of the business. The Bronfmans were shrewder merchandisers than most of their competitors, offering a better mix of price, quality, and dependability than buyers could find elsewhere. Their early experience in the hotel business made them particularly sensitive to customers' changing tastes. Like other importers, they soon began blending and bottling imported scotch whisky under their own labels. There is little foundation for stories of the Bronfmans selling rotgut whisky or having been bootleggers. The blending and "cutting" and branding of the high-proof scotch taught them important lessons in the production of saleable liquor. All the Canadian wholesalers sold to anyone who would buy. Most of the buyers from the Bronfmans' export stores in south Saskatchewan towns in 1920–22 ran the product into the United States; American enforcement of prohibition was almost non-existent in these early years.

Abe Bronfman and his young brother, Sam, set up similar distribution operations in other parts of Canada. When tighter regulations in Saskatchewan crippled the export trade, Harry moved to Montreal where the family established a major distillery. The Bronfmans' Distillers Corporation Limited continued to import large supplies of scotch and in 1926 the huge scotch whisky trust, Distillers Company Limited of Edinburgh, was persuaded to take a half-interest in their leading Canadian customer. In 1927 the Britishers bought control of the old Seagram family distillery in Waterloo, Ontario. A year later they reorganized the Canadian business, with the Bronfmans as their major partners, under the umbrella of a holding company, Distillers Corporation – Seagrams Limited. In one decade the Bronfman brothers had risen to the top of the Canadian distilling business. They suffered continuing harassments: charges of petty corruption from Harry's Saskatchewan days; the American government's outrage that it could not extend its laws into Canada; a major Canadian investigation launched as a result of manufacturers' complaints about traffic *into* Canada in smuggled cigarettes, radios, watches, and other high-tariff goods.

Many Canadians, especially the Protestants who believed in prohibition, looked on the liquor trade as an unsavoury business at the best of times, and positively immoral (however legal) now that it was flourishing as a supplier to American criminals. Aversion to the trade, or at least to the disreputability of some of the new people in it, partly explains why some established families left the industry in the 1920s. In Ontario both the Gooderham and Hiram Walker distilling businesses were purchased by another of the new entrepreneurs, Harry Hatch. Hatch was a Roman Catholic, the son of a Belleville, Ontario, hotelkeeper, who rose through storekeeping, mail-order selling, and the export trade in a career almost exactly parallel to that of the Bronfman brothers. He was more successful than the Bronfmans, in fact, having put together the largest distilling business in Canada by 1926. Both before and during prohibition, Hiram Walker's old "Canadian Club" brand of rye whisky (so good an Englishman would have it in his club) was one of the most popular in the United States.

In brewing, the Molsons had led a successful campaign in Quebec to keep their product flowing, and had few problems. Calgary's Cross family, owners of Calgary Brewing and Malting, continued to do business "contrary to the law" (it is not clear whether the law-breaking was in their distribution methods or their involvement in hotel ownership). London, Ontario's, old Carling Brewery was sold to some fairly notorious rum-runners, the group around Harry Low, who converted it into little more than a supplier to the export trade. The other London brewers, the well-established, Church of England, Labatt family, chose to turn over general management of the brewery, and a share of the profits, to an Irish-Catholic liquor and tobacco salesman, Edmund Burke. Burke cheerfully rose to the challenge of shipping the maximum amount of beer. Most of it flowed into the United States, as Burke's network of border agents got the maximum advantage from the brewery's location in the heart of Canada's southern peninsula. The Labatt family collected handsome dividends during prohibition and Edmund Burke became the proprietor of a substantial house and grounds outside London where he kept a private zoo and a mistress, and enjoyed saluting Labatt trucks as they passed by on the road to Windsor.

By the late 1920s beer and liquor was being poured into the United States by land, sea, and air from the Atlantic to the Pacific. The competition was so intense that Canadian exporters began to regulate it. In 1924 ten Ontario breweries agreed to fix prices and apportion the market for their export sales. Two years later they created a formal cartel, named the Bermuda Export Company. American importers used less formal methods to control competition. By the late 1920s, the most imaginative entrepreneurs in the Canadian industry, including Hatch, the Bronfmans, and a precocious Ottawa kid, Edward Plunkett Taylor, were beginning to think about the future of liquor and beer after prohibition. Every time the law-makers changed the rules of the game they created new opportunities for the nimble.

It was no accident that the Bronfmans and many of their associates in the liquor business were Jews. The poor emigrants from Central Europe who began arriving in Canada in the 1880s soon greatly outnumbered the handful of established Jewish families, and formed a community of high-achievers whose upward mobility, from the bottom rungs of society, began to be obvious by the 1920s. In the ghettoes of Montreal and Winnipeg there were thousands of Jewish-operated businesses: groceries, butcher shops, jewellery stores, every kind of garment trade, real estate offices, cinemas, car dealerships, hotels, whatever. The Bronfmans were among the first of the new Canadian Jewish entrepreneurs to break out into great wealth. As they and others like them gained visibility, Jewish invisibility in older businesses like banking became noticeable. So did the casual anti-semitism of WASPs defending their preferences for the old ethnic networks. In Saskatchewan in the early 1920s the prohibitionists' dislike of the Jews in the liquor trade was highly explicit. Half a century later their descendants lapped up journalists' highly coloured accounts of the "bootlegging" origins of the country's greatest Jewish fortune.

The booze business was a lucrative side show. When American businessmen came north in the 1920s their real interest was in the new Canadian resource industries which seemed to have unlimited twentieth-century potential: pulp and paper, mining, and hydro-electricity. They usually associated with Canadian groups interested in resource development, supplying risk capital and a knowledge of markets that the natives could not easily develop. One consequence of spectacular growth in these new resource staples was a fundamental, permanent shift in Canadian economic relations. In 1923 the United States replaced war-weakened Great Britain as the largest foreign source of capital for Canada; in 1926 it replaced Britain as Canada's most important trading partner.

The pulp and paper boom that had begun when American tariffs on newsprint were abolished in 1911–13 picked up momentum after the war, hardly paused as the weak producers crashed and were reorganized early in the decade, and reached a frenzied peak in 1926–27. By then almost every living stick of Canadian wood south of the Arctic circle had been capitalized by investors betting that the world's appetite for newsprint was insatiable. Provincial governments eagerly parcelled out their pulpwood forests on long-term leases sold at auction (accompanied by the usual whiffs of rigged bidding and political kickbacks) to investors who promised to pour millions into erecting big mills and bringing employment to some of the country's poorest regions. Investment in Canadian newsprint mills rose from approximately $157 million in 1918 to $580 million in 1928; production from

795,000 tons in 1919 to 2,725,000 in 1929, about 80 per cent exported to the United States. By the end of the 1920s Canada was the world's leading papermaker and papermaking was Canada's leading industry.

The old-fashioned lumber barons had disappeared with the broad axe, the camboose, and the spring drive. This new forest industry was run by promoters, financiers, and organizers – tamer versions of F.H. Clergue – who had never swung an axe or axe-handle in anger. Foremen, engineers, foresters, and pulpwood jobbers did the on-site work; the entrepreneurs met face-to-face with provincial premiers to arrange pulpwood concessions, talked money markets with the bond houses, and negotiated sales contracts in the United States. A few family names survived on mills and matchboxes in the industry, and even a few families, like the MacLarens and Prices, kept control of their enterprises. Most mills lost their distinctiveness or identity as they changed ownership in refinancings, reorganizations, and mergers.

Americans were active at every level in the industry, but the Canadian roots in older lumbering enterprises were very deep; primary financial support from the Canadian banks and bond houses was also important. American interests had about one-third of the equity in Canadian pulp and paper; the bonds were very widely held. To the beneficiaries of forest development, say the struggling farmers and fisherfolk of the North Shore of the St. Lawrence, it hardly mattered whether the engineers planning a big mill at a desolate place like Baie Comeau were Canadian or American. French-Canadian nationalists regretted that the newcomers' language tended to English, but they, like everyone else, were more interested in the colour of their money and the jobs they gave to Canadians and Canadiens.

Billions of board feet of Douglas fir clattered out of British Columbia sawmills onto world markets. The province consisted of mountains, trees, sawmills, a few orchards, and the odd mine. Even Vancouver was "a city of sawmills." As in the east, the greatest opportunities came to men who never met a tree in anger, notably the professional forester, Harvey Reginald MacMillan. Part of MacMillan's prewar job as a provincial civil servant was to tour the world looking for markets for British Columbia wood. In 1919, MacMillan and a British lumber importer founded the H.R. MacMillan Export Company to engage in timber brokerage, an aspect of the coastal industry previously dominated by Americans. They understood the new export possibilities created by the Panama Canal and worked furiously in the niches of the established trade – offering wood in smaller parcels than anyone else, for example – to build their business. As masters of the lumber market, MacMillan's traders sold BC wood around the world – in Britain, Australia, India (the Bengali railway-tie market was particularly important), Japan (where there was a huge rebuilding boom after the earthquake of 1923), and the eastern United States.

In 1924 MacMillan organized the Canadian Transport Company to charter lumber ships. Within a few years the CTCo. flag, a green fir on a white background, flew in ports all around the world as more than thirty vessels carried wood and grain. Sales of the H.R. MacMillan Export Company grew from $520,000 in 1920 to $15,785,000 in 1928, about 25 per cent of British Columbia's exports. A man of great restlessness, MacMillan was investing more money in sawmills, even as some of the mill-owners began objecting to the market power of his export company.

Mining's expansion parallelled the growth of the forest industries. Established mineral producers enjoyed steady growth through the decade, thanks to increasing world demand as well as technical improvements in the milling and marketing of Canadian products. New uses for asbestos fibre, notably in the brake linings of automobiles, led to increased production from mines in the Eastern Townships; they supplied 90 per cent of American demand. The development of selective flotation techniques for milling base metals, particularly by Cominco in British Columbia, brought down extraction costs, enlarging the Canadian share of world copper, lead, and zinc markets. Many of the older mines in the Kootenay were played out, but others, like Cominco's Sullivan, came into their own with the new technology. Vancouver mining men and brokers spawned a lively industry searching for more deposits.

The nickel companies of the Sudbury basin more than doubled production between 1919 and 1929 as the metal found new uses, ranging from auto parts to coins. Inco's major war-born competitor, British America Nickel, a final promotion of the Mackenzie-Pearson-Pellatt circle, could not meet serious price competition and failed in 1924. Four years later Inco took over the Mond Nickel Company, thus achieving a complete Canadian monopoly and control of 90 per cent of world production. There was no hope at all that the monopoly could last. A group of American and Canadian mining men, centring around Thayer Lindsley, were already beginning to develop the nickel deposits on the old Edison property in Falconbridge Township in the Sudbury basin.

The silver camp at Cobalt had seen its best days, but the great gold mines of Porcupine and Kirkland Lake were still expanding their output, and all the Canadian mining men and many outsiders were hunting for more ore. The use of aerial surveys and metal detectors seemed to have turned prospecting into dull routine, but there was nothing ordinary or predictable about the discovery of ore bodies good enough to become mines. Prospectors used dog sleds in the 1925–26 gold rush into Red Lake in northwestern Ontario. And one of the richest finds of the 1920s, or any other time in Canadian history, was made by an old-fashioned prospector, Ed Horne, of New Liskeard, who paddled and trampled through the wilderness moving east from Ontario's mineral belt into Quebec.

In 1920 Horne and the local men who grubstaked him found their fortune in a seventy-acre claim near Tremoy Lake in Quebec's Rouyn Township. The Canadians sold out to a syndicate of American mining experts who thought the property worthy developing. A secretary in the New Yorkers' office suggested that a mining company in *nor*them *Canada* could be named Noranda. It became a Canadian-American venture when the Hollinger group took a part interest in Noranda in return for early development money. The company's first president, J.Y. Murdoch, was a Toronto lawyer who understood the intricacies of incorporation and mining law. By 1927 railway branches had been built into the township, a state-of-the-art company town, Noranda, had been laid out next to the raw boom town of Rouyn, and Noranda's big smelter was beginning to process the rich copper ore of the Horne Mine. Murdoch planned to expand – into refining, the production of copper wire, and developing more mines. Ed Horne, a wealthy man, retired to his native Nova Scotia.

The misnamed "prairie" province of Manitoba found it too had northern treasures. Prospectors moving out from the line of the Hudson Bay Railway located promising metal deposits before and during the war. The same flotation process that made Cominco's Sullivan mine enabled a Canadian-American group, incorporated as Hudson Bay Mining and Smelting, finally to begin work on a big metals deposit at Flin Flon in the wilderness ninety miles north of The Pas. Further north at Lynn Lake development took longer, as both the Mond and Inco people let options on copper properties lapse. Finally the new men around Thayer Lindsley and his associates took over and in 1927 incorporated Sherritt Gordon Mines Limited. Carl Sherritt, who had staked the key claim, used part of his wealth to buy an aeroplane, the miner's new packhorse, and to learn to fly. During a demonstration at The Pas in 1928 he fell out of the plane to his death.

The big mines and the pulp and paper mills were heavy users of the hydro-electric power being generated at dozens of northern sites in the 1920s. But the waters of the Shield contained still more horsepower, attractive to anyone who needed large inputs of electricity in resource operations. The production of the wonderfully light metal, aluminum, from bauxite ore, depended on huge amounts of electricity. In the early 1900s America's leading producer, the Pittsburgh Reduction Company (soon to be renamed the Aluminum Company of America), moved into the Canadian north to erect a small aluminum smelter at Shawinigan on the St. Maurice River. Twenty years later Alcoa needed much more power and began investigating the potential of the Saguenay. The wandering American tobacco magnate, James B. Duke, had already "claimed" the best power sites, working in partnership with the old Price family. In 1925 Alcoa bought into the Duke-Price establishment and created the Aluminum Company of Canada to erect a huge smelter at the site of the cheapest hydro-electric power in eastern North America. The town Alcan built at the site was named after Alcoa's president, Arthur Vining Davis. Alcan's American origins were no more important to the people of the Saguenay, or to Quebec politicians, than the Scots birthplace of their region's original developers, the Prices.

By 1926 the northern resource boom was too big for anyone in Toronto or Montreal to neglect. Most other sectors of the economy had pretty well recovered from the slow years, so it was possible to begin feeling optimistic again. Bumper wheat crops on the prairies caused farmer grumbling about the iniquities of banks, railroads, and grain dealers almost to disappear (and how smart the farmers seemed to have been in creating their own wheat pools to market the crops instead of paying rake-offs to the leeches in the grain trade). The mid-decade increase in railway traffic was particularly noticeable, as was the renewed vitality of the giant transportation companies. Sir Henry Thornton was particularly visible as the flamboyant head of the CNR, a public entrepreneur cut from the same cloth as Adam Beck. Thornton thought he had a mandate from Canadian taxpayers to use their money to make the national railroad the greatest in the world. This was not a time for consolidation, penny-pinching, retrenchment; you made a railway great by expanding and competing all down the line.

"Canada has hit her stride," proclaimed the CPR's Beatty in 1927, a year when the railways raced to keep up with the demands of the country, the glowing prospects of the future, and each other. It was not simply a matter of buying new locomotives and cars, though there was a lot of that to be done; nor of building new hotels, though by 1929 it was a pretty poor Canadian city that could not boast of at least one palatial railway hotel, and Toronto's brand new Royal York was the largest hotel in the British Empire; nor of the CNR putting its *Lady* and *Princess* steamers up against the CPR's proud *Empresses*. Why, the railways were even building new branch lines, almost two thousand miles of them in 1928, with many more planned. This in a country that only a few years earlier seemed to have a century's supply of railways.

Where would it all end? To Beatty and Thornton and a swelling body of believers in these good years, there was simply no limit to Canada's potential. Even immigration had picked up and the railways were again running those old colonist cars to the West. It was like the good old days of '05 or '09 all over again. No, it was even better: Canada was booming on both its north-south and its east-west axes. All of the great primary industries and most of the important secondary ones were doing better than anyone had thought possible in the disruptions and doldrums of the early 1920s. The federal government ran budget surpluses, slashed the national debt, cut taxes every year, and still took in more money because of the wonderful prosperity. Canada had its present and its future back.

It was time for investors to get a share of Canada's future. Interest in Canadian securities picked up through 1926 and 1927, soared in 1928, and kept on rising through most of 1929. By today's standards there were still only a handful of players on very thin markets. At the peak of the boom a good day on the Montreal or Toronto stock exchanges saw two hundred thousand shares change hands (many other investors dealt through New York, often in Canadian stocks). To contemporaries this was a wave of investing beyond their experience. The fluctuations in paper values – hundreds of millions appearing out of nowhere, tens of millions wiped out in momentary setbacks – were staggering. The stock market itself became a new frontier for money-making. It was no longer just the preserve of the knowing insider, but apparently as open to the adventure-minded common man as the Klondike or Cobalt had been a quarter-century ago. Now you could strike it rich in your local broker's office.

Established brokers fed the demand for good-looking industrial securities by helping organize another wave of refinancings and mergers. Old family firms like Massey-Harris came on the market (as Vincent sold the last big block of family shares). Troubled industries like meat-packing were taken in hand and weak companies combined into well-financed giants: in this case J.S. McLean of Harris Abattoir took over the faltering William Davies Company and several others to create Canada Packers. New men were everywhere: young C.L. Burton raising the money to buy out the old management of Simpson's, pushy Roy Jodrey in the Annapolis valley peddling shares in Lilliputian power companies and pulp mills, T.P. Loblaw going to the market to expand his Canadian and American chains of "groceterias," Harry Hatch floating a $10 million stock issue to begin expanding into Scotland and the United States, Tip Top Tailors, and Honey Dew, and Laura Secord, and Goodyear Tire, and Canadian Marconi all peddling concepts in tune with the temper of the times.

Careful investors still wanted a mix of bonds and stock, but attention centred most often on the possibilities of common shares. Their prices had proven so volatile over the years that companies and brokers abandoned the fiction of "par value." Common shares were worth what people would pay for them. The twenties' fascination with paper values came partly from the new method of reckoning of a company's worth by the market value of its no-par common stock. What did the antiquated one dollar par value of Canadian Marconi shares mean in 1928, for example, when you could not buy them for less than $28? What did it mean when the stock market (in this case the New York Curb Exchange) valued this troubled, barely profitable little radio company, with no more than $5 million in assets, at about $130 million?

Five established securities houses – A.E. Ames and Company, Dominion Securities, Royal Securities, Nesbitt, Thompson, and Wood Gundy – dominated the new issues and underwriting business. I.W. Killam of Royal and Toronto's J.H. Gundy were the most visible of the new breed of self-proclaimed "investment bankers," active spirits in great industrial reorganizations ranging from Latin America (where Killam pulled all the bits and pieces of Aitken's old investments into a healthy utilities portfolio), through Cape Breton (Gundy decided to take the steel business in hand, floating a new Dominion Steel and Coal Company on the ruins of BESCO), and across the northern forests (where over-competition in pulp and paper was forcing rather more consolidations than the bankers would have liked). Some of the older players who had been burned in the past, notably A.E. Ames, were not willing to become quite so exposed.

Like Americans, the Canadian investment bankers found a strong market interest in the securities of companies formed for no other purpose than to hold interests in other companies. The holding company, through which an individual or a family consolidated its investments, evolved into an industry-wide vehicle (Canadian Pulp and Power Investments, Power Corporation of Canada, Hydro-Electric Bond and Share Corporation, among others), and very quickly grew into a general closed-end investment company. The former Conservative prime minister, Arthur Meighen, led the way as president of Canadian General Investment Trust Limited, formed in 1926. By 1928 it had spun out Second, Third, and Fourth Canadian Investment Trust[s] Limited. The investment companies soon found they could lever their holdings in interesting ways by using borrowed money. The profits they created for investors could be breathtaking. Common shares of Power Corporation, created by Nesbitt, Thomson to invest in and manage electrical utilities, were issued at $5 in 1925 and went to $139 in 1929.

Little Canadians who liked to speculate (gamble, take sporting chances, take flyers, throw away money) concentrated on the penny mines and oils hawked to them on suddenly energized local stock exchanges in Vancouver, Calgary, and Winnipeg, as well as Toronto's slick Standard Stock and Mining Exchange. The most hustling brokers and promoters went directly to the people, touting stocks by telephone and newsletter, installing tickers and "big boards" in storefront offices, and (as the bigger brokers had always done) carrying any good customer on margin – that is, on credit. I.W.C. "Ike" Solloway, an Englishman who had wandered around the mining areas of northern Ontario, emerged in 1926 as the wizard of retail brokerage when he and his partner, Harvey Mills, set up in a ground-floor shop in Toronto and began trading penny stocks out in the open where everyone could see and hear the action. Solloway, Mills and Company always seemed to give their customers the benefit of advantageous trades; they processed orders quickly, were wired to every exchange in North America, and spent a lot of money advertising their services.

As they moved west, opening offices everywhere, Solloway and Mills traded Manitoba mines, Turner valley oils, BC gold promotions, the whole gamut of Canadian resources. Solloway boasted of his success in persuading Canadians to invest in their own country instead of in American stocks. Yes, it was speculation and volatile and risky, but what was wrong with honest commercial speculations honestly transacted? By 1929 the single office and $17,000 capital had turned into a forty-office brokerage empire, fifteen hundred employees, and 13,500 miles of private wire linking Solloway, Mills and Company to fourteen exchanges. He and Mills spent much of their time in Alberta, touting the Mackenzie basin as Canada's last great resource frontier, "a veritable Eldorado for the prospector," organizing prospecting parties to go into the country, and setting up a fleet of aeroplanes "to solve the transportation problem from Edmonton to Aklavik."

The bull markets of the twenties symbolized the coming of age of the public corporation, at least as a vehicle for mobilizing money. The 1930 census showed that about half the business in the country was now transacted by corporations. But the big businessmen in the world of big corporations still scoffed at the penny mining people and the stock exchange gamblers – who were certainly not part of the established world of stable corporations and sensible investors. By 1929 every major bank president was on record as having warned against excessive stock market speculation. There was no doubt in their minds that the little people who flocked like lemmings to the market were going over the edge. It was simply a question of when and how far they would fall. Markets were bound to get down to sounder values. Because all the fundamentals were sound, though, with the country prospering as never before, the readjustment, when it came, would not be serious. Only the reckless and naive and ignorant would lose everything.

While the bulls and bears were thrashing about on the stock markets, the managers of Canada's great corporations concluded a decade whose last years more than compensated for the rough start. For some big firms, such as the life insurance companies, the whole postwar decade was good. The slaughter of the Great War seemed to have made people everywhere more conscious of the need for insurance. Many of them now had a savings base to build on, or were willing to give up a little of their pay every week for the cheap group life insurance that became the industry's most popular product in the twenties. For the men who managed the big life firms or the banks' head offices, or Bell Canada or the railroads, even the bigger manufacturing firms such as Ford or Massey-Harris, the most pressing problem of the decade in business was how to keep track of everything and keep all the workers in the office and the plant floors both happy and productive. In these biggest business organizations the 1920s was a decade of progress and innovation in the rational management of bureaucracy.

It was a decade when personnel managers were hired, serious recruitment and training programs instituted, aptitude and intelligence testing begun, house newsletters and employee cafeterias and company sports teams organized, pension, insurance, and sick benefit plans introduced. There were important experiments in company unions to try to keep outsiders out, and sustained attempts to do ongoing industrial research. Community service work, say through united charity appeals or leadership in board of trade or Rotary or Kinsmen clubs, became a favourite pastime for young bankers and managers, as corporate business tried to institutionalize the old personal sense of social responsibility. Standardizers and cost accountants seemed everywhere in the big firm.

Who could understand the line and staff operations of Bell or the CPR without an organization chart? Office managers organized and reorganized their armies of clerks along functional, increasingly specialized lines and tried to develop "scientific" standards to govern pay and promotion. Men and women worked together in more and more companies, but almost always worked at different jobs. The women did the most routine work for the lowest pay and with little prospect of promotion, though who could say that the stenographers or typists were unskilled?

The telegraph and telephone had been everyday business instruments for generations.* Mechanical work was facilitated in the big offices not only by the adding machines and typewriters, but by allocating them to special departments and pools to maximize their use. The next generation of office machines was already at hand: addressographs, cheque-writing machines, above all Hollerith tabulating machines to process data recorded on standardized punch cards. By 1920 the tabulators could even print out the results of their work.

A Canadian named St. George Bond who was interested in the Hollerith machines received a licence to establish the Canadian Tabulating Machine Company in 1910. His first customer was the Toronto Library Bureau. In 1917 the firm became incorporated in Canada as International Business Machines Company Limited, a subsidiary of Thomas Watson's Computing-Tabulating-Recording Corporation (which later appropriated the Canadian branch's name). By 1919 IBM had sales of more than $1 million of machines assembled in Canada. Several dozen of Canada's largest companies, led by the railways and life insurance firms, installed IBM Hollerith systems in the 1920s. "To say that these machines are 'human' in skill and intelligence is grossly to understate the case," the CPR staff bulletin reported in 1930. "They are actually superhuman, performing prodigies of involved arithmetic, sortation and compilation of records."

Many of the IBM and other advanced office machines used paper forms sold by the family of companies put together by the former printer for *Grip* magazine and now president of the Bank of Nova Scotia, S.J. Moore. A merger of three of these companies created Moore Corporation Limited, which began its existence on January 1, 1929. The era of the big corporation seemed to have arrived by 1929, in Canada and especially in Herbert Hoover's United States, where prosperity and big business seemed about to abolish poverty forever. Moore Corporation was completely international, virtually ignoring the border in its operations. These modern big businesses seemed far removed from whatever the grubby little stock speculators were doing with their moose pasture in the brokers'

---

* Toronto merchant and philanthropist Sigmund Samuel remembered that his family's metal-importing house began using the Atlantic cable service in 1869, three years after its completion. "I had thought the Atlantic cable would be a great boon to the business, but . . . it destroyed much of the advantage of our private information from Liverpool, since even the smallest importer was able to benefit from the cabled market reports which soon began to appear every day in the newspapers."

offices. Though it was probably a Moore group corporation that made the ticker tape.

The times were so good in 1929 that old Sir Henry Pellatt had managed to sell an option on his castle in Toronto to a group of Americans who planned to turn it into a luxury apartment hotel. During another late 1920s incarnation the castle was the nightclub setting for fine dining and dancing, often to the tunes of Glen Gray and the swinging band that became known as the Casa Loma Orchestra. The castle was the place to be on romantic summer nights, or to imagine as the magic of radio brought you the music, all across Canada.

Bennett-buggy, Saskatchewan (*Glenbow Archives*)

INSET LEFT: **Roy Thomson** (*NSL Archive*) CENTRE: **Samuel Bronfman** (*Toronto Star*) RIGHT: **Sir Herbert Holt** (*Royal Bank Archives*)

15

———————

Dark Years

Depression myths . . . a slow decline . . . the real crisis, 1931 . . . a bankrupt country? . . . black years . . . controlling competition . . . freezing enterprise . . . bankers against central banking . . . "funny money" . . . business and reform . . . new investment frontiers? . . . Eldorado . . . aviation . . . sparkplug entrepreneurs . . . "Call me Roy" . . . broadcasting . . . booze barons . . . E.P. Taylor builds Labatt's . . . C.D. Howe's toy airline

The big bull market died in October 1929. Billions in paper values disappeared. Thousands of speculators were wiped out. A decade of depression followed. The stock market highs of the 1920s did not recur until the 1950s. The Great Crash is so important in popular historical memory because it seemed to mark the end of a golden age, the beginning of a leaden decade.

We must not confuse symbol and reality. The stock market and its problems did not *cause* the Great Depression. Securities exchange problems were not fundamental to the business crisis of the 1930s. The black days of 1929 were not even the most alarming of the period. Much blacker ones lay ahead. The Great Depression was a phenomenon far transcending one big market break.

In both Canada and the United States the market collapse was a symptom of more fundamental underlying problems. Through the 1930s stock markets languished in confusion and depression and lack of investor confidence precisely because these fundamental problems had to be worked out. The greatest test of strength for financial institutions came in 1931 in Canada and 1933 in the United States when accumulated strains on debilitated systems threatened economic catastrophe. Canada's big banks, for example, worried about the solvency of some of their customers as the markets went down in the autumn of 1929. Two years later they had to worry about their own solvency and, in the darkest October days of 1931, the solvency of the Dominion government itself.

Canadian stock values went down with American ones, but the Great Depression had different causes and took somewhat different courses in the two countries. In Canada it would not have helped to have had Franklin D. Roosevelt and his New Deal to wrestle with the depression; nor would an earlier adoption of the new economics of John Maynard Keynes have made a great difference. Canada's was a far more open economy than the United States, highly dependent on international trade. The country could not recover its vitality until the major export industries regained their health. Canada depended on world markets which its government was virtually powerless to influence. By the late 1930s there were some who wondered if the world markets would ever recover. Perhaps Canada was doomed to permanent depression, they opined, because it had too many producers cutting and harvesting and milling products the world did not want.

The Great Depression was not the result of a business foul-up. It was not, as socialists like to suggest, a "crisis of capitalism" – though it certainly became a crisis for capitalism. Rather, it was an international crisis, rooted in the deep dislocations caused by the Great War of 1914–18 and its aftermath, then made worse by governments' nationalistic attempts to shelter their own producers at foreigners' expense. Historians still argue about the causes and course of the depression, but it was characterized (perhaps caused) by surplus productive capacity, particularly of primary products, and very low investment in the United States. Businessmen, like everyone else, were caught in winds of economic turmoil. There was almost nothing they could do, except try to hold on.

But who wanted to be a passive victim of havoc wreaked by invisible hands in the marketplace? Everyone – businessmen, farmers, the unemployed – believed something had to be done. Something, anything, to control or limit the disastrous effects of the decline, to begin to get the country moving again. During the 1930s large sectors of Canadian business supported the idea of replacing market mechanisms with administered prices. Business often looked to government for help with price control, and for help in other ways. Government spending on goods and services produced in the private sector seemed increasingly attractive to enterprisers starved for income.

It was not unnatural that there should be a general flight from free markets and private enterprise in years when there seemed no other way to cope with low prices, glutted markets, and "wasteful" competition. The Great Depression led businessmen and many other Canadians to increase their reliance on the state for the direction of the economy. As this reliance was reinforced by conditions of "war socialism" during the struggle against Hitler, and by the new economics after the war, the Canadian business climate became increasingly involved with and shaped by government action.

FEW SIGNS OF TROUBLE appeared before 1929. The market for Canadian newsprint crashed in 1927 when it became apparent that the rush to the forests had led to far more pulp and paper capacity than the world needed. That industry was deeply depressed as 1929 began. Prices for grain were also beginning to weaken, and the managers at the central selling agency of Canada's farmer-owned wheat pools, started to become a bit apprehensive about the marketing of the bumper 1928 crop. Through 1929 it seemed necessary to withhold wheat from the market until prices increased. But prices continued to soften.

All reputable financiers warned against excessive stock market speculation in 1928 and 1929. Some historians even blame bankers' insistence on pricking the market bubble, through tight money policies by the American Federal Reserve banks, for triggering the liquidation. When it finally came in October 1929, the decline was frighteningly steep. Wall Street was the centre of the turmoil, but there was also record turnover on the much smaller Canadian exchanges (500,000 shares in Montreal on October 29, 330,000 in Toronto; 16 million in New York.) Many Canadian investors traded directly with New York, and the losses caused headlines across Canada as well as the United States. But the banks were in good shape – "we have at no time in the history of the institution been more comfortable and liquid," the chairman of the Bank of Commerce wrote privately – and for every market plunger who was wiped out in his speculations, there was another who sold at a comfortable profit. And no one could say they had not been warned.

It was soon realized that several stockbrokers had been playing both sides of the street a little too closely. Led by Ontario, several provinces had passed securities fraud legislation in the late 1920s. Within weeks of the crash the *Financial Post* began exposing shady practices on Toronto's Standard Mining Exchange. A few weeks later police swooped down on many of the suspects, putting them out of business and, in a few cases, into jail. Solloway Mills and Company's store-front brokerage network was closed. I.W.C. Solloway spent several years in prison, protesting and publishing long accounts of his innocence and his heartfelt Canadian nationalism. He and most of the other condemned brokers had hedged their clients' long positions in many stocks by selling the same stocks short – in other words, they had bet against their customers. In the frequent absence of stock certificates to show that shares had changed hands, the brokers were actually running old-fashioned bucket shops. The arrest and conviction of these sharp operators seemed further evidence that the market excesses were mainly the creation of crooked brokers and gullible speculators. The Ontario Securities Commission and other provincial regulatory bodies were depression offspring.

It was more disconcerting when the markets continued to decline in November and December 1929, but businessmen still talked about the way the exchanges were returning to fundamental values. The fundamentals were sound. As Sir Charles Gordon, president of the Bank of Montreal, explained in his December 1929 annual address to the shareholders,

... the period of acute disturbance is now past .... There never was a time in the history of Canada when business as a whole has beeen at a higher peak than during the year under review, or when the developed sources of our wealth were more wide and varied than they are today, and never a time when the earning power of our people was sustained in so many channels of production. We must not allow a possible temporary reaction, the result of a collapse in a purely speculative orgy in the stock markets, unduly to distort our view. Fundamental conditions are sound, and there is no reason for apprehension as to the ultimate future of Canada.

Banks and other big companies could easily carry their customers through a season of adjustment. In 1929, for example, Imperial Oil decided to extend credit to farmers on their gas purchases. It was certain that the agricultural recession was only temporary.

The gradual decline or depression of prices, agonizingly evident as 1930 progressed, gave the decade its name. No one seemed to be buying in the world; no one wanted primary commodities. *Canada could not sell her wheat.* The most ominous price movements for Canadians in 1929 and 1930 were on commodity rather than stock markets, notably the Winnipeg Grain Exchange, where prices had edged and lurched and slid downward even as the wheat pools continued to stockpile wheat in anticipation of higher prices. Hardly anyone realized that in wheat, pulp and paper, minerals, and most other commodities, the world was awash in productive capacity. The build-up had originally been induced by demand during the Great War; it only partially slowed in the early 1920s, and was stimulated again by heavy American lending late in the decade.

If the stock liquidation had initially been triggered by bankers' tight money policies, the price decline of 1930 and 1931 seemed to have a momentum of its own. No national policies were able to arrest it. International organizations of commodity producers (OPEC's ancestors) failed in all their attempts to hold cartels together or create new ones. Canada's predicament was made worse by the national policies of other countries. The 1930 Smoot-Hawley tariff in the United States, the highest in American history, was designed to protect domestic producers from price-cutting foreign competitors. It severely hurt Canada's capacity to export to the United States.

The sickness spread from the forest and wheat economies to the railroads, retailers, and manufacturers – and the stock market kept sliding. Hiring stopped, then layoffs began. No national count of the unemployed existed in 1929, and at first there was sharp disagreement about the seriousness of the problem. Some sectors of the economy were misleadingly buoyant: the construction industry, for example, was busy well into 1930 on contracts let before the downturn. Mackenzie King's Liberal government was inclined to believe that most of the agitation about unemployment in the winter of 1929–30 was inspired by Conservative provincial governments trying to pry money out of Ottawa. His unfortunate remark that he would not give a "five-cent piece" to help a (Tory) provincial government deal with alleged unemployment cost him dearly in the general election of July 1930. The Liberals still seemed to doubt the seriousness of the problem in a summer when most Canadians were beginning to realize that something was seriously wrong.

The new Conservative leader, R.B. Bennett, was a millionaire businessman and corporation lawyer, an old crony of Max Aitken's who had stayed in the West, done well in promotions and flotations and politics, and inherited control of the E.B. Eddy Company from a former sweetheart, the widow Eddy. Bennett seemed to have a clearer grasp of the economic situation than Mackenzie King. He insisted that unemployment was a national problem and that he would end it "or perish in the attempt." Bennett's concern and dynamism – he was a powerful platform orator with an imposing physical presence – seemed in tune with the needs of a deteriorating situation. He was the businessman-politician as man of action. When he became prime minister in 1930, at the beginning of the worst economic crisis in Canadian history, no one could complain that business lacked political influence.

Bennett's recipe for ending unemployment was the old Conservative panacea of protection. A higher tariff would keep cheap foreign goods out of the country, thus preserving and increasing Canadian jobs. In a special session of Parliament after the election the new government raised the tariff to the highest levels ever. Manufacturers and some agricultural producers (such as central Canadian dairy farmers, who were in a losing battle with cheap New Zealand butter) were thereby able to maintain prices and market share. But for many goods the market shrank even faster as inelastic prices deterred purchasers. Generally, thanks to Bennett, the producers in Canada's protected industries succeeded in shifting more of the burden of the depression onto the already-stricken export sector (the tariff helped keep exporters' costs from falling as quickly as their income). Oh, there was to be a second effect of the new tariff, when Mr. Bennett would use it to "blast" Canada's way into world markets by forcing other countries to lower their tariffs. But neither the British nor the Americans were interested in negotiation, while Canada's other trading partners were moving toward protectionism just as rapidly as Canada herself.

By the summer of 1931 Canada was staggering under the double burden of a mounting trade deficit and huge foreign debts. The price of grain had fallen below all levels known to modern times. The wheat pools were hopelessly over-extended and were being carried by the banks. To keep them going the banks insisted on federal guarantees. Companies were beginning to reduce or eliminate dividends on common and preferred stock, and even default on bond interest, particularly in the devastated pulp and paper industry. Branch plants were under heavy pressure from their parents to repatriate profits and reserves During the good years corporations and governments of all levels had borrowed heavily abroad, mostly in New York, usually in foreign currency; some of them were still borrowing in early 1931. But as the export income needed to service foreign debts eroded, so did confidence in Canada's financial stability. Where would the money come from to pay the debts?

Other countries suffered similarly, even Britain herself. The pound came under tremendous pressure in the summer of 1931 when a general European liquidation was trigged by the failure of Austria's Kredit Anstalt. The country's Labour government collapsed, and so did the pound. On September 19, 1931, the new National Government suspended Great Britain's commitment to support its currency with gold. Overnight the pound dropped by almost 20 per cent against the American dollar.

Canada, too, had to face the full effect of the rush to hard currency. Technically the government had already abandoned the gold standard during pressure on the dollar early in 1929, but the notes had remained moored near parity with the U.S. dollar. Now Canada's currency sank in the worst crisis of confidence in the nation's history. On Monday, September 21, it lost 3.25 cents against the American dollar. On Tuesday it dropped 5.75 cents. Frightened bankers, brokers, and government officials had conferred through the weekend and decided that Canadian financial markets and institutions could not bear the full strain of the flight from Canadian paper. Stock exchanges in Canada were allowed to open on the 21st, but only for trading at prices *higher* than the Friday close. Short selling was prohibited. There were few transactions.

The artificial price-fixing was maintained for several months. Stocks traded at their real values anyway, in private deals on what came to be called the "gutter" market. But the fixed official values were important in maintaining the façade of solvency, for on a purely market valuation of assets they held as security for loans the banks might have driven a large number of their customers into liquidation. Most of Canada's leading investment houses and many brokers were, by normal accounting, insolvent. Some of the life insurance companies, especially the Sun, had plunged heavily into common stock in the 1920s. Result:

MEMORANDUM FOR RT. HON. MR. BENNETT

Sept. 19, 1931

RE: Sun Life Assurance Co. of Canada.

The declines in the New York market yesterday had the effect of reducing the market value of the assets of this Company below its liabilities....

The market value of the Company's holdings is less than the value on the basis of the September 15th quotations by at least $10,000,000, and at least $16,000,000 below the value on June 1st last . . . .

My belief is that the Company's assets are today less than its liabilities; that the capital is wiped out and, in addition, any shareholders' funds from which dividends to shareholders can be paid . . . .

Respectfully submitted
(signed): G.D. Finlayson
Superintendent of Insurance

There were other, more public signs that the house of financial cards could collapse. On October 5 and 6 three big Montreal brokerage firms – McDougall and Cowans (said to have done the largest stock brokerage business in the country), Greenshields and Company, and Watson and Chambers – all suspended payment to their creditors and petitioned for bankruptcy. Alarmed by the falling Canadian dollar, American banks had called in their loans.

The inner history of the Canadian financial crisis that autumn has yet to be written. It had both public and private dimensions. Leaders of the country's private financial institutions were apparently worried about the domino effect that could follow a devaluation of securities to unregulated market prices, or even a revelation of the plight of companies like Sun Life. Following precedents used in the war, and practices being implemented simultaneously in the United States, the Bennett government obliged the anxious financiers. It stretched the terms of the Unemployment and Farm Relief Act of 1931 to fantastic lengths to justify orders-in-council authorizing temporary changes in methods of valuing securities for reporting purposes: banks could report book value or market value on August 31, whichever was lower; life insurance companies could have special valuations of their common stock holdings by the superintendent and outside experts. Leading Canadian financiers may also have signed a "round robin" agreement (referred to in Lord Beaverbrook's memoir of Bennett, but as yet unlocated in the archives) to respect these artificial valuations. With these conventions in place – a general agreement to suspend market valuations – the erosion was checked.

The public dimension of the crisis that autumn was the inability of Canadian governments to borrow abroad. The New York market, devastated by the domestic liquidation, would not take more Canadian loans. Existing obligations had to be met in American dollars costing a premium that reached 20 per cent by December. Some Canadian municipalities and the western provinces were already at the limit of their resources and had to be helped by senior governments. But the Dominion government itself was stretched to the limit, had to borrow more, yet could not do it abroad. Major war bond issues were about to mature and a Conversion Loan campaign in May had been only partly successful. Where would the money come from to pay Canada's debts? There was serious talk in high business circles that the government of Canada might be forced to default. The collapse in values of even gilt-edged government bonds had been the final cause of the order-in-council affecting banks.

A worried Government of Canada went to the domestic market in November for a $150 million "National Service Loan." It was advertised and sold as though Canada were at war – the premiers of all the provinces, as well as the acting prime minister, went on national radio to urge support – and was a resounding success, raising a total of $221 million. The 5 per cent interest rate the government had to pay in a year when prices dropped about 15 per cent gave investors a very high return. Even so, the success of the campaign was R.B. Bennett's finest hour, for the nation had survived an immense test of confidence. We cannot know what failure would have meant. Bennett was worried enough that fall to threaten legal action against the *Financial Post* for daring to print news that New York financiers had lost faith in Canada. On the other hand, the recovery in bond values was such that the banks and the insurance companies made little use of the emergency valuation provisions (which were not unique to Canada, the Americans having had to make similar adjustments for their troubled financial institutions), which expired in the spring of 1932.

———

Nineteen thirty-two and 1933 were the worst years of the Great Depression. By some measurements the upturn began in the summer of 1932, but it was barely perceptible until 1934. Fairly rapid recovery after that ended suddenly in the "Roosevelt recession" of 1938, a very sharp downturn. At all times the wheat economy remained a problem because of low world prices and a new set of perils caused by drought and other natural plagues. Canada's recovery was still not complete when the outbreak of war in September 1939 changed everything. These statistics chart the course of the decade:

	1926	1929	1932	1933	1937	1939
Gross National Product (millions, current dollars)	5,152	6,134	3,827	3,510	5,257	5,636
Exports (millions)	1,261	1,152	490	529	997	925
Farm income (millions)	609	392	104	66	280	362
Gross fixed capital formation (millions)	808	1,344	444	319	809	746
Automobile Sales (thousands)	159	205	45	45	149	126

	1926	1929	1932	1933	1937	1939
Common stock prices (1935-39=100)	200.6	203.4	97.6	97.3	122.4	86.1
Unemployment: (thousands)	108	116	721	826	411	529
(% labour force)	3.0	2.8	17.6	19.3	9.1	11.4
Cost of living index (1935-39 = 100	121.7	121.6	98.9	94.3	101.2	101.5
Wage rates (1949 = 100)	46.1	48.5	43.8	41.6	47.3	48.9
Corporation profits (millions, before tax)	325	396	-98	73	280	362

SOURCE, *Historical Statistics of Canada*, first edition

The crude index numbers of stock prices are misleading, for they miss both the highs of 1929 and the low of May, 1932. The following table shows the figures for a representative sample of leading Canadian stocks.

Company	1929 high	1932 low	% decline
Abitibi	57¾	1	98.3
Bell Telephone	183	78	57.3
B.A. Oil	35⅞	8½	77.3
B.C. Power	60	15½	74.2
Canada Cement	36	2¾	93.8
Can. Bronze	94	9½	89.9
Can. Car & Fdry.	32¾	2¾	91.6
CPR	67½	8½	87.4
Cockshutt	53	3	94.3
Consumers Gas	196	142	27.6
Dist.-Seagram's	28½	3½	87.7
Dom. Bridge	117½	9	92.3
Dom. Stores	55	13⅜	76.5
Dom. Textile	118	39	66.9
Ford Canada	70	5¾	91.4
Hollinger	9.55	4.31	54.8
Imperial Oil	41¼	7⅜	82.5
Inter. Nickel	72½	4⅛	94.3

Company	1929 high	1932 low	% decline
Lake of Woods	65½	4	93.9
Massey-Harris	99½	2½	97.4
McColl-Frontenac	45	7¾	82.8
Montreal Power	90	20⅛	77.6
Nat. Breweries	38¼	9½	75.2
Noranda	69	12½	81.9
Quebec Power	99	9¼	90.7
Shawinigan	111	7¼	93.5
Sherwin Williams	65	7	89.2
Stelco	69¼	11	84.1
Winnipeg Electric	109½	2	98.1

SOURCE. *Canadian Annual Review, 1932*

The fifty leading stocks on Canadian exchanges lost 85.9 per cent of their value between the market high of October 1929 and the low of May 1932. Many serious investors who had bailed out before the crash and came in again afterwards to pick up bargains were wiped out in the downward slide. Annapolis valley entrepreneur Roy Jodrey is said to have "bought the bottom" of the market four times before being completely wiped out.

The severity of a firm's struggle to survive depended on how badly and for how long its industry was hit. Pulp and paper was in dismal straits for more than a decade. Most of the big firms, including Abitibi Power and Paper, Price Brothers, Great Lakes Paper, and Fraser Companies, went bankrupt and were reorganized by their bondholders; historic names such as Price continued, but now without any Prices (the first of several Price takeovers was by British press barons, led by Beaverbrook). Herbert Holt later said he was ashamed to admit how much money he had lost in the Canada Power and Paper Company failure, which included such historic mills as Laurentide Pulp and Paper.* Alcan had a difficult decade, closing

---

* In even the hardest-hit industries there were outstanding exceptions. The Ontario Paper Company was wholly owned by the *Chicago Tribune* interests of Robert R. McCormick, and existed solely to supply the newspaper. The ownership and marketing connection gave the firm much greater security than most of its competitors. In 1935 McCormick decided to proceed with a plan for a big new mill at the company's pulpwood concessions on the North Shore of the St. Lawrence. It had been delayed by the worst part of the depression, but was still an audacious project in 1935, when the industry was still wallowing in overcapacity. The spending and the five thousand jobs created by McCormick at Baie Comeau were like manna to the poor workers of northeastern Quebec. This American enterprise on the North Shore left a deep impression on young Brian Mulroney, whose father was employed as an electrician at the mill.

its smelters for years at a time, sometimes bartering its aluminum for Russian coal and oil. Inco suffered harshly in the early years, but had a quick recovery as world rearmanent increased the demand for nickel alloys. Massey-Harris lost $28 million between 1930 and 1935, operated its plants for almost two years at 10 per cent of capacity, and nearly decided to liquidate all of its foreign operations (a $6 million Russian tractor order in 1931 was certainly a godsend, more so because the firm had failed to develop a good tractor in the twenties, and never became a leader in that business).

Prices for base metals were disastrously low, but precious metals enjoyed their greatest boom ever because of the fixed price of gold. Gold not only held its value, at $20.67 an ounce, when everything else collapsed; but in 1934 was revalued by Franklin D. Roosevelt to $35 an ounce. There was no depression at all in Canadian gold mining: existing mines flourished, new deposits were developed (particularly in British Columbia), prospectors scoured the north country, and Canadians found spare dimes to keep the mining share market and their dreams of golden jackpots alive. Mining millionaires merged the faltering *Globe* and *Mail* in Toronto and tried to spread the doctrine of rugged individualism. Harry Oakes of Kirkland Lake was probably the richest man in Canada and came close to succeeding Henry Pellatt in the extravagance of his lifestyle, living in a semi-castle at Niagara Falls before fleeing for sunshine, low taxes, and a purchasable title in the Bahamas. Sir Harry Oakes, Bart., a participant in the social whirl of decadent aristocracy, was murdered there in 1943.

Companies like Noranda and Cominco, which owned composite ore bodies, were able to recover quickly by moving from copper, lead, and zinc into silver and gold. The life insurance business also held up well in the early years. Policyholders appreciated the security and borrowing rights life insurance offered in hard times; but the industry had a bad "second half" of the thirties as Canadians gave first priority to rebuilding their savings. At the largest company, Sun Life, there was an abrupt change in investment policy and senior management.

Canada's steel mills produced at less than 20 per cent capacity in 1932. For three months in the spring of 1933 no pig iron was made in the country for the first time in more than a century. Stelco's sales force found itself peddling coke as domestic furnace fuel. But the Hamilton company was now easily the strongest Canadian steel-maker and was the first to recover. By 1937 Stelco had surpassed 1929's production and profit levels. In the Maritimes the new Dominion Steel and Coal could not make any money. In northern Ontario Algoma fell into receivership and in 1935 was taken over by a spectre from the past, Sir James Dunn. Dunn turned himself from principal bondholder into controlling stockholder, and turned the company back into a proprietary steel firm, North America's last.

Algoma still lived and died on rail orders and other kinds of government help. Dunn urged his manager to "get the best part we can of the orders resulting from the Government relief finance and in this matter I hope to be of some use."

Whether Dunn's connections helped or not (he worked hard at it, treating Ontario's high-living premier, Mitch Hepburn, to "a grand time riding horses, flying dangerous planes . . . and shooting craps with Sam Goldwyn and other magnates of Hollywood" on an Arizona holiday), Algoma was too important an employer in northern Ontario to be shut down indefinitely. By 1934 the Bennett government was underwriting steel rail orders for both Algoma and Dosco as a relief measure. Dosco's coal mines also got large federal subsidies.

The railways were in no position to place new rail orders without help, for the depression stripped bare the facile, fragile assumptions that had passed for railway statesmanship in the late 1920s. There was no grain traffic to support those prairie branch lines, no immigrants to come to Canada on the brand new steamships, no travellers to stay in the splendid new railway hotels and lodges (the 1933 gross revenue of the CNR's showpiece, Minaki Lodge in northwestern Ontario, was $844.77). The CNR was particularly troubled, losing about $100 million a year by 1931 (its accounts were such a mess that no one could agree on the exact loss) and presenting the strained federal government with another terrible burden. The system's imaginative, expansive president, Sir Henry Thornton, came under intense criticism for what a royal commission called the "red thread of extravagance" of his administration (over which Parliament had not exercised effective control). Extravagant and troubled in his personal life, burdened by debt and rumours of scandal, stripped of his pension entitlement, Thornton was driven from office in 1932, and died a year later, railway flamboyance reduced to pathos.

Cars and trucks were by now making such heavy inroads on railway traffic that no one could guarantee a return to normality when – if – the depression lifted. Perhaps the railroads were fated to become a permanent sinkhole. By 1932 even the CPR was losing money on railroad operations for the first time in its history. It stopped paying dividends on its common and preferred stock, and needed a government loan guarantee in 1933 to avoid defaulting on its bonds. Beatty, the president, became deeply pessimistic and revived the idea of railway unification (under CPR management, with a guaranteed dividend) as the only permanent solution to Canada's railway problem. Governments tried to force cooperation on the railways as an alternative to monopoly, and placed the CNR under a special trusteeship. Royal commission recommendations to equalize competition in transportation by forcing users to pay the real cost of highways were derailed in the thickets of Canadian federalism.

Between 1929 and 1933 the two railways laid off sixty-five thousand workers, almost 10 per cent of Canada's unemployed. Their remaining employees had to take wage cuts of 10 per cent and then a further 15 per cent. Many other firms followed similar policies of layoffs and wage cuts, with the mix varying according to management's perception of the benefit of trying to retain a loyal work force. Work-sharing and discrimination in favour of men with dependants seems to have been common. At Alcan married men worked a five-day week, single men three days. At Moore Corporation many employees worked every other day, but married women with working husbands were laid off. Imperial Oil cut its work week to five days and introduced mandatory retirement at sixty-five for men, fifty-five for women. Wage cuts of 10 to 20 per cent were common at every level of business, but there was a 22.5 per cent decline in the cost of living between 1929 and 1933. The downward inelasticity of wage rates was such that most Canadians who kept their jobs during the depression enjoyed an improvement in their material, though not necessarily their psychic, standard of living. In the darkest year of the decade, the railway unions were prepared to stage a national strike rather than accept the wage cut proposed by management. A compromise was worked out when the prime minister personally intervened.

The railways were such important employers that the federal government began granting loans and subsidies to support maintenance, rail purchases, and new rolling stock, virtually as part of its public works and relief programs. Its tariff policy was also vitally important to many manufacturers. Thanks to tariffs and the inelasticity of demand for clothing, for example, employment remained high in the textile and leather industries. A new range of imperial preferences negotiated at the Ottawa Imperial Economic Conference of 1932 was about all that Bennett achieved in terms of access to world markets, and it was widely criticized as being too little, too late. But the preferences had striking effects in some areas. The timber preference, for example, saved the British Columbia industry in 1933 by suddenly shutting the competing U.S. and Baltic product out of the British and Dominion markets. It was a lifesaving rescue because earlier American tariffs had crippled British Columbian exports to the United States. Preferential food duties took the important British bacon market away from Danish producers and were probably the most important factor (along with ruthless accounting and cost-cutting) in Canada Packers' survival. The preferences also had the welcome effect of attracting more American firms to establish Canadian branches as a base for exporting to the other British countries. Great Britain herself was not suffering as badly in the depression as the North American countries, because of a mixture of low interest rates, the belated development of such new industries as cars and radio, a housing boom, new protective tariffs, and, for a time, the cheaper pound.

For the vast majority of businessmen it was a slow, grim, gruelling decade. Everyone was imperilled, no one saw easy answers to Canada's problems, business was less popular than ever, and as the depression years dragged on it became increasingly difficult to maintain optimism about Canada's future. Why was the CPR shop foreman proposing to spend scarce money on black paint, management asked? "To brighten up the place," he answered. The plight of businessmen who were wiped out in the depression cannot be compared with the troubles of the unemployed, western farmers, the aged, or the sick. But it was just as real a battle and often a losing one, particularly after the savings had gone. The skies did not rain despondent stockbrokers in 1929 (there is not a single case on record in North

America), but by 1932 many Canadians who relied on dividends and interest were in serious trouble.* Widows and retirees had to pinch pennies, cut back, hope for the best. One of the Montreal Molsons, Kenneth, had retired from the stock brokerage business at fifty with all the money he needed to maintain his sumptuous Montreal mansion and lifestyle. He was ruined by the spring of 1932. In despair, he shot himself.

———————◆———————

Depression business seemed to be one long exercise in cutting: cutting prices, cutting wages, cutting work force, cutting dividends, cutting costs and corners, and cutting back on personal expenses. Just as workers resisted wage cuts, businessmen naturally tried to resist having to cut prices. Their efforts to hold or restore price levels led to an immense resurgence of price-fixing and other restrictive devices. Cartels, trade associations, selling agencies, and other "stabilizing" bodies struggled to set floors on prices in domestic industries, to fix export prices, and to work with producers in other countries to fix world commodity prices. The deep-rooted anti-competitive instincts of economic actors whose greatest wants were security and cash flow in uncertain times came to the fore. "Competition" was a suspect term, invariably preceded by the adjectives "cutthroat" or "wasteful" – as in the orgy of wasteful competition between the CPR and CNR in the 1920s. Populist criticisms of free enterprise veered almost full circle from the old charge of monopoly. Now the problem with capitalism was that there was too much competition, too much freedom of enterprise. Competition drove down prices, drove down wages, demoralized and destroyed businessmen and workers alike.

It was possible to be against both competition and monopoly. Simply complain that excessive competition led to grinding monopoly. Small retailers had been making exactly this charge ever since the beginnings of the department–chain store revolution in the last decades of the nineteenth century. The competitive methods of the big stores and the chains, which proliferated during the 1920s, included volume buying, quick turnover, lower margins, loss leaders, and a growing reliance on self-service. These could not easily be met by independents, who resented the "unfairness" of practices that seemed to them to be rooted in something close to monopoly power, or that were certainly designed to obtain monopoly power after all the little men had been crushed.

* Your problems depended on your investments. Many conservative, well-managed firms were able to pay dividends out of reserves through several losing years. Then their problems began. Many of the new or recapitalized firms that had gone to the market in 1928–29 had taken on a debt load, premised on prosperity, that instantly became intolerable. Later in the thirties, and for many years afterwards, all managers tended toward conservatism, building or rebuilding reserves and financing expansion out of earnings, before borrowing or being generous to shareholders.

The Retail Merchants Association of Canada had been complaining about big retailers since its formation in 1898. During the depression its message found a warm response from thousands of desperately hard-pressed small businessmen and one important politician, Harry H. Stevens, Minister of Trade and Commerce in the Bennett government. In 1934 Stevens launched an investigation of price spreads in Canadian distribution. It quickly turned into a well-publicized witch-hunt against department and chain stores, as well as manufacturers thought to have excessive market power. The investigation became a royal commission, and garnered national headlines with revelations of the lowest wages and longest hours worked by those supplying goods to the powerful retailers. Eaton's and Simpson's were the inquiry's special targets, but, with enthusiastic support and documentation from his friends at the Retail Merchants Association, Stevens gradually became a neo-populist crusader against all big business. When Bennett tried to reign him in for publishing wild, unfounded attacks on the management of Simpson's, Stevens resigned from the cabinet. He formed his own political group, the Reconstruction Party, to contest the 1935 election.

Stevens's movement went nowhere. His "party of shopkeepers," as Graham Spry called it, got more votes nationally than any other third party in 1935, but it elected only Stevens, who soon made his peace with the Conservatives and abandoned his followers. The Royal Commission on Price Spreads and the Reconstruction Party were widely misunderstood at the time and afterwards. Because Stevens and his supporters attacked big business, monopoly, and market power, they were often cheered on by anti-business populists, including many in the new socialist party, the Co-operative Commonwealth Federation (or CCF, formed in 1932). In fact, the Reconstructionists' aim was to limit competition in retailing. Stevens's real agenda was to implement the Retail Merchants' Association's program of retail price-fixing and destroy department and chain stores' main competitive advantage. The most important recommendations of the Royal Commission on Price Spreads were for the legalization of price-fixing agreements among retailers, the banning of loss-leader selling, and various other controls on "predatory" competition.

The Stevens' agitation was the visible tip of a huge iceberg of small business and not-so-small business collectivism in the 1930s. The desire to get together and fix prices to stop the downward spiral – to combine to cut the strings binding sellers to the invisible hand of the marketplace – was massive and politically potent, endorsed in one form or another by almost all boards of trade, chambers of commerce, and trade associations in the country. Nor was it limited to traditional businessmen. The same sentiments were very important among agricultural producers, whose normal position as atomized sellers of identical products on almost perfect markets represented an extreme of producer helplessness. Since the early 1920s many Canadian farmers had supported plans to increase their market control through pools, cooperative selling agencies, and what came to be called marketing boards. In many areas of agriculture, producers began dreaming of a time when some kind of association or board would market their beans or barley or butter at levels high enough to give them a reasonable return on cost, would limit entry to the business to those who would accept its prices, and, if necessary, would limit production to maintain the prices. Such boards could never work without support from government. In 1934 the Bennett government responded to the agrarian attack on competition with a sweeping Natural Products Marketing Act that permitted and enforced the cartelization through marketing boards of any primary industry whose producers so desired.

The movement for marketing boards was part of the general flight from laissez-faire. In every industry there were similar pressures for price-fixing tending to cartelization. The Americans presented a powerful model of how to "codify" industry when Franklin D. Roosevelt's administration sponsored the National Industrial Recovery Act of 1933, the first major New Deal legislation. The NIRA encouraged producers in all industries to draw up binding codes of "fair competition." The real aim was to fix prices, wages, hours of work, and other conditions under government supervision. This remarkable experiment in freezing enterprise had overtones of European "corporatist" doctrines, rooted in the old medieval guilds and very popular on the political right. But it also seemed to involve elements of planning, state control, and abandonment of laissez-faire favoured by the socialist left. The common enemy was unfettered free enterprise, which seemed to have led to price cuts, depression, unemployment, and disaster.

The NIRA experiment was already breaking down under competitive pressures when it was declared unconstitutional in 1935. It deeply influenced Canadians anyway. Bennett himself became a convert to collectivism when in l935 he went on radio to denounce laissez-faire capitalism and announce a broad range of reforms, some of which appeared to make him a prophet of the welfare state. Actually, much of the thrust of Bennett's surprising "New Deal" (how could a millionaire capitalist be denouncing capitalism? Was it a case of Satan denouncing sin?) followed from the Natural Products Marketing Act and the recommendations of the Price Spreads Commission. The aim was to spread controls on competition throughout Canadian economic life. It was a corporatist, business-generated approach to reform.

Bennett got most of his program into law before the electorate replaced him with the Mackenzie King Liberals (who had considerable support from those businessmen worried about the future of enterprise in a highly controlled economy). The Liberals and the courts threw out most of the legislation, including the NPMA and the legalization of price-fixing by trade associations. But small businessmen carried on their crusade at the provincial level with more lasting success. Many provinces introduced marketing boards in various agricultural sectors, particularly dairy products. Some passed legislation to enforce resale price maintenance, the small retailer's best hope of avoiding price competition. Most provinces passed industrial standards acts, allowing small businessmen to set up price, hour, and wage codes which had the force of law. Many of the smallest businessmen, such as barbers, bakers, automobile repairmen, garment-makers, and others, stabilized their industries locally and provincially under this legislation. Licensing laws governing taxicabs, peddling, and many other trades were manipulated to the same effect. Municipalities and provinces levied discriminatory taxes on chain stores.

On a national level many trade associations carried on restrictionist activities just within, or without, the provisions of the Combines Act. "The Canadian associations perform scarcely any of the service functions which characterize trade associations in the United States," Lloyd G. Reynolds observed in 1940. "General statistical services, institutional advertising, cooperative research, and the like are very rare. The activities of the Canadian association center upon the maintenance of 'fair prices' and it is judged largely by its success or failure in this field. One trade association secretary, indeed, remarked that 'manufacturers up here wouldn't be bothered with an association that couldn't control prices.'"

It was not just small businessmen who disliked competition. In many industries effective control was exercised by one or more producers whose market power tended to increase as the weakest went to the wall; and there were few new entrants in a stagnant decade. State support through the tariff remained a vital limit on competition in many areas of manufacturing. The depression did begin to drive significant chinks in the old National Policy armour though, as the King government signed a reciprocal trade agreement with the United States in 1935. This successful completion of negotiations begun by Bennett was the first major trade liberalization between the countries since 1854. It was extended in 1938.

The newsprint industry became a classic case of public and private conspiracy to limit competition. Private attempts to regulate production and prices were tried repeatedly from the collapse of 1927. Most of Canada's biggest businessmen – Herbert Holt, J.H. Gundy, Beatty, Flavelle, Gordon, and many others – were involved in one or more of the associations, agreeements, and mergers, even an attempt to use NIRA codes, trying to restore order to the over-expanded industry. All failed. With each failure there was more condemnation of the madness of continued cut-throat individualism by a few independent or renegade producers.

"I have made up my mind that it is about useless to negotiate further with the newsprint companies.... Legislation is necessary and it is our intention to take such means as we may think proper to save this basic industry of Canada," Quebec's Premier L.A. Taschereau said in 1935. He was criticizing not the price-fixers, but the price-cutters. His government believed that only concerted action in the industry could restore employment to the north and health to the provincial treasury. Ontario and the other producing provinces agreed. Despite qualms about Ottawa's combines law, Ontario and Quebec finally used their law-making power to stabilize the industry. From 1937 no company was allowed to over-produce or sell below an established price; the Newsprint Association of Canada policed the cartel.

Governments were always the key to eliminating cutthroat competition. To the critics of unrestrained capitalism newsprint seemed a classic case of over-production and waste. "There must be planning, order and co-operation in economic affairs between individuals, groups and nations," the businessman Francis Hankin concluded in his 1933 book on the Canadian economy, *Recovery by Control*, " or disaster will overtake us all." The book's dust jacket showed human hands taking over economic strings formerly pulled by the invisible hand of Adam Smith's markets.

Manipulating the money supply seemed an important, probably a more effective alternative to price-fixing as a weapon against depression. Easier money – that is, lower interest rates – seemed an obvious nostrum for hard times. Get money into people's hands and they would start spending again. They would bid up prices, and the economy would be stimulated. These were almost commonsense sentiments, felt most deeply by hard-pressed debtors (particularly in the West) and by those who had sampled the most recent economic writing, notably the ideas about contra-cyclical monetary and fiscal policy being advocated in England by John Maynard Keynes. Governments could and should fight the depression by appropriately stimulating the financial system.

Who managed Canada's money? Apparently the chartered banks did, not the government. After years of discussion dating from before the Great War, Canada still had no central bank – no Bank of England, no Federal Reserve System. Was this another example of lack of control, of more laissez-faire? The bankers denied that they controlled the monetary system, portraying themselves as passive reactors to the needs of the economy. Canada's financial system was always flexible, they maintained, and had become more so after the 1914 Finance Act permitted the Department of Finance to enlarge the Dominion note issue in times of heavy demand for money. To most bankers, the demand for money was the critical variable. When demand was high the money supply naturally expanded; if it was contracting now, the reason was the lack of demand from good-quality borrowers.

To their critics the bankers seemed obtuse, narrowly self-interested, or worse. The demand for easier money was clearly present and they were not meeting it, many felt. Others argued that demand obviously varied with interest rates, was inflated or deflated according to the decisions of the money lenders. When bankers made interest-rate decisions, outsiders charged, they were always and invariably looking to their own advantage, not to their customers' or to the public interest. Why, just look at the fact that the big banks were still making profits when most of Canada was destitute. How dare they claim to be simply serving the community!

In good times the banking system seemed to have worked fairly well. In this great depression the money question seemed too important to be left in the hands of a few bankers sitting around a table at the Canadian Bankers' Association. It was

time to socialize banking, if only in the sense of making the monetary system subject to social control. As part of his government's response to intense pressure for a
more interventionist monetary policy, Bennett appointed a Royal Commission on
Banking and Currency in 1933 to consider the central bank issue.

Most bankers – the Royal Bank was the notable exception – did not believe
Canada needed a central bank. The banks did not want to lose income by surrendering their remaining note-issuing rights. Otherwise, their concern was more
general and principled. Some of it was well founded and poorly understood by outsiders who should have known better. The bankers had a defensible case, for example, in arguing that the Finance Act already gave the Department of Finance
most of the power it needed to manage the money supply; and it had shown this
with a compulsory loan to the banks late in 1932 to ease the contraction of their
reserves. They were also accurate in suggesting that no amount of money supply
expansion, the need for which they deeply doubted, could raise the price of
Canada's exports, or restore the confidence of investors to whom such policies
were a red flag.

In a way these doubts were beside the point. Apart from technical questions of
the limits of the government's manipulative ability under the Finance Act, it was a
simple political necessity in the 1930s that Canada be seen to have a real central
bank, just like England and the United States. Most of the country's bankers made
a major political misjudgment in not understanding the symbolic importance of a
central bank, and in being unnecessarily worried about government involvement in
banking (at least at that time; in later decades their fears of the inflationary bias of
government control of banking proved largely correct). They were afraid that a
government-owned bank would be staffed by patronage appointees and its policies
would reflect the demands of ignorant pressure groups. "If we were to create a
central bank in Canada," argued the president of the Canadian Bankers' Association, "it would create extravagant expectations in the minds of a great many
people." Best to leave banking where it naturally belonged, in the hands of the
bankers who, the bankers felt, had kept their houses in pretty good order through
the depression, to the immense benefit of the Canadian people.

"It is desirable to establish a central bank in Canada to regulate credit and currency in the best interests of the economic life of the nation, to control and protect
the external value of the national monetary unit and to mitigate by its influence
fluctuations in the general level of production, trade, prices and employment, so far
as may be possible within the scope of monetary action, and generally to promote
the economic and financial welfare of the Dominion," read the preamble to the
Bank of Canada Act, passed in 1934 on the recommendation of the Royal Commission on Banking. The Bank of Canada opened its doors in March 1935, began
management of the nation's money supply, and gradually took over responsibility
for the banknote issue. It was initially privately owned (with strict limitations on
share ownership and a strong government presence) to calm bankers' anxiety about

patronage; but even after it was fully nationalized by the King Liberals, the Bank of Canada stayed out of the political muck. Its first governor, Graham Towers, and most of his staff came from the private sector; they were sensitive to the views of bankers, well-insulated from politicians, and rocked no boats. The main effect of the big banks' opposition to central banking in Canada was to strengthen an image of their reactionary ignorance in the public's mind, then and in most of the history books later, particularly those written by confident Keynesians.

The strongest hostility to banks and other financial institutions came in debtor areas of the country. By 1931 the problem was not so much the need for more loans, as the complete inability of debtors to carry their existing obligations. The collapse of agricultural prices meant a doubling or tripling of the real burden of farmers' debts, and a welling insistence that some kind of relief be given. To many agrarians, steeped in a tradition of hostility to bankers and their power, it seemed positively obscene that those big eastern institutions, with their palatial head offices, their plump, well-dressed directors, and their slick lobbyists, should still be paying dividends of 10 and 12 and 14 per cent when thousands of honest ordinary Canadians were sweating blood to pay off a few dollars each month on the money they owed – haunted always by the fear of losing everything if they missed a few payments.

The chartered banks were short on elementary public relations sense, long on uncomprehending arrogance. They should have changed their anachronistic capital and dividend bases, which rested on $100 par value shares that had not sold nearly that low for decades. They should have made well-publicized write-downs of their formal reserves to advertise their sufferings, instead of carrying bad debts or covering them from internal contingency funds. They should have trumpeted their very considerable willingness to accommodate needy debtors; they were in fact more liberal than most municipalities were to delinquent tax-payers. Instead, the big bankers preached sermons to Canadians on sound money, the soundness of the banks, and the unsoundness of all ideas other than those held by bankers. To do this was to be right but irrelevant. By 1932–33 one provincial government after another was considering debt adjustment legislation to protect the little man from his creditors.

Partly to head off worse legislation, the federal government tried a national solution by passing a Farmers' Creditors Arrangements Act in 1934, establishing machinery for negotiated relief. More than forty thousand adjustments were made with the banks alone, and many more with the trust and mortgage loan companies that held the bulk of farmer mortgages. Maximum interest charges of 7 per cent were also imposed on the chartered banks. Many lenders voluntarily waived or reduced interest payments or, like Imperial Oil, pegged repayment schedules to the price of wheat. Several provinces went ahead anyway with legislated or negotiated debt moratoria, adjustments, and outright cancellations. In 1936, for example, the premier of drought-stricken Saskatchewan negotiated an agreement with the Dominion Mortgage and Investment Association, representing the mortgage loan companies, that involved the cancellation of $75 million worth of interest arrears and obligations.

All this was peanuts compared to the revolutionary credit arrangements advocated by the premier of Alberta, William Aberhart. In 1935 Aberhart's Social Credit movement swept the province with its doctrine that "poverty in the midst of plenty" could be ended if only the credit system was rearranged in accordance with society's needs, as outlined in the writings of the Scottish engineer, Major C.H. Douglas. The Douglasites were soft-money enthusiasts whose easy answers appealed to frontier regions that had always needed cheap money. Their Canadian prophet, Aberhart, was a high school principal and fundamentalist preacher gifted at organizing and simplifying. He believed that government should simply take control of credit away from Canada's "fifty big shots," give social credit dividends of $25 a month to all Albertans, and pass legislation requiring financial institutions to cooperate. Then prosperity would return. It was all so easy, Aberhart argued. Look at how those bankers gave credit: just wrote out cheques, creating money with the stroke of a pen. Why couldn't governments do the same? In a way, of course, that seemed to be what Keynes and the other pump-primers were saying.

Once elected, Aberhart veered erratically between his instinctive small-c conservatism and the Social Credit orthodoxy he had instilled in so many of his followers (unlike the CCF, Social Credit had no quarrel with the existing social order; it was only the credit system that was screwed up). A backbenchers' revolt in 1937 forced him to experiment with social dividends by issuing special Alberta scrip and to pass draconian legislation against the banks. All Alberta bank branches would pay special taxes, all banks and bankers would be licensed, and each bank in Alberta would be controlled by a local board, three members of which would be appointed by the government. Canada's major chartered banks were close to withdrawing from the province of Alberta when Ottawa dusted off its constitutional power of disallowance and threw out the legislation as interference with federal control of banking and commerce. The Social Credit scrip scheme had already collapsed, for Albertans were not interested in paper that even the issuing government would not accept in payment of taxes.

Bankers' troubles with farmers were ironic inasmuch as they still did not make loans on real estate and held very few of the hundreds of millions of farm mortgages outstanding in Canada. So much the better for scapegoating: damn the banks for not giving credit; damn them for collecting when they did give credit; damn them when anyone tried to collect. When ordinary Canadians thought of moneylenders they naturally thought of bankers. Some Social Creditors thought of Jewish bankers, and the fringe of their movement was tainted with anti-semitism. The truth of the 1930s was that Canadian chartered banks were run by Scotsmen and were still commercially oriented, offering neither mortgages nor personal consumer loans. In the later years of the decade some of the more far-sighted bankers began to wonder about the future of their business because of the shrinking demand for commercial loans. In recent decades corporations had tended to finance operations out of retained earnings and go directly to the market with bond and stock issues. If that trend continued, the banks would have to find new customers.* One of the unfortunate consequences of the more radical debt-adjustment legislation of the depression was that it tended to sour the commercial banks on real-estate based farm credit as a new source of business.†

———————

Except for the province of Alberta, which unilaterally reduced the interest it paid on its bonds, governments were among the best sources of business in the depression. They usually paid their bills, they could get money from taxpayers when no one else seemed to have any, and they were interested in supporting projects that would put people back to work. Many businessmen, particularly in industries traditionally reliant on government contracts, saw higher public spending as the best, possibly the only, road to Canadian recovery.

Construction work, for example, which buoyed the whole economy through 1930, had almost completely shut down by 1933. With more than two-thirds of the industry's labour force laid off and important firms like Dominion Bridge or C.D. Howe and Company (specialists in building grain elevators) reduced to office staff and a few secretaries, construction men began lobbying government for more

* In 1939 the general manager of the Bank of Nova Scotia outlined the situation to the annual meeting: "The big corporation finds it easier to obtain capital on the market than the small concern. With the development of domestic facilities for corporate financing – stock exchanges, the bond market and investment banking houses – the large enterprise has been able to obtain a greater proportion of its total capital requirements on a long-term basis than was the case in pre-War days. Moreover, big companies in particular have often tended to plow in profits, and establish large reserves, thereby further lessening their need for bank loans. As industrial processes have been speeded up and transportation has become more rapid, requirements for working capital have been correspondingly reduced, while the declining cycle of commodity prices from 1920 to 1933 was working in the same direction. In addition, the banks have been faced with a certain amount of competition in the commercial lending field, largely of an indirect character. One aspect of this has been the financing of Canadian subsidiaries of American corporations through the parent company in the United States and another has been the development of finance companies which are now an important factor in the short-term lending field."
† The overall effect of agrarian unrest between the wars was to convince governments that the capital markets did not well serve the farmer. A host of programs was implemented, at the time and later, to try to remedy this proclaimed shortcoming of private enterprise. Since the pattern of agrarian grievance tended to be contradictory – too little credit one year, too much debt another – it was not an easy situation to remedy.

public works projects. The Canadian Construction Association and the National Construction Council of Canada urged deliberate use of public works projects for contra-cyclical purposes. Construction spokesmen were among the first to introduce Keynesian ideas into their arguments, and became enthusiastic supporters of the notion that government monetary and fiscal policies, properly applied, could get the economy moving again.

It was not just a matter of building post offices or lighthouses, though the more of these the better, but of encouraging the government to stimulate house-building through mortgage support. The financial sector also stood to benefit: government support for private lending in housing could mean highly secure business. The first Dominion Housing Act, passed in 1935, directly reflected this interest in pump-priming and was supported by the construction industry, building materials suppliers, and companies dealing in mortgage loans. "This legislation is designed to cast out fear on the part of those investment institutions [the life insurance companies]," the Finance Minister said in bringing in a 1938 Housing Act, "and to encourage them, as partners with the Parliament of Canada, to make advances." During a depression, when opportunities were so thin and risky, Parliament was not a bad partner.

Parliament's ability to create purchasing power made the idea of expanded social programs attractive to many businessmen as well. The decade-long debate on national unemployment insurance was complicated by immense jurisdictional problems and huge regional and industrial differences in the country, but few businessmen objected in principle to coverage based on the well-understood principles of insurance. There was natural resistance to paying someone else's insurance premiums, and some concern that unemployment insurance might entail a high moral hazard (encouraging unemployment, instead of helping reduce it). But there was also the appeal of unemployment insurance as universal protection against hard times. Insurance meant continued consumer purchasing, a kind of floor or bottom line on destitution. Unemployment insurance could be actuarially sound; but even if it, or other programs, had to be financed by government deficits in some years, that was no particular problem providing that – as Keynes and his followers always said – the deficits were balanced by surpluses in good years. Business had no ideological aversion to responsible deficit financing.

Arthur B. Purvis, the president of Canadian Industries Limited (CIL), who served a long business apprenticeship in Britain before coming to Canada, achieved a considerable reputation as an industrial statesman for supporting unemployment insurance and other activist reforms in the 1938 report of the federally appointed National Employment Commission, which he chaired. The NEC's recommendations were a consensus of the views of the first generation of Keynesian economists in the universities, advanced trade unionists (the president of the Trades and Labor Congress was vice-chairman), and reform-minded businessmen. Its report helped pave the way for the adoption of a Keynesian approach to economic policy during and after the war and in 1938 received almost universal support from boards of trade, chambers of commerce, and other business spokesmen. Hardly anyone supported the old, discredited ideas of laissez-faire.

A few businessmen disdained some of the new enthusiasms, particularly the more collectivist approaches to price control, planning, and state supervision of economic life. Rugged individualists and tough competitors wanted to get on with their business and be left alone, particularly by the state. A few bankers, and other students of economics, had their doubts about pump-priming and government spending. In the open Canadian economy, dependent on resource exports, it was hard to see how any government could spend its way to lasting recovery. All the pump-priming in the world was not going to raise the price of the wheat that Canadian farmers grew for export, or make Americans pay more for newsprint, or put base metal miners back to work, and so on. Eventually, it would raise taxes further. They had already been rising steadily through the 1930s at both federal and provincial levels to help offset substantial government deficits. The provinces were particularly inventive with their income and corporation levies. Now the tax system was becoming horribly complex and reasonably onerous. If the spenders were unleashed, where would it all end?

A few reflective businessmen of the old school wondered whether any of the reform proposals could really address the heart of the problem. Sir Joseph Flavelle, still active in his seventies and one of the country's most dedicated exponents of eonomic individualism, tried to articulate the view that Canadians were hostage to a combination of unalterable market forces and the consequences of their greed in good times. Little could be done about the depression because the effects of past policies (excessive borrowing, excessive railway building) had to work themselves out. Most attempts to frustrate the movements of markets were either doomed to Canute-like failure, or would produce harmful unintended consequences. About all that businessmen could do in the depression was return to the old verities of hard work, thrift, and more hard work. But even many businessmen ignored such views as reactionary or irrelevant.* Flavelle died in 1939. He was buried the same day as

---

* One of Flavelle's friends who did not was H.R. MacMillan, whose letters to Flavelle bristled with unapologetic individualism. In 1935 MacMillan fought the battle of his business life to survive against a manufacturers' combine, the newly formed Seaboard Lumber Sales Company Limited, with which he refused to negotiate a quota deal. It was said that MacMillan's opponents called him a "buccaneer" for refusing to cooperate. "Sure," he replied, "I sink them all."

Another British Columbian entrepreneur who pushed individualism toward its limits was young W.A. Cecil Bennett of Kelowna, who started out in the hardware business in 1930 and later advised that depressions were the best time to create new businesses ("things get better; you can only go up. The people who go bankrupt are the people who start their business in good times. They think there is no end"). Bennett fortified himself for the struggle by springing out of bed each morning and loudly reciting Edgar A. Guest's poem, "It Couldn't be Done" ("He started to sing as he tackled the thing / That couldn't be done, and he did it").

Sir Henry Pellatt, whose old castle had been seized by the City of Toronto in 1934 for non-payment of taxes and turned over to the Kinsmen Club to operate as a public attraction.

———◆———

Business turned to government by the end of the 1930s because it alone seemed able to create the only important investment frontiers to be found. The depression's central problem, surplus world capacity and declining trade, was aggravated in North America by a coincidental pause in economic development, a blip in the application of new technologies, which meant a temporary dearth of opportunities, a shortage of new industrial frontiers. Canada had been a land of several economic frontiers: the agricultural frontier in the prairie West, the pulp and paper and mining frontiers across the north, the electrical utility frontiers in cities and by falling waters, the automobile frontier as that transportation revolution sopped up entrepreneurial talent, capital, and employment. Now in the thirties, new frontiers – big new opportunities – were hard to find.

But there were a few.

The far northern mining frontier held up best of all. In the Northwest Territories the depression was hardly noticeable as the exploration boom of the late 1920s began paying off. In 1930 a veteran Canadian prospector, Gilbert LaBine, finally found his pots of ore at the east end of Great Bear Lake. He developed the strike through an old gold mining company, Eldorado, left over from the Manitoba boom. But the ore was quite different; it was pitchblende, used to produce the magic anti-cancer substance, radium. (It also contained uranium, at that time tossed aside as a useless by-product.) The 1932 rush to radium country on Great Bear Lake did not lead to any more discoveries, but a useful gold strike was made on the northern Saskatchewan border, where the town of Goldfields appeared, and by 1934 the northern prospectors had fastened on the north shore of Great Slave Lake as a promising gold camp. A little community called Yellowknife took shape as claims began to be turned into mines. By this time all the gold towns in Canada were prospering as never before, thanks to the pegging of gold at $35 an ounce.

Eldorado Gold Mines, the radium producer, was just about the best stock in Canada during the market collapse – it went from 18.5 cents in 1930 to $8.10 in 1933 – and the LaBine brothers made a wonderfully romantic mine at Port Radium in the subarctic, along with a refinery at Port Hope on Lake Ontario. But like many other developers they had over-estimated the wealth of their mine and under-estimated the world competition. Radium had the glamour, but Eldorado would have been better off in gold. In 1934 its shares were back at 86 cents.*

* Robert Bothwell nicely describes the company's development in his history, *Eldorado*: "Between 1932 and 1940 Eldorado Gold Mines Limited grew in virtually every respect. Its output soared. Its staff doubled, doubled again, and did not stop there. It excavated a mine,

The job of getting men and freight to remote mining frontiers kept Canada's newest transportation industry in reasonable health. Dozens of little companies were formed in the 1920s to fly pontoon or ski-equipped planes wherever anyone wanted in the north (the first scheduled flights, from Haileybury, Ontario, into the mining town of Rouyn, Quebec, in 1924, were offered by Laurentide Air Services Limited, an offshoot of the forest survey arm of Laurentide Pulp and Paper). The industry was still crowded in 1930, but a dominant firm had emerged under the leadership of the expansive grain merchant of Winnipeg, James A. Richardson. In 1926 Richardson founded Western Canada Airways Limited to fly into the mining camps of Manitoba and northwestern Ontario (and up to Great Bear Lake when Gilbert LaBine went prospecting there); four years later it was the strongest outfit, merging with several eastern companies to form Canadian Airways Limited. Richardson's junior partners in CAL were a couple of big transportation outfits looking to the future: the CPR (which had obtained legislative permission to get into aviation back in 1919) and the CNR.

Government airmail contracts were used in all countries as seed funding to stimulate inter-city air service. Canadian Airways' long-range hopes were dealt a heavy blow when the Bennett government's economy drive included slashing the airmail contracts in 1931 and ending them in 1932. The huge volume of bush work – more air freight was being carried in Canada in the 1930s than in the whole of the United States – kept the company, and several competitors, flying through the darkest years. One reason for hanging on, despite serious losses, was the certainty that there would eventually be some kind of trans-Canadian airmail, freight, and probably passenger service. When it came, CAL would be the logical company to do the job – to become, as one pilot put it, "the CPR of the air transportation business."

Automobile sales collapsed in the thirties and the manufacturers suffered through a decade of severe excess capacity. Despite the appearance of a few well-publicized horsedrawn automobiles or "Bennett buggies," the cars on the road were still being used and had an enormous appetite for gas, parts, repair services, road maps, and more. People who did not own cars increasingly travelled by bus. Established companies such as Imperial Oil dominated some aspects of the transportation business, but there were many openings. It happened that Charles Trudeau of Montreal decided to get out of the industry in 1932, selling his thirty Montreal gas stations and his service club, the Automobile Owners' Association,

---

built a refinery, and bought its own transportation company. Its owners, the brothers La-Bine, became legendary pioneers of science . . . . Shareholders were attracted by the bedazzlement of science, and by a sense of participating in and profiting by one of the wonders of the age. Again and again, Eldorado's shareholders were told that prosperity, and a dividend, were just around the corner. Again and again, however, prosperity and profits were postponed."

to Imperial for $1.4 million. He reinvested enough of that money in common stocks at the market's low to support his family for several generations. He also instilled in his oldest son, Pierre, the urge to excel, though not necessarily in business. In Valcourt, Quebec, Armand Bombardier's son stayed with him in their curious snow-machine business, which began to soar ahead in 1936–37 on sales to northern bush operations. Instead of truck or car bodies on skis and tracks, the Bombardiers now produced a distinctive, enclosed, multi-passenger, tracked vehicle and were beginning to manufacture it year-round with assembly-line methods.

In Bouctouche, New Brunswick, young Kenneth Colin Irving was well supported by his father, but decided to expand on the family enterprises, and in the early 1920s added a gas station and Model-T dealership to the Irving general store. To get supplies in competition with Imperial Oil, he founded his own Irving Oil Company. He began supplying oil to other dealers, and added more garages and car dealerships to his network. By the 1930s Irving was centred in Saint John, where his car dealership, Universal Sales Limited, became the nucleus for expansion into providing bus and truck services around New Brunswick. Throughout the 1930s Irving bought up failing bus and truck companies, collected franchises, and developed new routes. By mid-decade he was the largest bus and truck operator in the province. In an old cotton mill in Saint John the manufacturing division of Universal Sales made bus bodies to supply the company's future needs. Over in the Annapolis valley, across the Bay of Fundy, where the market for apples held up fairly well in the 1930s, Roy Jodrey made his comeback from disaster by creating a similar chain of gas stations, car dealerships, and bus lines, the United Service Corporation.

The brothers John and Alfred Billes of Toronto concentrated on getting tires, batteries, and other auto parts to the car owner as cheaply as possible. In 1927 their original garage and parts depot, founded in 1922, was incorporated as Canadian Tire Corporation, had a couple of branches in the city, and was about to publish its first catalogue. The Billeses emphasized cut prices, their own brands, and direct selling (by-passing local garages). Like many of the early garagemen and car dealers, they experimented with other lines, especially radios and electrical goods, and found they could sell these and many other outdoor products. In 1934 they began franchising their concept and products through an "associate" store in Hamilton. By 1939 there were seventy-one associated Canadian Tire stores. It was a classic story of low-cost, price-cutting chain development, the kind of entrepreneurialism many established businesses hoped to limit through price-fixing.

One Toronto parts dealer who had less luck in the 1920s was a barber's son who had taken a year of high school and a little bookkeeping and shorthand at a business college before setting out to make a million. When Roy and Carl Thomson's auto supply business went under in 1925, they started up again in

Ottawa, doing just well enough to clear their Toronto debts. But there wasn't a good living, let alone a million, in the business, so Roy decided to hustle auto parts, radios, and anything else he could sell in the boom towns of northern Ontario. He moved to North Bay, named his shop Modern Electric, and began selling. "Name's Thomson – Call me Roy," the smiling fat man with the shiny, patched pants would introduce himself, as he hustled his goods, sold himself, angled for this or that deal, kited cheques, and made contacts. Modern Electric went down in the depression, but in 1931 Thomson had finagled his way into a licence to operate a local radio station and acquired some broken-down transmitting equipment. CFCH, North Bay, went on the air that March with a full fifty watts of power.

Thomson's interest in broadcasting apparently developed from the need to create a market for the De Forest Crosley radios he was peddling. He became fascinated by the idea of selling advertising on radio, hustled to get licences for new stations in the prospering mining towns of Timmins and Kirkland Lake, then let the logic of selling advertising lead him into the newspaper business by buying a flea-bitten weekly, *The Timmins Press*, in 1934. Thomson was a cheerful, uncomplicated salesman, an unreflective Willy Loman, who dreamed of becoming rich and socially prominent and cared little about the content of his broadcasts or newspapers. By the end of the decade he had moved the headquarters of his little media empire to Toronto, wore hundred-dollar suits, and left day-to-day management to his flashy protégé, Jack Kent Cooke, a former toothpaste salesman. At forty-five Thomson still did not have the million he had planned to make by thirty, but he had not had a bad depression.

Nobody became rich or prominent in Canadian radio, particularly after the government closed off the possibility of privately owned networks. As Thomson learned, you could use radio transmitters to sell radio receivers (the Canadian Marconi Company claimed that its CFCF in Montreal had been the world's first broadcasting station back in 1919; the founder's purpose of the most prominent Toronto station was implicit in its initials: C-F-R[ogers]-B[atteryless]). The proprietors of established newspapers were the first to see radio's advertising potential, and spun off many of the early stations. All of them were small, under-powered, and barely profitable. In 1930 the only strong operator in the Canadian business was Henry Thornton's Canadian National Railways, which in an inspired act of entrepreneurial imagination had established a radio department to entertain passengers on long-distance journeys. By 1929 the CNR produced several hours of programming weekly on a makeshift national network.

The trouble with Canadian radio was American radio. Powerful American stations had always covered Canada more thoroughly than home-grown transmitters. With the creation of national radio networks by the end of the 1920s, the Americans began broadcasting hugely popular entertainments that no Canadian producer could possibly match. Canadian broadcasters like E.S. Rogers of Toronto's CFRB responded to the network challenge by getting on the bandwagon and becoming a CBS affiliate. This seemed the future of Canadian broadcasting: stations would tie in with the American system as thoroughly as cinema owners (another new group of entrepreneurs relatively untouched by the depression) had done, becoming purveyors of American-produced entertainment. It would be good business, giving the Canadian people what they seemed to want.

Many articulate Canadians wanted alternative broadcasting, some system that would use radio for educational, national, and other non-commercial purposes. An intense lobbying campaign, building on the recommendations of a royal commission, led to the Bennett government's decision in 1932 to establish a Canadian Radio Broadcasting Commission. The CRBC was given power both to regulate the private broadcasters and go into station ownership and programming in its own right. Before and after its creation a major national debate raged on the merits of private versus public broadcasting. The private interests won some battles (the original Aird Commission on broadcasting thought radio was a natural monopoly and wanted to ban private stations), but lost their war against a state-owned broadcasting system. The problem was to create a Canadian alternative to the U.S. networks. No private group had any practical suggestion. The CPR came closest, proposing to create a national radio network of its own, but admitted it would require programming subsidies. The CPR was no more likely to be given a radio network monopoly in Canada than the railway monopoly Beatty also sought.

The CRBC had a stormy, mixed career before being changed into the Canadian Broadcasting Corporation in 1936. The CBC continued to regulate the private sector as well as compete with it, a conflict of interest which caused endless conflict with the private stations, whose growth it was determined to inhibit. Like every private broadcaster, the CBC found it could only attract listeners by carrying American network programs, a practice that caused more complaints about the state system intruding on commercial radio. On the other hand, the CBC was a safety valve for nationalism in broadcasting. Its presence lessened pressure on the private stations to give Canadians programming that was good for them instead of the programs they wanted.

The strangest entrepreneurs in commercial radio in the late 1920s were probably the managers of the old Gooderham and Worts distillery in Toronto, a subsidiary of Hiram Walker, who owned the city's "Cheerio Station," CKG(ooderham)W(orts). It is said that they intended to develop radio as a medium for advertising their illicit products in the United States. But the need was fast disappearing as the Americans gave up on the prohibition experiment, and prepared for the restoration of King Alcohol. Who would supply the booze when America went wet again in 1933? With bigger game afoot, Gooderham and Worts left radio, leasing CKGW to the CRBC. It later became the network's Toronto flagship, CBL.

Both Harry Hatch at Hiram Walker's and the Bronfman brothers at Distillers-Seagram had large stocks of aged whisky in their Canadian warehouses when American prohibition ended. But high American whisky duties effectively stopped the Canadians from flooding the new market. The U.S. government also raised the embarrassing question of back taxes on the Canadian booze imported during prohibition, forcing the foreigners to pay substantial settlements – without admitting complicity in smuggling – before they could get into the country legally. The Canadians had money as well as whisky though, so in the depth of the Great Depression in 1933 we find Hiram Walker spending $5 million to build the world's largest distillery at Peoria, Illinois. Distillers-Seagram soon followed, moving into Louisville, Kentucky, and other American centres.

The Canadian firms were not among the first on the market in 1933. While hordes of American liquor companies fell into ruinous price wars trying to sell raw green whisky, the Canadians blended aged, imported liquor with newer stuff at their American plants, then came on the market with good, dependable brands of light-bodied rye and bourbon. The marketing strategy may have reflected the entrepreneurs' early experience in the selling rather than the distilling end of the business. It worked beautifully. The American taste for scotch, largely created during prohibition, also proved permanent and highly advantageous for the Canadian importers. The liquor business was huge and steadily growing, worth about $500 million annually in the United States by the end of the decade. Distillers-Seagram and Hiram Walker were two of the big four liquor producers in North America. Hiram Walker's earnings grew from $250,000 in 1932 to $6.3 million (on sales of about $67 million) in 1938. Both Canadian companies developed reputations as being exceptionally well managed.

The domestic market was almost insignificant to the big distilleries, but for the brewers it was all there was. It began to open up in the late 1920s as the Protestant provinces gradually legalized the sale of real beer, usually under continuing government control. Markets were still highly fragmented and local, with Ontario by far the most important. Molson's had an Ontario agency, which helped secure a satisfactory share of that business, but the family still concentrated on dominating their home base in Quebec. The company engineered a vital adjustment in its product in the early thirties after deciding to use its advertising agency, Cockfield Brown and Company, as merchandising experts; their surveys revealed that taste was moving toward lighter ales and lagers. It was still unusual for any Canadian firm, let alone an old family business, to solicit and act on the advice of management consultants, of whom there were still hardly any in Canada. Corporation lawyers and accounting firms and advertising agencies gave advice on the side. Breweries needed advice in all these areas because their industry was now so highly regulated. One of them is said to have hired an advertising agency for the first time precisely because the law prevented it from advertising.

Molson's main competition in Quebec came from National Breweries, a widely held corporation created out of fourteen small breweries in the 1909 merger wave. Twenty years later, Edward Plunkett Taylor of Ottawa set out to create Ontario's equivalent of National Breweries. Born in 1901, Eddie Taylor was a

McGill-trained engineer, like his father, and after graduation followed his father into the securities business with McLeod Young Weir. Taylor found he had a knack for promoting companies, cutting his teeth on local bus and taxi firms, and then moving to Toronto to do bigger deals. He was a director of Ottawa's Brading Brewery, in which the family had a major holding on his mother's side; when sales of beer became legal in Ontario he became an ardent expansionist. Taylor's was the classic merger strategy: buy up a lot of little breweries, close the smaller, less efficient ones, consolidate marketing and other functions, and grow big enough to be the price leader in a not-very-competitive industry.

The buying binge began in 1930 under the umbrella of the Brewing Corporation of Ontario, soon to be reorganized as the Brewing Corporation of Canada Limited and in 1937 as Canadian Breweries Limited. Taylor paid for his acquisitions with common stock, notes, and, when absolutely necessary, cash supplied by a group of British investors. His methods were rough, capitalism at its most predatory. In 1931, for example, Taylor wrote to J.F. Cosgrave, president of the next company on his list, as follows:

> The cost of production and financial position of Brewing Corporation of Canada Limited are now such that it could meet a price war at any time and outlive practically all but a very few competitors. It could afford to sell its products at a price for a year which would either cause the failure or seriously cripple all but a very few of its competitiors in the province of Ontario. We believe that the time has now come when it will be in your best interests to seriously consider a proposal involving the exchange of the shares of your company for preferred and common shares of our company on an equity basis.

By some measurements, Brewing Corporation's growth was spectacular. In less than a decade Taylor absorbed sixteen Ontario breweries. His most important acquisitions were Kuntz of Waterloo, Carling of London, and the O'Keefe Brewery of Toronto. (Several soft drink companies were also acquired with their alcoholic parents; they included the Canadian branch of Orange Crush, which owned the Honey Dew chain of restaurants.) The expressed aim was to get 60 per cent of the Ontario business and by 1939 Canadian Breweries had acquired about that percentage of Ontario's brewing capacity. But sales were disappointing, stuck at a 30 to 40 per cent market share. Taylor's problem in his thrust for oligopoly was that his high acquisition costs and his surplus capacity made Canadian Breweries one of the least efficient producers in the shrinking industry. It did not turn its first profit until 1935.

The real beneficiary of E.P. Taylor's rationalization of the brewing industry was Labatt's, a tightly run firm (after the prohibition managers were replaced) producing at full capacity, with higher profit margins than CBL at any given price, and active in all forms of non-price competition. During the depression Labatt's saw its market share double, from about 15 to 30 per cent. Its net profits in the later years of the 1930s were three to ten times higher than Canadian Breweries'. The fact that beer sales in Ontario were closely regulated by the provincial government meant that competition between the big breweries never became too fierce. The Labatt family's only setback in the depression was the spectacular 1934 kidnapping of John S. Labatt, one of the heirs, by a gang of former bootleggers trying a new line of work. He was released unharmed.

Although E.P. Taylor's beer strategy was only partly successful, he won a considerable reputation in business-political circles as a young go-getter, ready to tackle any deal. Both his reputation and his ambition were evident in the scheme he, Harry Gundy, and other Torontonians concocted in 1936 to get the contract for a national airline service that Ottawa was about to let. Taylor was president of British North American Airways Limited, and his directors were drawn from the top ranks of Toronto business. They owned no airplanes and had never run an airline, but had good financial and excellent political connections with the Mackenzie King Liberal government. Their competition for the contract, of course, was Richardson's Canadian Airways Limited.

The Taylor-Gundy group were little more than promoters, much like the Toronto kibitzers who tried to stop the letting of the CPR contract in 1881. CAL was a proven aviation firm, which had flown mail and passengers in all parts of Canada and had pioneered in bush flying across the north. Aviation was not like radio. There was no need for governments to undertake a national service that private enterprise could not fill. Subsidies would be needed for a few years, but otherwise the carrier was at hand. Richardson's company was the equivalent of the CPR syndicate of the 1880s.

It did not become the CPR of Canadian aviation. Mackenzie King's Minister of Transport, in charge of getting a national airline off the ground, was Clarence Decatur Howe, an American-born engineer who had come to Canada to teach his specialty at Dalhousie University, drifted into consulting work, and then had a twenty-year career in the highly political business of grain elevator construction. When work disappeared in the depression, Howe considered starting again in Argentina, but instead succumbed to a proposal that he run as the Liberal candidate for Port Arthur in the 1935 election. In 1935 government service was an attractive alternative to a private sector that did not offer many opportunities for Howe's talents. Immediately on his election, Howe was taken into the cabinet.

As he laid plans for a national airline, Howe found the lobbying of the private companies bothersome. He preferred to learn about the business from the established operators in the United States, and basked in the glamour of America's commercial aviation pioneers. The government decided that Canada's national airline would be a new company, owned jointly by the railways and the public, with some provision for private shareholders. A reorganized CAL, already partly owned by the railways, was still the logical vehicle. But negotiations collapsed when Howe would not give the CPR protection in its minority role in the enterprise* or give CAL a role in the management of the new airline. Trans-Canada Airlines was to be an entirely new enterprise, wholly owned by the CNR, staffed by American aviation men chosen by C.D. Howe. Canadian expertise and experience was ignored by a minister who had become fascinated with both aviation and the exercise of power, who would treat the national airline, in his biographers' words, as "his favourite toy and chiefest concern."

Richardson and Beatty were outraged at what even senior Liberals considered a "breach of faith" on Howe's part. They were further offended by such stunting as Howe's dawn-to-dusk flight from Montreal to Vancouver on July 30, 1937, a media-distracting substitute for his failure to have met the deadline to begin the regular long-distance air service. Who was C.D. Howe anyway? Did he represent business in government? Not really. He was a highly political contractor from the Lakehead, who liked the exercise of power. "Howe's sudden acquisition of cabinet rank and power has gone to his head," the president of Canada's greatest corporation, the CPR, wrote Richardson. "He is not able to deal with ordinary individuals except on the basis of a superior being dealing with inferiors. However, he has undoubtedly been getting the breaks in many ways and as long as his luck holds out, we need not expect much change in him."

Howe's luck did hold, but there was more to his success than chance. By choosing to switch sectors in the middle of the depression – from private business to politics and government – C.D. Howe moved from the sidelines to centre court for the next several decades of Canadian development. The depression and the war shifted the focus of Canadian development from the private to the public spheres, and Howe had shifted too. He thereby established himself in the right place at the right time to become the most important public entrepreneur in Canadian history.

* Beatty and Howe clashed on the proportions of directors to be drawn from the various interests, with Beatty complaining that CNR-appointed directors were effectively government appointees. In an important letter of March 15, 1937, Howe sharply challenged Beatty's view of the CNR, writing that "the Government maintains only one very slight contact with the railway . . . it docs not undertake to direct the policies of management." Six weeks later Howe attended a CNR board meeting to (a) suggest that the CNR subscribe for all of the Trans-Canada Airlines shares; (b) announce that his department had already ordered planes for the new airline. A few weeks later he told the first TCA board meeting that he had a candidate in mind to head the airline. Howe's candidate got the job. Throughout his career Howe paid no attention to the formal independence of either the CNR or TCA.

TOP: **C.D. Howe receiving the 100 millionth projectile, a 25-pounder shell** *(Public Archives of Canada, #C7487)* ABOVE: **E.P. Taylor with his products** *(Herb Nott)*

16

Visible Hand:
The Years of C.D. Howe

*The Howe mystique . . . making war . . . controllers . . . "standing in the
need of prayer" . . . depreciation and taxes . . . dollar-a-year men . . .
business supports Keynes . . . "profit" a dirty word . . . decontrol . . . limited
free enterprise . . . flying into the future: Canadair, Avro, TCA,
CP Air . . . Canada's resource boom . . . iron, uranium, oil, heroic
engineers . . . Newfoundland . . . the Argus saga . . . "tycoon
Taylor" . . . Lord Thomson of Toronto . . . "C.D." and the personalization
of power . . . the pipeline debate . . . the Avro Arrow, a horrible
mistake . . . new myths*

The worst political crisis of C.D. Howe's career came in the autumn of 1940. In April of that year, as Nazi forces rolled across Europe, Howe was appointed Minister of Munitions and Supply, a new department designed to give Ottawa control of the commanding heights of the war economy. His mandate was to produce instruments of war. He went about it with apparently limitless energy – bringing in hordes of "dollar-a-year" men from private industry to help him, spinning them out as controllers and purchasers with unlimited powers to break the bottlenecks and delays of free enterprise, scattering war orders faster than anyone could count, buying, building, requisitioning factories for crown enterprises, and paying almost no attention to the cost of it all. "Hell, who's paying for anything these days?" he quipped.

The Minister of Finance, who did have to pay, was increasingly unimpressed by energy without accountability. Several of Howe's cabinet colleagues and many outsiders shared a concern that Munitions and Supply was out of control – disorganized, inefficient, wasteful, failing in its mandate. Partly to put the brakes on Howe, cabinet appointed a Wartime Requirements Board, headed by the outstanding industrialist H.R. MacMillan, to study the situation. MacMillan's analysis supported a view that the Canadian war effort needed an "industrial statesman" to clear up the mess, an industrial czar from the private sector who would function like J.W. Flavelle at the Imperial Munitions Board in the Great War. The logical man for the job, many felt (particularly the *Financial Post*, which was very critical of Howe) was Mac-Millan himself.

Howe was a tough man to bring down. He survived the torpedoing of the *Western Prince* carrying him to Britain in December, and then came back to Canada and fought off the MacMillan challenge. "You want my job, and I'm not ready to turn it over to you yet," he told the timber baron to his face. In the House of Commons he dismissed the *Financial Post'* s complaints, calling the newspaper (edited by Floyd Chalmers) "the number one saboteur in Canada since the beginning of the war." Munitions and Supply was reorganized to take account of some of the criticisms, and MacMillan was edged away into shipbuilding. By the end of 1941 the frantic organizing of 1940 was beginning to show results in busy factories, a mammoth and fairly smoothly running Munitions and Supply organization in Ottawa, and growing quantities of shells, guns, airframes, and other war materials to help the Allied effort. In the face of results, the grumbling about C.D. Howe subsided.

As the war went on, the results seemed more and more impressive and the minister's reputation as the man who organized Canada's war effort grew. Lord Beaverbrook, for example, called Howe "one of a handful of men of whom it can be said, 'But for him the war would have been lost.'" Howe's next job was to organize Canada for peace, as Minister of Reconstruction and Supply, then to expand Canada's economy as Minister of Trade and Commerce, and finally, as a result of the Korean War crisis of the early 1950s, to reorganize for war again as Minister of Defence Production. Howe seemed to be "Minister of Everything." He exercised more influence over Canadian economic development and Canadian business life than any politician or businessman in Canadian history. By the end of his career – he lost his seat in the 1957 election – Howe and his achievements had become legendary.

He was seen not just as the father of the Canadian war effort, but as the builder of modern Canada. C.D. and his boys had taken an underdeveloped, depressed country, and engineered an industrial revolution. After the war the dollar-a-year men had seized the commanding heights of the Canadian economy, and, in partnership with their leader in Ottawa, guided the young industrial giant through a generation of peace, prosperity, and handsome profits. The age of Howe seemed a golden age of business-government relations, when there was a real businessman with real power in Ottawa, a businessman who knew what Canada needed. Long before C.D. Howe died in 1960, even H.R. MacMillan hailed him as "the greatest organizer Canada has ever seen." Then his ghost haunted business and government for decades:

businessmen yearned for a reincarnation of Howe; politicians used the Howe legend, liberally spiced with bastard Keynesianism, to justify incursion after incursion into economic management.

Much of the Howe mystique was mythical. As an organizer he almost certainly was not indispensable to the war effort (Beaverbrook's comment reflected his estimate of his own contribution to the British war effort). Several others could have done Howe's job with about the same results, perhaps better. The real flaws in the ministerial and government's performance that caused so much criticism in 1940 were buried in the avalanche of war materials, covered with rationalizations about "cutting red tape" and the alleged failures of the private sector, and interred for decades by the wonderful Allied victory. Other Howe mistakes, misjudgments, and misuses of power were similarly obscured in the golden glow of postwar prosperity. The extent to which Howe's management methods were highly personal and highly political, to a degree questionable in his own time and intolerable a generation later, was seldom recognized.

Just as the minister's personal achievement was almost certainly exaggerated, so was the performance and potential of the Canadian economy in the Howe years. Canadians were carried away by their apparent wartime success and their real postwar resource boom. They came to believe in the Howe myth – that one man could work national industrial miracles. They believed in the Keynesian economic myths – that perpetual prosperity was mostly a matter of finding the right blend of government fiscal and monetary policy. Above all, they believed in the Canada myth – that the northern industrial giant, so wonderfully endowed with resources of all kinds, was growing up in the twentieth century to be the wonder of the economic world. Lucky country to have an organizer like Howe. Lucky Howe to have found a land like Canada, bursting with opportunities that only awaited his fine organizing hand.

I T IS OBVIOUS THAT in Canadian business history the years "Before C.D." were not totally dark. Canada's basic industrial plant was in place when war began in 1939. The steel mills and power stations, aluminum and chemical plants, textile mills and foundries and auto and implement factories that provided the bulk of the nation's war production had been created in a long developmental process extending over eight decades. They did not spring full-grown from the desks of bureaucrats in Munitions and Supply. Nor did the leading bureaucrats themselves, Howe's dollar-a-year men, leap from kindergarten to industrial statesmanship under his tutelage. Most were seasoned industrial veterans, already at or near the top of the executive ladder, whose careers would probably have been much the same if the war had never occurred. The idea that most of these men got their start or learned their skills in C.D.'s Ottawa is almost exactly wrong. It was C.D. and Ottawa who learned from them.

The war effort is often exaggerated in Canadian memory because it was such a radical change from the Great Depression. The war seemed to end the depression with its grey, aching unemployment, its insecurity, and its national drift. War brought full employment, fat pay cheques, busy-ness everywhere, a sense of national purpose – and for Canadian industry a huge surge of capital investment. And there was no depression after the war, only growth, growth, and more growth. So the war was the turning point, the birth of a new age for Canada. All the past could fade into memory as prologue, the dark years Before C.D. took everything in hand and the real boom began.

In fact the depression was gradually ending anyway. If Canadians had not had to make shells, tanks, and fighter planes in the early 1940s, many of them would have prospered making electric irons and washing machines, television sets, automobiles, and airplanes for civil aviation. The recovery would have been slower, and full employment much less likely. But war work for all was a long way from economic utopia. Canada's wartime "full employment" included the stationing of more than a million men and women in low-paying, numbingly tedious, and tragically hazardous jobs in the armed forces. To sustain the war economy and divert resources to war, extremely heavy taxes were levied and elaborate controls limited civilian purchasing power. More pay went in taxes and forced loans to the government than ever before; the remainder could not be spent on luxury goods because they were not available. The corollary of jobs for all in a war economy was sacrifice by all. Many more Canadians worked during the war than in the 1930s, and they worked longer and harder. But because so much of their production was used for battle, consumers' total disposable income did not rise from Depression levels. In the mid-1930s Windsor did not make many automobiles because so few could afford new ones. In the mid-years of the war it did not make *any* automobiles because it was directed to make troop-carriers instead. In either case the civilian did without a new car. In the war he could not get new tires or unrationed gasoline either.

The raw success of the wartime economic effort is undeniable. Canada's gross national product increased from $5.6 billion in l939 to $11.9 billion in 1945. The production of war materials totalled almost $10 billion. Among the allied countries, Canada was the fourth most important supplier. Its automobile factories turned out more than 800,000 transport vehicles, more than 50,000 armoured fighting vehicles. The most spectacular growth was in aircraft manufacture. In 1939 Canada's eight small aircraft plants employed 4,000 and produced about 40 airplanes a year in 500,000 square feet of factory space. In 1944 there were 116,000 employees in Canada's aircraft industry, which assembled more than 4,000 airplanes in 15 million square feet of plant. By the end of 1945 Canada had delivered 16,418 military aircraft. Statistics like these caused the Munitions and

Supply people themselves to believe the myth of wartime industrialization. Howe wrote in the foreword to the department's *History* that these had been "the years during which the country emerged from its position as a producer of basic supplies to that of a highly industrialized state."

A much larger percentage of GNP was devoted to making war in 1939–45 than in 1914–18, but with less damaging results on the home front. Inflation, the scourge of the Great War and its aftermath, was held to a minimum by a combination of high taxes and, after 1941, tight wage and price controls. During six years of war the consumer price index increased by a total of only 20.6 per cent, with most of the increase coming before the controllers got tough. Other government policies minimized inequalities, kept labour unrest to a minimum, and paved the way for a smooth transition to peacetime. Altogether a job well done by the government of Canada. Historians have traditionally applauded the Mackenzie King administration of the war years for having operated at an unusually high level of managerial competence.

The gross figures and the apparent magnitude and ease of the achievement were misleading. A country that was building tanks and destroyers and bombers and radar and advanced optics, that had created an important synthetic rubber plant, that had special crown corporations devoted to advanced research, and was refining uranium and pondering the development of nuclear energy, seemed to have made great strides toward industrial self-sufficiency. Canada had leaped onto the frontier of advanced technology. "Never again," Howe himself boasted in 1943, "will there be any doubt that Canada can manufacture anything that can be manufactured elsewhere."

This was not true. Canada's war effort caused the economy to surge forward along fairly traditional lines. It was primarily a raw materials producer (particularly a supplier of foodstuffs), and a manufacturer of small ships, ammunition, and small arms to British and American specifications. The main vehicular production was the assembly of motorized transport in the Canadian branches of General Motors, Ford, and Chrysler. Capacity existed in these plants because Canada was actually doing so little in the way of tank manufacture. The airframe factories were gigantic by prewar Canadian standards, ordinary by British or American (fifteen million square feet was not a huge amount of factory space), and there were many disappointing production delays, few of which were discussed in Parliament or described in official histories. After the foreign-designed Mosquitos and Lancasters and Hell Divers and M-4 tanks were assembled (and the Canadian-designed Ram tank, which was not deemed acceptable for combat), their imported engines were installed.

Great strides in engineering and technological sophistication did occur in Canadian industry as a result of the intensity of the effort, the willingness of government to help, and the pace of wartime technological change. These were matched in all other countries producing war goods. By learning how to run very quickly – a feat that astonished many Canadians, and often caused those who did it to sweat blood in the attempt and then feel justifiably proud of their achievement – Canada managed almost to keep up with Great Britain and the United States. It was true that by 1945 Canadian manufacturers had gained significant medium-term competitive advantage over formerly advanced producers in countries like Germany and Japan, whose factories had been bombed to rubble.

Wartime conditions could not be easily or desirably duplicated in peacetime. Most of the government's control programs were temporary, patchwork arrangements held together only by the glues of patriotism and the War Measures Act, adhesives that would both dissolve with the peace. Price control, administered by the Wartime Prices and Trade Board, was particularly fragile. The basic device was an attempt to freeze prices for the duration of the war at levels in effect in September and October 1941. It was soon realized that there were too many prices (hundreds of thousands in an economy which, by today's standards, was still fairly simple), too many levels, too many buyers and sellers, for the freeze to hold without all kinds of shaving and trimming and exhortation and exceptions. Manufacturers who were caught with raw material price increases they could not pass on simply cut back on quality, sometimes literally degrading their products. Retailers in the same boat cut back on service (no more home delivery, much more self-service, less credit). Primary producers whose 1941 prices were uneconomically low insisted on and got increases, sometimes through subsidies. Workers used strike threats to get wage increases.

For four years the WPTB, headed by a former banker, Donald Gordon, fought a complex and gradually losing holding action, offering subsidies here, rationing schemes there, exemptions somewhere else, hiring bureaucrats by the hundred to help plug leaks, running massive propaganda campaigns to increase compliance. Price control succeeded, more or less, because most citizens, including businessmen, voluntarily accepted the controls and because the war ended. Had it not ended in 1945, the sweeping control structure could not have been maintained much longer. Donald Gordon liked to settle down at night with his bottle of scotch, his accordion, and what he called the price board hymn: "It's me, it's me, O Lord, standin' in the need of prayer'." Talk of making wartime price control a permanent fixture in peace horrified most of the controllers, let alone the controlled.

Special methods were necessary to deflect Canadian industry abruptly into war work. The government minimized the risks of war production by offering loans, grants, and, most important, tax write-offs. Special capital cost allowances, also known as accelerated depreciation, gave producers a strong incentive to make investments for which there might be little need after the war. The idea of using the tax system this way originated in the 1939 budget as an early Keynesian pump-priming measure (give fast write-offs this year and you stimulate business spending, the economists thought; it never worked that quickly), and was then greatly extended to meet the needs of Munitions and Supply. Firms undertaking war contracts could be granted special depreciation rates by the War Contracts Depreciation Board, which offered a friendly forum ("the hearing consists of an informal round table discussion with the applicant as to his business problems, and as to the measure of relief to which he is entitled") and fairly generous relief. Through it and through other special arrangements, some negotiated directly with the minister and cabinet, more than one billion dollars' worth of extra depreciation was granted to encourage war work.

Some firms benefited spectacularly from the depreciation allowances. The Aluminum Company of Canada (which by 1945 was producing more aluminum than the whole world had used in 1938) was allowed instantly to write off $155 million of the $237 million spent enlarging its plant in Quebec, most of which went into the giant Shipshaw power development. Algoma Steel, the personal empire of the old financier Sir James Dunn, was fully modernized and expanded, receiving more than $20 million in capital assistance from the government, more than the other steel mills combined. Many other industrialists emerged from the war with enlarged, modern facilities fully paid for from untaxed proceeds of war work.

But their pay-off on that investment was still in the future, if it came at all. Accelerated depreciation only postponed tax liability. More important, during the war both the government as a matter of policy and Howe as a matter of personal principle worked hard to avoid profiteering scandals. The excess profits tax, imposed in 1939, used the previous four years as the profit norm, and by 1942 was creaming off 100 per cent of earnings above the 1936–39 average. The Department of Munitions and Supply tried to price its contracts to allow a profit of less than 5 per cent on costs. When it became apparent that falling costs gave contractors much higher returns, one of Howe's men was delegated to recapture the public's money, and the contracting system was reorganized and tightened.

There was a certain amount of business bitching about the EPT's effect in destroying what the *Financial Post* called the "basic human incentive to increased activity – the psychological vitamin of profit," and much use of accountants and lawyers to minimize tax liability (the Canadian Tax Foundation grew out of the wartime tax muddle). As with price control and the supply contracts, the excess profits taxes created so many complexities and inequities that the Minister of National Revenue had to create an independent board of referees to handle specific problems. It eventually processed thousands of claims, giving fairly generous relief, almost always on the reasonable ground that the depression years, 1936–39, were not a fair norm for profits.

The new taxes caused a few businessmen to pad their deductible expenses, but the general effect of the war situation was to encourage efficiency. With prices immobile and labour scarce, firms necessarily became cost-conscious, sharpening their accounting controls, improving managerial practices. There was a marked increase in the use of managerial consultants and schemes to improve worker productivity; often the government supplied both experts and exhortations to its contractors. There was a marked improvement in productivity in such labour-starved service industries as banking and life insurance, with much more use of office machinery, rationalization of jobs, and use of female workers. A few old-fashioned entrepeneurs – H.R. MacMillan was one – even found that the despised red tape of Ottawa bureaucracy had its good points. "On his return," an employee reminisced, "he was highly critical of the way HRMCo. did business and everybody was put to work making up organizational charts and setting out clearly areas of responsibility."

Most wartime controls and incentives and taxes were imposed as a temporary alternative to the free market system. The needs of war seemed to be too urgent to wait upon the sometimes cumbersome effects of relying on, say, tenders for munitions, or price signals to do the job of allocating the flow of materials, currency, or labour. The invisible hand of the market had to be replaced by visible hands, acting quickly and decisively.* Decisions made by impersonal market mechanisms were now made in person by controllers, regulators, trouble-shooters, civil servants, and their ministers, especially C.D. Howe. When the Minister of Munitions and Supply needed action, he still turned to the private sector because that was where the business expertise was. But to get fast action he cut through all the barriers separating the public from the private sector – creating new crown corporations, for example, when private firms were not immediately at hand for strategic purposes, and bringing private businessmen directly into government to run them.

Dollar-a-year wartime service in Ottawa could mean almost anything: one meeting of a volunteer fund-raising board; monthly consultations with civil servants about the state of an industry; a few months' hard work helping organize a new control program; years of eighteen-hour days as steel controller, oil controller, director of shipbuilding. Only a few prominent executives served for the duration. Wallace Campbell, president of Ford of Canada, was one of the first to come to Ottawa (in 1939, as head of the War Supply Board), and one of the first to leave, pushed aside by Howe after disregarding the political conventions and compromises governing the early semi-mobilization. James Duncan, vice-

---

* Such, at least, was the view of most war organizers, and has been the conventional verdict of history. Recently Joseph Lindsey has argued in his doctoral thesis that Howe had to do so much in 1940 partly because the government had so thoroughly bungled its war production planning in 1939. With more carefully thought-out and coherent use of carrot-and-stick incentives – i.e., more market-oriented planning – the government could possibly have achieved smoother, less disruptive and chaotic mobilization.

president and general manager of Massey-Harris, dropped everything in the 1940 crisis to serve a six-month stint as Deputy Minister of Defence for Air, setting up the British Commonwealth Air Training Plan. He then refused the offer of a safe seat in the House of Commons and a cabinet position (in which he would have instantly eclipsed Howe as a business spokesman) and went back to Toronto to assume Massey-Harris's presidency.

H.R. MacMillan, who made his peace with Howe and served for almost four years, brought Harry Carmichael, a vice-president of General Motors, to Ottawa for the Wartime Requirements Board and then levered him into the key position of production manager in Munitions and Supply. Carmichael became Howe's invaluable right-hand man and stayed for the duration. Prominent lawyers (Henry Borden), accountants (Gordon Scott), and engineers (R.A.C. Henry) also served on the team. Arthur Purvis of CIL, already noted for his public service in peacetime, was appointed head of Britain's North American supply organization, and was another industrialist who conceivably could have become more powerful than C.D. Howe. He died in a plane crash in 1941. No one actually was paid a dollar a year (the term was drawn from American practice in the Great War). Most of the businessmen who took full-time government jobs were paid for their efforts at the going rate; many of the volunteers on short stints continued to be paid by their companies.

E.P. Taylor was one of the fastest-moving of the dollar-a-year men, partly because the skills he brought to Ottawa were only suitable for certain kinds of service. After a surprise invitation from Howe over lunch at the Rideau Club to join Munitions and Supply, Taylor first served on its executive committee with almost complete free rein. His freewheeling approach to letting war contracts was one of the items in outsiders' indictment of the ministry in its early days. As it settled down into an administrative arm of government Taylor became something of an embarrassment. Howe gave him renewed scope for deal-making by appointing him head of War Supplies Limited, a crown corporation soliciting war orders in the United States. "Taylor positively thrived in the Byzantine atmosphere of wartime Washington," Howe's biographers write, "where achievement depended on putting together bizarre coalitions of antagonistic personalities and competing agencies." He attracted the attention of the most Byzantine of all Canadian entrepreneurs, Lord Beaverbrook, then serving as Britain's Minister of Aircraft Production; with Beaverbrook's help Taylor succeeded Purvis as president of the British Supply Council, placing war orders in North America. After a second year's frantic activity, Taylor left the service in the summer of 1942 to tend his private business affairs and position himself for postwar growth. Many other businessmen returned to private life at about the same time, feeling they had accomplished the job of getting the war organizations in place. As agencies settled into bureaucratic routine, there was neither need nor room for strong-minded, fast-moving entrepreneurs.

As soon as they knew the war would be won, Canadians began to worry about the postwar economic world. Would there be a hectic inflation followed by collapse, as in 1919–21, then by years of over-capacity? Would there be a gradual slide back into the stagnation and unemployment of the 1930s? How quickly would wartime controls and restrictions be abolished? Should they be abolished, if there was going to be trouble ahead? No one wanted to see anything like a return to the economic life of the depression. Everyone dreaded the possibility. Almost everyone, including many businessmen, supported the notion that government must now provide much more leadership in the management of the economy than it had in the days before central banking, Keynes' *The General Theory of Employment, Interest and Money*, and the apparent success of the wartime command economy. If nothing else, the wartime popularity of the socialist party, the CCF (in one of the early Gallup polls, taken in September 1943, the CCF narrowly led both Liberals and Conservatives; in 1944 it formed the government of Saskatchewan), demonstrated that ordinary Canadians also favoured a greater government role in the future. Government should intervene to protect Canadians from the worst consequences of the old free market system.

Mackenzie King's government was committed to unprecedented levels of state involvement in the economic order. In 1940 it had introduced a program of national unemployment insurance. In 1944 it threw the weight of government behind unions' thrust for collective bargaining, making it much easier for them to gain recognition and a place at the bargaining table. New programs that year ranged from the introduction of family allowances through loans to small business, export credit insurance, more aid to housing, and the creation of a new Department of Reconstruction under C.D. Howe. It was Howe himself who in 1945 presented to Parliament the government's landmark *White Paper on Employment and Income*, spelling out a commitment to Keynesian contra-cyclical budgeting. The new role of Canada's national government, another state paper announced, was to

> budget for the [business] cycle rather than for one fiscal year.... the Government will design both its spending policies and its tax policies throughout the cycle to levelling out the deflationary valleys and inflationary peaks. The growth in government revenues and expenditures made necessary by the war makes a responsible policy of this sort an obligation, and at the same time, with our increased knowledge of fiscal techniques, makes it a practical policy in the sense that it can have a really significant effect on the business cycle. The modern governmental budget must be the balance wheel of the economy; its very size to-day is such that if it were allowed to fluctuate up and down *with* the rest of the economy instead of deliberately *counter* to the business swings it would so exaggerate booms and depression as to be disastrous.

Business generally supported the new view of government's role, which seemed like little more than applied common sense. In 1943 the chairman of the Canadian Chamber of Commerce commented that businessmen had been "wrong ten or twelve years ago in their approach to government policies and fiscal policies and we are now taking exactly the opposite position, and we hope that if government in the future tries to encourage business in the days of depression, and tries to repress business in boom days, business on the whole will understand that [it is] a pretty sensible thing for the government to do, and won't make it any harder for government than possible." "One of the good things about a war," one of the Keynesian economists in the Department of Finance commented, "is that it leads to a process of general economic education." He might have added that the education was greater when the war came immediately after a crippling depression.

Still, there were *frissons* of anxiety that contra-cyclical government spending could get out of control. Suppose government began to crowd out private enterprise? Suppose its spending led Canadians to believe that economic and social security flowed freely from the public treasury? Suppose high levels of government spending started creating inflation? Where was the line between healthy carrot-and-stick type stimulation of private enterprise, and the unhealthy direct intervention and control that the socialists favoured? Another bothersome postwar factor, polls seemed to show, was the unpopularity of business. It had been a long time since businessmen had been seen as heroic nation-builders; during the long years of depression and war, "profit" had become an increasingly dirty word to many Canadians. "The simple unpleasant fact," the president of National Trust said in 1944, "is that they distrust us and regard us as selfish and incompetent." Opinion polls showed that Canadians, unlike Americans, were more willing to trust big unions than they were to trust big business.

Canadians were also forming big unions, as organized labour advanced in the immediate postwar years at a pace not seen since 1919. Industrial unionism had spread north to Canada through the Congress of Industrial Organizations in the 1930s. Labour militancy gradually increased as wartime labour markets tightened in an egalitarian social climate. Early in 1944 the federal government, by order-in-council, granted rights to organize and compel collective bargaining that had been won several years earlier in the United States. Immediately after the war unions flexed their newly reinforced muscles in several confrontations with organized employers. Some strikes, particularly in the auto industry, were accompanied by considerable violence.

Business was not happy with the new climate, and there was often strong, sometimes successful resistance to the organizing drives. Hardly anyone in business liked unions, but for most employers the nineteenth-century shock at labour "revolts" and strikes had long since faded. Labour problems had become another fact of business life, and the range of possible responses to most industrial relations' situations was clear enough. There was the usual apocalyptic rhetoric on both sides, but the big strikes of 1946–47 were more clearly "tests of strength" between protagonists who now understood the rules of the game, than old-fashioned life and death struggles over matters of high principle. If unions had to be recognized, then you hired industrial relations experts to tell you how to deal with them, and hoped for the best in each round of collective bargaining. Business strategists and statesmen seldom thought that industrial relations was the central theme or issue in either the evolution of their firms or the growth of modern capitalism.

Many in the CCF, and a few of the Liberal government's own civil servants, interpreted wartime controls as a great success and urged permanent control in peacetime. Why not use the methods that won the war against Hitler to make war on poverty, sickness, injustice, and all other evils? Did the experience of war socialism support the socialists' claim that the same methods would work in peace? Economists, philosophers, and politicians in the mid-1940s intensely debated the merits of free-market economies versus planning or control systems.

Most Canadian businessmen wanted no more than Keynesian indirect economic management. A few who had benefited from controls (especially price-fixing) and thought they could continue to manipulate government advantageously, were not unhappy to see the wartime order continue. The majority of businessmen abhorred state planners, who, as the *Financial Post* put it, "want the government to run nearly everything just as governments run nearly everything in totalitarian countries. These planners are saying that government has to carry a very big part of the burden of providing postwar employment; that the only way a comprehensive social security system can be got into operation is through major government spending and works projects, etc. This point of view ultimately, of course, can lead only to the end of the system of democracy and individual enterprise."

One early example of business resistance to government control came during the 1944 debate on the powers C.D. Howe would have as Minister of Reconstruction. The Montreal Board of Trade, the Canadian Chamber of Commerce, and the Canadian Manufacturers' Association all expressed reservations about the extent of the power that the government proposed to give to the minister, and succeeded in having it reduced. Writing in *Industrial Canada*, a British Columbia industrialist explained:

> I have great admiration for Mr. Howe, Minister of Munitions, who is doing great service for the country with conspicuous ability. He talks our language, as it were, and was a very successful technician in the atmosphere of free choice and opportunity.... The prolonged practice of unprecedented power, fully warranted at this time, can, you know, exercise a subtle influence over the very best of men.

Most of C.D. Howe's instincts, as he thought about the postwar world, were directed toward freeing enterprise. He saw free enterprise as Canada's engine of growth and was more sanguine than many Ottawa men about the private sector's ability to deliver postwar prosperity. Howe had opposed some of the most ambitious government spending and control programs (his chief economist in the Department of Reconstruction, W.A. Mackintosh, complained arrogantly that arguing with the minister was "an intellectual form of volley ball – bouncing ideas off Mr. Howe's battleship steel headpiece"). He wanted rapid decontrol rather than continued planning – there would be no five-year plans or grand industrial strategies in Howe's Canada – and moved quickly to dismantle much of the government's business apparatus. Most of the crown's war assets, including major operating companies, were sold for whatever they would bring, which was not very much on glutted markets, leading to good bargains for businessmen betting on an expanding economy.

Decontrol proceeded fitfully because of continued shortages and unforeseen market breakdowns. It was more orderly and slower than American decontrol, but much speedier than in war-torn countries like England, where rationing lasted into the 1950s. The Canadian resistance to decontrol was led by the CCF, who wanted a continuation of state socialism, by client groups who had developed strong vested interests (rent controls proved the hardest to abandon), and by spokesmen for a few business groups reluctant to see the end of wartime limits on competition. The freezing of the economy under wartime controls, eliminating many forms of competition (including, in many cases, new entries; business failures were very rare during the war years), was exactly what the small business lobbyists had been trying to achieve since the 1890s and particularly during the depression. The collectivists fought a bitter rearguard action to hold on to their favourite price-fixing tactic, resale price maintenance. It was finally outlawed by Ottawa in 1951. Only then, like forgotten Japanese soldiers on Pacific islands, did small retailers' associations begin to accept defeat in their long war against the market and the chains and the department stores. A few have never given up.

The postwar return to the market was not complete. There were distinct limits to the government's and C.D. Howe's commitment to private enterprise. Keynesian monetary and fiscal management, in itself a revolutionary development, shaded into more direct stimuli and controls. Manipulation of the tax system, for example, gradually evolved from a badly understood pump-priming device into the chief tool of industrial policy-making. Accelerated depreciation was introduced as a Keynesian device in 1939, then taken over as an instrument for creating war investment. In 1944, fearing a postwar slump, Ottawa announced double depreciation allowances for manufacturers completing capital projects by the end of 1946. Deadlines were pushed back, and back, into 1949; four-fifths of all manufacturing investment between 1945 and 1949 eventually qualified for the depreciation.

A very few businessmen questioned the need for the program and the way in which its administrative arrangements made government, usually through C.D. Howe, the arbiter of eligible projects. Others wondered whether the huge tax concessions were necessary and/or if they distorted priorities, overheating a postwar boom that actually needed little stimulus. Originally seen as a temporary stimulative measure in contra-cyclical budgeting, accelerated depreciation was finally institutionalized in the tax act of 1948. Now that high levels of taxation were a permanent fact of Canadian life, politicians were starting to discover the practically unlimited possibilities for taking action, giving favours, doing things, or appearing to do things, through tinkering with the tax system.

Most Canadian manufacturers still supported Canada's most fundamental industrial policy, tariff protection. After the beating that economic nationalism had taken in the depression and the way the war had discredited excesses of political nationalism, the National Policy was a tattered old standard to try to rally round. The federal government was, in principle, committed to free trade as a vital stepping stone to world prosperity. Canada's participation in the General Agreement on Tariffs and Trade (GATT), signed in 1947, meant the writing on the wall for many of the old National Policy tariff levels (though it proved to be dim writing and a long wall; the later rounds of GATT tariff negotiations lasted for years, and the actual tariff-cutting was similarly strung out). In 1947–48 it briefly appeared that the government might go much further: talks at the ministerial level with the United States led to serious discussion of a complete free trade agreement. Mackenzie King decided, however, that the lesson of 1911 dared not be ignored and killed the proposal. Free traders still feared the power and influence the organized manufacturers could bring to bear against any frontal attack on the grand old policy.

Howe had always been a free trader, and supported the maximum amount of reciprocity with the United States after the war. But his biographers, William Kilbourn and Robert Bothwell, argue convincingly that Howe's views were an extension of deep strains of Canadian economic nationalism. This immigrant from the United States had come to believe in Canada and its potential more deeply than many of the Canadians. His wartime experience had convinced him, Howe said in that important 1943 statement, that Canadians could manufacture any product on a competitive basis with the rest of the world. He favoured freer trade with the United States because he believed the new Canadian manufacturing capacity created in war could best be fostered by permanent access to the huge American market.

In contrast to his free trade beliefs, Howe was willing to use government to boost Canada's presence in certain frontier industries. He sold most of the wartime crown corporations, but kept Polymer Corporation Limited, the successful and nicely profitable synthetic rubber plant at Sarnia. There was a clear strategic reason for maintaining crown ownership of Eldorado Mines, the old LaBine operation on Great Bear Lake, which the government had nationalized in 1944 when its whole output of uranium was suddenly required for the Manhattan Project (to make an atomic bomb). Through Eldorado, and through the nuclear reactor the National Research Council had built at Chalk River, Ontario, Canada was obviously going to be an important participant in the nuclear age.

Most of all, Howe believed Canada had a major role to play in the air age, as a manufacturer of advanced aircraft. The country was strategically well placed in the new era because all the transatlantic flights had to use Canadian – or at least Newfoundland – airfields. It already had its own national airline, TCA, Howe's personal creation. And it had the big airframe assembly plants created during the war at Montreal, Vancouver, and Toronto. Here was the one wartime industry that could most easily be adopted to peace. (Canada's shipyards, which had arguably done a better manufacturing job, were bound to have trouble in flooded postwar markets because so much new merchant shipping had been built; military aircraft, however, could not easily be converted to peacetime use.) The big factories could be utilized by the best Canadian and foreign business talent available. With some help from the government, particularly to encourage Canadian design and engineering, the plants could manufacture new aircraft to meet Canadian and world needs in the certain postwar boom in civil aviation. They would give excellent jobs to tens of thousands of Canadians, perhaps repeating the growth of automobile factories after the First World War. Captured by the romance of flying in the thirties, Howe was as true a believer in aviation as the future of transportation as earlier generations of Canadians had been in railways. Howe's wartime Director-General for Aircraft Production, Ralph Bell, did not believe there would be peacetime markets for Canadian planes, but the minister went ahead anyway.

The government's Victory Aircraft plant at Malton, just outside of Toronto, was leased to the A.V. Roe Company of Great Britain, a subsidiary of Hawker-Siddeley, which promptly began work on a jet passenger aircraft. Ottawa supplied seed money and development contracts. A large government-built factory at Cartierville, Quebec, was bought by a group of its operating executives as Canadair Limited, and they were briefly successful, with Howe's help, in producing a four-engine passenger airliner of modified British and American design, the North Star. When Canadair ran out of money and markets for the plane, Howe arranged to have the company sold to the Electric Boat Company (predecessor to General Dynamics, already in the aviation business), while the RCAF and TCA placed orders for more North Stars. The American owners brought new expertise to the business, and the Canadian government supplied the market.

Howe's influence on TCA's equipment policy was typical of the control he maintained over the CNR-owned carrier. TCA was Howe's and the government's chosen instrument for Canadian transcontinental and international air service. A potential rival developed during the war in the form of Canadian Pacific Air Lines

Limited, a 1941–42 amalgamation of Richardson's Canadian Airways Limited and nine smaller, mostly bush outfits, arranged by the parent railroad. But the King government made clear its support for TCA's monopoly and, at Howe's insistence, in 1944 gave notice that CPR would have to divest itself of any interest in air transport. Intense lobbying got the decision reversed. Four years later, when TCA rejected the idea of trans-Pacific flying as uneconomic, Howe grudgingly allowed CP Air, still largely a northern carrier, to begin scheduled service to China, Japan, and Australia.* He required that the private firm buy equipment for the service from Canadair. The government-owned firm flew on through Canadian skies kept empty of competition by public policy. As its godfather moved from ministry to ministry, responsibility for the airline moved with him.

Howe's penchant for using power in aid of this or that industry became a matter of general parliamentary concern when the government imposed emergency import controls during a foreign exchange crisis in 1947. Howe was to exercise ministerial discretion over a broad range of commodities, granting or denying import permits at will. It was a fellow businessman and Conservative frontbencher, the respected former president of National Trust, J.M. Macdonnell, who complained that the arbitrary personal power made Howe "our new dictator" (leading promptly to the nickname, "Clarence Dictator Howe"). "The Minister of Reconstruction and Supply is quite a conundrum to me," Macdonnell told the House, "because I think he believes in energy, private initiative and all that kind of thing. What I am troubled about is that I think he still believes far more in his own personal power.... The Minister got his training in wartime, and I do not believe that kind of mentality is necessarily good for this kind of job." The shaft hit closer to home than Tory taunting of Howe for his alleged "What's a million?" comment, actually a remark in a 1945 debate that a million dollars cut from a $1,365 million War Appropriations bill would not be a very important matter.

Neither C.D. Howe's emergency powers nor the odd million of government spending seemed particularly worth worrying about as the good years of the late 1940s, fed by war-delayed consumer demand, fast-moving technological change, and heavy government pump-priming, faded into better and better years in the 1950s – another of those periods when Canada seemed to be the resource

---

* CP Air's breakthrough was a testament to the daring and the strange visions, drawn from his Mackenzie valley bush flying, of the airline's president, Grant McConachie. As head of Yukon Southern Air Transport before the merger and in the days of short-hop flying, McConachie had dreamed of developing a "Great Circle" route to the Orient across Alaska and the Behring Straits and down to Vladivostok and points east. He remained a Pacific man, ready to fly straight through this chink in TCA's monopoly. CP Air could have been ruined by the service; the outbreak of the Korean War in 1950 made it profitable.

cornucopia of the world. The forties were a time for new cars and nylons and frozen foods and new furniture for the veterans' new houses – all the consumer products that the stores and dealers were bulging with. By the fifties the shopping was not just from store to store, but at a shopping centre, set back from the street and surrounded by acres of free parking. And the centre was in the midst of a brand new suburban housing development where split-level ranch-style homes were being marketed like station wagons.

New fortunes were made in retailing, in land development, in urban construction and real estate, but the biggest developments of the 1950s continued to be on the resource frontiers. As the world recovered from war it was going to have an apparently insatiable need for Canada's wood, newsprint, metals, and other raw materials (food, especially wheat, was a significant exception. Grain sales continued to languish; Saskatchewan was Canada's most depressed province, and it was not clear that the country would ever again be the world's granary). The world's most powerful country, the United States, had special strategic needs for Canadian raw materials because its voracious industrial and military machine could no longer be fully supplied with U.S. resources. The bastion of the free world was running out of iron ore, seemed to have little uranium or nickel, and would soon be importing petroleum. The safest, most secure supplier of many of the goods America needed was good neighbour Canada. A new wave of American investment in Canadian resources had gotten nicely underway in 1950 when the outbreak of the Korean War added a new sense of urgency to North American industrial preparedness, causing more money to pour in. The Korean War also caused Canada to rearm, leading to more military spending and the creation of a new Department of Defence Production. C.D. Howe became its minister.

The resource boom in bountiful Canada included old minerals and new. For generations the Ungava-Labrador country had been known to contain huge deposits of low-grade iron ore, too remote from markets to be mined economically. Now the exhaustion of the American Mesabi ores made the Canadian reserves very attractive. Development of a big deposit at Steep Rock Lake, west of Superior, was the forerunner of massive investments to get ore out of Quebec. A consortium of six American steel companies, led by the Hanna interests of Cleveland, joined with the Hollinger and Timmins groups in Canada to form the Iron Ore Company of Canada, incorporated in Delaware in 1949. It invested about a quarter of a billion dollars in the rugged North Shore country, including the cost of a 357-mile railway from Sept-Îles on the gulf to the mines at Schefferville on the Quebec-Labrador border, before the first ore came out. Other mining companies joined the action. The need to move iron ore up the St. Lawrence to Great Lakes' steel mills was the final catalyst persuading Canada and the United States to invest hundreds of millions in deepening and re-canalizing the St. Lawrence. Publicists presented the St. Lawrence Seaway project as the culmination of centuries of struggle to strengthen the old commercial aorta of Canada.

The magic new mineral was uranium, the fuel supply for nuclear reactors and atomic weapons. Such was Canada's blessing that just as the old Great Bear Lake mine was running out of ore, Eldorado's prospectors found major new deposits at Beaverlodge near Lake Athabaska on Saskatchewan's northern border. And as soon as restrictions on private prospecting were lifted and the prices offered by governments became attractive, huge new uranium strikes were made, complete with the usual miners' tales of romance or adventure or intrigue. Incredible that the biggest uranium strike in the Beaverlodge area was made right under Eldorado's nose by Gilbert LaBine, whom C.D. Howe had squeezed out of Eldorado after nationalization. LaBine had another old mine on the shelf, Gunnar Gold Mines Limited, which he used to develop the property, dropping "Gold" from its name. It was better to have a uranium than a gold mine in the 1950s anyway; the still-frozen $35 price of gold was becoming uneconomic, production was falling, and the industry was pleading with governments for succour.

Even more incredible that the biggest uranium strike in Canadian history was made in an area of Ontario overrun with prospectors and already developed by highway and railway. And that the man who made the first big mine at Blind River, about seventy-five miles east of Sault Ste Marie, Joe Hirshhorn, was just another street kid from Brooklyn ("I've always wanted the sort of proposition that costs a dime and pays ten dollars"), who had come up to Canada during the depression to get in on Ontario's gold boom. "My Name is Opportunity And I Am Paging Canada," he advertised in the *Northern Miner*. Joe Hirshhorn eventually left Canada, and the Rio Tinto/Rio Algom organization that took over his properties, with tens of millions of dollars to invest in art and museums in the United States. The most incredible of the uranium stories belonged to Stephen B. Roman, Czech immigrant, class of 1937, who started in Canada as a tomato-picker, drifted from ethnic editing into mining promotion, and happened to take an option on some claims Hirshhorn missed in the Algoma basin. By 1957, when uranium sold to the United States government had become one of Canada's largest exports, Roman's Consolidated Denison Mines Limited had more reserves of ore than all the mines in the United States. How was that for striking it rich in North America?

The new place names told the story of the Canadian resource boom. Sept-Îles (not so new actually; it was named by Cartier in 1535) and Schefferville in Quebec, Wabush and Labrador City in Labrador, Uranium City in the Saskatchewan wilderness, Elliot Lake where the uranium miners worked in Ontario, Murdochville in the Gaspé where Noranda (J.Y. Murdoch, president) was opening up massive copper deposits, Kitimat in British Columbia, the site of another mammoth Alcan power development and the world's largest aluminum smelter, investment totalling $450 million. And there was the instantly legendary village of Leduc, Alberta, where in 1947 Imperial Oil's Leduc Number 1 well finally proved that Alberta really did float on a petroleum bed.

The postwar oil and gas story, to come in Chapter 18, did not exactly parallel the mineral boom because of problems with transportation and markets. Moving natural gas to eastern urban markets was particularly tricky. It took several years of intricate manoeuvring and negotiation, and was still not a firm deal, when Ottawa announced in 1956 its intention to support the construction of a natural gas pipeline from Alberta to the markets of eastern Canada. C.D. Howe, of course, was the minister responsible. The pipeline was going to be a big and important project, almost the equivalent of the construction of the CPR in the 1880s, following right on the heels of the equally grandiose St. Lawrence Seaway, and while the federal government was also helping the provinces build a transcontinental motor link, the Trans-Canada Highway.

Journalists often said that C.D. Howe personified business in government. This was not quite accurate. Howe was an engineer, apparently the first professional engineer to be a minister in a parliamentary government. The great projects of C.D. Howe's years – mines, power developments, new towns, pipelines, seaways, airports, highways – were all gourmand fare for engineers. These were the big jobs engineering students dream about at nights, engineering professors fondle in their memoirs. *Let me tell you how we diverted that river and drained that lake at Steep Rock.*

Even the job of re-equipping Canada's armed forces for Korea and beyond was made for engineers, because of the determination of government and industry that Canada's fighting men have distinctively Canadian equipment. By 1951 RCAF pilots were flying a Canadian-designed, Canadian-built jet interceptor, the Canuck, or CF-100, made by the A.V. Roe Company (Avro) in Toronto. Canadair in Montreal was building F-86 Sabre Jets being flown by the USAF in Korea, and Canada's third big aircraft producer, de Havilland, located in Toronto, had seized world leadership in the design of northern workhorses with its Beaver and Otter. Aircraft manufacture meant thousands more jobs for engineers in Canada (many of whom had to be recruited abroad). An engineers' country indeed. A country where government contractors would club together to finance a big picture book, *Canada at War*, dedicated to "The Rt. Hon. Clarence Decatur Howe, engineer and statesman," and with a chapter entitled "The Engineer as Hero."

There were few heroic engineers or aircraft manufacturers in Atlantic Canada, the region that profited least from the postwar resource boom. Mining and lumbering grew steadily in New Brunswick, and Dominion Steel and Coal managed to keep the Cape Breton industries going, more or less profitably, with the aid of federal subsidies. But Atlantic Canada lacked hydro-electric power, could not build on its wartime shipyard achievements, was poorly situated for manufacturing and marketing in the growing continental economy, and was once again being literally by-passed by the enthusiasts for the St. Lawrence Seaway. The old staple, fishing, seemed to be in long-term decline; it had become a highly competitive international industry in which Canadian producers had trouble holding old markets for cured and canned fish or developing new ones for frozen and fresh seafood.

A new maritime province of Canada developed in 1949 when the former Dominion of Newfoundland joined Confederation. The union was not a proud occasion for the people of a country that tasted independence in the 1920s before suffering the humiliation of national bankruptcy and the voluntary surrender of self-government back to Britain in 1934. For fifteen years the Island was ruled by an appointed commission. After the war Britain asked Newfoundlanders to decide their future. The options included returning to independence, some form of economic union with the United States, or joining Canada. A sometime pig farmer, journalist, and broadcaster named Joseph Smallwood led the Confederation forces that succeeded, narrowly, in obtaining support for the union.

The main impetus to Confederation was Newfoundlanders' desire to improve their standard of living. Since the 1880s the country had been trying to develop other resources besides the fishery and the annual seal hunt. Wave after wave of nation-building policies was implemented to try to stimulate agriculture, mining, forestry, transportation, and manufacturing in Newfoundland. As in Canada, merchants were among the leaders in investing in new industries, encouraging foreign investment, trying to cultivate new opportunities. Particularly after the collapse of fish prices in the 1920s there was a pervasive sense that the fishery could not provide Newfoundlanders with a modern standard of living. But two marginal pulp mills, the depleting iron mines of Bell Island, and an unprofitable trans-Island railway, were the only significant fruits of the diversification strategies. The 1930s were a horrible decade for Newfoundlanders, as the economy could not support the public debt, social services were almost non-existent, and the inhabitants of the hundreds of isolated outports became the poorest North Americans north of Mexico.

Few of the old fish merchants of St. John's were interested in pouring their resources into what seemed to be a dying industry. Over the years they concentrated on wholesaling and other merchandising, entered various service industries, or moved money elsewhere. Local businessmen were not among the leaders in the Confederation movement, partly for non-economic reasons (the Confederation debate became entangled with sharp geographic and religious divisions), partly for fear that they would not be able to compete as part of Canada. The head of the prominent Crosbie family was among the leading anti-Confederates, urging economic union with the United States as a better alternative. Smallwood's Confederates played on popular dislike of the St. John's establishment, suggesting that union with Canada would bring an end to their power. It would also bring Canadian veterans' benefits, unemployment insurance, family allowances, and development money – this last perhaps providing opportunities for Newfoundlanders to revivify their national life on a firm, more promising foundation.

After Confederation, Joey Smallwood's provincial government renewed the quest for economic diversification. When local businessmen still seemed oriented to trade rather than manufacturing (for example, the historic Bowring firm, dating from 1811, decided to specialize in retailing, and then narrowed their trade still further by concentrating on gift shops), Smallwood set out to use the power and resources of government to create new Newfoundland industries. The province had to "develop or perish," he proclaimed. To bring about the development, Smallwood hired a Director General of Economic Development, one Alfred A. Valdmanis, who before the war had served as Minister of Trade, Finance and Industry in the government of Latvia. It was C.D. Howe who recommended Valdmanis to Smallwood. With luck, Valdmanis and the Smallwood Liberal government might do for Newfoundland what Howe and the Liberals in Ottawa were doing for all of Canada.

While Canada's engineers were building monuments in stone and steel, the businessmen were organizing new corporate empires. There were more than sixteen million Canadians in 1956 and many more each year, thanks to a high birth rate and several waves of postwar immigrants. And the pace of enterprise had quickened along with the growth rate. Even the barest highlights of individual and corporate achievement after 1945 are hard to condense in short chapters. In food retailing alone the postwar decade saw the rapid expansion of Dominion Stores under William Horsey's brilliant management (the chain actually contracted in number of units, but unit sales soared), the growth of the Steinberg family's Montreal-based chain of supermarkets, the struggle of the American-owned Safeway chain to hold its own in western Canada, and the rise to regional prominence of a good-old boy from Stellarton, Nova Scotia, Frank Sobey, who brought the idea of the self-service, cash-and-carry supermarket, complete with automatic doors, to the Maritimes.

Entrepreneurs who got started in the 1930s – Irving in New Brunswick, the Billeses with their Canadian Tire stores, Roy Thomson and his string of newspapers and radio stations – flourished after the war (though Thomson's scrambling for opportunities took him out of Canada in 1954 to launch what seemed like an oddball attempt at founding private television in Scotland). New names such as Simard, Desmarais, and Bassett began to appear on the Quebec scene. In British Columbia H.R. MacMillan continued to tower, creating the largest integrated forest products firm Canada had ever seen, one of the largest in the world, with his 1953 amalgamation of the H.R. MacMillan Export Company (long on sawmills and shipping capacity, short on timber) and Bloedel, Stewart and Welch (large timber reserves) to form MacMillan-Bloedel. The Bronfmans of Montreal controlled the largest distilling company in the world, as Seagram had won the complex post-prohibition struggle for leadership in the American blended liquor market. Hiram Walker almost kept pace, both companies riding their marketing expertise and understanding of North Americans' thirst for brands of lighter, blended spirits.

The continued growth of Canadian Breweries Limited – it kept on gobbling up Ontario breweries, then took over National Breweries in Quebec, entered the United States, and began eyeing the western provinces – did not satisfy E.P. Taylor's hunger for deals, expansion, and mergers. A lone wolf in the thirties, Taylor first followed the logic of his brewing mergers. He integrated backward from brewing into malting and soy bean mills, then developed the food and soft drink sideline into a national web of bakeries, candy stores, cafeterias, and caterers under the umbrellas of Canadian Food Products Limited and Orange Crush. Next he diversified in directions apparently suggested by some of the friends he made in Ottawa and Washington. From discussions with J.S. Duncan, Taylor decided Massey-Harris might be a good investment, and began accumulating shares. H.R. MacMillan interested him in the British Columbia forests, where he began modestly by doing a small deal as a front for MacMillan, then made serious investments in sawmills and timber limits. He entered eastern forest industries by buying a controlling interest in a hardwood distillation outfit, Standard Chemicals, from the British group that had backed him in the 1930s. Taylor's partner in the chemical deal was Eric Phillips, a whiz at making auto glass (the family business) and then high-technology products for one of Howe's crown corporations. Tit for tat, Phillips brought Taylor into the interesting situation in Dominion Stores, where the company's dynamic president, William Horsey, was trying to out-bid Safeway to buy the chain from French investors. Horsey's original financial support in the deal came from J.A. (Bud) McDougald, a senior partner at Dominion Securities.

It was an American financier, Floyd Odlum, who suggested to Taylor the possibility of levering these assorted holdings through a special investment company, based on the model of Odlum's Atlas Corporation. The aim was to create more than just another holding company or investment fund. Like the Atlas group, the Argus folk would concentrate on a handful of growth situations, in each of which they would have a large enough holding to exercise managerial control if necessary, though not necessarily; ordinarily they would just watch the companies grow and collect dividends. Argus Corporation Limited was formed in September 1945, with the founding partners turning over their holdings in Canadian Breweries, Canadian Food Products, Orange Crush, Standard Chemical, Massey-Harris, and other companies, in return for Argus stock.

Public issues of Argus preferred and common shares were well received, giving the group more money to expand. Taylor originally had about a 50 per cent interest in Argus; other important investors included Phillips, MacMillan, Horsey, J. Wallace McCutcheon (a Toronto lawyer who had gone on the board of Canadian Breweries in the mid-1930s to watch Taylor on behalf of the Dominion

Bank), and E.W. Bickle. McDougald of Dominion Securities was not interested in an investment company, but was part of a separate entrepreneurial firm, Taylor, McDougald, and Company, that handled promotions and special deals for Argus. In 1955 he joined the Argus board.

The Argus group's gamble that postwar Canada would prosper was right. So was their sense that their companies could outperform the herd. Taylor seems to have worked largely by intuition. ("How did I know which companies were going to grow?" he once said. "It's a question of judgement. I remember in the old days the shares of streetcar companies were considered gilt edge investments. Well, they dried out. Then there was a time when the railroads were blue chip. Now they're all having a tough time, except the CPR. I never went into cither of those things. It's worked out pretty well for me.") The tax system helped. Heavy taxes on dividend income made it attractive for companies to retain earnings and then be sold, with the sellers taking their profits in tax-free capital gains. The buyers, like Taylor (and other entrepreneurs who understood the situation, including Walter Gordon in Toronto), often were able to pick up companies for little more than the firms' own reserves, sitting in the treasury. The other principle guiding the acquisitions seems to have been Taylor's notion, fairly commonly held, that all industries evolved toward monopoly and oligopoly. Successful entrepreneurs tried to be in on the process.

Argus Corporation was a fabulous success through the 1940s, 1950s, and into the 1960s. In its first ten years, from 1945 to 1955, the Canadian economy grew by 10.8 percent per annum in current dollars. Profits of Argus's three most important holdings, Canadian Breweries, Dominion Stores, and Massey-Ferguson, grew by 15.5, 20.8, and 21.8 per cent per annum respectively. Taylor's merger policy, plus expert management by George Black and some wartime confusion at Labatt, finally gave Canadian Breweries 50 per cent of the Canadian market. Its profits finally came to reflect its dominance of the rationalized industry. Much of Dominion Stores' growth came from internal rationalization. At Massey the main postwar job was simply to keep up with the North American demand for farm implements, particularly its self-propelled combine. It had been developed just before everyone else's planning was frozen by the war, giving Massey-Harris world leadership in the field. Massey's European network was quickly rebuilt, manufacturing commenced in Great Britain, and a new era began in 1953 when the Canadians purchased the British-based tractor company that a brilliant, eccentric Ulsterman named Harry Ferguson had developed. The new Massey-Ferguson was truly a full-line agricultural implement company, bigger than John Deere, second in the world only to International Harvester.

Argus sailed on. In 1946 the western forest companies were tucked into British Columbia Forests Products Limited, which continued to grow by the acquisition of smaller, often family-owned firms. Standard Chemical set its sights higher and by 1951 had completed an unfriendly takeover of another manufacturer of wood derivatives, the much larger Dominion Tar and Chemical (Domtar), to which was added the pulp and paper mills of St. Lawrence Corporation and Donnaconna Paper. There were some shoals and storms. The acquisitors envisaged major expansion in communications, for example, beginning with the interest they acquired in Standard Broadcasting Corporation Limited (mainly CFRB radio in Toronto) in 1946. But a few years later they were outbid by the Webster family for control of the *Globe and Mail* and then outmanoeuvred for control of the Toronto *Star*. Standard Broadcasting had applied for a licence to operate a television station as early as 1938; twenty-one years later the Toronto licence went to John Bassett, a transplanted newspaper publisher from Montreal. Taylor and J.H. Gundy finally did succeed in getting their own airline going, with Argus as a principal investor: Peruvian International Airways began offering passenger service from Montreal to Lima in 1946. It failed.

Taylor's entrepreneurial energies were not limited to Argus. He had been acquiring real estate north of Toronto for years, partly in support of his horse-breeding establishment, Windfields Farm. In the 1950s, as head of the Ontario Jockey Club, Taylor rationalized horse-racing in the province much as he had merged breweries. He was also adept at merging little parcels of land into big ones. One of these, northeast of the city, was to be the site of a company town for a new O'Keefe brewery. When the brewery decided to build in other provinces, Taylor developed the land anyway as a model residential/shopping community. The new city of Don Mills, created by E.P. Taylor's Don Mills Development Limited, was thought to be a model of advanced urban planning. It worked so well that Taylor began assembling land west of the city in an Erin Mills project.

By the mid-1950s E.P. Taylor had become the new symbol of the strengths and weaknesses of Canadian capitalism. He was the one Canadian businessman whose name was a household word, and whose physique, complete with top hat and full waistcoat, commonly graced the sports and gossip pages. To a public still suspicious of big business and great personal wealth, Taylor personified more weaknesses than strength. He was "big Eddie," "Excess Profits" Taylor, "the beer baron," "tycoon Taylor," and so on, much like one of those dreaded turn-of-the-century monopolists and plutocrats, taking a little sip from almost every glass or bottle of beer sold in Canada. Through the whole decade Taylor's actions in the creation of Canadian Breweries were under investigation by the federal combines commissioner; so was Domtar's role in an apparent combine in tar products. Finally, in 1959, the beer monopoly (and, by direct implication, the beer monopolist) went on trial for criminal offences against the Combines Investigation Act. The verdict was not guilty. There continued to be complaints that the Combines Investigation Act was too weak.

Taylor and Argus symbolized the new and the old worlds of Canadian business. They were devoted to big, corporate business. The family firm and the atomized, widely competitive industry seemed to have had its day. The way to be modern was to go public, grow, buy competitors, become one of the dominant firms in an industry. The widely held public corporation was the wave of the future, but the beauty of dispersed ownership was the control it gave to those, like Argus, who could muster a sizeable block of shares, say about 20 per cent. Management had not quite escaped shareholder control: the eyes of Argus were upon the executives, and sometimes the proprietors used their power to change horses on the teams.

Or, rather, the proprietorial corporation, Argus, flexed the muscles, for it was a second corporate buffer between the investors and the industries. Layers of corporations were spun out by these entrepreneurs and their lawyers: holding companies, trusteeship companies, investment companies, entrepreneurial companies, management companies, operating companies. Some existed for tax reasons, most existed to facilitate accounting and entrepeneurial flexibility. Argus and its lawyers were experts in using the corporate form as the everyday instrument of enterprise, the all-purpose way of approaching business needs. You set up these artificial persons to do business almost the way a later generation began installing robots on assembly lines. They were easy to create, durable, flexible, and had certain advantages in having no personality.

The American business historian, A.D. Chandler, has stressed how vital the big corporation became in replacing the market as a mechanism for making rational economic decisions – in supplying visible hands to manage the flow of goods and services from producer to consumer. Canadians' sense in the 1950s that the age of big business and the impersonal corporation was upon them was founded in the loss of personality by their own big firms. Did anyone outside of boardrooms know who ran the CPR or any of the banks? The auto companies and the oil companies were big, impersonal, and almost all American. There were no Masseys at Massey-Harris. The modern businessman seemed to wear a grey flannel suit and, according to William H. White's 1956 bestseller, had become "The Organization Man." Corporate capitalism was in full bloom.

Not quite. Impersonal corporate dominance and bureaucratic decision-making did not characterize the commanding heights of the Canadian economy in the 1950s. In the private sector it was still the age of Eddie Taylor and his buddies. You did business with the people you'd gotten to know – at school, at the club, in Ottawa during the war. Networks of contact, influence, power, ethnicity, and region were still in place and important. With the growth of big corporations in a small community the networks became neatly visible through memberships and interlocks on boards of directors, whose rosters became happy hunting grounds for socialist scholars and journalists tracing the filaments of capitalist power in Canada.

It was easy to make up a list of the top one hundred Canadian businessmen, and discover that many of them belonged to the same clubs and the same small circle of boards. They all knew each other, too. The public may not have known their names, but the heads of the big chartered banks and the railroads could get together around a small dinner table. Everyone knew Eddie Taylor and Bud Mc-Dougald, and Phillips and McCutcheon and their legal wizard J.S.D. Tory, the real successor to Z.A. Lash. Everyone knew the grand old men of Canadian business – J.W. McConnell in Montreal, Sir James Dunn of Algoma (who seemed to live everywhere), old I.W. Killam who carried on in Beaverbrook's tradition, and even the Beaver himself, still going strong in England, still radiating transatlantic influence and power.

Lord Beaverbrook had obtained his title so long ago that some of the youngsters would not know that he was originally plain Max Aitken, a bond salesman. Did it still happen, that ordinary Canadians got on in life and then got honoured and brought into the aristocracy? Not if they stayed in democratic Canada. It was said by his critics that E.P. Taylor's expanding interests in Great Britain and the Bahamas had something to do with an intense longing for a title. And while Roy Thomson had found a money machine in Scots television – "You know, it's just like having a licence to print your own money," he said, famously – and in modernizing British newspapers, the image of naive acquisitiveness masked a much deeper urge. Ambitious, insecure Canadian millionaires still liked to acquire title to their standing. "It's the best way I can prove to Canadians that I'm a success," Thomson told John Diefenbaker, pathetically. He had to renounce his Canadian citizenship to become eligible for the barony finally bestowed on him in 1964, and could not call himself Lord Thomson of Toronto because it would offend Canadians. So he became Lord Thomson of Fleet. Years earlier he had applied for a Thomson coat of arms. The Duke of Edinburgh commented nastily that it should include a cash register rampant on a field of fifty-pound notes. Thomson chose a beaver instead.

Everyone knew C.D. Howe. "C.D." knew every important businessman in the country. For fifteen years and more Howe's hand was visible in every major deal involving business and government in Canada. Through it all, the minister had had so much personal discretion in administering Canadian policy that his office was the decision-making centre for Canadian industry. They had been fifteen good years for business, and there was a generalized good feeling about Howe's achievements. Howe became "our man in Ottawa," particularly to the people who had worked with him during the war, grown up in business with him in Ottawa, or, as happened often, had had their careers advanced on his recommendations.

Howe liked dealing on a personal basis. He resembled the autocratic proprietor of a firm rather than a member of an executive team or a board (or a cabinet) or the head of a bureaucracy. He revelled in face-to-face negotiation, sought and gave favours, enjoyed flattery, promoted friends and lashed back at enemies. He despised debate in the House of Commons, scorned the opposition, and hated being criticized. He unashamedly and personally dunned government contractors for contributions to the Liberal party, serving as a political bagman and often handling large amounts of cash in bags and safety deposit boxes.* Young men who worked under Howe in Ottawa became his "boys," their careers advancing nicely on the minister's patronage (companies routinely asked Howe to recommend good people for jobs; his biographers note that his "personnel bureau" extended far beyond his "old-boy network"). Howe became close personal friends with many of the industrialists whose enterprises rose or fell according to his decisions, notably R.E. "Rip" Powell of Alcan, and Charles Wilson and George Humphrey of Hanna Mining and the Canadian iron ore developments. His closest friendship was with the notorious old charmer, Sir James Dunn, the caesar of Algoma Steel, a company made solvent and then prosperous by Howe's policies.

Howe is known to have turned down some of Dunn's offers of election cash, but he liked the cases of Krug 1926 champagne Sir James supplied, and enjoyed Dunn's company at their neighbouring summer places by the sea in St. Andrews, New Brunswick. In the 1950s he invested heavily in Algoma stock (the shares were held for him in trust). Dunn several times offered Howe the presidency of Algoma. When Dunn died in 1956, C.D. Howe, Canada's Minister of Trade and Commerce, became his executor. After arranging the sale of his own shares, Howe spent months working out the elaborate sale of Sir James's Algoma holdings to several Canadian corporations. "Nuts," he shouted across the House at Tories who persisted in charges that he had a conflict of interest.

Trafficking constantly in friendship and situations in which he had multiple interests, Howe was particularly thin-skinned about assaults on his honour. Critics ranging from the CCF to personal enemies like Cyrus Eaton thought Howe might be compromised by his friendships. The minister himself at least twice had second thoughts about his favours to Dunn: during the war a troubleshooter from

---

* The use of cash in political donations parallelled intimate personal contacts between businessmen and politicians. Details of the relations are, not surprisingly, hard to come by. The best picture of this *ancien regime* at work is provided in Conrad Black's biography of Maurice Duplessis, where he describes the mutual sycophancy of the premier and the industrialist, J.W. McConnell, and writes of how McConnell "showered Duplessis with little gifts – cigars, an 1890 $20 gold coin on his 68th birthday, *Star* photographs of Duplessis – with medium gifts, including the occasional Krieghoff, and big gifts, especially his election contributions. These . . . arrived within 48 hours of the dissolution of the Legislative Assembly in 1952 and 1956 and consisted of from $50,000 to $100,000 in wads of fresh bank notes delivered in cartons for the Prime Minister's own attention." Through the 1950s politicians toll-gated on government contracts, or expected systematic kickbacks, in most provinces. Howe's ex post facto fund-raising was the beginning of a looser system on the federal level. For every McConnell or Dunn, revelling in political contacts, there were other businessmen who despised the politicians' systems.

Munitions and Supply was sent to renegotiate one of Howe's sweetheart deals with Algoma ("Mr. Howe suddenly realized that if this were looked into," he said later, "this would look pretty damn bad"); later Howe destroyed some of his correspondence with Dunn, telling Beaverbrook that it might "be regarded by many as improper for me to have written such a letter." Dunn referred to Howe as "the Great White Father" in Ottawa.

Howe vigorously denied any serious improprieties in these relationships. He indignantly denied that decisions were made on the basis of personal friendship or his personal self-interest. He made decisions only on the basis of the national interest, and the man who questioned that questioned his integrity. There may have been smoke, at least in the eye of the beholder, but there was no fire. Howe's habits were close to the line for the 1950s, far beyond it by the tougher standards of a later generation. But they were characteristic of the way entrepreneurs and politicians had always operated in the small Canadian community. You could not avoid dealing with your friends (it was a big step forward from previous political generations that Howe did so little self-dealing; he had no connection with C.D. Howe and Company, the recipient of important government contracts, beyond the fact that it employed his son and son-in-law), and, while it was natural to want to help them out, there were many times when it was simply impossible. Everyone understood this. Most times something could be worked out, not least because Howe believed that his friends were the builders of Canada, men undertaking great national developments in the interests of all Canadians.

Howe worked in the public sector, but he seemed to have a bias in favour of private enterprise. He was not very reflective or consistent, but generally was happy to wield public power vigorously to help private enterprise achieve what seemed like national goals. But he used power personally, bluntly, more like an engineer blasting through rock than a finagling businessman or compromising politician. He also identified his goals and the national interest so interchangeably that it was not always clear how to decide between Canada's interest and C.D. Howe's interest. At times Howe seemed to be saying that the best interest for Canada coincided with the maximum power and influence for C.D. Howe. Progressive-Conservatives consistently opposed Howe and his approach to government and business. The CCF was often confused about Howe because he seemed to be such a fine leader of public enterprises. They were praising him one day in Parliament for apparently supporting their doctrinaire faith in public ownership. The minister drew an important line on the public enterprise question when he interjected, "This is different. This is my enterprise."

———————————◆———————————

Sir James Dunn's death in 1956, a few months after the passing of I.W. Killam, was widely noticed as the end of an age. Those who said Dunn was the last of the multi-millionaires were absurdly wrong. The idea that he was one of the last of the lone wolves, the old buccaneering breed, was closer to the truth (though one of the secrets of Dunn's survival and great success into the 1950s was his ability to hire and listen to expert managers, in Algoma's case, T.F. Rahilly and D.S. Holbrook). The disposition of his property was doubly symbolic of the coming of a new era. First, Howe decided that Algoma should not be controlled by any one shareholder, and sold Dunn's shares in several small blocks. Algoma would never again be a capitalist's personal corporation. Secondly, the government of Canada took a huge chunk of the Dunn and Killam estates in succession duties, a total of $100 million, which was virtually found money to an administration running budget surpluses. The politicians decided to use the windfall to support capital spending at Canada's universities and to endow a Canada Council for the encouragement of the arts, letters, humanities, and social sciences. The millions accumulated by the two old capitalists would be used philanthropically to support good causes, after they had been laundered through a new cultural bureaucracy.

The age of Howe ended soon after the years of Dunn and Killam. It was not a happy demise. Howe had become so habituated to his personal power, so confident in his judgment and rectitude, so contemptuous of his critics, in both Parliament and the cabinet, so rigid in his old age, that he was blind to forces gathering against him. In 1955 he began having trouble in cabinet over his plans for another great national development project, the construction of an all-Canadian natural gas pipeline from southern Alberta to Ontario. The emergency powers to control Canadian industry that he had been given as Minister of Defence Production during the Korean crisis in 1951 seemed to him still necessary because of the tricky and expensive armament orders just coming on-stream; but no one else in the country thought "Dictator" Howe needed such power in peacetime. He and the government suffered a thorough mauling in the House of Commons before accepting limits to the powers. Another example of the waning of his own influence in the government ("a government that has fallen into the hands of children," he grumbled) was the decision to appoint a Royal Commission on Canada's Economic Prospects under the chairmanship of Toronto accountant and businessman Walter Gordon. Howe deeply suspected Gordon, who was thought to be unsound on the issue of American involvement in Canadian economic development.

The American involvement in Howe's pipeline scheme was front and centre in the person of Texas oil and gas millionaire Clint Murchison, who had organized the company proposing to build the line. Trans-Canada Pipe Lines Limited was controlled by Texas interests. It intended to build an east-west Canadian pipeline, with Canadian government help. Other experts and entrepreneurs in the industry thought Canadian and American gas supplies should be rationalized on a continental basis, moving north and south to the most convenient markets. Instead, TCPL proposed to become the CPR of natural gas pipelines, building the longest system in the world, entirely in Canada, crossing even the semi-wilderness north of Superior. Howe was captured by the nationalist grandeur of the concept and determined to get the deal through as his last act of nation-building. Heavy government assistance was needed, as in the days of the CPR, to induce private investors to risk their capital. Howe could not understand opposition complaints about the American role in the deal. It was obvious that the Texans, not unlike Howe himself, were taking risks and spending their energies trying to build up Canada.

Howe's 1956 pipeline bills, which included a loan of up to $80 million to TCPL and a special crown corporation to build the northern Ontario section of the line, were introduced at a time of rising, and not entirely rational, Canadian nationalism. The American involvement in TCPL triggered some truly ugly Yankee-baiting in the country, and an almost completely negative opposition to the scheme by the Progressive-Conservatives. The CCF were at least consistent in calling for public ownership as an alternative. Howe's pipeline plan was a reasonable compromise between goals of energy efficiency on the one hand and political expediency (northern Ontario communities were particularly nationalistic in their desire for natural gas) on the other. The deal had been carefully structured to protect Canadian interests, and was delicately timed in relation to financing and construction schedules. Howe's pipeline plan served his adopted country fairly well, especially from the viewpoint of the less xenophobic of Canada's new nationalists.

But method and style came to outweigh substance. Howe decided that TCPL's options on scarce supplies of steel required the government to push the legislation through Parliament by using closure (the limitation of debate) at every stage. Howe personalized and personified the pipeline. His contempt for the opposition was already legendary. This use of closure, announced at the very beginning of the debate, was a step too far. It provoked furious, brilliant, and devastatingly effective resistance from the opposition parties. The Liberal majority rolled over them to pass the pipeline bills, but Howe's enemies won the war for public opinion. The whole government was tarred with the arrogance and insensitivity of the old minister, a bear at bay. In the 1957 general election Canadians repudiated the Liberals, their methods, and their Minister of Everything, electing a minority Conservative government led by John Diefenbaker. In his own riding of Port Arthur, C.D. Howe was defeated by a socialist high school history teacher, Douglas Fisher.

———————————◄►———————————

Defeat saved C.D. Howe from having to accept responsibility for the failure of one of the most grandiose of all the postwar economic projects, the enterprise that would almost have proved his 1943 boast that Canada could make anything.

Born in war, with an original aim of making warplanes for the Pacific theatre, the A.V. Roe Company of Canada made a bold but unsuccessful grab for peacetime leadership in aircraft design by producing one of the world's first jet-propelled passenger planes, the C-102 Jetliner. The project was funded by Howe's Department of Reconstruction and Supply. In 1949 a Jetliner began flying, shortly after the first flights of Britain's ill-fated Comet. No commercial airlines, including TCA, which refused to bend to the minister's pressure on this one, found the C-102 suitable for their needs. It was an impractical, premature leap onto a technological frontier, and was headed for the scrap-heap anyway when the Korean War provided an excuse for concentration on military aircraft.

Avro had good luck with a conventional jet fighter, the CF-100 Canuck, which it designed and built for the RCAF, manufacturing almost seven hundred of them, plus their Orenda engines, after 1951. The Canuck success led defence planners to commission Avro to design a successor, the project that became the CF-105, or Avro Arrow. After some years of preliminary studies, the Department of Defence let contracts with Avro in 1953 for production of prototypes of this supersonic, all-weather, jet interceptor. Originally the Arrow was to use imported engines, fire-control systems, and ground control systems. Gradually the military and the nationalists and the high-tech enthusiasts decided to have all these components manufactured in the country that could make anything, Canada. The first Arrows flew in 1958. Their Canadian-made engines and control systems were not yet ready, but the planes flew well and seemed to represent the state of the art in jet fighters.

By the time the Arrows flew, it was clear that the project was a horrible mistake. Avro Canada was not an experienced aircraft manufacturer; the CF-100 was its only success and it had been plagued with design problems and delays. For all his support of Canadian aircraft production, Howe was too good a businessman to buy all the items in promoter's, designers', and engineers' litanies of excuses. He distrusted Avro's management and admitted as early as 1952 that the Arrow project frightened him. When the more blindly nationalist Minister of Defence, Brooke Claxton, pressed on anyway, Howe told the House of Commons that the program "gives me the shudders."

While it was building the Arrow, A.V. Roe of Canada was using its huge revenues from cost-plus defence contracting to become a conglomerate, spinning out engine and steel and research components, buying foundries and railway car works, finally buying control of DOSCO, the holding company for all the Maritime steel and coal interests. In a few years in the fabulous fifties A.V. Roe turned itself into a single-company Canadian military-industrial complex. The firm's frenetic expansion, highly self-conscious publicizing of its commitment to high technology (its ultimate space-age product was the Avrocar, a doughnut-shaped vertical take-off and landing craft that resembled nothing so much as a flying saucer, which was developed for the U.S. Department of Defence: it was not practical), and very heavy reliance on government contracts, camouflaged serious managerial weaknesses. The evidence suggests that A.V. Roe was a classic promotional company, not unlike the enterprises of F.H. Clergue, built on wild optimism, taxpayers' money, media gullibility, and Canadians' naive patriotism. John Diefenbaker later commented that Avro "seemed horror-struck at the prospect of having ever to compete in a normal market-place situation." The promoters were Sir Roy Dobson of the parent Hawker-Siddeley group, and the Canadian president, the hard-drinking, abrasive Crawford Gordon, originally one of Howe's boys.*

Costs of the Arrow went straight up in a decade of comparatively little inflation. By 1957 aircraft originally estimated at $1 million each, would cost at least $8 million, probably much more. Arrows would cost six times as much as U.S.-designed interceptors. No one other than the RCAF wanted to buy the Arrow. Canadian salesmen found themselves victims of the same nationalist arguments that had been used to justify the Arrow: if Canada ought to have Canadian-designed planes, should not every other nation design its own planes? The Arrow was consuming a huge proportion of Canada's defence budget, and beginning to starve the other services for equipment. Even the Department of National Defence turned against it. Howe and the Liberal government decided to cancel the Arrow – after the 1957 election.

The Diefenbaker government inherited the Arrow mess. The final termination announcement, in February 1959, caused Avro instantly to dismiss its total Malton work force of almost fourteen thousand. Some were soon hired back; others were taken on by Canadair and de Havilland; many went to the United States. While there was criticism of both the government and Avro for mishandling of the Arrow scrapping, hardly anyone believed the program, which Canada simply could not afford, should be continued. Even citizen C.D. Howe, now collecting directorships like medals, told Lester Pearson, "There is no doubt in my mind that the CF-105 should be terminated – costs are completely out of hand." The Liberals' only criticism of the Conservative decision was that they had not taken it sooner.

If C.D. Howe had had to scrap the Arrow, his reputation as a dynamic builder might have been permanently tarnished. Since it was Diefenbaker, the bumbling

---

* "A large part of the inability of A.V. Roe to find a sympathetic response in government was due to the style of the company's president. Crawford Gordon had alienated not only the prime minister, but just about everyone in Ottawa, with his belligerent manner. There was probably nothing wrong with his preference for taking the night train for meetings in Ottawa, drinking and smoking into the early hours with his cronies, but it was hardly an intelligent way to prepare for an early meeting with Diefenbaker! Even people in the company found Gordon hard to bear. The vice-chairman of the board, Wilf Curtis, found Gordon's morals objectionable, his ethics questionable and his actions as president more a liability than an asset in dealing with the Conservatives." James Dow, *The Arrow*, p. 136.

prairie lawyer, who had done the deed, Howe's role in the Arrow débâcle – it developed almost directly from his over-rating of his own, the government's, and the nation's accomplishments during the war – could be largely forgotten. The fact that it was a wasteful sacrifice of Canadian taxpayers' money on suspect altars of economic nationalism and high technology could be forgotten. Then a whole new Arrow mythology could develop: the world's greatest fighter plane cruelly and mistakenly brought down by Canadians' lack of enterprise and vision. If Dief had only had the faith to stand by Crawford Gordon and the Avro team . . . just a few more million. . . .

The Arrow myth, like the Howe legends, flourished in the 1960s and afterwards because Canadians became so confident of their country's wonderful wealth and boundless future that they had trouble understanding that there were limits to the capacity of the northern economy. All those resources, all that growth, surely meant that government was doing something right. It must have succeeded. Canada was a land of big developments, big accomplishments. Unless they were frustrated by little men, disbelievers.

TOP: **The Bombardier Ski-Doo** *(Bombardier Company)* ABOVE: **Manicouagan Dam, Quebec** *(Province of Québec Film Bureau)*

17

———◆———

A Sense of Power

Triumph at Massey . . . affluence and power . . . Dief misses the boom . . . Canada's world banks . . . troubled banks in Canada . . . troubled life insurance . . . Zeckendorf and the development game . . . confident carmakers . . . Bombardier country . . . computers and hamburgers . . . Canadian conglomerates . . . MBA's . . . careers open to talent, but not women . . . fate of the "Queen Bee" . . . governments' sense of power . . . maîtres chez nous . . . businesslike government . . . Trudeau's confidence . . . economic nationalism . . . Canada in a world of global corporations . . . the need for more Masseys

The Argus group intervened decisively at Massey-Harris-Ferguson in 1956. The company was losing millions and seemed to have lost its sense of direction. To turn it around, Eric Phillips of Argus replaced James Duncan as chief executive officer, E.P. Taylor became chairman of the executive committee, and a Harvard-trained career manager, Albert A. Thornborough, was elevated to the presidency.

The new executives cleaned house. They hired top people from outside the company, even from outside the farm implement industry, who had been trained, often at business school, in running a modern multi-divisional, multi-national corporation. Phillips and Thornborough gave Massey a completely new structure, implementing the most advanced principles of "line" and "staff" responsibility, bringing organization charts, job definitions, statements of objectives, and modern planning procedures to the company, introducing the language of "profit impact," "rates of return," and "IPC" (Integrated Planning and Control) as tools for driving the grand old company to new heights of performance. When the new men faced special problems, such as the need for market research (previously done by intuition at Massey), they hired management consultants to give them the best advice money could buy. Massey's old self-made executives, high school graduates or less who had risen from the ranks because they knew their combines and hay rakes, were put out to pasture along with Duncan. They had had their day.

The organization's costs were brought under control, inventories were slashed, problems of duplication and confusion arising from the Ferguson merger were solved, and losses disappeared. Structural changes continued, as the Massey men moved to control production by reducing their reliance on outside suppliers. There were major acquisitions of engine and tractor firms; subcontracting was minimized as being too uncertain; company "sourcing" of parts, as fully interchangeable as possible, was implemented. Massey expanded its manufacturing operations in the United Kingdom, France, Germany, Australia, and South Africa, and began manufacturing in promising third world countries such as India, Brazil, and Turkey. A special operations division was created to explore and develop opportunities in new countries. Geographic diversification seemed to protect Massey from the vagaries of national business cycles, guaranteeing steady growth under almost all conditions. Product diversification was begun with an entry into construction machinery, and experiments in such growth products as snowmobiles. Massey's state-of-the-art organizational and control systems meant all its operations would benefit from first-rate management. The company could quickly identify and get out of bad situations (like snowmobile manufacture) but, most importantly, it now had the ability to manufacture and sell farm equipment anywhere in the world that opportunities could be found.

Sales, profits, dividends, all blossomed in the hands of Massey's professionals, operating during good years for the Canadian economy and the world. By the late 1960s the historic manufacturing firm, its name as Canadian as maple syrup, had annual sales of almost $1 billion, distributed remarkably evenly between North America, Europe, and the Third World. Head office was still in Toronto, but Massey-Ferguson had obviously, deliberately, become a full-fledged MNE, multinational enterprise, competitive with the great American multinationals. The Thornborough team were so proud of their achievements with Massey that they commissioned an economist, E.P. Neufeld, to write Massey's recent history. It was published in 1969 under the title *A Global Corporation* and was both a splendid account of the company's recent history and a celebration of modern management and the internationalization of business. The book concluded with observations about the Massey executive as "international man," who had transcended the limited outlook of performers in a purely domestic economy.

Massey seemed to symbolize the finest achievements of Canadian business in the 1960s, and it was not alone in having had a good decade. After 1957 the rate of growth fell, and unemployment rose, largely because business investment first declined and then remained sluggish. But revival came after 1961, creating the underpinnings of the fabulous sixties. By 1967, centennial year, Canada was riding the longest sustained boom in its history, quarter after quarter of uninterrupted expansion surpassing even the headiest of the

Laurier years. By the end of the decade inflation was becoming a problem in Canada and other industrialized nations, and there were troublingly high rates of unemployment, often concentrated in certain regions of the country. The 1970s were years of soaring energy costs, rampant inflation, and apparently high unemployment, producing a popular (and constantly media-fed) sense of unsatisfactory economic performance. But output and total employment regularly rose year after year – Canada's overall job-creation record was both impressive and little noticed – with real growth averaging 3 to 4 per cent per annum, a rate at which standards of living double every generation. The world wanted Canadian products; foreigners and Canadians rushed to invest in Canada; high levels of consumer confidence and spending kept domestic markets thriving; technological improvements in products from diapers to space stations fed consumer aspirations, revolutionized production and communications methods, and began to knit the world into Marshall McLuhan's "global village."

The decades after 1945 were the age of peace and prosperity that the builders of Canada had dreamed of and the veterans of two wars had fought for. Not since the Edwardian summer of Sir Wilfrid Laurier's Canada had the peaceable kingdom experienced such steadily rising levels of wealth combined with social and political stability. And now the progress was from a much higher base: the Canadian people shared with Americans, Scandinavians, and a few others, levels of mass affluence unprecedented in human history.

It became fashionable in quasi-intellectual circles to scorn material progress. A 1958 bestseller written by an expatriate Canadian economist, John Kenneth Galbraith, gave the world a catch-phrase for its new wealth, *The Affluent Society*. Galbraith's book, which made its author wealthy, oozed neo-puritanical contempt for unleavened materialism. Ordinary Canadians, and particularly people in business, knew that economic growth fostered freedom, because it increased individuals' range of choices and opportunities. Wealth, income, savings, gave power to people, organizations, and governments. Consumers could enjoy leisure activities, travel, or purchase better health and education; corporations could expand and diversify into new activities and services; governments could provide new services to their constituents.

A new sense of potentiality and power, largely the consequence of years of growth and affluence, began to affect Canadians and their institutions in the early 1960s. It was not seriously tempered, we will see, until the 1980s. For Canadian business, evidence of the sense of power was all around: in the maturing of Massey-Ferguson and other maple leaf multinationals; the creation of huge new industries, ranging from real estate development to telecommunications; heated competition and expansion in financial services; the ballooning development of oil and gas; the adoption of modern management techniques and the explosion of business schools; and the beginning of the end of the old ethnic exclusivity as networks and networking crumbled in a world of ready information, fast-moving competition, and ambitious, talented newcomers to business life.

Governments and politicians acknowledged few limits to their power. They came to believe they could give Canadians unprecedented levels of social service, create employment and industrial development, restructure the economies of whole regions and, if necessary, the entire country. Most notably, some Canadians inside and outside of government began to believe the country was so firmly in command of its destiny that the old reliance on outsiders for capital and entrepreneurial energy was no longer necessary. Instead of being helped by foreign investors, Canadians were being held back, even menaced by them, such critics came to believe. In a surge of economic nationalism that gathered strength through the 1960s and reached several climaxes during the 1970s, the newly confident, newly powerful Canadians moved to seize control of the commanding heights of their economy.

J OHN DIEFENBAKER anticipated the new Canadian confidence in his 1957 and 1958 election campaigns. His speeches resonated with images of Canada in the making, a fabulously rich northern kingdom reaching into its Arctic fastness to develop the minerals and water-power of the last frontier, processing its resources into manufactured goods, reducing its dependence on foreign enterprise; Canadians, young, vibrant, on the move, government and business working together to create hundreds of thousands of new jobs. "A new vision!" Diefenbaker proclaimed, "A new hope! A new soul for Canada!"

Then his government scrapped the Arrow, wrestled with the highest levels of unemployment since the war, fired the governor of the Bank of Canada, James Coyne, who insisted on running a tight money policy in years of slow growth, and was most innovative in designing new public works programs. The Chief's development visions were premature, especially in the North, where it took years to get railroads up to the known mineral deposits, and many more years to find other economic mines. The maturing of defence commitments affected more than aircraft, for the United States Atomic Energy Commission stopped stockpiling uranium in the late 1950s, imperilling the whole industry and threatening to turn Uranium City, Elliot Lake, and other bonanza communities into ghost towns. The trans-Canada gas pipeline was quickly built, and opened in 1958, but the wonderfully promising oil and gas industry of the West developed painfully slowly because of low prices. Through most of the fifties much of western Canada was still the "next-year country" of depression imagery. Only toward the end of its term of office did the Diefenbaker government score a marketing coup in negotiating huge wheat sales to the People's Republic of China and the USSR.

C.D. Howe thought Canada needed to have one or more great development projects under way to keep the economy stimulated, and the fifties had seen the St. Lawrence Seaway, rearmament, Labrador's iron, and then the pipeline. In 1957 it seemed as though there would be an incredible mega-project in British Columbia when W.A.C. Bennett announced the plans of the mysterious Swedish millionaire, Axel Wenner-Gren (Electrolux vacuum cleaners and Servel refrigerators), to develop the Rocky Mountain Trench. A forty-thousand-square-mile kingdom in the north-central interior would be transformed by a billion dollar 160-mile-per-hour monorail, pulp mills, and great hydro-electric projects. Wenner-Gren soon turned out to be another visionary promoter, cut from the F.H. Clergue cloth, and somewhat soiled for apparently having helped the Nazis with some of their visions during the war. Nothing came of the Rocky Mountain Trench dreaming – except Bennett's renewed determination to support railways, power dams, and anything else that would develop British Columbia's resources.

Came the 1960s and it seemed feasible to carry out all but the most fantastic of the developers' dreams. The mammoth power projects – on the Columbia, the South Saskatchewan, the Manicouagan, at Churchill Falls in Labrador, and eventually on the Peace – would have satiated an earlier generation's dreams. Now they only whetted engineers' appetites: James Bay would be next, and surely the harnessing of the tidal power of Fundy would be only a few years away. Neither mining nor forest developments had the glamour of the big dams and the artificial lakes, but that Pine Point mine of Cominco's, reached by the longest railroad built in Canada since the twenties, was the largest copper-lead-zinc producer in the world. And it was one of dozens of new Canadian base metals mines. Many were in British Columbia where low-grade copper and molybdenum deposits had become economic to exploit, bringing almost as much activity to the interior as Axel Wenner-Gren had envisioned. The mills and smelters and refineries at Trail, Sudbury, Flin Flon, and Noranda belched smoke and gases twenty-four hours a day creating metal for a hungry world. Uranium markets stabilized as the nuclear power industry needed food for its reactors, and when they threatened to collapse again in the early 1970s the government of Canada obligingly created an international cartel to help minimize the damage. Extractable iron ore seemed everywhere in Ontario now, not to mention soaring Labrador and Quebec production. Canada's forests were being torn down as never before to feed world demand for wood and paper; with the spread of pulp mills across the northern prairie provinces and up the North Shore of the St. Lawrence, it seemed as though the woodsmen would not stop until they reached the tree line in the Arctic. The oilmen were heading north too, as they began mining the tar sands of western Alberta and drilled holes in the high Arctic itself.

It was necessary in the sixties to rethink the traditional assumptions about the prairies as nothing but farm and ranch country. Apart from all the oil and gas,

whose future looked brighter year by year, there were such unexpected developments as the fantastic Saskatchewan potash boom. Saskatoon, it turned out, was
built roughly on top of the world's largest accessible deposits of potash. They
were just starting to be mined in 1958, the year of the Diefenbaker vision. In the
1960s the industry grew spectacularly – 25 per cent per year between 1962 and
1970 – to feed the world's fertilizer plants and nourish the "green revolution."
Profits were said to range "from significant to enormous." By 1969 Canada was
the world's largest potash producer. Saskatoon, the fastest growing city in the
west, called itself the "potash capital of the world." Poor, flat Saskatchewan, a
weak link in Confederation since the Great Depression, now seemed to have come
of age as a diversified producer of natural wealth: potash, uranium, pulp, oil, and
more wheat than ever before. And still more: by the early 1960s Saskatchewan
had its own steel mill, Interprovincial Steel and Pipe Corporation Limited of
Regina, the product of an alliance between entrepreneurial managers and an
enthusiastic NDP government. IPSCO's salesmen are said to have been trained to
refer to the chief competition, Stelco, as "the Eastern bastards."

(They needed to play the regional chauvinism card for all it was worth because Stelco and the other Ontario steel companies, Algoma and Dofasco,
provided powerful competition in most lines through the 1960s. As a result of war
and defence contracting and pipelines and steady industrial demand, the leading
Canadian steel companies had expanded and modernized their plants and become
among the most efficient producers on the continent. The sole exception was the
old DOSCO establishment at Sydney, Nova Scotia, taken over by A.V. Roe; it had
been running down for years and continued to decline along with its parent and
the rest of Hawker-Siddeley's Canadian assets. In 1966–67 Hawker-Siddeley gave
up: the Bell Island iron mines went to the government of Newfoundland, Cape
Breton's coal mines to a federal crown corporation, the Sydney steel mill to the
government of Nova Scotia. The Nova Scotians, for their part, tended to think of
their chief competitors as the Upper Canadian bastards.)

The big Canadian mining and resource companies – Inco, Falconbridge,
Alcan, Cominco, Abitibi-Price, MacMillan-Bloedel, Noranda, Hollinger, and
others – enjoyed a golden decade of high prices and growth. If they missed out on
opportunities to expand, newcomers, often from abroad, were there to seize them;
the Americans developed most of the potash mines of Saskatchewan, for example,
and the British and European consortium behind the British Newfoundland Company, BRINCO, brought in the huge Churchill Falls power project in Labrador.
Some of the biggest resource companies, undertaking the biggest projects, were
the provincially owned electrical companies. They usually had "hydro" in their
names, but, led by Ontario, many of their planners were designing the nuclear
power stations that everyone thought would dominate the twenty-first century.
The technology they bought, said by many to be the world's best, came from

Atomic Energy of Canada Limited, the crown corporation that intended to make the CANDU the world's most popular reactor.

The growth of Noranda Mines nicely symbolized Canadian achievement in natural resources. American money seeded its growth in the 1920s, but Canadians liked what they saw and bought its shares, achieving dominance in the 1930s. The giant Horne ore body at Noranda was so rich in copper, gold, and silver, that the company seemed to wallow in income no matter what happened in Canada or on world markets. Noranda never had a losing year. Its directors poured earnings into expansion – first into smelting and refining, then into secondary metal manufacturing, and soon into the acquisition of more mining properties. By the early 1960s Noranda was a mining giant, controlling copper, lead, zinc, molybdenum, silver, and gold properties from one end of Canada to the other. Then it spilled into other resource industries. A major property in Saskatchewan became one of the few potash mines developed by a Canadian company. Noranda went into aluminum manufacture in the U.S. midwest, where hydro-obsessed companies seemed to have neglected opportunities. The forests of British Columbia lured the eastern miners into one project after another: a few sawmills, then a joint venture in pulp with an American firm, then takeovers of British Columbia Forest Products, Fraser Companies Limited, and finally in 1981 control of MacMillan-Bloedel. Noranda operated only a few mines and other facilities outside of North America, but as a multi-divisional resource giant, exporting all over the world, and with sales that had grown from the tens of millions in the 1950s into the billions by 1967, Noranda had become a global corporation as surely as Massey-Ferguson.

The most truly global opportunities came in finance and were largely unrelated to the Canadian economy, but meant huge increases in business for the Canadian banks. International banking was given an enormous stimulus in the 1960s: world demand for working and investment capital soared just as American spending abroad led to the creation of huge pools of money that stayed abroad and came to be called Eurodollars. From their origins the Canadian chartered banks had specialized in international exchanges and at the turn of the century had become major forces in U.S. commercial banking and retail and wholesale banking in the Caribbean. International operations were neglected after the Great War and in some cases, especially in the United States, competitors edged out the Canadians. In the 1960s the Canadians renewed their search for foreign business, and found it everywhere – not only in the United States and Latin America, where old branches were revitalized and new ones opened, but in Great Britain, Europe, the Far East, the Pacific Rim, the whole non-communist world.

The old business of currency trading, servicing the foreign needs of Canadian customers, and serving as general Caribbean bankers revived and flourished

(Castro's Cuba, which nationalized banks in 1961, was a glaring exception; the Canadian banks, the Royal and the Bank of Nova Scotia, received better compensation than most), and developments like the expansion of tourism created important new business. But most of the growth came in Eurodollar intermediation. The floating American money was taken on deposit or otherwise borrowed, and was loaned to foreign corporations and governments, often in syndicated deals. As world capital markets evolved toward new levels of sophistication, the depositors, borrowers, the money, and the money-changers, operated with little regard for nationality or national interest.

The Canadian shareholders in the big five chartered banks – the Royal, Toronto-Dominion, Canadian Imperial Bank of Commerce, Bank of Nova Scotia, and Bank of Montreal – profited significantly from the large contribution that the international business made to profits. The Bank of Nova Scotia, which was the most active internationally in proportion to its total assets, saw its foreign currency business increase 10.5 per cent annually in constant dollars in the first half of the 1960s, 16 per cent in the second half. By 1970 the foreign deposits of the chartered banks had risen from less than one-fifth of their Canadian deposits to almost one-half. International banking offered both growth and glamour for Canada's world-class banks.

The big banks seemed the most powerful of all Canadian corporations. Their assets were incomprehensibly large, their branches were on every street corner, they seldom seemed to compete, and all banks and bankers emitted strong odours of formality, power, and conservatism. The few elements of truth in this image masked the fact that the chartered banks had failed to keep pace with the growing complexity and competitiveness of the financial system in the 1950s and 1960s. While they were expanding abroad, their dominance of the domestic market eroded.

The chartered banks had been conservative and defensive since the 1920s. Their last major innovation had been the development of the retail savings deposit business in the late nineteenth century. For many decades in the twentieth century they failed to take the next steps in retail banking. These would have been to expand retail lending through offering personal and mortgage loans, and to develop new debt instruments through which they could attract funds. To an extent the banks were crippled by regulation: for many years they could not take unsecured mortgages; the legal status of personal loans was unclear; in the 1950s the 6 per cent interest rate ceiling complicated attempts to make higher-risk loans. But, as Neufeld observed in his masterly study, *The Financial System of Canada*, the bankers had made few attempts to have the Bank Act liberalized. Content within their cages, happy to do business the old-fashioned way, they stayed out of household lending until the pressure of competition jerked them awake again in the 1950s and 1960s.

The sources of this banker conservatism have yet to be explained. They probably include the stultifying effects of oligopoly, decades of personnel recruitment along increasingly irrelevant network lines, over-reaction from the bank failures of the 1920s and the hard times of the 1930s, and the way in which years of concentration on banking as the accumulation of savings eroded the lending side of the business. The traditional branch manager of a chartered bank developed a mentality not unlike the community librarian: the books and the money were to be kept as safely away from the public as possible. And it was certainly unsettling that customers might shop around, daring to try to divide their banking. When Frank Sobey considered diverting some of his business from the Bank of Nova Scotia to the Royal Bank in the late 1940s a vice-president of the Royal – the Royal! – advised him "Frank, your bank is a bit like your church. If it lets you down, leave it. If it serves you well, stick with it."

The banks' inertia did not deprive Canadians of household credit, for other institutions sprouted to meet the demand, often with funds the banks loaned as credit wholesalers. Sales finance companies, which had emerged to finance automobile purchases in the 1920s, enjoyed spectacular growth after 1945, as did their near-neighbours, the personal finance companies. Caisses populaires in Quebec and credit unions in the rest of Canada dined on consumer discontent with the banks, and grew very rapidly in the postwar decades. Mortgage loan companies continued to do good business in the 1950s, though over the years a number of them had changed into trust companies. Mortgage and trust companies both had the power to do a near-bank business and they exercised it: founding branches wherever stagnant bank networks left an opening, taking demand and term deposits, writing a large volume of mortgage loans, selling mutual funds, finding ways to offer personal loans, and almost always staying open for business longer than the church-like bank branches.

The chartered banks finally entered the consumer credit field in the late 1950s, and soon reduced the finance companies to comparative insignificance. The 6 per cent interest ceiling was bothersome, but with the appropriate advance discounting, insurance and other charges, it was remarkable how easily 6 per cent could swell to 10 or 12. Bank funds started to flow into mortages by back and side doors: after 1954 National Housing Act-guaranteed mortgages were permissible, and, as with consumer credit, banks acted as wholesalers to mortgage-lending firms, sometimes controlling them. The banks gradually became aggressive competitors for funds at both ends of the market, offering many more instruments to meet the needs of big and small lenders, savers, and short-term depositers. In the 1950s they even started luring away each other's corporate parishioners, for special services.

Competition among financial institutions grew steadily during the 1960s boom. Trust companies stayed open on Saturdays and in the evenings, banks offered "Red Convertible" loans, finance companies raised capital directly by selling debentures paying unheard of 8 and 9 per cent interest. Aggressive entrepreneurs even prepared to enter Canadian banking itself. An alliance between the former governor of the Bank of Canada, James Coyne, and a Toronto financial whiz-kid, Sinclair Stevens, never quite worked in the promotion of the Bank of Western Canada, which got a charter but did not open. But a second Bank of British Columbia, god-fathered by W.A.C. Bennett's Social Credit government, did open in 1967 and managed to survive. As other chartered banks were proposed, promoted, opened, or merged, a new issue developed when the tiny Mercantile Bank of Canada was acquired by Citibank of New York and proposed to expand. Should foreigners or foreign banks be allowed into the country? Was Mercantile a camel with its nose in the tent? Should the government regulate numbers of camels or the size of noses, or should it open the tent to fresh air?

Parliament was not ready to create a wide-open banking marketplace. The 1967 Bank Act severely restricted foreign ownership of Canadian banks. It also restricted Canadian ownership, setting a 10 per cent cap on any individual holding, while banning interlocking directorships with other financial institutions. Banks would neither be controlled or controllers. Within those limits, they would be much freer to compete, for ceilings on interest rates and the ban on mortgage lending effectively disappeared. The decision to let interest rates be governed by competition among lenders marked government recognition that the market was now competitive.

It was so competitive, in fact, that some of the weaker or more reckless of the expanding finance and trust companies outran the limits of their resources and failed or negotiated death-bed mergers. The 1965 collapse of Atlantic Acceptance Corporation was the worst financial failure in the Dominion since the 1920s, and nearly dragged down an important trust company. The Prudential Finance Corporation went down in 1966, and when York Trust and Savings faltered that winter – depositors were staging runs on trust companies just like the old runs on banks – the federal government stepped in to create the Canada Deposit Insurance Corporation to protect most depositors (under $20,000) from loss. It seemed to stabilize the situation and the competitive game continued, with the fast-revitalizing banks starting to make the running at home as well as abroad.

———————

The biggest losers in the financial scramble of the 1960s were the life insurance companies. The insurance men faced a crisis that had been building gradually but inexorably since at least the 1930s, the obsolescence of their principal product. Life insurance per se was as popular as ever with Canadians, perhaps even more so, for the idea hardly needed selling any more. It was the savings component of traditional whole life insurance that had fallen out of favour. Canadians were happy to buy simple term life and lots of it, often through group plans. But growing numbers of them stopped looking to insurance plans for their security in old age.

The field was partly usurped by Ottawa's universal insurance – first old age pensions in 1951, then the Canada Pension Plan in 1965. Private pension plans did grow rapidly after the war, but a large slice of that business fell to trust companies as trustees, rather than to the life companies. The trust companies and many other firms also sold the mutual funds which became a popular personal savings alternative to whole life. The insurance companies were slow to revise their product to meet the competition and slow to offer new products, such as mutual funds or the registered retirement savings plans made attractive by tax changes in the late 1950s. They could not find important new kinds of insurance to sell, for the logical extension of life insurance was health insurance, where first provincial medical associations and then governments in the 1950s and 1960s staked out a near monopoly, leaving a few crumbs for specialists to ingest.

The life insurance industry's total assets grew steadily and impressively, yet its share of total financial assets declined steadily after the war. In the 1960s its share of the Canadian savings dollar plummeted, from 47 per cent of total personal savings in 1962 to 20 per cent in 1971. Entrepreneurial personalities like George Cox or the Macaulays, who had been attracted to life insurance companies as pools of capital, disappeared from management ranks in the highly regulated industry. They were replaced by actuaries and accountants, good at minding the store and computerizing the files (the industry was a Canadian leader in office automation), but not sure how to respond as the business weakened in an era of prosperity, two-income families, cradle-to-the grave social security, and competition from other financial institutions.

The picture was not entirely bleak. Term insurance sold well and the established companies earned substantial investment income. Like the banks, the insurance companies had not emphasized their foreign business after the First World War, but some stayed active abroad, where there were many opportunities. In the sixties the firms gradually began adjusting their Canadian product and changing the mix of their investments. Real estate, in which many of the Canadian life companies took substantial interests, was a good investment. Common stocks, to which they returned in 1965 after decades of conservatism and regulatory controls, yielded a very poor return.

The way Bill Zeckendorf told it, he had gone up to Montreal and shaken the backwoods Canadians out of their slumber. "Montreal had little wealth, dynamism, or modernity...I was the entrepreneur-risk-taker. I took the multi-million-dollar gamble, which nobody else in that country was willing to take...Montreal and Canada will never be quite the same again." Zeckendorf's gamble was that he could take a hole in the ground, owned by the CNR, and make it the site of one of the world's great office and shopping complexes. He succeeded. The stunning forty-two-storey cruciform tower adorning Place Ville Marie became an instant

Montreal landmark, a considerable commercial success, and the progenitor of dozens of steel and glass skyscrapers, office towers, shopping concourses, even forty-storey apartment buildings, in Canadian cities from Halifax to Vancouver.

Place Ville Marie was the first and one of the finest monuments to the skills of property developers in Canada, men and companies who in the 1960s literally shaped the urban growth of half the continent. There was no better symbol of the new Canadian affluence than the successes of these developers. They supplied houses, shopping centres, office towers, and high-rise apartments, and many combinations of these, to the inhabitants of one of the most thinly-settled countries in the world, who, fortunately for the developers, liked to cluster in cities.

Zeckendorf's choice of a Canadian city for big developments in the late 1950s reflected the northward movement of urban frontiers. American cities had a burst of growth between about 1945 and 1955, years in which Zeckendorf's firm, Webb and Knapp, became one of the world's largest developers. But then many of the older American cities entered troubled decades of continued flight to the suburbs, downtown decay, and violent racial problems. The newer sunbelt towns did not boom until the 1970s. When that happened, some of the most visible builders in towns such as Houston, Dallas, even New York itself, were big Canadian property development companies, moving south after years of gestation and growth in the post-Ville Marie boom. William Zeckendorf's American companies, on the other hand, overloaded with half-empty New York hotels, had collapsed in the early sixties. Only an infusion of British money and a metamorphosis of Webb and Knapp (Canada) into Trizec in 1960 had kept the Montreal project going.

The Zeckendorf version was wrong in implying that the Canadians contributed only the hole in the ground that started their boom. Land development was a very old Canadian business, rooted in the landholding propensities of the merchant-seigneurs of old Quebec. Generations of businessmen had provided accommodation for workers in their company towns, subdivided farmland on urban fringes, built houses in new suburbs like Maisonneuve, Lawrence Park, or Shaughnessy Heights, erected four- or six- or ten-storey office buildings in booming Winnipeg or Saskatoon. The railways were particularly important urban property owners and developers. They controlled huge tracts of prime land, and in their heyday had built palatial stations and regal hotels. Place Ville Marie was built on railway land first assembled for development by Mackenzie and Mann. Henry Thornton's CNR had been about to build on it when the depression ruined everything.

Almost twenty years of depression and war tore the heart out of Canadian land values, shattering continuity in the industry. But life returned before Zeckendorf came to Canada. Federal mortgage schemes supported the market for thousands of new homes built by ambitious contractors like Bob Keenan in Thunder Bay or Bob Campeau in Ottawa. E.P. Taylor's Don Mills, its origins in the Canadian company town tradition, was under way in Toronto, where another company town, Leaside, first planned by Mackenzie and Mann, was nicely complete. In half a dozen major cities family development companies, often Jewish, had learned the knack of putting together land, leases, and money to build shopping centres, the earliest of which (Park Royal near Vancouver and Sunnybrook Plaza in Toronto) were opened in 1950. "A man without land is nobody," Duddy Kravitz's grandfather told him; in 1950–51 the young hustler in Mordecai Richler's classic novel bought the land around Lac St. Pierre in the Laurentians which would become the basis of his resort development.

In fifties' Montreal, it was the CNR's Donald Gordon (the former price controller), starting up where Thornton had left off, who brought Zeckendorf to Canada. Place Ville Marie grew out of a creative collaboration between the railway company, the American developer, and the Royal Bank (the bank provided much of the money and leased the space in the main tower that made the deal viable). And Zeckendorf's disdain for Canadian enterprise was tempered during his Montreal experience by the performance of a local builder, Ionel Rudberg. Rudberg started and finished the CIL tower, kitty-corner to Place Ville Marie, while Zeckendorf was still building. Only a little-league building at thirty-four storeys, perhaps, but a case could be made for Rudberg's as the more handsome building.

Zeckendorf and his associates started a string of shopping centres across Canada (the most notable was Yorkdale on the outskirts in Toronto) but failed in a proposal to remodel the downtown of the fastest-growing city in North America. The Toronto-Dominion Bank, which had decided to locate a new head office in a prestige development, rejected Zeckendorf's presentation as too modest. Instead it formed a partnership with another Montreal-based group, Cemp Investments, to create a Toronto-Dominion Centre in Toronto. Cemp Investments had been founded by Sam Bronfman of Seagram to provide for his children, (C)harles, (E)dgar, (M)inda, and (P)hyllis. Aggressively managed by one of Charles's McGill classmates, Leo Kolber, Cemp got into shopping centre development as Fairview Corporation, built the T-D Centre (its first tower, opened in 1967 outdid Place Ville Marie by thirteen storeys and 300,000 square feet), repeated itself with the Pacific Centre in Vancouver, and for an encore brought in the Eaton Centre back in Toronto – another deal Zeckendorf had failed to close.

Zeckendorf-Trizec had to sell surplus Toronto properties in the early 1960s, including large chunks of the Flemingdon Park development south of Don Mills. One of the corners of Eglinton Avenue and Don Mills Road was bought cheaply by a central European Jewish family, reasonably well to do, who had been displaced by Naziism and wandered through several countries. The children of Samuel Reichmann came to Canada in the mid-1950s to manage tile companies in Montreal and Toronto. They started in construction when the bids on a warehouse they wanted seemed too high. The warehouse experience led to a separate business developing factory accommodation on the outskirts of Toronto. A family company, Olympia and York Developments Limited, was set up to handle the Olympia Square development at Eglinton and Don Mills, and soon got into other office buildings and shopping centres. None of the Reichmanns sought publicity in the early years. Albert and Paul, the most prominent of the brothers, were devoutly Orthodox. Their reputation for integrity, in an industry where the telephone handshake meant millions, combined with a mastery of construction and marketing techniques, helped foster Olympia and York's growth.

Unlike the Reichmanns, other developers, including E.P. Taylor, began going public in the 1960s. Most of the Taylor properties were bought by Fairview and by the city's most successful apartment builders, Cadillac Development Limited. In 1974 Cadillac and Fairview made a billion-dollar merger to become Canada's largest publicly held property company, Cadillac Fairview Corporation Limited.

The developers had mastered techniques of land assembly, found sources of short- and long-term money, and put together the sales forces or the lease packages that made projects go. Some accumulated balanced "portfolios" of houses, apartment buildings, shopping centres, and office complexes. Others specialized in one or two of the combinations, or, like Campeau Corporation in Ottawa, worked closely with government. In the early sixties they reaped handsome profits and/or capital gains as demand drove up urban property values in most Canadian cities. Then the inflation of the seventies seemed to make the industry even more attractive. Real estate was a classic hedge against inflation. The cost of land would go up, the value of the owed dollar would keep going down. Western Canada's seventies' resource boom created new fields of opportunity for both migratory easterners and home-grown builders. Alberta spawned the Nu-West Group and Carma Limited, Winnipeg's Great-West Life's interest in real estate led to the growth of Oxford Development, and Jack Poole's Daon Development Corporation became the British Columbian giant.

The development companies seemed unimaginably large, each controlling assets worth billions. Their liabilities were seldom mentioned. The developers were certainly much more powerful than any rinkydink contracting firm had been in the old days, not least because they seemed to have direct lines to big pools of capital in the banks and insurance companies. By the end of the 1970s, the old streets and avenues of Canadian cities enclosed a host of "Places", "Squares", "Courts", "Plazas" and "Centres". In a climate of gathering citizen resistance to excessive development, it seemed time to look for greener pastures to pave over, tunnel under, and build upon. The big, powerful Canadian companies started moving into the United States.

———————

The new arteries of movement were the concrete expressways linking the concrete cities. Canadians loved their cars and paid a kind of alimony to trains in the subsidies necessary to maintain minimal passenger service. The Canadian automobile market continued to be dominated by subsidiaries of the giant American carmakers. Superficially, it was coasting along placidly: three big firms, steady demand, entry costs so high that real competition by domestic producers was next to impossible. Only a few Canadians noticed that the world of automobile manufacturing was slowly beginning to shift, massively and permanently. European car manufacturing had begun to mature. Canadian automobile exports virtually disappeared in the depression and never recovered. Then importing began after the war, as British sports cars were followed by German beetles and several kinds of exotic French and Italian vehicles. None seriously challenged Canadians' love affair with Detroit's chrome and fins, and the Big Three quickly produced a line of "compacts" to stop slippage at the cheap end of the market. But the overall crowding effect – Canadian buyers could choose from over 350 models in 1960 – began to cause serious problems for manufacture in Canada. Production runs were simply too short for economic manufacture.

In the early 1960s the nation seemed headed for an unhappy automobile future characterized by a growing trade imbalance, higher tariffs (they were still in the 20 per cent range) leading to an even wider price disadvantage to Canadian motorists, taxpayer subsidies to try to encourage exports, or some combination of all of these. Finally, the Liberal government of Lester B. Pearson decided to approach Washington about rationalizing North American automobile manufacture under a free trade arrangement. In 1965 the governments signed an Auto Pact removing tariffs on cars and parts, but maintaining useful market-share guarantees for Canada. Free trade instantly stimulated the desired rationalization, gave an enormous boost to parts manufacture in Canada, created tens of thousands of jobs north of the border, and reduced the final price spread for automobiles between the two countries. By the end of the decade cars and parts had become Canada's largest export, statistically ending the myth of the Dominion as hewer of wood and drawer of water.

The Europeans were not driven away. Long-term prospects for challenging the American manufacturers on home ground, as it were, looked so good that the big Swedish automobile company, Volvo, began assembling cars in Nova Scotia in 1964. Renault and Peugeot entered Quebec a few years later. Some automobile promoters even talked about importing and someday assembling Japanese cars in Canada. Many thought the idea was silly. The little Japanese tin boxes with their puny engines would never stand up to the rigours of the Canadian climate.

Canadian nationalists hoped that someday someone would make a distinctive Canadian car, like Sweden's Volvo, to meet Canadians' special needs (and until someone did many of them bought Volvos). It was only occasionally noticed that a uniquely Canadian motor vehicle had been manufactured for years in Armand Bombardier's snowmobile factory in Valcourt, Quebec. Few Canadians had ever seen a real "Bombadeer," as they called the lumbering, tank-like carriers in the newsreels about the far north or snowbound Quebec. Except in the war, when Bombardier claimed he lost money on his contracts, use of the specialized, expensive vehicles was limited to construction, government projects, and the delivery of essential goods (including babies) in snow country. But in the late 1950s the Bombardier technicians perfected a design for a recreational snowmobile, running on a single continuous rubber tread. The Bombardier Ski-Doo hit consumers flush with money to buy new tools (it became everyman's work vehicle in the Canadian north), and new toys. Production soared. In 1964, the year of the founder's death, Bombardier sold more than ten thousand Ski-Doos, was flush with profits, and had a near-monopoly on Canada's contribution to motorized travel.

Were there any limits to the growth of demand for snowmobiles or to the growth of the new Canadian manufacturing giant? "Mon pays, c'est l'hiver," sang Gilles Vigneault, defining Bombardier country. The company's Ski-Doo sales doubled annually for several years. It became a $300 million business employing more than six thousand people. The key problem for the Canadians was to keep producing a better product than the hundred other North American companies attracted into snowmobile manufacture between 1965 and 1970. The Japanese were interested, too.

Another new motorized vehicle of the 1960s seemed distinctively Canadian. Steaming, clattering ice-resurfacing machines, named zambonis, became the intermission distraction at hockey rinks, the quintessential Canadian meeting places. As with hockey itself, however, Canadians had already lost their natural advantage in ice technology. Frank J. Zamboni invented the motorized resurfacer at his Iceland Skating Rink in Paramount, California, in 1947. His Canadian branch plant opened in 1965.

Just as the big automobile companies left snowmobile design to the tinkerers, similarly the giant business machine company, IBM, did not think there was any commercial future in the original "electronic brains" or computing machines. Pioneering in computers was left to other companies, notably Ferranti in England and the Univac division of Remington-Rand, and to tinkering scientists like the group at the University of Toronto, funded by the National Research Council, who built UTEC (the University of Toronto Electronic Computer) between 1947 and 1951. UTEC was a thousand-tube monster that flashed spectacularly in technicolour and generated enormous heat as it did mathematical tricks and played games for a few minutes at a time between breakdowns. The founders' dream that the university would become Canada's computer manufacturing centre died when the sponsors decided to replace UTEC with a British-made Ferranti. FERUT (FERranti-University of Toronto), the first computer purchased in Canada, began calculating in 1952.

The Ferranti group became Canada's early leaders in computer design (their most important commercial effort was to create TCA's reservation system), but were quickly overwhelmed by American multinationals. As soon as IBM realized the commercial potential of the computer, it set out to make the best possible application of the technology. The IBM 650, introduced in the United States in 1953 and Canada in 1956 (the first sale was to Manufacturers Life), was the Model-T of the computer industry. With it, IBM won 85 per cent of the North American market. UNIVAC machines continued to be competitive through the 1950s, and other American electronic firms, including Burroughs, RCA, Honeywell, and General Electric (all with Canadian branches) took a run at the leader, but by the end of the decade it was a competition between Gulliver and a host of Lilliputians, or, as the media described it "Snow White and the Seven Dwarfs."

IBM maintained overwhelming dominance of computer mainframe production through the 1960s and 1970s. The company combined technological leadership with legendary devotion to salesmanship, service, quality, and employee performance. IBM Canada grew as spectacularly as its parent, leasing and servicing its whole range of machines, gradually reorganizing its Canadian manufacturing to serve the company's worldwide needs. There was the usual talk about IBM as a "computer monopoly," but the firm could no more control all the opportunities flowing from the computer than car companies could make all their parts, sell gasoline to their customers, or design road maps. In Canada IBM became a classic "leaky bucket," offering valuable first-job training and experience to scores of bright entrepreneurs who slipped away to cultivate opportunities they had noticed.

Firms sprouted to install computers, program computers, sell time on computers, trouble-shoot with computers, advise firms on their computer needs, make systems components, and invent new ways of doing everything related to computers. Inventors everywhere always complain about lack of capital and support. The whining had no foundation in the highly publicized high-tech game of the 1960s as governments, venture capital firms, brokerage houses, and ordinary investors vied for the leadership, glamour, and expected profits of participation in the high-tech revolution. By 1967–68 the pioneer Canadian computer companies, sporting high-tech names like Computel Systems, AGT Data, and Systems Dimensions, began going public. Investor enthusiasm turned their founders into instant paper millionaires. Everyone wanted to be a charter shareholder in the next IBM.

The steam and internal combustion revolutions had slowed after the first breakthroughs. In computers the pace of change accelerated. By the 1970s data processing was giving way to data communications as the industry's new frontier (instead of just making computers you started communicating with and through computers). Would this be an important territory for Canadians to claim? The country had been a leader in long-distance communications from the days of Alexander Graham Bell and the building of the CPR. Established firms such as Bell Telephone and Bell's manufacturing subsidiary, Northern Electric, were top firms in their industries. Canadian entrepreneurs were among world leaders in such new communications industries as cable television. And the country had an impressive pool of scientists and computer-oriented intellectuals, ranging from

Ph.D.s in the federal Department of Communications to Professor Marshall McLuhan, the University of Toronto's pop prophet of the world as global village.

The enthusiasts clamoured for an all-out Canadian effort in the transition to the new world, the new civilization, in which paper and print and pens and books – everything that had happened in the five centuries since Gutenberg – would become obsolete in the next few years. And Canada was definitely an international leader. Witness, for example, the success of its flagship telecommunications company, Telesat Canada (owned by the federal government, CN/CP Telecommunications, and the major telephone companies), launching in 1972 the world's first commercial domestic geostationary communications satellite, Anik A-l (named from the Inuit word for "brother"). Witness the emergence of Northern Electric, later Northern Telecom, as a world-class telecommunications research company, developing switching devices for an insatiable American telecommunications market.

Northern researchers were on the ground floor of the next revolution (the revolutions were occurring simultaneously rather than serially), the creation of computing power on grains of sand following from Intel's introduction of silicon chip microprocessors in 1971. Like IBM, Northern started leaking personnel and companies to exploit the miniaturization revolution. Was Canada's answer to the California microprocessing industry going to be its own Silicon Valley North in Kanata, outside Ottawa? Perhaps it would be the "Silicon Flats" research complex near Saskatoon, or Silicon Hills in the Eastern Townships (where Mitel Corporation was locating a big assembly plant). And what about this possibility: that as the computer revolution became worldwide, with computers in every home and office, all talking to each other and their owners, the "language" used to move messages back and forth in videotex would be the uniquely Canadian system, Telidon? A global village with Canadian wires, eh?

And American hamburgers. The IBM of the fast food industry – of the fast-growing service sector generally – became McDonald's, a worldwide restaurant chain that began to evolve in the late 1950s from a California hamburger stand. Unlike IBM, which pre-existed the computer, McDonald's grew from nothing, rising as older restaurant chains stagnated and rotted. A similar process occurred in Canada. The food services giant of the 1950s, the Argus-controlled Canadian Food Products Limited, was ideally situated to advance in the restaurant industry. It owned the Honey Dew chain of about thirty limited-menu restaurants, and strings of bakeries, candy and ice cream shops, cafeterias, and catering services. In the early 1950s E.P. Taylor and his associates decided the restaurant business was too easy to enter to have much of a future. ("You know, there are more failures in the restaurant business than in any other business in the world," Taylor told his biographer. "People who are not informed say, 'The public has to eat, therefore I'll open a restaurant and get into the food business.' A great many men who retire go into the food business and lose their capital.") Argus gave Canadian

Foods low priority, and eventually sold it piecemeal. The leading food conglomerate to emerge in the 1960s, George Weston Limited, manufactured fast foods (Weston's and McCormick's biscuits and confectionaries, Neilson chocolate bars and dairy products), and sold them (Loblaw's and several subsidiaries), and diversified into many vaguely related industries, but stayed away from restaurants.

The doors were open to new entrepreneurs, and to one old company that had been handling prepared food for decades. The Canadian Railway News Company, founded by T.P. Phelan, had been peddling newspapers, selling sandwiches, and running station lunch-counters for the railways and steamships of Canada since the 1880s. Logically it ought to have run down along with the railways, but CRNCo discovered a new market for its skills in the 1940s when the airlines needed someone to prepare box lunches. The company's airline catering and airport concession business grew faster than its old specialties declined. In 1961 the founder's grandson, Paul Phelan, reorganized the firm as CARA Operations, brought in outside managers, and expanded into restaurants and fast foods. CARA was not able to make a better hamburger – its Zumburger chain failed – but it knew when to buy into restaurant chains that worked. By the time of its 1982 centennial, the oldest food service company in Canada was doing $400 million a year's business in Harvey's hamburgers, Swiss Chalet barbecued chicken dinners, the provision of 55,000 in-flight meals a day to Canadian airlines, and the operation of newstands in airports and train stations.

What CARA did not do in the sixties was obtain Canadian franchising rights for McDonald restaurants. This opportunity was left to a peripatetic Chicago lawyer, George Cohon, who picked up the eastern Canada rights for $70,000 in 1968 and parlayed them into the presidency of McDonald's Restaurants of Canada and a handsome personal fortune. As the golden arches rose over Canada in the 1970s, Ronald McDonald became a better-known public figure than Sir John A. But American burger wars also spilled over the border, pitting Burger King and Wendy's against the champion, with Harvey's and other indigenous chains scrambling for the leftovers. The renewed popularity of franchising (expansion by granting rights to sell products or services, a method as old as Singer sewing machines, car dealerships, gas stations, and soft drink bottlers) infected industries from hotels to shoeshine parlours. It seemed an ideal way of grafting the energies and entrepreneurship of the small Canadian proprietor onto the trunk of experience, expertise, and advertising capacity possessed by big business, whether domestic or foreign.

————————

With even hamburger stands trumpeting sales in the millions and billions, and books being written about Canadian global corporations, big business seemed to have conquered Canada. Companies such as Massey and Noranda had grown too big to be confined to their old industrial homesteads, and had diversified geographically or into related businesses. For many years Canadian Pacific had led the way in diversification, as the railroaders went into steamship service, hotelkeeping, mining, aviation, and, to meet competition in the 1940s, trucking. In 1962 Canadian Pacific Limited spun out Canadian Pacific Investments to hold its non-transportation assets. This was a mighty portfolio that by the end of the decade included control of Cominco, Algoma Steel (which controlled Dominion Bridge), Marathon Realty (a major developer thanks to the CPR's urban property holdings), Great Lakes Paper, Canadian Pacific Hotels, oil and gas and coal properties, leasing, consulting, and securities companies. And it continued to grow as CPI began raising money through stock issues to make new investments.

It seemed particularly sensible to diversify out of industries where growth opportunities seemed limited. Through the 1950s and 1960s the big three beer companies swallowed their remaining regional competitors, knew that further concentration through merger would be prohibited, and found there was nowhere to go in Canadian beer except as demography and consumer tastes permitted. For years Canadian Breweries Limited tried to grow in the American and British markets. Labatt's and Molson's chose to diversify, the former into related food and drink companies, the latter wherever there were attractive investments. CBL's strategy did not work well; in fact nothing worked well for the erstwhile monopoly as its share of the Canadian market began to decline. In 1968 the company's founder, E.P. Taylor, allowed the Argus interest in Canadian Breweries to be sold to Rothmans of Pall Mall, a tobacco company embarking on deliberate diversification. When the writing about the health hazards of smoking appeared literally on their packs, Rothmans, Imperial Tobacco (later Imasco), and the other cigarette companies knew it was time to head toward new businesses.

The big firms were everywhere, even in the Maritimes, especially in New Brunswick. K.C. Irving had decided to limit the growth of his firms to the region, so instead of expanding geographically he went into one industry after another. By the 1960s the Irving group of oil companies (tankers, refineries, and hundreds of service stations), lumber and pulp and paper mills, shipping and drydock operations, newspapers, and other firms – one hundred separate enterprises – was more prominent in New Brunswick than any firm in a province since the days of the Hudson's Bay Company. Irving was a household word in New Brunswick. Outside it, K.C. Irving replaced E.P. Taylor in the Canadian consciousness as the new symbol of monopoly capitalism.

No wonder, since the Irving interests owned *all* the daily newspapers in New Brunswick. Journalists and politicians were particularly sensitive about concentrated ownership in the media, so there was great interest in the 1972 trial of the Irving newspaper companies for contraventions of the Combines Investigation Act. Some thought it might be a first step toward tighter control of the growing media giants, including Southam Publishing and Maclean-Hunter, which was now an imperial power in magazines and broadcasting. Long gone from Canada, Lord Thomson of Fleet continued to buy newspapers and supporting enterprises wherever they were available, including in Canada. He even bought a weekly paper in New Brunswick. The Irvings had no dailies for sale.

Firms that grew or fled out of their original industries invested money and management expertise in new fields. As Canadian Pacific discovered, the strategy often led to the creation of a holding or investment company not unlike such older vehicles as Argus or Power Corporation, or the Sam Bronfman family's Cemp Investments, or the Alan Bronfman family's Edper Investments. Holding companies had great flexibility for raising new money and for organizing forays into industries that might be unrelated to a firm's original operations, leading, in theory, to a steadier, less cyclical flow of earnings. In the sixties it became fashionable to hopscotch into quite unrelated lines of business, putting together conglomerates of enterprises. Sometimes conglomeration was just a matter of making shrewd investments in well-run firms in other industries; in other cases the conglomerators took their lead from American pacesetting entrepreneurs like Harold Geneen of ITT or Jimmy Ling of Ling-Temco-Vought and boasted of the "synergy" created by applying their management skills in different fields. Synergy was supposed to make the whole greater than the sum of the parts.

Some firms had little choice but to conglomeratize. That old Canadian investment in the Brazilian Traction, Light and Power Company was finally approaching termination as the giant utility company's tramways, gasworks, telephone systems, and generating plants in Brazil were taken over by various levels of Brazilian government. Most of the compensation and continued earnings had to be reinvested locally, but a portion could be brought back to Canada, now a considerably more stable home for capital than Brazil. In 1967 Brazilian made its first major Canadian investment, buying a 25 per cent interest in Labatt's (from the Joseph Schlitz Beer Company, whose Canadian acquisition had just been blocked by U.S. antitrust laws). The utility's directors formed a close working alliance with Labatt's management, led by J.H. Moore. The Labatt group eventually moved over to the renamed Brascan, and began directing a program of Canadian expansion. As more capital was repatriated from South America, Brascan commanded increasing attention as a powerful new player in the small world of big Canadian holding companies.

The old player that still got most of the media attention, Argus, had tired of the game during the sixties. The original partnership gradually disintegrated as Wallace McCutcheon went into politics in 1962, Eric Phillips died in 1964, and E.P. Taylor and Bud McDougald began to disagree on strategy. Observers who saw only the paper power of Argus, or its good record in Massey, Dominion Stores, and Hollinger, tended to ignore the decline of Canadian Breweries, the failure in food services, Taylor's inability to keep going in Toronto property development, and Argus's weakening earnings record. E.P. Taylor was at the height of his notoriety in 1960 when Canadian Breweries' gift to Toronto, the O'Keefe Centre, opened with a production of Rogers and Hammerstein's *Camelot*. In the next decade, the most prosperous in Canadian history, the most famous Canadian capitalist of the 1950s found his Camelot in the Bahamas, where there was resort land to develop, a very favourable tax regime, and titles for distinguished achievers. In 1975 E.P. Taylor became a citizen of the Bahamas. He had already sold most of his Canadian hold-ings, leaving McDougald and associates in control of Argus.

———————————

The Argus-installed management of Massey-Ferguson made it a matter of policy in the late 1950s to replace "self-made" implement executives with trained profes-sional managers. This was the new orthodoxy in corporate recruiting. High school dropouts who started on the shop floor or as bank tellers, graduates of second-storey business "colleges" with a smattering of bookkeeping and stenography, even chartered accountants and old-fashioned bachelors of commerce from the universities, seemed ill-equipped to handle the complex strategic and tactical, financial, production, and marketing problems of multi-divisional, multinational enterprises. Canadian businessmen needed more education in the science of man-agement, the kind of advanced business training that Americans were getting at their country's flourishing business schools. Canada needed more masters of business administration.

Many of the MBAs hired at Massey and other firms had American degrees, either because they were Americans or were Canadians who had done time at the Harvard Business School. A fair approximation of the Harvard degree, complete with training by case study, was available from the University of Western Ontario by the late forties. The University of Toronto, whose bachelor of commerce program, created in the 1920s, had been very successful, was not eager to shed its belief that business training was a minor supplement to a liberal education, but finally allowed specialization in management studies at the graduate level. In the late fifties, higher education of all kinds was sold to Canadians as the only way to develop the nation's "human capital." The sixties' boom in undergraduate and graduate business schools at new universities and old was as spectacular as any of the other educational developments in the decade. In years when the young were popularly supposed to be rejecting the work ethic, competition, and business values, the number of full-time undergraduates seeking business degrees in Canada rose from approximately fifty-five hundred (in 1959–60) to sixteen thousand (in 1969–70). MBA candidates went from two hundred to more than two thousand. In 1970 eighteen Canadian universities offered MBA programs.

After-dinner speakers still talked about the virtues of literacy and liberal education, but company recruiters went for highly trained business specialists. As in the United States, they bought their college-educated executives with huge starting salaries and the promise of fast-track promotion. Western's faculty of business administration remained the best-known Canadian business school, with York University's faculty of administrative studies the most energetic newcomer.

The highest starting salaries and fastest tracks were still reserved for the Harvard graduates.

The new executive knew a great deal about organizational theory, rate of return accounting, and planning techniques. Often his business education capped university training in mathematics, behavioural sciences, law, accounting, or, in the 1970s, computers. Equipped with the tools of modern management, the graduate could go into the business world, chose an industry or a company, and go with it. Not much attention was paid to concepts of entrepreneurship in business schools – what was the starting salary for entrepreneurs? who recruited entrepreneurs? The intimate knowledge of manure-spreaders or bacon or the special accounting techniques of the bacon business that men who actually made and sold these products developed over the years was not too important either. The chief executives of the conglomerates of the future would have to be able to sell bacon, manure-spreaders, and manure all at the same time, not to mention crude oil and perfume and geodesic widgets. If they got into trouble in any of these divisions, they would call on the management consultants – the trouble-shooters, firefighters, head-hunters, terminators, specialists for every management problem.

So everyone went to college. Even the raw recruits chosen to manage McDonald's restaurants took courses at the firm's Hamburger University in Illinois. Was the company running a ridiculous parody of trends in business education? Or was it giving its people a more practical, more job-oriented, and more entrepreneurial training than they could find in many MBA programs?

The new emphasis on education for business coincided with declining concern for ethnicity and social class in recruitment. Old network credentials of family, school, church, and clan were gradually superseded by diplomas and degrees. These were the new tokens of merit and potential; the smartest recruiters stopped looking beyond them into a man's nationality, or his father's income. In the post-Hitler era, the old ethnic consciousness was a fading embarrassment. Its passing was hastened by the rise to prominence of powerful Canadian businessmen with names such as Bronfman, Hirshhorn, Roman, Desmarais, Gerstein, Levy, Bata, Sarlos, Koffler, Cohen, and Reichmann. "It's a good thing for word to get out that you're not against doing business with people of my faith," Duddy Kravitz comments to old WASP money in the Richler novel, published in 1959.

For the pioneers, like the Bronfmans, it had been a struggle upward from the ghetto through marginal industries, and against WASP exclusivity and contempt that took many years to die. The building of Place Ville Marie was a fair symbol of breakthrough. It was a collaboration between an American Jew, William Zeckendorf, his Chinese-American architect, I.M. Pei, and two Scots-blooded Canadians, Gordon of the CNR and James Muir of the Royal Bank, to erect a building with a French name. By the 1960s Jewish and other non-WASP names (particularly Czech and Hungarian, as a result of Soviet rule in Eastern Europe) were appearing on the boards of even the most conservative Canadian banks.

Networking as a recruiting system would not completely die – non-WASPs in their own firms, and new players in big ones, often drew on their own networks – but was slowly submerged in the large organization's tendency to hire more on merit.

Gender was another matter. Not many recruiters or promoters in the 1960s thought that women wanted to be in business or would make very good businessmen. They seldom rose above the lowest ranks of management. In 1968 the Bank of Nova Scotia had two women branch managers. That was progress, for they were the first two. Widows and daughters were sometimes active in family firms, and a few entrepreneurial women were able to make careers in shops and services catering to women's interests (or, like Elizabeth Arden, leave the country and do well in the United States). But the typical Canadian businesswoman was still the supervisor of the secretaries or the head of Simpson's Shoppers' Service. The good news was that universities began to allow and encourage women to enter regular business programs instead of limiting them to secretarial science ghettoes. The bad news for businesswomen in search of role models in the 1960s was the conviction of Canada's most prominent female entrepreneur, Viola MacMillan, for "wash" trading in connection with the Kidd Creek/Windfall Mine scandal of 1964. The "Queen Bee" of Ontario prospecting ended her career in a woman's reformatory.

The MacMillans, of course, were old-fashioned entrepreneurial types, increasingly anachronistic in the age of the global corporation. Viola's conviction was part of a general clean-up of the mining promotion game as the Toronto Stock Exchange finally put its house in order and became a market catering to institutional investors and sophisticated public corporations. In 1965, during that modernization, John Porter wrote in his study of Canadian society, *The Vertical Mosaic*, that "Entrepreneurial capitalism has been replaced by corporate capitalism." Two years later in *The New Industrial State*, John Kenneth Galbraith dazzled a mass readership with his argument that the "technostructure" in charge of North America's giant corporations was now able to manage demand and plan production and innovation so effectively that it had won control of markets from consumers and the forces of competition. Modern business was manager-driven, not market-driven. Eventually even chroniclers got into the act: in 1977 North America's leading business historian, Alfred D. Chandler, swept away an older interest in the entrepreneurial drive by celebrating the triumph of professionally managed big business in his Pulitzer Prize-winning study, *The Visible Hand: The Managerial Revolution in American Business*.

Many economists and thoughtful businessmen, including most managers trained in marketing, knew that outsiders were exaggerating the power of the corporation. At least they knew it in theory. From the vantage point of, say, 1968, when sales and profits and dividends set new records for the fifth or sixth year in a row, it was not easy to find the weaknesses in Canada's huge corporations, dynamos of jobs and prosperity for a whole nation. In the boardroom of, say,

Massey-Ferguson, where you talked sales in the billions, jobs in the hundreds of thousands, markets, and factories, and sales forces and Special Ops on every continent, it was hard not to think that the visible hands of your managers were in control. You had mastered the marketing, the production, the planning so thoroughly that your future was secure and predictable.

———————◆———————

The new sense of corporate power was exactly parallelled by governments' new sense of their power. Political organizations grew much like businesses, doing more for their clients, working with record revenues, expanding into new areas, hiring more professional managers, growing steadily in assurance, apparently serving citizens' demands. It was a process with deep roots in Canadian political development. From colonial days governments had tried to stimulate economic growth, juggling resource and subsidy and tariff policies to try to overcome Canada's disadvantages and keep up with the United States. During the Great Depression, the focus shifted from promoting growth to supplying a safety net of minimum standards of social security. The delayed result was Canada's basic social welfare system, introduced between 1941 and 1951. Before and during the war governments believed they had the tools to avoid repetition of 1930s-style unemployment thanks to the Keynesian economists. The apparent success of wartime economic management enormously stimulated politicians' and civil servants' confidence in their ability to control the course of economic events. Were governments really at the mercy of uncontrollable economic forces, as they had seemed in the dirty thirties? Look at wage and price controls during the war. Government had exerted its will over markets in the most basic and direct ways and thought it had triumphed. C.D. Howe and his boys also thought they had triumphed. Hadn't they shown how the vigorous use of the power of government could change the very structure of the Canadian economy?

Through the mid-1950s federal intervention was mainly in the area of social policy and Keynesian fiscal and monetary management, supplemented by Howe's propensity to collect and use power directly. In the late 1950s Canadian governments began expanding their welfare consciousness into the geographic realm of regional disparities, claiming it was time to intervene more actively to minimize income gaps among the provinces. Similarly, as apparently Keynesian fiscal and monetary policies (devout Keynesians, like Christians, maintain that the beliefs have never been properly followed in the real world, except by the founder) failed to produce high growth and full employment during the Diefenbaker "recession," more direct structural manipulation seemed required to help Canadians toward a prosperous future. If jobs in traditional manufacturing were threatened by a combination of slow growth and "automation," for example, the federal government should train new workers and retrain old workers for new, high-tech jobs. And/or it should try to create new manufacturing jobs in regions of high unemployment, such as the Maritimes. There were only a few odd cases – the automobile industry was finally recognized as one – where the best growth strategy seemed to be to back away and let free trade supply the stimulus.

Provincial governments became strikingly expansionist in the early sixties. They had been eclipsed by Ottawa during and after the war, but by the late fifties they found themselves having to provide schools, hospitals, highways, universities, and other social services for the swelling ranks of the baby-boom generation. The provinces' interest in regional growth predated Ottawa's because they were the regions that wanted the growth. Joey Smallwood's former nation of Newfoundland led the way in "province-building" with its early fifties' attempts at government-led diversification. Eventually all of the provinces hired industrial development experts, launched development funds and industrial estates, sponsored trade crusades, and experimented with public-private partnerships in industrial development. Party labels meant little. The passion for forcing the pace of growth infected socialists in Saskatchewan, Social Crediters in British Columbia, Conservatives in Manitoba and Ontario and Nova Scotia, and, above all, Liberals in Quebec. In that province, the expansion of government activities was the keystone of a "Quiet Revolution" with massive implications for all of Canada.

The Quebec government's burst of interventionism and entrepreneurship during the Jean Lesage administration of the early 1960s was not unique. All the provinces, including Ontario, increased their spending, their bureaucracies, and their demands on Ottawa for more power and money to provide more services for their people. The difference in Quebec was that the Lesage government quickly identified its policies with the advancement of Canada's second-largest ethnic group. While other governments talked vaguely about serving all the people, the Quebec government set out to be the agent for elevating French Canadians in Quebec life and in Canada. It intended to make them, as René Lévesque and Lesage's other nationalist ministers liked to put it, *maîtres chez nous*.

To a large extent in Quebec, anglophone business was the enemy. French Canadians catalogued their absence from the commanding heights of Quebec-based business, and looked to the state for change. At first it seemed difficult to exercise more than moral suasion over private companies in Quebec. A government-owned firm like the CNR seemed a special case, in several senses. Its Scots president, Donald Gordon, seemed particularly insensitive to the French fact in Quebec. During the mid-1950s the CNR's insistence on naming its new Montreal hotel, "The Queen Elizabeth/La Reine Elizabeth," was a running insult to Quebec nationalists, who favoured names like Château Maisonneuve. In 1962 Gordon caused a storm of outrage by telling a parliamentary committee that none of the railway's eighteen vice-presidents was French Canadian because there had not been any qualified French-Canadian candidates. During both affairs demonstrators burned Gordon in effigy. His insistence that the CNR's promotion policies were based solely on merit was seen as a front for traditional Anglo-Scots networking. Quebec's nationalists thought it was time to do some networking of their own, were determined to use the state and the newly expanded Hydro-Québec for that purpose, and would not be satisfied until the CNR and other federal companies, and then the private companies in Quebec, made room at the top for French Canadians. Years later, when the fully biculturalized CNR subsidized Gordon's biography, he was *The Great Scot* in the English title, *Un grand patron* in French.

Quebec government institutions carried out world-scale hydro-electric projects, launched a provincial steel industry, devised pension plans to fund a potentially very large provincial investment agency (the Caisse de dépôt et placement du Québec), and encouraged Jean Drapeau's breath-taking modernization of Montreal for the 1967 centennial and world's fair, and then his plans to host the 1976 Olympic Games. Many French-Canadian nationalists concluded that it was feasible and desirable for the provincial government to keep adding to its power until Quebec became an independent state. As it took form in the 1960s, Quebec separatism represented a provincial sense of the possibilities of power taken to an ultimate conclusion. The French-Canadian cultural and economic nation in Canada could achieve expression through the activities of a French-Canadian political nation.

When Pierre Elliott Trudeau succeeded Lester Pearson as prime minister in 1968, Canadian optimism about the possible uses of political power was approaching fever pitch. Since 1945 the welfare state and Keynesian economic management in Canada had been accompanied by year after year of growth, confounding all the sour alarmists who had complained about excessive government spending and power. The country had never been wealthier, its people and politicians never readier for new challenges. And of course the inexhaustible supplies of natural wealth in the north guaranteed that the Canadian economy could ride through any periods of strain or temporary recession without real worry. The land and its economy were very strong.

The state-organized centennial celebrations were a happy triumph, culminating in the universally acclaimed excellence of Jean Drapeau's world's fair, Expo '67. It directly followed the abysmal failure of the New York World's Fair, intended as a showcase performance by U.S. private enterprise. American enterprise seemed hardly a showcase of anything in the late 1960s. The United States became trapped in a tragic, losing war in Vietnam while wracked by urban decay, racial violence, and extreme political protest at home. Americans did not believe in big government. Canadians in the late 1960s could see little wrong with the performance of their governments compared with the American version. Even history seemed to show the difference: Conservative historians wrote of the successful nation-building of the National Policy in the days of Sir John A. Macdonald; the Liberal and NDP view of Canada's past emphasized nation-building by crown corporations, wise Keynesians, dedicated civil servants, and C.D. Howe. If the bottom line in the past had been so favourable, the directors of the body politic were surely justified in moving aggressively into new fields now and for the future. As well, Canadians told themselves that governments had to become bigger and more powerful in an age of bigness and power. How else could government cope with big business and big labour? If there was any hope of bringing the industrial state's "technostructure" under social control, Galbraith taught, it was through government.

Pierre Trudeau went into politics to use the power of government to create a new ethnic balance in Canada. But in the 1968 election he also talked about creating a "just society," mainly, it seemed, through greater emphasis on regional equalization. The late sixties were heady times everywhere in Canada, with a youth-swollen society shucking off restraints, taboos, and limits of all kinds. Canadians' aspirations for the Age of Aquarius became increasingly utopian. Everything was possible, in both the personal and the political realms. Pierre Trudeau, a politician who literally soared above the old-fashioned political crowd (during his first campaign he gave a well-photographed high-diving exhibition), was destined to lead a government more open to experimentation and innovation and participation than Canada had yet seen. It would try to solve racial problems, end regional inequities, maybe give all Canadians a guaranteed annual income. It would introduce industrial policies to modernize the economy, science policies to stimulate research and development, cultural policies to aid the country's infant cultural industries. Regulatory agencies would protect consumers from predators in the private sector. There would be regulations and agencies to make politicians honest and women equal to men. There would be programs to make all Canadians fit and celebrations to make them happy and human rights commissioners to make them good and environmental programs to keep them clean. Just as business conglomerates boasted of being able to operate in any market, now the conglomerate of government was ready to act on any voter need. What Richard French calls "the pervasive state" had arrived.

Did it have the organizational capacity to handle its new responsibilities? In 1962 the Royal Commission on Government Organization, headed by Grant Glassco of Brazilian Traction, recommended the modernization of government in accordance with the best practices used in the private sector. In the United States Robert McNamara, former president of Ford, was introducing modern management systems to the Pentagon as Secretary of Defense in the John F. Kennedy administration. When Canada's Kennedy, Pierre Trudeau, took office, considerable impetus toward organizational change had accumulated. It was not toward the meaningless "participatory democracy" some of the Trudeauites fantasized about, but involved a managerial revolution parallelling the changes taking place in the largest private corporations.

The old mandarins of the traditional departments of government, who had entered External or Finance or Trade and Commerce out of school in the thirties, served loyally, and were content to finish their careers with a few years as an ambassador or deputy minister, were shunted aside by a new generation of public administration specialists, planners, forecasters, systems coordinators, experts in administrative affairs, and other specialized generalists. One of their aims was to centralize the reins of bureaucratic power in the Privy Council Office and Prime Minister's Office, thus breaking down old departmental fiefdoms. Another was to rationalize cabinet planning and decision-making through an elaborate committee system. Planning and "prioritizing" were to receive high priority. The flow of inputs, decision-making, and legislative action would be systematized according to optimal criteria. Senior civil servants no longer made departmental careers. They were to become mobile generalists, masters of managerial process. All levels of government were more conscious of planning and coordination, and the need for expertise. To get it, they drew freely on forecasters, management consultants, and others, to supply the best advice taxpayers' money could buy.

By the mid-1970s most of these ideas had been implemented in Ottawa. There had been similar revolutions in the larger provinces. The trained public administration specialist became almost as desirable an item in government as the MBA in business. These public sector changes had many parallels to private events like the Argus revolution at Massey-Ferguson, and seemed to signify an advance to new levels of civil service competence, control, and power to carry out its responsibilities.

Hardly anyone remembered that the Glassco Commission had also called for the elimination of unnecessary services, greater reliance on the private sector, and the privatization of several crown corporations. There was not much sympathy in Camelot North for Mr. Glassco's view of government as "a necessary evil." Trudeau, the child of the age, set the new tone in a 1969 speech: he talked about political parties as "society's radar," and proclaimed that "the techniques of cybernetics, by transforming the control function and the manipulation of information, will transform our whole society." The creative use of political power was at hand. "With this knowledge," Trudeau boasted, "we are wide awake, alert, capable of action; no longer are we blind, inert pawns of fate."

Business spokesmen were uncertain, often divided in their views on the course of Canadian government in the sixties. It was hard to quarrel with the completion of the welfare state, at least in theory, or with the need to find ways of reducing dissatisfaction in Quebec. The Liberal governments of Lester Pearson and Pierre Trudeau retained a considerable constituency of businessmen who had been involved with the party since Howe's day; Ottawa did little to alienate powerful interests, and now and then seemed to have found a new Howe in this or that business-friendly minister. Conservative political thought, as a serious body of practical ideas, hardly existed in Canada.

Firms responded to new pressures from government and the public by attempting to become more "socially responsible." It was not very clear what was meant by the term beyond such practical matters as pollution control. Public relations specialists became important support staff in large firms. Corporate support for Canadian culture began to eclipse personal philanthropy, if only because the p.r. staff made sure the donations were acknowledged and publicized. Otherwise there was little effective communication. The popular media paid little attention to business except when journalists were angry at it, which was fairly often in the utopian climate of the late sixties. General business periodicals, such as the *Financial Post* and *Financial Times* preached mainly to the converted, and did so without eloquence, wit, or power. And there was one steadily growing issue that sowed division and confusion in business ranks. It was the new nationalism and its hostility to foreign ownership.

High levels of foreign ownership had been a fact of Canadian economic life since French and English traders first arrived to take over from the aboriginal peoples. Through the nineteenth century the crown's resources were gradually domesticated as Britain gave the North American provinces self-government, but outside investors remained vital to the health of both public and private sectors. As the twentieth century developed, the outsiders were increasingly American (from 13.6 of all foreign investment in Canada in 1900 to 75.5 per cent in 1950, and growing; the British share declined proportionately), and their investments were commonly direct – that is, through ownership of branch or subsidiary firms operating in Canada.

The inrush of American money, corporations, and managers was particularly noticeable during the post Second World War boom, partly because of its concentration in mining, manufacturing, and, above all, the petroleum industry. By the late 1950s more than 60 per cent of Canada's oil and gas industry was controlled by foreign firms, mostly American, as was more than 50 per cent of mining and almost 50 per cent of all manufacturing. In some of Canada's largest industries, such as automobile manufacture, it was impossible to find a single Canadian-controlled firm. In some Canadian cities, such as Calgary, it was impossible to escape American accents at work or play. Americans continued to come north, cash in hand, looking for interesting opportunities. In the early 1950s, for example, there was considerable American interest in Canada's life insurance companies, control of whose big pools of capital seemed to be available for the low market price of their shares.

The Communist Party of Canada objected loudly to American "economic imperialism" in Canada from the beginning of the Cold War. A few lonely Canadian nationalists tried the same refrain, but no one listened. It was the 1956 pipeline issue – there was the government of Canada, and its American-born minister, apparently underwriting an American company's control of Canada's transcontinental gas pipeline – that first unleashed widespread criticism of the "sell-out" of the country to foreigners. A year later this xenophobia was given a veneer of respectability when the report of the Royal Commission on Canada's Economic

Prospects, chaired by Walter Gordon, catalogued nationalists' worries about the high levels of direct foreign investment in Canada. "There is concern that as the position of American capital in the dynamic resource and manufacturing sectors becomes ever more dominant, our economy will inevitably become more and more integrated with that of the United States," the commissioners wrote. "Behind this is the fear that continuing integration might lead to economic domination by the United States and eventually to the loss of our political independence."

The Diefenbaker Conservative government attempted some nationalist initiatives between 1957 and 1963. It promised, for example, to divert 15 per cent of Canada's trade from the United States to Great Britain, a practical impossibility. It fully supported initiatives already afoot to protect the life insurance industry from foreign takeovers (the magic remedy was mutualization, in other words, the purchase of the companies by their policyholders; aided by friendly legislation, the Canada Life, Sun, Manufacturers, Confederation, and Equitable Life all mutualized in 1957-58), but was otherwise not inclined to deter foreign investments at a time of slow growth and heightened consciousness of regional disparities. When the Liberals returned to power, however, Canada was booming again, there seemed plenty of investment to go around, and the businessman chosen by Lester Pearson to be Minister of Finance happened to be his old friend Walter Gordon.

The extreme nationalist proposals in Gordon's 1963 budget (including a 30 per cent "takeover tax" on the sale of publicly held Canadian companies to foreign investors) created a storm of indignation in business circles and had to be withdrawn. Along with his other fumblings, they almost cost the minister his job. The fat was in the fire, though, and nationalist sentiment began flaring on one issue after another. Should the Rockefeller-owned Mercantile Bank be allowed to expand in Canada? Was it fair that *Time* and *Reader's Digest* could garner the lion's share of Canadian magazine advertising by recycling their American editorial copy in cheap Canadian editions? Were Canadian authors, Canadian culture itself, menaced by McGraw-Hill's takeover of the venerable old Ryerson Press, a leading Canadian publisher? The media noticed such foreign takeovers, and they noticed instances of Canadians losing jobs when branch plants shut down. It was widely believed that American-owned firms in Canada would sacrifice their Canadian operations to protect their U.S. interests, and would, of course, do the bidding of the U.S. government (everyone cited the notorious case of Ford Canada having been prevented from selling trucks to Castro's Cuba). It was feared that parent companies stopped their Canadian subsidiaries from being very competitive, vetoing any tendency to aggressive exporting or exploitation of high technology.

Specific concerns about foreign ownership were reinforced and heightened by a more general upsurge of Canadian nationalism in the late 1960s. Canada was becoming richer, more successful every year, a country whose infant cultural institutions and whose sense of distinctiveness were thriving as never before. The

United States, on the other hand, seemed to be declining: mired in Vietnam, racked by racial violence and ugly crime; at home, led by unpleasant men such as Lyndon Johnson and Richard Nixon. The border seemed more real and more important in the late 1960s than it had at any time since the War of 1812. To many Canadians, particularly young people and intellectuals, it seemed a good idea to supplement the customs houses with other barriers to excessive American influence. If Canada was becoming an economic colony of the United States, it might also become a cultural colony and then a political colony. Its history would have been an evolution from colony to nation to colony. A 1964 Gallup poll revealed that 46 per cent of Canadians thought the country had enough U.S. capital; by 1972 the figure had risen to 67 per cent.

In the mid-1960s the nationalist tide began to have important legislative consequences in the evolution of a new protectionism. It was an elaboration and extension of the old tariff-based economic nationalism of the National Policy. Now there were new policies to forbid significant foreign penetration of such key sectors of the Canadian economy as broadcasting, the press, and financial services. Canadian branch plants were told to abide by new codes of corporate citizenship. Government programs discriminated in favour of Canadian-owned companies, particularly in culturally sensitive industries like publishing and motion-picture distribution. In 1971 the federal government implemented one of Walter Gordon's favourite ideas by creating the Canada Development Corporation, a publicly controlled vehicle with a mandate to mobilize resources to "buy back" Canada (the popular image was that the CDC would be a kind of national "white knight" in takeover battles with Americans).

In 1973 Parliament created a special screening agency to oversee all new and expanded foreign direct investment in the country. The Foreign Investment Review Agency (FIRA) would prevent foreign investment that did not bring "significant benefit" to the Canadian economy; civil servants, and ultimately the cabinet – not the market – would judge the proposed benefit. As FIRA began operations in 1974, nationalist critics complained that the agency was too little, too late. The new target of their interest was petroleum, where the foreign multinational oil companies dominated the Canadian scene. How could their grip on Canada be broken in a time of world energy crisis?

It was fashionable in nationalist circles to portray Canada as a piece of real estate that the Americans were buying up lot by lot. Soon there would be nothing left. That the Americans did not own the oil, the gas, or the timber, almost all of which was crown property, was rarely mentioned. Strong measures had to be taken to resist the Americans because their grip on the country was increasing.

A few businessmen and economists knew that the Canadian reality was almost exactly the reverse of nationalist hand-wringing. The country was becoming less rather than more reliant on outside investment. "Canada's overall dependence on foreign capital relative to total Canadian capital formation has declined from the

first decade of the century to the third to the seventh as domes/
savings have expanded," the Task Force on the Structure of Can
(chaired by Melville Watkins, later a guru of socialist nationalism) ... ,
1968.

The popular media publicized the most visible foreign takeovers and repeated
the most alarmist statistics, both of which were highly selective. It was true that
American direct investment had recently increased sharply as a percentage of all
foreign investment in Canada. But the overall picture, for the few who bothered to
notice, was of steadily growing Canadian financial strength, considerable postwar
patriation through investment in such formerly foreign-owned firms as the CPR,
Hudson's Bay Company, Inco, and Alcan, and much lower foreign ownership
figures than the public realized. (Percentages plummeted sharply when sectors like
finance and transportation, almost 100 per cent Canadian-controlled, were added
in; neither agriculture nor real estate was considered by nationalists; statistical
measurements of the "ownership" or "control" of widely held firms were noto-
riously imprecise.) Nor did many people notice the very substantial Canadian
investments in other countries, including the United States. The economic
nationalism of the 1960s reflected a revolution of rising expectations rather than a
rational response to a worsening problem. The alarm about foreign ownership was
not a function of its seriousness as a national problem. That seriousness was
decreasing. Instead, it was a function of Canadians' growing belief that they could
and should do something about foreign ownership, beyond their long tradition of
reciprocating with their own very substantial investments abroad, particularly in
the United States. Fear of foreign ownership was a perverse expression of
Canadians' sense of power in the 1960s.

Most businessmen were appalled at the crudities of the new nationalism: the
media sensationalism, the distorted statistics, the belief that Canada no longer
needed foreign capital, the rejection of internationalism, above all the assumption
that successful firms, domestic or multinational, could or should base decisions on
non-market, nationalist considerations. But the issue was more complex than a conflict between internationally minded businessmen on the one side and an alliance
of nationalist intellectuals, populists, civil servants, and the young on the other.
For many years there had been frictions and competition within the business world
that had created stress along national lines. Within foreign-owned firms there had
sometimes been competition for jobs or directorships. Business-oriented nationalists such as Walter Gordon resented what seemed like the intrusion of American
networking into Canada, denying Canadians equal opportunities. Wholly owned
foreign firms operating in Canada also seemed to be denying Canadians the opportunity to buy into their operations. This raised the mid-sixties spectre of a shortage
of equities on Canadian securities markets, a concept widely discussed though
seldom analysed. The newly flush, newly aggressive Canadians wanted to move in
on those companies and get a piece of the action, as employees or as owners.

Other Canadian businessmen wanted to cripple competitors and/or create new opportunities for themselves. It seemed a rational business strategy for Canadian entrepreneurs to support certain measures that would limit or eliminate the possibility of foreign competition, make it possible to buy assets cheaply in the absence of foreign bidders, get special subsidies or loans from government, and expand into opportunities vacated by the foreigners. Canadian book publishers, for example, were pleased to support a growing gamut of controls on foreign-controlled firms; the controls turned the market over to them. The two big magazine publishers, Southam and Maclean-Hunter, lobbied strenuously in favour of the contentious legislation that eventually drove *Time* Canada and other split-run magazines out of business (fierce counter-lobbying resulted in special consideration for *Reader's Digest*). As soon as it was passed, Maclean-Hunter stepped smartly into the vacuum with an all-Canadian substitute for *Time's* Canadian edition. No one, least of all the journalists at the new *Maclean's*, paid any attention to the Canadian firms, some with deep roots, that were driven out of business by the legislation.

Canadian film makers were delighted at the opportunities that special subsidies and tax write-offs gave them, and lobbied hungrily for more. Eventually, imaginative entrepreneurs like Garth Drabinsky saw the possibilities for growth in tackling the U.S.-owned theatre chains that controlled motion picture distribution in Canada. The new protectionism of the 1970s had many parallels to the rise of protected manufacturing in the 1870s and 1880s. None was clearer than in the way producers in the "cultural industries" (a term once used only to refer derisively to state culture in communist countries) seized opportunities to mobilize the state and play on Canadians' nationalism in their own interest. Their demands for taxpayer assistance, their mobilization of a broader constituency of job-hungry Canadian performers, their flag-waving to the point of national blackmail, was all reminiscent of nineteenth-century manufacturers' support for the National Policy. In neither case were the beneficiaries of protection insincere in their identification of their activities with the national interest. They were simply in the fortunate position of being entrepreneurs whose principles and interests coincided.

The critics of foreign ownership, whether they were nationalist-socialists or nationalist-capitalists, always stressed how difficult it was for Canadians to make headway in a world of American multinational enterprises. The Americans had led the world in the creation of big business. Their enormous corporations combined the best of modern management, superb technology, an all-out commitment to research and development, vast capital resources, and, in a pinch, the muscle of the U.S. government. These were the corporations Galbraith described as being almost beyond control: they had conquered the market; it was not clear whether they had conquered government. The whole world, not just the United States or Canada, had to face up to the challenge of the multinational corporation. Europe, too, would have to respond to what the bestselling French author, Jean-Jacques Servan-

Schreiber, described in 1966 as *La Défi Americaine*, "The American Challenge."

Perhaps Canada could be a world leader in meeting the American challenge. A rich North American country, wonderfully endowed with natural resources, blessed with political wisdom and social systems that compared favourably with anything in the United States, it might use the power of government creatively to build its own multinational firms. It already had several of them: Inco, Alcan, Northern Telecom, Noranda, Seagram's, Hiram Walker, the Big Five banks, the Bata shoe empire, and its giant global manufacturing firm, Massey-Ferguson. One national priority for the 1970s would be to create more, particularly in the newly vital area of energy. To many Canadian politicians, nationalists, and politically-sensitive entrepreneurs, it would be a fine thing in the menacing world of OPEC and the Seven Sisters if an energy equivalent of Massey-Ferguson could be created in the western Canadian oil patch.

TOP: **Guests at Leduc Number 1, February 13, 1947** *(Imperial Oil Archives)*
ABOVE: **Atlantic Number 3 on fire, 1948** *(Calgary Herald Collection, Glenbow Archives)*

18

Western Energy

Two oil wells began the postwar boom. The way they came in symbolized the past and future struggles of the petroleum industry.

The famous Leduc Number 1, drilled by Imperial Oil near the village of Leduc, south of Edmonton, was always under control. Vernon "Dry Hole" Hunter's crew found indications of oil in the drilling mud at about five thousand feet and on February 3, 1947, got a small gush that was easily handled. Imperial decided to run a production test and invited five hundred influential Albertans to the site on February 13, 1947. Swabbing techniques were used to draw the oil to the surface. The flare pit was lit to burn off gas and give the crowd a thrill. A provincial cabinet minister turned the valve to begin production. Imperial immediately began drilling the "step-out" wells that soon proved Leduc was a major find.

Thirteen months later, on March 8, 1948, the Atlantic Oil Company's third well, drilled about a mile from Imperial's discovery well, burst out of control. It had hit the main reservoir in the prehistoric rocks. A surge of pressure drove oil, gas, and mud in an arching geyser over the rig. When workers sealed the main hole, new geysers broke out around it. A lake of oil, growing by fifteen thousand barrels a day, formed at the site; hundreds of millions of cubic feet of natural gas polluted the air. Canadian roughnecks and hired American trouble-shooters spent months stuffing the hole with cement, mud, sawdust, even feathers. They got nowhere. Mile-deep relief wells were almost finished on September 8 when the Atlantic Number 3 crater ignited. A roaring six-hundred-foot column of fire, spewing smoke visible a hundred miles away, seemed like an atom bomb explosion. Two days later the relief wells were used to seal the hole, and the fires went out.

Photos and newsreel coverage of the rogue well publicized Alberta's new oil patch everywhere, especially in the United States. All that runaway oil, millions of barrels of it, certainly showed the Canadians had something. The Atlantic Oil Company's proprietors, Frank and George McMahon, a couple of drillers and promoters from British Columbia who had been scratching around in gas and oil fields for years, were not hurt by the publicity either. It probably made fund-raising easier for more exploration. And Atlantic made a cool million anyway from collecting and selling the oil while the rig was out of control, a time when other wells in the field were shut down. Adventures like this did not happen to big American outfits like Imperial. Canadian independents like the McMahons needed very bit of luck they could get, making money on the fires of hell, to stay in the play with the big boys.

IMPERIAL OIL was legally a Canadian company, had some Canadian share holders, and liked to identify itself with the Dominion. Its executives tried to limit public knowledge of its real ownership because its owner, Standard Oil, was the hated oil trust, John D. Rockefeller's attempt to monopolize the distribution of petroleum products in the United States, North America, and as much of the rest of the world as possible. Standard bought control of Imperial from struggling Canadians in 1898, swallowed other Canadian refineries, and ran the firm as a completely *un*autonomous Canadian branch. Anti-monopoly sentiment in these years, on both sides of the border, focused on Rockefeller and S.O. as arch-villains. Imperial never had a monopoly in Canada, but it was the only national distributor; for several decades its control was so nearly total that its executives did not need the added incubus, as it were, of being seen as a tentacle of Standard. For years they resisted parental suggestions that the company's gasoline brands be changed from Imperial to Esso.

There was new opposition from the beginning. In 1901 several maverick Ontario producers merged as the Canadian Oil Refining Company. In 1908 it was taken over by Americans, reorganized as Canadian Oil Companies Limited, and expanded into a national distributor. In Toronto a former Standard Oil accountant, E.L. Ellsworth, started British American Oil in 1906 to peddle kerosene and lubricating oils, and in 1908 cobbled together a couple of second-hand stills as his first refinery. A few other Petrolia-based Canadian independents struggled on. Another major outsider entered Canada in 1911 when the Royal Dutch–Shell group, an Anglo-Dutch consortium formed to combat Standard, began bringing Borneo oil into Montreal and distributing it through the Shell Company of Canada.

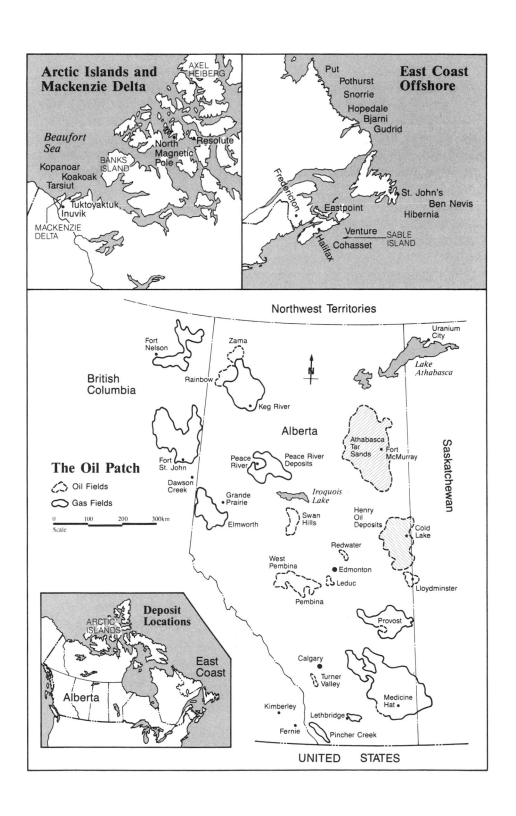

Arctic Islands and Mackenzie Delta

AXEL HEIBERG

Beaufort Sea

Kopanoar
Koakoak
Tarsiut

BANKS ISLAND

North Magnetic Pole

Resolute

Tuktoyaktuk
Inuvik

MACKENZIE DELTA

East Coast Offshore

Put
Pothurst
Snorrie
Hopedale
Bjarni
Gudrid

Frederiction

Eastpoint

St. John's
Ben Nevis
Hibernia

Venture
Cohasset
SABLE ISLAND

Halifax

Northwest Territories

Fort Nelson
Zama
Rainbow
Keg River

British Columbia

Uranium City

Lake Athabasca

The Oil Patch

⌐ Oil Fields

⌐ Gas Fields

0   100   200   300km
Scale

Alberta

Fort St. John
Dawson Creek

Peace River
Peace River Deposits

Athabasca Tar Sands
Fort McMurray

Saskatchewan

Grande Prairie
Elmworth

Iroquois Lake

Swan Hills

Henry Oil Deposits

Cold Lake

West Pembina

Redwater

Edmonton

Leduc

Pembina

Lloydminster

Provost

Deposit Locations

ARCTIC ISLANDS

Alberta

East Coast

Calgary

Turner Valley

Medicine Hat

Kimberley

Lethbridge

Fernie

Pincher Creek

UNITED STATES

There would have been more Canadian oilmen if there had been more Canadian oil. Petrolia's production, which had once been adequate for Canada's modest needs, dwindled steadily after 1900 (though there are still a number of producing wells in the region). No new fields were found. Petrolia-trained oilmen left the country and the supply was not renewed. Canadian consumers depended on imported oil and a new generation of imported oilmen who knew the business and had money to invest. The consumer did not yet use oil for home heating, relying on coal instead. Most of the coal was imported.

Everyone knew, of course, that nature had deposited more hydrocarbons than anyone would ever need in certain regions of the old Northwest Territories, especially the Alberta district. Knowledge of the tar sands dated from the days of Peter Pond and Alexander Mackenzie. But the Geological Survey of Canada, which drilled some experimental wells in the Athabasca sands in the 1890s, found that the mucky tar did not, as they had hoped, sit on top of pools of light oil. The tar sands themselves were commercially useless. So was most of the natural gas that disappointed CPR men in 1883 when they were drilling for water near Langevin, in southern Alberta. It could be used locally: gas lit the streets and homes of Medicine Hat (the city with "all hell for a basement," Rudyard Kipling remarked) early in the new century, and the little community dreamed that its cheap fuel would make it "the Pittsburgh of Canada." But the steel mills did not relocate, and the gas could not be piped economically more than a few miles from wellhead. Besides, electricity seemed the energy of the future. Imperial refined a few thousand barrels a week of Ontario oil at Sarnia, but left Alberta to a few Canadian drifters and dreamers, notably William Stewart ("Never-Sell") Herron and Archibald Dingman. They, and not the Americans, began Alberta's oil age. It started on May 14, 1914 in the Turner Valley near Calgary when the Dingman well of Calgary Petroleum Products Company Limited began flowing clear naphtha.

The Turner Valley discovery, plus Shell's activity, caused Imperial to begin serious exploration of the western sedimentary basin in 1917. "Imperial entered the search for oil with a cautious wait-and-see attitude, embarked on its first major operation largely because of competitive pressure, secured the services of a reputed drunkard and dope addict as its first field manager, and undertook an exploration campaign which was as defensive as it was energetic and extensive," concluded John S. Ewing, in a commissioned history of the company that was never published. Imperial's one strike, at Fort Norman on the Mackenzie River in 1920, caused immense initial excitement. *Saturday Night* magazine suggested Fort Norman had enough oil to wipe out the national debt. Officials in Ottawa suggested development of the oil under public ownership rather than by the gouging "Oil Trust." Believing that Canada's oil future lay in the remaining Northwest Territories, Ottawa gave little thought to the mineral rights on Alberta lands which it then controlled. In 1930 the lands and the rights were given to the province. Both Imperial and Ottawa soon found that the northern oilfield was too far from any market to be economic. It was completely unproductive until a few barrels were supplied to LaBine's radium mine on Great Bear Lake in the 1930s.

Imperial also moved quickly into the Turner Valley. It bought mineral rights, producing wells, and independents' production. Imperial's Royalite Number 4 well, flaming out of control, ignited the valley's second petroleum boomlet in 1924. But during that decade and most of the next, more than 95 per cent of the petroleum burned in Canada was imported. The real struggle among oil companies was in distribution. Starting with a garden hose attached to a tank in Vancouver in 1908, Imperial was the first company to create service stations for Canadian automobiles. By 1930 it had a national chain of 628 units. The industry grew so fast that the company had no hope of holding its market dominance, which slipped from 79 per cent of petroleum products in 1921 to 61 per cent in 1931 and continued to fall. British American rose impressively in the 1920s to rival Imperial nationally, importing gasoline from refineries it owned in the United States. Jobbers and local retailers like K.C. Irving and Charlie Trudeau could not be kept out of the industry. Competition at the pumps became particularly severe in the thirties as independents such as Joy Petroleum ("Joy is Better than Ethyl") took aim at fat markets like Toronto. By 1939 Imperial's market share was down to 47 per cent.

Imperial never lost money, even in the depression, but by the late thirties its gasoline distribution was relatively less profitable than British American's. The company suffered from unenergetic, Toronto-bound management (its president from 1933 to 1944 never travelled east of Montreal or west of Sarnia) and the incessant demands of the parent for more dividends. Its refinery domination slipped too, as rivals such as Shell built cheap new refineries during the depression. The hard times killed some oil companies – including Canadian Oil's American parent – but Canadians stepped in to buy its stock and keep the White Rose brand gasoline flowing. And there were tough, depression-born newcomers, such as the Texas Corporation, which came into Canada through McColl-Frontenac (an old Petrolia firm) in 1938 and gradually converted its stations to Texaco brands. When the third Turner Valley boom of the late 1930s finally led to significant Canadian production, the big oil companies stepped up their exploration activities. Wartime demand spurred exploration further.

Nobody had much luck during the war and in the first months of peace. The Turner Valley was almost played out, and only a few small gas fields had been found in its place. The country again imported almost 90 per cent of its needs. Shell became discouraged and suspended exploration. Calgary refineries considered importing American crude. Some was shipped up from the United States by rail and there was talk of importing oil through Churchill on Hudson Bay. Tar sands extraction had been tried by several entrepreneurs and promoters over the years, often with government support. Petroleum could be obtained from the bitumen, but even if your plant did not burn down after a few weeks of operation, the processes were all wildly uneconomic.

In 1946 Imperial was investigating techniques for synthesizing oil from natural gas, a technology used by the Germans during the war. In thirty years of Canadian exploration it had drilled 133 dry holes in the Canadian provinces. It had only found oil up in the far north, near the Arctic circle, too far from civilization to be useful. (War had been slightly different. In 1943–44 the U.S. army spend $135 million building the 4½-inch Canol pipeline from Norman Wells to a refinery at Whitehorse to supply oil for the Alaska Highway. The cost was exorbitant even by war standards. Canol was an extended white elephant, probably uneconomic even in wartime, that died as soon as peace broke out). The company was mainly interested in gas fields south of Edmonton when it decided to explore an anomaly that seismographic data indicated near Leduc.

———————

The Dingman "discovery" of 1914 set off "the wildest, most delirious, most uproarious, most exciting time that had ever entered into human imagination to conceive," according to the *Calgary Albertan*. The local men who had backed Herron and Dingman, including lawyers R.B. Bennett and James Lougheed, the ranching, brewing Cross family, and various real estate promoters, had apparently struck it rich. All the other locals in Calgary and for miles around wanted a piece of the action. The prospect of wildcat drilling in far-off fields ("out among the wildcats") did not attract little investors then or later. The best oil land was the land nearest the discovery rig, so promoters rushed to buy Turner Valley rights (mineral rights had been reserved by the crown after 1887 and could be leased; they were privately owned and transferable on land granted before 1887), or at least to advertise that their acres leaned right up against the Dingman derrick. As in mining booms, the appeal was to the small investor, in for a few dimes or dollars. Put the cash in one basket, take your shares out of the other. So many shysters infested Calgary in that first boom that the whole industry was given a bad name. Its reputation worsened when the play petered out in a trickle of gas condensates, many dry holes, and the 1920 sale of the discovery company, Calgary Petroleum Products, to Imperial Oil.

The Turner Valley strikes of the mid-1920s and the late 1930s featured more producing wells, Imperial's domination of production and purchasing, and the formation and survival of a few new Canadian companies. The twenties' rush to get close in to Imperial's Royalite properties was the usual promoter's delight. (James Gray in *The Roar of the Twenties* writes of the "lawyers' oil companies, doctors' oil companies, merchants' oil companies, farm implement dealers' companies, ranchers' oil companies, car dealers' oil companies, officers corps' oil companies, and school teachers' oil companies," plus a few senators' oil companies, formed to strike it rich.) For some serious promoters, such as W.S. Herron, whose Okalta Oils had several producing wells, years of dreaming and scheming finally paid off.

The flow was still tiny and consisted mostly of gas condensates, but the stocks of genuine producers such as Home Oil (formed in 1926 in Calgary by "Major" Jimmie Lowery, previously a real estate salesman, who hustled up blue-ribbon Vancouver backing) had a terrific ride on the decade's bull markets. Home sizzled with insiders' profits all the way up from a dollar to a 1929 high of $29. How big was the twenties' boom? Big enough for Calgary's first million-dollar deal. Ike Solloway, the stockbroker, bought a million dollars' worth of Home shares and Lowery spent the money to buy a quarter-section Turner Valley property from R.A. Brown's United Oils. No oil was found, but everyone's stocks gushed and flared. Then everything but a few small wells dried up in the depression. In 1932 you could pick up Home Oil shares for 15 cents. It was still a producing company, but petroleum markets everywhere were glutted and they were finding millions of barrels more of the stuff down in Texas and Oklahoma. At less than a dollar a barrel, western oil was sometimes cheaper than water.

R.A. Brown, Senior, an electrical engineer who had run Calgary's streetcars and other municipal utilities and invested his savings in oil companies, began the final Turner Valley play in 1936. Brown looked for oil under the valley's west slope when most others had given up. Nobody had loose cash to give away to oil stock salesmen in the depression, so Brown and his friends brought royalties' financing to Canada: they sold investors units entitling them to portions of a producing well's revenues. It was a marginally less risky way to invest. To keep drilling, though, Brown had to use his family's savings and get backing from Imperial and British American.

Turner Valley Royalties Number 1 came in spectacularly on the same summer day in 1936 that the city of Calgary defaulted on its municipal bonds. Almost every other well drilled in the next two years, most of them financed on a royalties' basis, became a producer. By 1938, with a total production of over six million barrels, Alberta was self-sufficient and was shipping oil into neighbouring provinces. The problem of price competition among oil producers, which in the nineteenth century had been solved by Rockefeller's combines, was solved for Alberta by the provincial government. Its regulatory board, based on Texas models, controlled wellhead prices and prorated (rationed) production to give everyone a share. Imperial and British American were the largest purchasers of crude oil. There was still only a local market for natural gas, most of which simply burned away in flare pits. It is said that hobos kept warm by the gas fires in the thirties.

Home Oil effectively left Alberta to prospect for minerals in British Columbia in the thirties. It came back to Turner Valley in 1938 and made the biggest strike of all, up in the north end. Another British Columbian who got in on the play was Frank McMahon, a scrambling hard-rock driller from the Kootenay country who spent the thirties failing to develop any of the gas and oil prospects that looked so good in the Fraser delta, the Flathead country, and up north on the Peace River. British Columbia's mining boom created the money to finance oil and gas speculations, but when nothing paid off and with the government locking up the best land for itself (Premier Duff Pattullo believed it should drill its own wells), McMahon and his backers decided to go wildcatting in Alberta.

The leases he picked up looked mostly like moose pasture and McMahon spent years searching for money to finance his drilling. His West Turner Petroleums Number One came in handsomely in 1938 and the follow-up wells were almost all good, but prices were so low and debts so high that McMahon could barely keep going. In 1939 the British Columbians consolidated their properties as Pacific Petroleums, the valley's second most important independent. Criticized for extravagance in his drilling contracts, McMahon left Pacific to chase new wildcats.

Oil-finding was never a simple matter of doing geological sums. Geologists had too little knowledge of netherworld topography to make anything add up, and at most times you could hire a geologist to prove anything. Hunches were important. Fund-raising was all-important. And when the movies are made about the early days of the petroleum industry, the most dramatic shots will be of "scouts" spying on drilling operations to get inside knowledge, and then of frantic kitchen-table bargaining for mineral rights on hot properties. The way to break Imperial's hold on Turner or Leduc was to go after the freehold rights held by farmers on land granted before 1887. Jim Lowery knew that Leduc looked good before almost anyone else did; so his professional "land man" locked up the rights on Ukrainian farmer William Sycz's quarter-section early on. Sycz, who kept a picture of Stalin in his living-room, became an affluent capitalist on royalties from the eight producing wells Home drilled on his land.

Imperial thought it had the rights to the Bronislaw Rebus quarter-section at Leduc locked up through the widow Rebus. But Frank McMahon's lease-broker got to the eldest son, John Rebus, who had a claim under the badly drawn will, hid him away for a week in a Calgary apartment, and got his signature on an option for the same rights Imperial was after. Imperial got 100,000 barrels of oil for dropping the issue. John Rebus got $200,000 plus royalties, the highest price yet paid in Leduc; the rest of the family was somehow pacified. McMahon brought some of his old friends, including Pacific Petroleums, into the deal, creating the Atlantic Oil Company to do the drilling. John Rebus was irate when the black lake around Atlantic Number 3 ruined his land for farming, but $366,000 in royalties from the spill was more than ample compensation – and the land was eventually put back in cultivation.

Leduc was a 200-million-barrel field, turning Turner Valley into a secondary field of largely historical interest. Better yet, the Leduc oil came from reefs that recurred all along Alberta's Devonian trend, a strip two hundred miles wide by one thousand miles long running diagonally from northeast to southwest Alberta. In 1948 Imperial brought in the discovery well in the Redwater field, northeast of

Edmonton. Redwater's 750 million barrels made Leduc look tiny. Every year through the mid-1950s the oil-finders brought in at least one new Devonian field the size of Leduc. In 1953 a Socony-Seaboard (later Mobil) wildcat in the rugged Drayton Valley west of Edmonton opened up huge new possibilities by finding a vast oil reservoir in Cardium sandstone. The Pembina field, as it came to be called, contained about 2,000 million barrels of recoverable crude. No wonder the Alberta oilmen used to say that extra zeros would take care of themselves.

Between Dingman Number 1 in 1914 and Leduc Number 1 in 1947 about $200 million was spent exploring for oil in western Canada. After Leduc that much and more was spent every year in the hunt for more black gold. Alberta was the centre of things, but exploration and minor discoveries spilled into Manitoba, Saskatchewan, and British Columbia. A few visionaries wondered about the far north. Oil companies came in all sizes and in several nationalities. The American industry had been growing fat on new discoveries for decades while the poor Canadian cousins watched Petrolia decline to insignificance. Given the overwhelming size of their companies and the favourable tax treatment Americans got for exploring for the strategic resource in foreign countries, it was not surprising that Americans dominated the Canadian oil patch. The foreigners put up the money for exploration, supplied many of the rigs and roughnecks, brought in engineers and geologists, built their own companies as wholly owned branches, bought Canadian ones, sometimes got into joint ventures with Canadian partners.

By 1956 more than twelve hundred firms were exploring for oil in western Canada, servicing the industry, refining and distributing oil and gas, mobilizing capital, and brokering oil and gas leases. Alberta's Social Credit government fed the boom with a cautious, honest, and, for the provincial treasury, highly profitable regulatory regime. After Leduc, Edmonton was the provincial centre for drilling and exploration, but Turner Valley days had made Calgary the permanent head office of the industry. By the early 1950s its eight- and ten-storey skyscrapers towered over the prairies, as up to date as anything in Tulsa or Kansas City.

Four big integrated oil companies – Imperial, Shell, Texaco, and British American – dominated the Canadian industry. Then British American bought Canadian Gulf Oil Company from its U.S. parent in 1956 for treasury stock. It was gradually realized that deal was in fact a Gulf Oil takeover of the largest Canadian-owned company. The old BA signs at gas stations were converted to Gulf, joining McColl-Frontenac as gas-station Canadiana. The new Fina stations of the mid-1950s were owned by a Canadian subsidiary of the Belgian oil giant, Petrofina, SA, which had decided to join the other multinationals in Canada.

Petrofina's 1955 acquisition of Western Leaseholds Limited supplied the icing for the first big Canadian oil fortune. In 1944 Eric L. Harvie, a Calgary lawyer who had been active on the fringes of the Turner Valley plays, bought half a million acres of freehold mineral rights from some dying pre-1887 immigration companies. A few years later he found himself sitting on some of the best acreage in both the Leduc and Redwater fields. By selling to Petrofina (for about a $20 million capital gain), Harvie abandoned any plans he might have had for a great Canadian oil company. Instead he used large chunks of his fortune (which continued to grow on royalties and rents from other properties) to enrich Calgary, Alberta, and Canada, with the Glenbow Foundations and various parks, zoos, and other public facilities.

The broad middle-range of exploration and production companies included the most agile of the Canadian independents, notably Pacific Petroleums (which had absorbed Atlantic), and Home Oil, control of which had passed from Jim Lowery to R.A. "Oil Baby" Brown, Jr. There was room for a small, international and integrated company, Husky Oil, which was largely the personal creation of a border-country rancher, Glenn Nielson. Nielson started up a small refinery in Wyoming in the late 1930s, sold bunker oil to the U.S. navy, then saw the opportunity to be the first to refine the heavy oils in the Lloydminster field on the Alberta-Saskatchewan border. Husky sold a lot of asphalt as a by-product, and gradually developed a major chain of western gas stations.

Scouts and geologists for upstarts like Husky jostled with agents of the venerable Hudson's Bay Company and Canadian Pacific Railway, both of which owned mineral rights to millions of acres of pre-1887 land grants. Until the 1960s the CPR usually leased its rights and paid little attention to the industry. In the 1920s the HBC went into a joint venture with Americans to explore its lands; the moribund Hudson's Bay Oil and Gas Company, controlled by the Continental Oil Company, revived and became very active after Leduc. By the 1950s HBOG was growing much faster than its old Canadian parent, the department store and fur company, which retained a one-quarter interest.

The little exploration outfits chased the big companies and each other in and out of the oilfields, punching down a few holes where they could get close-in land, risking outrageous wildcats, hawking shares to knowledgeable Albertans, blue-serge Torontonians, and Americans looking for tax shelters. An oil well could be drilled in Alberta for less than $100,000 in the early 1950s, so there was still room for the small company. In fact there always had been in an industry whose growth had constantly created more opportunities, in production, distribution, even retailing, than Imperial or the other integrated firms could handle. Promoters never thought outsiders appreciated investment opportunities in the West, but in fact all sorts of easterners and outsiders had been funnelling risk capital into oil opportunities since at least the late 1920s. It was only the uninformed man on the street, perhaps misled by the ubiquitous Esso, Shell, Texaco, and Gulf logos on Canadian service stations, who equated the petroleum industry with a few big companies.

Dome Exploration (Western) Limited was not untypical of the new firms. It was created in 1950 as a vehicle for the American owners of Dome Mines, the Ontario gold producer, to dabble in oils. The endowment funds of several Ivy League universities chipped in. The company's first employee was a Manitoba-born geologist, Jack Gallagher, who had decided to make his career in Canada after several years' exploring abroad for the multinationals. Dome made a few finds in the early 1950s, went public, and in 1958 became Dome Petroleum. Its head office moved from Toronto to Calgary, but, naturally, Gallagher still spent days on airplanes going to see his backers. Dome was just another small-to-middling Alberta oil company, pouring its earnings back into exploration, hoping for a big strike.

Oil and gas were discovered in western Canada faster than they could be brought to market. Pipeline planning was fraught with complications. Were reserves big enough to justify the huge cost of pipelines? Were markets adequate and secure? Should regulatory boards grant pipeline monopolies or encourage competition? If so, at one end or both? Most important, where should the lines run? Should they connect major North American markets with the closest, or cheapest, source of supply? Or should Canadians follow a Canada-first policy to benefit their own producers and for greater national security? But suppose the extra-costs of more secure lines made the product non-competitive with competing fuels, like coal or electricity: should the pipelines be subsidized?

Perhaps pipelines were instruments of nation-building, like the railway network. Perhaps they were just conduits of energy, like electrical transmission lines. Perhaps pipelines were just pipelines. Finally, who should build them? Pipeline promoters came out of the woodwork with a dazzling variety of schemes, arguing six sides of every issue, promising to build loops to the moon if they could only get regulatory approval. While regulators pondered and politicians debated, producers emitted a rising whine of complaints about their capped wells, prorationed production, and low prices.

Oil was easier to move than gas. Oil flows smoothly through relatively small-diameter pipe, which can be relocated if necessary. Oil is piped only to refineries; the gasoline and other products are normally distributed by train and truck. The knack of refinery location was to balance access to crude against proximity to markets; Canadian refineries tended to be scattered along the Great Lakes and at seaboard. Imperial Oil was the natural leader in planning pipelines to bring western crude to its Sarnia refineries. There was only minor, passing protest at Imperial's plan to lay its pipe along the cheapest route, through the United States south of Lake Superior. Conservative worries about the security of Canada's supplies of its "vital fluid" seemed unimportant. Canada had imported oil (and coal) through most of its history, and parts of the country would probably always use imports, mainly because domestic crude tended to be expensive and foreign crude very cheap. In 1950 Interprovincial Pipe Line, in which Imperial was the largest shareholder, built 1,130 miles of pipeline from Edmonton to a Lake Superior port in Wisconsin. Two years later the line was extended through Michigan to Sarnia.

In the same years the Trans Mountain Oil Pipe Line Company, another oil company consortium led by Imperial, laid pipe from Edmonton over the Yellowhead Pass and down the Fraser to refineries in Vancouver.

Gas was a different kettle of fish. It had always been a wonderfully cheap and efficient fuel for Albertans lucky enough to be able to tap into a local gas line, and they wanted to keep it that way. There was powerful sentiment in the province that no gas should be shipped out of Alberta until Albertans' present and future requirements were satisfied. Other Canadian fuel consumers wanted Albertans' advantages and looked forward to the coming of natural gas. This meant, unlike oil, that pipelines would have to run their way. Gas pipeline location became much more contentious than with oil.

If the main east-west line followed the oil pipeline south of the Great Lakes, for example, the communities of northern Ontario would have no supply of natural gas. American towns along its route probably would, meaning that the precious fuel would be heating American homes while Canadians used more expensive coal or oil. On the other hand, the high cost of building and operating a gas pipeline north of Superior might make the fuel uneconomic in its final market, Ontario's Golden Horseshoe. It was the old CPR dilemma all over again, complicated by new possibilities like the idea of piping eastern Canada's gas up from U.S. fields, while sending Alberta gas south in a fully continental pattern. But nothing could be done until Alberta made up its mind that it had surplus gas to sell.

While eastern pipeline discussions dragged on, Frank McMahon and his partners staged an entrepreneurial coup in their successful promotion of a pipeline to the Pacific coast. Since the 1920s McMahon had been sniffing for gas up in the Peace River country straddling the Alberta–British Columbia border. He was literally first in line to file for permits when the area was finally opened for exploration in 1947. Before, during, and after his companies' hunts for gas up there, McMahon promoted the idea of a trunk pipeline from the Peace to bring gas to Vancouver and the cities of the U.S. Pacific coast, one of the last major North American markets without access to gas. His Westcoast Transmission Company Limited was among the first pipeline companies chartered in 1949, the year that pipelines began to seem practical.

It eventually took Westcoast only two years to build a $160 million, 650-mile pipline down the spines of British Columbia to Vancouver and the border. The real struggle came in the six years' of hearings, investigations, deal-making, and political arm-bending required to get the licences and money to start construction. McMahon and his friends (he was backed by Pacific Petroleums, many of his old supporters in Vancouver, and new American contacts) bucketed back and forth across North America from one regulatory hearing to another, presenting themselves now as Canada- and BC-firsters (better to pipe gas on Canadian soil from the north, serving all of British Columbia in passing, rather than take it out of southern Alberta through the United States), now as sensible continentalists

(Canadian gas was the best way to supply the U.S. northwest; high volume exports kept gas costs to Canadians down), always as convivial Canadians simply trying to tap the limitless gas resources of the north. To make the deal work, it was necessary to stretch reserve estimates beyond most limits, go to bed with the same American companies Westcoast fought tooth-and-nail at Federal Power Commission hearings, write sweetheart export contracts with U.S. customers, pull all available political levers, and always entertain and celebrate lavishly.

McMahon's pipe dream was pretty fantastic. Bigger and more credible companies stood in the way at every turn, the Canadians' claims and promises were highly suspect ("Boys, our only strength in Washington is our breath," McMahon quipped), and their applications were several times rejected. In 1951, when prospects still looked minimal, Westcoast's promoters gave themselves an option on 500,000 treasury shares at 5 cents each. In 1957, with all hurdles cleared and its pipeline a-building, Westcoast offered its shares publicly at $5. They eventually sold at a peak of $57, giving the original $31,247 in nickel shares a market value of $35,625,000. Frank McMahon's other lucky strikes in the 1950s included a major share in the Broadway musicals, *Pyjama Game* and *Damn Yankees*, and the victory of his horse, Majestic Prince, in two-thirds of the Triple Crown.

The Frank McMahon of eastern pipelines was a Texas oilman, Clint Murchison. He was almost the only promoter who thought it possible to build a trans-Canada gas pipeline on Canadian soil. Murchison also began his campaign in 1949. The key to his success was C.D. Howe's growing conviction that an all-Canadian line was both practical and necessary. Almost all experts and investors thought either a southern route or a continental grid was the only economical way to supply gas to southern Ontario. For Howe this economic logic was submerged by a mixture of sentimental nationalism and political pragmatism: the voters wanted an all-Canadian gas pipeline and there would be no Liberals elected in northern Ontario if the region did not get gas. Howe and Clint Murchison became good friends; Howe used power outrageously to further the Trans-Canada plan and block un-Canadian alternatives. At one stage the federal government used its control over navigable waters to block a plan to bring U.S. gas to Canada across the Niagara gorge at Niagara Falls; the line apparently threatened the purity of the *Maid of the Mist*.

Murchison's Trans-Canada Pipe Lines Limited was threatened by suppliers', purchasers', and investors' lack of confidence in the project's viability. It could not close deals with producers in Alberta, customers in Ontario, or suppliers of the capital needed to build the line. Against the better judgment of many in the federal government, Howe persisted in his support. He agreed to create a special crown corporation to build the northern Ontario section of the pipeline. Then, as problems continued, Howe decided that Canada would loan Trans-Canada most of the money it needed to finish its main line. These two proposals were the essence of the pipeline bill that caused Howe so much trouble in the House of Commons in 1956.

Those of Howe's critics who did not get sidetracked on the closure issue (see p. 474), tended to favour public ownership of the pipeline as the best alternative to so much aid to an American-controlled company. The government's strongest counter-argument was its fear of politicizing the contentious problem of setting natural gas prices. Under nationalization the gas price issue would surely become a very hot potato. It seemed better to let private companies and markets resolve the conflicting interests of eastern consumers and western producers. The usual last-minute charter-hunters appeared offering to build a more Canadian pipeline. One of these was Frank McMahon, dreaming up a new scheme in his spare time. Howe quickly convinced him it would not be in Westcoast's interest to pursue the matter.

The pipeline debate helped destroy Howe and the Liberal government. The waves of Canadian nationalism it released continued to build and crash and batter for the next quarter century. Ironically, it was soon clear that almost all of the nationalists' criticisms of the Trans-Canada project were unfounded. Canadians sat on the board and participated in the public financing of Trans-Canada. The company did not find a way of siphoning gas off to the United States. It was only modestly profitable, never issued anything like 5-cent shares, and settled down as another utility operator; ownership and control quickly passed into Canadian hands. The only real scandal generated in pipeline promotion broke in 1958 when several Ontario Conservative cabinet ministers left office in disgrace after revelations of their insider trading in the launching of Northern Ontario Natural Gas, the company that distributed the gas Trans-Canada delivered to northern Ontario.

Trans-Canada did not pipe gas from the wellhead in Alberta. The provincial government, which had only approved exports after exhaustive inquiry, determined not to let the resource slip out of Albertans' hands on home ground. In 1954 it chartered the Alberta Gas Trunk Line Company to gather and move natural gas within the borders of the province. AGTL was owned and controlled by residents of Alberta; it delivered gas to the Trans-Canada line at the Saskatchewan border. Trans-Canada's main line, finished in 1958, was supplemented nine years later by an even larger line south of the Great Lakes, operated as a joint venture with several American gas companies. Nationalist objections were countered with the argument that it was still uneconomic to pipe the nation's gas entirely on Canadian territory.

Canadians switched from coal to oil and gas as their principal fuel in the 1950s, but the western producers did not get fabulously rich as a result. Canada's postwar petroleum boom was almost trivial compared with worldwide discoveries, especially in the Middle East. A few acres of semi-populated Arabian desert gushed more oil, better-quality oil, and much cheaper oil than all of the Canadian prairies. By the end of the fifties the world was awash in oil. At US$2.50 a barrel, Canadian producers received almost 30 per cent less for their product than at the time of

Leduc. A difficult struggle for the domestic market developed between Alberta crude and cheap foreign oil brought in by supertanker.

It was a confusing struggle because it was largely internal to the integrated, multinational oil companies. The Seven Sisters of the oil business (Exxon, Shell, British Petroleum, Texaco, Gulf, Mobil, and Standard Oil of California) bought crude all over the world and allocated it to various markets according to their internal planning systems. Many suspicious outsiders thought the multinationals marketed their oil collusively to get the highest possible prices, while paying the lowest possible prices to producers. Either that or they rigged their cartel to operate in the interests of their parent countries, which for five of the seven was the United States. To some Canadian nationalists, for example, it seemed suspicious that none of the multis supported the campaign for a national fuel policy in the 1950s led by Bob Brown of Home Oil. None of Canada's big four – Imperial, Gulf, Shell, and Texaco – endorsed Brown's idea of eastward oil pipeline extensions to bring Alberta oil to Quebec and the Maritimes. All were happy to see eastern Canada supplied with Venezuela crude. It must have been more profitable to them, or perhaps it was important their worldwide political manoeuvring.

In fact, it was more profitable to supply eastern Canada with imported oil than domestic because the offshore product was cheaper. If all oil companies had been independent, if the whole industry had been owned by Canadians, the debate would have been little different. A louder clamour by domestic producers for control of the market would have been met by importers' lobbying for cheaper Venezuelan crude. The fundamental economic fact, unaffected by corporate organization or sororital machinations, was that western Canadian oil was non-competitive in eastern Canada. The campaign for a national fuel policy was old-fashioned protectionism, aimed at securing import controls and an artificially high price in eastern Canada. It got little support from any Canadian consumers.

A National Oil Policy did emerge from the recommendations of the Royal Commission on Energy, chaired by Henry Borden. The Borden Commission suggested reserving markets west of the Ottawa valley for Canadian oil, while permitting imports east of the line. With the NOP's inception in 1961, Ontario consumers paid a few cents a barrel above world prices, as a measure of aid to Alberta producers. Another Borden recommendation led to the creation of the National Energy Board to regulate the oil and gas industry, particularly to handle the thorny question of exports to the United States. Exports became an issue in the 1960s as western producers pressed for more markets for their huge surpluses. By the late sixties western Canada was shipping almost a million barrels of oil a day south to the United States, about the same amount that eastern Canada imported. About half the country's gas production was also exported.

Neither the NOP nor the exports (which had to be at low, competitive prices), gave producers incentives to continue aggressive exploration. Canadian independents were increasingly squeezed for cash. The largely foreign-owned integrated companies were in slightly better shape because they could balance low production income against profits from their refining and retailing operations. In the age of the global oil company, the little man seemed doomed to go the wall or sell out. The strengthening grip of the foreigners was most noticed in 1962 when the last signifi-cant Canadian-owned integrated oil company, Canadian Oil Companies was taken over by Shell Canada for $162 million. With three thousand service stations, the company's White Rose briefly became a national symbol on its way to the ash can.

Frank McMahon's principal oil company, Pacific Petroleums, gobbled up several smaller Canadian outfits, but in 1960 it sought strength and stability through affiliation with Phillips Petroleum of Bartlesville, Oklahoma. Manage-ment's decision to link up with the Americans was part of its ongoing struggle to tame an organization still infected with McMahon's extravagant promoter's spirit. The hard-nosed oilmen who took over from McMahon and his cronies cut back on the wildcatting, sold the executive jets and the fancy executive suites, trimmed staff, installed budget systems and financial controls. Westcoast Transmission went through a similar shakeout (the c.e.o. who turned both companies into efficient organizations was Kelly Gibson, a former field hand from Broken Arrow, Oklahoma), but was fundamentally in worse shape from the promotional era. McMahon had promised Westcoast's customers more gas than he could find or deliver, and had locked the company into ruinously low export prices. Westcoast's stock sold far below its euphoric high of the early days. The company did not become solidly profitable until the 1970s when an NDP provincial government insisted on new export contracts and gave Westcoast a guaranteed return on its domestic sales. By then Frank McMahon was an almost forgotten character from the old days, the man who made millions bringing gas to Vancouver. He spent most of his time in Palm Beach, Florida, a wildcatters' Valhalla.

Home Oil, the largest Canadian independent, did not shed its promotional style so easily. Bob Brown's Gulfstream II, with the gold-plated dolphin taps in its wash-room, was thought to be the world's most luxurious executive jet. Brown jetted everywhere, drinking heavily all the way, looking for deals to keep Home growing and reduce his own load of debt (principally to the Canadian Bank of Commerce, which had great faith in Brown and a Canadian role in the oil industry). Brown wanted to expand everywhere. Not content with increased oil sales at low prices, he tried to take Home into pipelines (it was for several years the largest shareholder in Trans-Canada), gas distribution, and, most successfuly, the processing of natural gas to obtain natural gas liquids and other saleable by-products. Pacific and other producers went in the same direction. Jack Gallagher's Dome Petroleum was among the fastest-moving and became the largest producer of natural gas liquids in Canada. It was a very profitable sideline, partly because there was no prorationing on sales of these products.

Home was burdened with debt because Brown kept wildcatting to find more oil. But the pace of Canadian discovery slowed markedly after the Swan Hills find of 1957. By the mid-sixties there was a growing feeling in the oil patch that the easy finds had all been made. The new action would probably be in more remote regions or in developing heavy oil deposits like the tar sands. Several of the multinationals began planning big tar sands extraction plants. Fearing competition with its conventional production, Alberta allowed only one scheme, Sun Oil's Great Canadian Oil Sands plant, to go ahead. More ambitious plans (the ultimate proposal was Atlantic Richfield's idea of using nuclear explosions to cook oil from the tar sands), were put on hold.

In the meantime, a few Canadian independents started looking to the far north, to the attractive sedimentary rocks of the Mackenzie basin and the Arctic islands. The first Arctic well was drilled at Winter Harbour on Melville Island in 1959; Dome Petroleum operated the rig on behalf of a consortium of Canadian independents. It was a dry hole, but several Calgary visionaries kept a dream of Arctic oil alive through the sixties. They eventually organized an exploration company, Panarctic Oils Limited, to carry out northern drilling. When the majors showed little interest in joining Panarctic, the federal government decided in 1967 to keep the project going by taking a 45 per cent interest. Some Canadian companies, including Home, went farther afield, all the way to Britain and the North Sea – a play that ingested many North American oilmen (and created such unlikely oilmen as Lord Thomson of Fleet, who just happened to be on the spot with money to invest).

Faith in the Arctic seemed spectacularly vindicated in 1968 when Atlantic Richfield announced a huge oil and gas strike at Prudhoe Bay on Alaska's North Slope. The investors in Canada's Panarctic, including the federal government, seemed to be in on the ground floor of petroleum's northern future. Others rushed to join the play. Home Oil, for example, paid huge sums for North Slope acreage and for ARCO stock. Brown, now sick and befuddled by drink, staked everything on new discoveries or some fantastic takeover of ARCO. When the fantasies collapsed into dry holes and falling stock markets, Home and its promoter were deeply troubled. Brown had to sell out. With nationalist stormclouds gathering everywhere, Ottawa was in no mood to see a major Canadian energy corporation pass into foreign hands (it had just stopped Stephen Roman's attempt to sell Denison Mines to U.S. interests). Several politicians and senior civil servants thought Home should be taken over and run as a state oil company. In 1971 the government blocked Brown's attempt to sell his Home shares to an American firm. It was prepared to take the company over itself, using Eldorado Nuclear as its vehicle, when Brown finally sold to Consumers' Gas, the Toronto-based distributor. The last of the pioneering promoters went down in the lean years of the sixties and the Alaska boom and bust.

Strange clouds gathered over the Canadian industry in the early 1970s. Demand for Canadian oil and gas began growing faster than new reserves were discovered. Gas sales to the United States became a touch-point, as exporters petitioned the National Energy Board for huge increases. A simmering, spreading debate developed, as Canadian consumers and distributors began to ask whether the industry's optimistic estimates of reserves could be fully trusted. Was the producers' argument that more exports led to more exploration, discoveries, and reserves, necessarily sound? Was Canada exporting too much of the fossil fuel essential to its future? By the early 1970s the bureaucrats in the new federal Department of Energy, Mines and Resources felt an intense need for estimates of Canada's real energy resources that did not come from a self-interested, secretive, and largely foreign-owned industry.

Were Canadians selling their oil and gas too cheaply? As North American fuel markets tightened and prices edged upwards, deals made a year or two earlier, often to break into a competitive market, seemed too favourable to American consumers. Who made these deals? Often American-owned petroleum companies, the foreign owners more and more Canadians were beginning to distrust. To nationalists they were draining away the country's vital fluids and gases, and making sweetheart deals or using their internal transfer-pricing systems to minimize the return to Canadians. Canadians were the ultimate owners of most of the oil and gas, for, except on the pre-1887 land grants, the companies leased oil rights from the crown and paid royalties on production. Perhaps the time had come to renegotiate the terms of oil and gas leases, or even to levy new taxes, to ensure that windfall profits in this evolving market went to the real owners.

There was an important technical question, in fact a fundamental question, about ownership. All crown resources in Canada's provinces belonged to the provincial governments, not the federal government. Alberta's oil and gas belonged to the government and people of Alberta, not Canada. It was an Alberta politician, Conservative leader Peter Lougheed, who made an issue of the distribution of oil and gas revenues in the 1971 election that brought him to power. The people of Alberta needed a larger share of the rents from oil and gas sales, Lougheed argued, so they could get on with the job of province-building and avoid the boom-and-bust fate of American oil states like Oklahoma. He wanted to diversify Alberta's economy so it would no longer depend on a resource industry whose future was in question because of declining reserves. In Ottawa, on the other hand, there was a growing sense that the national government was responsible for the nation's fuel supply, and that it had a responsibility to manage the industry for the benefit of all Canadians.

No one had any idea of the energy storm that was about to break over the whole world. But in 1973, with oil having moved up by more than 50 per cent to about $3 a barrel from a mid-sixties price of less than $2, both Alberta and Ottawa began jockeying for control and profit. Alberta simply raised royalties, infuriating the industry by violating past commitments. In September, the Trudeau government reacted to rising world prices with a special tax to seize windfall profits in

Canada's oil exports. It also placed a six-month freeze on the domestic price of crude to protect Canadian consumers. Alberta and Ottawa clashed sharply over control of the resource. The industry complained loudly about being trapped in the middle. Then the world broke in and set the Canadian industry and its landlords on a wild ride through economic country populated by monstrous price changes, revenues, profits, costs, risks, and conflicts.

———————

The Arab-based Organization of Petroleum Exporting Companies (OPEC), which had been at the mercy of market forces since its formation in 1960, finally conquered the market during the Yom Kippur war of October 1973. Production cutbacks showed the cartel had near-monopoly power, and it began charging monopoly prices. Led by OPEC, the international price of oil had quadrupled by January 1974, rising from $3 a barrel to $11.65. The world energy "crisis" had begun.

Some Canadians and their media fell prey to nightmares of freezing in the dark and predictions of gathering global catastrophe. But OPEC's actions did not necessarily imply a crisis for resource-rich Canada. The country produced about as much oil and gas as it consumed, and was thus effectively self-sufficient in these forms of energy. If imports were to continue, their increased cost could be covered by higher prices for exports. They could be reduced, of course, by using more Canadian fuel in Canada. OPEC seemed to have such a hammerlock on the world's dwindling oil reserves that it would be able to hold all petro-poor countries to ransom through the 1970s and 1980s and into the indefinite future. But Canada could probably develop enough new supplies to remain at least self-sufficient indefinitely.

In 1973–74 the Trudeau government announced a set of national energy policies designed to foster self-sufficiency. Conservation was encouraged by a variety of programs. The Interprovincial oil pipeline was to be extended from Toronto to Montreal to bring domestic crude to eastern Canada. Oil and gas exports were more tightly controlled by quantity and price. Ottawa would foster frontier exploration and development, and was strongly in favour of new initiatives in the tar sands, particularly the Syncrude project for which plans were developed. And it supported a pipeline down the Mackenzie valley to bring to North American consumers the natural gas of the Arctic, both Alaska gas and the huge supplies Canadians were bound to find.

If the government had stopped there, its response to the energy crisis would have been relatively non-controversial. But a government driven by confident, activist politicians and bureaucrats, imbued with nationalist zeal, suspicious of big business – and, between the 1972 and 1974 elections, dependent on NDP support in Parliament – had no intention of leaving an essential Canadian industry in the hands of the companies that had created it. There was too much money at stake:

why should private producers get all the windfall profits created by the "artificial" energy price rise? And there were too many non-Canadian players in a game that now had to be specially responsive to Canadian interests.

Ottawa decided that only some of the benefits of the price increases would accrue to the industry. It was going to get some of the windfall itself through its tax regimes. It would hold Canadian oil and gas prices below world levels to ensure that the Canadian consumer profited too. Finally, to give government a better grip on the industry, it would create a national, publicly owned oil company. Such an organization would be a "window" to the inside affairs of petroleum; it would respond directly to the government's desires in such areas as frontier exploration; and it could represent Canada in the nation-to-nation oil negotiations that OPEC seemed to have made the style of the future. A few nationalists thought the national oil company could also be a vehicle for "buying back" Canada's energy industry, funnelling the profits to Canadians instead of foreigners.

The confident, activist government of Alberta, zealous to build the province, suspicious of Ottawa and resentful of a century of eastern domination, was outraged at Ottawa's attempts to seize control of provincially owned resources. Peter Lougheed's high-handed royalty policies were mightily offensive to the industry, but at least the companies and Alberta were in the energy-producing business together. Ottawa's use of price controls in the interest of Canadian consumers, and export taxes in the interest of the federal treasury, offended everyone in the West. Ottawa would not let either the oil companies or the people of Alberta (or of other producing provinces; Saskatchewan and British Columbia shared Alberta's outrage) collect the world price for the oil and gas. No one had ever stopped the lumber and mining companies of central Canada, or the landlord governments, from getting world prices for wood or newsprint or nickel or asbestos or copper. And it had been national policy since 1879 to force all Canadians to pay more than world prices for manufactured goods produced largely in central Canada. Now, when resource prices had finally turned in favour of the western provinces, a huge exception was being made. To oilmen and westerners alike, it seemed that the federal decision to insulate Canadian consumers from prices being paid by everyone else was another act of eastern oppression.

It certainly was what C.D. Howe and the Liberals had dreaded during the pipeline debate: the politicization of energy-pricing disputes. Now that the state had stepped in, producer-consumer haggling would be the stuff of politics, not of normal commercial markets. The inevitable result of this politicization of energy was escalated rhetoric and heightened sectional antagonism, creating an immediate and lasting climate of bitterness and distrust.* Within the borders of their

---

* The climate was further poisoned by a parallel debate on the Crow's Nest Pass grain rates, unchanged since 1922, which were now absurdly low. Eighty years after Laurier's politicization of national freight rates, the struggle to change the Crow rates helped undo

own country, in legislatures and on television, Canadians replicated the great international struggles between energy producers and consumers. "Let the eastern bastards freeze in the dark," read the famous, if little seen, Alberta bumper sticker of the early 1970s. In central Canada there seemed no reason to accept one province's desire to unbalance Confederation in its favour (on some projections oil royalties would make Alberta Canada's only "have" province; all the others would be "have-nots"). Independent, confident Canadians, led by a Liberal federal government and a Conservative government of Ontario, refused to pay homage to foreign oil sheiks, or foreign oil corporations, or to the "blue-eyed sheiks" of their own oil-producing areas.

The energy crisis and governments' response to it caught the industry off balance. The Seven Sisters had never been particularly popular. OPEC's price increases gave them such huge inventory profits in the last quarter of 1973 that they became even more unpopular and were widely accused of engineering the whole affair for their own benefit. They seemed to have misled the world in general and Canadians in particular about prices and reserves, for none of their public forecasts had suggested anything like OPEC's price hikes, or the supply shortages they now predicted. Big oil was widely thought to have been either dishonest or incompetent in the run-up to the energy crisis.

In Canada big oil was foreign-controlled, hardly a trustworthy vehicle, it seemed, to implement policies aimed at protecting Canada's national interest. In the early stages of the energy crisis, a confused, discredited industry sometimes took to advertising its Canadianism and its commitment to exploration and development, sometimes just laid low, and sometimes literally ran for cover. When the Ottawa-Alberta tax squeeze reached an absurd peak in 1974 (Ottawa announced that provincial royalties would be non-deductible for federal tax purposes, creating certain situations in which marginal tax rates surpassed 100 per cent), many companies diverted staff, drilling rigs, and exploration programs to greener pastures in the United States.

———————

In a year or two the market turmoil and political manoeuvring began to subside, as the players adjusted to the new energy game. The key to the new era was that in self-sufficient Canada everyone could appear to get a share of the energy loot. Even at prices well below OPEC's levels, there were massive new revenues for both the public and private sector. Yet the Canadian consumers who coughed up the money could hardly complain, since they were blessed with lower gasoline and fuel oil prices than almost anyone outside of OPEC. By 1975 Alberta and Ottawa had reached a working compromise on royalty-tax-pricing issues, bumping the wellhead price gradually toward world levels. Edmonton's intense resentment

———————

four generations of well-meant political rhetoric about the need for Canadian unity. The Crow rate structure was abolished by Parliament in 1983.

at the power grab by Ottawa and central and eastern Canada was tempered by the flow of hundreds of millions in excess oil royalties into its Heritage Trust Fund, a highly visible reward-cum-safety net for the citizens of the fortunate province. Energy companies large and small, foreign- and Canadian-owned, were vitalized by higher prices and cash flow. They began planning their long-term accommodation to high prices, active government, and the need to find more Canadian oil and gas.

Imperial and Gulf settled down to hard bargaining with Alberta and Ottawa over the terms of their partnership in the Syncrude tar sands project. Construction began in 1975 and the plant was operational within three years. More complex studies and lengthy hearings were necessary on the Mackenzie valley pipeline question, largely because of concern for the environment and native rights. No one doubted that it would eventually go ahead, almost certainly under the aegis of Canadian Arctic Gas, a blue-ribbon syndicate of all the leading firms. New tar sands and heavy oil extraction plants were planned. Panarctic Oils upped its drilling program on the Arctic islands. The geologists and exploration men and offshore drilling experts began thinking about the hydrocarbon possibilities of the Grand Banks and the Scotian Shelf. Dome Petroleum, growing fat on revenues from natural gas liquids, began acting on Jack Gallagher's belief that the greatest Canadian "elephant" of all, probably larger than the oil reserves of Arabia, lay just off the mouth of the Mackenzie River under the shallow waters of the Beaufort Sea.

The western sedimentary basin was not played out either. In 1976 the drillers for Canadian Hunter, a wildcat vehicle for Jim Masters and John Gray, made one of the most spectacular gas finds in Canadian history in the Elmvale area of west-central Alberta. The next year one of the lesser sisters, Chevron Standard, led in the deep drilling that poked into the West Pembina pools, another billion or so barrels of oil, the largest find in the province in a decade. The investors and brokers who played Canadian oil and gas stocks through most of the seventies struck money at least as often as the drillers found oil. Every new announcement drove the market up. Bells literally rang in Calgary, where a broker mounted a bell outside his office and clanged it whenever he did a big trade.

The new national oil company, Petro-Canada, began operating early in 1976 under the leadership of a politically astute entrepreneur, Maurice Strong, and two nimble Ottawa men, Joel Bell and William Hopper. The money they spent came from Canadian taxpayers. Petro-Canada's original mandate was to be a leader in frontier exploration. With preferential back-ins (favourable reversions of exploration rights) arranged by Ottawa, the company quickly became active in most of the plays and in tar sands and heavy oil development. Every whiff of gas or oil was the occasion for press releases claiming the vindication of the experiment in public ownership, but Petro-Canada did not have unusual exploration luck. To give their company producing assets and cash flow, management engineered the

1977 acquisition, for $242 million, of Atlantic Richfield Canada. Some nationalists were disappointed that Petro-Canada did not stalk bigger game, like Shell or Gulf or Imperial. Most oilmen were angry that the company was in the field at all, using public money to compete with real energy entrepreneurs.

Petro-Canada's head office, of course, was in Calgary. Everyone's head office was in Calgary, the energy capital of Canada and all its hinterlands. Edmonton, the capital of Alberta, was the supply base for most western and northern exploration. The rebuilding of the two Alberta cities was the most visible consequence of the energy boom. Five years of OPEC made the fifties' skyscrapers and towers seem like quaint and endangered symbols of pioneer days. Calgary became a forest of cranes, standing on every corner, drawing forty-storey office towers out of deep holes in the ground. Edmonton was not far behind. Oilmen's imagery was often sexual, and it was hard to avoid believing that the macho-driven companies were not consciously vying for the largest erection (a contest they all lost to the CN Tower in Toronto). But the prairie towers of the New West were also symbols of the permanence of the boom. This time prosperity had come for good.

The skyscrapers were also symbols of the West's new presence in urban, financial Canada. Generations of oilmen had made endless pilgrimages to the big eastern cities looking for money. At last the bastards in the big banks, and even the politicians in Ottawa, and even the premier of Ontario, were getting off their asses and onto planes themselves. Easterners were trekking west. Soon they were setting up western offices, moving staff and whole corporate divisions. Westerners were creating their own new institutions to service the boom, ranging from drilling firms and oil supply companies, to restaurants, newsmagazines, and new chartered banks. Make no mistake, the balance in Canada was changing. The West was changing from hinterland to heartland, and the new urban geography of Alberta showed it.

Other neglected Canadian hinterlands shared the resource boom of the 1970s. Coal, electricity, even cordwood, soared in price along with oil and gas. Most other raw materials and foodstuffs increased in price as world demand kept growing. Consumers and people on fixed incomes suffered from the inflation and governments tried to stop it (after opposing wage and price controls in the 1974 election, the Trudeau government levied them in 1975, with mixed results). But the other side of the inflation coin in lucky Canada was one of the greatest and best resource booms of the century. It meant huge foreign investments, often Japanese, in the coal seams of the British Columbia Rockies and the railways needed to reach them. It meant a revival of potash in Saskatchewan, new copper and base metals mines in half a dozen provinces, good times for precious metal producers, and soaring revenues for provincial electrical utilities. Even the hydro men moved north, as Hydro-Québec made Robert Bourassa's dream of bringing power from the James Bay watershed come true in a mega-development rivalling the mining of the tar sands. Other countries and the Canadian media might complain of "stagflation" in the seventies. For Canada it was actually a decade of inflation combined with constant economic growth.

Among producing provinces, only Newfoundland was deprived of a reasonable share of the energy bonanza. In the 1960s the British Newfoundland Company entered into some of the most short-sighted contracts in Canadian history by agreeing to sell most of the power from its giant Churchill Falls development to Hydro-Québec at long-term, reducing rates. As the price of electricity soared in the 1970s, Hydro-Québec made hundreds of millions in windfall profits from Newfoundland's resource and refused to renegotiate the contracts. The one powerful consolation for Newfoundlanders as the decade wound on was a revival in their oldest industry, the fishery. Under the new umbrella of the two-hundred-mile limit, the fish supply improved while world demand drove prices up. With good times in the fishery, perhaps the most steadily depressed Canadian resource industry in the twentieth century, history had come full circle. And a bit more: the one new hazard on the fishing banks was offshore drilling rigs. The oil and gas that were making western Canada rich was going to be found in the Maritimes too. Canada's Atlantic waters would feed the world with fish and hydrocarbons.

———————◆———————

Canada's energy future did not unfold as smoothly in the late seventies as the planners expected. The Mackenzie valley pipeline scheme, for example, was delayed again and again by royal commission and regulatory board hearings. In 1977 the Berger Royal Commission on the northern environment and the National Energy Board surprised almost everyone by coming out against a Mackenzie valley pipeline and against the Canadian Arctic Gas proposal, for largely ecological reasons. A competing scheme to pipe northern gas down the Alaska Highway was favoured. The chief backer of this Alcan project was Robert Blair, president of Alberta Gas Trunk Lines, a distinctively Albertan corporation. This triumph of the western underdogs (Blair's principal support came from another distinctively western source, the Pacific Petroleum–Westcoast Transmission group) was heralded as another milestone in the rise of the New West. Unfortunately there were further delays in planning the world's greatest pipeline, as potential investors asked hard questions about natural gas supplies and markets. The Americans, in particular, were not so sure that Arctic gas was really needed just yet.

There were similar nagging doubts about more tar sands and heavy oil plants. The senior staff of the federal Department of Energy, Mines, and Resources found negotiations with Shell about terms and conditions for the $5 billion Alsands project it was leading, and with Imperial about the $6 billion Cold Lake upgrading plant, deeply frustrating. The oilmen would not commit their companies without better tax and pricing guarantees. Unconventional oil was high-cost oil. As Syncrude and Great Canadian Oil Sands discovered, there was little profit in the oil sands at prices under about US$17 a barrel. The world price was usually below that figure, and, while Ottawa was impatient, it was not ready to take the risk of guaranteeing a price higher than OPEC's.

The big, romantic, expensive quest for new energy reserves in the Arctic and off the coasts, which had been going on since the 1960s, was taking longer to pay off than many enthusiasts had expected. The visionaries at Dome Petroleum liked to begin each season's Arctic drilling with predictions that this would be the year of the elephant. Rumours emanated each mid-season that Dome had hit it, and its stock soared. A few months later Dome would explain that while the oil was certainly there and the drill results were excellent, another season's work was necessary to firm up the field . . . and that the super-depletion tax allowance under which it raised money for Beaufort drilling (some investors could profit on dry holes thanks to Ottawa) was absolutely essential to stimulating Canadian frontier exploration. Of course there was no doubt, Dome implied, that Canada's Arctic oil would be flowing to the world by 1984 or 1985 at the latest.

At Petro-Canada some good prospects arose from back-ins on Mobil's work off Nova Scotia and Chevron's off Newfoundland, but the exploration money kept draining away in dry or capped holes. The national oil company was going to be a perpetual money-loser unless it got more of the industry's gravy: revenue from selling crude oil and natural gas, refining, and pumping gasoline. The Ottawa policy-makers were frustrated by how much of this mainstream action continued to be Alberta-centred, supporting Peter Lougheed's bulging Heritage Fund and his strident provincialism.

In 1978 Petro-Canada, backed by the financial power of Ottawa, decided to buy its way in. It approached Husky Oil, one of the most Canadian of the integrated companies, was rebuffed by the Nielson family, and was then embarrassed by the brilliant open market manoeuvrings of Bob Blair, who won control of Husky for AGTL. Trying again, Petro-Canada offered $1.5 billion to the shareholders of Pacific Petroleum, foreign-controlled but one of the most historically Canadian firms in the industry. The takeover, at that time the largest in Canadian history, succeeded, partly due to Petro-Canada's use of financial loopholes (the issuance of tax-friendly term preferred shares) just before the government closed them. The government did not oppose the crown corporation's expansion. Nationalists still chafed at the failure of Petro-Canada, Blair, or any other Canadian, to go after the truly big foreign-owned firms that still dominated the Canadian scene.

On the other hand, at least Petro-Canada was becoming a major Canadian force in the industry, along with the other dynamically entrepreneurial Canadian firms, Blair's AGTL, and Jack Gallagher's Dome. Or, rather, Jack Gallagher and Bill Richards's Dome, for "Smilin' Jack" had become Dome's chairman in 1974 after grooming a deal-making lawyer, William Richards, to succeed him in the presidency. While Gallagher's visions underlay Dome's exploration in the Beaufort, Richards determined that the company would grow by acquisition.

Beginning in 1978, Dome went on the biggest buying spree in Canadian history, spending hundreds of millions at a crack to acquire oil and gas properties, plus control of Trans-Canada Pipe Lines. Its rapid growth and its highly touted Beaufort drilling made Dome the darling of investors and governments alike. Maybe Dome, rather than Petrocan or AGTL, would be the first great Canadian oil company.

Hopper and Bell at Petro-Canada moved quickly on the Pacific takeover in order to defeat the Conservative party's promise to dismantle their corporation. The Tories had opposed Petro-Canada from its inception, just as they had opposed most aspects of Liberal energy policy. Led by an Albertan, Joe Clark, the opposition questioned both the economic wisdom of holding Canadian energy policies below world levels (cheap energy was a disincentive to conservation and exploration) and Ottawa's disregard for Alberta's ownership rights in a Canadian federation that Clark characterized as a "community of communities." Petro-Canada was unnecessary, chauvinist, and inefficient. A Conservative government, Clark promised, would mean fundamentally new directions in energy policy and an end to Petro-Canada.

When Joe Clark ended sixteen years of Liberal rule in the May 1979 general election, it seemed as though a political revolution had come to Canada. But the more important revolution of 1978–79 was in Iran. The tough new regime of Ayatollah Khomeini led OPEC into its second price revolution, raising the cost of a barrel of oil from about US$14 to more than $28 in the spring of 1979. In Canada the new prices instantly reopened the Pandora's box of producer-consumer conflict. Having still not returned to market-pricing, politicians had to decide how much of the enormous increase would accrue to consumers, to private producers, to the Alberta public through its government, to the Canadian people through their government – and how to free the country from this bondage to a cartel apparently growing ever more powerful. Consumers were understandably opposed to any quick move to world prices. Alberta was understandably determined not to be robbed of its patrimony a second time by Ottawa. And the new climate of international insecurity and market disruption hardly seemed propitious for dismantling Canada's national oil company.

Energy policy became a stinking, clawing albatross, largely responsible for the destruction of Clark's minority government. The stench of the past lay in the way Canadians had been spoiled by controlled prices, far below world levels. Used to their cheap gasoline and fuel oil, they had no desire to bear the burden of anything like the real price of their fuel. The active clawing came from the arrogant, assertive Lougheed government, which turned down all of Ottawa's proposals for a new pricing regime, barely disguising its contempt for fellow Conservatives in Ottawa.

With Ontario's Conservative government doing all it could to sabotage national unity on energy policy, and the management of Petro-Canada working almost openly to defeat the government of Canada's announced policy toward the company, the inexperienced federal Tories bounced from pillar to post. They were finally defeated in the House of Commons on a budget that proposed a new 18 cent a gallon federal excise tax on gasoline. It was a triflingly modest proposal in a world of doubled energy prices. In the parochial world of Canadian insularity and lust for cheap energy, it was politically unacceptable. In the 18-cent election of February 1980, the Liberals resurrected Pierre Elliott Trudeau and ran what their chief organizer called a "brilliantly cynical" campaign in favour of cheap energy and Canadian nationalism. They won a new mandate, and set out to secure their place in Canadian history.

The National Energy Program was introduced by the Minister of Finance as part of his budget speech on October 28, 1980. Its real parents were Energy Minister Marc Lalonde and a group of senior civil servants, based in Energy, Mines, and Resources, who had been developing ideas for a grand Canadian energy strategy over the past several years. Longer, actually, for their thought reflected approaches to economic policy-making and intervention practised by Liberal governments since the days of C.D. Howe. The opportunity to put it all together seemed to have been lost with the 1979 defeat. Now the politicians and planners were determined to use their reprise to get clear, forceful policies in place. No more dithering, no more half-measures. Strike while the iron is hot. Let history be the judge.

The NEP was a bewilderingly complex set of policies involving taxes, prices, grants, charges, and nationality. They were all based on the government's assumption, provided by the best planners and forecasters in Ottawa, that the international energy cartel, OPEC, would continue to control world petroleum markets. Market forces, the workings of the law of supply and demand, the effects of competition, et cetera – all those laissez-faire principles from the old days – would continue to be irrelevant in energy economics. The cartel was in control and it would continue to raise real prices through the 1980s. They would rise from about C$40 a barrel to C$80 in 1986 and continue to go up. The rest of the world would be held captive by the monopolists, but lucky Canadians would be protected by the policies of their national government. "If a way can be found to share more equitably the benefits of Canada's energy resources, it may be possible to insulate Canada from some of the shocks emanating from the world economy," the NEP stated, "and to build upon this energy strength an industrial base in all parts of Canada that will provide for sustained economic growth."

"Equity," as the NEP conceived it, was to be achieved by wrenching power and resources away from the provinces in favour of the one government that spoke for all Canadians, and by wrenching power and resources away from foreign-controlled petroleum companies in favour of companies owned or controlled by Canadians, especially companies owned by the government of Canada. New national taxes on natural gas and on petroleum limited the revenues that would go to the producing provinces. In the longer term, the provinces' role in both production and policy-making would shrink, for Canada's energy future was certain to lie under the "Canada Lands" of the north and the offshore continental shelf. To help make that future unfold, Ottawa offered special exploration grants, Petroleum Incentive Payments, which would cover up to 80 per cent of the costs of drilling in the Canada Lands.

The full PIP grants would be available only to companies that were 75 per cent Canadian-owned. Less than 50 per cent Canadian ownership disqualified a company from producing on Canada Lands. All companies active on Canada Lands would have to surrender a 25 per cent interest in their holdings to Petro-Canada or some other crown corporation. Several new crown oil companies might be created to handle this development and buy out foreigners. A special Canadian Ownership Account – a new federal tax – was to be levied to make such purchases possible. Private Canadian companies were also encouraged to buy foreigners' assets, and the foreign owners' ability to diversify or expand in Canada would be limited by FIRA as well as the NEP. Ottawa wanted to achieve 50 per cent Canadian ownership of oil and gas assets within the decade. "Some firms may regard the new conditions as unsatisfactory," the government stated. "The Government's acquisition program provides an answer to them. The Government of Canada is a willing buyer, at fair and reasonable prices."

Ottawa would use its command of the industry to continue to insulate Canadians from world energy prices (the Liberals claimed, dishonestly, that the new taxes would be less than the Tories' rejected 18 cents a gallon). A complicated "blended" pricing regime under the NEP would give producers more profit on new discoveries, prevent profiteering on old oil and gas, and, though tending upward, maintain Canadian prices below world levels. More conservation programs would encourage greater efficiency in Canadians' energy use. The huge revenues created by even slowly increasing prices – a total of more than $150 billion in the first five years – would be spent, in part, on imaginative industrial policies to benefit all Canadians. There would be a special $4 billion Western Development Fund, for example, as an Ottawa gesture to mollify producing provinces for its takeover of the revenues from their resources.

The NEP was greeted by storms of criticism. It was hard to know who was more outraged: the Alberta government at Ottawa's smash-and-grab; foreign oilmen at becoming the subjects of systematic discrimination (John Masters of Canadian Hunter claimed they were being treated like Jewish businessmen in Hitler's Germany); or the junior Canadian companies, expected to be prime beneficiaries of the NEP, who realized that the tax numbers added up to disaster.

None of the criticisms significantly influenced a government with a parliamentary majority and a lemming-like determination to hold its course. Peter Lougheed, whose bungling of the chance to make a deal with the Clark government now appeared to be a calamitous sacrifice of Alberta's interests, raged against Ottawa and announced retaliatory cutbacks in oil exports from the province. American oilmen turned to Washington for help with the renegade Canadians. Junior oilmen shut down their rigs and looked south. Ottawa pressed on. The civil servants hammered out the details of the NEP and began implementing the grand design.

They had allies in business. Within four months of the announcement of the National Energy Program, an unprecedented expansion of Canadian ownership took place. Foreign owners of Canadian-based oil and gas companies decided to get out while the market was good. The "big three" Canadian firms were among the leading purchasers. Petro-Canada paid $1.5 billion for the assets of Petrofina Canada. Nova, An Alberta Corporation, (the old AGTL with a Yuppie name), used its Husky Oil subsidiary to spend $800 million buying several firms from Americans. In the biggest deal in Canadian history, Dome Petroleum repatriated Hudson's Bay Oil and Gas from Conoco for just under $2 billion. Other dynamic Canadian companies, such as fast-growing Turbo and Sulpetro, joined the acquisition binge. So did the Canada Development Corporation, still largely owned by the federal government, which paid $1.2 billion for Aquitaine Company of Canada from the French government, its owner. Even the government of Ontario got into the act, buying a 25 per cent interest in Suncor from its American parent for $650 million.

The big Canadian banks were happy to finance these acquisitions where necessary (Petro-Canada got its money directly from the taxpayer under the NEP). They shared the common assumption that the price of energy would go up indefinitely, and they were impressed by the federal government's vigorous support for acquisitive nationalism. The buying spree grew and grew, reaching a total of $6.6 billion by July 1981. The outflow of Canadian dollars created downward pressure on the exchange rate. At the end of July the Minister of Finance had to ask the banks to limit their lending for energy takeovers. "Canadianization has exceeded the government's most optimistic expectations. We're the victims of our own success," Marc Lalonde stated.

Dome Petroleum was first off the mark in the race for PIP grants to support its highly publicized Beaufort drilling. Dome had an embarrassingly large number of American shareholders, so Gallagher and Richards spun out a special exploration vehicle, Dome Canada, which met the NEP's criteria. Its March 1981 sale of $400 million in common stock was the largest equity issue in Canadian history – the man in the street's opportunity to be part of the great Canadian energy adventure. The fact that Chevron and Mobil had found a billion-barrel pool of oil at the Hibernia site off Newfoundland made frontier exploration that much more attractive.

Hibernia would bring unprecedented wealth to the poor Newfoundland people, all the Newfoundlanders thought – just as the Nova Scotians thought the Venture discoveries near Sable Island meant the end of generations of decline. In the rest of Canada Dome Petroleum was the company to conjure with. Its work in the Arctic had led it into buying a navy of drilling ships, and icebreakers, and northern work boats, and into buying one of the largest Canadian shipyards, the Davie complex in Quebec City. Jack Gallagher, the smooth-talking, always-smiling, northern explorer, was the prophet of breathtaking developments to come. In his Calgary office, with its Eskimo carvings and the Alan Collier paintings of the high Arctic, Gallagher treated visitors to a dazzling slide show of the spectacular developments ahead. I saw the presentation in 1982; at the same time Dome closed the second-stage of its HBOG transaction (buying out the minority shareholders for another $1 billion) and became by some measurements the largest oil and gas company Canada had ever seen, bigger even than Imperial.

After Dome had finished finding the oil in the Beaufort it was going to become the world leader in Arctic transportation. Canada's oil would move to market along the historic Northwest Passage, the route those early explorers, like Martin Frobisher, had come to the New World to find. Having finished Frobisher's job by making the Passage a commercial reality, Dome would go on to the next stage and use high-tech icebreakers to create the most direct route of all across the top of the world, a North Pole Passage to Europe and Asia. Of course it was all practical, Gallagher always explained, so long as Canadians had faith in their resources and their future.

Simply believe.

Canada's National Energy Program was proclaimed one week before Ronald Reagan was elected president of the United States. With his advent to power the Americans embarked on an era of free-market economics, deregulation, tax reduction, attempts at downsizing government, and enthusiasm for small business and individual entrepreneurship.

Canada was taking another course. The Liberal government of Canada believed, as a 1981 strategy paper on economic development put it, "that a fundamental and essentially permanent shift has taken place during the 1970s, one that strengthens Canada's traditional comparative advantage in the production of basic commodities, related manufacturing, products, and high productivity, high technology manufactured goods." The government believed that the world's demand for Canadian resources, especially Canadian energy, would support the launching of dozens of "major projects," some $440 billion worth of them by the year 2000. They would include gas and oil pipelines from the north, tar sands and heavy oil extraction projects, refineries, natural gas processing plants, dozens of new hydro-electric dams and generating stations and transmission lines, coal mines, lead and zinc mines, copper mines, uranium mines, potash mines, aluminum smelters, pulp and paper mills, automobile plants, airplane plants and airport expansions, railways to resources, and tankers to ply the Northwest Passage and the Polar Passage.

The mega-projects, as they were called, were very big business. A federal government task force on the mega-projects (chaired by Robert Blair of Nova and Shirley Carr of the Canadian Labour Congress) titled its 1981 report *Major Canadian Projects: Major Canadian Opportunities*. "The Canadian economy is about to embark on one of the most significant periods of investment spending in its history," the task force announced. Its report showed how the development of the opportunities would be scheduled, assisted, monitored, encouraged, and Canadianized, by government. "Major projects can provide a chance to grasp opportunities Canadians have not realized in the past." All those opportunities had slipped by in the old days of unregulated, private enterprise. Now big business would go to work in a planned, systematic way with the encouragement of big government, overseeing developments as a kind of benevolent big brother.

TOP: **Launching of Anik 1, 1972** *(Telesat Canada)* ABOVE: **Oil refinery, Come-by-Chance, Newfoundland** *(Canadian Press)*

19

"Less Place to Hide"

*World-class failures: Massey, Dome, Canadair . . . bank failures . . . the
inflation mentality . . . dancing faster . . . mega-lending . . . the energy
collapse . . . foreigners win . . . world surpluses . . . a sunset country? . . . the
world breaks in . . . the crisis of corporate management . . . dinosaurs
downsize . . . the entrepreneurial revival . . . government as
Leviathan . . . reckless debt . . . "interfacing" . . . concentration and
competition . . . business lifestyles . . . businesswomen . . . free trade*

CANADA'S WELL-KNOWN GLOBAL MANUFACTURING CORPORATION, Massey-Ferguson, was the first to crumble. In 1976 it was still the darling of investment analysts, earning US$118 million on record sales of $2.8 billion. For the first quarter of 1978 it reported a loss of $38.7 million, more than twice the total loss in the worst year in the company's 131-year history. The 1978 results established a new record for all companies in Canadian history. Massey lost an astonishing $262 million.

Bud McDougald still controlled Argus Corporation, Massey's principal shareholder. The other founders of Argus had died or, like E.P. Taylor, sold out. McDougald became Taylor's successor in public notoriety in 1976 when Peter C. Newman portrayed him as "the archetype of the tycoons" in his bestselling book, *The Canadian Establishment*. McDougald died in March 1978, a day after his seventieth birthday. With his last breaths, Newman reported in a later book, McDougald called for Al Thornborough of Massey. The tycoon's last words were, "I've got to speak to Al. Get him down here. Tell him only I can fix Massey."

In the summer of 1978 McDougald's heir at Argus, Conrad Black, assumed the chairmanship of Massey-Ferguson; a few months later he became its chief executive officer. It was widely believed that Black, whom *Fortune* called the "boy wonder" of Canadian business, had staked his reputation on his ability to turn Massey around, not unlike the way Eric Phillips had saved the situation in 1956. Black and the man he chose to succeed Thornborough, Victor A. Rice, set out to fix Massey by cutting costs, getting rid of money-losing operations, keeping the firm's large number of creditors at bay, and developing a plan for a major infusion of equity.

The new boys' optimism about their ability to turn Massey around seemed warranted by the $37 million profit it reported in 1979. In the spring of 1980, though, the roof fell in. Sales collapsed and interest rates on the firm's huge floating debt soared. Black stepped down as chairman and chief executive officer, but told the press that Argus had taken the roller-coaster all the way down with Massey and would ride it all the way up. There were rumours of impending bankruptcy and that Massey was asking governments to bail it out, much as troubled Chrysler had just been aided in the United States and Canada. In October Black suddenly announced that Argus was getting out of Massey; Argus gave its Massey shares, which it had written off as valueless, to the Massey pension fund. Massey's 1980 loss was $225 million.

Rice persuaded Massey's bankers and the governments of Canada and Ontario to keep the company out of bankruptcy. In early 1981 a $700 million refinancing package was put together in which creditors exchanged some debt for equity and the governments guaranteed $200 million in preferred shares. Within twelve months of the bailout, Massey failed to meet dividends on the new shares and the governments of Canada and Ontario had to honour their guarantees. The worst year was 1982, in which Massey lost $413 million. Massey never went bankrupt, but that was only a technicality. The investors who had believed in Massey-Ferguson – shareholders and bankers, and then governments – lost a total of $1.2 billion between 1978 and 1984. By 1986 when it decided to change its name to Varity Corporation the firm had shrunk to about one-third of its size in the glory years and was barely breaking even. A stated reason for the change was the company's desire to make acquisitions outside of the farm implement business. With the name change, the word "Massey" disappeared from the centre stage of Canadian business. It would only survive in association with several prominent educational and cultural institutions. "Varity" was derived from the old Verity Plow Company, acquired by Massey-Harris in 1892.

Dome Petroleum's shares began to slip in value in 1981, during the height of the buy-outs stimulated by the National Energy Program. Dome's $2 billion purchase price for the 53 per cent of Hudson's Bay Oil and Gas owned by Conoco seemed high, and so was Dome's total debt, then standing at $5.3 billion. It seemed that no company in history, certainly none in Canada's history, had ever incurred so much debt so fast. Perhaps if inflation were taken into account, Mackenzie and Mann's Canadian Northern had borrowed about as much as Dome. But Dome had to keep on borrowing. In the summer of 1981 management realized that Dome could not cover its interest payments without access to the cash flow of HBOG. As 53 per cent owner it was only entitled to dividends. So Dome had to obtain another $1.8 billion to buy the rest of HBOG from its remaining shareholders, principally the Hudson's Bay Company. A syndicate of foreign banks, led by New York's Citibank, lent Dome the money.

Within weeks of closing the final HBOG deal, in March 1982, Dome had to ask its bankers for emergency loans. The largest oil and gas company ever put together by Canadians was insolvent. Much of its problem seemed to lie in the floating interest rates on much of its debt. These were rising towards 20 per cent and beyond in a year of horrendous inflation and grim tightening of money markets. One commodity that had certainly stopped inflating in value, however, was petroleum. OPEC managed to get the price of a barrel of crude oil up to the US$36-40 range in 1981, but could not hold it there. Through 1982 prices on the world's spot markets were consistently below OPEC's benchmark price. The highly inflationary price forecasts that had informed Canada's National Energy Program and the planning of companies like Dome became more unrealistic by the month.

Dome and its Canadian bankers turned to Ottawa in the summer of 1982 for assistance in averting the firm's bankruptcy. On September 29, one day before a huge chunk of principal was due to the Canadian banks, a complex, billion-dollar Dome bail-out was announced. Debt terms were to be extended, creditors would take interest in shares, and the Canadian taxpayer would kick in $500 million. When Dome shareholders balked at some of the terms of the deal (their remaining equity would be severely diluted), the chief executive officer of the Canadian Imperial Bank of Commerce, Russell Harrison, urged them to "get down on their knees and thank God that we came to an agreement." Otherwise their shares would have been totally worthless, and Canada would have experienced what Harrison called "the biggest bankruptcy in the history of the world . . . I shudder to think of it . . . . The credit of the Canadian banking system – and the Canadian government itself – would be in question." Dome's net loss for 1982 of $370 million was almost as high as Massey's.

The bail-out agreement was never fully implemented. Dome and its bankers kept rescheduling payments, while the company scrambled to sell assets and generate cash flow. As effectively bankrupt as Massey-Ferguson, Dome was systematically stripped of its shipyards and navy, its drilling rigs, and its imperial pretensions. First Jack Gallagher and then Bill Richards were forced to leave the company. Dome's exploration declined, though it continued work on the Canada Lands because the NEP's PIP grants made the work very cheap. The continued slippage in world oil prices – early in 1983 OPEC had to drop its benchmark price to US$29 – kept cash flow tight, but it was often adequate to cover interest payments. Various proposals for injections of equity were not well received by investors.

When glutted oil markets finally caused a world price collapse in 1986, Dome was an early casualty. It suspended interest payments on a debt load still over $5 billion, and continued to negotiate with its creditors. There were many rumours of immanent bankruptcy. In 1986 Dome Petroleum's five-year-old offspring, Dome Canada, whose founding shareholders had lost millions because of their faith in Gallagher, Richards, and company, changed its name to Encor Energy Corporation to distance itself from the moribund parent.

Ten years earlier the management of Canadair Limited, the aircraft manufacturer, had asked Ottawa to help free it from what the Canadians thought was the dead hand of its American parent, General Dynamics. In 1976 the government of Canada bought Canadair for $38 million, with the aim of preserving Canada's ability to produce advanced aircraft, saving jobs, and stimulating high-technology manufacturing. Ottawa planned to stabilize the situation at Canadair, which had been declining with shrinking markets for military aircraft, and then sell the company back into private hands. Canadair's management decided to make a major entry into civilian aircraft by producing a new executive jet, the Challenger. Ottawa and the province of Quebec provided most of the seed money for the project.

There were no financial analysts or shareholders scrutinizing the quarterly or annual results of operations at the state-owned company. Few Canadians, including members of Parliament, had any awareness of the price they were paying for the Challenger until April 1983, when CBC television's *Fifth Estate* revealed that Ottawa had supported Canadair to the tune of $1.5 billion and more. These Challenger development costs had not been clearly delineated in Canadair's accounts and there was no hope that they would ever be recovered in sales. Canadair decided it had to write off these costs and in June 1983 announced a loss of $1,414.9 million. The loss was a new record for a Canadian corporation, surpassing Dome's $1.1 billion in the same year. There was no danger of a formal Canadair bankruptcy, of course, for its owners, the Canadian people, could borrow or tax themselves to cover the loss. In 1986 Canadair was sold to Bombardier, its debt having been written off.

Massey, Dome, and Canadair were not everyday corporate basket cases. Apart from the staggering size of their losses – these were Canada's world-class corporate failures – each was a show-case company, at one time or another thought to represent Canadians' best aspirations and energies as entrepreneurs, managers, manufacturers. Nor are we considering three completely exceptional cases. All of Canadian business suffered hard punishment in the deep, international recession of 1981–82, the worst turndown since the Great Depression of the 1930s. Tough going. And even tougher going throughout the 1980s for old-fashioned manufacturing companies, like Massey, or the automobile companies, which lacked the flexibility to adjust to changed conditions, particularly a sharp intensification of international competition. The Dome failure was the most spectacular and insoluble of the troubles of a host of Canadian energy and resource companies in the 1980s. Glutted world markets and collapsing commodity prices eroded even the strongest Canadian resource producers, as blue-chip firms such as Inco and Noranda lost hundreds of millions in the worst years and wondered if they could ever regain "normal" levels of prosperity. Canadair was the worst-managed Canadian aircraft manufacturer; the better-managed one, de Havilland, also under government ownership, lost about $400 million in its own right. In the mid-1980s the only profitable Canadian manufacturer of complete aircraft was Fantasy Sky Productions Incorporated of Kitchener, Ontario, maker of the Labatt Blue and other hot-air balloons.

Were other symbols of trouble needed? Three generations of Canadians had been brought up to believe that the Canadian banking system, resting on massive pillars of Scots-Canadian prudence and rectitude, was invulnerable. Canadian banks did not fail. They could not fail. They were too powerful. They could save each other, or, if the unthinkable happened, government could save them all. In the autumn of 1985 no one saved the Canadian Commercial Bank and the Northland Bank of Canada, two 1970s-born chartered banks based in Alberta. These were the first banks to fail in Canada since the Home Bank collapse of 1923. Their demise took place a few months before the 1986 collapse in energy and grain prices imperilled the whole economy of western Canada.

Businessmen who were forced through the crucible of recession, who faced unprecedented competition in their traditional markets from offshore producers, who saw commodity prices collapse to levels no one thought possible, knew that the cosy assumptions of the boom years were shattered. Canada could not isolate or protect itself from the workings of world markets. Canada's resources were not necessarily a cornucopia of natural wealth. Big Canadian corporations were no more immune from market forces than small ones. The Galbraithian world of controlled markets, planning systems, and perpetual profits was a naive fantasy. Canadian governments' confidence in their ability to anticipate the future and shape economic events was pathetically absurd. Neither public nor private organizations had the power to control their destinies. Markets, competition, great economic forces frustrated all the visible hands of the managers, planners, politicians, and forecasters. No one knew what the price of a barrel of oil would be next week.

The best business practice in response to the tough going of the 1980s was to return to fundamental values: market sensitivity, entrepreneurship, emphasis on leanness, motivation, and the maximum use of human resources. At the same time many Canadian businessmen wondered whether governments and ordinary citizens understood the seriousness of the challenges facing the country. It was a tough, unfriendly world, that might never again need so many raw materials from northern North America. There were no guarantees of security or survival, and inside the country there were stunning costs of optimistic mismanagement, including imperilled national finances. As the Royal Commission on the Economic Union and Development Prospects for Canada, chaired by Donald S. Macdonald, noted in its 1985 Report, "the message is that there is less and less place to hide."

Inflation had been counted on to hide a lot. The inflation mentality, in which risks are taken on the premise, hardening to certainty, of continuing price increases, had infected business in all previous Canadian booms – during the nineteenth century, in the later Laurier years, the Great War, and at the end of the 1920s. It became particularly deep-seated in the 1970s for several reasons, not least being an assumption that the lessons of previous business cycles (if anyone remembered anything about the pre-Keynesian dark ages) were irrelevant.

INFLATION

Annual percentage changes in the Consumer Price Index:

1966:	3.7	1973:	7.7	1980:	10.2
1967:	3.6	1974:	10.9	1981:	12.5
1968:	4.0	1975:	10.8	1982:	10.8
1969:	4.6	1976:	7.5	1983:	5.8
1970:	3.3	1977:	7.9	1984:	4.4
1971:	2.9	1978:	8.8	1985:	4.0
1972:	4.7	1979:	9.2	1986:	4.2

SOURCE: Statistics Canada

Prices simply did not fall any more, it seemed. Their rate of increase might change, but the tendency was forever upward. Some economists thought that inelastic wages gave modern economies an inflationary bias; Keynesian monetary policy, as applied by employment- and vote-conscious politicians – probably tended in the same direction. So did the scarcities that pundits thought they saw everywhere in the 1960s and 1970s. It was widely believed that the surging economies of the industrialized nations were gobbling up finite and shrinking supplies of natural resources – metals, fossil fuels, even agricultural land and fresh water. Whether or not the world reached the much-publicized "limits of growth" forecast by a think-tank called the Club of Rome in 1972, it seemed that the collision of growing demand with shrinking supply was bound to lead to perpetual price increases.

The energy crisis of the 1970s seemed to be the proof of the prophecies. OPEC's control of the world's oil market only existed because demand was greater than supply. So the suppliers took monopoly prices and profits. Assume constantly increasing demand and steadily shrinking supply (every mile you drove meant that much less fossil fuel in the world), as a few experts had done in the late 1960s, and you have the price shocks of 1973–74 and 1979–80. Continue the projections indefinitely into the future and you have the high price assumptions underlying the National Energy Program and the growth of Dome Petroleum.

Whether it was oil or oysters that was inflating in value, home heating oil or houses and lots, the sensible strategy seemed to be to acquire commodities on credit now and pay for them in depreciating paper later on. Buy assets whose worth was increasing. Spend dollars quickly and borrow more to spend because they can be paid back cheaply. The real commodities will never again be so cheap. It made sense for corporations with access to cash or credit to spend it on growth by acquisition or merger. To inflation bugs, the shares of many companies whose sales and profits were bound to increase with inflation were being under-valued by skittish investors. Time to buy them now.

The NEP-induced takeovers of 1981 were the most visible examples of infla-tion-bred growth strategy. Many other resource companies, ranging from Noranda through Inco and Denison Mines to the British Columbia Resources Corporation, were pursuing similar expansions, buying ore and trees and coal and oil and gas and shares of companies that owned these scarce resources that were bound to in-crease in value. Other firms joined the dance, especially in real estate and devel-opment, where the successes of the sixties seemed to show that land and the buildings on it were an inflation-proof waltz to wealth. Old firms and new, large and small, became acquisitors. The Hudson's Bay Company, for example, still a major fur trader, but not a dominant force in Canadian retailing, embarked on a major program of expansion by takeover in 1978 when it acquired the Zellers chain of discount department stores; the next year it took over Simpsons, one of its leading competitors in eastern Canada. Then, to its surprise, the Bay itself was taken over when the International Thomson Organization Limited outbid Weston's for a controlling interest. Roy Thomson, who had died in 1976, would have been thrilled at the thought that his aristocratic heirs, complete with beaver on their coat of arms, governed Canada's most historic corporation.

It was not really a surprising development. At about the same time the proprietors of the 150-year-old Abitibi-Price forest empire became the Reichmann brothers, whose Olympia and York had become the largest property development firm in the world thanks to breathtakingly successful gambles in Manhattan office towers. A few years later the Reichmanns also became the effective proprietors of Gulf Canada, then of Hiram Walker Resources. In 1979 the proud managers of Brascan, rooted in old London, Ontario, and Labatts, found they had no defence against a takeover by Edper Equities Limited, a holding company controlled by Allan Bronfman's sons, Edgar and Peter. While the big Bronfman company, Seagram's, manoeuvred daringly in the United States, becoming the largest shareholder in blue-blooded Du Pont chemicals, Edgar and Peter and Brascan, and their brilliant lawyer-entrepreneur, Trevor Eyton, moved to centre stage in corporate Canada. Within months of the Edper takeover, Brascan acquired a major interest, amounting to control, in Noranda Mines, a company that for more than half a century had been the wonderfully rich pride of Canadian mining. The com-panies kept their old names; the age of the old entrepreneurs and the old families passed away.

The pace became most frantic in real estate and property development, an in-dustry anyone could enter with a few dollars for a down-payment on a house or lot. Buy empty land, buy houses, take a piece of a strip mall, get into a MURB deal (in 1974 Ottawa created special tax shelters to encourage the construction of multiple unit residential buildings), flip the properties at a profit, and go on to more. Access to mortgage money was all-important in the property game, and often the hardest part of deals to put in place. For the real estate entrepreneurs there were many advantages in being able to shortcut the normal route of arm's length borrowing from established financial institutions. So they bought or built their own money suppliers, often trust companies because they had such broad deposit-taking and lending powers.

By the end of the 1970s there were a host of new rags to riches stories in real estate and development and finance, most in the booming West. Dr. Charles Allard's real estate–based Edmonton empire (including North West Trust) was virtually old wealth, compared to the mushrooming fortunes of, say, Nelson Skalbania in Vancouver (more deals than he bothered to count), or the Ghermezian brothers (a gargantuan Edmonton shopping centre) or young Peter Pocklington (Fidelity Trust, Wayne Gretzky). Were the Belzburgs, poor Polish Jews whose father worked on the floor of Pat Burns's slaughterhouse, going to be Canada's next Bronfmans? From business origins in furniture stores and dog food companies, the Belzburgs of Calgary and Vancouver had built western Canada's largest financial institution, First City Trust Company, and were moving on to the big leagues of corporate acquisition in the United States.

Of course the Belzburgs kept in touch with the next stage in the evolution of western Canadian enterprise, the creation of the West's own banks. The second Bank of British Columbia was already on the scene and growing. In 1976 it was joined by the Canadian Commercial Bank and the Northland Bank, headquartered in Edmonton and Calgary respectively. Other new banks were in the works, including Allard's long-planned Bank of Alberta, which opened in 1983 and, in Vancouver in the same year, the Western and Pacific Bank of Canada. Put the new banks and the trust companies and the confident financial wizards behind them all together – most of them worked the same western energy and property development fields, and did a lot of related deals – extend the ties to the east, say with the real estate–financial empire that Leonard Rosenberg was creating through the Greymac family of mortgage and trust companies, and you could see the outlines of a new financial order struggling to emerge in the Dominion.

Trust companies seemed peculiarly on the cutting edge of the reshaping of Canadian finance. The 1967 Bank Act revisions had cut many of the older trust companies loose from their affiliations with chartered banks by prohibiting interlocking directorates. Trust companies possessed almost all of the powers and flexibility of chartered banks, without the banks' handicap (also imposed in 1967) of the 10 per cent limit on individual sharcholdings. It seemed as though they could be the most entrepreneurial financial institutions in the scramble to meet Canadians' ever-growing demands for financial services.

In the early 1980s almost everyone seemed to be angling for control of a trust company or more trust companies: all the new players in the West; blue-ribbon Toronto financiers like Hal Jackman, building from a family base in insurance; life insurance companies like Manufacturers, trying to position itself as a general provider of financial services; established eastern developers like Campeau Corporation and real estate entrepreneurs like George Mann; up-and-coming Montreal financiers like Reuben Cohen and Leonard Ellen; and an assortment of other go-getters, some of whom were thought to have paid little attention to the law in their scramble to succeed. There were highly publicized takeover battles for control of trust companies, including several rounds in an ongoing struggle for Crown Trust, an old but honoured orphan after being cut loose by Argus. By the summer of 1982 it seemed that Crown had found a home at last, when it was taken over by Leonard Rosenberg's Greymac group. Once again the torch had passed from the old establishment to the new players.

The major chartered banks had no intention of being left behind by faster-moving competitors, including the several dozen foreign banks that entered Canada after 1980's Bank Act revisions. Banking conservatism and contentment were traits of the past, long since abandoned. The modern banker was aggressive, fast-moving, market-oriented, growth-conscious. Bankers met the evolving competition of the seventies by introducing new deposit instruments and offering new kinds of loans (all intermediaries adjusted to inflation by moving toward shorter terms and floating interest rates), strengthening their hold on consumer credit (they had particular success with their credit card network), and expanding their merchant banking and international activities. The big five chartered banks were determined to become "universal" banks, offering every possible kind of banking service. In the gathering debate on deregulation of financial services they made known their impatience with regulations limiting their entrepreneurial capacity. They showed their new entrepreneurship by competing vigorously all over the world in the bankers' rush to lend to less-developed countries, and in their willingness to finance corporate growth in Canada, especially in the energy sector.

At the height of inflation, the banks' willingness to hand out their money was a wonder to behold, especially to westerners who for years had cursed bankers six ways to Sunday as they rode pullmans and North Stars down to Toronto. Now you just got on the phone, said how much you wanted, got the okay, and set the underlings to work on the paper. Sometimes the bankers even came to you and asked to be let in on a deal. Charles Allard took one afternoon from his Edmonton office to raise $150 million to build a methanol plant in Medicine Hat, and five minutes more to arrange an extra $25 million. Joel Bell of Petro-Canada asked the Royal's man in Calgary, by telephone, for "one and a quarter" for the Petro-Canada takeover – one and a quarter billion. And Bill Richards and Jack Gallagher of Dome might as well have had the keys to the vaults. They seemed able to walk in and carry away the banks' money. Total Canadian chartered bank support for the petroleum industry in Canada was estimated to be about $300 million in 1970. By 1978 it had risen to about $3 billion.

Then the mega-lending began. This was an age of big business and shrinking dollars, but it was still a rare thing anywhere in the world for a single bank to lend a single private customer a billion dollars. Not in Canada. By the middle of 1981 Dome Petroleum had billion-dollar loans from *each* of the Bank of Montreal, Toronto-Dominion Bank, and Canadian Imperial Bank of Commerce. The Royal was not far behind, and in 1981 the Bank of Nova Scotia lent a Dome subsidiary $350 million to buy a mine in the Yukon. The chartered banks' total exposure to Dome, approximately $4 billion, was well over half the total capital invested in Canadian banks. No Canadian bankers had ever before risked so much money on a single client. The loans were so big that the Inspector General of Banks stepped in to remind the bankers of the need for prudence. The intervention must have been humiliating. It was nothing compared to the troubles ahead.

From time immemorial the fundamental merchant skill has been knowing when to buy and when to sell. Buy cheap and sell dear and you succeeded. If you misread the market, bought dear and had to sell cheap, you were buried in potter's field. The state of any market depended on the relationship between supply and demand.

Everyone in Canada who was still betting on continuing energy inflation for the 1980s misread the market. "Everyone" included Dome Petroleum, Nova, Petro-Canada, the Canada Development Corporation, the governments of Alberta and Canada, and the stewards of Canada's banking system. Their fundamental mistake was to believe the conventional myths of energy shortage and permanent crisis. These were simply wrong. Eight years of high energy prices triggered exactly the global adjustments in world supply and demand that would occur on any unimpeded market – and that had been predicted by some market-oriented observers when the crisis began. Supply increased because high prices led to more exploration which led to more discovery. Demand decreased because high prices induced conservation and conversion to alternative sources ranging from coal to nuclear power. As world oil supply caught up with and edged past demand, the producers' cartel struggled with increasing difficulty to hold prices.

The collapse came in two stages: the more or less orderly retreat from $40 a barrel oil in 1981 to an official OPEC price of $29 in early 1983; then the complete breakdown of price agreements in 1986. During the summer of 1986, a season when Canada's energy planning for the 1980s had forecast a world price of oil of c$79.10 a barrel, the real price gyrated wildly in the neighbourhood of c$14, not far from its historic norm. As the former monopolists struggled to sop up the tide of oil, onlookers slowly awoke to the realization that the visible hands of OPEC were powerless. The cartel was drowning in its own, and its competitors', oil.

The tragedy of Dome, the tragedy of Canadian energy policy, was that the merchants had bought at the peak of the market. The Canadian expansionists had loaded themselves with debt, mortgaging the farm, the store, perhaps the country's future, to buy and buy and buy. Now the market turned against them, and many were ruined. The desperately hard times that descended on the oil patch in 1986 were a simple function of the price collapse. At $14 a barrel, at anything less than c$20-25 a barrel, huge chunks of the Canadian petroleum industry were uneconomic. Companies could not carry the huge debt load they had acquired in good times (Dome was the most spectacular of the basket cases, but not the only one; half a dozen other mushroom firms with assets once valued in the hundreds of millions also collapsed, never to become even footnotes to Canadian business history), or were crippled for years to come.

Who dared gamble against a glut? One by one, the energy mega-projects that had been expected to drive Canada's economy into the twenty-first century were postponed or abandoned. After all that planning and investigation and corporate manoeuvring, there was no Arctic gas pipeline, only a "pre-built" section up to northern Alberta to help producers increase cash flow with more exports. Instead of planning on new tar sands' plants every two or three years for decades, companies and governments had to worry about the viability of the two existing operations, as Syncrude and Suncor lost money on every barrel they produced. All the expensive frontier exploration of the past decade had led to the discovery of several billion barrels of oil under the Canada Lands, including even the Beaufort Sea – though it was left to Gulf and Shell and Esso, picking up Dome's pieces and Ottawa's PIP grants, to make the strikes. Not one barrel of it was worth producing unless world prices recovered. The window to the future that OPEC and the energy crisis seemed to have opened to the people of Newfoundland, Nova Scotia, and the Arctic, was crashing shut.

The big winners in the energy bull market had been those who were smart or lucky enough to sell out at the top. The supreme irony of Canada's National Energy Program was that it stimulated Canadian buy-outs of foreign oil interests at the highest prices of the century. The greatest beneficiaries of Canadian energy nationalism were foreign capitalists: the shareholders of Conoco when they got rid of HBOG, the Belgian owners of Petrofina who were astounded at the price Petro-Canada paid for their Canadian company, the treasury of the Sun Oil Company, which received $650 million from the astonishingly inept government of the province of Ontario* for assets worth less than $100 million five years later.

The losers were not just the visionary businessmen and energy experts who made or recommended the disastrous deals, but all the shareholders who had had faith in their judgment, as well as Canadian taxpayers, who had had very little say in the matter. Taxpayers were multiple losers. They had to bear the cost of bad energy investments by governments and the companies they owned, as well as most of the costs of frontier exploration, underwritten by tax breaks and the NEP's PIP grants. At the same time, and possibly for years into the future, Canadians' royalty and tax income from the natural resources themselves, the oil and gas they owned, was imperilled by the collapse of world prices. There was little the national government could have done about the latter problem; the former mess was almost entirely of its own making. The utter failure of Canada's National Energy Program, based as it was on complete misunderstanding of energy markets, was a policy disaster for the Dominion whose only historical parallel was the tragic over-building of railways in the early years of the twentieth century.

———————

An even more serious problem lay in the fact that the rise and fall of the price of oil was not an isolated phenomenon. As the inflation of the seventies ground to a halt, the prices of many other commodities softened or declined. Virtually the whole of Canada's natural resource economy had to adjust to lower prices for its products. In 1986 Inco had to sell its nickel at US $1.85 to $1.90 a pound; in 1980 it had been $3.14. The prices Noranda got for its copper in the mid-eighties – about 65 cents a pound, down from an inflation high of about $1.25 – were among the lowest in recorded history. Cominco could not make money with zinc at 35 cents a pound, lead at 18 cents, or silver at $5 an ounce. Weakness in the price of wood products in the early eighties meant losses for forest companies. All energy prices were interrelated, of course, and the idea of developing Rocky Mountain coal mines as a way of participating in the permanent energy boom turned into a nightmare for several major firms, including Denison Mines, which wrote off $241 million on its disastrous Quintette adventure in British Columbia when coal expected to sell for $125 a ton fell to $70. No one in the 1950s would have believed that Canada's iron ore adventure in Labrador would drift to an end in only thirty years, as mines were closed and workers paid off, the company towns were razed, and some of the executives moved on to other jobs.

* Ontario was the naive latecomer, last to buy just before the break, and at a price immediately seen to be absurd. Its energy fiasco was parallelled by a wild adventure in government land speculation, as it accumulated huge amounts of acreage to service growth and take inflationary profits that never came. The initial write-down after the Conservatives were defeated in 1985 was $271 million. The land bankers had fallen prey to one of the oldest but least probable of all Canadian myths, the idea that the country was short of land.

TROUBLED RESOURCE COMPANIES, 1979–85

Company	1979	1980	1981	1982	1983	1984	1985
Alcan: Revenue(millions)	4,195	4,992	4,732	4,353	4,969	5,272	5,511
Net income:	406	542	264	-58	58	216	-216
Algoma Steel	1,081	1,149	1,426	874	860	1,104	1,177
	112	109	165	-40	-127	-46	-10
B.C. Resources	359	520	859	694	856	1,060	1,051
	41	48	42	-3	6	-14	-471
Canada Development Corp.	2,015	2,359	3,136	4,011	3,835	4,180	3,257
	113	189	85	-126	-45	81	171
Cominco	1,274	1,443	1,417	1,235	1,375	1,590	1,458
	204	169	65	-49	-39	24	-97
Inco	2,489	3,036	1,886	1,236	1,173	1,468	1,491
	142	219	-5	-204	-234	-77	52
MacMillan Bloedel	2,180	2,436	2,210	1,843	2,044	2,128	2,354
	155	113	-27	-93	3	19	43
Noranda	2,485	2,889	3,030	2,630	3,100	3,400	3,439
	410	361	106	-140	-35	-4	-254
Stelco	2,091	2,229	2,174	2,020	2,033	2,401	2,435
	157	132	83	-41	-14	48	78

SOURCE: Financial Post Corporation Service

The sickness of the resource sector spread inexorably into linked industries, affecting construction, real estate, home values, and finance. As the economy of western Canada sank into recession and then depression in the 1980s, it was only a matter of time before the weakest of the region's new financial institutions went down. At the wholesale level, there were real, old-fashioned "runs" on financial institutions. Several trust companies and credit unions failed along with the Canadian Commercial Bank and the Northland Bank. Others, including several of the weaker banks, were swallowed up in mergers. In 1986 the Hongkong Bank of Canada had to be paid $135 million to take over the Bank of British Columbia. So much for economic nationalism – or regional nationalism. All of these institutions had made substantial loans to energy companies or for western property development that were only viable at the top of the market. Excessive concentration in the vulnerable industries of a vulnerable region was as fatal to banks and trust companies in the 1980s as it had been in the 1880s. But no one had paid any attention to the lessons of the past.

The death-throes of Dome, the failed banks, and the other mushroom organizations and entrepreneurs became the stuff of fascinating reportage. The titles
of the books – *Other People's Money; A Matter of Trust; Public Money, Private
Greed; Massey at the Brink; Breaking the Banks* – spoke to the principles and
practices of the great inflation, and to the morning after. The post-mortem descriptions of the inflationists' desperate attempts to bail out sinking companies often
read like accounts of the *Titanic's* last night. The difference was that the great ship
was a well-built vessel, destroyed by bad luck and bad seamanship. As time sharp-
ened the focus of Canadians' hindsight on the seventies, it became increasingly
clear that many of the creatures and creations spawned by the inflation had never
been sound. The inflationary mind-set had blinded politicians, planners, accountants, bankers, and many other businessmen to the weaknesses, often glaring
and fundamental, of organizations whose growth they had supported and
entrepreneurs with whom they had done business. Some of the wildest promoters
in Canadian history, advancing schemes reminiscent of Martin Frobisher, the
Grand Trunk Railway, F.H. Clergue, and the most extreme fantasies of Mackenzie
and Mann, had won all-out backing from businessmen who prided themselves
professionally on hard-headedness and prudence. Dome Petroleum, for example,
was probably less sound in its careening growth, less well managed, and less controlled by its bankers, than the old Canadian Northern Railway.*

It was natural for businessmen and forecasters who had grown up in an age of
growth and inflation to predict a speedy return to high prices and prosperity. The
strong 1983–85 national recovery from the recession, despite the troubles of mining and some of the other resource industries and the whole province of British

---

* Dome was the biggest, but not the most bizarre of the promoters' creations. When the big
development firm, Cadillac Fairview, needed liquidity in November 1982, it sold eleven
thousand Toronto apartment units to Leonard Rosenberg's Greymac Credit for $270 million.
Greymac immediately sold the units to Kilderkin Investments, owned by William Player,
for $312 million. Kilderkin immediately resold the units, apparently, to a consortium of
Saudi Arabian investors for $500 million. Greymac Trust, Andrew Markle's Seaway Trust,
and Crown Trust advanced most of the mortgage money to finance the deal. In the winter of
1982–83 the government of Ontario passed emergency legislation enabling it to seize the
trust companies, and did so.

At the end of "the trust companies affair," as it was called, the entrepreneurs' companies
and reputations were in ruins, and one of the trio, Player, finished 1986 in jail. The Canada
Deposit Insurance Corporation was trying to recover more than $700 million in depositors'
losses that it had had to cover.

Columbia, seemed to vindicate the optimists. Lower inflation and interest rates caused stock markets to soar. But with the energy crash of 1986, the spreading consciousness of continuing problems in mining and other resource industries, and the growing realization that the world was now awash in surplus protein and carbohydrate, as well as hydrocarbons, it was no longer so clear that growth would continue in the old channels that had been so favourable to the Dominion of the north.

By the mid-eighties there was unsettling evidence of deep historic shifts in the world's uses of and demand for raw materials. High-technology industries, and even traditional ones like automobile manufacture, used much more silicon and plastic and glass, much less iron and steel and nickel. Most of the growth industries of the future, centring on electronics, biotechnology, microtechnology, and the provision of services, seemed likely to need even fewer traditional raw materials. What would happen to copper wire in the world of fibre optics? Who used lead for anything (except batteries) any more? Asbestos fibres were a health hazard. World demand for many traditional metals seemed to be in absolute decline, at the same time as more and more of it was met by low-cost producers in Third World countries. Even where demand seemed assured, for, say, newsprint and other kinds of paper, a rush of new suppliers began crowding the market. Most significantly perhaps, the world would always need food, but there had been such a concerted and successful attempt to increase production, combined with policies to subsidize and stimulate surpluses in areas such as the European Economic Community, that markets were bulging with wheat, dairy products, and other foodstuffs. With the government of the United States subsidizing grain sales to the Soviet Union, Canadians faced the toughest international competition in agricultural markets since the Great Depression.

Canada's traditional industries, many of its largest firms, whole regions of the country, were based on the nation's historic role as a supplier of raw materials to the hungry world economy. What if the world stopped wanting Canadian raw materials? From the beginning of the commodity downturn in 1977 through the mid-1980s the natural wealth of Canada – the one-time treasures of its rocks and trees – was literally devalued. In 1986 raw material prices stood at their lowest levels in history in relation to manufactured goods and services, as low as they had in the Great Depression. "It is quite unlikely," Peter Drucker concluded in an influential article on the changing world economy, "that raw material prices will ever rise substantially as compared to the prices of manufactured goods (or high-knowledge services such as information, education or health care) except in the event of a major prolonged war."

If that judgment was correct, the implications for Canada were staggering. A treasure house of resources that were losing their value! Drop the price low enough and the black gold and the bountiful forest and the glittering ore turned into worthless goo and rocks and trees, the northern cornucopia became a northern wilderness again, *cap de nada*. Ominous signs of it were already there in the closing of the Labrador mines, the shrinking of Sudbury, the decimation and worse of mining towns and logging camps of British Columbia, the bust in Alberta, the end of frontier drilling. Pessimists talked of all of Canadian mining as a "sunset industry" – though a tremendous surge in gold sales, production, discoveries, and exploration offset many other metallic woes. Just as it had in the Great Depression. The gold boom was no help to dying base metal refiners or to secondary metal producers like Canada's steel companies, who began suffering serious problems in their major markets. The big old steel mill at Sydney, Cape Breton Island, was a tragic failure, of course; it had seldom been viable at any time in its history. But it had been a long time since there had been serious questions about the viability of the Algoma establishment at Sault Ste Marie. In the mid-1980s they were asked again. "Perhaps this *was* Canada's century," the *Globe and Mail* commented after a worried editorial survey of the plight of Canadian agriculture. The dollar had dropped from par in 1976 to less than 70 cents US in early 1986, a record low. There was a net loss of foreign direct investment in Canada. Was Canada fated to become a sunset country?

Developments in the resource economy parallelled and were related to long-term shifts in other kinds of production. In the 1960s and 1970s North America's strength in key areas of manufacturing began eroding. The slippage was twofold. Traditional labour-intensive production tended to locate in developing countries where low wages gave significant competitive advantage. At the same time, leadership in manufacturing innovation, particularly the development of high-technology products and factory automation, came increasingly from abroad. For a time the most dynamic Pacific rim communities – Japan, South Korea, Hong Kong, and Singapore – benefited from *both* trends, though by the eighties all were being pressed by lower-cost producers. From the point of view of North American producers, the source of the imports did not matter so much as the fact that wave after wave of them poured into domestic markets, flooding over the sandbars and seawalls of tariff and non-tariff protection. Both Americans and Canadians began wondering about the future of their smokestack industries and blue collar workforces. How could they stay competitive in manufacturing?

For some Canadian industries, such as textiles and footwear, the pressure was not new. For more than a hundred years their history had been a story of protection behind National Policy dikes that had to be plugged and reinforced constantly. Large chunks of such industries had never been truly competitive and probably never would. Their lobbyists' pathways to Ottawa were well worn; the pleas to protect Canadian jobs just a little longer while plans were implemented to modernize this or that industry were uncanny echoes of the 1880s. Producers in other light manufacturing industries, ranging from traditional electronics (radio and television sets and parts) to bicycles and most other sporting goods, had neither the lobbying clout nor significant hope of ever attaining competitive advantage, and declined drastically as domestic employers.

The most dramatic and visible and important offshore challenge came in automobiles. The Europeans had made permanent inroads on North American car markets in the sixties. In the conserving seventies those once-improbable little Japanese cars – Datsuns, Toyotas, Hondas, Mazdas – proved cheaper to buy and operate than the overpowered gas-guzzlers made in Windsor, St. Thomas, or Oshawa. Detroit's response to the import challenge, the Big Three's introduction of their own lines of sub-compacts, was only partially effective, and was very costly. It was not clear whether the Japanese car-makers enjoyed structural cost advantages, or whether they were particularly well-managed firms that had the good luck to be going up against a trio of lumbering dinosaurs named Ford, Chrysler, and General Motors. Probably a little of both.

By the 1980s other car-makers were not far behind the Japanese in their attack on North America. If the cheap Russian Lada did not turn the capitalists into believers in socialist value, perhaps the Yugoslavian Yugo would. South Korean Ponies and Stellars and Excels from Hyundai slipped through every opening in Canadian quota systems. Brazilian cars were going to be next. When would the Taiwanese follow? Who would have believed this paragraph in, say, 1955? Who would have believed it possible that poverty-stricken India would be producing surpluses of food in the mid-1980s? Would it take another thirty years for the first Indian-made automobiles to be imported into Canada?

Rationalization of the automobile industry through continental free trade had been an effective approach to the problem of high costs and limited markets in Canada in the 1960s. By the end of the 1970s, with Chrysler on the brink of collapse and Ford losing money, even the Americans had to protect their market, mainly by the use of quotas on Japanese imports. Canada did the same. Within one generation the most secure North American manufacturing industry, thought to epitomize corporate power and managerial skill (Galbraith used it in *The New Industrial State* as his model of advanced corporate planning power), had become, in the eyes of many, a basket case. All the old verities had broken down. The wily foreigners could compete in anything. Was any industry or company safe?

———————

Through the 1970s the most remarked-upon response to the globalization of business had been the creation of the global corporation. The logic was this: Business had first gone overseas to sell. It could just as easily go abroad to produce. Corporations could outgrow nations, and, it seemed, could keep on internalizing production and distribution functions without limit. Big business could just keep on getting bigger.

Some Canadian firms were able to produce successfully abroad. For several generations the family-owned Bata shoe empire, headquartered in Canada after the Batas left Czechoslovakia before the Second World War, had been making and selling shoes in practically every non-communist country in the world. Other Canadian manufacturing firms adjusted to offshore sourcing by buying or assembling abroad, and, as the Cohen family of Winnipeg discovered, some very big businesses could be built as distributors for the new imported products. In their case a Canadian's good judgment and/or good luck in obtaining the franchise to distribute Sony products in Canada in the 1950s (hard on the heels of a minor triumph importing the Paper-Mate ballpoint pen), was the crucial catalyst in turning a family cigar-store supply business into a major Canadian corporation, Gendis, in one generation.

But the fate of Massey-Ferguson was a cautionary tale for all who believed in the myths about the power of big, multinational business. After its spectacular turn-around and expansion in the 1960s, Massey thought itself invulnerable: it sold in so many markets around the world that it was surely sheltered against a cyclical downturn in the farm equipment market on any continent. It did not foresee a post–green revolution downturn on all continents. Massey had begun to diversify into heavy construction equipment without realizing that it lacked the expertise to compete in that field. In its transnational expansion it had bet that nation states would continue to favour domestic manufacturers, and found itself with too many branch factories producing for limited markets. It had minimized subcontracting to integrate its manufacturing operations, and found itself saddled with high-cost, inflexible, internal supply systems. Above all, as the firm expanded through the 1970s in quest of world dominance, it loaded itself with bank debt at floating rates. As the rates floated upward and sales turned down, the crunch began.

"The Massey-Ferguson management presided over and tolerated a completely unacceptable and noncompetitive degree of inefficiency and general corporate slothfulness," Conrad Black wrote of his predecessors. In its final years the Thornborough regime at Massey, once thought to be on the creative frontier of advanced management, failed utterly to anticipate the firm's problems or take steps to solve them. All the cost control and product planning and communications and trouble-shooting systems introduced by Thornborough's men failed. The men themselves failed, their company becoming the least competitive performer in an industry where there was still room for at least one well-run giant, Deere, to survive and prosper. Massey's chief executives became caught up in the inflationary mentality, failed to understand the intricacies of the global farm implement business, and, above all, became trapped in their own corporate hubris. They had succeeded so well in the past, and, after all, their company was so big and powerful. "A young manager arriving in the Toronto plant was told not to concern himself too much with inefficiencies in production and delays in deliveries and shipments," Peter Cook wrote in *Massey at the Brink.* "Massey was a company that could not fail to make money."

It became fashionable to blame Massey's problems on the lack of strong proprietorial leadership at the firm. There was actually a stronger proprietorial presence in Massey than in most big, widely held corporations because of the Argus interest. Perhaps the proprietorial failure actually occurred at Argus, whose partners' strength had never been in attention to management. Black later characterized Bud McDougald as "a man who had everyone believing he was a supremely capable executive when it was all an absolutely brilliant con job." One of McDougald's failures was that he had not brought along successors at Argus with the experience, detailed knowledge, and time to arrange the managerial revolutions needed in several of the companies it controlled. After clawing his way to the top of Argus, Conrad Black was a latecomer to the affairs of its troubled corporate empire who himself had little managerial experience. He eventually found it in the best interest of the Argus shareholders to liquidate the investments in Massey, Dominion Stores, Standard Broadcasting, and the other firms, and less than a decade later seemed to have taken a not untrodden path into British media proprietorship. "Nobody is going to hang this one on me," Black told his biographer, Peter Newman, of the Massey débâcle.

Whether or not Argus should have been more committed to saving Massey, the other failure had been by Massey's other proprietors, the firm's own top management. A debate about the ownership of financial service corporations that developed a few years later – would a firm be more responsibly managed if its ownership was concentrated or widely dispersed? – generated intense argument about what was largely a non-issue. It was certainly true that ownership and control had been separated in the modern widely held corporation, a phenomen popularized in the 1930's by Berle and Means's classic, *The Modern Corporation and Private Property.* But that very divorce had freed management to wield proprietorial power, exercising as firm (or infirm) control as any of the old fashioned owner-managers. All proprietors, whether owners, managers, or owner-managers, had the potential to ruin an organization if they managed it in their own short-term self-interest or just managed it badly. Massey's real problem was not in its ownership structure, but in the difficulties all managers were experiencing with mammoth corporations in the rapidly changing business world of the 1970s and 1980s.

The Massey failure reflected bad management practices writ large. Other gigantic Canadian corporations suffered from similar if milder illnesses. In the 1970s the management of Inco, for example, cost its shareholders hundreds of millions in ill-conceived attempts at geographic diversification (into Guatemala) and downstream integration (into the battery business). Hiram Walker Resources' determination to ride the energy bandwagon led to an almost risible purchase of

American oil and gas properties in 1981 without checking their (very high) valuation. The chartered banks' problems with Dome and other energy-related clients, not to mention their problems with their $20 billion in loans to less-developed countries (where they were at least in the company of all the leading American banks), represented stunning executive mistakes in what many had thought were some of Canada's best managed institutions.

Whose business judgment was worse? Was it the management of the Hudson's Bay Company in its takeover of Simpson's, which turned out to be a quagmire of a company? Or was it the management of Thomson International, in its takeover of the Bay, a company messed up by the burden of Simpson's and other managerial misjudgments? Noranda fared little better in its takeover of MacMillan-Bloedel or Brascan in its investment in Noranda. Power Corporation and Canadian Pacific Investments did not achieve high returns from their acquisitions. In fact hardly any of the diversifiers and conglomerators of the 1960s and 1970s produced impressive results. The Bryce Royal Commission on Corporate Concentration reported in 1978 that the Canadian conglomerates, like their American cousins, gave shareholders returns below the market average.

An apparently more careful strategy of expanding along familiar lines into the rich United States market led to heavy losses for several Canadian firms, ranging from real estate development companies caught in the downturn to respected retailing chains like Canadian Tire, Peoples Jewellers, and Dylex Limited. In the fast-moving, market-driven world of retailing it was difficult for some of the older, larger firms to hold their own even in Canada. What had gone wrong with Dominion Stores, once the largest supermarket chain in the Dominion? If it was just another example of Argus-Black mismanagement, why was Safeway also losing market share and prestige? Had all the department store chains, Eaton's and Woodward's as well as Simpson's and the Bay, become dinosaurs in the face of changed conditions in retailing, especially the rise of the mall-based specialty chain? Had the managerial errors of the heads of Canada's chartered banks turned them into dinosaurs in the heightened competition with the trust companies and the rejuvenating insurance firms?

In the heady days of the fifties and sixties, corporation managers had believed that the commonsense maxims about the difficulty of maintaining the impressive growth rates of a firm's youth no longer held. By the eighties some of the same managers, or their successors, had to forget about growth and worry about survival.

———————◆———————

Such problems were not unique to Canadian corporations or managers. In the United States the successes of offshore competition in the seventies caused an unprecedented crisis of confidence in American management, a sense of business leadership gone drastically wrong. American management was supposed to lead the world. Now "the American Challenge" was to catch up with the Japanese!

North American business became obsessed with discovering the secrets of Japanese success at the same time as it turned inward in intense scrutiny of home-grown strengths and weaknesses. The runaway success of the 1982 book, *In Search of Excellence: Lessons from America's Best-Run Companies*, by Thomas J. Peters and Robert H. Waterman, Jr., reflected popular and well-founded anxiety for better management practices, for a new set of guidelines to help in the running of the modern, competitive firm. Americans were being jolted into the need to relearn their own game much the way Canadians had been taught some home truths about hockey by the Europeans in the 1960s.

In more ways than Peters and Waterman and the Japan-watchers realized, the best ways were the old ways. At one level it was becoming clear that the management orthodoxies of the postwar era were inadequate. Emphases on accounting, organization, and planning, "number-crunching," executive mobility and higher education, and the traditional staples of business school curricula had become passé. A company certainly had to get its numbers right and know what its employees did, but it needed much more. The truth underlined in *In Search of Excellence* was that competitive edges could only be maintained by constant, intense sharpening. Fundamentals like customer service and marketing, quality control and production organization, were at least as important as accounting and high-level planning. Most fundamentally, companies had to maximize the performance of their only real resource, their people. The members of an organization had to be so motivated and so skilled that they outperformed their competitors. They had to work harder, more productively, and more creatively.

Eighties' management revived such old-fashioned notions as mastering one's business and sticking to it, and valued practical training and experience over paper-chasing at business school. The main lesson drawn from Japanese corporate practice, and from high-performing North American firms like IBM, was of the need to strengthen corporate culture, the environment of traditions, values, and in-centives in which employees worked and performed. In the heyday of the old in-dustrialism, giant organizations emphasized notions such as control, discipline, hierarchy, and command – metaphors and precepts drawn from military experience and/or the scientific management movement – as tools for getting the maximum effort from thousands of poorly motivated employees doing routine factory or clerical work. These were now being gradually replaced by concepts tailored to the aspirations of a more highly educated, self-motivated, and fluid workforce, expected to be more skilled, versatile, and independent in the daily work rhythm.

There were no magic answers in creating good firms to work for. Management might be centralized or decentralized, or a little of both. Performance standards, job descriptions, compensation packages, might be rigidly prescribed or highly flexible, or a little of both. A corporation might be lean and hungry, travelling economy fare, or it might decide its high-performing employees deserved the best of everything. It was often shocking when blue-ribbon companies made their first layoffs in the 1980s, but there was a knack of wielding the knife humanely and cementing the loyalties of those who stayed. The lesson of the *Financial Post's* 1985 book on *The 100 Best Companies to Work for in Canada* seemed to be that management respect for the employee as an individual was the single most important attribute of a happy, productive workplace. The idea of showing wise personal concern for the people you worked with, treating them with near-familial regard or affection, rewarding achievement and offering security and a shared value-system, had deep roots in the enlightened paternalism of the best nineteenth-century employers.

Above all, big firms struggled to regain the knack of being entrepreneurial. They tried to become more innovative, fast-moving, and market-responsive. The idea of research and development had been around for generations, of course, and to many outsiders, particularly in government, it seemed that more research and development was the whole answer to the problem of survival in an age of technology-driven change. Throw more resources into labs, computers, and planners.

Insiders knew that the problem was how to obtain *better* R&D and better performance in everything else. How could firms generate truly brilliant ideas? How could they invent products and services that had never existed before and get these on the market before anyone else did? How could they use existing technology more economically (obtaining innovations by licensing or joint venture, for example, rather than pouring money into attempts to do it themselves)?* How could they find and keep the people who would come up with the better ideas for doing any and every facet of the business?

Some trends suggested that, despite brilliant success at certain firms, big business in many industries was fighting a losing battle. In both the United States and Canada small business enjoyed a renaissance of apparently unprecedented proportions. New corporations were created by the tens of thousands. Virtually all new job creation was in the small business sector. The idea of going independent, building your own business, putting your own ideas into practice, became more fashionable, even among business school students, than the quest for lifetime security with a big corporation. Courses in entrepreneurship began to appear in MBA programs, business journalism rediscovered small business and the aspiring entrepreneur, and success stories about little folk who made good (Canadian titles included *Wildcatters; Money-Makers!; The Entrepreneurs; Money-Rustlers*) became popular. All the prophets of the age of big business, socialist and capitalist alike, had disdained the small business sector as old-fashioned, shrinking, propped up by government favouritism. Suddenly the small business world was trendy, growing, creative, the new frontier of capitalist enterprise.

---

* The snowmobile company, Bombardier, used this strategy as part of its post-1970 evolution into a manufacturer of transportation equipment ranging from locomotives to subway cars and airplanes. In the late 1980s it was considering a joint venture with a Japanese firm to produce a distinctive (Japanese)-Canadian automobile.

The small business resurgence of the 1980s appeared to have both spiritual and structural roots. Big corporations could make executives rich, and sometimes even famous. But generations of high-achieving entrepreneurs had testified to more important satisfactions of business life relating to the joys of ownership – the sense of having created an ongoing organization, of having built something useful, of having been one's own boss, subservient to no man. As large organizations struggled to accommodate and nurture the entrepreneurs in their midst, thus creating *intra*preneurs, the haunting possibility was that no amount of stock options or profit-sharing could substitute for real ownership, no amount of freedom within a tolerant, caring organization could truly accommodate a thorough-going individualist or self-starter. By definition the individual was not an organization man, or woman.

Structurally, the business organization was, in most cases, a mechanism for internalizing transactions that would otherwise be conducted on open markets. The integrated corporation evolved as organizations found it advantageous to do things themselves: do their own manufacturing, or distribution, or selling, rather than rely on other firms; hire permanent staff rather than buy labour on a spot basis; create in-house service systems ranging from legal departments to garbage collection; and so on. Integration was economic and the key to success in certain industries at certain time periods, but was not invariably or necessarily a substitute for market transactions. Where markets were busy and thick and efficient, as in the construction industry for most of this century, there were few advantages to corporate size. The better strategy might be to stay small: go after contracts one by one and borrow, lease, rent, or subcontract to get them done. As markets evolved, it often became cheaper to buy services on a contract or spot basis: go outside to get your freelance writers and copy editors, your window-washers or maintenance or security staff, your computer-hackers and food vendors, the firms to manufacture your software, even the people who thought about your management structure and your future. By the 1980s, with markets becoming deeper and more sophisticated in practically every area of enterprise, many companies were faced with the option of literally dis-integrating. One function after another could be profitably farmed or contracted out because efficient, lower-cost suppliers could be found externally.

So small business also grew because of corporate downsizing, the transfer of functions from big businesses to external suppliers. Some big organizations were broken up entirely, as the sum of their parts proved greater than the value of the whole. Conrad Black's complex strategy with the Argus empire finally amounted to selling it off in chunks. Gulf Canada and Hiram Walker were effectively broken up as part of their acquisitors' strategy. For every firm in the sixties or seventies that had tried to increase profits by acquisition or merger, building on the supposed synergy of managerial excellence, there was an eighties' company that maximized profits by shedding units and divisions so that scarce managerial resources could be concentrated to best effect. Leanness to the point of corporate anorexia was the new North American business style.

To the market-oriented, this was not a surprising development. Businessmen had always argued that a market system produced and distributed goods more efficiently than political organizations. The same reasoning in fact applied to markets and economic organizations, i.e., corporations. Theoretically the invisible hand of unimpeded market forces was more efficient than the visible hands of corporation managers. As markets became more perfect the theory became practice. The emerging triumph of the market jeopardized many kinds of big business. Some of the dinosaurs grew lean and quick and agile, but the furry little creatures got to the new food supply first, and ate it all, and the dinosaurs starved and died.

It was still too soon to know the long-term significance of these tendencies. As usual, the trends were more marked in the United States, where the Reagan years saw a remarkable surge of conservatism, individualism, and entrepreneurship in American life. It was not clear whether the phenomenon, often reminiscent of America's mood in the twenties, was permanent or cyclical. Rapid shifts in economic conditions could easily poison the new wells of entrepreneurship. A prolonged recession, for example, might daunt the spirit of the hardiest entrepreneurs, as it had in the thirties. A protectionist route might be taken to reduce market fluidities and strengthen the staying power of established big business. No one familiar with the surprises of the past could feel confident about easy projections of the present into the future.

The Canadian prospectus was even murkier. The country experienced the business trends of the Reagan years, but with less than perfect resonance. It was widely felt, probably accurately, that average Canadians were less interested in enterprise and risk-taking than Americans, less distrustful of authority and organizations, more interested in security and a quiet life. Perhaps the business bestsellers told the comparative story: *In Search of Excellence* in the United States, *The 100 Best Companies to Work for in Canada.*

Attitudes toward government and the recent adventures of government in the two societies were a more concrete ground for comparison. The United States was a country born in a revolution against authority. Americans retained a suspicion of external government amounting sometimes to an anarchist strain in their national life. Ronald Reagan's presidency fed on anti-Washington feeling and a conservatism that led to a major attempt to scale down the size and activities of governments, which were already proportionately smaller at federal, state, and municipal levels than their Canadian counterparts. Canadians, on the other hand, were the ambivalent heirs to forty years of consistently activist government. They were at the end of a long era of wartime management, Keynesian "fine-tuning," C.D. Howe's love affair with public power, the province-building of the 1960s, economic nationalism, industrial strategies, controls, the National Energy Program, and the expansion of universal social welfare programs.

It would take another book to analyse the impact of all of these policies, but by the time of the federal election held in 1984, the year George Orwell's novel about Big Brother's totalitarianism had etched in everyone's consciousness, there was widespread dissatisfaction with the recent record of Canadian governments.

The ruins of the National Energy Program were palpable, though many of the costs were still hidden. A decade of economic nationalism had hurt Canada's reputation abroad, produced a discredited, protectionist Foreign Investment Review Agency and a debt-burdened Canada Development Company, and hindered performance in every industry where decisions had been made on the basis of nationality rather than efficiency. It had been accompanied, we shall see later, by greater Canadian dependence on the United States. As a specific case study of government involvement in business, the Canadair débâcle, carried out under public ownership, was the final legacy to the Canadian people of the C.D. Howe mystique, the notion that Canada could manufacture anything, and the misreading of the history of the Avro Arrow. War-bred and nationalist dreams of being on the cutting age of aerospace, of pioneering in high technology, and using government to foster world-class research and development, had all contributed to the Challenger disaster. They had been fed by the easy assumptions of the sixties and seventies and by the institutionalization of highly articulate lobbies in such organizations as the Science Council of Canada.

Other examples of failed support for high technology included much of government aid to Canada's "knights of the new technology," the computer wizards. The list of fiascos and disasters included failed computer companies (Consolidated Computer Inc., bailed out and taken over by Ottawa and a $125 million sink hole), the failed Canadian videotex system, Telidon, and the failure of the distinctively Canadian personal computer, Dynalogic's Hyperion. Few of the firms whose growth had been hastened and hyped by Ottawa money made a successful transition to the tough real world of markets. The most publicized of the Canadian high-tech mushroom companies, Mitel Corporation, of Kanata, Ontario, lost $270 million between 1983 and its 1986 sale to British Telecommunications. The concept of nationalism was as difficult to apply to computers as it was to aerospace because the industries had become almost completely international and specialized. "Since the essence of high technology is the defiance of time and geography through instant communication," David Thomas concluded in his history of Canada's computer industry, "it reduces traditional nationalisms . . . to folkloric anachronisms." Canadians would have to be content to contribute components to hardware, perhaps some good software, and, in aerospace, a helping arm to the American-dominated program.

The most spectacular institutionalization of the ideals of the high-tech nationalists came in a special tax scheme, introduced in 1983, to give credits for Canadian research and development activities. The Scientific Research Tax Credit was suspended in 1984 after it had cost the Canadian people upwards of $2.8

billion in forgone revenues, with no discernible benefits and considerable evidence of widespread fraud. Its failure was also part of mounting evidence that four decades' use of the tax system to influence investment and other business decisions had created a monstrously confusing and inequitable regime, despised even by most of the people it was designed to benefit.

Beginning with C.D. Howe at the national level and the Smallwood-Valdmanis regime in Newfoundland in the early 1950s, government obsession with jobs and development had led to multitudes of attempts to second-guess or divert market forces. Billions were poured into keeping dying industries and firms alive, and their workers in dead-end jobs, particularly in Quebec and the Maritimes. More billions, in every region of the country, had been poured into schemes for creating flashy new industries, luring this or that manufacturing plant, beefing up disadvantaged areas with infrastructure (industrial parks, railroads, highways, harbours, airports), and otherwise trying to create "winners" that might someday stand on their own.

Some of the more notorious adventures in what Philip Mathias called "forced growth" included Nova Scotia's unworkable heavy water plant on Cape Breton Island and its support of Clairtone electronics in the sixties; New Brunswick's ludicrous partnership in the seventies with the American promoter who was going to build a better automobile, Malcolm Bricklin; virtually all of the Quebec government's state enterprises, ranging from its money-gobbling steel mills to the state-owned auto assembly plant, and the asbestos company, purchased just as the market collapsed; the Ontario government's IDEA corporation of the eighties as a general proposition, its land banks as a particular fiasco in development planning, and Minaki Lodge as an individual absurdity; Manitoba's losses with Churchill Forest Industries and the Flyer bus company; almost all of the components of the British Columbia Resources Corporation; extensions of the British Columbia Railway; and Consolidated Computer Inc. And then there was the oil refinery at Come-by-Chance, Newfoundland.

Come-by-Chance had been Joey Smallwood's last attempt at subsidized industrialization of the Newfoundland economy. Neither Smallwood nor any of the other provincial enthusiasts had learned from the results of Newfoundland's post-Confederation pioneering in the development business: failed factories, money wasted, and an economic "expert," Valdmanis, who went to jail for taking kickbacks. The Come-by-Chance refinery opened in 1973, and went bankrupt in 1976, with debts of $600 to $700 million. The Newfoundlanders would have been more prosperous had they concentrated their resources on modernizing the old industry in which they still had a chance at competitive advantage, fishing. In 1986 Petro-Canada, $42 million poorer for having bought the refinery from Newfoundland, sold it to Americans for two dollars. A $38 million federal wharf, built to service the refinery, went for one dollar.

Other government disasters like Mirabel airport in Quebec and the national postal system were constant reminders and irritants of the inability of Ottawa to plan and deliver efficient services. On the other hand, Canadians were far less contemptuous of their social welfare system. They accepted and clung to their entitlements with a mixture of justified pride and naked self-interest. Government aid to individuals – and whole industries – helped distinguish Canada from the United States, they thought. But the aid was often indiscriminate and expensive, with few clear distinctions between bathwater and babies. The huge costs of unemployment and health "insurance," old age pensions, and social assistance, combined with governments' penchant for subsidizing regions, industries, and many special interest groups, led to enormous spending commitments at the federal and provincial levels. At Confederation governments spent about 5 per cent of Canadian gross national product; in 1962 the proportion was still less than 30 per cent. Twenty years later it was over 45 per cent and still rising.

Because the tax system was also regarded as a mechanism for "spending" potential revenues to please interest groups, including business, and under the extra stimulus of perverted Keynesianism (the idea that deficit spending was justified at all times when economies were performing at less than 100 per cent of capacity), it became politically impossible to balance revenues and expenditures. After a budget surplus of $481 million in 1972–73, the government of Canada incurred public accounts deficits that mounted from $673 million the next year to $38,500 million in 1984-85.

FEDERAL SURPLUSES OR DEFICITS (millions of dollars)

1972–3:	481	1979–80:	-12,054
1973–4:	-673	1980–1 :	-12,816
1974–5:	-1,146	1981–2 :	-13,372
1975–6:	-4,021	1982–3 :	-24,340
1976–7:	-6,301	1983–4 :	-32,353
1977–8:	-10,036	1984–5 :	-38,500
1978–9:	-11,707	1985–6 :	-34,500

SOURCE: *Canadian Statistical Review; Globe and Mail*

These huge debts, the highest of any industrial nation except Italy, had no parallel whatever in Canada's peacetime history. By 1986 the $250 billion debt burden and its nearly $25 billion in annual carrying costs lay across Canadians' route to the twenty-first century like an enormous pile of rocks, growing higher by the minute. All Canadian taxpayers of future generations would have these loaded onto their backs (per capita debt had risen from $795.60 in 1970 to $6,049.40 in 1984), unless inflation or repudiation ruined the creditors instead. This would be their inheritance from the years when the Canadian people opted for a free lunch, billed to their children.

In the age of big organizations, government had become the biggest organization of all. It had become the Leviathan Hobbes had envisaged, or, in dinosaur imagery, tyrannosaurus rex. Through the seventies there were glimmers of popular and political realization of the limits of government (Prime Minister Trudeau and his ministers alternated between promising to satisfy the most extravagant public expectations and complaining that the public's expectations were unrealistic), but the 1980s saw the distinct onset of the new mood. It was first evident in the William Bennett government's austerity program for British Columbia in 1982–83, then reflected in the Mulroney Conservative landslide in the 1984 general election, and, perhaps most interestingly and surprisingly, in the sharp reaction against big government that seemed to sweep Quebec in the aftermath of the Liberal party's 1985 defeat of the Parti Québécois.

The sense of the need to curtail Leviathan crossed traditional party lines because so many of the governors, whatever their party loyalties, had lost confidence in the possibilities of political and bureaucratic action. Most of the administrative reforms catalogued in Chapter 17 were no more effective in Ottawa than the parallel processes had been in large corporations like Massey-Ferguson. Many led to inefficiences, overload, and demoralization. Serious planning of the future proved next to impossible. The public saw Ottawa posit a new era of comparative resource advantage and mega-project investment for the Dominion just when Canada's resources began declining in value. We saw Ottawa base national planning and budgeting on predictions of a 1986 oil price five times higher than actually transpired. Could civil servants and politicians chart a course for the future? Who could tell next week's price of a barrel of oil?

If the big corporation was a troubled organization as it faced the market, governments were even more perplexed. The idea that governments should downsize, turning functions and responsibilities back to the private sector, parallelled the notion of downsizing by big private corporations. The idea of "privatization," or government withdrawal from many of its business enterprises, was not just ideological conservatism, but was grounded in years of lessons about the problems organizations encountered trying to handle rapidly changing, competitive situations in the marketplace.* Similarly, interest in "deregulation," a

---

* Of course privatization was no magic answer. One of the first firms to leave government hands, the British Columbia Resources Investment Corporation, which was literally given to the people of British Columbia by the provincial government in 1978, then decided to expand and become a resources conglomerate. Its management misjudged the markets as thoroughly as any government would have and by 1986 the firm had become an extremely sick resource reptile.

concept that spread slowly into Canada from the United States, was rooted in decades of experience with regulatory regimes that became captured by the regulatees, stifled competition and innovation, and led to gross inefficiency and high costs.

Whether Canadian governments could seriously shrink, or even stop growing, was still in question as the country faced the challenges of the last years of the twentieth century. The national record through 1986 was spotty and ambiguous. Prime Minister Mulroney declared that the country was "bankrupt" and his government put an end to PIP grants and some of Canada's energy adventuring even before markets completed the job. The Conservatives sold de Havilland and Canadair and seemed serious about privatizing other major government enterprises. The breezes of deregulation began to create healthy turbulence in air travel and trucking, and the fresh air began to drift toward Canadian broadcasting. The Foreign Investment Review Agency was rotated through 180 degrees to become Investment Canada, charged with beckoning foreigners to enter the country's reopened doors.

On the other hand, the government of Canada engineered inept and costly bail-outs of banks that failed anyway, had no will to end scandalously expensive subsidies to Canadian travellers who used Via Rail, lacked the courage to close Mirabel airport (which cost Canadian taxpayers more money every day it stayed open), could not make the postal service work efficiently, and apparently dared not rein in Petro-Canada. In 1985 Petro-Canada expanded further as part of the Reichmanns' complex "Canadianization" of Gulf Canada, a takeover and carve-up (Petro-Canada bought many of Gulf's downstream assets, including the service stations) reminiscent of the NEP excesses of 1981. While all the other monuments to the energy fantasies of the seventies were collapsing or, in the case of Calgary skyscrapers, lowering their rents, Petro-Canada replaced Dome and Imperial as the country's largest oil company. William Hopper's achievement in building Petro-Canada through good times and bad made him one of the most successful public entrepreneurs in Canadian history. "I don't give a shit," he said in response to critics who wondered if the country profited from Petro-Canada.

Ottawa's most worrisome failure was its inability to break its own and the country's addiction to $30 billion dollar a year deficits. It was not totally surprising, for even staunchly conservative regimes in other countries had difficulty making more than token assaults on Leviathan's ability to feed on itself and grow in the coldest, most hostile waters. The Reagan administration itself not only failed in many of its anti-government aspirations, but achieved much of its domestic popularity by making tax cuts that created monstrous $200 billion American deficits and credit and financial distortions that potentially menaced the whole world. In Canada the government did rather worse: the deficit through 1986 was proportionately 50 per cent larger than Washington's. It had to be supported by an economy less diverse, self-sufficient, and resilient; and Canadians and their governors seemed less anxious than Americans to do anything at all about the problem. In worst-case scenarios, the reckless spending policies of the government of Canada under both Liberal and Conservative regimes had gravely imperilled the nation's ability to cope with recession. A situation had been created reminiscent of the Dominion of Newfoundland's financial problems as it faced the Great Depression of the 1930s.

———————————

Business attitudes toward the problems of government in the 1980s were varied, ambiguous and uncertain. Through the years of government expansion most general business comment had been negative and hectoring. At its best, business tried to alert Canadians to the distortions and inefficiencies brought about by government intervention in the market and to the costs of big government. In the Trudeau years the ineffectiveness of this stance had several causes. One of the most important was that the particular interests of corporations and entrepreneurs and trade associations led them to beg endlessly for the very grants and subsidies and tax breaks and contracts and bail-outs that they condemned in theory. To outsiders, the self-interested hypocrisy of these "corporate welfare bums" (as the NDP's David Lewis called them) seemed palpable, and tended to destroy the credibility of all business rhetoric.

As well, government spending created a kept business constituency. Thousands of firms, from advertising agencies to oil companies and book publishers and aerospace suppliers, relied for nourishment on a steady flow of government contracts, subsidies, loans, or other kinds of support. Most were understandably reluctant to appear to bite the teat that fed them; many turned aside and opened their mouths only to beg for more. For a time in the early 1980s there seemed to be few significant Canadian firms whose public positions were not being gradually influenced by the need to keep on the good side of big brother in Ottawa or the provincial capitals. Canadian merchants catered to government as they had two centuries earlier, but in those days there had been more plain talking and open (and mutual) contempt.

A radical change in the nature of businessmen's contacts with government had taken place by the 1980s. Politicians and businessmen had become more segregated than at any previous time in Canadian history. Fewer businessmen became politicians and fewer politicians cultivated business contacts while in office. This situation helped stimulate and was reinforced by new and much tougher conflict-of-interest concepts. There was less room for the gifted amateur in politics, and less willingness by successful entrepreneurs to sacrifice their private interests for the intense stresses and limited satisfactions of the political world. It was doubtful that there could ever be another C.D. Howe in Canadian government. Business people who did venture into politics found that the slightest misstep in the relation between their public and private affairs led to trial by headline, exhaustive and exhausting inquiries, and career-menacing controversy.

In everyday business-government relations much less cash changed hands under tables or through old-fashioned bagmen than had been common through the 1950s. Politicians took fewer junkets to corporate fishing lodges and private mansions on company planes, and firms stopped routinely doling out cases of scotch or sherry to civil servants and political friends at Christmas (unless they did business in less developed countries where such practices were still the norm; it was also true that some regions of the Canadian political world were less developed than others). Business and politics no longer meshed; instead they "interfaced" through the mediation of government affairs specialists, lobbyists, and on ritual social occasions like fund-raising dinners and other planned events. Platoons of trade associations, chambers of commerce, and other formal organizations, led by the Business Council on National Issues, pronounced professionally on issues of interest, and jostled politely to obtain non-compromising access to opinion-leaders and policy-makers. Politicians became welcome elder statesmen and luncheon-organizers on boards of directors after they had been beaten, retired, or otherwise left office.

In the 1980s business issues seemed to be more widely publicized and better understood in the country. Newspapers, radio, and television had all steadily expanded coverage of business news. There were more and better business papers and magazines. Book publishers had discovered a steady market for profiles of business success, dissections of failure, and investigations of arcane industries. In many ways the country seemed more knowledgeable and literate about business affairs, more willing to listen to positions advocated by business. Young Canadians were flocking to business courses and business schools, particularly in Quebec. Gallup polls showed a steady decline in public distrust of big business compared to big government or organized labour.

The popular notion of a Canadian "business community" still made little sense. How could firms or entrepreneurs whose aim was usually to drive each other out of business be considered a community? The jungle metaphor was more appropriate. There was some evidence, though, that the private sector was approaching a consensus on certain vital issues. Business spokesmen were more apt in the 1980s to oppose selective tax breaks and government subsidies, even for business. There was virtual unanimity on the menace of the deficit, and on the need to reform the social welfare system so that it served the needy rather than rich and poor indiscriminately. As we see later, a near-consensus had also formed around the desirability of free trade.

The private sector operated in a climate still disrupted by periodic storms of anti-corporate, dogmatically egalitarian populism. Many Canadians lacked understanding of the operations of a market system, the forces of competition, or the nature and uses of profits. Myths of Canada's unlimited natural wealth and of the ability of governments to solve all problems with laws, regulations, or controls died hard. Groups with powerful vested interests, including trade unions, civil servants, tenured academics, and courtesanal cultural producers, perpetuated a hostility toward business enterprise rooted in their own fear of competition on open markets.

Canadians were still confused in their cultural values: they tended simultaneously to honour and tax success, acknowledge self-interest but deplore materialism, preach individualism and collectivism, and, in the traditions of Governor Simcoe and his lady, turn fastidious noses up at the odours of crass, sweating, hustling profit-seeking. The strength of nationalism as a secular religion in a country whose people had little else in common also meant that the economic nativism of the 1960s and 1970s – a deep and damaging Canadian prejudice against foreign businessmen and their companies – continued to limit wealth creation.

———

The single greatest gulf between those who understood the workings of a market economy and those who did not was reflected in the incessant debate on competition and concentration in the Canadian economy. The old cries of monopoly still issued from the populist media and the NDP every few months. In 1976 an attempt by Power Corporation to purchase effective control of Argus Corporation led to the appointment of a Royal Commission on Corporate Concentration in Canada which found that concentration had been declining in the Canadian economy by practically every possible measurement. While its report and several dozen supporting studies gathered dust, the worriers continued to view with alarm every well-publicized manoeuvre by successive business barons and to call for beefed up anti-combines laws.

Was Conrad Black strengthening his stranglehold on the business life of Canada? Were the Reichmanns becoming too powerful? What about the Brascan-Bronfman empires and that lawyer of theirs whom *Toronto Life* said was the most powerful man in Canada's greatest city? Were the American multinationals really running Canada? Or had Canada's six or nine or twenty-one big business families taken over all the assets on the TSE? When would these big interests stop fixing the price of gas at the pumps? When would this endless wave of takeovers and mergers that created fewer and fewer companies, more and more concentration, end? If the trends continued, a few powerful people would wind up owning everything. Probably they already did.

The real trends were all the other way. This chapter and all the preceding ones have been about the effects of constant growth, discovery, innovation, and entrepreneurship in the Canadian and world economies. More and more players have entered the dance as new industries and technologies have enriched and complicated and sometimes replaced old ones, dooming one establishment after another to stagnation and decline.*

If anything, the pace of change and the competitive scramble speeded up in the 1980s. Communication and transportation revolutions and ongoing technological change, the astonishing growth of sophisticated international capital markets, and the constant, restless growth and migration and multiplication of enterprises and industries around the world eroded barrier after barrier, natural and man-made alike, to competition. For Canadians, like Americans, Japanese, and most Europeans, the business world of the 1980s and 1990s would be desperately competitive, domestically and internationally. Competitive advantage would become harder and harder to find and maintain. Monopoly's moments – almost always produced and sustained by governments – would be fewer and shorter. Old dynasties would go down, and new ones would be shorter lived. There would be less place to hide.

While politicians, the media, and historians looked back to analyse the follies and disasters of the Great Inflation, the next generation of entrepreneurs and entrepreneurial corporations was struggling to set the course for Canada's future. It was not a future that belonged to Massey-Ferguson, Dome Petroleum, government-

---

* Almost all alarmist comment on corporate concentration stressed shrinking numbers of firms or expanding market share as a result of mergers or acquisitions. Concern for temporary shrinkage in some industries was seldom balanced by awareness of immense growth, including the creation of thousands of new firms, in other industries and often in the no longer shrinking industry itself. Assumptions about static industries and markets took no account of shifting boundaries and new competitive pressures, say from new products or non-Canadian firms. Finally, virtually all attempts to capture the monopoly sasquatch statistically neglected to make the temporal, Canadian comparisons necessary to show a growing problem. When the statistics were applied carefully, as in the *Report* of the Royal Commission on Corporate Concentration, they showed a lessening one. The most common journalists' fallacy was to make comparisons between concentration in Canada and in the United States – an economy more than ten times as large as Canada's, and considerably more sophisticated.

Effective monopoly powers cannot be long exercised on efficient markets. The smaller and more imperfect the market, the longer monopoly can have its day. Would-be monopolists know that the most effective, longest-lasting interference with markets is brought about by the law-making capacity of governments. Most cases of effective use of monopoly power in Canada, such as the operation of agricultural marketing boards, organized collective bargaining, firms in regulated industries, and professional organizations, rest firmly on laws and regulations originally thought to be matters of public interest.

owned aircraft companies, the promoters and bounty-hunters who still haunted the corridors of power, or banks that had loaded their portfolios with unproductive loans. It would not belong to Argus Corporation, or Avro, or firms spoiled by the good life of the old regulatory systems and tariffs, or other pridefully dozing corporations. The future would not belong to publicity-courting tycoons, whose prominence and arrogance would inevitably make them symbols of plutocracy and targets for populist retaliation. It was probably not a future that belonged to Reichmanns, or Bronfmans, or Thomsons – at least not after a generation or two as families ran short on entrepreneurs and conglomerates settled down to typically low rates of return. Perhaps in Canada there would always be Molsons and Eatons and, if it survived the losses of the 1980s, the Hudson's Bay Company.

Canada's business future belonged to new firms, driven by ambitious entrepreneurs with bright ideas, and to old firms with the hunger and nimbleness and ingenuity to become young and entrepreneurial in spirit. It belonged to ordinary men and women, driven by ambition or other demons, or by the pressures of competition, to find ways of achieving extraordinary things. There would always be rags-to-riches stories, and spectacular adventures in acquisition: scores of them had kept on occurring right through the worst of the recession. Thanks to inflation, the billionaire had replaced the millionaire as the symbol of capitalist achievement, and the lives of the rich and famous would continue to fascinate gossip columnists and establishment-watchers. The days of castles and titles had almost ended,* and Canadian boardrooms would never again by dominated by Scots accents or Methodist piety.

The business world had become far more diverse, lively, and crowded. Most of the eight hundred thousand Canadians who were in business in one way or another were ordinary people, but "ordinary" is never the right word to apply to a cross-section of humanity. The world of Canadian enterprise was and would be peopled by geniuses and klutzes, hustlers and dimwits, workaholics and layabouts, ruthless sons-of-bitches, improbable saints, and workaday dullards. The main twenty-first century tendency in business lifestyles seemed to be in the direction of personal fitness and asceticism, as life became too fast-paced and precious to be frittered away over three-martini lunches and cigars. In populist demonology the bloated, heel-grinding oppressor was about to be replaced by lean and hungry Cassius-types, wielding daggers.

Eventually there would even be a Lady Macbeth. The spectacular influx of women into Canadian business in the 1980s was bound someday to produce a

---

* There was widespread "street" speculation that Conrad Black's decision to become a newspaper proprietor in Great Britain might lead eventually to his becoming Sir Conrad or Lord Black in the Mountstephen/Beaverbrook/Dunn/Oakes/Thomson tradition. It was not thought that his replacement in the Toronto business limelight, Brascan's Trevor Eyton, harboured any such ambition.

ruthless tycooness, whose power and resources would be seen as a menace to all Canadians of both sexes. But it would take time. The first generation of female MBAs and entrepreneurs and salespersons and career-oriented bankers, brokers, and other professionals faced a long struggle before the most successful of them reached the top.

In some ways it was wonderfully exciting to see business, and other spheres of public life, finally start drawing on the abilities and energy of the other half of the human race. Those grizzled European fishermen who first sailed into the northern waters in the fifteenth century seeking riches had left their women at home. Five centuries later women themselves had become treasure-seekers and adventurers, embarking on long voyages into strange waters. But, as women's mere business presence in the 1980s began eroding the male trappings of Canadian business life, there remained a host of unanswered questions about career prospects for the female stockbroker, manufacturer, banker, or manager.

Perhaps their progress to the top was so slow because men still blocked female participation in business, especially at the highest levels. Many critics, especially in the feminist movement, called for affirmative action to clear the way. Perhaps more significantly, it was not clear how many of the new career women could or wanted to endure the rigours of business life. Did they have the necessary personal drive, amounting often to workaholism and cruel self-exploitation, to reach the top? Would businesswomen's conscious "networking," revived by some of them just as men were abandoning the practice, make a difference? Did businesswomen have family support systems, including sacrificial husbands, to keep home fires burning and supply sanity and stability? The trouble with enterprise, from the first transatlantic voyages to risk-taking at the computer console, was its high casualty rate. Most women, and many of the men, probably preferred to stay at home.

Women's participation is one of three important themes in the next chapter in Canadian business history, being written every day in the real world. The second theme, in which many businesswomen are already playing a role, is the remarkable competitive battle in so many areas of the Canadian marketplace.

In the eighties, for example, the old, slow struggle among providers of financial services finally turned into hot business warfare. Traditional boundaries confining banks, insurance companies, trust companies, investment dealers, and other money-movers lost much of their meaning as entrepreneurs and innovators probed shifting opportunities in the marketplace. Non-Canadian competitors began breaking into the most sheltered recesses of Bay Street and Main Street, sometimes with a big bang. The financial wars were fought in the marketplace, in the hallways of government, and in the courts of public opinion. The struggles had ethical as well as entrepreneurial implications, for they became entangled by complex questions about self-dealing and interlocking ownership. Some of the questions were new; many were echoes of the days of the Cox family of financial companies, the age of the private banker, and the one-man financial general store.

It was not yet clear how they would be answered by the market, governments, or the players themselves.

No one could confidently chart the course of competition in most other industries. Which computer firm would be next month's darling? Who would invent the software that would make the home computer really part of the furniture? Were IBM and General Motors staggering at last? When would McDonald's stop growing? Would deregulation in the peculiar Canadian climate help or hinder the entrepreneurial airlines, Wardair and PWA? When would Air Canada be privatized? What would the old CPR group, no longer flying high, sell off next? How many food stores would Provigo open? Would the new apparel entrepreneurs – selling canvas bags and coats, high-tech skiwear, the best in leather boots – be able to fend off imitators and foreign competitors? Who would win the corner store wars, the department store wars, the drugstore and the super-store wars, and would the storekeepers ever again agree not to stay open on Sundays? Was the outburst of French-Canadian entrepreneurship and the Montreal Revival a deep-rooted phenomenon or a passing fad, about to wither in winters of hard times? How would the car wars sort themselves out now that the Japanese had decided to move to North America, and everyone thought it a good time to invest in low-cost Canada? How would Lavalin, Bombardier, and Magna International, favourite firms of Canadian governments, fare in the marketplace in the long term? Could Bombardier, for example, make the Challenger fly across national boundaries? Would the people who knew the answers to these questions know when to take their stock market profits and move on to the next growth situation?

The third and most important theme for the future was the effort to obtain a free trade agreement with the United States. Throughout the twentieth century north-south trade had steadily increased, both absolutely and as a percentage of Canada's total foreign trade. Britain lost its place as Canada's principal trading partner in the 1920s; in the 1970s, after joining the European Economic Community, it became less important to Canada than Japan. By then Canada's trade with the United States was three times as important as its trade with all of the rest of the world's countries combined. In the 1980s approximately three-quarters of all of Canada's foreign trade was with the United States.

Thanks to the agreements of 1935 and 1938, GATT, the Auto Pact, and other liberalizing steps, most trans-border transactions were no longer seriously impeded by tariff barriers. The ranks of Canadian exporters had thickened to include thousands of manufacturers and service companies, as well as the natural resource producers. Virtually all Canadian businessmen looked on the mammoth United States market, the world's richest, as the opportunity of the future. Without easy access to a large market, Canadian business could not sustain degrees of specialization, efficiency, and diversity attainable by the producers of every other industrialized country in the world. All other industrial countries had unimpeded access to markets of more than one hundred million consumers. It was unrealistic to think that Canada could find any market other than the American one in which it would be allowed and able to compete.

A wave of free trade sentiment was born in the recession of 1981–82 and resulted in the Mulroney government's initiation of negotiations with Washington in 1986. The idea of continental free trade had deep historic roots, all the way back to the Reciprocity Treaty of 1854, and it had been neglected, revived, rejected, half-tried, but always kept alive throughout the next 120 years. The 1980s incarnation of free trade reflected Canadian business's deep concern about security of access to the American market. Protectionist lobbies in the United States had the potential to cripple Canadian companies, industries, even whole provinces, if they succeeded in persuading Congress to rebuild tariff walls to anything like historic American norms – let alone the "Chinese wall" levels of the Great Depression. Proponents of a free trade agreement hoped that it would thwart American protectionism, protect existing trade relationships made more secure, and open immense opportunities for future growth.

There were important pockets of deep concern about the implications of free trade, notably among the cultural industries. But support for freer trade by Canadian businessmen and their organizations was remarkably strong. With even the Canadian Manufacturers' Association reversing its century-long defence of the National Policy, there had been an historic shift in the climate of business opinion. It was related not only to the desire to protect an important status quo in trade relations, but also to the newly dominant belief by Canadian business that there was no future in trying to hide from competition and the rigours of the marketplace. Canada had to be competitive to survive even in its own market, where there was no hope whatever of keeping efficient foreigners indefinitely at bay. The country had to stop believing it could become a second United States – gargantuan in population, diversity, and wealth – and realize that its best hope was to emulate the Scandinavian countries in their relationship to Europe. Specialize, find and exploit comparative advantage, look outward, choose quality instead of quantity, let culture grow in the fresh air of economic freedom.

The free trade debate became tied up with broader concerns for the country's independence and future. In an interdependent world, old ideas of unhampered national sovereignty made little sense; they implied an economic self-sufficiency that simply did not exist. As the Great Depression had shown, all trading countries depended for their well-being on the foreigners who bought their products. Canadians' prosperity and national well-being were more dependent on the whims of Congress and the American electoral system without free trade than they might be under a comprehensive agreement. Trade wars and the lobbying of special interests, playing on Canadians' and Americans' deep nationalist sentiments, might well frustrate free trade initiatives in the short and/or long terms. So might the obstructionism of provincial governments, whose parochialism had already eroded the Fathers of Confederation's dream of free trade within the Dominion. Few businessmen or economists thought that a reversion to protectionist hiding places, with concomitant reliance on government to induce entrepreneurial excellence, would be anything but disastrous for Canadians' standard of living and their real independence. The one sure prescription for the eventual failure of the Canadian experiment in nationality would be to create an ever-widening gap in standards of living between the two North American democracies.

Tough economic times in the mid-1980s underlined the urgency of the free trade negotiations and other measures to maintain Canadian foreign markets and business competitiveness at home and abroad. If the country faced even a protracted period of low resource prices, with the prospect of permanent devaluation of its natural wealth, the adjustment process could be severe and wrenching, perhaps next to impossible in the context of the crippling debt load placed on the country by its government. Many Canadian businessmen, who lived in a world of constantly changing markets, accountability, and relentless measurement of success or failure, seemed more aware of these challenges than either politicians or the public at large. With exceptions, Canadian businessmen supported the lifting of the dead hand of past policies, so they could be free to compete, expand, and maximize the wealth and opportunities available to the Canadian people.

Sources and Further Reading

I consulted many more sources during the research for this book than it would be possible to list here. This essay is a guide to the important literature in the field, both the works that most influenced these chapters and the most useful books and articles for further reading. Early drafts of the chapters which contain citations for all quotations have been deposited in the University of Toronto Archives. Anyone still puzzled about my sources should contact me directly.

Unless otherwise noted in the following entries the place of publication is Toronto.

ABBREVIATIONS:

CHAR: Canadian Historical Association, *Annual Report* (after 1972, *Historical Papers*)
CHR: *Canadian Historical Review*
CJEPS: *Canadian Journal of Economics and Political Science*
DCB: *Dictionary of Canadian Biography*
HS/SH: *Histoire Sociale/Social History*
JCS: *Journal of Canadian Studies*
M&S: McClelland and Stewart
OH: *Ontario History*
RHAF: *Revue d'Histoire de l'Amérique française*
UTP: University of Toronto Press

GENERAL

There are no other surveys of the history of Canadian business. The only work that appears to do so even partially is *The History of Canadian Business, 1867-1914* by Tom Naylor (2 vols., Lorimer, 1976). It is an eclectically Marxist work, factually unreliable, and was of no use in the preparation of this history. Three anthologies – David S. Macmillan, ed., *Canadian Business History: Selected Studies, 1497–1971* (M&S, 1971); Robert Cuff, ed., *Enterprise and National Development: Essays in Canadian Business and Economic History* (Hakkert, 1972); and Tom Traves, ed., *Essays in Canadian Business History* (M&S, 1984) – contain several important articles as well as useful bibliographic comment, but no good introductory overviews. The autumn 1985 issue of the *Journal of Canadian Studies* contains a sampling of the most recent scholarly articles in the area, originally presented to the first Conference on Canadian Business History, at Trent University in 1984. In "Canadian Company Histories: A Checklist,"*Communiqué*, spring 1981, Paul Craven, Anne Forrest, and Tom Traves list 599 publications dealing with the histories of individual companies.

The standard history of Canadian economic development was W.T. Easterbrook and Hugh G.J. Aitken, *Canadian Economic History* (Macmillan, 1956), but it gradually became dated and was replaced by *Canada: An Economic History* (Macmillan, 1980), by William L. Marr and Donald G. Paterson, an almost inaccessible book to the non-specialist. Richard Pomfret's *The Economic Development of Canada* (Methuen, 1981) went to the other extreme and is short and shallow. The most recent trends in the writing of Canadian economic history are displayed in Duncan Cameron, ed., *Explorations in Canadian Economic History: Essays in Honour of Irene M. Spry* (Ottawa, U. of Ottawa Press, 1985). An older anthology, *Approaches to Canadian Economic History* (M&S, 1967), edited by W.T. Easterbrook and M.H. Watkins, is still useful. All historians are indebted to the economists and statisticians who produced the two editions of *Historical Statistics of Canada* (Macmillan, 1965: Ottawa, Statistics Canada, 1983), an invaluable basic source (except for the fact that most Canadian statistical series date only from the 1920s). The two most general collections of documents relating to Canadian economic history are H.A. Innis and A.R.M. Lower, eds., *Select Documents in Canadian Economic History*: vol. I, 1497–1783; vol. II, 1783–1885 (UTP, 1929, 1933).

There are many single-volume general surveys of Canadian history. The Canadian Centenary Series, a history of the country in nineteen volumes published by McClelland & Stewart (the first volume was published in 1963; in 1987 one volume remains to be published) is widely used for basic reference. Some of the Centenary volumes are much better than others. For detailed guides to writing in all fields of Canadian history, consult *A Reader's Guide to Canadian History* (2 vols., UTP, 1982; vol. I: *Beginnings to Confederation*, ed. by D.A. Muise; vol. 2, *Confederation to the Present* ed. by J.L. Granatstein and Paul Stevens). All such guides quickly become dated; specialists keep up through the quarterly *Canadian Historical Review* (CHR), particularly its "Recent Publications Relating to Canada" lists.

Special attention should be given to the magnificent *Dictionary of Canadian Biography* (DCB), published by the University of Toronto Press. It is a twelve-volume encyclopedia of detailed, authoritative biographies of all historically important Canadians, organized according to death dates, who died before 1900. The first volume of the DCB was published in 1966, the twelfth is scheduled for 1990. Merchants and businessmen are given due attention in the volumes, and many of the entries, long and short, were important sources for these chapters. The most useful of the many other encyclopedia-like research tools for Canadian scholarship has been the *Canadian Annual Review*, single-volume surveys of national life for each of the years from 1901 to 1938 and 1960 to the present. The current CAR series has become almost exclusively devoted to the affairs of governments, perhaps a sign of the times. The three volumes of *The Canadian Encyclopedia* (Edmonton: Hurtig, 1985) are a handy reference guide to Canadian topics past and present. There are many other more detailed sources of knowledge and statistics, notably the publications of Statistics Canada.

CHAPTER 1. THE ORIGINAL BUSINESS: FISHING

The *cap de nada* anecdote was found in Joseph-Noel Fauteux, *Essai sur L'industrie du Canada Sous Le Régime Français* (Quebec, Imprimateur du Roi, 1927). Otherwise the chapter was built from the standard sources for the subject. Details of exploration are drawn from Tryggvi Oleson's *Early Voyages and Northern Approaches* in the Centenary Series (1963), and the writings of David Quinn, particularly his authoritative survey, *North America From Earliest Discovery to First Settlements: The Norse Voyages to 1612* (New York: Harper, 1972). Patrick McGrath's "Bristol in America, 1480–1631" in K.R. Andrews, ed., *The Westward Enterprises* (Liverpool University Press, 1978) was also useful. Most of the works of Harold Adams Innis, Canada's best-known economic historian, are now better read about than read. They are all dated and have no redeeming literary merit. His study of *The Cod Fisheries: The History of an International Economy* (UTP,1940) is almost an exception, particularly useful as a source of fact and illustration. Modern scholarship on the development of the Atlantic fishery is best sampled in John Gilchrist's chapter, "Exploration and Enterprise – The Newfoundland Fishery, c. 1497–1677," in Macmillan, *Canadian Business History,* and Gillian T. Cell's monograph, *English Enterprise in Newfoundland, 1577-1660* (UTP, 1969). For the development of Newfoundland I relied on Cell and C. Grant Head, *Eighteenth Century Newfoundland: A Geographer's Perspective* (Ottawa, Carleton Library, 1976). The DCB, vol. 1, provided biographical detail on the Cabots, Frobisher, and most of the other explorer-entrepreneurs.

CHAPTER 2. INDIANS AND THE FUR TRADE

The notion that native people initially profited from trade goods and were skilled traders is a commonplace of modern scholarship. The history of European-native encounters and interaction has been completely rewritten in recent decades to try to minimize ethnocentric bias. The new views, as well as the historical literature, are masterfully presented in Bruce G. Trigger's synthesis, *Natives and Newcomers: Canada's "Heroic Age" Reconsidered* (Kingston and Montreal: McGill-

Queen's UP, 1985). The chapter also draws on his earlier work, *The Children of Aataentsic: A History of the Huron People to 1660* (2 vols., Kingston and Montreal: McGill-Queen's, 1976) and some of his article literature. Of the many other scholars exploring native trading patterns and attitudes, the most influential has been the historical geographer, Arthur J. Ray. Ray and Donald Freeman, *"Give Us Good Measure": An Economic Analysis of Relations Between the Indians and the Hudson's Bay Company Before 1763* (UTP, 1978), and Ray, *Indians in the Fur Trade: their role as trappers, hunters, and middlemen in the lands southwest of Hudson Bay, 1660–1870* (UTP, 1974) have been key sources for both this chapter and Chapter 4. Conrad Heidenreich's *Huronia: A History and Geography of the Huron Indians: 1600–1650* (M&S, 1971) was also useful, along with Alfred G. Bailey's seminal *The Conflict of European and Eastern Algonkian Cultures, 1504–1700* (UTP, second ed., 1969), and L.F.S. Upton, *Micmacs and Colonists: Indian-White Relations in the Maritimes 1713–1867* (Vancouver: UBC Press, 1979). Calvin Martin, *Keepers of the Game: Indian-Animal Relationships and the Fur Trade* (Berkeley: U. of California Press, 1978) has some valuable insights into native attitudes, but grossly overstates a contentious thesis. The best assessment of natives as traders may still be E.E. Rich's "Trade Habits and Economic Motivation Among the Indians of North America," CJEPS, 1960.

There is no satisfactory single-volume history of the fur trade. Innis's *The Fur Trade in Canada: An Introduction to Canadian Economic History* (UTP, 1930, 1956) is no longer worth reading. For some of its failings, see W.J. Eccles "A Belated Review of Harold Adams Innis' *The Fur Trade in Canada,*" CHR, December 1979, and the ensuing controversy. Paul Crysler Phillips' exhaustive two-volume history, *The Fur Trade* (Norman: U. of Oklahoma Press, 1961) has many flaws but also contains detail available nowhere else; its continental perspective is a useful corrective to Canadian parochialism in fur trade studies. E.E. Rich's survey, *The Fur Trade and the Northwest to 1857* in the Centenary Series (1967) is sweeping and authoritative, but can usefully be supplemented by his short volume *Montreal and the Fur Trade* (Montreal: McGill UP, 1966). Recent conferences on the fur trade have produced several volumes of articles on all aspects of the business, particularly native roles. These include *Selected Papers of the 1965 North American Fur Trade Conference* (St. Paul, Minnesota: Historical Society, 1967); *People and Pelts: Selected Papers of the Second North American Fur Trade Conference* (Winnipeg: Peguis, 1972); and Carol M. Judd and Arthur J. Ray, eds., *Old Trails and New Directions: Papers of the Third North American Fur Trade Conference* (UTP, 1980). One starting place for all Canadian fur trade reading might be J.F. Crean, "Hats and the Fur Trade," CJEPS, August 1962.

For the early trade in New France I relied on Marcel Trudel, *The Beginnings of New France, 1524–1663,* and W.J. Eccles, *Canada Under Louis XIV, 1663– 1701,* in the Centenary Series (1964); the H.P. Biggar edition of *The Voyages of*

Jacques Cartier (Ottawa, 1924); and Biggar's *The Early Trading Companies of New France* (UTP, 1901). The origins of the Hudson's Bay Company are authoritatively discussed in E.E. Rich's masterly three-volume *Hudson's Bay Company* (M&S, 1960), which is the standard history for the firm's first two centuries. Again, the *DCB* is an invaluable source of biographical detail; Eccles's assessment of Perrot, for example, comes from his biography of the governor in Volume I.

CHAPTER 3. DOING BUSINESS IN NEW FRANCE

There are no general surveys of commerce or the economy of New France. Jean Lunn's 1942 Ph.D. thesis, "Economic Development in New France, 1713-1760," written at McGill and never published, remains the best overview, comprehensive in detail and still sound in its interpretations. By contrast, Jean Hamelin's *Economie et Société en Nouvelle-France* (Québec: Les Presses de l'Université Laval, 3rd ed., 1970), is insubstantial and obsessed with the wrong questions. James Pritchard provides a good short survey in "Commerce in New France," in Macmillan, *Canadian Business History,* and presented a mine of detail in his 1971 University of Toronto Ph.D. thesis, "Ships, Men and Commerce: A Study of Maritime Activity in New France." The Lunn-Pritchard view of a colony with relatively little trade and many disadvantages strikes me as more convincing than Jacques Mathieu's argument in *Le commerce entre le nouvelle-france et les antilles au XVIIIe siécle* (Montreal: Fides, 1981) to the effect that trade flourished. For the organization of the fur trade and the administrative history of New France, I have relied on Guy Fregault's studies in *Le XVIIIe Siècle Canadien* (Montreal: Editions Hurtubise, 1970). Christopher Moore's writing on Louisbourg, particularly "The Other Louisbourg: Trade and Merchant Enterprise in Ile Royale 1713–1758," *HS/SH* no. 24, May 1979, has drawn attention to its importance as a trading centre.

I have drawn heavily on the detailed portrait of merchant traders in Dale Miquelon's excellent study, *Dugard of Rouen: French Trade to Canada and the West Indies, 1729-1770* (Montreal-Kingston: McGill-Queen's UP, 1978), and his article, "Havy & Lefebvre of Quebec: A Case Study of Metropolitan Participation in Canadian Trade, 1730–1760," *CHR*, March 1975. Much has been written about the merchants of New France as a collectivity, ranging from the chapters in Louise Dechêne's *Habitants et marchands de Montréal au XVIIe siècle* (Montreal: Pion, 1974) through Cameron Nish's portrayals of *Les Bourgeois-Gentilhommes de la Nouvelle-France, 1729–1748* (Montreal: Fides, 1968), or his "The Nature, Composition, and Functions of the Canadian Bourgeoisie, 1729–1748," *CHAR*, 1966; and José Igartua's studies of Montreal merchants at the end of the French regime, presented most accessibly in "The Merchants of Montreal at the Conquest: Socio-Economic Profile," *HS/SH*, no. 16, 1975. The standard work on the seigneurial system is R.C. Harris, *The Seigneurial System in Early Canada* (Madison: U. of Wisconsin Press, 1966).

The *DCB* was a particularly important source of detail on the entrepreneurs of New France, male and female. It should be the first source of reference for studies of everyone mentioned in the chapter. More biographical data on Marie-Ann Barbel is contained in Lilianne Plamondon, "Une Femme d'Affaires en Nouvelle-France: Marie-Ann Barbel, Veuve Fornel," *RHAF*, September 1977, and on La Chesnaye in Y.F. Zoltvany, "Some Aspects of the Business Career of Charles Aubert de la Chesnaye (1632–1702)," *CHAHP*, 1968. The Desaunier sisters are described in Jean Lunn's important article, "The Illegal Fur Trade out of New France, 1713-1760," *CHAR*, 1939. John Bosher's *DCB* articles on Bigot and Cadet, along with his many other articles on the administration and trade of New France, have been particularly influential in shaping my understanding of concepts of networks and the use of public office for private gain. See, for example, "The French government's motives in the Affaire du Canada, 1761–1763," *English Historical Review*, January 1981; "French Protestant Families in Canadian Trade, 1740–1760," *HS/SH*, May 1974; "French Colonial Society in Canada," *Transactions of the Royal Society of Canada*, 1981; "The Paris Business World & the Seaports Under Louis XV: Speculators in Marine Insurance, Naval Finances & Trade," *HS/SH* , no. 24, 1979. Montcalm's view of the last days of the colony is published, along with many other useful documents, in Adam Shortt, ed., *Documents Relating to Canadian Currency, Exchange and Finance During the French Regime* (2 vols., Ottawa: King's Printer, 1925).

CHAPTER 4. "A MERE BUSINESS OF FUR TRADING," 1670–1821

Most of the works on the fur trade mentioned in Chapter 2 were also used in this chapter: Ray's work on natives, Phillips and Innis on the fur trade, and particularly the writings of E.E. Rich, whose history of the Hudson's Bay Company is unrivalled in fur trade company studies. There is an enormous wealth of detail in A.S. Morton's magnum opus, *A History of the Canadian West to 1870–71* (UTP, 1939), and, by contrast, an excellent short survey of "The Hudson's Bay Company and the Fur Trade: 1670–1870" by Glyndwyr Williams, in the special autumn 1983 issue of *The Beaver.* The huge body of fur trade literature ranges from many volumes of trader correspondence, published by the Champlain Society and the Hudson's Bay Record Society, to popular histories by amateurs and journalists such as Douglas MacKay and Peter C. Newman. MacKay's *The Honourable Company: A History of the Hudson's Bay Company* (orig. pub. 1936; rev. ed., M&S, 1949) was well received by historians of the fur trade; Newman's *Company of Adventurers* (Penguin/Viking, 1985) was harshly criticized for, among other failings, its perpetuation of racist stereotypes. Scholars are now producing important new studies in native-white trading relations in the various regions of the country; one of the best and most useful is Daniel Francis and Toby Morantz, *Partners in Furs: A History of the Fur Trade in Eastern James Bay 1600–1870* (Kingston and Montreal: McGill-Queen's, 1983).

Most of the quotations in the chapter are fairly well known and come from the standard sources. My understanding of the HBC was also influenced by Richard Glover, "The Difficulties of the Hudson's Bay Company's Penetration of the West," *CHR*, 1948, and two articles by K.G. Davies, "The Years of No Dividends: Finances of the Hudson's Bay Company, 1690-1718," in *People and Pelts* and "From Competition to Union" in *Selected Papers of the 1965 North American Fur Trade Conference*. The North West Company awaits its historian. In the meantime Marjorie Wilkins Campbell did a passable job of popularization in *The North West Company* (Macmillan, 1957) and a useful biography, *Northwest to the Sea: A Biography of William McGillivray* (Clarke Irwin, 1975). It is still necessary to use basic documentary collections, particularly W.S. Wallace, *Documents Relating to the North West Company* (Champlain Society, 1934), and L.R. Masson, ed., *Les Bourgeois de la Compagnie du Nord-Ouest* (Montreal, 1889–90). Wallace's collected articles in *The Pedlars from Quebec and Other Papers on the Nor'Westers* (Ryerson, 1954) were helpful, and the *DCB* was again a gold mine, most notably for Fernand Ouellet's entry on Simon McTavish and Kaye Lamb on Alexander Mackenzie. There is extensive biographical literature on Mackenzie, beginning with Roy Daniells, *Alexander Mackenzie and the North West* (London: Faber & Faber, 1969).

The most important of Ouellet's writings on the fur trade, offering stimulating perspectives on the competition for labour between agriculture and the fur trade, is "Dualité économique et changement technologique au Québec (1760–1790)," *HS/SH*, no. 18, 1976. This most distinguished of French-Canadian historians has published enormously on Lower Canada generally in his major volumes, *Histoire économique et sociale du Québec, 1760–1850* (Montreal: Fides, 1966; English translation, Carleton Library, 1980), and *Lower Canada, 1791–1840* (1980) in the Centenary Series, but the great debate between Ouellet and many others on the fate of the French-Canadian bourgeois after the Conquest now seems to have been overdone, for the questions lend themselves to the fairly obvious answer provided in the text. For those still interested in the literature, it can be approached through Dale Miquelon, ed., *Society and Conquest: The Debate on the Bourgeoisie and Social Change in French Canada, 1700–1850* (Copp Clark, 1977), and a continuing, seemingly endless stream of articles in the *RHAF*. D.G. Creighton's *Commercial Empire of the St. Lawrence*, commented upon below, has not worn well.

For two of the lesser fur trading companies it was necessary to consult unpublished theses: Edward H. Borins's 1968 McGill M.A. dissertation on "La compagnie du nord, 1682–1700," and Richard Anthony Pendergast's, "The XY Company 1898 to 1904," a 1957 Ph.D. thesis at the University of Ottawa. Recent writings of Ann Carlos – "The Birth and Death of Predatory Competition in the North American Fur Trade: 1810–1821," *Explorations in Economic History,* 1982; "The Causes and Origins of the North American Fur Trade Rivalry: 1804–1810," *Journal of Economic History,* December 1981 – confirm the notion that the NWC and the HBC tried to limit their rivalry. The recent tendency of fur trade research to emphasize the distinctive society created by the interchange is well represented in Sylvia Van Kirk's *"Many Tender Ties": Women in Fur-Trade Society in Western Canada, 1670-1870* (Winnipeg: Watson & Dwyer, 1981), and Jennifer S.H. Brown, *Strangers in Blood: Fur Trade Families in Indian Country* (Vancouver: UBC Press, 1980).

CHAPTER 5. MERCHANTS' NETWORKS, 1749–1814

D.G. Creighton's study of the Montreal commercial class in *The Commercial Empire of the St. Lawrence* (Ryerson, 1936; 2nd. ed., Macmillan, 1956) does not stand up well to a critical reading, being stronger on literary devices, author's suppositions, and political history than as an analysis and description of the real merchant group after the Conquest. Nor does Ouellet's work, useful as it is, probe particularly deeply into the formation and activities of the merchant community. The single most comprehensive overview of the creation of the foundations of British North American business is David S. Macmillan's long article "The 'New Man' in Action: Scottish Mercantile and Shipping Operations in the North American Colonies, 1760–1825," in Macmillan, ed., *Canadian Business History.* It can usefully be supplemented by his chapter, "The Scot as Businessman," in W. Sanford Reid, ed., *The Scottish Tradition in Canada* (M&S, 1972), and his DCB article (with A.J.H. Richardson) on James Dunlop. The entries in volumes IV to VI of the DCB comprise a nice collective portrait of the merchants, with David Roberts's biography of William Grant, Denis Vaugeois's of Aaron Hart, and Donald Chard's of Joshua Mauger being particularly useful.

The descriptions of the influx of merchants and their conflicts with the Quebec administration are based mainly on A.L. Burt's *The Old Province of Quebec* (Ryerson, 1933; Carleton Library, 2 vols., 1968), Hilda Neatby's *Quebec: The Revolutionary Age, 1760–1791* (1966) in the Centenary Series, and merchants' complaints published in Adam Shortt and A.G. Doughty, eds., *Documents Relating to the Constitutional History of Canada , 1759–1791* (Ottawa: King's Printer, 1918). The observation of "great animosities between the English" comes from W.S. Wallace, ed., *The Masères Letters, 1766–1768* (UTP, 1919); and Lymburner's 1791 prophecy from Ouellet's *Lower Canada.*

For the Nova Scotia merchant community I relied on J.B. Brebner, *The Neutral Yankees of Nova Scotia* (New York: Columbia UP, 1937; Carleton Library, 1969), W.S. MacNutt, *The Atlantic Provinces: The Emergence of Colonial Society, 1712–1857* (1965) in the Centenary Series, and on David Alexander Sutherland's important 1975 University of Toronto Ph.D. thesis, "The Merchants of Halifax, 1815–1850. A Commercial Class in Pursuit of Metropolitan Status," in addition to DCB entries. For the evolution of the fishery and "merchantocracy" in Newfoundland, I used Shannon Ryan, "The Newfoundland Salt Cod Trade in the Nineteenth Century" in James Hiller and Peter Neary, eds., *New foundland in the Nineteenth and Twentieth Centuries: Essays in Interpretation* (UTP, 1980), Rosemary E. Ommer's "'All the Fish of the Post': Resource Property Rights and Development in a Nineteenth-Century Inshore Fishery,"*Acadiensis*, spring 1981, and M.E. Smith's unpublished 1968 Memorial University M.A. thesis, "Newfoundland 1815–1840: A Study of a Merchantocracy," from which the quotation on merchant despotism was drawn.

The importance of government contracting for the post-Conquest merchant community was suggested in Eccles's article on the military in New France, leaps out of DCB entries, and is elaborated in greatest detail in Bruce Wilson's meticulous study, *The Enterprises of Robert Hamilton: A Study of Wealth and Influence in Early Upper Canada, 1776–1812* (Ottawa: Carleton UP, 1983). Wilson's work, which breaks new ground in pre-Confederation business biography, is the source of most of the detail on Hamilton and Cartwright, but Donald C. MacDonald, "Honourable Richard Cartwright, 1759-1815" in *Three History Theses* (Ontario Department of Public Records and Archives, 1961) is still useful.

CHAPTER 6. WOOD, BANKS, AND WHOLESALERS

The writings of A.R.M. Lower used to be the starting point for most studies of the forest industries in Canada. There is a wealth of detail in his principal books, *Great Britain's Woodyard: British America and the Timber Trade, 1763-1867* (Kingston and Montreal: McGill-Queen's UP, 1973), *Settlement and the Forest Frontier in Eastern Canada* (Macmillan, 1936), and *The North American Assault on the Canadian Forest* (Ryerson Press, 1958), but the interpretive framework is idiosyncratic, rickety, and dated. Lower's forest writing can also be sampled in his article "The Trade in Square Timber," reprinted in Easterbrook and Watkins, eds. *Approaches to Canadian Economic History*. Lower's work has now been superseded for New Brunswick by Graeme Wynn's sophisticated monograph, *Timber Colony: A Historical Geography of Early Nineteenth Century New Brunswick* (UTP, 1981) and for the Ottawa valley by Sandra J. Gillis, *The Timber Trade in the Ottawa Valley, 1806–54* (Parks Canada, National Historic Parks and Sites Branch, Manuscript Report no. 83). For the origins of Canadian forest industries, Robert G. Albion's *Forests & Sea Power: The Timber Problem of the Royal Navy* (Cambridge, Mass.: Harvard UP, 1926) is still useful. An eccentric but rich history of Pollack, Gilmour and Company was published in 1921 by John Rankin, *A History of Our Firm* (Liverpool: Henry Young & Sons). The DCB entries for Joseph and Samuel Cunard, by W.A. Spray and Phyllis Blakeley respectively, were particularly useful, as was Louise Dechêne's article on William Price (which is extended in "Les enterprises de William Price, 1810–1850," HS/SH, no. 1, April 1968). For detail on the Wright family I drew upon John W. Hughson and Courtney C.J. Bond, *Hurling Down the Pine* (Old Chelsea, P.Q.: Historical Society of the Gatineau, 2nd ed., 1965) and for the Calvins on D.D. Calvin, *A*

Saga of the St. Lawrence: Timber and Shipping Through Three Generations (Ryerson, 1945). Michael Cross's 1968 University of Toronto Ph.D. thesis, "The Dark Druidical Groves: The Lumber Community and the Commercial Frontier in British North America to 1854," contains valuable factual detail as well as provocative interpretations.

Energetic historians in Atlantic Canada have recently produced a mass of scholarly writing on many aspects of shipbuilding and shipowning in the region. Their findings are summarized in two publications by Eric W. Sager and Lewis R. Fischer, "Atlantic Canada & the Age of Sail Revisited," CHR, June 1982, and *Shipping and Shipbuilding in Atlantic Canada, 1820-1914* (Ottawa: CHA, Historical Booklet 42, 1986), both of which contain guides to the literature. As noted in the text, F.W. Wallace's *Wooden Ships and Iron Men* (London: Hodder & Stoughton, 1924) is still a useful guide to the origins of the industry.

Everyone who studies the history of financial services in Canada begins with E.P. Neufeld's magisterial study, *The Financial System of Canada: Its Growth and Development* (Macmillan, 1972). It has influenced my argument in several chapters as well as guided me to sources and useful quotations. Canadian banking has had several historians, the most accessible of whom is R. Craig McIvor in *Canadian Monetary, Banking and Fiscal Development* (Macmillan, 1958). R.M. Breckenridge's old books *The Canadian Banking System, 1817–1890* (Toronto, 1894) and *The History of Banking in Canada* (Washington, 1910) are still worth consulting, as is A.B. Jamieson, *Chartered Banking in Canada* (Ryerson, 1955), and two series of articles by Adam Shortt: "Founders of Canadian Banking," in the *Journal of the Canadian Bankers' Association*, vols. 29–32; and "The History of Canadian Currency," in vols. 7–14. Bray Hammond's article on "Banking in Canada Before Confederation, 1792–1867" in Easterbrook and Watkins, eds., *Approaches to Canadian Economic History*, is particularly useful for comparisons with the United States.

Half-decent histories exist for three of Canada's five major chartered banks. Victor Ross and A. St. L. Trigge, *A History of the Canadian Bank of Commerce* (3 vols., Oxford University Press, 1920–34) contains a mass of detail on the Commerce to 1929 as well as lengthy histories of the banks it absorbed. The journalist Merrill Denison, who pioneered in the writing of commissioned corporate histories in Canada, was not at his best in *Canada's First Bank: A History of the Bank of Montreal* (2 vols., M&S, 1966–67), but his chapters present more facts and more challenges to conventional wisdom than his critics have tended to notice. Similarly, the newest in-house bank history, *The Scotiabank Story: A History of the Bank of Nova Scotia, 1832-1982* (Macmillan, 1982), is both fairly comprehensive and a good source of anecdotal material. One professional business historian, Ronald Rudin, has broken new ground in Canadian banking history with his monograph *Banking en français: The French Banks of Quebec, 1835–1925* (UTP, 1985); for a short version, see his article "Banking in Quebec: The French Banks, and the Mobilization of French Funds, 1835-1925," in the autumn 1985 *JCS*.

Two books, both written by specialists in business history, are essential for the evolution of nineteenth-century merchants and have greatly influenced these chapters: Gerald Tulchinsky's *The River Barons: Montreal Business and the Growth of Industry and Transportation, 1837–1853* (UTP, 1977); and Douglas McCalla, *The Upper Canada Trade, 1834–1872: A Study of the Buchanans' Business* (UTP, 1979). The Sutherland thesis, "The Merchants of Halifax," was also helpful, and an accessible short analysis of the trading networks is contained in T.W. Acheson, "The Nature and Structure of York Commerce in the 1820s," CHR, 1969. For the coming of free trade, see Gilbert N. Tucker, *The Canadian Commercial Revolution, 1845–51* (New Haven: Yale UP, 1936; Carleton Library, 1964). There is an excellent chapter on the insecurity of the mid-nineteenth century businessman's life in Michael B. Katz, *The People of Hamilton, Canada West* (Cambridge, Mass.: Harvard UP, 1975).

CHAPTER 7. THE STEAM REVOLUTION

The general history of Canadian transportation is surveyed in G.P. deT. Glazebrook's old but still useful *A History of Transportation in Canada* (Ryerson, 1938; Carleton Library ed., 2 vols, 1964). Tulchinsky's *The River Barons* has several good chapters on the coming of steam transportation to the St. Lawrence. For the impact of the railway on Canadians' consciousness T.C. Keefer's contemporary pamphlet, *Philosophy of Railways*, has become a classic. It was republished by UTP in 1972 under that title, along with several other Keefer essays and an excellent introduction by H.V. Nelles.

There are no good general histories of steamboating or canals. For the Molson family's enterprises I have used Merrill Denison's conventional business history, *The Barley and the Stream: The Molson Story* (M&S, 1955), supplemented by Shirley E. Woods Jr.'s uneven *The Molson Saga, 1763–1983* (Doubleday, 1983). In addition to the Cunard entries in the DCB, I used Kay Grant's short biography, *Samuel Cunard, Pioneer of the Atlantic Steamship* (London and Toronto, 1967) and Francis E. Hyde's substantial scholarly study, *Cunard and the North Atlantic, 1840–1973: A History of Shipping and Financial Management* (London, Macmillan, 1975). There is a splendid biographical article on Hugh Allan by Brian J. Young and Gerald Tulchinsky in the DCB, XI; it was supplemented by Thomas E. Appleton, *Ravenscrag: The Allan Royal Mail Line* (M&S, 1974). Tulchinsky's chapters on steamer lines in *The River Barons* are very good. My account of the Welland Canal derives from Hugh G.J. Aitken's pioneering monograph, *The Welland Canal Company: A Study in Canadian Enterprise* (Cambridge, Mass.: Harvard UP, 1954).

Canadian railroading still awaits a comprehensive historical overview. Robert F. Legget's *Railways of Canada* (Vancouver: Douglas & McIntyre, 1973) is very slight. But G.R. Stevens's two-volume *Canadian National Railways* (Clarke Irwin, 1960, 1962) contains histories of all of the lines eventually absorbed in the national system, i.e., practically all Canadian railways other than the Canadian Pacific. Stevens is witty and opinionated but usually reliable. There is much more fact, balance, and dullness in A.W. Currie's thick study of *The Grand Trunk Railway of Canada* (UTP, 1957). The antiquarian approach to railway history is typefied by Nick and Helen Mika, *Canada's First Railway: The Champlain and St. Lawrence* (Belleville, Ont.: Mika Publishing, 1985), and the professional business historian's by Peter Baskerville's publications arising from his doctoral thesis. These include: "Americans in Britain's Backyard: The Railway Era in Upper Canada, 1850–1880," *Business History Review*, autumn 1981, and "Professional vs Proprietor: Power Distribution in the Railroad World of Upper Canada/Ontario, 1850–1881," CHAR, 1978.

There is an abundance of biographical studies of the early railway builders, but only a few are still useful. The best is Donald R. Beer's *Sir Allan Napier MacNab* (Hamilton: Dictionary of Hamilton Biography, 1984). *Sir Casimir Stanislaur Gzowski: A Biography* by Ludwig Kos-Rabcewicz-Zubrowski and Wm. E. Greening (Clarke Irwin, 1959) is not very good but was helpful *faute de mieux*. Of the several biographical works on the Galts, only Andrew den Otter's *Civilizing the West: The Galts and the Development of Western Canada* (Edmonton: U. of Alberta Press, 1982), which deals mainly with a later period, captures Galt's developer's vision. There are no good published studies of the Canada Company; I used Roger Hall's 1973 Cambridge Ph.D. thesis, "The Canada Company, 1826–1843." Another helpful thesis was Henry C. Klassen's "Luther Hamilton Holton: Montreal Businessman & Politician, 1817–1867" (University of Toronto, 1970).

Much of the literature on the coming of the railway also deals with the relationships between politicians and railway promoters. Gustavus Myers's muckraking *A History of Canadian Wealth, vol 1* (Chicago 1914; repub. Lorimer, 1981) became the standard for all left-wing attacks on railway promoters and other Canadian entrepreneurs. There are now many more sensitive and useful studies of politicians' business connections, such as Brian Young's excellent short biography, *George-Etienne Cartier, Montreal Bourgeois* (Kingston and Montreal: McGill-Queen's, 1981) or his equally good history of one of the most troubled political railways: *Promoters and Politicians: The North Shore Railways in the History of Quebec, 1854–1885* (UTP, 1978). John A. Macdonald's entrepreneurial interests have been probed revealingly in J.K. Johnson's "John A. Macdonald, The Young Non-Politician," CHAR, 1971, and the most publicized railway scandal of the day is given exhaustive analysis by Paul Romney in "'The Ten Thousand Pound Job': Political Corruption, Equitable Jurisdiction and the Public Interest in Upper Canada 1852–1856," in David H. Flaherty, ed., *Essays in the History of Canadian Law*, vol. II (Osgoode Society, 1983). There will soon be more studies of Hincks, arguably the most important business mind in Canadian political history. Michael J. Piva has begun the re-evaluation with great insight in "Continuity and Crisis: Francis Hincks and Canadian Economic Policy," CHR, June 1985.

CHAPTER 8. WESTERN EMPIRE, 1821–1885

Canadian merchants' lack of interest in Confederation was discovered many years ago by my colleague Robert Bothwell in a research paper that he chose not to publish. Promoters' and developers' interest in the far West is well known, and can be approached through many sources, one of the best being Douglas Owram, *Promise of Eden: The Canadian Expansionist Movement and the Idea of the West, 1856–1900* (UTP, 1980).

This chapter's argument about the erosion and lack of flexibility of the HBC is based on the work of several authors, none of whom takes the thesis as far as I have. Without quite realizing it, John S. Galbraith portrays a company beset by competition on all sides, and often retreating in its face, in his splendid study, *The Hudson's Bay Company as an Imperial Factor, 1821–1869* (UTP, 1957). Alvin G. Gluek Jr. writes from the point of view of the most aggressive and menacing competitors in *Minnesota and the Manifest Destiny of the Canadian Northwest* (UTP, 1965). And my understanding of several aspects of the western transportation situation, as well as national railway strategy, has been heavily influenced by the writings of Andrew den Otter. These include "The Hudson's Bay Company's Prairie Transportation Problem," in John Foster, ed., *The Developing West* (Edmonton: U. of Alberta Press, 1983); "Transportation & Transformation: The Hudson's Bay Company, 1857–1885," *Great Plains Quarterly*, summer 1983; and "Jay Cooke and the Pacific Railway," paper presented to the Business History Conference, Trent University, 1984. E.E. Rich's history of the HBC and his survey, *The Fur Trade and the Northwest*, continued to be useful, as was A.S. Morton's *History of the Canadian West* and J.S. Galbraith's exemplary biography of George Simpson, *The Little Emperor: Governor Simpson of the Hudson's Bay Company* (Macmillan, 1956). For the company's early attempts to develop its storekeeping and land businesses I relied on the introductions and documents in Hartwell Bowsfield, ed., *The Letters of Charles John Brydges, Hudson's Bay Land Commissioner* (Winnipeg: Hudson's Bay Record Society, 1977, 1981).

The beginnings of economic activity in British Columbia are authoritatively described in Robin Fisher's *Contact and Conflict: Indian-European Relations in British Columbia, 1774–1890* (Vancouver: UBC Press, 1977). The HBC's activities in the area were further illuminated for me, and the quotation on page 202 supplied, in an unpublished UBC research paper, "'A Most Curious Compound of Professions': The Hudson's Bay Company on Coastal British Columbia, 1849–1858," kindly made available by its author, Richard Mackie. H. Keith Ralston's good article, "Miners and Managers: The Organization of Coal Production on

Vancouver Island by the Hudson's Bay Company, 1848–1862," in E. Blanche Norcross, ed., *The Company on the Coast* (Nanaimo Historical Society, 1983) was useful, as were two of J.M.S. Careless's articles: "The Business Community in the Early Development of Victoria, British Columbia," in Macmillan, ed., *Canadian Business History*; and "The Lowe Brothers, 1852–1870: A Study in Business Relations on the North Pacific Coast," *B.C. Studies*, 1969.

Further light on the free traders of Red River is cast in Irene M. Spry, "The 'Private Adventurers' of Rupert's Land," in Foster, ed., *The Developing West*. The later western trading networks are nicely outlined in Donald Kerr, "Wholesale Trade on the Canadian Plains in the Late Nineteenth Century: Winnipeg and its Competitors," in Howard Palmer, ed., *The Settlement of the West* (University of Calgary, 1977), and J.M.S. Careless, "The Development of the Winnipeg Business Community, 1870–1890," *Transactions of the Royal Society of Canada*, 1970. James G. MacGregor, *Edmonton Trader: The Story of John A. McDougall* (M&S, 1963) is a helpful biography of that pioneering Edmonton businessman. The authoritative history of the development of the Alberta ranching economy is David H. Breen, *The Canadian Prairie West and the Ranching Frontier, 1874–1924* (UTP, 1983).

The origins of the CPR and its construction are colourfully and readably portrayed as Canada's national epic in Pierre Berton's two volume study, *The Great Railway* (M&S, 1970–71). While Berton's popularization is unusually good, especially in the second volume's account of the actual construction, scholars need to dig more deeply. Den Otter's "Jay Cooke" paper, for example, undercuts many of Berton's assumptions about nationalism and the CPR, as does Leonard Irwin's *Pacific Railways and Nationalism in the Canadian-American Northwest, 1845–1873* (New York: Greenwood Press, 2nd ed., 1968). The most complete account of the origins of the syndicate and the building of the Manitoba line is contained in Albro Martin's *James J. Hill and the Opening of the Northwest* (New York: Oxford, 1976), a splendid biographical saga of North American business. It is much better than Dolores Greenberg, "A Study of Capital Alliances: The St. Paul & Pacific," CHR, March 1976. For the general history of the CPR, W. Kaye Lamb's *History of the Canadian Pacific Railway* (New York: Macmillan, 1977), is thorough and authoritative, and has been useful in several chapters. Several of the articles in Hugh A. Dempsey, ed., *The CPR West: The Iron Road & the Making of a Nation* (Vancouver: Douglas & McIntyre, 1984) are first-rate studies. The only remaining value of Innis's published doctoral thesis, *A History of the Canadian Pacific Railway* (UTP, 1923, 1971), lies in Peter George's introduction to the 1971 edition in which he questions the need for the large subsidies to the line. Except for Martin, the biographical literature on the railway builders is slim and dated. Heather Gilbert's *Awakening Continent: The Life of Lord Mount Stephen, vol 1, 1829–1891* (Aberdeen UP, 1965) is of some value, which is more than can be said of volume 2. Walter Vaughan's old *The Life and Work of Sir*

William Van Horne (New York: Century, 1920) is still the best source on the renaissance man of Canadian business; a new Van Horne biography is badly needed. Most of my impressions of the CPR's first two presidents come from their correspondence in the Public Archives of Canada.

CHAPTER 9. PROTECTING THE MANUFACTURERS

There are no histories of the growth of manufacturing in Canada. The discussion of tariff policy in the latter parts of this chapter profits immensely from the research of Ben Forster, published as *A Conjunction of Interests: Business, Politics, and Tariffs, 1825–1879* (UTP, 1986). Forster's conclusions about the emergence of the National Policy, somewhat more cautious than mine, are summarized in his article, "The Coming of the National Policy: Business, Government and the Tariff, 1876-1879," JCS, autumn 1979. His work almost, but not entirely, supersedes O.J. McDiarmid's *Commercial Policy in the Canadian Economy* (Cambridge, Mass.: Harvard UP, 1946).

As general sources on the early development of various manufacturing industries, I found Tulchinsky's *The River Barons* invaluable on Montreal to supplement Denison and Woods on the Molsons. T.W. Acheson's "The Great Merchant and Economic Development in St. John, 1820–1850," *Acadiensis*, spring 1979, subsequently expanded upon in *Saint John: The Making of a Colonial Urban Community* (UTP, 1985) is revealing if not always convincing on early Maritime manufacturing, and is partly parallelled for Halifax by L.D. McCann, "Staples and the New Industrialism in the Growth of Post-Confederation Halifax," *Acadiensis*, spring 1979. The relationship of agriculture and manufacturing is nicely illuminated for central Canada in John McCallum's important *Unequal Beginnings: Agriculture and Economic Development in Quebec and Ontario until 1870* (UTP, 1980). Further data on Ontario manufacturing can be found in Jacob Spelt, *Urban Development in South-Central Ontario* (1955; M&S ed., 1972); D.C. Masters, *The Rise of Toronto, 1850–1890* (UTP, 1947, 1974); and Gregory S. Kealey, *Toronto Workers Respond to Industrial Capitalism 1867–1892* (UTP, 1980). The notion that merchants and banks were not interested in supporting manufacturing was advanced in Tom Naylor's books and articles and was briefly taken seriously by a few historians. The most exhaustive of the several works demolishing the argument is Christopher Inwood's *The Canadian Charcoal Iron Industry* (New York: Garland, 1986).

Many of the early millers, distillers, and manufacturers have now found their way into the pages of the DCB; the entries for Gooderham, Van Norman, and furniture-makers Jacques and Hay were particularly helpful. There is a substantial article literature on the miller-industrialists, including W.P.J. Millar, "George P.M. Ball: A Rural Businessman in Upper Canada," OH, June 1974; Jean-Claude Robert, "Un Seigneur Entrepreneur, Barthélemy Joliette, et la Fondation du Village d'Industrie (Joliette), 1822–1850," RHAF, *décembre* 1972; and Françoise

Noel, "Chambly Mills, 1784–1815," CHAR, 1985. The contents are not as good as the title of Sidney Thomson Fisher's *The Merchant-Millers of the Humber Valley: A Study of the Early Economy of Canada* (NC Press, 1985). The best study of an early company town is R.G. Hoskins, "Hiram Walker and the Origins and Development of Walkerville," OH, September 1972.

A businessman/history buff, George Carruthers, published all the facts he could glean on his industry's world and its Canadian origins in *Paper-Making* (Garden City Press, 1947), and it has been mined by historians ever since. Only J.A. Blyth, "The Development of the Paper Industry in Old Ontario, 1824–1867," OH, June 1970, goes beyond him. While the history of Canadian textiles has yet to be written, there is a useful beginning for woollens in Richard Reid's "The Rosamond Woollen Company of Almonte: Industrial Development in a Rural Setting," OH, September 1983. On garment-making I relied on Gerald Tulchinsky, "Aspects of the Clothing Manufacturing Industry in Canada, 1850s to 1914," paper delivered to the Business History Conference, Trent University, 1984. For early footwear manufacture, Joanne Burgess, "L'industrie de la chaussure à Montréal: 1840–1870 – le passage de l'artisanat à la fabrique," RHAF, 1977 was helpful.

The nineteenth-century origins of Canadian iron and steel production are surveyed in considerable detail in W.J.A. Donald, *The Canadian Iron and Steel Industry: A Study in the Economic History of a Protected Industry* (Boston: Houghton Mifflin, 1915), and with more literary grace in William Kilbourn, *The Elements Combined: A History of the Steel Company of Canada* (Clarke Irwin, 1960). There is material on the early Montreal iron works in the Tulchinsky and McCallum volumes, and on St. Maurice and the other charcoal furnaces in the Inwood thesis. The considerable literature on the St. Maurice forges is also discussed in Louise Trottier, *Les Forges: Historiographie des Forges de Saint-Maurice* (Montreal: Boréal Express, 1980). One of the most important articles published on early Canadian manufacturing in recent years is Paul Craven and Tom Traves's demonstration in "Canadian Railways as Manufacturers, 1850–1880," CHAR, 1983, of the railway companies' major presence in heavy manufacturing.

The early history of Massey-Harris was written by Merrill Denison in another commissioned work, *Harvest Triumphant: The Story of Massey-Harris* (M&S, 1948), which contains much data available nowhere else. The implement industry is given slim, but professional, treatment in W.G. Phillips, *The Agricultural Implement Industry in Canada: A Study of Competition* (UTP, 1956). For meat-packing, see E. Sherwood Fox, ed., *Letters of William Davies, 1854–1861* (UTP, 1945) and my biography of Sir Joseph Flavelle, listed in Chapter 10. Ian McKay's article, "Capital and Labour in the Halifax Baking and Confectionary Industry during the Last Half of the Nineteenth Century," in Traves, ed., *Essays in Canadian Business History*, is an excellent account of the emergence of that industry in one city.

For the problems of shipbuilding, in addition to titles mentioned in Chapter 6, I used Albert Faucher, "The Decline of Shipbuilding at Quebec in the Nineteenth

Century," CJEPS, 1957. The paragraphs on oil and Petrolia derive from a research study prepared for me by Gene Allen; the principal published sources are Robert Page, "The Early History of the Canadian Oil Industry, 1860–1900," *Queen's Quarterly*, winter 1984; and Edward Phelps, "Foundations of the Canadian Oil Industry, 1850–1866," in *Profiles of a Province* (Ontario Historical Society, 1967)

CHAPTER 10. THE GROWTH OF FINANCIAL SERVICES

My debt to Neufeld's *The Financial System of Canada* is most evident in this chapter. McIvor, Breckenridge, and the bank histories listed in Chapter 6 were also valuable, especially Ross on the Bank of Commerce and the institutions it acquired, including the first Bank of British Columbia and the Eastern Townships Bank. Joseph Schull's *100 Years of Banking in Canada: A History of the Toronto-Dominion Bank* (Copp Clark, 1958) is slight but helpful. The regional bases of bankers' rivalries are well described by D.C. Masters in "Toronto vs Montreal: The Struggle for Financial Hegemony," CHR, June 1941. Ron Rudin's work on the French banks parallels the argument of the chapter, as does his article "Naissance et Déclin d'une Élite Locale: La Banque des Cantons de l'Est, 1859–1912," in the autumn 1985 JCS; and James D. Frost's "The 'Nationalization' of the Bank of Nova Scotia, 1880–1910," in Traves, ed., *Essays in Canadian Business History*. The history of McDonald's Bank of Victoria is told in R.L. Reid, "The First Bank in Western Canada," CHR, 1926, and the private bank of Alloway and Champion is described by Peter Lowe in "All Western Dollars," *Historical and Scientific Society of Manitoba, Papers, 1945–46*. The history of Prince Edward Island banking has now been written by Douglas O. Baldwin in "The Growth and Decline of the Charlottetown Banks, 1854–1906," *Acadiensis*, spring 1986.

The literature on all non-bank financial institutions in Canada is very weak. For mortgage companies there is only Neufeld plus a couple of thin pamphlet histories of the Canada Permanent and the Lambton Loan and Investment Company. No serious research has been done on the history of life insurance. The one half-decent book-length study is Joseph Schull's *The Century of the Sun: The First Hundred Years of Sun Life Assurance Company of Canada* (Macmillan, 1971). My account of the Canadian industry is built from this source and from privately published anniversary histories, none of them very good, of the Canada Life, North American, Manufacturers, Confederation, Sun, London Life, and the Dominion of Canada General Insurance Company. To get a sense of life insurance as an industry it was necessary to use Morton Keller's scholarly work on the American industry, *The Life Insurance Enterprise, 1885–1910: A Study in the Limits of Corporate Power* (Cambridge, Mass.: Harvard UP, 1963).

The literature on stock exchanges and brokerage and investment houses is even worse. The shining exception is John Fraser Whiteside's 1979 Trent University M.A. thesis, "The Toronto Stock Exchange to 1900: Its Membership and the

Development of the Share Market," which is partly summarized in his article, "The Toronto Stock Exchange and the Development of the Share Market to 1885," *JCS*, autumn 1985. It stands alone as a model history of the evolution of the TSE and the Toronto brokerage community. For George Cox and his financial networking, consult my study, *A Canadian Millionaire: The Life and Business Times of Sir Joseph Flavelle, Bart., 1858-1939* (Macmillan, 1978), or an article based on it, "Getting On In Life: The Saga of George Cox," *Canadian Journal of Life Insurance*, May 1979.

CHAPTER 11. A NATION IN BUSINESS, 1880–1900

The contents of chapters 11 to 13 rest more often on archival and other primary research than other sections of the book. For Timothy Eaton and Robert Simpson, for example, I am drawing on credit reports in the Dun and Bradstreet collection at the Baker Library of the Harvard Business School and on some of my own studies of Eaton Company documents and the diaries of John Macdonald. But I have also profited from discussions with Joy Santink, whose University of Toronto thesis on Timothy Eaton should become the standard work on the evolution of the department store in Canada. In the meantime the only useful published works on Eaton are an old, unsatisfactory biography, *Timothy Eaton*, by G.G. Nasmith (M&S, 1923) and a thin anniversary history by William Stephenson, *The Store that Timothy Built* (M&S, 1969). In 1965 Alan Wilson published a pioneering study in Canadian storekeeping history in his good biography, *John Northway: A Blue Serge Canadian* (Burns & McEachern). For the Woodwards, see the commissioned history, *The Woodwards*, by Douglas Harker (Vancouver: Mitchell Press, 1976). For retailing-wholesaling patterns, the D.G. Kerr article, cited in Chapter 8, was helpful, as was an unpublished University of Toronto research paper by Gene Allen, "Competition and Consolidation in the Toronto Wholesale Trade, 1860–1880"; and Gaetan Gervais's "Le commerce de détail au Canada (1870–1880)," *RHAF*, 1980.

The account of the CPR's early operations rests on Lamb, the Stephen and Van Horne biographies, Albro Martin on J.J. Hill, G.R. Stevens on the competitors, and articles in Dempsey, ed., in *The CPR West*, along with my reading of the Stephen-Macdonald correspondence in the PAC. A review of Berton on the CPR by H.V. Nelles in the November-December 1970 issue of *Canadian Forum*, and the ensuing controversy, helped shape my understanding of the CPR as a premature railroad. Gathering western opposition to the CPR is best presented in the early pages of T.D. Regehr's excellent railway history, *The Canadian Northern Railway: Pioneer Road of the Northern Prairies 1895–1915* (Macmillan, 1976). For the early growth of Vancouver I used Robert A. McDonald, "City-Building in the Canadian West: A Case Study of Economic Growth in Early Vancouver, 1886–

1893," *BC Studies*, autumn 1979, and Norbert MacDonald, "The Canadian Pacific Railway and Vancouver's Development to 1900," *BC Studies*, autumn 1977.

The discussion of the impact of the National Policy is rooted in research for my doctoral thesis, published as *A Living Profit: Studies in the Social History of Canadian Business, 1883–1911* (Toronto, M&S), with a subsidiary article, "Canadianizing American Business: The Roots of the Branch Plant," in Ian Lumsden, ed., *Close the 49th Parallel: The Americanization of Canada* (UTP, 1972). My general views on the tariff's impact follow the distinguished economist John H. Dales, whose 1966 argument in *Protective Tariff in Canadian Development* (UTP) has not been significantly challenged. The National Policy's impact on the Maritimes is described in T.W. Acheson, "The National Policy and the Industrialization of the Maritimes," *Acadiensis*, 1972; Peter DeLottinville, "Trouble in the Hives of Industry: The Cotton Industry Comes to Milltown, New Brunswick, 1879-1892," CHAR, 1980; and L.D. McCann's "The Mercantile-Industrial Transition in the Metal Towns of Pictou County, 1857–1931," *Acadiensis*, 1981. For further detail on coal and steel in Nova Scotia, see Don MacGillivray, "Henry Melville Whitney Comes to Cape Breton: The Saga of a Gilded Age Entrepreneur," *Acadiensis*, autumn 1979; and David Frank, "The Cape Breton Coal Industry and the Rise and Fall of the British Empire Steel Corporation," *Acadiensis*, 1977. The origins of Hamilton steel production are described in Donald, *Canadian Iron and Steel Industry*, and Kilbourn, *The Elements Combined*.

The sorry effect of tariffs and other industrial strategies on Canadian exports of manufactured goods has been studied in Glen Williams, *Not for Export: Toward a Political Economy of Canada's Arrested Industrialization* (M&S, 1983). For Massey and Harris, Denison's *Harvest Triumphant* contains enough detail to induce the fact of oligopoly. For Pat Burns and western meat-packing I used Grant MacEwan, *Pat Burns, Cattle King* (Saskatoon: Western Producer Press, 1979), and for Flavelle and the William Davies Company my 1978 study, *A Canadian Millionaire: The Life and Business Times of Sir Joseph Flavelle*.

The saga of F.H. Clergue and the Sault industries is related in both an excellent scholarly work by Duncan McDowall, *Steel at the Sault: Francis H. Clergue, Sir James Dunn, and the Algoma Steel Corporation, 1901–1956* (UTP, 1984), and in fiction – one of the rare Canadian novels about a businessman, Alan Sullivan's *The Rapids* (1906, UTP reprint 1972).

CHAPTER 12. "TRUSTING SOMEWHAT THE FUTURE"

The turn-of-the-century blossoming of the Canadian resource economy, the emergence of railway and utility magnates, and the maturing of the financial system have been the subject of considerable historical attention. There is no better starting place for the opening of the new resource frontiers than Morris Zaslow's volume in the Canadian Centenary Series, *The Opening of the Canadian North, 1870–1914* (1971), a book which has enriched my understanding of post-Confederation Canada. Another rich and important book, but limited to Ontario, is H.V. Nelles, *The Politics of Development: Forests, Mines & Hydro-Electric Power in Ontario, 1849–1911* (Macmillan, 1974). After its publication, Nelles began a collaboration with Christopher Armstrong to study the communication, transport, lighting, and power utilities of modern Canada in their formative years. It led to many articles and, recently, to a major book, *Monopoly's Moment: The Organization and Regulation of Canadian Utilities, 1830–1930* (Philadelphia: Temple University Press, 1986), from which I probably ought to have drawn more in the way of emphases and interpretation.

Armstrong and Nelles's work treats the utility entrepreneurs at several points. In their railroading incarnation, as builders of the Canadian Northern, Mackenzie and Mann have been definitively studied in the best book written in Canadian railway history, Regehr's *The Canadian Northern Railway*. The links with finance and utility promotion at home and abroad are discussed in my biography of Flavelle, *A Canadian Millionaire*, and in McDowall's *Steel at the Sault*. McDowall has also written a detailed history of Canada's Brazilian companies, "The Light: A History of the Brazilian Traction, Light and Power Company Limited, 1859–1878," soon to be published, to which he generously gave me access and on which I have relied for most of the details of the Sao Paulo promotion. In 1962 Ian M. Drummond published a seminal article on several aspects of the development of Canadian capital markets in "Canadian Life Insurance Companies and the Capital Market, 1890–1914," in CJEPS. Donald G. Paterson's *British Direct Investment in Canada, 1890–1914* (UTP, 1976), is also useful.

There is a huge body of literature on almost all aspects of Canadian mining and resource development. The most useful general overview of Canadian mining history is still D.M. LeBourdais, *Metals and Men: The Story of Canadian Mining* (M&S, 1957), but for Ontario there is now a well-written non-academic history by Philip Smith, *Harvest From the Rock: A History of Mining in Ontario* (Macmillan, 1986). Zaslow's chapter on the Klondike is excellent; for Joe Boyle, I used William Rodney, *Joe Boyle: King of the Klondike* (McGraw-Hill Ryerson, 1974). The Canadian pulp and paper industry still awaits its historian. Some problems of adjustment in the forest industries are well discussed in Robert Peter Gillis, "The Ottawa Lumber Barons and the Conservation Movement, 1880–1914," JCS, February 1974. For the transition from lumbering I used Lower's work; G.W. Taylor, *Timber: History of the Forest Industry in B.C.* (Vancouver: J.J. Douglas, 1975); James Hiller, "The Origins of the Pulp and Paper Industry in Newfoundland," *Acadiensis*, spring 1982; William F. Ryan, *The Clergy and Economic Growth in Quebec, 1896–1914* (Québec: Les Presses de l'Université Laval, 1966); and Jorge Niosi, "La Laurentide (1887–1928): Pionnière du Paper Journal au Canada," RHAF, décembre 1975.

The idea of the railroad as a northern development line is best portrayed in Albert Tucker's history of the Ontario Northland Railway, *Steam Into Wilderness* (Fitzhenry & Whiteside, 1978). Regehr on the Canadian Northern is the best source for the orgy of railway-building in the Laurier period, supplemented by Stevens on the CNR and Lamb on the CPR, and Patricia E. Roy, "Progress, Prosperity and Politics: The Railway Policies of Richard McBride," *BC Studies*, autumn 1980. Regehr has also published a good article comparing Mackenzie and Herbert Holt, "A Backwoodsman and an Engineer in Canadian Business: An Examination of Entrepreneurial Practices in Canada at the Turn of the Century," CHAR, 1977. For the history of the railroad that perhaps most perfectly realized Canadians' naive northern visions, see Howard Fleming, *Canada's Arctic Outlet: A History of the Hudson Bay Railway* (Berkeley: U. of California Press, 1957).

In addition to the sources cited for the utility entrepreneurs – McDowall, Armstrong and Nelles, Regehr, Bliss – the biography of Max Aitken by A.J.P. Taylor, *Beaverbrook* (London: Hamish Hamilton, 1972) is good, though unlikely to be the last word. Christopher Armstrong tells what it was really like to peddle bonds in the pioneer years in "Making a market: selling securities in Atlantic Canada before World War I," *Canadian Journal of Economics*, August 1980. Armstrong and Nelles have explored the Mexican involvements in "A Curious Capital Flow: Canadian Investments in Mexico, 1902–1910," *Business History Review*, summer 1984; and there is a useful overview of the Latin American experience in J.C.M. Oglesby, *Gringoes From the Far North, Essays in the History of Canadian-Latin American Relations, 1866–1968* (Macmillan, 1976).

For the history of newspapers and the media generally in Canada, see Paul Rutherford, *The Making of the Canadian Media* (McGraw-Hill Ryerson, 1978); for the nineteenth century see his specialized study, *A Victorian Authority: The Daily Press in Late Nineteenth-Century Canada* (UTP, 1982). Charles Bruce's *News and the Southams* (Macmillan, 1968) is a superior commissioned history. For the rise of J.B. Maclean's publishing empire I used Floyd Chalmers's good biography of the founder, *A Gentleman of the Press* (Doubleday, 1969).

The collapse of F.H. Clergue's dream is described by McDowall and in Sullivan, *The Rapids*.

CHAPTER 13. AT WAR WITH BUSINESS

This chapter is based most extensively on my previous research. It draws on my 1972 University of Toronto Ph.D. thesis, "A Living Profit: Studies in the Social History of Canadian Business, 1883–1911," on the 1974 book by that title (which considerably abridges the thesis), and on *A Canadian Millionaire*. Various aspects of the discussion are fleshed out from other sources. The chapter on Flavelle's generosity in *A Canadian Millionaire*, for example, is the only analytical study of a philanthropist's givings, but much can also be learned from G.P. deT.

Glazebrook's *Sir Edmund Walker* (UTP, 1933). For the givings of Sir William Macdonald I used Stanley B. Frost, *McGill University*, vol. II (Kingston and Montreal: McGill-Queen's UP, 1984), and John F. Snell, *Macdonald College of McGill University: A History from 1904–1955* (Montreal: McGill UP, 1963). The public service–reform tradition among Ottawa lumber barons is well set out by Peter Gillis in "Big Business and the Origins of the Conservative Reform Movement in Ottawa, 1890–1912," *JCS*, spring 1980.

Denison on the Molsons and Masseys was helpful for the understanding of dynastic values, as are the memoirs of both Vincent and Raymond Massey, and the first volume of Claude Bissell's biography, *The Young Vincent Massey* (UTP, 1981). Henry Pellatt's absurd side is well displayed in Carlie Oreskovich, *Sir Henry Pellatt: the King of Casa Loma* (McGraw-Hill Ryerson, 1982), a book not unlike its subject. Easily the most revealing of the family histories, however, a triumph of will against both threats of libel and the temptations of strong drink, is James F. Audain's account of the history of the family into which he married, *From Coalmine to Castle: The Story of the Dunsmuirs of Vancouver Island* (New York: Pageant Press, 1955). He followed it with several sequels, the best of which was *Alex Dunsmuir's Dilemma* (Victoria: Sunnylane Publishing, 1964). Dola Dunsmuir's lack of panties is revealed in Sherrill MacLaren's saga of slightly, though not altogetherly, more restrained western *arrivistes: Braehead: Three Founding Families in Nineteenth Century Canada* (M&S, 1986).

Little has been written on the history of management practices in Canadian business. Most of the comments here come from my study of Flavelle, with other material from corporate histories, especially Schull and Gibson on the Bank of Nova Scotia. After J.P. Buschlen published his muckraking, potboiling novel, *A Canadian Bankclerk* (William Briggs, 1913), he tried to organize a union of Canadian bank clerks. Nothing came of it.

There is, of course, an enormous amount of historical literature on Canadian labour, both unorganized and organized – now probably more than there is on the history of Canadian business. For an introduction to it, see the survey and bibliography in Bryan D. Palmer's *Working-Class Experience: The Rise and Reconstitution of Canadian Labour, 1800–1980* (Butterworths, 1983), or the pages of the journal of Canadian labour history, *Labour/Le Travailleur*, or the bibliographic essay by Irving Abella in J.L. Granatstein and Paul Stevens, *A Reader's Guide to Canadian History , vol. 2* (UTP, 1982). An abridged version of the proceedings of the Royal Commission on the Relations of Labor and Capital was published by the University of Toronto Press in 1973 under the title, *Canada Investigates Industrialism*, edited by Gregory S. Kealey. For business response to the challenge of trade unions, I use the chapters in *A Living Profit*. There is some interesting material on the growth of scientific management in Canada in Craig Heron and Bryan D. Palmer, "Through the Prism of the Strike: Industrial Conflict in Southern Ontario, 1901–14," *CHR*, December 1977, but they tend to exaggerate the movement's importance in Canada.

All of the material on business attitudes to competition comes from *A Living Profit* and its earlier version. For the 1889 origins of Canadian combines laws, see my article, "Another Anti-Trust Tradition: Canadian Anti-combines Policy, 1889–1910," in Porter and Cuff, eds., *Enterprise and National Development*. For the development of rural-based populism in Canada there is a large body of literature on farmer protest, including W.L. Morton, *The Progressive Party in Canada* (UTP, 1950), and Paul Sharp, *The Agrarian Revolt in Western Canada* (Minneapolis: University of Minnesota Press, 1948); the best and most economically literate of the works on agrarian protest is Vernon C. Fowke's *National Policy and the Wheat Economy* (UTP, 1957). Urban populism and its consequences has now been given exhaustive treatment by Armstrong and Nelles in *Monopoly's Moment*; one of their articles, "The Rise of Civic Populism in Toronto," in Victor Russell, ed., *Forging the Consensus: Essays on the History of Toronto* (UTP, 1984) is a particularly useful elaboration. The reformers' attack on the private interests is discussed in *Monopoly's Moment*, Nelles's *Politics of Development*, and my *A Canadian Millionaire*. There is a good case study of tactics that forestalled populism in Patricia Roy's, "The Fine Arts of Lobbying and Persuading: The Case of the B.C. Electric Railway," in Macmillan, ed., *Canadian Business History*.

The Centenary series volume covering 1896–1921, *A Nation Transformed*, by R. Craig Brown and Ramsay Cook (1974), has particularly good chapters on reform movements and the economy during the Great War. Regehr's work on the Canadian Northern is the best coverage of the sorry railway mess. For the Imperial Munitions Board and the travails of J.W. Flavelle, see *A Canadian Millionaire*. My reconsideration of the IMB experience, which helps explain the relatively brief coverage of the war economy in this book, is "War Business as Usual: Canadian Munitions Production, 1914–1918," in N.F. Dreisziger, ed., *Mobilization for Total War* (Waterloo: Wilfrid Laurier UP, 1981).

CHAPTER 14. THE STUTTERING TWENTIES

There is no good overview of the Canadian economy or Canadian business between the wars. The best of a bad lot are the relevant chapters in John Herd Thompson and Allen Seager, *Canada, 1922–1939*, in the Centenary series (1985). Tom Traves's *The State and Enterprise: Canadian Manufacturers and the Federal Government 1917–1931* (UTP, 1979) studies several important themes of the decade, stressing the complexities of events. Much of my chapter was shaped by primary research done for the Flavelle biography. For all students of the period the volumes in the *Canadian Annual Review* are particularly useful; I draw on them, for example, for details of the banking crisis, as well as on Schull's history of the Toronto and Dominion banks for the run on the latter.

David Frank's article on BESCO, and Ernest R. Forbes's important monograph, *The Maritime Rights Movement, 1919–1927: A Study in Canadian Regionalism* (Kingston and Montreal: McGill-Queen's UP, 1979) are the principal sources for the discussion of the Maritimes. My sense of the region-nation tension in the decade has been influenced by Andrew den Otter's pioneering article, "Railways and Alberta's Coal Problem, 1880–1960," in Anthony Rasporich, ed., *Western Canada Past and Present* (Calgary: M&S West, 1975). The railway mess of the 1920s and 1930s is covered by Lamb, *Canadian Pacific Railway*; by G.R. Stevens in a single-volume condensation and extension of his earlier work, *History of the Canadian National* (New York: Macmillan, 1973); in an eccentric but useful biography by D'Arcy Marsh, *The Tragedy of Henry Thornton* (Macmillan, 1935); and in *A Canadian Millionaire*. The standard history of taxation in Canada is J. Harvey Perry, *Taxes, Tariffs and Subsidies: A History of Canadian Fiscal Development* (2 vols., UTP, 1955).

The literature on the coming of the automobile to Canada is thoroughly inadequate. The most useful source is the material on Ford of Canada in Mira Wilkins and Frank E. Hill, *American Business Abroad: Ford on Six Continents* (Detroit: Wayne State UP, 1964). Nothing of importance has been written on the McLaughlins and GM of Canada; I was able to find useful factual material in a slim popular history by Robert Collins, *A Great Way to Go: The Automobile in Canada* (Ryerson, 1969). C.H. Aikman's old monograph, *The Automobile Industry of Canada* (Montreal, McGill Economic Studies, no. 8, 1926), was also useful, as was the chapter on the automobile tariff in Traves, *The State and Enterprise*.

There is no good history of the prohibition years in Canada and their effect on enterprise. The activities of the Bronfman family during prohibition were given immense publicity in Peter C. Newman's shallow, misleading study of the family, *Bronfman Dynasty: The Rothschilds of the New World* (M&S, 1978). Virtually all of Newman's material on the 1920s was based on the research James H. Gray did for his earlier book, *Booze: The Impact of Whisky on the Prairie West* (Macmillan, 1972), and this work is deeply influenced by the unexamined assumptions of a Protestant prohibitionist who disliked almost everything about the Bronfmans. The useful literature on Bronfman success is listed in Chapter 15. For breweries in the 1920s I was fortunate to have access to Albert Tucker's excellent history of the Labatt enterprises, which is scheduled for publication in 1987. The Cross family's brewing activities are touched on in MacLaren's *Braehead*.

The boom mentality of the late 1920s is well captured in James H. Gray's good popular history of the decade, *The Roar of the Twenties* (Macmillan, 1975), which includes chapters on oil and the Solloway brokerage empire. Donald MacKay's detailed history of MacMillan Bloedel, *Empire of Wood* (Vancouver: Douglas & McIntyre, 1982) is particularly useful for MacMillan's rise in the twenties. LeBourdais, *Metals and Man*, and Smith, *Harvest from the Rock*, on mining were helpful, as well as the commissioned history, *Noranda*, by Leslie Roberts (Clarke Irwin, 1956). Competition and monopoly in nickel are studied by an economic historian in O.W. Main's, *The Canadian Nickel Industry: A Study in Market Control and Public Policy* (UTP, 1955), and Alexander Dow has published several scholarly articles which begin the serious study of the evolution of Canadian base metals production. These include "Prometheus in Canada: The Expansion of Metal Mining, 1900–1950," in Cameron, *Explorations in Canadian Economic History*; and "Finance and Foreign Control in Canadian Base Metal Mining, 1918–1955," *Economic History Review*, February 1984. Robert Armstrong's article on asbestos in the Cameron volume is also helpful. For aluminum I used Duncan C. Campbell, *Global Mission: The Story of Alcan, Volume 1, to 1950* (Ontario Publishing Company, 1985), and José Igartua, "Corporate Strategy and Locational Decision-Making: The Duke-Price Alcoa Merger, 1925," JCS, autumn 1985. French-Canadian nationalists' confused but generally favourable attitudes toward American investment during the decade are well treated in Yves Roby's, *Les Québécois et les Investissements Américains (1918–1929)* (Québec: Les Presses de l'Université Laval, 1976).

The history of the management of the white-collar workforce, with particular concentration on the 1920s, is beginning to become accessible thanks to Graham Stanley Lowe's 1979 University of Toronto Ph.D. thesis, "The Administrative Revolution: The Growth of Clerical Occupations and the Development of the Modern Office in Canada, 1911–1931." Lowe's publications include "The Administrative Revolution in the Canadian Office: An Overview" in Traves, ed., *Essays in Canadian Business History*, and "Women, Work and the Office: The Feminization of Clerical Occupations in Canada, 1901–1931," *Canadian Journal of Sociology*, 1980. Other details on the rise of big business are drawn from a variety of sources. Biographies of entrepreneurs who came to prominence in the 1920s include Douglas How, *Canada's Mystery Man of High Finance: The Story of Izaak Walton Killam and His Glittering Wife Dorothy* (Hantsport, N.S.: Lancelot Press, 1986), and Harry Bruce, *R.A.: The Story of Roy Jodrey, Entrepreneur* (M&S, 1979).

CHAPTER 15. DARK YEARS

Next to nothing has been written about Canadian business during the Great Depression. There are two technical studies of the Canadian economy: A.E. Safarian, *The Canadian Economy in the Great Depression* (UTP, 1959); and Edward Marcus, *Canada and the International Business Cycle, 1927–1939* (New York: Bookman Associates, 1954). One study of business activities, *Business and Social Reform in the Thirties* (Lorimer, 1979), by Alvin Finkel, tries to hold businessmen responsible for practically everything that happened during the decade, but does not convince. Journalist Doug Fetherling wrote a once-over-lightly account of the stock market crash in *Gold Diggers of 1929* (Macmillan, 1979). There is more substance in several of the chapters of Floyd S. Chalmers's memoirs, *Both Sides of the Street: One Man's Life in Business and the Arts in Canada* (Macmillan, 1983). Much of the material in this chapter comes from the standard corporate histories, such as Kilbourn on Stelco and Lamb on the CPR, my

Flavelle research, the *Canadian Annual Review*, and various primary sources – including the PAC (with special thanks to Glenn Wright) for the 1931 crisis generally and the Sun Life memo in particular.

The flight from laissez-faire during the 1930s has not been well understood. It is discussed in *A Canadian Millionaire* and the introduction to L.M. Grayson and Michael Bliss, eds., *The Wretched of Canada: Letters to R.B. Bennett, 1930–1935* (UTP, 1972). The most useful older source for the flight from competition is Lloyd G. Reynolds, *The Control of Competition in Canada* (Cambridge, Mass.: Harvard UP, 1940). On price-fixing in the pulp and paper industry see T.D. Regehr, "Entrepreneurs and the Canadian Newsprint Industry, 1923–31," paper presented to the Canadian Business History Conference, Trent University, 1984; and Nelles, *Politics of Development*.

The coming of the Bank of Canada and bankers' attitudes toward it are described in several of the standard sources. The most useful of several special studies are Irving Brecher's *Monetary and Fiscal Thought and Policy in Canada, 1919–1939* (UTP, 1957) and T.D. Regehr, "Bankers and Farmers in Western Canada, 1900-1939," in John E. Foster, ed., *The Developing West* (Edmonton: U. of Alberta, 1983). The business conversion to Keynesianism, led by the construction industry, is adequately analysed by Finkel in *Business and Social Reform*. The footnoted comment by H.R. MacMillan on his opponents is from MacKay's *Empire of Wood*; W.A.C. Bennett's individualism is taken from J. David Mitchell, *W.A.C. Bennett and the Rise of British Columbia* (Vancouver: Douglas & McIntyre, 1983).

For the LaBines, radium, and uranium, I used Robert Bothwell's excellent corporate history, *Eldorado: Canada's National Uranium Company* (UTP, 1984). The development of civil aviation in Canada has been surveyed in J.R.K. Main, *Voyagers of the Air: A History of Civil Aviation in Canada 1858-1967* (Ottawa: Queen's Printer, 1967); and, with particular reference to CAL, in K.M. Molson, *Pioneering in Canadian Air Transport* (Winnipeg: James Richardson & Sons, 1974). The founding and first fifty years of TCA/Air Canada have now been ably chronicled by Philip Smith, in *It Seems Like Only Yesterday* (M&S, 1986). The semi-official biography of C.D. Howe was written by Robert Bothwell and William Kilbourn, and published by M&S in 1979 as *C.D. Howe: A Biography*. My view of Howe is generally more critical than theirs.

The best book on the political struggles about Canadian broadcasting is Frank W. Peers, *The Politics of Canadian Broadcasting, 1920-1950* (UTP, 1969). For the advent of radio generally, see E. Austin Weir, *The Struggle for National Broadcasting in Canada* (M&S, 1965). A great deal of material on Roy Thomson's early career can be found in the remarkably candid biography, *Roy Thomson of Fleet Street* (Collins, 1965) by Russell Braddon. Russell Hunt and Robert Campbell's unauthorized biography, *K.C. Irving, The Art of the Industrialist* (M&S, 1973) is sketchy for Irving's early career, and Richard Rohmer's official biography, *E.P. Taylor* (M&S, 1978) tends to be uncritical.

On brewing in the thirties I was helped by Denison on the Molsons, Tucker on Labatts, and a 1968 Northwestern Ph.D. thesis by Frank Roseman, "The Canadian Brewing Industry: The Effect of Mergers and Provincial Regulation on Economic Conduct and Performance." The discussion of the competitive struggle for the American liquor market and the strategies of the Bronfmans and Hiram Walker is based on "Whiskey," *Fortune*, November 1933; "Liquor in America: An Interim Audit," *Fortune*, October 1934; and "Seagram in the Chips," *Fortune*, September 1948.

CHAPTER 16. THE YEARS OF C.D. HOWE

Bothwell and Kilbourn's biography, *C.D. Howe*, is, of course, the main source for the events of the minister's life. It replaces an older, more adulatory biography by Leslie Roberts, *C.D., The Life and Times of Clarence Decatur Howe* (Clarke Irwin, 1957). For overviews of the war economy, see J.L. Granatstein, *Canada's War· The Politics of the Mackenzie King Government, 1939–1945* (Oxford UP, 1945); C.P. Stacey, *Arms, Men and Governments: The War Policies of Canada 1939–1945* (Ottawa: Queen's Printer, 1970); and Robert Bothwell, "'Who's Paying for Anything These Days?' War Production in Canada 1938–45," in N.F. Dreisziger, ed., *Mobilization for Total War* (Waterloo: Wilfrid Laurier Press, 1981). As well, J.D. Lindsey prepared a special research paper on Canadian business during the war and reconstruction periods, which utilized a wide range of primary sources and has been drawn upon freely; Lindsey's revisionist views of the war economy, roughly parallelling some of my criticisms of Howe and war-born nationalism, will now be found in his 1987 York University doctoral thesis, "Reconstructing Capitalism: Business-Government Relations during the Keynesian Revolution, 1939–1950."

The best overview of the postwar economy and economic management is contained in the relevant chapters of Robert Bothwell, Ian Drummond, and John English, *Canada since 1945: Power, Politics, and Provincialism* (UTP, 1981). For the Howe-Dunn relationship in both war and peace, McDowall's *Steel at the Sault* was constantly helpful. Another important biography of a bureaucrat-businessman who spanned the Howe era is Joseph Schull's *The Great Scot: A Biography of Donald Gordon* (Kingston and Montreal: McGill-Queen's UP, 1979). James S. Duncan, a dollar-a-year man and the head of Massey-Harris, wrote his own memoirs in *Not A One-Way Street* (Clarke Irwin, 1971). The account of the Argus group is built up from the Rohmer biography of Taylor; Taylor's only published reminiscence, in Sue Baptie, *First Growth: The Story of British Columbia Forest Products Limited* (Vancouver: privately pub., 1975); and H. T. Seymour, *Argus Corporation Limited, A Corporate Background Report* (Ottawa, Study No. 1 of the Royal Commission on Corporate Concentration, 1977). Conrad Black, who appears in later chapters under another guise, proved himself a more than competent historian in his massive 1977 biography of the Quebec premier, *Duplessis* (M&S), a book that greatly illuminates notions of economic development and business-government relations in the 1940s and 1950s. A good sense of the business climate of Atlantic Canada is conveyed in Harry Bruce's biography of Jodrey and its successor, *Frank Sobey: The Man and the Empire* (Macmillan, 1985)

The postwar development of Canadian aviation is described in the Howe biographies, Smith's history of Air Canada, and, for CP Air, Ronald A. Keith, *Bush Pilot With a Briefcase: The Happy-Go-Lucky Story of Grant McConachie* (Doubleday, 1972). Historians lean to an unusual consensus on the wisdom of cancelling the Avro Arrow, with the context for that decision best presented in Jon B. McLin, *Canada's Changing Defense Policy, 1957–1963: The Problems of a Middle Power in Alliance* (Baltimore: Johns Hopkins Press, 1967). The best history of the Arrow, James Dow's *The Arrow* (Lorimer, 1979), arrives at the opposite conclusion, but presents evidence pointing the other way.

The mining boom of the fifties is described by LeBourdais and Smith, with Bothwell's *Eldorado* being the best introduction to the new strategic material and the industry. The recent economic history of Canada's new province, Newfoundland, is described in many sources, the most important of which is the work of David Alexander: *The Decay of Trade: An Economic History of the Newfoundland Saltfish Trade, 1935–65* (St. John's, Memorial University, 1977); and *Atlantic Canada and Confederation: Essays in Canadian Political Economy* (UTP, 1983). Another overview of the fishery is Rosemary E. Ommer's "What's Wrong with Canadian Fish?" *JCS*, autumn 1985. Joey Smallwood's post-Confederation development strategy is defended, unconvincingly, by Gerhard P. Bassler in the spring 1986 *Acadiensis*, "'Develop or Perish': Joseph R. Smallwood and Newfoundland's Quest for German Industry, 1949–1953."

The impaling of C.D. Howe and the government on the pipeline issue is given careful, balanced study in William Kilbourn's excellent history of Trans-Canada Pipe Lines, *Pipeline* (Clarke Irwin, 1970).

CHAPTER 17. A SENSE OF POWER

The Argus-managerial revolution at Massey is celebrated in E.P. Neufeld, *A Global Corporation: A History of the International Development of Massey-Ferguson Limited* (UTP, 1969). The Axel Wenner-Gren plans for British Columbia are mentioned in David A. Mitchell's biography of W.A.C. Bennett. The new sense of Saskatchewan's riches is best described in John Richards and Larry Pratt, *Prairie Capitalism: Power and Influence in the New West* (M&S, 1979). The revival of international banking in an era of heightened domestic competition is described partially in Neufeld's *Financial System of Canada* and in the Schull-Gibson history of the Bank of Nova Scotia. Ben Forster did special research papers for me on the evolution of life insurance and the growth of business schools.

Like most of the subjects treated in this chapter, the property development industry is too recent to have been the subject of detached historical consideration. William Zeckendorf's version of his career is colourfully presented in *The Autobiography of William Zeckendorf* (New York: Holt, Rinehart, 1970). The development industry received critical but not unadmiring treatment in James Lorimer's *The Developers* (Lorimer, 1978); and enthusiastic, uncritical coverage by Susan Goldenberg in *Men of Property: The Canadian Developers Who Are Buying America* (Personal Library, 1981). In 1986 the Reichmann family were the subject of Peter Foster's detailed and critical, The *Master Builders: How the Reichmanns Reached for an Empire* (Key Porter). There is much less substantial literature on the Canadian motor vehicle industry. My references to Bombardier are based on a good overview by Alexander Ross in his 1975 book, *The Risk-Takers* (Financial Post/Macmillan, 1975), and a scholarly paper, "Bombardier's Mass Production of the Snowmobile – The Canadian Exception?" by Chris de Bresson and Joseph Lampel, read to the Canadian Science and Technology Historical Association in 1982.

Historical writing about the coming of computers to Canada began with the 1982 publication of *Entering the Computer Age: The Computer Industry in Canada: The First Thirty Years* by Beverley J. Bleackley and Jean LaPrairie (Agincourt: Book Society of Canada). The Royal Commission on Corporate Concentration produced a useful research report, IBM *Canada Ltd., A Case Study* by Marcel Coté, Yvan Allaire, and Roger-Emile Miller (Ottawa, 1976); and the situation to 1983 was outlined by David Thomas in *Knights of the New Technology: The Inside Story of Canada's Computer Elite* (Key Porter, 1983). Little has been written about the food services industry in Canada; my comments rely on Rohmer's biography of E.P. Taylor and the interesting commissioned history, *Cara: 100 Years* (Cara Holdings, 1983), by Kenneth Edwards.

Canadian fears that big business was becoming too big led to an exhaustive analysis of the causes, extent, and consequences of concentration, diversification, and conglomeration in the 1978 *Report of the Royal Commission on Corporate Concentration* (Ottawa: Minister of Supply and Services) and two dozen supporting research studies. Journalists and others criticized the commission for not supporting their own preconceptions, but no one has seriously challenged its arguments or statistical analyses, which are important to the interpretations presented here and in Chapter 19. For some years previously, academics and journalists had been fascinated by the interlocking directorates of public corporations and the networking such relations revealed. John Porter was the first academic sociologist to write about a Canadian "power elite" in *The Vertical Mosaic: An Analysis of Social Class and Power in Canada* (UTP, 1965). His work was later followed by Marxist sociologist Wallace Clement, in *The Canadian Corporate Elite* (M&S, 1975), and several other dreary tomes; and most recently by a revisionist though no less turgid

Marxist sociologist, William K. Carroll, in *Corporate Power and Canadian Capitalism* (Vancouver: UBC Press 1986). In the meantime journalist Peter C. Newman achieved great popular success with the "establishment" concept in his fact-filled profiles, *The Canadian Establishment, Volume One* (M&S, 1975); and *The Canadian Establishment, Volume Two: The Acquisitors* (M&S, 1981). Even as these authors and their researchers charted and counted directors, the evolving, expanding economy was dating their work and old networking practices were becoming increasingly anachronistic in business itself.

Similarly, Canadians began ringing alarm bells about foreign ownership about the time that it began to decline. Leftist-nationalist viewers-with-alarm generated bushels of literature about evils of the foreign capitalists, perhaps the most famous polemic being Kari Levitt's *Silent Surrender: The Multinational Corporation in Canada* (Macmillan, 1970). The quiet scholarship of thoughtful economists such as A.E. Safarian (see, among many writings, "Foreign Investment in Canada: Some Myths," *JCS*, 1971) tended to be ignored in the clamour against the non-Canadians. Walter Gordon's several books, including his memoirs, are rich veins of business-oriented nationalism, as are the chapters in James H. Gray's memoir, *Troublemaker: A Personal History* (Macmillan, 1978), about Canadian resentments in the oil and gas industry. I have described the emergence of nationalist restrictions on foreign investment at greater length in "Founding FIRA: The Historical Background," in James M. Spence and William P. Rosenfeld, eds., *Foreign Investment Review Law in Canada* (Butterworths, 1984), and give a fuller account of the historical literature on foreign investment in a bibliographic essay in Granatstein and Stevens, eds., *A Reader's Guide to Canadian History, volume 2*. The Bothwell, Drummond, and English history, *Canada Since 1945*, contains a judicious evaluation of the nationalism of the 1960s and 1970s and correctly anticipates its waning in the 1980s.

The growth of big government has not been given anything like the popular critical scrutiny lavished on big business. A few political scientists and economists have catalogued the expansion of government activities and the introduction of "modern" management in research studies published by Canada's small flock of think-tanks. The most influential and accessible of these, which well captures the utopianism of the Trudeau years is Richard D. French, *How Ottawa Decides: Planning and Industrial Policy-Making, 1968–1980* (Ottawa: Canadian Institute for Economic Policy, 1980). On a popular level, both that utopianism and its corruption when it confronted economic reality and its adherents' lust for power and security, is beautifully illuminated in Christina McCall-Newman's *Grits: An Intimate Portrait of the Liberal Party* (Macmillan, 1982). In *Where Business Fails* (Montreal: Institute for Research on Public Policy, 1981), James Gillies captured business's confused response to the shifting Ottawa scene.

CHAPTER 18. WESTERN ENERGY

There are no comprehensive histories of the petroleum industry in Canada. Two slim journalistic overviews are presented in Earle Gray, *The Great Canadian Oil Patch* (Maclean-Hunter, 1970) and Ed Gould, *Oil: The History of Canada's Oil & Gas Industry* (Victoria: Hancock House, 1977). Natural gas processing has been surveyed by Fred Stenson in *Waste to Wealth: A History of Gas Processing in Canada* (Calgary, Canadian Gas Processors Association, 1985), and there have been several books on the history of the tar sands, including J. Joseph Fitzgerald, *Black Gold With Grit: The Alberta Oil Sands* (Sidney, BC: Gray's Publishing, 1978), and Barry B. Ferguson, *Athabasca Oil Sands: Northern Resource Exploration, 1875–1951* (Regina: Canadian Plains Research Centre, 1985). Otherwise, the industry, like so many others in Canada, awaits its historian.

Three commissioned company histories have been used extensively in this chapter. Imperial Oil chose not to publish the enormous – and indeed unpublishable – manuscript John S. Ewing delivered to it in 1951 on "The History of Imperial Oil Ltd.," but made a copy available to me in their library (as it has to other historians). It contains a wealth of detail. The McMahon family and their companies were well served by Earle Gray in *Wildcatters: The Story of Pacific Petroleums and Westcoast Transmission* (M&S, 1982), as was Home Oil by Philip Smith's *The Treasure-Seekers: The Men Who Built Home Oil* (Macmillan, 1978).

Articles about the nineteenth-century Ontario origins of the industry are mentioned in Chapter 19. The historian David H. Breen has recently begun academic study of the Western industry with his introduction to the documents in *William Stewart Herron: Father of the Petroleum Industry in Alberta* (Calgary: Historical Society of Alberta, 1984) and an important article, "Anglo-American Rivalry and the Evolution of Canadian Petroleum Policy to 1930," *CHR*, September 1981. James H. Gray added rich anecdotal material on the twenties and thirties in *The Roar of the Twenties* and *Troublemaker*. The first post-Leduc decade of development in Alberta was usefully discussed in Eric J. Hanson's *Dynamic Decade* (M&S, 1958); and the pipeline debate, as well as the general history of TCPL, is given excellent analysis in Kilbourn's *Pipeline*.

The boom of the seventies sparked innumerable academic and popular studies of all aspects of energy policy, though few with much historical perspective. John N. McDougall did set fuel policy in historical perspective in *Fuels and the National Policy* (Butterworth, 1982); while Richards and Pratt became historian-analysts of the postwar growth of the resource-rich region in the well-received (but now dated) *Prairie Capitalism*. Pratt also wrote useful articles on the origins and early years of Petro-Canada: "Petro-Canada," in Allan Tupper and G. Bruce Doern, eds., *Public Corporations and Public Policy in Canada* (Montreal: Institute for

Research on Public Policy, 1981); "Oil and State Enterprises: Assessing Petro-Canada," in W.T. Stanbury and Fred Thompson, eds., *Managing Public Enterprises* (New York: Praeger, 1982). From a more popular perspective, journalist Peter Foster profiled the oil and gas elite of the seventies in *The Blue-Eyed Sheiks, The Canadian Oil Establishment* (Collins, 1979), which is also now dated.

Works on Dome and the NEP appeared after the ball was over, and chronicle both the apparent triumph and the real disasters. Peter Foster became much more incisive and angry in his history of the genesis of the NEP, *The Sorcerer's Apprentices: Canada's Super-Bureaucrats and the Energy Mess* (Collins, 1982), and his account of the rise and fall of Dome, *Other People's Money: The Banks, the Government, and Dome* (Collins, 1983). Jim Lyon also covered the débâcle, somewhat thinly, in *Dome: The Rise and Fall of the House that Jack Built* (Macmillan, 1983). All of Foster's books use interview material available nowhere else, but for scholars the NEP study has been superseded by G. Bruce Doern and Glen Toner's exhaustive *The Politics of Energy: The Development and Implementation of the NEP* (Methuen, 1985). For mega-projects, see *Major Canadian Projects, Major Canadian Opportunities: A Report by the Consultative Task Force on Industrial and Regional Benefits from Major Canadian Projects* (Ottawa: Department of Supply and Services, 1981), as well as G. Bruce Doern, "The Mega-project Episode and the Formulation of Canadian Economic Policy,"*Canadian Public Administration*, summer 1983.

CHAPTER 19. "LESS PLACE TO HIDE"

Much of this chapter is current history, derived from close reading of the daily, weekly, and monthly business press, discussions with business people, and reflection on past and present trends. None the less, there are some important guides to the course of recent Canadian business history. Peter C. Newman's biography of Conrad Black, for example, *The Establishment Man: A Portrait of Power* (M&S, 1982) contains accounts of the struggle to save Massey and Argus infighting that are available nowhere else. The Massey mess was also set in the context of the company's history by Peter Cook in *Massey at the Brink* (Collins, 1981). The Foster and Lyon histories of Dome include the collapse and early years of the death throes. There is a good chapter on Canadair in volume 2 of Michael J. Trebilcock, *et al.*, *The Political Economy of Business Bailouts* (Ontario Economic Council, 1985).

Journalists and other writers were particularly quick off the mark in attempting to come to terms with the problems of troubled financial institutions in the 1980s. One of the best books ever written about business in Canada, one that illuminates the inflation mentality, *arriviste* capitalism, and many other themes, is Terence Corcoran and Laura Reid's *Public Money, Private Greed: The Greymac, Seaway and Crown Trusts Affair* (Collins, 1984). The next year a less insightful, though more general and very informative study of trust companies, Patricia Best and Ann Shortell's *A Matter of Trust: Power and Privilege in Canada's Trust Companies* (Penguin, 1985), was the first winner of the new National Business Book Award. My understanding of the recent history of Canadian banking was helped by Gordon Boreham's articles on "The Changing Nature of Canadian Banking," *Canadian Banker and ICB Review*, February-June, 1983, but no one has satisfactorily explained the shameful banking failure that produced the lending to Dome.

Canadians' interest in business and the lives of the rich and famous led to a continuous flow of profiles, success stories, and self-help books, most of which were ephemeral, but often useful in publicizing little-known entrepreneurs and their achievements. Newman's *The Acquisitors*, for example, casts light on the boom mentality in its portrait of Nelson Skalbania, a man who will otherwise be ignored by history. There were useful short biographies in Paul Grescoe and David Cruise's *The Money Rustlers: Self-made Millionaires of the New West* (Penguin, 1985); and Keith Barnes and Everett Banning's *Money-Makers: The Secrets of Canada's Most Successful Entrepreneurs* (M&S, 1985); as well as Allan Gould's *The New Entrepreneurs: 80 Canadian Success Stories* (M&S Bantam, 1986). The indefatigable Susan Goldenberg wrote fact-filled profiles of corporate giants, *Canadian Pacific: A Portrait of Power* (Methuen, 1983); and *The Thomson Empire* (Methuen, 1984) without quite realizing their vulnerability. And a little gem of Canadian business history was created when Albert Cohen, head of Winnipeg's Gendis Inc., set down his family's rags to riches story in *The Entrepreneurs* (M&S, 1985).

As early as 1971, Philip Mathias of the *Financial Post* had begun probing the disasters caused by government attempts to subsidize new industries. His book, *Forced Growth: Five Studies of Government Involvement in the Development of Canada* (James Lewis & Samuel), can still be read profitably and seems prophetic. Almost a generation later the literature generated by the Clairtone, Bricklin, Mirabel, Canadair, and other disasters, fills a small bookshelf. For the bail-out phenomen, see the Trebilcock study. For government as dinosaur, see French, *How Ottawa Decides*; the essays in George Lermer, ed., *Probing Leviathan: An Investigation of Government in the Economy* (Vancouver: Fraser Institute, 1984); and on the fate of bright hopes for a well-managed civil service, see Paul A. Pross, "From System to Serendipity: The Practice and Study of Public Policy in the Trudeau Years," in Kenneth Kernaghan, ed., *Canadian Public Administration: Discipline and Profession* (Butterworths, 1985).

The work of the Royal Commission on Corporate Concentration remained a guide, also proving somewhat prophetic, to the strength of competitive forces in the Canadian economy. As its publications gathered dust, journalist Diane Francis proved that populism was still alive and well (and living at the Toronto *Star*), and almost thoroughly out of touch with Canadian business reality in *Controlling Interest: Who Owns Canada?* (Macmillan, 1986).

Even as the government of Canada began negotiations looking to a free trade agreement with the United States, scholars were still perusing the three thick volumes of the 1985 *Report* of the Royal Commission on the Economic Union and Development Prospects for Canada, a mid-1980s state-of-the-nation report which reflected the new free trade consensus on the part of concerned businessmen and economists. Good academic comment on the Macdonald Commission's Report was contained in the February 1986 supplement to *Canadian Public Policy*. For those whose appetite for knowledge about Canadian economic, political, and institutional life was still not satiated, the commission published seventy-two volumes of academic research studies covering the past, present, and future of topics ranging from industrial strategies to high technology, multilateral trading agreements, and the harmonization of business law in Canada. Many of these studies were sampled during research for this book. A few were useful; many were not. Most suffer from painfully bad prose.

PERMISSIONS

Canadian History, A Chronology

1497	John Cabot's voyage
1534–35	Voyages of Jacques Cartier
1608	Champlain founds Quebec
1663	New France a royal province
1670	Hudson's Bay Company chartered
1713	Treaty of Utrecht gives Acadia (Nova Scotia) to Britain
1759	Quebec captured
1763	British conquest confirmed by Treaty of Paris
1774	Quebec Act
1776–83	American Revolution
1791	Quebec divided into Upper and Lower Canada
1812–14	War of 1812
1821	Merger of Hudson's Bay Company and North West Company
1837	Rebellions in Upper and Lower Canada
1841	Upper and Lower Canada reunited
1846	Britain adopts free trade
1849	Annexation Manifesto
1854	Reciprocity with United States
1861–65	U.S. Civil War
1867	Confederation creates Dominion of Canada
1879	National Policy
1885	Canadian Pacific Railway completed
1896	Laurier defeats Conservatives
1906	Alberta and Saskatchewan become provinces
1911	Liberals and reciprocity defeated
1914–18	World War One (Great War)
1929	Onset of Great Depression
1939–45	World War Two (Hitler's War)
1947	Leduc oil discovery
1949	Newfoundland joins Canada
1957	Diefenbaker defeats Liberals
1967	Centennial; Expo '67
1968	Trudeau becomes Prime Minister
1973	Onset of world energy crisis
1981	National Energy Program
1984	Conservatives regain power

Index